The Abacus and the Sword

DATE DUE

JE 9 '10			

A

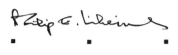

B O O K

The Philip E. Lilienthal imprint
honors special books
in commemoration of a man whose work
at the University of California Press from 1954 to 1979
was marked by dedication to young authors
and to high standards in the field of Asian Studies.
Friends, family, authors, and foundations have together
endowed the Lilienthal Fund, which enables the Press
to publish under this imprint selected books
in a way that reflects the taste and judgment
of a great and beloved editor.

Twentieth-Century Japan: The Emergence of a World Power
Irwin Scheiner, Editor

1. General Terauchi Masatake, the new resident-general (seated in carriage), passing through Kotobuki-chō, Seoul, on the way to his official residence in July 1910.

The Abacus and the Sword

The Japanese Penetration of Korea,
1895–1910

Peter Duus

UNIVERSITY OF CALIFORNIA PRESS
Berkeley · Los Angeles · London

University of California Press
Berkeley and Los Angeles, California

University of California Press, Ltd.
London, England

© 1995 by
The Regents of the University of California

First Paperback Printing 1998

Library of Congress Cataloging-in-Publication Data
Duus, Peter, 1933–
      The abacus and the sword: the Japanese
   penetration of Korea, 1895–1910/Peter Duus.
         p.   cm.—(Twentieth-century Japan; 4)
      "Lilienthal book."
      Includes bibliographical references and index.
      ISBN-13 978-0-520-21361-6 (pbk.: alk. paper)
      ISBN-10 0-520-21361-0 (pbk.: alk. paper)
      1. Japan—History—Meiji period, 1868–
      1912.   2. Korea—History—1864–1910.
   3. Japan—Relations—Korea.   4. Korea—
   Relations—Japan. I. Title. II. Series.
   DS882.D88   1995
   951.9'02—dc20   94-6118
                                        CIP

Printed in the United States of America

08   07   06
9 8 7 6 5 4

Contents

Illustrations

Plates 2–15 follow page 241

Acknowledgments

It has been a dozen or more years since I first embarked on this study, and I am thoroughly grateful that it is now out of the house. Its preparation has not been made any easier by the computer revolution. Since I first set keyboard (or is it chip?) to paper, I have gone through two generations of computer architecture, two sizes of floppy disks, and three versions of word-processing software. Even as I write, my software is becoming a dim memory in the marketplace, as I recently discovered when I had to call a 900 number in Georgia to find out how to pummel my footnotes into endnotes. Progress is painful.

Doing history, fortunately, is not. Not only is there pleasure in chasing down the evidence, but helping hands always speed the pursuit. In doing research for this book I have enjoyed the assistance of librarians and staff of the East Asia Collection of the Hoover Institution on War, Peace, and Revolution, the National Archives in Washington, D.C., the New York Public Library, the National Diet Library in Tokyo, the libraries of the Faculty of Economics and the Institute for Social Science at the University of Tokyo, and the Yūhō Kyōkai in Tokyo. Along the way Kajimura Hideki, Kobayashi Hideo, Lew Young-Ick, Moriyama Shigenori, Yui Tsunehiko, and several other scholars offered helpful suggestions about what kind of materials were available and what kind of questions might be asked. And I must not forget to acknowledge the valuable assistance of several students who have engaged in various types of drudgery for me: Rob Eskildsen, Roseanne Fiore, Andrew

Goble, Thomas Kierstead, Michael Lewis, Jennifer Nogaki, Martha Tocco, and especially Kweon Sug-in for her translation of Korean-language material.

At various stages in my work I have been blessed with generous financial assistance from the Japan Foundation, the Fulbright Commission in Japan, the Hoover Institution, the School of Humanities and Sciences, and the Center for East Asia Studies at Stanford University. I am grateful to Professors Komiya Ryūtarō and Ishii Kanji for arranging affiliation with the Faculty of Economics at the University of Tokyo in 1981–82 and to Professor Bannō Junji for doing the same at the Institute of Social Science in 1986–87. And, of course, the staff at International House of Japan in Tokyo were warmly supportive and exceptionally tolerant of pipe smoke during the months when I used a study carrel there. (I have since given up the habit.)

I must express thanks to Irv Scheiner, editor of this series, and to three anonymous readers for their penetrating comments on an earlier manuscript. Their critical perspectives forced me to rethink several important sections of the book, and while they may not entirely agree with my revisions I think their suggestions helped me to improve the coherence of the argument and to avoid what might have appeared to be an endorsement of Japanese imperialism.

Final words of gratitude are due Dan Gunter for his painstaking copy editing of the manuscript, Augean footnotes and all, and Betsey Scheiner for manhandling it through production with thoughtfulness and efficiency.

Abbreviations

CDU	Kim Chŏng-myŏng, ed. *Chōsen dokuritsu undō*. 6 vols. Tokyo: Hara Shobō, 1966–67.
FMA	Foreign Ministry Archives, Tokyo.
HI	Hoover Institution on War, Revolution, and Peace, Stanford California
HL-Korea	Residency-General Archives, Hoover Institution.
HRCKS	Itō Hirobumi and Hiratsuka Atsushi, eds. *Hisho ruisan: Chōsen kōshō shiryō*. Rev. ed. 3 vols. Tokyo: Hisho Ruisan Kankōkai, 1934–36.
JNN	*Jitsugyō no Nihon.*
KKR	Mutsu Munemitsu. *Kenkenroku: A Diplomatic Record of the Sino-Japanese War, 1894–1895.* Trans. Gordon M. Berger. Tokyo: University of Tokyo, 1982.
KNSKK	Tabohashi Kiyoshi. *Kindai nissen kankei no kenkyū.* 2 vols. Tokyo: Bunka Shiryō Chōsakai, 1963–64.
KSH	Kensei Shiryō Hensanshitsu, National Diet Library, Tokyo.
KSSH	Ōsaka Shōkō Kaigisho. *Kankoku sangyō shisatsu hōkokusho.* Osaka, 1904.

NA   National Archives, Washington, D.C.

NGB   *Nihon gaikō bunsho.* Tokyo: Nihon Kokusai Renmei
          Kyōkai, 1936–.

NGNSB   Gaimushō, ed. *Nihon gaikō nenpyō oyobi shuyō bun-
          sho.* 2 vols. Tokyo: 1955.

NKGS   Kim Chŏng-myŏng, ed. *Nikkan gaikō shiryō.* 10 vols.
          Tokyo: Hara Shobō, 1979–81.

NKGSS   Kim, Chŏng-myŏng, ed. *Nikkan gaikō shiryō shūsei.*
          10 vols. Tokyo: Gannando, 1962–67.

SEDS   Ryūmonsha, ed. *Shibusawa Eiichi denki shiryō.* Tokyo:
          Shibusawa Eiichi Denki Shiryō Kankōkai, 1955–65.

YAI   Ōyama Azusa. *Yamagata Aritomo ikensho.* Tokyo:
          Hara Shobō, 1966.

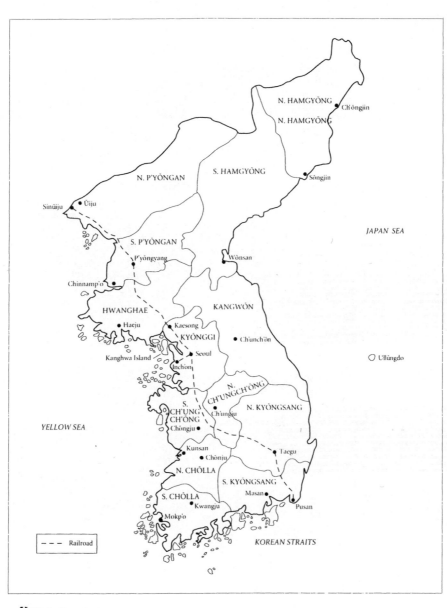

Railroad

Korea, ca. 1910

The Origins of Meiji Imperialism

Why did Japan begin to acquire an overseas colonial empire in the late Meiji period? After all, there was little precedent in Japanese history for a deliberate program of overseas territorial expansion. Throughout most of their recorded past the Japanese had remained in splendid isolation from their continental neighbors, making very few attempts to expand their political power abroad. No dynastic marriages had linked the Japanese with the continental monarchies, nor had the imperial or shogunal regimes ever established a stable territorial foothold there, as, for example, the English monarchy had in France during the twelfth and thirteenth centuries. The only exception to this tradition of relative political isolation—Hideyoshi's brief, costly, and unsuccessful invasion of Korea in the 1590s—did not inspire imitation. Neither was there any sustained tradition of exploration abroad nor any outward migration like the Chinese diaspora in Southeast Asia. Of all the nineteenth-century imperialist powers, Japan therefore had the least experience in dealing with alien peoples overseas, let alone exercising domination over them. As Takekoshi Yosaburō complained in 1913, "Nurtured by history and limited in vision, the [Japanese] people have lacked the intellectual heritage of a maritime country, the idea of national expansion."[1]

Indeed, for most of the three centuries that separated Hideyoshi's in-

1. Takekoshi Yosaburō, "Keizai gunji futatsu hōmen yori mitaru hantō," in Aoyagi, Chōsen, 262–63.

vasions of Korea from the Sino-Japanese War, the Japanese had lived at peace with their neighbors, carrying on trade and occasionally exchanging emissaries, but firmly avoiding sustained contact. If any East Asian country was "imperialist" during these years, it was Ch'ing China, whose armies marched and countermarched across the Inner Asian frontier, shoring up old areas of domination on the steppes of Mongolia and establishing new ones in the highlands of Tibet. If "tradition" or "historical precedent" have any explanatory value, it should have been China, not Japan, that emerged as the first Asian imperialist power. Indeed, for a brief period in the 1880s and early 1890s the Ch'ing leadership pursued an imperialist program in Korea, but they ultimately failed, in part because of reluctance to abandon practices associated with the tribute system, China's traditional form of exercising domination over alien peoples.

For the Japanese, a policy of external expansion, like so much else in the Meiji period, was new and unprecedented. And like so much else that was new and unprecedented, it had its origins in Japan's new contacts with the West. It is no coincidence that until intrusions by the Russians in the late eighteenth century and by the British and the Americans in the early nineteenth century, the notion of overseas colonies found no place in Japanese political discourse. Only in the wake of these contacts did visionaries and reformers like Hayashi Shihei, Satō Nobuhiro, and Yoshida Shōin, all later touted as "precursors" or "forerunners" of modern Japanese expansion, begin to spin schemes for Japanese colonial expansion. These men were "precursors" or "forerunners" only in the sense that they were the first to imagine new relationships with the outside world, based on a hazy understanding of what the Westerners were doing. With the emergence of the Meiji government, what had been visionary and hypothetical became a national goal. Within a generation after the Meiji Restoration, the Japanese leadership had shifted from a traditional policy of peaceful and passive isolation to a radically new policy of active expansion.

THE INTERNATIONAL CONTEXT
OF MEIJI IMPERIALISM

The adoption of an expansionist policy was intimately linked to the timing of Japan's decision to modernize. The Japanese chose to tread the path toward "civilization and enlightenment" at precisely the moment in history when the nation-states of Western Europe were in the midst of frenzied territorial expansion across the globe. Between 1800 and 1900 the Europeans acquired control over territory eight or nine times the size of Europe itself. Indeed, this Western surge to seize dominion over lands and peoples historically and geographically remote from Europe was the most salient feature of international politics during the Meiji era. The global reach of Western imperialism could not help but influence both the character of Meiji modernization and the thrust of Meiji foreign policy. It provided the context in which the Meiji leaders acted and a model for them to follow.

The imperialism that the Japanese encountered in the nineteenth century was quite different from the imperialism they had encountered two and a half centuries earlier. The Portuguese, the Spanish, the English, and the Dutch who arrived in Japan during the sixteenth and early seventeenth centuries had been the vanguard of early modern trading empires, interested less in acquiring territory than in inserting themselves into regional trade networks in East Asia and establishing small trading outposts to sustain their commercial activities. Theirs was an entrepreneurial expansionism, bolstered by crown or church in most cases but spearheaded by bold explorers, adventurous merchants, or enterprising courtiers, often operating within the framework of a chartered company. Indeed, these early empires may be seen as trade diasporas, involving only a handful of Europeans, driven by dreams of gold and personal glory, but only tenuously linked to the metropolitan society. By contrast the Western empires confronting Meiji Japan forged far tighter links between metropole and periphery and engaged far broader social participation.

Nineteenth-century Western imperialism was *postnationalist* as well as *postindustrial*. The main agent of expansion was not the adventurous entrepreneur, nor the freebooting trading company, but the nation-state itself. Whatever tangle of private motives or initiatives may have prompted expansion, it was the nation-state that ultimately undertook the responsibility for the acquisition of new territories and new privileges abroad, that provided the military and financial resources to build new colonial regimes, and that provided a cloak of legitimacy for expansion. The acquisition of colonies or other overseas territories became one of the attributes of international status, state power, and even modernity. At the beginning of the nineteenth century the European "powers" had been dynastic regimes whose strength was measured by the size of their standing armies and who sought to dominate one another, but by its end they were ranked as well by the size of their navies, the output of their manufacturing sectors, and the extent of their non-European possessions.

What gave the nineteenth-century nation-state its political cohesion was the belief, though not necessarily the reality, that political boundaries conformed to ethnic or cultural boundaries. In Benedict Anderson's terms, they were "imagined communities" whose internal coherence rested on the presumption of linguistic or cultural unity and whose elites were assumed to share a common culture and language with the mass of the population. Since the modern nation-state was a "participatory" state in the sense that a mass public was seduced rather than coerced into supporting the incumbent regime, these new and often fragile feelings of shared tradition and destiny enabled political leaders to conscript mass armies and send them to war in the name of a higher "national" cause. And as the political franchise expanded, political leaders discovered that an imperialist foreign policy, festooned with appeals to "national ideals," "national pride," "national mission," or "national destiny" that promised some collective good, could be a powerful means to build popular political support.

The literate, enfranchised, newspaper-reading political publics in late nineteenth-century Europe were stirred by news of far-off jungle explorations, colonial battles, and naval encounters. Association with successful imperialist enterprises offered an empowering identity to the emerging mass publics. What glorified the nation glorified the national populace, no matter how dimly that glory was reflected in their own lives. Victories over the "natives" in far-off lands placed the low and powerless in the metropolitan society above the high and mighty in the colonial domains, and the acquisition of overseas territories appeared to add to the collective national wealth. Leaders as different as Napoleon III, Disraeli, and Bismarck all used jingoism to build support among the new mass publics, who vociferously applauded and consistently supported imperialist policies.[2] Indeed, some historians have argued that Western leaders deployed expansionist policies in order to divert attention from domestic social conflicts generated by industrialization—conflicts between countryside and city, capital and labor, or small enterprises and large—and to reintegrate conflicting forces in a grand national enterprise.[3]

While governments in the European imperialist powers could deploy

2. Cf. Hayes, *Generation of Materialism*, 228.
3. Cf. Wehler, "Bismarck's Imperialism, 1862–1890," 119–22.

common symbols—flag and country—to mobilize support for expansionist policies, the prenationalist societies they encountered could not. Their elites, often set apart from the masses by ethnic, religious, intellectual, or cultural barriers, found it difficult to mobilize broad resistance to the Europeans. They were also put at a disadvantage by their unfamiliarity with the framework of "international law" under which the European imperialist nations operated. This system of law was assumed to be universal among the "community of nations." When leaders in non-Western states ignored or "violated" international law out of ignorance, the Westerners frequently seized the moment to impose sanctions, including the establishment of their own dominion. Societies with no state organization at all were even more vulnerable since only nation-states were considered subject to international law. Many Western international legal theorists took the position that "backward" or "uncivilized" peoples had no sovereign rights over the territories they inhabited and that territorial rights should be recognized only if held by states able to protect its inhabitants. Such arguments, for example, sanctioned the European partition of sub-Saharan Africa.[4]

The imperialist powers would have been far less successful in imposing their dominion on others had they not been industrialized. The projection of state power overseas always moved in one direction—from the industrialized states of Western Europe and North America to the preindustrial regions of the globe. The technological and economic changes wrought by the industrial revolution empowered the Europeans to impose their will on others. Without the steamship and the railroad, the breech-loading rifle and the modern cannon, the telegraph line and the undersea cable, the dynamite charge and the steam engine, it is unlikely that the Western imperialist powers would have been able to expand as quickly as they did or perhaps even expand at all. As Daniel R. Headrick has noted, "There is no reason to believe that late nineteenth century imperialists were any more strongly motivated than their predecessors. The reason for their sudden success was a shift in technology, similar to the development of ocean-going ships some four centuries earlier."[5]

4. "Territorial sovereignty bears an obvious resemblance to ownership in private property.... As a result of this resemblance early international law borrowed the Roman rules for the acquisition of property and adapted them to the acquisition of territory, and these rules are still the foundation of law on the subject." Brierly, *Law of Nations*, 150.

5. Headrick, *Tentacles of Progress*, 5.

Industrialization upset the technological balance of power between the European powers and the rest of the world, and this imbalance made possible the rapid European successes in conquest and domination. Once European colonial empires disintegrated, often within a generation or two of their creation, it was easy to see how transient and fragile their technological advantage was. But in the early stages of industrialization, the possession of superior technologies, and the sense of superiority they conveyed to both dominator and dominated, made the encounter between the Western societies and the rest of the world a lopsided one. In the early seventeenth century the Japanese had thrown the Spanish, the Portuguese, and even the English out of their country without much fear of retaliation, but Commodore Perry and his four black steamships posed a threat that threw the country into a panic.

Industrialization not only extended the reach of Western political power but also enabled the Western economies to dominate the new global market. According to some estimates, between 1750 and 1913 the value of world trade increased more than fiftyfold, most of it in the hands of the Europeans and the North Americans. The peoples of Africa, South and Southeast Asia, and Oceania were no more able to withstand the impact of Western traders bearing machine-spun cotton yarn than they were able to resist Western troops armed with repeating rifles and Gatling guns. The penetration of distant markets went hand in hand with the expansion of European political dominion. Indeed, the first steps toward political dominion often began with attempts to force open doors to markets barred by restrictive political or institutional barriers intended to keep foreign goods out. The Westerners also began to consume a larger and larger volume of goods from the non-Western world. At first, with the exception of items like tea or spices, raw materials were imported to feed the burgeoning textile industry—cotton, silk, and even wool; then, as technology advanced came new types of raw materials—palm oil, rubber, tin and mercury, and eventually petroleum not found in Europe; and finally imported foodstuffs became increasingly important to the Western diet—not only exotic tropical goods like coffee, cocoa, and bananas but even wheat, beef, and dairy products.

The expansion of external markets helped to sustain economic growth in the industrial economies. In the early part of the century the British, who had the most advanced industrial economy, discovered that manufacturing output eventually reached the point where it ran ahead of domestic demand and required external markets for surplus production. Usually the most important outlets for exports were to be found in other relatively industrialized economies, but for mass-produced goods, particularly cotton textiles, the British began to seek more distant markets in Latin America, Africa, and Asia. At the same time, the growth of manufacturing and the shift of workers out of agriculture created new demands for foodstuffs and raw materials that could be satisfied by imports from these new customers.

The search for new markets and new sources of raw materials became more intense during the pan-European "great depression," a long-term slowdown in economic growth in the Western European economies that lasted from the 1870s down through the 1890s, more or less coinciding with the era of "new imperialism." Visions of "overproduction" at home led officials, manufacturers, merchants, and other businessmen to argue that vigorous export policies, protective tariffs, and colonial expansion were essential to national prosperity.

As trade expanded, so did Western investment in the world outside the West. The new world market required the improvement of harbors, the building of interior roads and tunnels, new networks of rail lines, and underseas cable systems. For example, between 1825 and 1920 world railway mileage expanded from 5,000 miles of track to 675,000, most of it concentrated in Europe and North America but nearly one-quarter of it in Latin America, Asia, Africa, and Australasia. Like the world trade system, this world railway system was devised for Western ends to increase access to markets and raw materials, to extend political and military reach, or to facilitate the migrations and settlement of Western colonists. There was also much investment in extractive industries—mines, plantations, and oil fields that produced the raw materials Europe was consuming in ever greedier portions. By contrast, since the Westerners saw no need to stimulate competition for their own exports, relatively little Western capital flowed into manufacturing facilities in the non-Western world.

Industrial technology, and the wealth and power it created, gave the Western imperialist nations the novel idea that they were entitled to dominate the rest of the world. In earlier centuries the Westerners had seen themselves as morally superior to non-Western peoples, particularly those who had been conquered, but they had not necessarily seen themselves as materially or politically superior. In the sixteenth century Portuguese and Spanish missionaries described Japan as a "heathen" country, but they also found its people as intelligent, courteous, industrious, and vigorous as any in the world; and in the seventeenth century a Dutch visitor like Engelbert Kaempfer marveled at the flourishing commerce revealed in the bustling ports, highways, and towns he encountered on the road to Edo. By the mid-nineteenth century, however, "progress" came to be measured in terms of material wealth, and technological mastery became a touchstone to separate the "advanced" from the "backward," and a new sense of inherent European superiority opened a yawning gulf between imperialists and imperialized.[6] The social distance between the Westerners and subordinate peoples was underlined by obvious differences in physique and skin and hair color and magnified by the pervasiveness of race thinking and social Darwinism.

THE ADVANCE OF WESTERN IMPERIALISM IN EAST ASIA

In East Asia the first stage of imperialist penetration took the form of "informal empire," or what John Gallagher and Ronald Robinson have called the "imperialism of free trade." As this term suggests, the goal was not to establish direct political control or formal colonies but instead to exercise less direct and visible forms of domination.[7] In East Asia the essence of British policy was, as Gallagher and Robinson suggest, "trade with informal control if possible; trade with rule when necessary." States such as China, Japan, and Korea were too weak to resist Western demands for trade, but they were strong enough to deter conquest or occupation by force. The British therefore chose to negotiate trade agreements under the threat or limited use of force rather than to attempt military conquest or subjugation. In any case, since British military and naval power was finite, and indeed was stretched rather thin as the empire expanded in the nineteenth century, the technique of "informal imperialism" was a parsimonious means of extending domination.[8]

As in other parts of the world outside the West, when the British encountered "closed" markets but did not wish to bear the costs of governing the local population, they advanced their commercial interests under the cloak of free-trade ideology. Arguing that the laws of economics—and sometimes the law of God—required societies to trade

6. Cf. Strachey, *End of Empire.*
7. Gallagher and Robinson, "Imperialism of Free Trade."
8. As Grover Clark observed many years ago, "Where economic advantage could be secured without actual annexation of territory, it was felt perhaps as well to avoid the complications and responsibilities which went with political control." Clark, *Place in the Sun,* 28.

freely with one another, the British negotiated treaties that gave them privileged trading enclaves.[9] Such treaties—usually called "treaties of free trade and friendship"—were signed with China in 1842, 1858, and 1860, with Japan in the 1850s, and with Korea in the 1880s. Essentially these treaties were "unequal contracts" signed under duress—the explicit or implicit threat of force—which gave the British and other Western powers rights and privileges that went unreciprocated. This asymmetrical structure, later dubbed "the unequal treaty system," was a classic expression of "informal empire." And while these treaties were later viewed as a matter of national humiliation, at the time they checked more predatory forms of imperialist penetration.

By the last third of the century, however, the Western imperialist powers turned to more aggressive tactics. To be sure, Western powers continued to be interested in opening markets, but beginning in the 1870s they began a frenetic competition for the acquisition of colonial territory, particularly in Africa but in Southeast Asia and the Pacific as well. "Between 1876 and 1915," notes Eric Hobsbawm, "about one quarter of the globe's land surface was distributed or redistributed as colonies among a half-dozen states."[10] Astonishingly, the European colonial powers acquired an average of about 240,000 square miles (an area somewhat larger than France) per year between the late 1870s and World War I. This new phase of European expansion was probably triggered by changes in the political map of Europe.[11] The redrawing of national boundaries on the continent left little room for further redivision or redistribution of territory, and the intra-European rivalries that had occupied the Western countries for centuries were displaced to other parts of the world, where weaker states and less developed economies remained easy prey to the growing military and economic strength of the Europeans. The territorial partition of sub-Saharan Africa among the major European powers during the 1870s and 1880s was the rawest and most immediate expression of this "new imperialism."

As the Western powers expanded in Africa, they not only brought new colonies under their control, they also developed new techniques of "informal empire": the "protectorate," the "sphere of influence," and

9. Gallagher and Robinson, "Imperialism of Free Trade."
10. Hobsbawm, Age of Empire, 59.
11. As C. J. Hayes noted many years ago, "[The new imperialism] followed hard upon the national wars which created an all-powerful Germany and a united Italy, which carried Russia within sight of Constantinople, and which left England and France eclipsed. It expressed the resulting psychological reaction, an ardent desire to maintain or recover national prestige." Hayes, Generation of Materialism, 220.

the "concession" or "leasehold." All were created in "international law" to minimize the likelihood of direct military conflict between competing imperialist powers. Under a "protectorate," such as the French deployed in Tunis and the British in Egypt, the imperialist state promised to guarantee the security of a dominated state; a protectorate was usually created by negotiated agreement and fell short of full colonial control. The "sphere of influence" (also called a "sphere of action" or a "sphere of interest") received general recognition at the Berlin Conference of 1884–85, which declared that the territory of a state might be under the "influence" as opposed to the "protection" or "sovereignty" of another. "Spheres of influence" were created by boundary-marking agreements among the imperialist powers, often without the consent of the dominated people, to forestall or to resolve standing disputes among them.[12] "Leaseholds" or "concessions," by contrast, were established when a dominated state agreed to let a dominant one "occupy and administer" part or all of its territory for a specific period. Like the "treaty of free trade and friendship," the leasehold was a temporary and unequal contract, but it was often a preliminary step toward long-term cession of territory.[13] The development of the Suez Canal in the 1850s and 1860s provided a model of how concessions could serve a complex set of military, economic, and diplomatic interests simultaneously.

By the time the "new imperialism" reached East Asia its territorial appetite had been sated to some degree. During the 1870s the Russians moved into the Ili River valley in Chinese Turkestan, and the British began to extend political control over the Malay Peninsula and into Burma. By the end of the 1880s the French, who had already conquered Cochin China and established a protectorate over Cambodia, had brought Annam and Tongking under its colonial control.[14] Although the Europeans were greedy enough to nibble on the borders of the

12. Agreements setting up "spheres of influence" might take any number of forms: agreements of one power to abstain from taking any actions that might lead to the acquisition of territory allotted to another; recognition by two powers of the special interest of one in the territory of a third; or an agreement by a subordinate state not to dispose of a piece of territory except to the dominant one. Lindley, *Backward Territories in International Law*, 207–46.

13. In 1890, for example, the Sultan of Zanzibar granted leaseholds to the British East Africa Company; in 1895 the company transferred its leasehold to the British government.

14. Shinobu Seizaburō, *Nihon gaikōshi*, 1:129. In late November the Japanese minister in Peking, Enomoto Takeaki, informed the government in Tokyo that the French were demanding the cession of Taiwan. Fearful that a French occupation of Taiwan would pose a threat to the Ryukyu Islands, the Japanese government offered to mediate between the French and the Ch'ing court on the condition that the Chinese fend off demands for Taiwan by agreeing to an indemnity payment and a grant of railroad concessions on the island. Needless to say, the Chinese refused the offer.

Ch'ing empire, none dreamed of swallowing China, where their main interests continued to be trade and markets. In any case, China was too vast to bring under control. But just as imperialist competition had escalated elsewhere by the 1890s, it escalated in East Asia too. Instead of pursuing formal empire, the Europeans sought leaseholds, concessions, and spheres of influence that would give them exclusive rights to raw materials, markets, or naval stations. In a sense, this "concession imperialism" was halfway between the "imperialism of free trade" and direct colonial rule.

The "free-trade imperialism" of the 1840s and 1850s had been a collective enterprise. The inclusion of "most favored nation" clauses in the early treaties with China and Japan assured that the gains enjoyed by one power would be enjoyed by all the others. In this sense, the imperialism of free trade in East Asia rested on a multilateral structure, with all of the powers sharing the same set of privileges. But in the 1890s the European competition that had produced the partition of Africa manifested itself as a "race for concessions" in China, with all the major powers trying to secure an economic or political enclave from which it could exclude the others. The runners in this race were driven by economic motives, as they always had been, but the urge to primp the national plumage by acquiring what their rivals got was no less important. As one American observer later described concession diplomacy:

> A concession was in effect a business favor granted by the conceding nation to the government of the diplomat who asked for it. An immediate result of granting to one foreign nation a business favor ... is to excite competition and jealousy among all other national representatives in that place. Each must succeed in wresting a similar profitable privilege ... or the prestige of his own nation is diminished.[15]

The mingling of nationalist with economic goals served to intensify the competition.

THE IMPERIALIST IMPULSE IN JAPAN

A world dominated by Western imperialism provided both context and model for the agents of Meiji modernization—the bureaucrats and politicians, the generals and the admirals, the entrepreneurs and financiers, the ideologues and intelligentsia. In much the same way that they imported, assimilated, and transformed other cultural and institutional

15. Sands, *Undiplomatic Memories*, 197–98.

structures from the Western world, they adopted imperialist practices as well. Given the successful example provided by the Western nations, it was natural to conclude that acquisition of overseas possessions, like building a modern army and navy, was essential to establishing Japan's bona fides as "civilized" state and society. Indeed, one is often struck by the absence of doubt about the appropriateness of imperialism as a policy or as a way of life. With the exception of a handful of dissidents like Kōtoku Shūsui, hardly a voice was raised in protest against a program of expansion. Disputes revolved around the speed, direction, and management of expansion, not its legitimacy, which was no more questioned than was the legitimacy of steam-driven machinery or constitutional systems. In this sense, the pursuit of an expansionist agenda was part and parcel of the larger mimetic project of the Meiji elites.

THE SEARCH FOR STATUS

The intrusion of the Western imperialists introduced the Japanese to a new way of defining their relationships with other societies. The imperialism of free trade provided their first, and rather ambiguous, lesson in the culture of imperialism. On the one hand, the "civilized countries" refused to recognize traditional practices of interstate relations within East Asia that rested on notions of suzerain-vassal relations and elaborate rituals of exchange. Instead, they insisted on a new system of "international law" (*rekkoku kōhō* or *bankoku kōhō*) that assumed that all members of the "community of nations" would deal with one another on the basis of equality and reciprocity.[16] By the mid-1860s works like Wheatley's *International Law* had been translated into Japanese, and the Japanese leadership accepted it as a fixed and universal system ("*tenri jindō no kōhō*," as Iwakura Tomomi put it) upheld by all "civilized nations."[17] They may have had an easier time accepting this new system than Ch'ing dynasty officials because traditional relations with

16. As Sanjō Sanetomi observed in a memorial to Iwakura Tomomi in 1871, "The purpose of treaties among the powers is both to maintain equal rights and refrain from mutual insults or aggression and to exchange the profits of trade under their procedures and regulations; moreover, since all countries, as a matter of course, enjoy equal rights, it goes without saying that these treaties must be based on equal rights.... It is the law of nations (*rekkoku kōhō*) that guarantees good will in intercourse and regulates the profits of trade. On the law of nations depends the maintenance of equal rights among countries by restraints on [national] strength, regulation of disparity in size, and support of the just principles of the laws of Heaven (*tenri*) and the Way of Man (*jindō*)." See Sanjō, "Iwakura tokumei zenken taishishi teimei kakkoku hōmon ni kansuru ken," in *NGB*, 4:67.

17. "Bei-ō shisetsudan haken no riyūsho," in Shibahara, Ikai, and Ikeda, *Taigaikan*, 17.

other countries did not place Japan at the center of its own world system. Rather, the *bakufu* had organized relations with Korea, China, the Ryukyus, and the Dutch on an ad hoc basis, dealing with each in a different fashion rather than trying to fit them into a ceremonial matrix designed to underline Japan's centrality.

On the other hand, gunboat diplomacy made it clear that some nations were more equal than others. While the Westerners denied the old ritual hierarchies, they created a new hierarchy of power, and the more "civilized" a country was, the higher it stood in that hierarchy. The Western nations gave lip service to the "equality of nations," but in practice they regarded themselves as on a higher level than those nations with whom they had concluded unequal treaties, including Japan. The Westerners justified extraterritoriality and consular jurisdiction, for example, on the ground that the laws of Japan were too "barbarous" and "uncivilized" for Westerners to submit themselves to. As the Japanese leaders came to understand better the nature of the imperialist world order, they realized what a considerable affront to national amourpropre the treaties with the Westerners were. Visceral xenophobes had rejected foreign intercourse in the 1850s and early 1860s because they thought that consorting with Western barbarians was polluting, defiling, and disgusting. By the late 1860s, however, the treaties came under criticism because they revealed national weakness and ignorance.[18] The Meiji leadership was acutely aware that the treaties with the Westerners had placed Japan in a subordinate place in the hierarchy of power. Needless to say, they put the blame on the *bakufu*. Even the departing shogun, Tokugawa Yoshinobu, in his letter of resignation as shogun, expressed the hope that a change in regime would enable the country "to maintain its rank and dignity among the nations of the world."[19]

18. For example, when the Ministry of Foreign Affairs urged the Dajōkan to bring the matter of treaty revision before the Shūgiin in January 1871, officials argued that existing treaties had been concluded at a time when the Japanese knew little about conditions abroad and the people lacked unity. The *bakufu* had no choice but to sign the treaties as a temporary expedient. But conditions had changed, the authority of the emperor had been restored, and the country was making progress toward "enlightenment," so it was appropriate to raise the question again. In any event, *ūchū no kōgi* required that Japan be established on equal and parallel standing with the Western powers. Shimomura, *Meiji shonen jōyaku kaiseishi.*

19. Center for East Asian Cultural Studies, *Meiji Japan,* 2:65. Similar sentiments were expressed in a memorial on foreign intercourse presented by the daimyos of Echizen, Tosa, Choshu, Satsuma, Aki, and Kumamoto, who urged that the country rid itself of narrow-minded xenophobia "in order to restore the fallen fortunes of the empire and to make imperial dignity respected abroad." Ibid., 2:79.

While the new government enjoined the populace to abide by the treaties and to refrain from antiforeign activity, privately its leaders brooded over how best to restore "imperial prestige" (kōi), "national prestige" (kokui), or "national power" (kokken). After all, many of them had begun their political lives as antiforeign jōi activists, and they chafed against the inferior international status of Japan. To be sure, the Meiji leaders worried about foreign economic domination or potential foreign territorial intrusions on the borders of the archipelago, but their early foreign policy was shaped by an almost obsessive concern with enhancing "national prestige" or "national rights."[20] Wherever the leaders might stand on other issues, they agreed that the achievement of symbolic and legal parity with the West through treaty revision was of the highest priority. Less than a year after the Restoration the foreign affairs office sounded out the Western diplomatic community about the possibility. As they quickly learned from rebuffs at the hands of Western diplomats like Sir Harry Parkes, however, treaty revision was a long-term task, requiring a program of massive self-strengthening, institutional change, and cultural reform. The Iwakura mission, originally intended to launch treaty revision negotiations with the Western powers, was transformed into a mission to explore the secrets of Western wealth and power firsthand.

Failure in this early effort at treaty revision did not deter the Meiji leaders from attempting to retrieve a degree of national dignity by restructuring relationships with China and Korea. Given its limited fiscal, political, and military resources, the Meiji government was in no position to embark on an expansionist policy in the 1870s and 1880s, but it could notch itself higher in the international hierarchy by doing to their neighbors what the Westerners had done to Japan. When the Meiji government sought diplomatic relations with China in 1870, it tried—unsuccessfully, to be sure—to extract an "unequal treaty" from the Ch'ing government modeled on Western treaties with China. Their assumption was that Japan, having embarked on a reform program, had clambered one or two rungs higher than the Chinese on the ladder toward "civilization." The Chinese, needless to say, did not share this assumption and rebuffed the Japanese demands. And when the Meiji leaders sent an expedition to "open" Korea in 1876, not only were they consciously mimicking the Perry expedition of twenty years before, but

20. In 1943 Ōkawa Shūmei observed that a policy to spread "the imperial dignity" was a positive expression of the "expel the barbarians" idea. Ōkawa, Ōkawa Shūmei zenshū, 2:780.

afterward they were eager to show the Koreans how easy it was to assimilate the benefits of "civilization."

The pursuit of international status continued to consume the Meiji leadership down through the 1890s. Indeed, as Itō Hirobumi noted in 1899, "the hope of competing with the Powers for leadership" lay behind the post-Restoration development of the country.[21] The Meiji leaders constantly fretted about how their policies would affect "national prestige." Whatever benefits or harm a particular policy might entail on other grounds, its effects on Japan's international standing always figured in the debate. And when the Japanese leaders were confronted with a "national humiliation," such as the Korean refusal to enter into Western-style diplomatic relations in the early 1870s or the Triple Intervention that forced a victorious Japan to return the Liaotung concession to China in 1895, they renewed their effort to establish Japan's "proper place" in the international order. Significantly, it was only when Japan consolidated its colonial empire that the Meiji leaders finally felt that Japan had been accepted as a full-fledged power by the Western nations.

STRATEGIC ANXIETY

The encounter with Western imperialism aroused a perennial anxiety over national security. In the 1850s, as young men, the Meiji leaders had watched helplessly as the gunboats of Commodore Perry sailed brazenly under the coastal defenses at Edo, and as *jōi* activists they had fulminated at the intrusions of the foreigners into the newly opened treaty ports. Even after the Restoration they still felt Japan to be at risk. As Iwakura Tomomi noted in a memorandum to Sanjō Sanetomi in 1869:

> Although we have no choice in having intercourse with the countries beyond the seas, in the final analysis those countries are our enemies. Why are they our enemies? Day by day these countries develop their arts and technology with a view to growing in wealth and power. Even a little country like Holland remains independent among the powers and submits itself to no other power. That is because the people's hearts, high and low, are united in revering their monarch and loving their state. Thus, every foreign country tries to place itself over other countries. Country A directs its efforts at country B, country B at country C—they are all the same. That is why I say, all countries

21. Komatsu, *Itō-kō chokuwa*, 332.

beyond the seas are our enemies. Therefore, henceforth, in dealing with foreign countries our great objective must be neither to sully the emperor's glory nor to impair our national rights.[22]

From the beginning, Meiji foreign policy was thus characterized by a "paranoid style"—a predilection to see outsiders, and particularly Westerners, as hostile.

This paranoid style may well have been nurtured by the *bakuhan* system, which functioned as an interstate system not unlike that of the Western "community of nations." While the domains lacked the sense of solid cultural or ethnic identity that characterized the nineteenth century Western nation-state, domain officials often saw themselves in direct competition with other domains, whether for preference at the *bakufu* court or for access to the national market centers of Osaka and Edo. In larger domains with stable boundaries and ruling dynasties, like Satsuma and Chōshū, strong feelings of domain autonomy—what Albert Craig once called "han nationalism"—encouraged them to maneuver for position at the *bakufu* court during the *bakumatsu* years.[23] The experience of working within the *bakuhan* system, where domains tried to push their way to the fore and domain leaders constantly looked over their shoulders at the competition, may well have fostered a paranoid style in foreign policy.

As Henry Kissinger once observed, however, even paranoiacs have enemies. The Meiji leaders were not haunted by groundless fantasies or empty apparitions. Throughout the 1870s and 1880s a series of events— Russian encroachments on the Chinese border, French seizure of Indo-China, British expansion into Burma and Malaya—reminded them that an aggressive Western imperialism was on the march in Asia. The war between France and China in 1883–84 was particularly worrisome, for it prefigured the imminent breakup of China, a possibility unimaginable a decade before. An 1884 cartoon in the *Marumaru chinbun*, for example, showed a foreigner (unidentified by nationality) dreaming of a grand banquet where the European powers carved up a Chinese pig, a favorite visual metaphor for China. But the dismemberment of China would likely be a bloody slaughter, not a peaceful feast, and the Jap-

---

22. *NGB*, 2.1, pp. 370–71. See also Oka Yoshitake, "Kokuminteki dokuritsu to kokka risei," in Takeuchi and Karaki, *Kindai Nihon shisō kōza*, 8:12.

23. See Albert Craig, *Chōshū in the Meiji Restoration*, passim. Even after the Restoration, Inoue Kaoru complained, local loyalties impeded the establishment of a unified nation: "It is nearly a decade since the Restoration, but the people still do not know what the change to monarchical rule means. Every time a law is issued they look back and think about their domain lord." Quoted in Yui and Obinata, *Kanryō Keisatsu*, 88.

anese were rightly concerned about how it would affect their own future.

By the 1880s anxiety about Western imperialism was common among the politically articulate. For example, a study of leading Tokyo newspapers, most associated with the "popular rights" movement, has shown that at the beginning of the 1880s their view of world affairs was highly pessimistic. International relations, their editorials emphasized, were governed not by law or morality but by force. The "civilized nations," it was clear, were engaged in a "struggle for the survival of the fittest," extending their dominion over non-Western peoples openly and without shame, and in this context the Japanese had to be prepared for the worst.[24] Foreign Minister Inoue Kaoru summed up this consensus in a long memorandum in 1887:

> The [European] countries are all devoting their power more and more to the colonization and development of overseas territories.... In India, Cambodia, Cochin-China, and elsewhere, the weak become prey for the strong.... During the past three or four years the European countries have expanded their power into Asia and Africa more than ever before, and they are brandishing their power in the Far East as well. Ah, the continents of Africa and Asia are about to become the cockpit of conflict among the Europeans.

The contest for overseas empire had become a "fixed policy" of all the European countries, who were willing to sacrifice men and millions to expand. And, what was most worrisome, independent Asian countries like Persia, Siam, and Korea were becoming the object of the "colonial policies" of the Westerners.[25]

While no longer fearful of direct Western aggression against Japan as they had been in the 1850s, the Meiji leaders were deeply concerned about the fate of neighboring countries. If Korea or China were to fall under the dominion of the Western imperialist powers, Japan would find itself increasingly vulnerable to Western pressure. In this sense, the late Meiji impulse to expand was aimed as much at denying territory to others as in acquiring it for Japan. As Yamagata Aritomo put it in the early 1890s, Japan had to maintain not only a "cordon of sovereignty" but a "cordon of interest," and this "cordon of interest" included the weaker neighboring countries that might become the object of Western imperialist aggression.

In its preemptive character Meiji expansionism reflected the strategic

---

24. Oka Yoshitake, "Meiji shoki jiyūminkenronsha no me ni eijiru tōji no kokusai jijō."
25. Shibahara, Ikai, and Ikeda, *Taigaikan*, 60–65.

impulses that lay behind much Western imperialism. In a provocative essay John Gallagher and Ronald Robinson have described the partition of Africa as the result of the desire of European leaders not to let rivals steal a march on them. What advanced were not the "frontiers of trade and empire, but the frontiers of fear." "A perpetual fumbling for safety in the world at large," they observed, "drove the powers to claim spheres, to proclaim protectorates, to charter companies; but in almost all cases this was done with no purpose other than to keep out others whose presence could conceivably inconvenience a national interest, no matter how speculative or unlikely."[26] The calculus of the European leaders, like that of the Meiji leaders, assumed that the worst would always happen: if one's own country did not establish dominion over a particular territory, then a rival or enemy would. When one European state took action, the others were prompted to respond in kind, with paranoia feeding on paranoia. The result was an escalating rivalry driven by fervid imaginings that saw enemies on every side, and an international competition in which the play became the goal. It is not surprising that the Japanese leaders, aspiring to join the great game, became caught up in this peculiar psychology.

INCORPORATION IN THE WORLD ECONOMY

Contact with the imperialist West incorporated Japan into the Western-dominated world economy. For a society that had managed to feed, clothe, and shelter itself for centuries without extensive external economic contacts, this was a wrenching experience, but it also gave the Japanese access to all the modern technology that had made possible the sudden explosion of Western domination. Before the Restoration the *bakufu* and the domains had imported foreign gunboats, small arms, and munitions in a desperate attempt to build up the country's defenses against Western intrusion; they had even attempted to build steam engines and smelting furnaces. Military technology transfer continued under the new government, which invested heavily in the production of weapons, munitions, and ships. In the near term the new technology permitted the Meiji leaders to unify the country and crush internal dissent, but in the long run it enabled them to project Japanese power abroad.

26. John Gallagher and Ronald Robinson, "The Partition of Africa," in Bury, *New Cambridge Modern History,* 11:615–17.

The acquisition of advanced technology also created new needs and demands that could be satisfied only by increased contact with the outside world. For centuries the Japanese had been content to haul goods and travelers overland on either the backs of animals or the backs of men; after contact with the West they suddenly found themselves in need of iron rails, steam engines, and rolling stock, all of which had to be obtained from the West. As the result of such new demands, the economy was suddenly inundated with finished goods and processed raw materials, which accounted for more than half of Japan's imports even at the turn of the century. Indeed, it was not until the eve of World War I that the Japanese were able to approach self-sufficiency in the production of military and naval weapons. Ironically, the program to defend Japan against Western economic and political encroachment thus threw Japan into greater dependence on the West.

The Japanese paid for imports by exporting agricultural products like tea and silk, but in the long run Japanese political and business leaders realized that Japan could survive in the Western-dominated global market only if the country became an exporter of manufactures as well. To acquire the machinery, technology, and raw materials required for continued industrial growth, and hence national prosperity, it had to sell higher-value-added products to the outside. By the 1890s government officials, businessmen, and even military leaders spoke of the need "to build Japan as a commercial and manufacturing country (*shōkō rikkoku*)" by shifting Japan's role in the world market from an exporter of agricultural goods to an exporter of manufactured goods. And this shift required Japan to find not only markets for its goods but also sources of raw materials to feed its burgeoning manufacturing sector.

None of this compelled the Japanese to acquire a colonial empire, but it did add another dimension to the strategic anxieties induced by Western imperialism. Neighboring countries like China and Korea were not only essential to the security of Japan but were also promising markets for Japanese goods; if these territories were to come under the exclusive control of the Western powers, then Japan would suffer economically as well as strategically. At the very least, incorporation in the world economy gave the Japanese a stake in maintaining free access to neighboring markets in East Asia, the only region in the world where they might compete with the more advanced Western economies. As Sakatani Yoshio, a key official in the Finance Ministry, observed in the late 1890s, "If one looks at the whole world today, there is no place for Japan to secure commercial and industrial profit but Asia. . . . If one asks where the products of our country are preferred and welcome, the answer is: China and Korea."[27]

The Meiji leaders were well aware that industrialization and expansion went hand in hand. They knew that European leaders invoked economic benefits to justify the acquisition of colonial territory (even when there was little evidence to support such claims) and that the European powers used trade, loans, and investments as an entering wedge for political penetration. By the 1890s the significance of economic penetration had crept into all Japanese discussions of regional foreign policy. In Asia Japan confronted not only the territorial ambitions of the Western powers but their commercial aggressiveness as well. In 1902 Foreign Minister Komura Jūtarō warned that Japan was lagging behind the Westerners in the race for economic advantage in Asia. "Competition through commercial and industrial activity and through overseas enterprises," he wrote, "is a phenomenon of grave importance in recent international relations. Its emergence has been most prominent in the Far East. For a number of years the Western countries ... have been zealous in expanding their rights in mining, in railroads, in inland waterways, and in various other directions on the Asian continent, especially in China."[28] Even though Japan had the most important interests in the area, it seemed to be doing little to meet the Western competition.

In short, the top Meiji leaders, like the leaders of other imperialist states, saw an inextricable linkage between economic competition and political competition, between economic penetration and territorial expansion. As Prime Minister Ōkuma told a group of businessmen and high officials in 1898: "If you ask what international interests are most fought over today, it is commerce."[29] It thus becomes difficult to disentangle the economic motives behind Japan's expansion from its search for international prestige and its strategic anxieties. Political and business leaders, who feared that opportunities for trade and investment would slip into the hands of the Western powers unless Japan were more aggressive in East Asia, feared a loss of political influence as well. For political as well as economic reasons, it was important that Japanese rather than Russians or Frenchmen build railroads in Korea, that Japanese as well as Englishmen build cotton mills in Shanghai, or that Japanese rather than Americans dominate the textile market in Man-

27. Daisankai nōshōkō kōtō kaigiroku, 652–53.
28. NGNSB, 1:206.
29. Daisankai nōshōkō kōtō kaigiroku, 42.

churia. And if political as well as market forces had to be brought to bear to secure these advantages for Japan, then that too should be an aspect of foreign policy.

OPPORTUNITIES FOR EXPANSION

In recent years historians of imperialism have drawn attention to the importance of conditions on the periphery in shaping the timing and direction of territorial expansion—what Ronald Robinson has called "peripheral" or "excentric" interpretations of imperialism.[30] While it is important to emphasize the ways in which Western imperialism pushed Meiji Japan toward an expansionist policy, it should be remembered that the acquisition of a colonial empire requires not only a motive but an object, that is, territory vulnerable to outside domination. To put the matter crudely, a successful policy of imperialism requires an available victim—a weaker, less organized, or less advanced society or state unable to defend itself against outside intrusion. For example, when Western nations encountered countries able to put up resistance, they eschewed a policy of direct domination. The ability of Japan to maintain its independence is a case in point. Had the country failed to modernize during the era of new imperialism, it might have suffered the fate of its neighbors in East Asia, subjected to ever deeper penetration of its economy and ever growing compromise of its sovereign independence by the Western powers. But because the Meiji leaders embarked on a program of self-strengthening to defend Japan against foreign encroachment, the European powers never attempted to exercise more direct domination over it.[31]

By contrast, the Western intrusion into East Asia revealed the weakness of China, traditionally regarded by the Japanese as the region's "great power." The defeat of the Ch'ing at the hands of the British during the Opium War was a profound shock to the samurai elite, who had long seen the country as a source of culture and learning. At first the revelation of Chinese weakness promoted the idea that Japan and China, which were "as close as lips and teeth," should stand together to defend East Asia against the intrusions of the predatory Western na-

30. Ronald Robinson, "The Excentric Idea of Imperialism, with or without Empire," in Mommsen and Osterhammel, *Imperialism and After*, 267–89.
31. An alternative explanation is that the Westerners were not as interested in incorporating Japan into the capitalist "world system" as they were in incorporating China. See Moulder, *Japan, China, and the Modern World Economy*.

tions. But gradually, since China remained unable to prevent the Western nations from nibbling away at its borders, the Meiji leaders grew more ambivalent toward their largest neighbor. From the late 1870s they began to regard the Ch'ing empire as their principal hypothetical enemy. And by the 1890s, after seeing China suffer a new series of defeats at the hands of the French and the Russians, the military high command had become confident it too could win a war with the Chinese.

Not surprisingly, many apologists of Japanese imperialism have suggested that if China had managed to carry out a capitalist revolution in the late nineteenth century as Japan had, then Japan might not have become an imperialist power. Hosokawa Karoku, the leading prewar historian of Japanese colonialism, argued that the modernization of China would have posed a "fatal obstacle" to Japanese expansion and the whole character of Sino-Japanese relations would have developed differently. But, he said, such was not the case. Preexisting economic and political conditions in each country resulted in quite different responses to Western intrusion. In "feudal Japan" the maturation of a "civil society" (*shimin shakai*) provided the foundation for a firm centralized government structure; in China, by contrast, a "feudal" structure had been abandoned two millennia before, yet feudal elements persisted in the densely populated countryside, blocking the emergence of a "civil society" or a strong centralized state. Japan's pattern of development enabled it to modernize; China's left it vulnerable to intrusion.[32] While it is tempting to dismiss this line of argument as blaming the victim for the assault, one should also recognize that uneven development played a significant role in creating a context for Japanese expansion.

Inevitably, then, the analysis of Meiji imperialism leads back to the question of why Japan was the first East Asian society to succeed at modernization, or to put it another way, why China, Korea, and Vietnam were less prompt in response to the challenges posed by the intrusion of nineteenth-century imperialism. The debate on this issue, which has intrigued historians and other observers for decades, has reached no resolution, and certainly none will be offered here; but the debate does serve to remind us there is no simple answer to the question of why Meiji Japan adopted a policy of colonial expansion and certainly no theoretical passe partout that can reduce its "causes" to internal factors. The Meiji leaders, no less than the leaders of the Western imperialist states, lived in an environment of conflicting impulses, fleeting oppor-

32. Hosokawa, *Shokuminchi*, 39–41.

tunities, and historical accident. About all that can be said with certainty is that by responding to the intrusion of Western imperialism by reconstructing Japan as a modern nation-state and by undertaking the industrialization of the economy, the Meiji leaders set themselves on the road to imperialist expansion.

THE IMPERIALIST COALITION IN MEIJI JAPAN

Whatever the shared characteristics of modern imperialist states, it is a truism that every case of imperialist expansion in the nineteenth century was a separate case, requiring separate analysis. What led the Gladstone cabinet to dispatch a military expedition to Egypt in 1882 was not precisely the same set of motives and circumstances that led King Leopold to acquire the Congo in 1885 or the French government to create the Indochinese Union in 1887. The reason for this diversity is clear: the adoption of an expansionist policy involved a coalition of groups or individuals, each with something quite different in mind. For example, the proselytizing missionaries, ambitious naval officers, and opportunistic politicians who promoted French expansion into Indo-China had common goals but not necessarily common interests. Nor did they pursue a common course of action. Yet the synergy of their parallel efforts created the momentum that finally led the French government to extend its dominion over Indo-China. Imperialism, in other words, is a collective enterprise, a bandwagon ridden by a diverse band of passengers who climb aboard at different times with different destinations but who are all heading in the same direction.

To understand any particular case of imperialist expansion, we must disaggregate the imperialist coalition. My purpose in this book is to carry out such a disaggregation. I will argue that Meiji imperialism, and more specifically expansion into Korea, was the product of a complex coalition uniting the Meiji leaders, backed and prodded by a chorus of domestic politicians, journalists, businessmen, and military leaders, with a subimperialist Japanese community in Korea. The Japanese annexation of Korea in 1910 will be described as the result of two separate but interlinked processes, one political, the other economic. The political process entailed the gradual extension of influence and control over the Korean state by the Meiji leadership; the economic process entailed the gradual penetration of the Korean market by an anonymous army of Japanese traders, sojourners, and settlers. The two processes were linked, each reinforcing the other. Every increase in Japanese political influence licensed new advantages for the Japanese expatriate community in Korea, and every new push of Japanese economic interests into Korean trade networks, landholding, or production buttressed, and sometimes justified, further advances in Japanese power. Symbiotic ties linked the two processes. Each was propelled by an independent energy, yet each nourished the other: the sword was the servant of the abacus, the abacus the handmaiden of the sword.

This book is therefore organized, perhaps somewhat artificially, into two narratives, one focused on the Japanese metropolitan leadership and their policies toward the Korean state, and the other on the Japanese expatriate community and their activities in the Korean market. The main actors in the first narrative are the oligarchs, bureaucrats, diplomats, generals, and business tycoons; the main actors in the second are ordinary travelers, settlers, sojourners, and petty businessmen. Since the mise-en-scène is the same, and since historical experience is more complex than historical monographs, actors from one narrative often wander into the other. But there is a point in keeping the two narratives separate: that is, the possibility of imagining that one could have taken place without the other. More specifically, it is possible to imagine that the Japanese penetration of the Korean market might have taken place even if the Japanese leaders had failed to expand their influence over the Korean state. To be sure, the reshaping of the Korean political economy, particularly after 1905, facilitated Japanese economic penetration. But in the long run the rapid modern economic development of Japan, and the relative lack of it in Korea, guaranteed that the economic relationship between the two countries would be asymmetrical.

The fundamental premise of this book is that the industrialization of Japan did not impel the Japanese leaders to adopt an imperialist policy in Korea but merely empowered them to do so. It is possible to imagine an industrialized Japan that was not imperialist, but it is difficult to imagine an imperialist Japan that had not been industrialized. As I have already argued, the industrialization of Japan can be taken as a given in any explanation of Japanese expansion into Korea, or indeed into other parts of East Asia, but it must be thought of as a necessary, not a sufficient condition. Neither narrative will include an analysis of why and how the Meiji leadership decided to industrialize; that is, in any case, a well-known story. Rather, I will attempt to peel apart the various layers of motivation that brought the Japanese to Korea and induced them to stay there. The purpose is the reconstruction of a mental world, not a material one.

By and large, one significant element is missing from both narratives —the Koreans themselves. Any complete understanding of why and how the Japanese succeeded in annexing the peninsula must consider the behavior of the Korean elite and ordinary population. As Ronald Robinson and others have pointed out, the analysis of imperialism should look at the periphery as well as the metropolis. Often what happens, or does not happen, on the periphery is the driving force behind imperialist expansion. There is a simple explanation of why the Koreans remain largely in the background, only occasionally thrust forward in this historical account: I cannot read Korean. The result is that both narratives reflect a Japanese perspective rather than a Korean one. By "perspective," however, I do not mean an interpretive perspective, which is solely my responsibility. Rather, I merely mean, quite literally, the vantage from which events are observed. For example, in 1905 the city of Seoul might have looked primitive, inconvenient, and backward to a Japanese newly arrived from Tokyo, but with its electric tram line and its scattering of Western-style buildings it might have seemed quite impressively modern to a Korean visitor from Ŭiju. This book will more often reflect the perspective of the traveler from Tokyo than the visitor from Ŭiju. In short, both narratives will deal with Japanese history rather than Korean history, or even Japanese-Korean history, if one can imagine such a thing.

PART ONE

■　■　■

CHAPTER I

The Korean Question, 1876–1894

In the minds of the feisty young Meiji leaders the treaty settlements of the 1850s had tarnished the national honor—or as they often put it, the "imperial prestige" (*kōi*). Iwakura Tomomi noted in late February 1869 that "it is extremely humiliating to our imperial land that foreign troops land in our ports and that foreigners in the treaty ports are punished by their own officials when they violate our country's laws."[1] But how best could the Japanese overcome their national humiliation? One obvious answer was to restore legal parity with the Western nations by seeking revision of the "unequal treaties," an effort that began less than a year after the establishment of the new government. But even before the departure of the Iwakura mission, sent to North America and Europe ostensibly to renegotiate the treaties, top government leaders realized it would take a program of far more sweeping reforms to convince the Westerners that Japan's laws were no longer in contradiction with the "public law of nations" (*bankoku kōhō*).[2]

In the early days of the new government, however, many officials, fired by antiforeign zeal and anxiety over national unity, favored more aggressive ways of reestablishing national prestige, even the use of military force, in order to rally the population behind a common cause that would overcome petty regional differences and interests. Even Ōkubo Toshimichi, who later enjoyed a reputation as the coolest realist within

1. *NGB*, 2.1, pp. 370–71.
2. *NGB*, 4:67–73; Ian Nish, *Japanese Foreign Policy, 1869–1942*, 18–20.

the Meiji leadership, was not immune to this view. In September 1869 he urged war with Russia over the Sakhalin question. At stake, he said, was not merely the territorial question but the nation's morale. A war with Russia would not only provide an opportunity to "rouse the hearts of the people of the realm," it would reassert "imperial prestige." The most urgent tasks of the day, he wrote, were to "erect the foundations of stability and unity in the empire, to shed the contempt of foreign countries, and to spread the glory of the Imperial House to the outside world."[3] In short, an aggressive foreign policy, even if it meant a military showdown, was essential to restoring national dignity and creating national unity.

It was in the context of this desire to restore national prestige and create national unity that Japan's early policy toward Korea took shape. During the Edo period the *bakufu* had carried on "neighborly relations" with Korea mediated by the Sō family, the daimyo of Tsushima. Until the middle of the eighteenth century the Korean court periodically sent ceremonial missions to the *bakufu* court at Edo, usually at the accession of a new shogun, and the Sō family, dependent on Korea for food supplies, had dispatched trade missions to the peninsula. The relationship had not been without its frictions, especially over questions of protocol. In 1711 the Koreans had been affronted when Arai Hakuseki, an adviser to the shogun, proposed to put the Korean monarch and the shogun on an equal ceremonial level by changing the shogun's title in official documents from *taikun* to *kokuō*. No Japanese, moreover, were allowed to travel to the Korean capital at Seoul, and the Japanese traders who came to Korea, as well as the representatives of the Sō family, were confined to the Tongnae *waegwan*, a small outpost near Pusan not unlike the Dutch factory at Deshima.

As part of its efforts to restore "imperial prestige," the new Bureau of Foreign Affairs proposed to change these arrangements. In late 1868, a retainer of the Sō family was dispatched to Pusan to inform the Korean authorities that a new imperial government had been established and that an envoy bearing a letter from the new emperor would be arriving shortly to arrange for a goodwill mission between the two countries. The Korean response revealed that the Korean court was firmly wedded to established protocol and was offended by the introduction of new symbols and new language into Japanese-Korean relations. The Korean authorities found it unacceptable that the documents brought by the mission bore a seal issued by the Meiji government instead of one the

3. Toyama, "Meiji shonen no gaikō ishiki," 135–39.

Korean court had authorized the Sō family to use. The documents also used the character *kō* [皇] rather than *taikun* [大君] to refer to the emperor. Since the Koreans used this character only to refer to the Chinese monarch, and since it implied ceremonial superiority to the Korean monarch, whose title was *ō* [王] (or *wang* in Chinese), it would mark the Korean monarch as the vassal or subject of the Japanese ruler. An Dong-jun, the local official charged with handling Japanese affairs (*waehak hundo*), thought the Japanese guilty of extraordinary arrogance and informed the Sō envoy that he could not countenance the arrival of a Japanese mission that in any way departed from the usual procedures.[4]

The Meiji government, confident that it was acting in accordance with the new "law of nations" introduced by the Westerners, saw itself as simply adjusting the relationship to the new domestic political situation. From their point of view, the emperor was not being renamed at all but simply inserted into the ceremonial relationship now that the shogun was gone; the name given the Japanese monarch should be a matter of no importance. As a Japanese memorial to the mayor of Tongnae pointed out in late 1869, many independent countries addressed the ruler of China as *huang ti* [皇帝] without becoming his vassal, so there was no reason why the Koreans should not use the character *kō* to refer to the Japanese ruler if that is what the Japanese wanted to call him. The Japanese leadership, in short, adopted a kind of cultural relativism, whereas the Koreans remained in a world of absolutes dominated by the "universal" system of interstate relationships centering on China.[5] Having failed to entice the Koreans into that system, the Tokyo government turned instead to reformulating its ties to China; but the Korean response, easy to construe as a "national insult," played into the hands of those who favored an aggressive foreign policy.

THE ORIGINS OF THE "SUBDUE KOREA" POLICY

From the outset the Korean problem was a magnet for those obsessed with Japan's international status. The Ministry of Foreign Affairs (and its predecessor, the Bureau of Foreign Affairs) was heavily populated with former loyalist (*jōi*) activists intensely sensitive to questions of

4. Key-hiuk Kim, *East Asian World Order*, 116–19; *NGB*, 2.1, pp. 205–8.
5. The cultural impasse was epitomized in an exchange between Sada Hakubo, a Japanese Foreign Ministry official, and An Dong-jun, the Korean inspector of Japanese affairs at Tongnae (Pusan). "Your code of ceremonies must be very old," said Sada. "Is it based on the T'ang and Ming examples?" "Not so new," replied An. "It is based on the precedents of Chou." Sada, "Sei-kan ron no kyūmondan," 45.

national prestige. From 1869 to 1871 the foreign minister was Sawa Nobuyoshi, one of the court nobles who had persuaded the Kōmei emperor to withhold his approval of the Harris treaty in 1858 and who had fled to Chōshū along with Iwakura and Sanjō in 1863 after Satsuma forces expelled the loyalist factions from Kyoto. In the lower echelons of the ministry were other less prominent though no less militant loyalists, some of them veterans of the imperial forces that overthrew the *bakufu* and waged campaigns against resistance to the Restoration. The ministry also attracted men who had advocated a forward policy toward Japan's neighbors. For example, Moriyama Shigeru, a Satsuma retainer who plotted with other comrades to occupy Ullŏng Island in 1869, was rewarded with a post in the ministry for his efforts and later played an influential role in the formation of policy toward Korea.

Officials in the Foreign Affairs Bureau (and later the Ministry of Foreign Affairs) made the earliest proposals for a policy of "subduing Korea" (*sei-Kan ron*) modeled on Western "gunboat diplomacy." By dispatching an emissary backed by military and naval forces, they hoped to force the Korean government into negotiations. There was no consensus, however, about what the ultimate goal of "subduing Korea" should be. For some advocates of *sei-Kan*, the dispatch of a military expedition was simply a way of forcing the Koreans to accept trade and diplomatic relations as they were understood under the "law of nations"; for others, a military expedition was intended to restore the old "tributary" relationships that allegedly had once linked Korea to Japan; and for still others, it was aimed at establishing a "fraternal alliance" between the two countries to present a united front to the foreigners. Few if any of the early advocates of "subduing Korea," however, appear to have envisaged the seizure of Korea as a colony or the establishment of direct control over Korea such as Japan maintained over Hokkaido. The purpose of "subduing Korea" was not conquest but the reordering of formal relationships.

The most prominent early advocate of a *sei-Kan* policy was Kido Takayoshi, the senior Chōshū leader in the new government and a junior imperial councillor.[6] In response to the "discourtesy" of the Koreans

6. In the early 1860s, under the influence of Yoshida Shōin, whose vision of Japan's future included the restoration of Korea as a tributary state, Kido had thrown himself into efforts to secure *bakufu* permission for Chōshū to colonize Ullŏng Island and to promote an invasion of Korea by Tsushima with Chōshū and Satsuma backing. Undoubtedly Kido expected such bold initiatives would enhance Chōshū's position in *bakumatsu* politics, but he also feared that one of the foreign powers, perhaps the French, would take over the peninsula if Japan did not. Key-hiuk Kim, *East Asian World Order*, 94–97.

toward overtures from the new government, Kido called for a forward policy. As he told Iwakura in late January 1869, if the Koreans did not acknowledge the error of their ways, Japan should condemn them publicly and launch an attack to establish Japanese influence in Korea. The question of national prestige was of great concern to Kido, but he saw other and perhaps more compelling reasons for launching an expedition. "If [the expedition is sent], the reactionary traditions of our nation will be altered overnight," he wrote in his diary. "By fixing our goals on an overseas land, we shall make advances in developing all sorts of practical skills and technology; and we shall wash away our undesirable practices of spying on one another, criticizing and reproaching each other, rather than reflecting each on his own self."[7] In short, Kido linked a military adventure in Korea to the solution of what he thought to be the most critical internal political problem: how to end the fragmentation of loyalty and authority inherited from the *bakuhan* system.

If deflecting political energies from domestic squabbles to foreign glory was one important rationale for a Korean expedition, another was a desire to preempt penetration of Korea by one of the Western powers. The Japanese knew in great detail about the abortive French and American expeditions to open Korea in 1866, and they were aware of continuing foreign military interest in the region. Of particular concern were the long-term intentions of the Russians, especially after the *Possadonick* incident in 1861, when a Russian warship put in at Tsushima demanding that the *bakufu* lease land there for a naval base. This incident convinced Katsu Kaishū, among others, that the Russians planned to use the island for future operations in Korea.[8] Anxieties persisted after the Restoration. In October 1869 a French adviser to the Ministry of Foreign Affairs wrote a memorandum warning that the Russians intended to establish a military base in Sakhalin to strengthen their strategic position in East Asia; if the Russians made their next move into Korea, the Japanese would find it impossible to maintain their independence.[9] Iwakura was sufficiently alarmed by this opinion that he consulted with Sir Harry Parkes, the British minister, as to whether it would be advisable to take military action against the Russians.

In 1869 Miyamoto Okazu, a lower echelon Foreign Ministry official,

7. Brown and Hirota, *Diary of Kido Takayoshi*, 1:167–68. For Kido's memorial on Korean policy, see *NGB*, 2.1, pp. 205–8.

8. Key-hiuk Kim, *East Asian World Order*, 90–95.

9. *NGB*, 2.3, pp. 70–73.

advanced similar concerns about the intentions of the foreigners in Korea. He warned that not only Russia but other Western powers had their eyes on Korea and that if one of them swallowed up Korea it would inflict "everlasting harm" on Japan. Since Japan at the moment had neither the military power nor the wealth to annex Korea itself, he suggested that a Japanese emissary backed by gunboats be sent to negotiate a "fraternal alliance" with Korea and that the "semi-independent" Korea be joined in a "united federation" with Japan. Under such an alliance Japan would take charge of Korean diplomacy as well as reform of its calendar, its era names, its finances, and its military affairs, and it would work to "wash away the stain of out-moded customs" in Korea.[10]

In late 1869 militants in the Ministry of Foreign Affairs recommended that the Dajōkan authorize the dispatch of an imperial envoy escorted by gunboats to establish a pact with Korea. As a preliminary step, however, it was decided instead to send a mission to Korea to find out, among other things, whether Russia was poking its "venomous snout" into the peninsula.[11] The official chosen to head the fact-finding mission was Sada Hakubo (Motoichirō), a former loyalist from Kurume who had served briefly in the new imperial army after the Restoration and who had long been a vocal advocate of a strong policy toward Korea. Like Kido, Sada had been obsessed with the Korean problem since the 1860s. Imprisoned for alleged ties with the Chōshū loyalist movement, he whiled away his days discussing the foreign problem with his fellow prisoners. In Sada's view Korea was a traditional "vassal state" or "dependency" of Japan, and it was time to reassert Japan's dominion there. After his release Sada remained obsessed with the Korea question and twice memorialized the Dajōkan to take action. Since the days of Ōjin, he argued, Korea had submitted itself to Japan, and it was appropriate to take advantage of the Restoration to extend Japan's hand there once more. "Those who are early," he warned, "control others; those who are late are controlled [by others]."[12] For the hawks in the ministry, Sada's views made him the ideal leader of the mission to Korea, and he was accompanied by Moriyama Shigeru and Saitō Sakae, two Foreign Ministry officials with equally aggressive views on Korean policy.

After its return in spring 1870 the Sada mission produced a long in-

10. *NGB*, 2.2, pp. 862–64.
11. *NGB*, 2.3, pp. 265–68.
12. Sada, "Sei-kan ron no kyūmondan," 38–39.

telligence report on Korean politics and military strength, trade opportunities, and relations with China. The report also recommended a plan to dispatch a military expedition if the Korean court did not apologize for its earlier insolence toward Japan. The plan was elaborate and specific: a force of thirty battalions was to launch a coordinated attack. A main force of ten battalions landing on Kanghwa Island was to strike directly at Seoul while subsidiary forces moved south through the provinces of Kyŏngsang, Chŏlla, and Ch'ungch'ŏng and north through Hamgyŏng, P'yŏngan, and Hwanghae. Once these forces converged on Seoul, the Korean government was sure to collapse; if the Chinese intervened, the Japanese forces could handle them easily. The whole operation, Sada opined, would take only fifty days; to finance it, he modestly proposed that Japan sell its territorial rights in Sakhalin to the Russians. This wildly unrealistic plan, based on wishful thinking rather than cautious assessment of Japan's capabilities, found few strong supporters other than Moriyama and Saitō in the Ministry of Foreign Affairs, and none at the highest levels of government.[13]

While Sada's memorial reveals no purpose other than chastisement for Korean insults, and certainly no long-term plan for control or annexation of Korea, it does provide a useful summary of the arguments advanced in support of a "subdue Korea" policy. First, he raised the specter of foreign penetration. The French, licking their wounds after their unsuccessful attempt to open Korea in 1866, were likely to try again, and both the Russians and the Americans were interested as well. "If Imperial Japan passes this great opportunity to the foreigners," Sada wrote, "we will lose our lips [i.e., Korea] as a consequence, and one day our teeth will surely suffer from the cold." Second, a military expedition would reap more concrete economic rewards than colonizing Hokkaido. "Korea is a gold mine, and rice and wheat are abundant. With one sweep we can mobilize the manpower, the mineral resources, and the grain [in Korea] and use them in Hokkaido." Finally, as Kido had argued earlier, the dispatch of an expedition against Korea would ease social and political unrest brought on by the abolition of the domains and the displacement of the samurai class. Japan "is suffering from the problem of too many military men rather than a shortage thereof.... The belligerent, when discontent, contemplate revolt. At this time when there is fear of civil war in our country, if we undertake the Korean expedition and make the bitter cup of samurai grievance spill

13. NGB, 3:131–43.

[in Korea], we can massacre Korea with a single stroke, polish our military system, and demonstrate to the world the imperial glory (kōi)."[14]

Although the Foreign Ministry did not forward Sada's plan to the higher levels of government, a military expedition against Korea was one of the three alternative policies it recommended to the Dajōkan in May 1870. The first alternative was to break off relations with Korea and withdraw all Japanese living on the peninsula until Japan built up its strength to deal with the problem; the second was to send a gunboat mission, headed by Kido Takayoshi, to negotiate a new treaty and to go to war with Korea if it rebuffed the mission; the third was to send an envoy to China to negotiate a treaty with the Ch'ing court as a first step toward asserting Japanese superiority over Korea.[15] Foreign Ministry officials were unenthusiastic about breaking off relations since it would leave Korea exposed to a takeover by Russia or some other foreign power, and they argued that the dispatch of a mission to China was too great an expense. Clearly sentiment within the ministry favored the dispatch of a gunboat mission to Korea—and so did Kido Takayoshi. "If the Koreans do not yield to universal principles (kōri)," he wrote in July 1870, "we must make a resolute decision, and therefore we must quickly prepare soldiers, warships, military supplies and weapons."[16]

Ōkubo Toshimichi, whose influence within the government was growing, opposed the idea, and so did Iwakura. Instead, the government chose the third alternative, dispatching Yanagiwara Sakimitsu, a former court noble who favored some sort of preemptive action in Korea, to begin negotiations with the Chinese.[17] In frustration and disappointment, the hawkish Kido offered his resignation as an imperial councillor, but with the departure of the Yanagiwara mission to China, the discussion of a military expedition to "subjugate Korea" receded from the top of the diplomatic agenda, which shifted to other vexing issues— the revision of the foreign treaties, the mission to the West, the negotiations with China over the Ryukyu Islands, and the handling of the Sakhalin question.

Instead of trying to force the Koreans into accepting a new set of

14. NGB, 3:138–43.
15. NGB, 3:144–45
16. NGB, 3:145–146.
17. Yanagiwara thought that the Russians might well take advantage of the Franco–Prussian War to extend their power over Korea. NGB, 3:149–50.

diplomatic symbols and practices, the Japanese government began to change them unilaterally. To a degree, this shift in tactics resulted from the abolition of the domains, including Tsushima, in August 1871. This meant that it was simply no longer possible for the Sō family to act as intermediaries with the Koreans. But equally important was the appointment of a new foreign minister, Soejima Taneomi, a loyalist from Hizen who had briefly studied law at Nagasaki with Guido Verbeck. Familiar with the "law of nations" through his acquaintance with W. A. P. Martin's translation of Wheaton's treatise on international law, Soejima pursued a strong forward policy in East Asia, using the new international rules in his dealings with the Chinese and the Koreans and with the Westerners. During his tenure as minister of foreign affairs, the Japanese slowly began to shut down the old apparatus managed by Tsushima, laying the groundwork for the opening of trade and the establishment of "normal" diplomatic relations.

In September 1872 Hanabusa Yoshimoto, a foreign ministry official, was assigned the job of transferring control over the *waegwan* from the Sō family to the Foreign Ministry. Sending home all but a handful of local functionaries, he renamed the *waegwan* as the legation of Japan. In April 1873 Hirotsu Hiroshima, a foreign ministry official in charge of Korean relations, arrived at Pusan to take up office as the new "Commissioner of the *Waegwan*." Since trade had fallen off sharply as a result of the frictions generated the previous year, agents of the Mitsuigumi, disguised as merchants belonging to a Tsushima trading house, arrived shortly after Hirotsu to revive business with local merchants. From the Japanese point of view, the symbolic transformation was complete. No longer a symbol of traditional subordination of the Sō family to the Korean court, the *waegwan* had become a foothold for the new "civilized" set of institutions through which the Japanese intended to conduct their formal relations with Korea.

This blatant defiance of precedent elicited a new barrage of objections from the local Korean authorities. In late May 1873 a wall notice posted on the residence of the chief guard (*sot'ongsa*) of the *waegwan* attacked the Japanese for their outrageously aberrant behavior:

[The Japanese] do not feel shameful in adopting institutions from the foreigners and changing their appearance as well as their customs. We should not consider them as "Japanese" any more nor should we admit them into our territory. We should not allow [the Japanese] to enter our territory on a steamer, which is also a violation of established rules. . . . We have set forth rules and regulations with Tsushima concerning trade, and both [Korea and

Japan] should prohibit illegal trade. Judging from how the Japanese behave recently, we may call [Japan] a lawless country.[18]

In a dispatch to Tokyo, to which a copy of the wall poster was attached, Hirotsu reported that local Korean officials were making it difficult for the Japanese in the *waegwan* to obtain food and other daily necessities and were obstructing the activities of Japanese merchants. This report brought the Korean problem once more to the attention of the highest levels of the Japanese government, provoking a debate on Korean policy that rumbled on into the fall of 1873.

THE "SUBDUE KOREA" DEBATE, 1873

To understand the 1873 debate over Korea, we must remember, first, that the Korean question was simply one of many issues the top leaders of the government were grappling with, and for many it was by no means the most important; and second, that the substance of the Korean question was of less moment to many participants in the debate than the question of how it might affect political alliances and alignments in the highest echelons of the government. These observations should be borne in mind lest one leap to the easy conclusion, which many historians seem to take for granted, that a Japanese invasion of Korea might have taken place in 1873. The evidence suggests to the contrary that the "subdue Korea" policy was at best a minority view and that the composition of that minority shifted often and significantly. Not everyone who left the government in protest in October 1873 had supported a "subdue Korea" policy in the early summer, nor did all of its early advocates support it until the very end. In other words, the crisis of 1873 was less a turning point in the direction of Japanese foreign policy than a turning point in the makeup of the national leadership. The most important consequence of the debate was not the annexation of Korea in 1910 but the samurai revolts and protest movements of the late 1870s.

It is difficult to imagine why the Korean issue suddenly became the focus of such heated debate at the highest level of the government. The Korean response to the unilateral Japanese attempts to establish a diplomatic outpost and regular trading relations at the *waegwan* hardly represented an escalation of their rhetoric, let alone a change in attitude. Until the arrival of Hirotsu's report, the most pressing foreign policy issue before the government had been how to respond to the slaughter of fifty-four Ryukyu Island fishermen by Taiwanese aborigines in 1872.

18. *NGB*, 6:282–83; translation according to Limb, "Sei-Kan Ron," 139.

Indeed, the top government leaders in Tokyo were moving slowly toward a decision to launch a punitive expedition against Taiwan. Saigō Takamori, with the backing of Ōyama Tsunayoshi, the governor of Kagoshima, had agreed that a Taiwan expedition was necessary, perhaps as a "way to give vent to [anger over the reduction of samurai pensions] outside the country." When the Hirotsu report arrived, Foreign Minister Soejima was in China trying to ascertain the status of China's relations with Taiwan as well as Korea and the Ryukyus.

The news of fresh insults by the Koreans deflected attention away from the Taiwan problem. Perhaps, as Ōkuma Shigenobu later suggested, a Korean insult was less tolerable to the Japanese leadership than was Taiwanese violence,[19] or perhaps these insults provided the advocates of an assertive diplomacy an excuse to precipitate a resolution to the Korean problem. With Soejima out of the country, Ueno Kagemori, the acting foreign minister, asked the Dajōkan how to respond to the Koreans. Stressing the gravity of the recent incidents as an infringement on "imperial dignity" and "an insult to the nation," he proposed that army and naval vessels be sent at once to protect the Japanese residents in Tongnae and that an emissary backed by military force be dispatched to carry out negotiations in accord with "the principles of public justice and reason" (*kōri kōdō*).

A proposal to send a military expedition against Korea came up for discussion in the Dajōkan on June 12, 1873. At issue, however, was not a "conquest" of Korea but a show of military force for limited diplomatic purposes: the protection of the Japanese at Tongnae and the opening of treaty negotiations. Itagaki Taisuke called for a military expedition, arguing that the government had a responsibility to protect its nationals. While sentiment at first favored Itagaki's view, Saigō Takamori, usually seen as the fiercest advocate of *sei-Kan* policy, spoke against it. A military expedition would arouse suspicion not only in Korea but in the rest of the world, he said, and the foreigners might well intervene to protect Korea. It would be better to send an imperial emissary before resorting to military action; if the Koreans harmed or killed the emissary, only then would Japan have a legitimate excuse to take

19. "We, as a nation, were more infuriated over Korea than Taiwan. Why? As far as Taiwan is concerned, the aborigines are uncivilized tribes and their murder of shipwrecked aliens and robbery are acts common to barbarians, or so we could comfort ourselves; but Korea had been our subject country for more than two thousand years, although our past regimes neglected to control the country; now Korea became boldly contemptuous, looking down on us as if it were a superior country." Ōkuma Shigenobu, as quoted in Limb, "Sei-Kan Ron," 151.

military action. Convinced by these arguments, Itagaki withdrew his original proposal, and together with Etō Shimpei and Gotō Shōjirō, gave his support to Saigō's plan.

When Foreign Minister Soejima returned from China, he was surprised to learn that his colleagues were contemplating an expedition to Korea rather than one against Taiwan. Neither he nor Sanjō thought it would be a good idea to send Saigō as imperial emissary to Korea. Soejima, who considered himself well acquainted with the Korean problem, probably wanted to go himself, hoping to cap his triumphant negotiations with China with success in Korea. Although he did his best to put off resolution of the issue, Saigō continued to lobby for the job.[20] Rumors circulating in the capital suggested that many within the military, especially among the Satsuma men, favored military action. In the fall of 1873, after Saigō left the government, Itō Hirobumi told Kido Takayoshi that "army officers from Satsuma have insisted on the attack on Korea from the start and they have agitated for this policy all over the country" and that "two-thirds of the men in the Imperial Guard lean toward the view that Korea should be subjugated."[21] What Saigō himself really had in mind remains a mystery. He may simply have hoped for a triumphant negotiation at Seoul which would bring him the same personal glory that the mission to Peking had brought Soejima. The chance that he might be assassinated was remote, and Saigō's declaration of his willingness to die was a bit of hyperbole to strengthen his candidacy.[22] By contrast, Itagaki Taisuke appears to have been a much stronger advocate of military force.

As is well known, although the Dajōkan decided on August 17 to

20. Mori, *Meiji rokunen seihen no kenkyū*; a shorter version of the study was published as *Meiji rokunen seihen*. Mori argues that it is a mistake to take at face value Saigō's declared willingness to die. In his view, Saigō suspected that Ōkuma, Etō, and Ōki would support the appointment of their countryman Soejima as imperial emissary. To win Itagaki's support for his own candidacy, Saigō tried to demonstrate his sincerity, even to the point of self-sacrifice, by suggesting that the emissary might be assassinated. His admission of willingness to die was peculiar since Itagaki was not personally close to Saigō and had often disagreed with Saigō on policy issues; it was only in his letters to Itagaki that he talked about assassination. In fact, Saigō frequently suggested that tensions with Korea might be resolved through negotiation. Although he had built a reputation as a bold and fearless military leader, Saigō had more often resorted to negotiation than to force to resolve political conflict. The most famous example, of course, was his negotiation with Katsu Kaishū to arrange a peaceful surrender of Edo castle in 1868. Mori, *Meiji roku nen seihen*, 124–26.
21. Brown and Hirota, *Diary of Kido Takayoshi*, 2:386–87.
22. In his report to the Dajōkan on October 15, Saigō insisted that throughout the crisis his main interest had been the improvement of relations with Korea, not conquest, and certainly not annexation or colonization. Mori, *Meiji roku nen seihen no kenkyū*, 121–23.

appoint Saigō as imperial envoy to Korea, the next day Sanjō informed Saigō that the appointment was not to be announced until Iwakura and the rest of his mission arrived home in September. For Iwakura, however, the Korean question was not of the highest priority. On his return he found a host of other issues waiting for him: difficulties created by the resignations of Inoue Kaoru and Shibusawa Eiichi from the Ministry of Finance, the troublesome behavior of Shimazu Hisamatsu, the continuing friction between Japanese settlers and Russian soldiers on Sakhalin, and the resolution of the Taiwan problem. It was not until a month after his return that Saigō's appointment as imperial emissary to Korea once again came before the Dajōkan.[23]

The oft-described debate finally took place on October 14–15. The issue, framed by Sanjō in a memorial to Iwakura on October 4, was the purpose of the imperial mission.

> Is the object of the mission to Korea to wipe away the national insult and restore our national honor by restoring our traditional friendship and improving neighborly relations with Korea, or is it to make it ultimately into a dependent country (fuyokoku)?
>
> As a separate question, will it lay a careful basis for future foreign policy, or is it no more than a temporary tactic related to domestic affairs?
>
> Will the mission anticipate the outbreak of hostilities, or will it not? And even if it does not anticipate hostilities, if they should prove unavoidable, will we engage in war?
>
> What are the advantages in hostilities with Korea? Will the goal of hostilities be the acquisition of territory, or will it simply be to chastise the Koreans?[24]

Iwakura, Ōkubo, Ōkuma, and Ōki Takatō insisted on postponing the mission, but the rest of the Dajōkan, including Sanjō, decided to confirm the earlier decision to appoint Saigō as emissary. Iwakura thought settlement of the Sakhalin problem should have priority, and Ōkubo feared that a gunboat expedition would provoke a war that Japan was unprepared for. The next day Saigō, who absented himself from the meeting, sent a memorial arguing against a military expedition to protect the Japanese at Tongnae; it would be better to send one to improve relations. In other words, Saigō did not seem to share Ōkubo's assumption that the mission would inevitably result in war or that its purpose should be to provoke Korea.[25]

Whether Saigō's mission to Korea would have resulted in hostilities

---

23. In a letter to the Japanese minister in Paris, Iwakura expressed the view that there was no particular need to act quickly in resolving the Korean issue. Ibid., 150, 160–61.
24. Ibid., 164–65.
25. Ibid., 184

remains an unanswerable question. On October 23, after a week or so of behind-the-scenes maneuvering, Iwakura told the emperor that Saigō should not be sent. His brief was a simple one: "Upon serious consideration, I venture to say that it is not more than four or five years since the Restoration, the foundation of the nation is not very solid, political institutions have not yet been well organized, and, though internal security seems to be maintained, there is no telling what trouble may occur. Under such circumstances dealings with foreign countries should not be viewed lightly."[26]

Ōkubo and other key officials, wary of embarking on a foreign adventure when internal reform was far from complete, backed Iwakura's position on practical grounds. Katsu Kaishū, the navy minister, told Sanjō that the navy was not ready to fight Korea and that he would resign if war were declared; only after the navy acquired additional warships abroad would it be possible to embark on an expedition. Similarly, Yamagata Aritomo thought that the army was unprepared for an overseas expedition, and other important figures in the army including Saigō's brother Tsugumichi, Torio Koyata, and Yoshii Tomosane were opposed as well. In September Kuroda Kiyotaka, an influential Satsuma leader, told Saigō that he thought the Sakhalin question deserved priority over Korea and asked him to support that view. And key younger officials like Itō Hirobumi (Ministry of Industry), Inoue Kaoru (Ministry of Finance), and Terashima Munemori expressed their opposition to the expedition.

Perhaps most interesting was Kido Takayoshi's turnabout on Korean policy. In mid-August he sent Sanjō a memorial arguing against military expeditions to Taiwan or Korea. While he agreed that it would be appropriate to punish Taiwanese violence against the Ryukyu islanders and to chastise the "insulting" behavior of the Koreans, the country was facing more urgent problems, especially ordering national finances and building national strength. By early September he was deeply worried that the government would decide to send expeditions to both places. As he noted in his diary:

> At present our common people are undergoing hardships; they are bewildered by a myriad of new ordinances; and several times last year they have risen in revolt.... To speak of planning for the present, nothing is more urgent than proper management of domestic affairs; and to mention our
>
> obligations in foreign affairs, nothing is of greater moment than protection

26. Center for East Asian Cultural Studies, *Meiji Japan*, 2:114.

for the people of Karafuto.... Why must we harp on speedy punishment of those guilty of "infringing on our national honor"? At this time the proper management of internal administration must have the first priority.[27]

This was a complete change of heart for a man who a year before had railed against the "stupidity and obstinacy" of the Koreans.[28]

The "subdue Korea" debate of 1873 may have split the government leadership, but otherwise it ended exactly as similar discussions had since 1869—in a decision not to send a military expedition to Korea. Even if Saigō or Soejima had led such an expedition, it probably would not have been much different from the one led by Kuroda Kiyotaka and Inoue Kaoru less than three years later. It would have resulted neither in an occupation or annexation of Korea nor the extension of Japanese sovereignty over the peninsula. Members of the Dajōkan who advocated a *sei-Kan* policy did so for the same reasons that those at a lower level had: as a safety valve for discontent that was building among the former samurai class, as retribution for Korean "insults" against Japan, or as a means to negotiate a new formal relationship with Korea. There is no evidence that they contemplated the projection of Japanese power for any other purpose. Despite all the attention historians have lavished on the incident, it was neither a defining crisis nor a commitment to annexation but simply a step toward further attempts at "opening" Korea.

THE OPENING OF KOREA

The final decision to impose Western-style diplomatic practices on Korea came in 1876. The chain of events that led to it is well known. On the morning of September 20, 1875, the *Un'yo*, a Japanese naval vessel surveying the Western coast of Korea, put ashore a party on Kanghwa Island to request water and provisions. When Korean shore batteries fired on the *Un'yo*, the Japanese response was swift and severe. After bombarding the Korean fortifications, the *Un'yo* landed a shore party that torched several houses on the island and exchanged fire with Korean troops. The Japanese, armed with rifles, made quick work of the Koreans, who carried matchlock muskets, and thirty-five Korean soldiers were left dead.[29] News of the incident did not reach Tokyo until September 28, but the next day the Dajōkan decided to dispatch gun-

27. Brown and Hirota, *Diary of Kido Takayoshi*, 2:370–71.
28. Ibid., 2:206–7.
29. Kang Je-on, "Kwangwha jiken zengo."

boats to Pusan to protect Japanese residents there, and began deliberating whether or not to send a mission to Korea to settle the incident.

In reporting the incident to the public, the government alleged that the Korean bombardment of the *Un'yo* had been unexpected, and it informed the British and the French ministers that the Koreans were to blame. That version of the event strains credulity. While there is no documentary evidence that the incident was a direct and deliberate provocation by the Japanese, circumstantial evidence suggests that it was. It is difficult to understand why a Japanese naval survey vessel did not plan its provisioning sufficiently well enough not to run out of water off Kanghwa Island, a key strategic point at the mouth of the Han River, guarding the western approach to Seoul. It is also difficult to understand why the Japanese commander could not have foreseen trouble when it was well known that Korean shore batteries had earlier fired on naval probes by the French and the Americans. Indeed, the *Un'yo* carried charts used by the commander of the American Far Eastern fleet. If the Japanese vessel was not looking for trouble, it was certainly not trying very hard to avoid it. It is also significant that the *Un'yo* had been ordered to sea on its survey mission several days after Moriyama Shigeru, who had been carrying on negotiations with the Koreans at Pusan since early 1875, was ordered to break them off and come home.[30]

In fact, Moriyama, a longtime hardliner in the Ministry of Foreign Affairs, had argued that a show of force was necessary to expedite negotiations with the Koreans and to obtain the best possible terms from the Koreans. The court, he surmised, was weakened by a struggle between the anti-foreign Taewŏn'gun and his opponents, the Min family; with the Taewŏn'gun out of power, the moment was opportune to extract concessions.[31] Three Japanese naval vessels, including the *Un'yo*, had been dispatched to Pusan in early April 1875. The Korean authorities protested. When a Korean official and his assistants boarded the vessel for an inspection in early June, the Japanese commander, in a classic show of force, rattled the harbor with gunnery exercise. The Korean authorities, however, were not sufficiently impressed to make any concessions to Moriyama. Discouraged by his failure to make any headway in July and August, Moriyama asked to be called home and

30. Key-Hiuk Kim supports the argument that the Kanghwa incident was the work of the Satsuma men and that Ōkubo Toshimichi used the Korean problem to deflect attention from efforts to prevent the reduction of his personal influence by prohibiting members of the Dajōkan to serve in ministries simultaneously. Key-Hiuk Kim, *East Asian World Order*, 226–27, 232–37.

31. *NGB*, 8:70–73.

recommended that sterner measures be adopted to break the impasse. It is not hard to conclude that the mission of the *Un'yo* was intended to set these sterner measures in motion.

The readiness of the Japanese leadership to dispatch a gunboat mission to Korea in 1875, in contrast to its reluctance to respond forcefully to the "insults" of 1873, undoubtedly had to do with the more serious character of the Korean "provocations." Military forces had been engaged, and lives had been lost, as they had not been earlier. More important, changes in the international situation had reduced earlier anxieties about the foreign reaction. First, the "Russian threat" was receding. In early May 1875 the Japanese had signed the Treaty of St. Petersburg with the Russians exchanging Japan's rights in Sakhalin for sovereignty over the central and northern islands of the Kurile chain. In the course of his negotiations, Enomoto Takeaki, the Japanese representative, had concluded that the Russians would not interfere if conflict broke out between Japan and Korea, and he even suggested that Japan sign a secret agreement guaranteeing Russian neutrality in the event of such a conflict.[32] Second, the 1874 military expedition against Taiwan, involving more than three thousand troops, had also succeeded without any foreign intervention. Not only did the expedition extract indemnities from the Chinese for the slaughtered Ryukyu islanders, but it also maneuvered the Ch'ing court into tacit recognition of Japanese suzerainty over the Ryukyus. Both the British and American ministers in Tokyo had initially expressed disapproval of the expedition, but the British minister to China mediated the final settlement. Significantly, once Japanese troops had withdrawn from Taiwan, Charles LeGendre, an American adviser to the Ministry of Foreign Affairs, urged the Japanese to move on to Korea.[33]

The Japanese leaders took their time in organizing the expedition to Korea. In early October Kido Takayoshi, the former advocate of a full-scale military expedition, once again volunteered his services as an emissary to Korea, but he struck an appropriately cautious note. The Kanghwa incident, he thought, was far more serious than the Taiwan incident, and there could be no question of abandoning the Japanese residents in Korea. But even though appropriate action ought to be taken "for the glory of the empire and the security of our people," he suggested that the government should approach China to see if it would

32. Key-Hiuk Kim, *East Asian World Order,* 218–19; Lensen, *Russian Push Toward Japan,* 442–46.
33. Key-Hiuk Kim, *East Asian World Order,* 190–200, 217.

represent Korea; if not, then Japan could deal directly with the Koreans. If the Koreans refused to respond, Japan would have to hold Korea accountable for its actions, but before resorting to military force the government should carefully consider the question of timing and the strength of government finances.[34]

The fiscal impact of a military expedition worried the Japanese leaders. Ōkubo continued to insist on the importance of domestic development over foreign adventures and the need to recover tariff autonomy.[35] Matsukata Masayoshi, his major subordinate in the Ministry of Finance, made similar protestations all through 1874 and 1875. In the summer of 1875 Matsukata wrote a memorial opposing a military expedition to Korea on the grounds that internal reform should have first priority and urging that tension with the outside be avoided. If a military expedition were sent to Korea on the heels of the Taiwan expedition at a time when specie reserves in the national treasury were low, he argued, the government might very well bankrupt itself. He also took pains to point out that the Korean question was not a matter of life and death to Japan and certainly not as important as treaty revision. The unequal treaties were just as much an "insult" to Japan as anything the Koreans had done, and they also weakened Japan economically.[36]

Only in November, nearly three months after the Kanghwa incident, did the Dajōkan decide to send a mission headed by Kuroda Kiyotaka, a Satsuma man, as minister extraordinary and plenipotentiary, with Inoue Kaoru (Chōshū) as his deputy. Its ostensible purpose was to settle the Kanghwa incident, but its real goal was to "open" the country. Kuroda's instructions, issued in December, charged him to demand indemnities for the attack on the Un'yo but noted that his principal task was to negotiate a treaty based on the "law of nations" and that such a treaty might be considered as indemnity. The treaty was to provide for ceremonial parity between the two countries; the right of Japanese to carry on trade freely in Pusan; the opening of an additional port for Japanese trade and settlement in Kanghwa or Seoul; permission for the Japanese to travel freely between Seoul and Pusan; the right of Japanese naval or commercial vessels to survey Korean waters; the exchange of diplomatic representatives on an equal basis; and the right of Japanese consuls to regulate trade in the open ports.[37] In short the proposed

34. NKGS, 1:14–16.
35. Bannō, Kindai Nihon, no gaikō, 27.
36. Ibid., 15–16

treaty resembled the "unequal treaties" the Americans and other foreigners had imposed in Japan.

The parallel did not escape notice. An editorial in the *Chōya shinbun* likened Kuroda and Inoue to Perry and Adams.[38] While the comparison was apt, the Japanese mission was not simply a reenactment of the American expedition. Korea was far more important to the Meiji leaders than Japan had been to President Millard Fillmore. It is also unlikely that the United States was planning a war to open Japan. Commodore Perry bluffed the Japanese with hints of military action, but in the end his gunboats were more important for their symbolic power than for their firepower. In contrast, evidence suggests that the Meiji government was prepared to use military force against Korea if the Kuroda-Inoue mission were rebuffed, insulted, or attacked.

Before his departure Kuroda set forth a plan of action for the dispatch of troops to Korea in the event that negotiations broke down.[39] Four days after the mission arrived in Pusan, Yamagata Aritomo and Torio Koyata prepared a long memorandum laying out contingency plans in the event of hostilities: an army division and a convoy of four or five warships were to be mobilized to go to Korea if needed; ammunition, weapons, food, and stores were to be stockpiled at Shimonoseki; strategic points within Japan were to be secured by the transfer of the Kumamoto garrison to Kokura and the units from the Hiroshima garrison to Chofu; and a second division was to be formed in reserve if the first division was defeated by the Koreans or if the Chinese became involved in the fighting.[40] These contingency plans indicate the seriousness with which top government leaders took the possibility of war with Korea.

In fact, the Japanese had to rely on bluff just as much as Perry had. The show of naval force was pure sham. The Japanese navy was larger than it had been in 1873, but it was still nothing to boast about. The Kuroda-Inoue mission sailed on three warships and three cargo ships, two of which were captained by foreigners. The whole flotilla had trouble staying together since the vessels sailed at quite different speeds. Had the Koreans refused to parley, it is doubtful that the Japanese could have brought much force to bear. But the Japanese were able to play on

37. *NKGS*, 1:59–61.
38. Yamada Shōji, "Jiyūminken undō to Chōsen."
39. *NKGS*, 1:92–93.
40. Yamabe, *Nihon no Kankoku heigō*, 30–32; Tokutomi, *Kōshaku Yamagata Aritomo den*, 2:426–28.

Korean anxiety and ignorance just as the Americans had played on
Japanese anxiety and ignorance twenty years before. When they established their headquarters on Kanghwa Island in early February, they
were accompanied by a mere four hundred troops. But Kuroda made it
clear that Korea might well face an invasion if it did not sign a treaty
with Japan, and when a supply ship arrived a few days later with a new
force of eight hundred men, Kuroda told the Korean authorities it had
brought four thousand.[41]

From the Japanese perspective the Treaty of Kanghwa accomplished
a major change in relations with Korea. It ended once and for all the
traditional system of ceremonial exchange mediated through the Sō
family on Tsushima. Korea was declared to be an independent state,
Japan was pronounced to be its equal, and their intercourse was to be
based on the "law of nations." At the same time, the treaty granted the
Japanese many of the same privileges in Korea that were regarded as an
affront to "national dignity" at home. Its provisions included elements
from both the first and second treaty settlements of the 1850s. On the
model of Perry's "wood and water treaty" it provided for the opening of
two ports in addition to Pusan, the establishment of Japanese consuls in
these ports, and the right of distressed ships to put into shore for wood,
water, and shelter; on the model of the Harris treaty, it called for the
exchange of diplomatic representatives, the right to survey Korean
coastal waters, and the right of extraterritoriality. The treaty did not
include a "most favored nation" clause, nor did it deal with the question
of tariffs and other trade regulations; nevertheless, it was clearly an
"unequal treaty."

The supplementary treaty and trade regulations negotiated during the
summer of 1876 were even more "unequal" than the commercial treaties the *bakufu* had signed with the Western powers. First, the Japanese
were allowed to purchase Korean goods with their own currency at face
value; second, the Koreans agreed to a complete exemption of tariffs on
Japanese imports and exports; and third, the Japanese agreed not to levy
duties on goods coming from or going to Korea. This settlement made it
much easier for Japanese to trade in Korea than foreigners could in
Japan. Japanese merchants were not allowed to own land in the Korean
treaty ports or travel more than ten Korean *ri* (about 2.5 miles) outside
the ports, but otherwise they could do business much as they did at
home. Their imports were not restricted by tariffs even at the modest

41. Key-Hiuk Kim, *East Asian World Order*, 247.

level the Japanese collected on Western imports, nor did they have to convert their national currency to Korean currency in order to buy goods. The Japanese had discovered how to improve on the practices of "free-trade imperialism."

To sum up, the Meiji government's early policy toward Korea was part of a larger effort to incorporate Japan into the matrix of interstate relations constructed by the Western nations to accommodate the needs and interests of free-trade imperialism. On the one hand, this drive involved seeking legal and symbolic parity with the Western nations by revising the unequal treaties; on the other, it involved establishing an asymmetric symbolic and legal relationship with its Asian neighbors by negotiating unequal treaties with them. It is a mistake to interpret this early Korean policy in light of later events. The "subdue Korea" debate, and the subsequent opening of Korea, did not spring from any long-term desire to assert Japanese political control over the peninsula or to acquire territory there. Rather, it was the beginning of a long, difficult, and complicated process that nurtured a sense that Japan had more tangible political, strategic, and economic interests at stake in Korea than elsewhere in East Asia.

SINO-JAPANESE RIVALRY IN KOREA, 1880–1894

During the 1880s, as the "new imperialism" intruded ever more ominously into East Asia and even China became a possible object of Western territorial ambitions, the discourse over the Korean problem refocused on the issues of Korean reform and Japanese national security. The two were linked. The Korean Peninsula was, as Major Jacob Meckel, a German military adviser to Japan, put it, a "dagger pointed at the heart of Japan; but what made Korea of strategic concern was not merely its proximity to Japan but its inability to defend itself against outsiders. If Korea were truly independent, it posed no strategic problem, but if Korea remained "backward" and "uncivilized," it would remain weak, and if it remained weak, it would be inviting prey for foreign predators. The "maintenance of Korean independence," a litany invoked by popular rights activists as well as by the Meiji leaders, required a program of Korean self-strengthening like the post-Restoration reforms in Japan.

What worried the Japanese was the activities of the Chinese, who appeared to be thwarting the fragile growth of forces backing "progressive" reform in Korea. The Ch'ing government, beset by internal rebellion and foreign intrusion in the 1860s and 1870s, had loosened its hold over Korea. When the Japanese succeeded in establishing a legal basis for Korean "independence" in 1876, the Chinese government complacently accepted it as a fait accompli. However, many Ch'ing high officials—the most important being Li Hung-chang, the powerful and influential governor of Chihli Province—were alarmed by the Japanese annexation of the Ryukyu kingdom. What had happened to this former tributary state could happen to another as well. In an ironic echo of earlier Japanese anxieties about Russia, the Tsungli Yamen noted in August 1879: "Relying on cunning tricks, Japan is trying to master the Orient. Judging from the circumstances, we believe that she will surely turn her expansionist design to Korea in some future day."[42] To forestall this turn of events, the Ch'ing government began to reassert its influence on the peninsula.[43]

The Chinese relied at first on the time-honored tactic of "using barbarian against barbarian" by encouraging the Korean court to establish relations with the Western countries. When a swarm of foreign ships arrived in Korea with requests to "open" the country during the spring and summer of 1880—the Russians in April, the Americans in May, the French in June, and the Italians in August—Li Hung-chang, hoping to counterbalance the growing Japanese presence, counseled the Korean court to oblige them by signing trade agreements. In the spring of 1881, after Korea signed unequal treaties with the Americans, the British, and the Germans, not only was the Japanese monopoly over trade broken, but the Japanese found themselves confronted with a new kind of political competition as well. The Chinese were no less able to mimic the Western imperialists than they were.

The aggressive policies promoted by Li Hung-chang and his circle infected and redefined the Chinese relations with Japan. When the humiliation of the "unequal treaty" settlement was still fresh in the 1860s, Japanese leaders had noted that Japan and China were as close as "lips and teeth," but the reassertion of Chinese hegemony in Korea eroded any sense of Sino-Japanese solidarity. From the perspective of the Meiji leaders, since China itself remained attached to its traditional ways and was no longer capable of fending off foreign intrusion, Korea was more

---

42. Chien, *Opening of Korea*, 63.
43. There is a large and detailed literature in English on Chinese policy in Korea during the 1880s. In addition to Chien, *Opening of Korea*, see Lin, "Li Hung-chang"; Nelson, *Korea and the Old Order*; Wright, "Adapability of Ch'ing Diplomacy"; Yur-bok Lee, *West Goes East*.

vulnerable than ever before.[44] This turn of events, regarded as extremely ominous for Japan's long-term interests, provoked widespread alarm outside the Meiji government as well. As a group of Kaishintō members noted in an 1884 memorial to Itō Hirobumi: "If by some stroke of ill fortune, Korea becomes a base for foreign naval vessels, our country will not be able to maintain the peace of the Japan Sea.... Hence, to help Korea achieve complete independence, and to deepen the friendship between our nations, is ultimately to protect our own independence."[45] In this construction of the Korean problem, much more was at stake than "national prestige." The fate of Korea was entwined with that of the peninsula in ways not imagined ten years before.

THE JAPANESE AND
THE KOREAN REFORM MOVEMENT

The political consensus in Japan was that the road to independence for Korea lay, as it had for Japan, through the importation of "civilization" from the West. As a *Hōchi shinbun* editorial noted in early June 1894:

> The independence of Korea does not refer simply to its relations with foreign countries. In the widest sense it means independence in diplomacy and internal affairs; internally it means the spread of education, the promotion of agriculture and the development of commerce, the organization of military affairs and impartiality in laws. All these things are indispensable to [Korean] independence, but without encouragement and help from our country [Korea] will not be able to acquire them.[46]

As this editorial suggests, the Japanese interest in the reform of Korea was not purely altruistic. Not only would it enable Korea to resist foreign intrusion, which was in Japan's direct interest, but it would also offer Japan the opportunity, as a conduit of change, to play a larger role on the peninsula.

The key question, and the most vexing one, was not whether Korea

44. As a *Nichinichi shinbun* editorial noted at the time of 1884 coup: "We have no desire to possess the peninsula. As the possession of Korea, however, by any other power would be a matter of considerable importance to us, we should force our nearest neighbor to govern herself, and, if China could only be brought to understand that, it should not be difficult for her to desist from her policy of interference in Korean affairs, and treat Korea as an independent country." Quoted in *The Japan Weekly Mail*, Jan. 10, 1885.

45. *HRCKS*, 2:126–27. These sentiments were by no means new. As a *Chōya shinbun* editorial observed in December 1880, "Korea is our northwestern gate. If we do not guard that gate our own independence is not at all secure.... If Korea comes under the occupation of another people, we must not abandon it even for a day." Oka, "Kokuminteki dokuritsu to kokka risei," 58.

46. Quoted in *Kokumin no tomo*, June 23, 1894, p. 958.

should be reformed but how reform might be accomplished. Should Japan adopt a passive role, nurturing reformist elements within Korea and rendering them assistance whenever possible? Or should it adopt a more aggressive policy, actively interfering in Korean politics to assure that reform took place? While some advocates of reform swung between these two poles, fulminating over Korean backwardness in one breath, urging the promotion of "progressive forces" with the next,[47] the Meiji leaders adopted a passive policy, cajoling the Korea court to follow the Japanese model but offering little concrete assistance except for the dispatch of a small military mission headed by Lieutenant Horimoto Reizō to train a newly organized modern-style military unit, the *pyŏlgigun*.[48]

By the early 1880s the Meiji leaders saw the best hope for reform in the emergence of a small group of Korean officials committed to a program of self-strengthening. The nucleus of an "enlightenment" faction had taken shape well before the arrival of the Japanese, but its influence grew in the late 1870s. Young scholars and officials like Kim Yun-sik, Kim Hong-jip, Ŏ Yun-jung, and others began to talk about the need to open up the country and learn the sources of Western power. In 1880 a number of these reform-minded officials accompanied the second Korean mission to Japan, where they received encouraging advice from Japanese leaders as well as members of the Chinese legation in Tokyo.[49] Their direct observation of what was happening in Japan convinced them that continued isolation was impossible. After returning home, Kim Hong-jip presented the king with a treatise by Huang Tsunhsien, an official at the Chinese legation in Tokyo, who urged Korea to establish close ties with China and Japan and to strengthen itself by adopting Western institutions and technology. Conservative scholars

47. Fukuzawa Yūkichi is a case in point. In the heat of the moment after the Imo mutiny, he urged the establishment of a Japanese protectorate in Korea to promote "progressive elements" and spread "the felicity of civilization." Minister Hanabusa, he said, should be made "protector general of Korea" (*Kankoku kokumu kantokukan*), empowered to oversee all national affairs and to appoint "enlightened persons" (*kaikokushugi no hito*) to assist him in governing the country. By the fall of 1882 Fukuzawa had returned to his earlier position that Korea ought to be "civilized" by the force of ideas rather than the force of arms. Cf. Aoki, "Fukuzawa Yūkichi no Chōsenron," 32–35.

48. *NKGS*, 2:57ff.; *KNSKK*, 1:747–49.

49. For example, Inoue Kaoru told the group that Korea should promote production and make trade flourish, and since good relations between the two countries depended on good communication, the Koreans should establish language schools and send students to Japan. Shortly before their return to Korea, he also warned them to take measures to deal with the eastern advance of the Russians and urged them to open relations with the outside world. Inoue Kaoru Kō Denki Hensankai, *Segai Inoue Kaoru Kō den*, 3:442–43.

accused Kim of heterodoxy, but King Kojong appears to have been persuaded by Huang's arguments. In early 1881 a new government office, the T'ongni kimu amun, heavily staffed by members of the Min clan, was charged with undertaking reform measures, and in February the king dispatched the so-called gentlemen's mission to study conditions in Japan.[50]

For nearly four months members of the "gentlemen's mission" led by Pak Chŏng-yang, Ŏ Yun-jung, Hong Yŏng-sik, and Cho Chun-yang visited military facilities, schools, government ministries, factories, libraries, post offices, museums, arsenals, hospitals, and shipyards. Their voluminous reports, not unlike those of the Iwakura mission a decade earlier, were suffused with admiration for the institutional and material changes the Japanese had accomplished since the Restoration. The arrival of the Korean mission in 1881 encouraged many Japanese political and intellectual leaders to think that Korea was on the verge of major change. Fukuzawa Yūkichi, for example, saw in these young Koreans a reflection of his own recent past. As he noted in a letter to a friend, "In the early part of this month, a number of Koreans arrived to observe conditions in Japan, and two of them are enrolled in our academy.... When I think about myself twenty-odd years ago, I cannot help feeling sympathy and compassion for them.... When I hear them talk, it is Japan of thirty years ago."[51]

While all the mission members returned home committed to change, two of its junior members, Kim Ok-kiun and Sŏ Kwang-bŏm, who had close ties with Pak Yŏng-hyo, a brother-in-law of King Kojong, became the nucleus of a more radical "independence" movement, recruited from young yangban officials as well as a few chungin and commoners. Convinced that the Japanese might provide support for efforts to bring about "enlightenment" at home, in the winter of 1881–82 Kim and Sŏ returned to Japan, where they met with a roster of distinguished Japanese leaders—Inoue Kaoru, Shibusawa Eiichi, Gotō Shōjirō, Ōkuma Shigenobu, and Itō Hirobumi.[52]

In July 1882 the forces of reform suffered a setback when rebellious soldiers from traditional Korean army units, angered over unpaid wages and resentful of the attention lavished on the new modern-style force trained by Lieutenant Horimoto, staged a mutiny. After killing Horimoto, the mutineers attacked the Japanese legation, forcing the Jap-

50. KNSKK, 1:740–46.
51. Kamigaito, Nihon ryūgakusei to kakumei undō, 7.
52. KNSKK, 1:740–46.

anese minister and his staff to flee for their lives to Inchon. The conservative Taewŏn'gun, then serving as King Kojong's regent, used the mutiny to stage a coup against his rivals at court, members of the queen's family, the Min clan; however, the Ch'ing government staged a countercoup. Chinese troops dispatched to Seoul spirited the Taewŏn'gun off to confinement in Tientsin, where he nursed his resentments for the next three years. With the Taewŏn'gun out of the way, a pro-Chinese faction led by members of the Min clan resumed ascendancy at the Korean court, and Chinese influence on the peninsula was firmly reestablished.

In the wake of the 1882 incident—known as the Imo mutiny—the Ch'ing government began to turn its most loyal tributary state into a semi-colony by deploying the tactics of "informal empire." As one Korean historian has put it, "China's policy toward Korea substantially changed to a new imperialistic one whereby the suzerain state demanded certain privileges in her vassal state."[53] In early October 1882 the Korean government agreed to a new set of trade regulations that gave the Chinese substantial advantages over the Japanese and the Westerners. Not only did the document reassert Korea's dependency on China, but it also granted the Chinese unilateral extraterritoriality privileges in civil and criminal cases. To establish firmer control over the Korean court, Ma Chien-chung, one of Li Hung-chang's lieutenants, arrived in Seoul to serve as an adviser to the government. Wu Ch'ang-ch'ing, together with a staff of Chinese officers, took over the training of the Korean army, which the Chinese provided with 1,000 rifles, two cannons, and 10,000 rounds of ammunition. At the suggestion of the Chinese the Koreans hired Paul Georg von Mollendorf, a former employee of both the German consular service and the Chinese Maritime Customs Service, to head the new customs administration in Korea. All these moves were intended to parry the "cunning tricks" of the Japanese.[54]

The resurgence of the conservatives at the Korean court after the Imo mutiny raised the question of whether the Japanese should take a more active role in the reform of Korea. In October 1882 another mission headed by Pak Yŏng-hyo and Kim Ok-kiun, and composed mainly of members of the proreform, proindependence faction, arrived in Tokyo,

53. Park Il-keun, "China's Policy Toward Korea," 61.
54. For example, Li Hung-chang confided to Kim Yun-sik, a proreform official, that he was recommending Mollendorf to spite the Japanese. "The Japanese fear Germany the most and dislike Mollendorf, so we will send him to Korea in order to prevent their licentiousness." Chien, *Opening of Korea*, 42–44.

eager to win official Japanese support for their reform efforts. The government, informed by Minister Hanabusa that the mission should be treated with special courtesy, decided to defray all its expenses. In long discussions with Foreign Minister Inoue, both Kim and Pak urged the Japanese government to help the "independence" faction.[55] Inoue, initially won over by their arguments, recommended that Japan give more direct aid to the reform elements in Korea, in hopes of securing the country's independence. While his proposal had the backing of Itō, then off on his "study tour" of Europe, the more cautious Iwakura Tomomi warned against providing any aid that might arouse the suspicions of the Chinese. Inoue, unwilling to risk a clash with China that might not secure Korean independence, ultimately decided to refrain from direct intervention in Korean politics.[56]

The government's only concrete gesture of support was the advance of a small loan to the Korean government. Evidently without any previous discussions at home or any documented authorization from the king, Pak Yŏng-hyo asked his Japanese hosts for ¥170,000. Anxious to win the good will of the young reformers without alarming their conservative opponents at home, the government arranged a low interest loan through the Yokohama Specie Bank, which borrowed the money from the ministry of finance. Part of the loan (¥50,000) went for an indemnity payment to the Japanese, but the rest (¥120,000) was apparently used to support the efforts of the "independence" faction.[57] When a small group of Japanese, several of them Fukuzawa's disciples—Inoue Kakugorō, Ushiba Takuzō, and Takahashi Masanobu—arrived in Seoul in January 1883 to oversee the expenditure of the loan, they discovered that the conservatives at court had managed to outmaneuver the young reformers. Pak Yŏng-hyo had been assigned to Kaesong, and Kim Ok-kiun had been placed in a remote provincial post. Inoue Kakugorō decided to stay in Korea, serving as an adviser to the T'ongni kimu amun and helping to publish the Hansŏng sunbo, the first Korean gazette; Ushiba, though, returned to Japan with a group of forty-odd young Korean students, whose expenses probably were defrayed by part of the ¥170,000 loan.[58]

55. Cho, Kindai Kankoku keizaishi, 183–85.
56. KNSKK, 1:902–6.
57. Cho, Kindai kankoku keizaishi, 185–87; KNSKK, 1:912; Chien, Opening of Korea, 137–39.
58. Hardly any of these students were from families of important government officials. More than half came from politically marginal strata—provincial yangban, chungin, or even commoner families—for whom foreign study offered a chance for upward mobil-

Beyond this, however, the increasingly cautious Meiji leaders were unwilling to offer more substantial financial backing for reform efforts. In June 1883 Kim Ok-kiun traveled to Japan again to seek a loan of ¥3 million, an amount roughly equivalent to the annual revenue of the Korean government, to tide it over current financial difficulty. His appeals fell on deaf ears. Shibusawa Eiichi, head of the Dai-Ichi Bank, told him that it would not be difficult to raise ¥100,000 or ¥200,000 if he had the backing of the Foreign Ministry, but a larger amount was out of the question.[59] Gotō Shōjirō helped Kim raise funds from well-to-do Jiyūtō supporters in Shikoku and Kansai, but the effort to secure an official loan came to naught.[60] The amount requested, equivalent to about half of the Japanese government's land tax revenues or about one-third of its income from official enterprises, was a staggering sum, well beyond the capacities of either the Japanese government or private banks to provide. Had the government been interested in supporting the cause of the reformers, it might have been able to come up with a smaller loan, but by the middle of 1883 the Japanese leadership was no longer entirely sure that the future lay with the reformers.[61] Indeed, Foreign Minister Inoue did not take the time to meet with Kim; after

---

ity. About half the group enrolled in the Toyama Military Academy to be trained as officers for new-style military units. Following Fukuzawa Yūkichi's advice, the rest entered various schools to learn commerce or other technical skills needed for the development of industry and production at home. *KNSKK*, 1:918.

59. Members of the Min family had proposed to deal with the government's financial problems by debasing the currency, but Kim objected that this would make the financial situation worse in the long run. Kim proposed instead to raise a foreign loan secured by timber-cutting rights on Ullŏngdo, an island off the eastern coast of Korea, and whaling rights in Korean waters. Since it was clear that Japan would be the only country likely to make such a loan, the Min faction opposed the idea for fear it would open the way to greater Japanese influence, and they pointed out that it would be difficult to repay a foreign loan in the current financial situation. King Kojong resolved the controversy by authorizing a de facto debasement of coinage while allowing Kim to raise money in Japan. With the help of the American minister to Japan, John A. Bingham, Kim got an introduction to an American businessman in Yokohama, James R. Morse, who offered to act as his agent raising money in London and New York, an effort that ultimately proved fruitless. Cho, *Kindai kankoku keizaishi*, 188–92.

60. Omachi, *Hakushaku Gotō Shōjirō*, 542.

61. Only Fukuzawa seems to have offered any public support for Kim's loan project. In a series of editorials lauding Korean reform efforts, he argued that the most effective way to induce change in Korea was to supply the country with capital. A loan of three to four million yen, secured by treaty or official collateral, could be used to promote "civilized enterprises" in Korea—modern shipping, schools, publishing, mining, harbor construction, and the like. The advantages to Japan would be substantial: since China could not provide this level of financial help, a loan would make Korea more dependent on Japan; and the support of "civilized enterprises" would provide employment for trouble-making excess intelligentsia (*chishikijin*) in Japan, who could go to Korea as advisers. Aoki, "Fukuzawa Yūkichi no Chōsenron," 41–44.

several fruitless months in Japan, Kim finally went home empty-handed.[62]

The new Japanese minister to Seoul, Takazoe Shinichirō, sensing that Kim and his group were losing ground, proposed that the Japanese government try instead to win the favor of the court by forgiving the ¥400,000 indemnity required by the Treaty of Chemulpo. If collaboration with the reformers promised little, it made sense to mend fences with the court. The gesture would do Japan no particular harm, said Takazoe, and it might nurture a sense of gratitude toward Japan. In early November 1884 the Japanese minister informed the Korean king of the Japanese government's decision to "donate" the indemnity payments to Korea and suggested that the money be used to undertake modernization projects like the establishment of a postal service or reform of the military establishment. If countries like Japan, China, and Korea wanted to reach the level of the Western countries, he said, then they would have to change their ways of living and governing themselves.[63]

By late 1884 the government in Tokyo seemed to be losing interest in working with the "independence" faction. Nevertheless, Takazoe, who was aware that its leaders (Kim Ok-kiun, Pak Yŏng-hyo, Hong Yŏng-sik, and Sŏ Kwang-bŏm) were planning a coup against the conservatives, thought the situation in Seoul was like that of the Tokugawa *bakufu* on the eve of the Restoration. Takazoe asked the home government if he should provide military assistance to the plotters by protecting the palace and expelling Chinese troops by military force if the Korean king requested. However, he was instructed to adopt a hands-off attitude: "Our government will not support one Korean political faction, nor will it openly intervene. It will be to our advantage to try, insofar as possible, to encourage the so-called Japan faction to bring about the enlightenment of their country by peaceful means."[64] Unfortunately the cable from home arrived too late to check Takazoe's covert support for the coup.[65] In the end the coup failed, the young reformers were forced into exile, and the Min faction resumed control of the court.[66]

62. Cho, *Kindai kankoku keizaishi*, 188–92.

63. *KNSKK*, 1:924–25.

64. *HRCKS*, 3:265–68, 295.

65. It was symbolic of the Japanese government's halfhearted support for the reformers that when the coup collapsed on December 6, Takazoe was willing to take its leaders only as far as Inchon. He refused to take them back to Japan on the *Chitose-maru*. Only with the help of Inoue Kakugorō were they smuggled on board.

66. The fullest account in English is found in Cook, *Korea's 1884 Incident*, 247.

While the Japanese government refused to return Kim and Pak to Korea for punishment as "traitors," the signing of the Tientsin Convention made it clear that the reformers could no longer expect direct official Japanese help. Willy-nilly, the Japanese would have to deal only with the Korean court. Pak Yŏng-hyo, Sŏ Kwang-bŏm, and Sŏ Chae-p'il departed for the United States, perhaps with Japanese government travel funds channeled to them through the good offices of Fukuzawa. Kim Ok-kiun, by contrast, remained in Japan with financial help from Fukuzawa, Gotō Shōjirō, Inoue Kakugorō, Toyama Mitsuru, and others, but his continuing presence became an embarrassment to the Japanese government, especially after Korean assassins were sent to Japan to kill him. After being ordered out of Tokyo, he took up residence at the Grand Hotel in Yokohama, where he was able to resist the Japanese cabinet's decision to throw him out of the country in 1886. Eventually he was spirited off to the Ogasawara Islands, where he remained for two years, his living expenses provided by the Japanese government; after a subsequent two-year stay in Sapporo, he was finally allowed to live in Tokyo under the assumed name of Iwata Shusaku.[67] The fate of Pak Yŏng-hyo was less ignominious. In 1889, after spending a few years in the United States, he and Sŏ Kwang-bŏm returned to Japan, where he led a quiet but peripatetic life. Not long after fleeing into exile, Pak had become estranged from Kim, and there was little communication between the two even after Kim returned from Hokkaido. Most Korean exiles in Japan clustered around Pak, whose most important Japanese patron was Gotō Shōjirō.[68] But other former official friends, like Foreign Minister Inoue Kaoru, who was deeply involved in the treaty revision question, kept him at a distance.[69]

In the meantime the Chinese tightened their control in Seoul. The new Chinese representative in Seoul, Yuan Shih-kai, a clever and dynamic protégé of Li Hung-chang, bullied the Korean court into accepting Chinese control over its foreign policy, and in November 1885 Yuan proclaimed that as the Imperial Chinese Minister Resident he had charge of Korea's foreign diplomatic and commercial relations. In the

67. *KNSKK*, 2:167.
68. Gotō had been interested in the the reform of Korea since 1880, when he met with members of the official mission. Gotō had promised, but not delivered, financial backing for Ōi Kentarō's harebrained scheme to send a band of Japanese activists to Korea to stage a countercoup against the Min faction and the pro-Chinese conservatives, and he continued to maintain contact with the Korean exiles.
69. *KNSKK*, 2:184.

meantime, King Kojong, worried about the growing influence of the Chinese, had made secret overtures to the Russians, hoping for assistance to keep the Chinese at arm's length. In the summer of 1886 the Chinese government, aware of the king's initiatives, ordered Yuan to depose the royal couple, intending to replace the king with the Taewŏn'gun, who was returned from exile in Tientsin, or his grandson, Yi Chun-yong. While this intrigue ultimately failed, Yuan was able to force Kojong to dismiss or punish his pro-Russian ministers.[70]

The Korean court showed signs of inching its way toward "civilization and enlightenment," but its reform efforts—gas lights for the palace, a postal system, the establishment of a national mint, and the like— did little to enhance Korean national strength or independence. The Korean government did not address the endemic problems of official waste, corruption, and inefficiency, nor did it do anything to increase national wealth. So fragile were the Korean government's reform efforts that in 1888 the Chinese were even able to force the Korean government to shut down one of its more effective enterprises, the Hamsŏng sunbo, a mixed-script (hangŭl and Chinese characters) gazette published by the government. With the exception of a few high officials like Kim Hongjip, who favored "self-strengthening," or certain members of the Min family like Min Yŏng-ik and Min Kyŏm-ho, the Japanese could discern little support for reform in Seoul. With the Chinese firmly entrenched at the Korean capital, the Japanese government could only exhort the Korean court to make changes, and with the radical reformers discredited and in exile, private Japanese supporters of Korean reform had little leverage.

From the Japanese perspective, the likelihood of vigorous reform in Korea seemed to be dwindling. In June 1893 Sugimura Fukashi, a second secretary in the Seoul legation, offered a gloomy assessment:

> In a pitiful state, everything in Korea is in collapse—a government bereft of control, people without vitality, a lack of military and naval preparation, stagnation in scholarship, crafts, and agriculture, and so forth. . . . Our commentators often compare [Korea] to bakumatsu Japan but this is not correct. Korea resembles bakumatsu Japan only to the extent that it has had open relations with foreign countries for some years; its apparent progress in politics, in crafts, and in production hardly matches that of bakumatsu Japan at all. On the contrary, the minds of its people remain immature, debilitated by

70. Yur-bok Lee, West Goes East, 156–65; Denny, China and Korea; Palmer, Korean–American Relations, 2:11–13.

time, and they lack the vital spirit of *bakumatsu*. In short, it must be said that Korea at this stage in its development is like Japan a millennium ago, and over the past few years it has gradually deteriorated.[71]

But Sugimura proposed no remedies other than to suggest that the government continue to do what it had always done.

As we have seen, the Meiji leaders, despite their initial optimism about the the "independence" movement in Korea, had failed to provide it any substantial support, either financial or military. The reasons are clear: first, Japan lacked sufficient military and naval capability to back the reformers by force; second, budget retrenchment limited the government's capacity for financial support; and third, the Meiji leaders wished to provoke neither the Chinese nor the Korean court. A cautious policy, however, had not won the Japanese any friends. On the contrary, even the limited protection the Japanese provided the exiled reformers, who were regarded as "murderers" and "traitors" by the Korean court, served only to deepen suspicions toward Japan. As Sugimura Fukashi lamented in 1894, "When the Koreans speak of foreign enemies, they first point to Japan; they seem to regard the Japanese as wild beasts."[72] It was this failure to find a basis for collaboration with the Korean reform movement that made the resort to force a more likely alternative for dealing with Chinese influence on the peninsula.

PREPARATIONS FOR WAR WITH CHINA

As the Meiji leaders lost hope in Korean self-strengthening efforts in the late 1880s, their attention shifted to a military buildup for a possible confrontation with China. The original mission of the Japanese army had been to quell or control domestic disturbances, but after the successful suppression of the Satsuma rebellion in 1878 the likelihood of a major internal uprising receded.[73] The changing international environ-

71. *HRCKS*, 3:200–201.
72. *HRCKS*, 3:203, 207.
73. Matsushita, *Meiji gunsei shiron*, 2:32. To the extent that the early Meiji leaders worried about conflict with a foreign power, Russia was seen as the main threat. In December 1872 the army projected Russia as the country's chief hypothetical enemy as a basis for planning the size of forces needed, the composition of its armaments, and the disposition of its troops. The army leadership did not expect to engage the Russians on their own territory, however; rather, they were contemplating domestic defense against a possible Russian incursion into Hokkaido. To that end military colonists (*tondenhei*) were dispatched to the northern island, equipped with axes to clear the land and rifles to fend off invaders. After the Japanese reached an agreement with the Russians in May 1875 to cede rights over Karafuto (Sakhalin) in return for Russian recognition over Japanese claims to the Chishima (Kuril) Islands, worries about the threat from the north began to recede.

ment of the 1880s, especially developments on the peninsula, induced the newly organized general staff to call for the development of a military force capable of external warfare. For example, in a joint memorial urging the adoption of a strategy of *défense à outrance*, Katsura Tarō and Kawakami Sōroku, two key general staff officers, observed:

> The nations of the world, whether great or small, have two choices in establishing an army. They can simply defend themselves against enemy invasion or preserve neutrality. This is the goal of second-rate nations in the West. Alternatively, they can display military power and, in times of crisis, field a nation in arms, thus taking insult from no one. To do this, a force capable of acting overseas is necessary.... Although it is just a short time since we built our military system and reforms remain to be carried out, we are not looking to stand with the second-rate Western nations, but to rank with the leading powers.[74]

While this basic shift in military policy might have occurred in any case, the developments in Korea no doubt made it easier to convince civilian leaders.

Not surprisingly, the army leadership regarded the Ch'ing empire as the chief hypothetical enemy and assumed that any major external war would be fought there. In 1879–80 several reconnaissance missions dispatched to China produced a six-volume survey of the size, quality, and morale of the Ch'ing military forces.[75] On the basis of this report, Chief of Staff Yamagata Aritomo recommended expanding Japanese military forces to maintain parity with its big neighbor. Given the growing instability of the East Asia region, he pointed out, war with China was becoming a greater likelihood. Although traditional Chinese fighting units like the Eight Banners and the Green Banners were ineffectual, modern arsenals and shipyards had been built at Shanghai, Tientsin, and Foochow. If China adopted a European-style conscription system, it would be able to raise a force of 8.5 million men in time of war, making it a formidable military power. To deal with that contingency, Yamagata urged a buildup of Japan's own forces.[76]

74. Quoted in Lone, "General Katsura Tarō," 26. See also Osawa, "Emperor Versus Army Leaders."

75. Shinobu Seizaburō, *Nihon gaikōshi*, 2:106. On his return from China, Lieutenant Colonel Katsura also drafted a contingency plan for a possible conflict. It envisaged landing three divisions to occupy Dairen and attack Fukien in preparation for a direct attack on Peking.

76. Nakatsuka, *Nisshin sensō no kenkyū*, 70; Matsushita, *Meiji gunsei shiron*, 32.

Despite Yamagata's persistent lobbying, civilian leaders were at first reluctant to go along with his proposals. Faced with rampant inflation, climbing interest rates, expanding imports, and an outflow of specie, the Meiji leadership decided in late 1880 to stabilize the currency by increased taxation and financial retrenchment. In the late summer of 1882, however, the Imo mutiny underscored the urgency of military expansion. In contrast to the Chinese, who had quickly dispatched an expeditionary force to Seoul where they controlled the situation by establishing military superiority, the Japanese, with their limited military and naval power, had been forced to pursue a reactive or passive policy. The lesson was clear, argued Yamagata: a conscript army of forty thousand men was no longer adequate to Japan's needs, nor was a navy lacking transport ships to dispatch Japanese troops abroad.

The crisis in Korea persuaded top civilian leaders that it was unwise to postpone expenditure on a bigger army and navy. In September 1882 Iwakura told the Dajōkan that increased naval strength was essential for a maritime country like Japan. Were hostilities to break out with Korea or China, he said, the country would be in grave difficulty. If Japan tried to attack either country, it would not have enough vessels to protect the home islands; and if it used its fleet to protect the home islands, it would not be able to mount an attack on China or Korea. The Chinese were building up their fleet, and the day might come when Japan would be unable to defend itself against China's scorn—a thought he "shuddered at." It was of the utmost urgency to spend more on the navy, he said, even if this meant raising taxes.[77] Even Finance Minister Matsukata Masayoshi, author of the fiscal retrenchment policy, agreed that financial resources had to be found for a military and naval buildup if the international situation required.

Spurred by anxieties over China, military expenditures grew steadily in the 1880s. In 1880 the share of military spending had amounted to 19 percent of total government expenditures; by 1886 it had risen to 25 percent; and by 1890 it stood at 31 percent. In 1883 army plans called for a substantial expansion of land forces: twenty-eight infantry regiments (including four imperial guard regiments), each regiment to consist of three battalions; seven cavalry battalions, each consisting of three companies; seven field artillery battalions, each consisting of two field-gun battalions and one mountain-gun battalion; seven engineer battalions; and seven transport battalions. The proposed composition of

77. Matsushita, *Meiji gunsei shiron*, 36–37.

forces was clearly intended to reshape the army as a force capable of fighting on the continent. If internal defense had been the main mission, the plan would have included more fixed artillery units and fewer cavalry, engineer, or transport units. The navy developed its own plans for expansion of the fleet to forty-two vessels, thirty-two of which would have to be newly constructed. Within the next two years twelve new vessels were purchased or put under construction.[78]

The general staff also moved ahead with contingency plans for a war on the Asian mainland. The army's main China expert, Colonel Ogawa Masaji, chief of the second bureau, had traveled to China in 1879 and again in 1886; with this background, he drew up a plan intended to protect Japan's "independence" by dividing China into small pieces and bringing it under Japanese influence before the Western imperialists carved it up. He anticipated that it would take about five years to prepare for a war with China and urged that an attack should then be mounted whenever an appropriate opportunity presented itself. The Ogawa plan projected the landing of eight divisions on the continent: five for an attack on Peking in the north, and three to occupy strong points in the Yangtze Valley and to prevent the Hunan army from moving north. Since it did not take into account the possibility of either popular Chinese resistance or foreign intervention, the plan remained a naive and unrealistic paper exercise, unlikely to be executed in reality.[79] More significant were large-scale joint army-navy maneuvers, involving 31,759 troops, 4,266 horses, 20 warships, and 3 transports, carried out in Aichi prefecture in the spring of 1890; similar joint maneuvers were staged in Tochigi in the fall of 1892. These exercises rehearsed landing operations, the use of rail transport, and the mobilization of reserves. The army also proceeded with the organization of logistical support for overseas operations.[80]

What was the significance of the military buildup of the 1880s for Japanese policy toward Korea? On the one hand, there can be little doubt that it made the Japanese leadership more confident of success in any clash with the Chinese. An enhanced state of military readiness reduced inhibitions about using force to back a forward policy in Korea. In the early 1880s the Japanese government had hesitated to challenge the Chinese in Korea for fear of provoking a losing fight; by the early

78. Nakatsuka, *Nisshin sensō no kenkyū*, 72.
79. Ibid., 77–80.
80. Ibid., 80–82.

1890s army leadership was sure that it could win.[81] On the other hand, military preparedness did not necessarily push the Japanese leaders in one direction or another. It made the use of military force in Korea a more plausible option, but it did not impel them to choose that option. There remained diplomatic solutions to the Korean problem, and indeed to the growing instability in East Asia.

Few documents illustrate this better than Yamagata Aritomo's 1890 memorial on foreign policy, often cited as an example of the strategic analysis behind Japan's expansionism. Yamagata began with the assumption that a "cordon of interest" as well as a "cordon of sovereignty" was indispensable to Japan's "independence and self-defense." In his view Korea, a country within the "cordon of interest," was perilously close to losing its independence. Once the trans-Siberian railway was completed, a time of "great upheaval" would begin in East Asia, and the wealth and resources of the region would become like a "pile of meat among tigers." Not only would the Europeans have easier access to the region, but China was likely to strengthen its military and naval position in Korea, perhaps even forming alliances with a Western power. Should that happen, it would be difficult for Korea to maintain its independence. Were Korea to suffer the same fate as Annam, Japan's "cordon of sovereignty" through the Straits of Tsushima would be threatened.

It is interesting, however, that Yamagata's analysis did not lead him to conclude that a preemptive military seizure of the peninsula was required. Predictably enough, he called for more naval power and seven divisions to protect the "cordon of interest." But significantly, in confronting the question of how to deal with the threat to Korean independence, he suggested not a military solution but a diplomatic one—an international agreement to guarantee that Korea would not come under foreign domination. Japan should attempt to persuade Great Britain and Germany, both of which had an interest in Korea, to mediate a joint Sino-Japanese protectorate over Korea, creating a balance of power in East Asia and reducing the risk of conflict. The result would be an independent Korea, under a joint Sino-Japanese tutelage and committed to "permanent neutrality," just like Switzerland, Belgium, Serbia, or Luxembourg.[82]

81. The leadership of the navy, by contrast, was rather more cautious since they were not entirely confident of the ability of the Japanese fleet to defeat the larger and better-armed Peiyang fleet.

82. YAI, 196–200.

To be sure, some army leaders, including Vice Chief of Staff Kawa-kami Sōroku, who had been preparing for a war with China for more than a decade, were not loath to test their newly strengthened forces in a contest with China over Korea. Indeed, Kawakami's confidence that Japan could whip the Chinese was bolstered by a tour of Korea and China in the spring of 1893, and on the eve of the Sino-Japanese War he consistently advocated meeting the Chinese with superior force in order to drive them out of Korea and bring the peninsula under Japanese control.[83] But civilian leaders like Prime Minister Itō and Foreign Minister Mutsu Munemitsu, worried about the possibility of foreign intervention, were much more cautious and much less enthusiastic about a military solution. It was a path they chose only when Korea seemed to be on the verge of complete breakdown.

83. Matsushita, *Meiji gunsei shiron*, 359–62; Tokutomi, *Rikugun taishō Kawakami Sōroku*, 126–27.

CHAPTER 2

The Failed Protectorate, 1894–1895

What finally brought war with China was fear that the Korean monarchy was on its last legs. In 1893 unrest had begun to spread among the peasantry in the southern provinces of Chŏlla and Ch'ungch'ŏng. Farmers angry at heavy taxes, the intrusion of foreign-made cotton textiles, and usurious loan rates were drawn in larger and larger numbers to a new religious sect, the Tonghaks, who promised sweeping social change. By the spring of 1894 full-scale rebellion had broken out in the south. In early May Tonghak rebel troops, pitifully armed with cudgels, swords, lances, and a few rifles, overwhelmed a much smaller but better-armed government force at Changsong. Marching north toward Seoul, the Tonghak rebels met no major resistance, and by the end of May they had occupied the capital of Chŏlla Province, Chŏnju, where the founder of the Yi dynasty had been born. Seizure of the city was ominous, and so was the demonstrated inability of the government at Seoul to stop the rebel advance.[1]

The flare-up of the rebellion deepened Japanese apprehension about the ability of the Korean court to maintain the country's independence. The Tonghaks were known to be antiforeign, but that was of less concern to the Japanese than the court's failure to put the rebellion down. A year before the Korean court had announced the successful suppression of the Tonghaks, but the events of May belied that claim. In a *Jiji shinpō*

---

1. Lee Ki-baik, *New History of Korea*, 283–88; Pak Jong-keun, "1894-nen ni okeru Nihongun teppei," 30–32.

editorial, Fukuzawa Yūkichi expressed the fear that if the government were unable to suppress the Tonghaks, the country might well plunge into anarchy, giving either the Westerners or the Chinese an excuse to send in military forces. In either case, Korean independence would be lost, a turn of affairs with enormous consequences for Japan's prestige. To forestall such a crisis, Fukuzawa urged the dispatch of gunboats and troops to protect Japanese residents and to put the rebellion down if Chinese troops were called in.[2]

The earliest official calls for military intervention came from the legation at Seoul, whose staff members were anxiously monitoring the progress of the rebellion. The recently appointed Japanese minister, Ōtori Keisuke, a venerable *yōgakusha* concurrently serving as minister to China, was out of the country, but on May 22 Sugimura Fukashi, chargé d'affaires at Seoul, recommended that Tokyo send in troops to maintain military parity if the Koreans appealed for Chinese help. Sugimura, an old Korean hand, had first come to the peninsula when Hanabusa had been minister, serving as vice-consul at Inchon, then rising steadily to the post of first secretary at the legation. Ministers had come and gone but Sugimura remained, and his views as a Korean expert were respected, influencing even Foreign Minister Mutsu Munemitsu. On May 31 Ōtori Keisuke echoed Sugimura's proposal, suggesting to Mutsu that a rebel invasion of Seoul would provide an opportunity to force the Korean government to undertake reform.[3] In anticipation of intervention, Assistant Chief of Staff Kawakami Sōroku had already ordered preparations for the mobilization of an expeditionary force.[4]

The Itō cabinet's decision to send in troops was shaped by memories of the not-so-distant past. In 1882 the Japanese government had planned to dispatch a mixed brigade to Korea, but the Chinese had moved troops in more quickly to restore order. Had the Chinese tarried, the Japanese would have had the glory of occupying the capital, ousting the Taewŏn'gun, and bringing the rebellion under control. Again in 1884, the timely arrival of superior Japanese forces might have prevented the ruthless suppression of the Kapsin coup, leaving in power a government committed to Japanese-style reform.[5] These lost opportunities made the Japanese leadership aware that they had to put superior military forces

2. *Meiji nyūsu jiten*, 5:443–44.
3. *NGB*, 27.2, p. 154.
4. Nakatsuka, *Nisshin sensō no kenkyū*, 110–12; Pak Jong-keun, "1894 nen ni okeru Nihongun teppei."
5. *KNSKK*, 1:897ff.

on the ground in Korea promptly if they wished to turn the Tonghak crisis to Japan's advantage.[6]

A telegram announcing the departure of fifteen hundred Chinese troops for Korea arrived at the Chinese legation in Seoul during an official dinner on June 4. Horace Allen, then a secretary at the American legation, later recalled, "The jubilation of the Japanese was so evident that the gloom seemed at once to rest most heavily upon our Chinese hosts, as a realizing sense was forced upon them of what the step might mean."[7] The gloomy Chinese knew that a direct confrontation loomed, and the jubilant Japanese knew that soon they would control events in Korea. The next day the Japanese army general staff mobilized the Fifth Division and requisitioned several transports from the NYK line. On June 10 Ōtori, who had landed at Inchon the day before, marched into Seoul with a force of several hundred marines.[8] The Korean government protested vigorously, but the Japanese legation brushed their protests aside, insisting on their right to protect their own citizens in time of trouble.

Aware of the Pandora's box they had opened, Korean officials at Seoul tried desperately to negotiate a truce with the Tonghak leaders at Chŏnju. Chŏn Pong-jun, the chief rebel leader, agreed to an armistice in return for government assurance that official abuses would be ended and the activities of foreign merchants would be curbed. In the face of outside intrusion the internal crisis resolved itself, for the moment at least, and the rebel army at Chŏnju began to disperse. The Korean government could now argue that there was no longer any threat to foreign residents, and in mid-June the Koreans asked both Yuan Shih-kai and Ōtori to withdraw their troops. Two days later Ōtori, who had already informed Tokyo that danger had passed, worked out an agreement with Yuan to begin a reduction in both forces.[9]

The Itō government was determined not to let a golden opportunity slip. The dispatch of a military force was no longer to be debated. The

6. As Itō Hirobumi later told his old friend Sir Ernest Satow, the Japanese had decided to send a larger force than the Chinese because of "the disadvantage in which [Japan] had been placed on a former occasion by her forces being numerically inferior to the Chinese." Lensen, *Korea and Manchuria*, 45.

7. Allen, "Acquaintance with Yuan Shih-kai," 114.

8. Pak Jong-keun, "1894 nen ni okeru Nihongun teppei," 32–40.

9. Ōtori met with Yuan on June 13 to discuss troop withdrawals, and on June 15 they agreed to reduce the Japanese force to 250 men at Inchon and the Chinese force to 400 men at Asan. Other legation officials, among them Sugimura, Motono Ichirō, and Matsui Keishirō, argued against any withdrawal of Japanese troops, and so did the representatives of the Japanese army. Pak Jong-keun, *Nisshin sensō to Chōsen*, 24–31.

armistice at Chŏnju had brought temporary peace, but rebellion might flare up again, and if it did the Chinese could take advantage of the situation.[10] By the end of June the Japanese government had put eight thousand men into Korea, a force several times as large as the Chinese, crossing a line difficult to retreat from without considerable loss of face. Even without the arrival of the Chinese troops, it is conceivable that the Japanese government might have seized on the rebellion to expand its political presence as the Chinese had in 1882 and 1884. Article 5 of the Treaty of Chemulpo allowed the Japanese to protect the Japanese legation and the Japanese community. Had the Tonghak army reached the capital or threatened Japanese residents there or at Inchon, there can be little doubt that the Japanese government would have sent a military expedition. But the real motive would have been to establish a dominant position on the peninsula before any other power could.

THE JAPANESE MOTIVES

Just what did the Japanese leadership expect to accomplish in Korea? It is evident that the top leadership at first had no well-defined idea other than countering the Chinese. While there was general agreement that Japan should keep Korea from falling under the control of another power, just how to do that was far from clear. Was it enough to induce the Koreans to reform themselves to maintain their independence? Should the Japanese establish Korea as a quasi protectorate and involve themselves directly in reform? Was it better to bind Korea to Japan by a denser web of economic and military ties? Or should the Japanese simply seize control of the country and bring it under their direct domination? At no point during the next year did the government in Tokyo resolve these questions in any formal way. Indeed, as we shall see, when Foreign Minister Mutsu Munemitsu asked the cabinet to adopt an overall policy in mid-August, they were unable to reach a conclusion. Thus, there exists no document that could be called a master plan for Korea.

Nevertheless, if actions speak as loudly as words, it is clear that the Itō cabinet and its representatives in Korea sought two goals: one was to bring about a basic reform of Korean institutions; the other was to acquire economic privileges for Japan. Both of these goals were linked in their minds to the preservation of Korean "independence," by which the Japanese meant both formal independence in terms of international law

10. *NGB*, 27.2, pp. 192–200.

and independence from any outside political influence or political domination other than their own. Needless to say, from the perspective of Korean leaders and other outside observers, the Japanese position appeared self-contradictory. If the Japanese were so interested in Korean independence, then why were they interfering so officiously in Korean politics? The contradiction was apparent to some Japanese leaders even before the outbreak of the war. As Matsukata Masayoshi observed in mid-June, "Since we have already recognized Korea as an independent country, let's stop interfering in its internal affairs as best we can. If we rashly interfere in their internal affairs, this will damage the appearance of Korea's independence."[11] The contradiction eventually became clear to others too.

Few contemporary observers doubted that the Japanese wanted to establish a paramount economic position in Korea during the Sino-Japanese War. The strongest advocate of this goal was Matsukata, who did not relish the idea of a war with China or even a program of internal reform but saw the presence of Japanese troops in Korea as an opportunity to press economic demands on the Korean government. In mid-June he wrote Kuroda Kiyotaka, minister of transportation, urging that Japan acquire "real rights and real interests" in Korea: "The first [way to accomplish that] is to seize the opportunity to open three new ports and establish settlements there; the second is to secure mining rights in Korea; the third is to acquire the privilege of laying telegraph lines; and the fourth is to secure the right to build a railway line between Seoul and Pusan."[12] In effect, Matsukata was proposing that Japan expand its trade enclave, acquire access to underground resources, and develop a basic system of transportation and communication in Korea. Since other foreign powers were equally interested in developing Korea as a market, he thought that they would see these policies in their own interest. No doubt that was true, but not all the other powers wished to see Japan take the initiative in opening the country wider.

Prime Minister Itō and Home Minister Inoue Kaoru also wanted to expand Japan's economic presence in Korea, but at first they gave higher priority to reforming the Korean government. It has been argued that their commitment to reform was merely an effort to put Japan's actions in a positive light. Foreign Minister Mutsu later noted in his memoir: "I myself never saw any significance in the issue of Korea's reform other

11. Tokutomi, *Kōshaku Matsukata Masayoshi den*, 2:499–500, 510–24.
12. Ibid.

than its being a matter of political necessity. Furthermore, I saw no need whatsoever to launch crusades in the name of national chivalry." There were others, he added, who wanted to use reform "as an excuse for expanding our frontiers" and "to make Korea a protectorate completely subservient to Japan."[13] Many historians have interpreted this passage to mean that reform was a cynical cover for territorial and political aggression. But the Japanese insistence on reform was too persistent, and in execution often too politically inept, to support this interpretation. Had the commitment to reform been cynical, the Japanese would have abandoned it early on.

To be sure, the Japanese leaders thought a reform program would serve Japanese interests. In March 1895, for example, Inoue Kaoru, then serving as Japanese minister in Seoul, observed that unless "fundamental reform" were undertaken it would be impossible to realize Korean independence or maintain it permanently.[14] A weak and complaisant court, a rapacious class of officials, endemic bribery and corruption, mismanaged finances and chaotic currency, and technological backwardness—all these kept Korea weak and unable to resist outside pressure. Unless these abuses were overcome by a program of intense self-strengthening, Korea could not act as a strategic buffer between Japan and its powerful neighbors, China and Russia. Without reform the Korean polity would remain easy prey, leaving Japan's flanks dangerously exposed. The Japanese made no secret of this rationale for reform and indeed presented such arguments to the Koreans themselves.[15]

The urgency of reform was reinforced by pleas from the legation staff in Seoul. Typical was a long dispatch from Uchida Sadatsuchi, the consul at Seoul, who painted a bleak picture of Korean politics corruption in the central government ministries, struggles among selfish and self-interested factions to curry royal favor, steady deterioration of the popular energy (*minryoku*), and economic stagnation. *Yangban* bribed their

---

13. *KKR*, 29.
14. *NGNSB*, 1:158.
15. Ōtori presented this rationale to the Koreans in late June. For more than a decade the country had been racked by military revolts and popular disturbances, unable to maintain domestic peace, and so weak that it had been reduced to calling in foreign troops to restore public order. The country lacked the military strength either to keep internal peace or to protect its independence. This situation, Ōtori explained, was of grave concern to the Japanese, who were separated from Korea by only a narrow strait, and whose political and trading ties with Korea were so substantial that they could not sit idly watching disturbances in Korea that were bound to influence Japan's interests. To be sure, this rebuke was self-serving, but it made sense. *NGB*, 27.1, pp. 578–80, 586–91.

way into office, then proceeded to squeeze the local population to enrich their families as quickly as possible. Local officials lined their pockets by exacting bribes from lower functionaries, selling monopolies to local merchants, levying exorbitant taxes, extorting money from local land-owners and merchants by throwing them in prison on trumped-up charges, using grain embargoes to corner the local market for them-selves, and so forth. This rampant corruption, argued Uchida, weakened the very fabric of Korean society. The people normally tolerated it, but when it became excessive, they exploded into rebellion, as they had in Chŏlla, attacking local yamens and killing local officials. Even if the people did not rebel, corruption stifled their ambition and initiative, and those who managed to accumulate wealth tried to conceal it, living fru-gally and austerely to avoid being preyed on by local officials. The result was stagnation in agriculture, commerce, and manufacturing. Only if "fundamental reform" were undertaken could the economy be revived, foreign trade flourish, new government revenues be developed, official corruption ended, the rights and duties of the people be clarified, the lives and property of the populace secured, the "teachings of enlight-enment" spread among the population, and a policy of *shokusan kogyō* be adopted.[16]

No doubt arguments like Uchida's were persuasive because they em-bodied an ideology of progress internalized by the Meiji leadership. If not as naively zealous about the benefits of "civilization and enlight-enment" as Fukuzawa Yūkichi and his disciples, the Meiji leaders nonetheless thought the Koreans would be better off following the path already taken by Japan. Proud of their own efforts at modernizing, they wanted the Koreans, in effect, to carry out their own Meiji Restoration. Reform, in other words, was not merely a matter of political expediency or political advantage for Japan; rather, it would benefit the Koreans themselves, especially the benighted commoners squeezed and extorted by *yangban* officials. The first priority was to reform the Korean gov-ernment, a warren of sinecures, riddled with patronage, nepotism, favoritism, and corruption and populated by an army of greedy and self-interested functionaries. In its place the Meiji leaders hoped to see a rationally organized modern bureaucratic structure, not so very differ-ent from the one they had erected.

Abstracted from a series of documents in the summer of 1894, the Japanese program for the reform of Korea may be summarized as

16. *NKGS*, 10:4–8.

follows: (1) the creation of a modern specialized bureaucracy, with functionally defined offices filled by technically competent officials, adequately paid and free from the abuses of nepotism and the sale of office; (2) a rationalized governmental structure, shorn of sinecures and unnecessary offices, centering on a cabinet made up of functionally specialized ministries; (3) a new judicial structure with permanent professional judges and a hierarchy of appeals courts, capable of conducting fair and open trials, to replace an outmoded judicial structure and process conducted by nonspecialized local officials and magistrates; (4) a rationalized system of central government finances, with clear and complete accounting of revenues and expenditures, a regular budget, checks on the misappropriation of funds, a reformed tax system, and a uniform system of currency; (5) modernized police and military forces; (6) a modern transportation and communication system, including telegraph lines, a railroad system, and a postal service; and (7) a modernized educational system, from primary school through high school.

THE JAPANESE COUP DE MAIN

The key question was, Would the Koreans be able to carry out such reforms all by themselves? The consensus in Tokyo was that they could not. In mid-June Prime Minister Itō proposed to the cabinet that the Japanese join with the Chinese in a cooperative effort to bring about change in Korea. His plan was simple: the Chinese and Japanese troops would put down the Tonghak rebels, and then both countries would send several dozen "commissioners" to Korea to launch an overhaul of the central government. The cabinet backed Itō's proposal, but Foreign Minister Mutsu doubted that the Chinese would accept it. At its meeting the next morning the cabinet agreed to two provisos suggested by Mutsu: the first was that Japan would not withdraw its troops from Korea until negotiations with China had reached some conclusion; and the second was that if China refused to cooperate in a joint reform effort, Japan alone would try to "compel the Korean government to undertake administrative reform."

When the Chinese rejected the joint reform proposal, as Mutsu had predicted, Itō began to countenance the possibility of a conflict with China. Early in the morning of June 22, he gloomily told Matsukata that since the Ch'ing appeared to be making military preparations, there was probably "no policy but to go to war." The cabinet agreed later in the day to press ahead with a reform effort in Korea even though that was likely to antagonize the Chinese. "We are bound now to do single-handed what we proposed to the Chinese government," said Mutsu. The reform of Korea was emerging as a key issue, not simply a rationale for some other objective. As Lord Curzon later observed, "The Japanese anxiety to apply the purge [of reform], though only a secondary motive of the war, has been of no make-believe character, but has been pushed with the professional earnestness of the physicians enforcing a disagreeable medicine upon some refractory patient."[17]

The Korean court resisted the medicine stubbornly. When Ōtori presented Kojong with a set of reform proposals on June 26, the king ignored him, responding with a demand that the Japanese immediately withdraw their troops. For the next few weeks the Koreans continued to insist on troop withdrawals and the Japanese continued to insist on reform. In early July the Koreans formed their own reform commission, headed by Home Minister Sin Jung-hui; even then the legation staff doubted that it was a sincere effort. Ōtori cabled Mutsu that since the Korean government was only paying lip service to reform, the time had come to resort to "exceptional measures": Japanese troops should seize control of the capital and the royal palace, and then the Japanese should "carry on relentless negotiations with the Korean government until they consent to our recommendations." Otherwise there was little hope that the Koreans would do anything by themselves.

Whether a military coup de main was Ōtori's own idea or not, it certainly enjoyed the full support of the legation staff, who wanted to use force to prod the recalcitrant Koreans toward change. Sugimura Fukashi had already suggested that Japanese troops oust the conservative pro-Chinese Min faction and replace them with an "enlightened" government of anti-Min or neutral officials. In late June Uchida Sadatsuchi proposed a more radical alternative: the establishment of a Japanese protectorate. If Japan wanted to lead Korea toward "enlightenment and national strength" (kaimei fukoku), it would have to intervene directly in the country's internal and external affairs; the Koreans should be forced to sign a treaty putting the country under Japanese control and permitting Japan to assist in internal reforms. The policy that finally emerged incorporated elements of both proposals.

The Japanese military forces made an ostentatious show of strength on the streets of Seoul, partly as a matter of preparedness, partly as a

17. Curzon, Problems of the Far East, 373.

means of psychological intimidation. Japanese troops paraded through the city streets, Japanese sentries were posted at intervals along Chongno, the main east-west artery, and Japanese soldiers stood guard at the city gates. An infantry battalion was dispatched to secure the high ground near the great South Gate, and six artillery emplacements were set up at Namsan, on heights commanding the whole city. The Japanese legation justified these troop dispositions as necessary to protect the legation and the Japanese community in Seoul, but clearly they were intended to forestall any sudden military moves by the Chinese and to prevent the flight of the king to Chinese protection or some other refuge where he might rally resistance to the Japanese.[18] The mistakes of 1882 and 1884 were not to be repeated. The Japanese were well positioned to seize control of the capital and the court if Tokyo decided to do so.

The more difficult question was where to find Korean collaborators. It was impossible to expect support from the Min faction under the leadership of Min Yŏng-jun, who was wedded to a policy of "relying on the powerful" (i.e., the Chinese). And the few remaining reform-minded officials, who could remember that death or exile had been the fate of the reformers of 1884, were not likely to take the initiative. In any case, as Ōtori reported to Mutsu, none of them appeared to be strong leaders. The only other alternative, suggested by proreform officials such as Kim Ga-jin, An Tong-su, and Yu Kil-chun, was to turn to the Taewŏn'gun, long a rival of the Min and an enemy of the Chinese. But the Taewŏn'gun, a deeply conservative Confucian defender of traditional ways, was suspicious of all foreigners, including the Japanese. Having returned from his exile in Tientsin to virtual confinement in his residence at Seoul, he was also reluctant to take political risks, and when Sugimura sent an emissary to sound him out in late June, he remained noncommittal. Nevertheless, the legation staff, operating on the misguided assumption that the Taewŏn'gun would become Japan's friend since he was an enemy of their enemies, saw no way to assure that the Korean government would undertake reform except to install in power an unlikely coalition between the crusty old Confucian and a cadre of proreform "enlightened officials."[19]

The government in Tokyo was not enthusiastic about a coup since it was likely to upset the foreign powers. Even more to the point, it would beget a contradiction in Japanese policy: how could Japan claim it was

18. Pak Jong-keun, "Nisshin kaisen ni okeru Nihongun no Chōsen ōkyū senryō," 41–42.
19. NGB, 27.1, pp. 635–36.

protecting the independence of Korea if it were to seize control of its government?[20] But since it had become clear that the British, the Americans, and the Russians were not going to intervene in support of the Chinese, the Itō cabinet was inching its way toward a decision for war. In this new context, on July 19 Mutsu cabled Ōtori to take whatever steps he thought necessary to compel the Korean government to carry out a reform program. He added a cautious proviso: "You may take such steps as you think proper but carefully avoid complications with other foreign powers, as previously instructed. It is hoped that you will not actually besiege the Royal Palace or the capital, as such an act is considered unwise and impolitic."[21]

A seizure of the palace to oust the Min faction was precisely what Ōtori and other legation staff members were planning in tight secrecy with Major General Ōshima Yoshimasa, the commander of the mixed brigade. To avoid "complications with the other powers," the change in government was to be portrayed as a coup by the Taewŏn'gun against the Min faction, and the involvement of Japanese troops was to be portrayed as a response to a call for help from the Taewŏn'gun to overcome resistance by pro-Min Korean troops. The plan unfolded on the morning of July 23. At dawn a Japanese infantry regiment marched into the Kyŏngbok palace, where it quickly overcame resistance. Commanding access to the palace interior, Japanese guards barred members of the Min faction from entering. To foil a countercoup, Japanese troops were dispatched to maintain surveillance of the residences of key government officials. By 8:10 A.M. Ōtori was able to cable Mutsu that the royal palace was under control. But the clockwork precision of the coup had been marred by the absence of the one person critical to its success—the Taewŏn'gun.

On the previous evening, as the Japanese were preparing for the assault on the palace, a group of legation officials—Okamoto Ryūnosuke, Hozumi Torakurō, Kokubun Shōtarō, and Hagiwara Shujirō—arrived at the Taewŏn'gun's residence with a Japanese infantry company to escort him to the palace. The old man, who earlier had rebuffed several secret approaches both by reform-minded Korean officials and Japanese legation staff members, refused to budge. Foreigners, he told his visitors, had no business meddling in the affairs of the Korean court. The flustered Japanese huddled. Hagiwara, anxious to keep the operation on sched-

20. *KKR*, 81. Mutsu continued to worry about this contradiction even after the coup of July 23. See *NGB*, 27.1, pp. 640–41.
21. *KKR*, 82.

ule, wanted to drag the Taewŏn'gun to the palace by force, but Oka-moto suggested reasoning with him. Sugimura, who was summoned from the legation to resolve the impasse, first entreated, then threatened. The Taewŏn'gun finally agreed to cooperate, saying that no matter how distasteful the Japanese demands were, he would have to countenance them since the fate of the country and the royal family was at stake. But he insisted on a written assurance from Sugimura that Japan would not demand a single piece of territory from Korea and he refused to go to the palace without an order from the king. It was 11:00 A.M. by the time the Taewŏn'gun reached the palace, escorted by a company of Japanese troops and about twenty Japanese policemen.[22]

While the legation officials wanted the Taewŏn'gun as the nominal head of the new government, they did not want him to exercise any real power. His ideas about Korea's future were quite different from theirs, and it was likely he would do his best to thwart the Japanese reform effort. To bypass him the Japanese suggested setting up a special deliberative council to expedite change. Four days after the coup, two of which were spent winning the Taewŏn'gun over to the idea, a Military Deliberative Council (*Kun'guk Kimuch'ŏ*), a new and unprecedented policymaking body, was empowered to discuss and draft new laws and regulations concerning official appointments, administrative procedures, tax and fiscal regulations, the school system, the military system, and matters relating to industry and commerce—in short, everything the Japanese wanted to reform. The deliberative council could also discuss all matters relating to defense of the country.[23] While its decisions were to be presented formally to the regent, they required only the sanction of the king.

The Japanese hoped that the new deliberative council would be dominated by proreform officials. The failed reform coup of 1884 had broken the radical wing of the Korean enlightenment movement, but a small cadre of reform-minded moderates not directly involved in the coup plot continued to serve in the government, often in middle-echelon posts, quietly but actively introducing and propagating "new knowledge" from the outside world by establishing modern-style schools, teacher training institutes, agricultural experimental stations, modern minting facilities, and so on. Like the "self-strengthening" Ch'ing officials of the 1860s and 1870s, they focused on technological and educational

22. Pak Jong-keun, *Nisshin sensō to Chōsen*, 58–62.
23. Sugimura, *Kushinroku*, 63–64.

change rather than major institutional reform. Their ranks were swelled by a number of officials who had come to realize the enormous dimensions of the foreign challenge while traveling abroad on study missions or serving as diplomatic representatives in Korea's new legations in Tokyo, Washington, and elsewhere. It was in these officials that the Japanese placed their hopes, and it was from their numbers that key members of the deliberative council were recruited.[24]

The most important of the reform-minded officials on the council was Kim Hong-jip (1842–96), who had been impressed by Japan's progress when he visited there as a member of the second official mission in 1880. It was doubtless his reputation as a forward-looking official that prompted the conspirators of 1884 to recommend that he be appointed governor of Seoul, and even after the Min faction was restored to power, Kim continued to hold important official positions. Known as a gradualist who favored prudent reform, he was precisely the type of political ally the Japanese sought. So were Kim Yun-sik and Ŏ Yun-jung, both of whom had been sent on major missions to explore the reform efforts of Korea's two neighbors in 1881. Kim headed a mission to Tientsin, then the center of the Li Hung-chang's "self-strengthening" efforts, and Ŏ Yun-jung had gone to Japan with Cho Chun-yŏng, Pak Chŏng-yang, Hong Yŏng-sik, and others. All three men—the two Kims and Ŏ—were trusted by the Japanese. Indeed, in 1885, at the time of secret negotiations between the Russians and the Korean court, Inoue Kaoru had proposed to the Chinese that the three men be installed at the head of a proreform government to replace the pro-Russian Min faction to head off Korean rapprochement with Russia.[25]

Within the council were other stronger advocates of change, willing to experiment and cut to the root of the institutional structure. The best known is Yu Kil-chun, who had studied "enlightenment" ideas under Pak Kyu-su before traveling to Japan as an assistant to Ŏ Yun-jung in 1881. After enrolling briefly in Keiō Gijuku, he returned to Korea, where Pak Yŏng-hyo asked him to manage the Hansŏng sunbo with help from Inoue Kakugorō. After Pak was dismissed as governor of Seoul in 1883, Yu went abroad to study in the United States, where he acquired a cosmopolitan acquaintance with the outside world rare among his contemporaries. When he returned to Korea in 1885, he devoted himself to promoting knowledge about the West and advo-

24. Pak Jong-keun, "Kim Hong-jip seiken," 2–4.
25. Pak Jong-keun, Nisshin sensō to Chōsen, 77.

cating change according to the Western model. In 1895 he published *A Journey to the West (Soyu kyonmun)*, a comprehensive introduction to Western civilization similar to Fukuzawa Yūkichi's *Seiyō jijō*. Like Fukuzawa, Yu argued that superficial absorption of Western customs was less important than understanding the principles of Western civilization and that true "civilization and enlightenment" required adaptation of these principles to the realities of Korea. Some reforms he suggested—the adoption of a constitutional monarchy and the introduction of free enterprise—were quite radical by Korean standards of the time.[26]

In principle all decisions within the deliberative council were to be made by a majority vote. Ōtori assured Itō that the council was dominated by "the Japan faction, that is to say, the reform faction." In fact, its composition was more complex. As the result of political compromise within the court it included not only moderate reformers (Kim Hong-jip, Kim Yun-sik, Ŏ Yun-jung) and younger "enlightened" officials (Kim Ka-jin, Cho Hŭi-yon, An Kyŏng-su, Kim Hag-u, and Yu Kil-chun) but also supporters of the queen, familiars of the Taewŏn'gun, and several neutral officials. The proreform elements took the lead in the preparation of legislation, but the peculiar composition of the council was to cause political difficulties, particularly as the Taewŏn'gun, angry and frustrated at the flood of reform pouring out of the council, politicked behind the scenes to sabotage its work.

TOWARD A PROTECTORATE

The war with China, formally declared on August 1, was more than two weeks old before the Itō cabinet tried to define its goals in Korea. No one at the highest levels questioned the need for reform in Korea, and no one questioned the goal of Korean independence, but there were deepening doubts that the Koreans could be expected to accomplish either by themselves. With Japanese troops pouring into the peninsula and early victories behind them, the Japanese had new opportunities to squeeze concessions from the Korean government, consolidating a more active and permanent role for Japan on the peninsula. Diplomatic and military officials in Seoul also began to call for intervention in Korean affairs. On August 4 Uchida Sadatsuchi even urged Mutsu to conclude a protec-

26. Pak Jong-keun, "Kim Hong-jip seiken," 7–11; Lee Ki-baik, *New History of Korea*, 297–98; Harada Tamaki, "Chōsen no kindaika kōsō," 10–68.

torate treaty permitting the Japanese to become directly involved in the reform program. If the cabinet thought a protectorate premature, he said, than at the very least it ought to persuade the Korean government to employ Japanese advisers as "prime movers."[27]

On August 17 Mutsu, hoping to clarify political objectives in Korea, presented four policy alternatives to the cabinet: (1) a hands-off policy, refraining from direct interference in Korea's internal affairs (and preventing other countries from interfering), letting the Koreans pursue reform on their own initiative; (2) the establishment of a Japanese protectorate with the Japanese assisting and supporting Korean independence, directly or indirectly, for an unspecified period of time; (3) the establishment of a joint Sino-Japanese guarantee of Korean independence and territorial integrity: and (4) an internationally guaranteed neutralization of Korea by agreement among Japan, China, and the Western powers. All had been discussed and debated during the spring and summer of 1894, but as Mutsu carefully pointed out, all had substantial shortcomings. A hands-off policy might mean a return to power of the conservative Min faction backed by the Chinese; a protectorate would invite the suspicion and censure of the foreign powers; a Sino-Japanese guarantee might founder on disagreement over questions of diplomatic status and domestic reform in Korea; and an international guarantee might provoke political trouble at home since it would involve no substantive or material gains for Japan.[28]

With the outcome of the war still in doubt, and the reaction of the foreign powers to events in Korea uncertain, the cabinet was unable to reach a provisional decision, let alone a formal one. "We simply agreed for the time being," recalled Mutsu, "that the second of the four options I had suggested [i.e., a protectorate] should serve as our general goal, and that sometime in the future, we should make a definite decision on the policies we wished to pursue over the long term."[29] The failure to decide on a firm policy goal disappointed Mutsu, but it did leave open the opportunity to improvise a de facto Japanese protectorate in Korea. This course of action had the support of the legation staff in Seoul, and it was also likely to play well with the domestic political audience. As Mutsu warned the cabinet, "If nothing substantial comes after dispatching a large force and spending an enormous amount for military

27. NKGS, 9:57–59
28. Kajima, *Diplomacy of Japan*, 1:109–11.
29. KKR, 99.

expenses, can the Imperial Japanese government escape attack from public opinion?"[30]

On August 20 Minister Ōtori signed a provisional agreement with the Korean government based on a draft treaty presented at the end of July to Kim Ka-jin, the vice-minister of foreign affairs and a member of the proreform faction.[31] While the Koreans rejected a clause calling for the hiring of Japanese advisers and excluded any reference to Japanese "protection" of Korea, the agreement paved the way for a substantial increase in Japanese economic and political influence. It gave the Japanese rights to construct railroad trunk lines linking Seoul to Pusan and Inchon, promised the opening of a new treaty port in Chŏlla Province, and provided for the signing of a treaty allowing the Japanese to control the military telegraph lines laid down between the capital and the two major ports. It also promised the future establishment of a joint Korean-Japanese reform commission to "meet and decide upon those matters necessary to consolidate Korea's independence and autonomy." If this agreement did not establish a Japanese protectorate in a formal sense, it moved in that direction by setting up a "dyarchic" reform commission; and if it did not guarantee Japanese economic predominance, it gave the Japanese a powerful hold on the development of the country's transportation and communication system. During the next year the document was to provide the Japanese grounds for demanding increased involvement in the reform program.[32]

Six days later the Korean government signed a treaty of alliance with Japan permitting the Japanese to take military action against China and promising Korean assistance in facilitating the movement and provisioning of Japanese troops. Since only the Japanese had a significant military force, this was a curiously one-sided alliance. Its main purpose was to assure that the Koreans would not switch sides in the middle of the war, a turn of events that would be a diplomatic and political fiasco for Japan but was not beyond the bounds of possibility. As Ōtori reported to Mutsu, the Taewŏn'gun, the titular head of the Korean government, did not seem very interested in the war or Korea's role in it, except to complain to the Russian minister that a prolonged con-

30. Kajima, *Diplomacy of Japan*, 1:111.
31. This draft had provided for Japanese construction of railroad lines linking Seoul to Pusan and Inchon, Japanese control over telegraph lines connecting Seoul with Inchon and Pusan, the opening of a new port in Chŏlla Province, the employment of Japanese military, political, and legal advisers, and the establishment of a joint Korean-Japanese commission to oversee the reform effort. *NGB*, 27.1, pp. 633–34.
32. *NGB*, 27.1, pp. 652–55.

flict would upset peace in East Asia, a tacit invitation for Russian intervention.[33]

THE FLOUNDERING OF REFORM

Doubts about the ability of the Koreans to carry out reforms by themselves fortified arguments in favor of deeper Japanese involvement in Korean internal affairs. Since its establishment in late July the deliberative council had been surging ahead with the promulgation of reform measures. This was the beginning of the so-called Kabo reforms. By late August it had approved sixteen laws fundamentally reorganizing the central government, and it had presented to the king 106 resolutions calling for everything from the transliteration of Western proper nouns into *han'gŭl* through the legalization of remarriage for *yangban* widows to the establishment of a royal guard (*ch'inwigun*) staffed by Japanese-trained noncommissioned officers. There was no question about the efficiency of the deliberative council; its effectiveness was another matter.

The Taewŏn'gun, never an enthusiast for Western-style or Japanese-style reform, was angry at the flood of reform documents pouring out of the council. He agreed with none of the changes, and he refused to approve any of them. He was further irritated when the council began to forward their memorials directly to the king, bypassing him completely. To thwart the reform effort, he decided to encourage factional splits by carefully cultivating men like Yu Kil-chun, Pak Jun-yang, and Yi Wŏn-kyun and by intimidating ardent proreformers like Yi Yun-yong, An Kyŏng-su, Kim Ka-jin, and Kwon Yung-jin, who turned for support to the royal couple. Caught in the middle of this internal squabbling were the gradualists, Kim Hong-jip, Kim Yun-sik, and Ŏ Yun-jung, who tried to maintain neutrality. By the middle of August, however, the two Kims and Ŏ had begun to move into the Taewŏn'gun's orbit, and Kim Hong-jip was appointed to head a newly created cabinet (*naegak*) manned by fellow moderates.

The basic difficulty with the reform program was that it attempted too much too quickly in a chaotic political setting. It was easy enough to draft paper reforms, secure royal approval, and promulgate new laws and regulations, but it was difficult to make sure that they were carried out. Lower-echelon officials in Seoul did not change their ways easily, and neither did officials in the provinces. The outbreak of war made the

33. *NGB*, 27.1, pp. 638–39.

problem worse. While the Japanese were landing forces at Pusan and Inchon, the Chinese were pouring in troops from the north, concentrating them at P'yŏngyang. The country was a battlefield divided between a Chinese-controlled north and a Japanese-controlled south. "Inasmuch as the central authority of the Korean government scarcely extended beyond Seoul and its environs," Mutsu later observed, "Korea's leaders had neither the opportunity nor the wherewithal to carry out domestic reforms anywhere, however loudly they might declare their intentions to do so."[34] Conservative senior officials, fearful that the reforms were undermining the monarchical order, began to submit antireform memorials to the king.

In Japan, by contrast, the prevailing mood was impatience over the desultory pace of change. Even as the Japanese were sacrificing lives and money for Korean independence, complained the press, the Koreans appeared obdurately resistant to Japanese guidance and obstinately unwilling to shake off the lethargy and backwardness that had weakened Korean independence in the first place. In the *Jiji shinpō* Fukuzawa fumed that Korea was a "barbarian country" whose people had no idea of what "civilization" was and whose stubbornness could be overcome only by "intimidation" (*kyōhaku*).[35] Fukuzawa's wrath was directed mainly against the Taewŏn'gun, but others felt that the Koreans were basically incapable of putting their own house in order.

Much blame for the failure of the reform program fell on Ōtori, who had already been criticized by the Japanese military command in Korea as being "old" and "indecisive."[36] In fact, Ōtori was a supporter of gradual change, but he was also reluctant to interfere deeply or directly in Korean politics for fear that too aggressive a posture might push the Koreans into the arms of the Chinese or invite the intervention of Russia or another power.[37] Even if he had pushed a reform program more aggressively, however, it is not likely that he could have exercised much influence over the deeply divided Korean elite. Neither a major Japanese political figure nor an expert on Korean affairs, he had been appointed minister to Seoul largely because of his knowledge of China and his connections in Peking. Although Mutsu was inclined to defend Ōtori, pressures to remove him mounted.

As victories rolled up for Japan on land and sea, Mutsu and Itō once

34. *KKR*, 97.
35. Pak Jong-keun, *Nisshin sensō to Chōsen*, 124.
36. Ibid., 124–27.
37. FMA, File 3.8.4.16-3, Ōtori to Mutsu, Aug. 14, 1894.

again began to worry that the foreigners might intervene. If that were to happen, the Japanese representative in Korea had to be a person of grander stature who could act on his own initiative in response to rapidly changing conditions.[38] What was needed was a proconsul, not an emissary.[39] Mutsu himself may have harbored ambitions, but the choice finally fell on Home Minister Inoue Kaoru, a close political ally of Itō. Among the top Japanese leaders, no one else had as much experience in negotiating with Korea. In 1876 Inoue had accompanied Kuroda to Seoul as vice-plenipotentiary during the negotiation of the Treaty of Kangwha; he had presided over the negotiations of the Treaty of Chemulpo as foreign minister in 1882; and he had served as plenipotentiary in the negotiations of the Treaty of Seoul in 1885. Over the years he had built up a wide circle of connections within the Korean elite, many of whom he knew personally. Whenever Korean diplomatic or cultural missions arrived in Tokyo, their itineraries usually included a visit with him. And Inoue was also a Chōshū man, an important consideration since the early Japanese victories at P'yŏngyang and in the Yellow Sea had been the work of Satsuma generals and admirals. If glory on the battlefield went to Satsuma, then Chōshū should have a chance at the glory of transforming an independent Korea into a "civilized" country.[40]

OUSTING THE CONSERVATIVES

For eight months after his arrival in Seoul in late October 1894, Inoue made a bold but ultimately unsuccessful effort to turn Korea into a political and economic dependency of Japan, a protectorate in fact if not in name. Abandoning the conciliatory style of Ōtori, he deliberately adopted a lordly manner to impress the Korean leadership with his own importance. Like the recently departed Chinese proconsul, Yuan Shih-kai, Inoue insisted on being treated differently from the other foreign representatives in Seoul, and he demanded immediate audiences with the king whenever he wished. At his first meeting with Kojong—a

38. *KKR*, 101–2, 112.

39. Rumors had been circulating since late August that Gotō Shōjirō, a prominent Jiyūtō leader with close ties to Kim Ok-kiun, Pak Yŏng-hyo, and other Korean political refugees, was to be invited to serve as an adviser to the Korean government, but Mutsu thought it would be unwise to turn someone of Gotō's political stripe loose in Korea. FMA, File 3.6.4.16-3, "Gaikoku kanchō ni oite honpōjin kankei zakken. Kankoku no bu," Mutsu to Ōtori, Aug. 22, 1894; Ōtori to Mutsu, Aug. 23, 1894; Mutsu to Ōtori, Aug. 30, 1894.

40. Pak Jong-keun, *Nisshin sensō to Chōsen*, 127–28; Inoue Kaoru Kō Denki Hensankai, *Segai Inoue-Kō den*, 4:389–99.

meeting that no Korean officials other than the foreign minister and the royal household minister were allowed to attend—Inoue bluntly told the king that he was not an ordinary diplomat but had come to Korea at the special request of the Japanese emperor to advise the king on his country's affairs.[41]

The first task on Inoue's ambitious agenda was to clear away the thickets of conservatism at the Korean court. While critics at home might blame the general "backwardness" of Korea for the slow pace of reform, Inoue saw more specific political obstacles—the queen and her faction, the Taewŏn'gun, and Yi Chun-yong, the Taewŏn'gun's favorite grandson. The chief obstacle was the Taewŏn'gun, whom Inoue thought a cunning "China worshiper" more interested in reasserting his influence than in reforming the state.[42] During his first few weeks in Seoul Inoue did what he could to undermine the Taewŏn'gun's political standing, pointedly suggesting to Prime Minister Kim Hong-jip that there was no need to consult with the Taewŏn'gun on policy matters. He also tried to substantiate rumors that the old man had been behind the renewed outbreak of local disturbances in the south. While it is unlikely that a staunch Confucian conservative like the Taewŏn'gun would have conspired with rebels, and no connection with them was ever established, Inoue had rebel leaders and suspected intermediaries closely interrogated.[43]

As matters turned out, it proved far easier to discredit the Taewŏn'gun than expected. In late August he had sent a secret letter to the commander of the Chinese forces in Korea asking for help against the Japanese. Even though a military alliance had been signed with Japan only a few days before, similar letters had also been sent by King Kojong, Kim Hong-jip, and the royal household minister. It was by no means clear at the time what the outcome of the fighting would be, and the Korean leaders, accustomed to thinking of China as an invincible power, expected the Ch'ing army to win the battle at P'yŏngyang. If the Chinese then moved south toward the capital, the Korean leaders wanted to make clear they had signed the military alliance with Japan under pressure. Indiscreet though these secret messages may have been, sending them was a sensible recourse for a government helpless to defend itself against either belligerent. The Taewŏn'gun's letter, however, was the most impassioned and the most bluntly anti-Japanese.

41. Pak Jong-keun, *Nisshin sensō to Chōsen*, 128ff.
42. *NGB*, 27.2, pp. 25–34.
43. Pak Jong-keun, *Nisshin sensō to Chōsen*, 129–40.

When P'yŏngyang fell, the documents were discovered by the Japanese. On November 18 Inoue confronted Kim Hong-jip, Kim Yun-sik, and Ŏ Yun-jung with this godsend. Aghast at the discovery, Kim Hong-jip fumbled to make excuses for the king. Two days later Sugimura suggested to the three cabinet ministers that if the Taewŏn'gun were to take responsibility for the affair, the Japanese would not pursue the question of the king's communications with the Chinese. While the delicacy of this proposal may have been intended to buy the king's gratitude, the Japanese were also reluctant to retaliate against him for fear of provoking foreign intervention. In any event, under heavy pressure from the Korean cabinet the Taewŏn'gun grudgingly agreed to retire. Inoue was not confident that the old man would cease his intrigues. "We cannot rest assured," he cabled Mutsu, "because what Koreans do is not always what they say and they can not be trusted."[44] Inoue was not off the mark. Unceremoniously dumped from power after four months, the Taewŏn'gun continued to use his influence against the Japanese whenever he could.

Neutralizing the influence of the queen and her faction was trickier. A general purge of the Min faction from office had already taken place under the Taewŏn'gun's auspices, but the queen herself still had her husband's ear. It would be impossible to remove the queen without removing the king as well, and that was out of the question. The alternative was to put an end, in the name of reform, to the royal couple's direct involvement in the work of the government. That, in large part, was the intent of the twenty-article reform proposal that Inoue presented to the king on November 19–20. Most of the document reiterated reform proposals that the Japanese had been pressing on the Koreans since July, but it also addressed the position of the royal family explicitly by proposing that the king become a constitutional monarch whose exercise of power would be constrained by law. Deploring the commingling of court and government as the source of many abuses, the document also called for a clear separation of the two, with the prime minister and other cabinet ministers responsible for the government's affairs and the palace ministry handling the court's affairs.[45] Since the queen had no standing outside the palace, the separation of the court from the government would reduce her influence.

Although the king agreed to move forward with reform, on No-

44. Kajima, *Diplomacy of Japan*, 1:122.

45. *NGB*, 27.2, pp. 100–111. For Inoue's comments on the reform proposal, see *NKGS*, 4:208–37.

vember 28 the official gazette announced the appointment of four new vice-ministers, all members of the Min faction. Having failed to persuade the royal couple, an outraged Inoue decided to intimidate them. At an audience on December 1 he told the king that since there was no hope that the Korean government would reform itself, he would order the withdrawal of Japanese troops fighting the Tonghak rebels in the south; there was no need for Japanese soldiers to sacrifice their lives for the Korean government if it was not willing to put itself in order. The king, surprised at Inoue's outburst, promised to keep the queen from interfering in government affairs.[46] A week later, in return for assurances that the Japanese would support the king, the queen, and the crown prince against intrigues to dethrone the royal family, the queen promised not to meddle in political affairs anymore.[47] And in his solemn oath before the royal ancestors on January 7, 1895, the king pledged not only to consult with his ministers before making decisions but asserted that the queen and her relatives should not interfere in government decisions.

By late December Inoue, apparently satisfied that he had been successful in ousting the conservatives from political influence, cabled home: "I am in the saddle. [The king and queen] have confidence and reliance in me."[48] In fact, he had merely won a temporary victory. The queen's faction was no easier to contain than was the Taewǒn'gun, and both continued to intrigue behind the scenes. Inoue perhaps hoped that rivalry would weaken them, but both factions remained resilient, ultimately seducing and dividing the collaborationist cabinet that Inoue maneuvered into power at the end of 1894.[49]

BUILDING A COLLABORATIONIST COALITION

Since concern about foreign intervention committed the Japanese government to scrupulously maintaining the appearance of Korean independence, its best hope for the success of reform was to place known reformers in power. That had been the reason for installing the moderate reformer Kim Hong-jip as prime minister. But Kim had not been as effective as hoped, even with more visionary officials like Yu Kil-chun in important subministerial posts. The alternative was to turn to political

46. Inoue Kaoru Kō Denki Hensankai, *Segai Inoue Kō den*, 4:422–32.
47. *NGB*, 27.2, p. 120.
48. *NGB*, 27.2, p. 124.
49. *NGB*, 27.2, p. 109.

exiles like Pak Yŏng-hyo and Sŏ Kwang-bŏm, who had been forced to flee Korea after the collapse of the 1884 coup. Since the summer the Japanese legation had been working to restore both men to political respectability. By December Pak and Sŏ had been pardoned and their court ranks restored. On December 17 the cabinet was reorganized to create a coalition between the two returned political refugees and the moderate reformers already in power (Kim Hong-jip, Kim Yun-sik, Ŏ Jung-yung). Late Yi politics often produced strange bedfellows, and this coupling was as peculiar as the one between the Taewŏn'gun and the moderate reformers.[50]

Only thirty-three years old when appointed to the cabinet, Pak Yŏng-hyo had spent much of his adult life outside of Korea. Born into a *yangban* family in Suwŏn, he had been adopted into the royal family at the age of eleven as the consort of King Ch'ŏlchong's only daughter. Although Pak's child bride died soon after the betrothal, his ties to the royal family gave him a status and prestige that guaranteed a successful official future. His appointment as the chief envoy of the 1882 mission to Japan was a turning point in his life. Returning home an enthusiastic advocate of Japanese-style modernization, he plunged into a series of reform projects—the creation of a police office, a new road system for Seoul, a newspaper, and a modern-style military unit while serving as a local magistrate in Seoul and Kwangju. Eyed with suspicion by members of the Min faction, he was soon ousted from his official post. Frustrated by the stubborn conservatism of the court, the disgruntled young man joined with Kim Ok-kiun and others in the conspiracy to oust the Min from power in 1884.[51]

In 1888 Pak composed an "Eight-Point Proposal" addressed to King Kojong, listing 114 suggestions for reform. The document was a visionary blueprint inspired by the Korean *sirhak* school, the Chinese "self-strengthening" movement, and the Japanese model of "civilization and enlightenment." Although politically moderate, the document was socially revolutionary. As a framework for change Pak proposed a modernized monarchy, with the king's power limited by law and backed by a political party dedicated to the state and the dynasty (presumably

50. Sugimura, *Kushinroku*, 108–12.

51. In late 1893, with the nominal backing of prominent figures like Soejima Taneomi, Ōkuma Shigenobu, Itagaki Taisuke, Shinagawa Yajirō, and Tani Kanjō, Pak announced plans to set up a dormitory and private academy, the Shinrin Gijuku (Ch'inrin Uisuk), for a selected group of young Koreans in the fashionable Ichiban-chō section of Tokyo. *Tōkyō nichinichi*, Nov. 22, 1893, quoted in *Meiji nyūsu jiten*, 5:744.

similar to the "party" that had backed the 1884 coup). Under the aegis of a benevolent and paternalistic monarch, Korea was to be transformed into a more rational, more egalitarian, and more liberal society. Much of the document was a catalogue of measures to sweep away the evils and abuses of the past that kept Korea weak and backward. Class distinctions were to be eradicated, controls over the economy loosened, and social practices radically altered. On his list of reforms were abolition of concubinage, lifting the prohibition on the remarriage of widows, ending child marriage, prohibitions of the mistreatment of wives, universal primary education for both sexes, a universal system of medical treatment and relief, and the regulation of house sizes in major cities. The ultimate goal was the "national wealth and strength" required for survival in a hostile and competitive world.[52] While the sincerity of Pak's commitment to reform is not to be doubted, his sense of the possible was limited, and his political imagination far outran his political acuity.

Until the outbreak of the Sino-Japanese War, the Korean government regarded Pak as a dangerous radical, no different from Kim Ok-kiun. Indeed, in March 1894 he narrowly escaped an attempt on his life, allegedly ordered by the king. To the Japanese, however, Pak represented the best hope for Korea's future. Shortly after the occupation of the royal palace in late July the authorities in Tokyo, perhaps with prodding from Tani Kanjō and Pak's other political friends, arranged for his return to Korea. It was clear after his arrival in August that he was still persona non grata. When he petitioned for clemency and an audience with the king, a group of high officials, including Kim Hong-jip, denounced him as a traitor. Even the American and Russian ministers protested his return.[53]

It does not appear to have bothered Inoue that he had brought Pak into a government with men who had called him a "traitor" and a "murderer" only a few months before. Inoue blithely urged the new cabinet to work together for the national good, confident that he had put in place a new leadership that in the main was pro-reform, pro-Japanese, and amenable to Japanese goals.[54] The deliberative council, which had served its purpose, was abolished in mid-December, and in

52. Lew, "Park Young-hyo," 21–26.
53. Sugimura, *Kushinroku*, 104.
54. *NGB*, 28.1, pp. 398–99.

early January the cabinet was given principal powers as the decision-making body within the national government.[55]

Inoue's optimism may have been due to his success in persuading the Korean government to employ Japanese advisers, an idea that Japanese legation officials like Uchida Sadatsuchi had been pushing since the summer. With Japanese advisers in place, the Japanese could assure satisfactory progress on reform while maintaining the fiction of non-interference in Korea's domestic affairs. Uchida had suggested that the Koreans be given no discretion in hiring advisers and that they be placed under the supervision of the Japanese minister to ensure that they would pursue the aims of the Japanese government. In effect, he was proposing to place agents of the Japanese government at the heart of the Korean decision-making process, a major step toward the creation of a de facto protectorate.[56] Needless to say, the Korean government resisted the idea.

Shortly after arriving in October, Inoue once again raised the issue of Japanese advisers with Kim Hong-jip. Without them, he told Mutsu, "all my efforts will remain mere explanations of principles without practical results."[57] While Kim Hong-jip once again showed little enthusiasm for the proposal, after several weeks of continuing pressure from Inoue the Koreans finally agreed to hire Takehisa Katsuzō, a police sergeant at the Japanese legation, as an adviser to the Korean metropolitan police.

By the spring of 1895 a total of forty Japanese advisers, assistant advisers, and secretary-clerks had been hired by the Korean government. Eight key advisers were placed in the royal household, four cabinet ministries (finance, home, justice, and war), the metropolitan police, and the postal service. Several were police or military officials previously attached to the Japanese legation; others were former high-ranking civilian officials brought in from Japan; and one was Hoshi Tōru, an influential Jiyūtō politician. Like foreign advisers to the Meiji government, all of them were extremely well paid, earning more than the Korean prime minister, but they were given much more sweeping powers. Under the ministerial regulations issued in April 1895, all ministries and offices were required to present proposed new regulations to the advisers for

55. On the model of the Japanese central government structure, a royal household ministry was created to handle the royal family's affairs, and a privy council was established to provide an honorary place for senior nobles and conservative officials.

56. NGB, 27.1, pp. 637–38; NKGS, 9:57–59.

57. FMA, File 3.8.4.16-3, Inoue to Mutsu, Nov. 22, 1894.

examination, and all public papers had to flow through them as well. The advisers were also permitted to attend cabinet meetings and to present their views there. These regulations positioned them to block or veto policies contrary to Japanese interests and to serve as a channel for Japanese policy initiatives. And few official secrets could be kept from them.[58] The Korean government continued to retain the services of several other foreign advisers such as Clarence R. Greathouse, a legal adviser to the Foreign Ministry, but they neither served as agents of their home governments nor exercised any supervisory control over their Korean colleagues.[59] The Japanese advisers, by contrast, were put in place to consolidate the de facto Japanese protectorate.

THE PUSH FOR CONCESSIONS

By early 1895 the easy optimism that Inoue had expressed in late December had begun to dissipate. Korean collaborators proved harder to deal with than expected, and even putatively "pro-Japanese" Korean leaders turned out to be more patriotic than anticipated. "Independence" meant something quite different to them than it did to the Japanese. While they tolerated Japan's prodding for institutional reform, they were less willing to place their country under its economic yoke.

As we have seen, the expansion of economic rights was an important goal of Japanese policy. In December Inoue emphasized once again that economic concessions would ensure Japan's position in Korea even if the reform effort failed. He urged the Tokyo government to secure firm commitments from the Koreans on rights to construct railway lines connecting Seoul with Inchon and Pusan, to operate the telegraph system, to lease a naval base, and to open a new treaty port in the Taedong River valley. He also proposed that the Japanese lend the Korean government ¥300,000 in return for the employment of a Japanese national as the superintendent of customs and ¥5 million in gold or silver specie secured by tax revenues from the three southern provinces (Chŏlla, Kyŏngsang, and Ch'ungch'ŏong) to be collected under the supervision

58. Lew, "Minister Inoue Kaoru," 14–15; Pak Jong-keun, *Nisshin sensō to Chōsen*, 148–56.
59. American advisers hired at the request of the Koreans often turned out to be an embarrassment to the American legation. In 1893 Horace Allen even suggested that "American influence would be increased, rather than lessened, if we were to content ourselves with keeping in American hands, the one position of Government Adviser." Palmer, *Korean-American Relations*, 2:181.

of Japanese officials. These skeins of profit, he said, would bind Korea more tightly to Japan.[60]

In arguing for this policy, Inoue was taking a cue from Western imperialist practice. As the British had demonstrated in Egypt, deepening economic involvement in a country provided leverage for deeper political involvement.

> Up to the present our country has helped Korea by strengthening its independence and demanding its internal reform simply in the name of friendly relations. As a result our position in Korea has been weak and we have not had adequate pretexts with respect to the foreign powers.
>
> What was England's pretext for intervening in Egypt? Was it not in the fact that England had obtained a position of real interest there by supplying Egypt with capital? I firmly believe that if we wish to solidify our position in Korea and establish a pretext for intervention in its internal affairs, we must obtain real interests there, whether through railroads or through loans, and by financial means create pretexts for extending our intervention to other kinds of relationships.[61]

As the experience of the Westerners had shown, it was not necessary to conquer a country by military force in order to control it; there were subtler means of doing so. If the Korean government were to renege on its promises to reform, Japan would have an excuse, as a last resort, to cease its military operations against the Tonghaks, withdraw its troops to Seoul and the treaty ports, and offer no assistance if the Tonghaks attacked the capital. That would force the Koreans to plead for help from the Japanese, and that would give the Japanese an opportunity to institute an effective program of reform.

In suggesting that Japan "Egyptianize" Korea, Inoue also had short-term goals in sight. The advance of a loan to Korea was critical to the reform program. Large sums were needed to build up new military, police, and educational systems, and to pension off redundant officials. The government was in disastrous financial condition, barely able to keep afloat let alone embark on new ventures. In December Inoue reported that army wages had not been paid for four months, ministerial salaries had been cut in half, and the budget of the metropolitan police had been reduced as well. Tax collection was difficult if not impossible in the northwest, where fields had been trampled during the fighting between Chinese and Japanese troops, and in the three southern provinces that had been overrun by Tonghak rebels. The only reliable revenues came

60. *NGB*, 27.1, pp. 476–78.
61. *NGB*, 27.1, p. 477.

from just three provinces: Kyŏnggi, Kangwŏn, and Hamgyŏng. If the Japanese did not come to the financial rescue of the Korean government, Inoue warned, official morale would collapse, the military might revolt, and the reform effort would be doomed.[62]

The reform faction had already approached the Japanese for a loan in October 1894.[63] To deal with short-term financial difficulties, Inoue suggested that a loan of ¥300,000 be used for current needs and an additional ¥240,000 to pay off other foreign lenders. When he got no encouragement from the Itō government, he turned to the managers of the Dai-Ichi Bank in Seoul and Inchon. The bank headquarters in Tokyo responded that ¥300,000 was much too large, but in early January it instructed the Inchon branch to loan the Korean government ¥200,000 at a rate of 10 percent. Inoue thought that too high, but toward the end of the lunar year, when debts were traditionally settled, the Korean government was becoming desperate. At the end of January, with Inoue's mediation, the Dai-Ichi Bank, sharing half the principal with the NYK line, lent the government ¥130,000 at 8 percent.

The grander scheme for a loan of ¥5 million in specie fared less well. In late December Mutsu, who was reluctant to use public funds for the loan since it would require debate in the Diet, approached two leading businessmen, Nakamigawa Hikojirō, executive director of the Mitsui Bank, and Sasaki Yūsaburō, about raising a private loan. Neither was particularly enthusiastic, objecting that the loan was too large and insisting on a 10 percent rate.[64] Inoue Kaoru was appalled. The Chinese government had not asked for any interest at all on their loans to the Korean government, and a 10 percent interest rate would be "inconsistent with our apparently paternal declaration to help this poor nation to independence and development."[65] But the Japanese bankers were less interested in advancing Japanese influence in Korea than in assuring a safe return on their investment.[66]

The Mitsui interests finally offered to put up the loan on condition that the Mitsui Bank be permitted to print gold-backed paper currency for circulation in Korea and to tie the exchange rate to the yen. They

62. *NGB*, 27.1, pp. 480–81; 27.2, pp. 123–24.
63. Yu Kil-chun discussed such a proposal with the Japanese leaders at Hiroshima. Moriyama Shigenori, "Kabo kaikaku shakkan mondai," 115–16. Yu returned to Korea with Inoue.
64. *NGB*, 27.1, pp. 479–80.
65. *NGB*, 27.1, p. 480.
66. As Inoue noted, "Just think how inconsistent we are to charge such high interest considering that this Government is now practically in our hands. . . . It is my object as well as yours I suppose to take whole financial power into our hands." *NGB*, 28.1, p. 139.

also wanted the Korean government to let Mitsui take over the management of the Korean treasury. Had these concessions been granted, Mitsui would not only have taken control of the public finance system in Korea but would have displaced the Dai-Ichi Bank as the principal foreign bank in Korea. Needless to say, these conditions were not met, and the Mitsui Bank did not make its loan. The general reluctance of the Tokyo financiers to make loans to Korea or to finance the public debt reflected doubt about the Korean government's ability to repay or even to manage its own financial affairs. Big capital was less prepared for the "Egyptianization" of Korea than Inoue was.

Since private businessmen seemed to put private profit ahead of public purpose, Itō and Mutsu decided to appropriate loan money as part of the emergency military budget. The supplementary budget approved by the Diet in late February provided for a loan of ¥3 million (or ¥2 million less than Inoue had proposed) to be lent at 6 percent through the Bank of Japan with Korean tax revenues as collateral. The Bank of Japan had its own agenda. It proposed to the Korean government that the loan be made not in specie but in Bank of Japan convertible notes that would circulate as the country's sole paper currency until the loan was repaid. The circulation of Japanese currency as legal tender, a goal the Japanese had sought since the opening of the country, would allow Japan to dominate the currency system and thus the market. The Japanese military forces were already paying for porters, horses, and provisions with paper money as well as metal currency, creating a temporary yen bloc within Korea, and the proposal of the Bank of Japan would have prolonged this monetary intrusion.[67]

The Korean leaders were appalled at these terms. Prime Minister Kim and Finance Minister Ŏ protested that the circulation of Japanese banknotes as legal tender would damage the national prestige and stymie currency reform. But since the Koreans were desperate for money, the loan negotiations with the Bank of Japan stumbled on. On March 30 the Koreans finally signed an agreement providing (1) that half of the ¥3 million would be made in convertible notes and half in specie; (2) that the loan would be repaid in two installments by the end of 1899; (3) that as collateral the Japanese would have first lien on national land tax revenues; and (4) that the Korean government would raise no other loans secured by tax or customs revenues without permission from the

67. NGB, 8.1, pp. 347–48, Mar. 14, 1895; Moriyama, "Kabo kaikaku shakkan mondai," 119–26; Nakatsuka, Nisshin sensō no kenkyū, 212–14.

Bank of Japan.[68] The loans did not win new friends for the Japanese. As Yun Ch'i-ho noted in his diary, "The littleness of the Japanese is contemptible. The Japanese representatives here know what a shabby trick they have practiced on poor, hopeless, and helpless Korea. They have not got the cheek to tell the American[s] about the wretched loan."[69]

The negotiations over the "wretched loan" became entangled with Inoue's attempts to conclude a treaty giving Japan the economic concessions promised in the provisional agreement of August 20. In early January treaty drafts approved by the Privy Council were sent to Inoue in Seoul.[70] While no published draft exists, it seems likely that its content is the same as that of a document in the Mutsu papers.[71] Since the bleak financial situation of the Korean government would not permit it to undertake large-scale capital intensive projects, the draft treaty proposed to give Japan the right to build two railway trunk lines linking Seoul with Inchon and Pusan. The Korean government would be vested with ownership of the railroad lines, but until the Korean government repaid Japan for construction costs, the Japanese government would control their operation and pay the Korean government a percentage of the profits. Since the treaty specified that the Koreans were not to fully reimburse the Japanese until fifty years after the opening of the lines, it is clear that the Japanese had long-term control in mind.[72]

It was not until late February, when Inoue received the good news that the Diet had approved the ¥3 million loan proposal, that he approached the Koreans about railroad and telegraph concessions. This suggests that he viewed the concessions as a quid pro quo for the loan. At first the Korean leaders made no objection to the railroad concession, but they were reluctant to cede control over telegraph lines. Inoue, who was much more interested in getting a commitment on railway lines, proposed a compromise: the Koreans could manage their own telegraph line on the understanding that the Japanese could use it in time of emer-

68. Moriyama, "Kabo kaikaku shakkan mondai," 124–126; NGB, 30:329.
69. Lew, "Minister Inoue Kaoru," 173.
70. NKGS, 4:257, 259.
71. KSH, Mutsu Papers, vol. 26, doc. 17 (2).
72. Nakatsuka argues that Inoue may also have negotiated a secret treaty with the Koreans giving Japan substantial control over the development of their military forces. In the Mutsu papers he discovered a draft document of such a treaty, and Young-Ick Lew seems to accept that a final version was signed ("Minister Inoue Kaoru," 166) However, Nakatsuka points out that there is no documentary evidence that such a treaty was ever proposed to the Koreans, let alone concluded. It may be that Inoue vetoed the idea. The secret agreement is not mentioned, for example, in Inoue's early December 1894 dispatch to Mutsu even though the two proposed loans and the economic concessions later negotiated with the Koreans were. Nakatsuka, Nisshin sensō no kenkyū.

gency.[73] But as the talks on the economic treaty dragged on, overlapping with the loan negotiations, divisions emerged in the Korean cabinet.

Far from having won friends for Japan, Inoue's heavy-handed tactics had alienated potential collaborators. Opponents of the treaty began to fulminate about the loss of "national prestige" and the compromise of "national rights." As the American minister John M. Sill noted in early March, "Hatred toward the Japanese, always intense and hereditary, has grown more and more bitter, and the people are in a condition to welcome a conqueror of some other kind than this detested nation whose connection with Korea is written in blood.... The Koreans cannot believe the Japanese to be sincere in their professions of good will."[74] Rumors circulating in Seoul hinted that the Russians might play the role of that other "conqueror," and the exchange of Japanese dispatches between Seoul and Tokyo all through the winter and spring revealed growing apprehension over Russian intentions on the peninsula. The leaders of the Korean government, aware that the hovering Russian presence put a powerful trump in their otherwise weak hand, did their best to put the Japanese off.

In early April, as the signing of a peace treaty with China drew near, Inoue saw himself caught in the same dilemma the Japanese had faced since the outbreak of the war. On the one hand, he felt that the reform program should be pushed aggressively and that economic concessions should be extracted from the Koreans. On the other hand, he realized that any perceived attempt to compromise the independence of Korea was likely to invite foreign suspicion that Japan wanted to reduce Korea to a dependency. He asked Tokyo for guidance not only on what to do about the negotiations for an economic treaty but also on how to deal with the reform program and the stationing of Japanese troops in Korea after war's end.[75] The buoyant aggressiveness of his mood on arrival in Korea a half year before seems to have dissipated.

What took the wind completely out of Inoue's sails was the Triple Intervention. On April 23, less than a week after the signing of the treaty with China, Russia, Germany, and France "advised" the Japanese government to restore the Liaotung peninsula to China in return for a reduced indemnity payment. The psychological and diplomatic impact in Korea was enormous. It demonstrated that despite their military victory over China, the Japanese still had to bend to the wishes of the Western

73. NKGS, 4:333–34.
74. Palmer, Korean-American Relations, 2:353.
75. NGB, 4:386–88.

powers. With the country's independence reconfirmed by the Treaty of Shimonoseki, Korean leaders saw a way to fend off Japanese pressure by appealing for help to the Westerners. The Triple Intervention significantly weakened Japanese influence in Korea, as the Itō government was well aware. In its wake Mutsu warned Inoue against using "strong methods" in his negotiations with the Koreans, doubtless out of concern about Western response.[76]

All hope of securing railroad or telegraph concessions vanished on May 5, when the American, German, British, and Russian ministers sent a message to the Korean foreign minister protesting Japan's attempts to secure special concessions. As Minister Sill observed,

> It seemed to be the determination of the Japanese to force from the Koreans, prior to the settlement of the present difficulties by the pending peace negotiations all manner of exclusive concessions for railroads, telegraphs, mines and other industries, as well as special treaties for open ports to be occupied by the Japanese exclusively, the garrisoning of Korean cities by Japanese troops, and the exclusion of all foreign employees except the Japanese, several of whom are now employed in every Governmental department.

Together with the Russian minister, Karl Waeber, Sill asked the Korean foreign minister to "call us in for conference before doing anything to militate against the 'most favored nation clause' of each of our treaties."[77] Given this show of solidarity by the other foreign powers, the end was in sight for Japan's attempt to establish a de facto protectorate in Korea. The Korean leaders now realized that they once again could use the other powers as an effective counterbalance against Japan.

During the winter and early spring the Korean collaborators in the cabinet had buckled under to Inoue's demands not because he was politically adept or persuasive but because Japan had demonstrated its military prowess in the fighting with China. But once the end of the war was in sight, they were less amenable to Japanese pressure. As Inoue himself observed, the Koreans were "smart enough to see that as soon as peace has been declared Japan alone cannot have free play" and that if the Japanese tried to put heavy pressure on the Koreans they could "merely look for help to foreign representatives."[78] That is precisely what happened after the Triple Intervention.[79]

76. NKGS, 4:365.
77. NA, Dispatch Book, U.S. Legation to Seoul, no. 111, May 11, 1895, Sill to Gresham.
78. KSH, Mutsu Papers, vol. 28, pp. 104–7, Inoue to Mutsu.
79. Pak Jong-keun, Nisshin sensō to Chōsen, 145–46.

THE COLLAPSE OF JAPANESE INFLUENCE

While the Triple Intervention accelerated the erosion of Japan's political position in Seoul, it was the failure of the Japanese to find reliable political allies that ultimately doomed the wartime effort to create a de facto protectorate. Since early winter Inoue had seen his influence slipping. The collaborationist coalition he had maneuvered into power not only failed to respond to his importuning on a variety of issues but also fell to internecine squabbling. In style, outlook, and experience the moderate reformers and returned refugees who were joined in the cabinet were worlds apart. A few weeks after its formation the new ministers (presumably Pak Yŏng-hyo and Sŏ Kwang-bŏm) began to complain that the incumbents (presumably Kim Hong-jip, Kim Yun-sik, and Ŏ Yung-jung) made all decisions by themselves without consulting the others.[80] These moderate leaders, they said, might give lip service to reform, but they were basically pro-Chinese and continued to have close ties to the Taewŏn'gun. For their part the moderate leaders distrusted Pak and Sŏ, who had returned only with Japanese backing. The collaborators were unable to cooperate with either the Japanese or each other.

The most miscalculated choice turned out to be Pak Yŏng-hyo, whom a number of Japanese officials in Seoul, including Inoue Kaoru, saw as the most promising supporter of an aggressive reform program. Saitō Shuichirō, the Japanese adviser to the home minister, and Hoshi Tōru, the Japanese adviser to the justice minister both wanted Pak to assume full control of the government; with their encouragement, he continued to intrigue against the influence of the more moderate members of the cabinet. Deprived of a domestic political base by his long exile, Pak at first used his pedigree and marriage ties to the royal family to ingratiate himself with the king and queen, whom he regaled with stories about his experiences in the outside world. Pak used his special access to the palace, shared with none of the other ministers, to get business done and to establish his political precedence within the cabinet. No doubt the royal couple saw advantages to cultivate him. The American minister even reported that Pak had become the queen's "tool" and that she was using him "against his friends and his friends against him."[81]

Open hostility between Pak and his fellow cabinet members erupted in early February, when Pak opposed the promotion of Sin Ung-hui as

80. *NGB*, 28.1, p. 299.
81. Palmer, *Korean-American Relations*, 2:352–53.

commander of the *hullyŏndae*, a new military unit organized with the help of Japanese advisers. Pak objected that in 1884 Sin had served as a cat's-paw of the Chinese by leading an attack on the palace that brought down the reform government. The war minister, Cho Hŭi-yon, replied that as home minister Pak had no business interfering in military personnel matters, but Pak undermined Cho by placing his own followers in key positions in the War Ministry.[82] Pak also clashed with Kim Hong-jip and other moderate reformers on symbolic issues, such as whether to change the year name or to tear down a stele honoring the Ch'ing monarch. The American minister reported that since "these people cannot differ politically and be good friends at the same time, . . . various factions were not on speaking terms with one another."[83]

Exasperated at this squabbling, Inoue gave the cabinet a harsh dressing down in early February, urging both factions, the moderate reformers and the returned exiles, to cooperate in addressing the important issues of reform and independence. At the suggestion of Pak, the entire cabinet resigned three days later, the Pak faction hoping that Inoue would ask them to form a new government and the Kim faction under the mistaken impression that Inoue had asked for their resignations. Even though Inoue convinced the king not to accept the resignations, the government was shut down for more than a week, and the intrigues continued. In a move to weaken the Taewŏn'gun's influence, for example, Sŏ Kwang-bŏm directed the police to arrest Yi Chun-yong, the old man's favorite grandson, for alleged involvement in the assassination of Kim Hag-u, a moderate reformer, as well as plots against several other officials.

Pak's intrigues against War Minister Cho finally brought down the collaborationist coalition. At a cabinet meeting on May 13 the government split on a vote to remove Cho from office. Kim Hong-jip, Kim Yun-sik, and Ŏ Jung-yung voted against the proposal, and Pak Yŏng-hyo, Sŏ Kwang-bŏm, Pak Chŏng-yang, and Kim Ka-jin voted for it. Inoue tried to patch things up, but Pak Yŏng-hyo, anxious to consolidate his power and increasingly confident that he no longer needed Japanese support, refused to cooperate. No reconciliation was reached, and when Cho was forced to resign, Kim Hong-jip decided to do so as well. The uneasy coalition between the moderate reformers and the returned exiles was at an end.

82. Sugimura, *Kushinroku*, 131–36.
83. Palmer, *Korean-American Relations*, 2:352–53.

In analyzing the failure of the coalition, Inoue placed the blame on the political exiles, Pak and Sŏ. Recently returned from abroad, publicly branded as criminals or traitors, and lacking the experience and reputation of senior officials like Kim Hong-jip, the political exiles had tried to consolidate their power too quickly, thereby inviting the distrust of the moderate reformers. By allying himself with the royal couple and cloaking himself in the king's authority, Pak excited suspicion that he intended to establish himself as an autocrat, and the moderate reformers retaliated by turning to Inoue for help. Absolving himself of any responsibility for the failure of the coalition, Inoue observed that he had not been able to help either side in their internecine struggle and so remained on the sidelines, letting matters take their course. No doubt he was miffed by the assertiveness of Pak Yŏng-hyo, who since March had become increasingly truculent toward the Japanese, criticizing the terms of the ¥3 million loan, resisting the granting of railroad and telegraph concessions, and opposing the expansion of the Japanese settlement area in Seoul.

The cabinet, reorganized with Pak Chŏng-yang at its head, included the moderate reformers Kim Yun-sik and Ŏ Jung-yang, but most observers regarded it as a Pak Yŏng-hyo government. What was most unusual about the new cabinet was that nearly all its members had some foreign experience as diplomatic representatives, students, or political refugees in Japan or the United States. The same was true of nearly all the vice-ministers. Not since 1884 had the country been led by a group so well acquainted with the outside world or so committed to reform. A torrent of reform decrees continued to pour out of the government. Increasingly they dealt with the internal machinery of power—the military, the police, and the local government system. There was little doubt that the political exiles, committed to rapid and radical reform, were in the saddle.

The reorganized reform government lasted less than two months, however. The ties that Pak had so carefully nurtured with the palace began to unravel as the queen's family reasserted its influence. Even though abruptly removed from the palace inner circle by the Taewŏn'gun during the previous summer, the Min faction remained active behind the scenes. Pak Yŏng-hyo, evidently worried about the stability of his position, decided to secure firm control over the court by having the Japanese-trained *hullyŏndae*, now under the command of a supporter, replace the palace guard. The king rejected the idea. With his influence at the court eroding, Pak tried to patch up his relations with the Japanese, but Inoue, whom he had alienated by his assertiveness and independence, was not inclined to help. In an attempt to renew his alliance with the Japanese, Pak had approached Sugimura Fukashi with a plan to assassinate the queen. It is not clear whether this was his true intention or whether it was simply a way to insinuate himself into the good graces of the Japanese. In any event, word leaked back to the king, sealing Pak's political fate.[84]

In early July a gathering of high officials—including Kim Hong-jip as well as the incumbent prime minister, Pak Chŏng-yang, and several other cabinet ministers—decided that Pak should be arrested on charges of treason. Warned of his imminent arrest, Pak left his residence under an escort of Japanese guards to board a Japanese steam launch waiting for him on a dock at the Han River. At Inchon he was shepherded aboard a Japanese gunboat to go once more to exile in Japan. According to Minister Sill, Pak had taken care to place "a large sum of money to his credit in the bank," much of it earned presumably through distribution of government patronage during his months in power.[85] Even reformers could find value in time-honored customs.

By the early summer of 1895 the attempt to turn Korea into a de facto protectorate, administered by Korean collaborators with the support of Japanese advisers, had clearly failed. In part the failure can be attributed to the Triple Intervention, in part to the poor choice of collaborators, and in part to the instability of the collaborationist coalition. But Inoue, the principal agent of the policy, pointed out a more fundamental contradiction in the policy: How was it possible to consolidate Japanese economic and political privilege in Korea while publicly proclaiming a commitment to Korean independence? In a report to the cabinet he expressed impatience at Japanese who returned from visits to Korea thinking only of the benefits or profits the Japanese might obtain there—the opening of mines, the obtaining of fishing rights, the acquisition of commercial or manufacturing interests, or the bringing in of Japanese settlers. To concentrate exclusively on Japan's economic interests in Korea, he said, undermined the foundations of Korean independence. In the future, Japan should adopt goals that would neither harm Korea's interests nor result in a loss of Japan's; rather, both countries should move forward to the mutual profit of both. These were sober words from a man who had advocated the "Egyptianization" of Korea a half year earlier.

84. Sugimura, Kushinroku, 143–51.
85. NA, Dispatch Book, U.S. Legation to Seoul, no. 123, Sill to Uhl, July 7, 1895.

The home government was equally gloomy. In the wake of the Triple Intervention it was clear that Russia was emerging to replace China as Japan's most powerful rival on the peninsula. Anxious to salvage what he could from this diplomatic setback, Mutsu called for an international guarantee of Korean independence, a policy option mooted before the Sino-Japanese War by Yamagata and others, but on May 25 Itō vetoed the idea. He had not abandoned his interest in reforming Korea, and he felt it important to keep Japanese advisers in place to spur the Koreans on. To reassure the other powers about Japan's benevolent intentions, the government issued a vague statement of self-denial on June 4, publicly announcing a "passive policy." Since the Chinese formally recognized Korean independence in the peace treaty, and since the Russians had been assured that Japan was committed to Korean independence in both name and reality, future policy toward Korea "should take as its goal to refrain as much as possible from interfering in its internal affairs and promoting its independence." Specifically, this meant that the Japanese would no longer forcibly pursue the acquisition of railroad and telegraph concessions.[86] This cabinet decision signified a temporary retreat from an aggressive policy of expanding Japanese influence in Korea. Even though Japan had lost the opportunity to maintain a dominant position there, it still had interests to protect and political ties to maintain. Over the next few years the Japanese pursued those ends in a more low-key fashion.

86. *NGB*, 28.1, p. 441. See also Sakeda Masatoshi, "Nisshin sengo gaikō," 5–7.

CHAPTER 3

Japanese Power
in Limbo, 1895–1898

Having fought a war for the "independence" and "reform" of Korea, the Japanese leadership found the postwar situation little better, and in many ways worse, than it had been a year before. The Triple Intervention had seriously damaged Japan's prestige, and it had encouraged the Korean leadership to resist Japanese pressures. To be sure, reform was still underway, but with the fall of the Kim Hong-jip government Japan could no longer count on reliable collaborators in Seoul. Rather more ominous was the eruption of a new kind of European imperialism in East Asia—"concession imperialism." Before the war the Japanese had confronted only the relatively weaker and more backward Chinese; after the war they faced the European powers, particularly the Russians. The leaders in Tokyo watched anxiously as they began to seek special rights and privileges in Korea denied to the Japanese. While a "race for concessions" in China consumed the attention of the powers in the late 1890s, a smaller and perhaps less dangerous race was already underway in Korea.

The Korean race for concessions began in early May 1895, when the American, British, German, and Russian ministers in Seoul formally protested the Japanese attempt to secure railroad and other economic concessions. Clearly this protest was intended to keep opportunities open for all foreigners, and the Western representatives soon began to press the cause of concession hunters from their own countries. For example, in June 1895, with help from the American legation, James

TABLE I   FOREIGN CONCESSIONS IN KOREA,
1896–1900

Year	Concession	Concessionaire
1896	Inchon–Seoul railroad	American
1896	Mines in N. Hamgyŏng	Russian
1896	Mines in N. P'yŏngan	American
1896	Seoul–Ŭiju railroad	French
1896	Timber rights in Yalu basin and Ullŭng Island	Russian
1897	Mines in Kangwŏn	German
1898	Streetcar line in Seoul	American
1898	Electric plant in Seoul	American
1898	Waterworks in Seoul	American
1898	Mines in N. P'yŏngan	British
1900	Mines in N. P'yŏngan	German

Morse, an American businessman with experience in the Japan trade, secured from the Korean government timber-cutting and mining rights in P'yŏngan Province. During the next few years the Korean government and the Korean court was engulfed by a swarm of concession seekers, usually acting with the implicit or active support of their local diplomatic representatives. As the American minister Horace Allen, an active promoter of his own country's interests, noted in 1899, concession hunters were "getting as thick as fleas in a Korean blanket."[1]

Leaders in Tokyo sat helplessly watching the other powers, notably Russia and the United States, demonstrate their ability to win friends and influence in Korea (table 1). Yet what were the alternatives? Neither a renewed resort to force of arms nor a return to the strong-arm tactics of direct intervention in Korean court politics was possible. The country did not have the political or the economic strength to pursue either option. The war had taken a heavy toll on the nation's resources, and the occupation of Taiwan required a heavy commitment of military force. When Ernest Satow visited Tokyo in the fall of 1895, he found that the Japanese leaders were not eager indeed, were not prepared to fight another war in the near future. As Ōkuma Shigenobu told him, Japan had neither the power to manufacture weapons nor the fiscal base to support

1. Harrington, *God, Mammon, and the Japanese*, 193.

land forces, and it would take years to develop the men and officers to staff an enlarged navy.[2]

Chastened by their inability to turn aside foreign pressure, the Japanese leadership had only two practical alternatives in Korea. The first was to continue pushing the Korean government to reform and modernize, and the second was to find a Western power willing to share in guaranteeing Korean independence. Neither alternative, however, looked promising in the summer of 1895. With the royal couple and their entourage back at the helm, the reform effort was blunted, and the Russians and the Americans were more intent on advancing their own interests than in cooperating with the Japanese. By inertia, or by default, the Japanese therefore continued their efforts to buy the friendship of the Korean leadership through generous gestures.

THE ABORTIVE LOAN PLAN

Despite the cabinet's decision on June 4 not to interfere in Korea's internal affairs, both Itō and Inoue wanted to continue the wartime policy: pressuring the Koreans to reform and extracting from them economic concessions to buttress Japan's political presence. Japan's hand was no longer as strong as it had been in the early days of the war, but Inoue was still committed to a policy of "Egyptianizing" Korea. Although he was quick to criticize Japanese who sought to gratify selfish interests in Korea, Inoue remained full of plans for continuing the economic and political penetration of that country. He urged the construction of a Seoul-Inchon railway line with machinery, supplies, and technicians brought from Japan; he wanted Japanese technicians to supervise the operation of the Korean telegraph system; he wanted the Korean court to permit the stationing of Japanese troops in the peninsula; he wanted controls over Japanese immigration to Korea to keep out political troublemakers, greedy traders, and other self-seeking types; and he wanted new treaty ports opened in Mokp'o and Chinnamp'o.[3]

After the Triple Intervention, however, Korean leaders knew that they could turn to one of the Western powers to counterbalance the Japanese. Inoue therefore proposed to win cooperation from the Korean government by persuasion rather than bluster, threat, or pressure. His

2. Lensen, *Korea and Manchuria*, 46–48.
3. *HRCKS*, 3:687–99.

main project in the summer of 1895 was to offer a financial "contribution" to the Korean government. If not precisely a bribe, the
"contribution" was intended to win over the Korean leadership with
generosity. Inoue had two proposals: The first was to use five to six
million yen from the Chinese indemnity to make a "contribution" to
Korea, with ¥3 million to pay off the equivalent Korean debt to Japan,
another ¥1 million to ¥1.5 million as a gift to the Korean court; the remainder would be invested in profitable enterprises such as the Seoul–
Inchon railway line, with any shortfall in construction costs to be covered by private Japanese loans. The second alternative was to offer
softer terms for the ¥3 million loan offered in February 1895. The purpose of the first proposal was to buy the "obedience" and to increase the
"dependence" of the Korean government, preempting other countries
from establishing close economic and political connections with Koreans. The second proposal, admittedly less effective than the first,
would assuage any resentments spawned by the earlier loan negotiations.[4] This was "Egyptianization" in a gentler form.

With the malleable Kim Hong-jip reinstalled as prime minister in
early July, the Japanese cabinet agreed to extend the terms of the ¥3
million loan to a period of fifteen to twenty years and to provide the
Korean government with a "contribution" of ¥3 million to establish an
enterprise that would serve as a "permanent memorial" to the Japan–
Korea relationship.[5] When Inoue returned to Seoul later in July, he carried the good news of Japanese generosity to the king and queen and
assured them that Japan was interested only in the "independence of
Korea" and the "safety of the royal family." As a mark of his good faith,
and in a complete reversal of his tactics the preceding winter, he encouraged the queen to stand at the king's side in attending to affairs of
state. Even more astonishingly, he paved the way for restoring the Min
faction to power by urging the king to issue an amnesty for faction
members who had been incarcerated or exiled by the Taewŏn'gun; and
he encouraged the king to include members of the queen's faction in the
cabinet. Having failed in his efforts to mate the moderate reformers with
the Taewŏn'gun and with the returned political exiles, in desperation
Inoue finally turned to the only other major force in court politics.

This attempt at buying the cooperation of the Korea leadership ran
afoul of domestic politics in Japan. In the summer of 1895 the Itō cab-

4. NGB, 28.1, pp. 367–68.
5. NGB, 28.1, p. 368.

inet was under heavy attack from jingoist critics inside and outside the Diet who deplored what they regarded as an inept and pusillanimous Korean policy. The battlefield successes of the imperial army had excited an ebullient patriotism, and in the final days of the war the more extreme hawks called for a grandiose peace settlement. In the Diet the Kakushintō and the Kaishintō demanded Japanese occupation of Shantung, Kiangsu, Fukien, and Kwangtung Provinces, while the Jiyūtō called for the occupation of the three northeastern provinces of China. In anticipation of the peace negotiations, Gotō Shōjirō submitted to the government a lengthy memorandum calling for the occupation of Manchuria, sole control over Korea, the occupation of Peking, the building of a railway line from Pusan through Seoul and Mukden to the Amur River, and the signing of an alliance with France and Russia against Great Britain.[6] News of the Triple Intervention, and the Itō cabinet's supine response, dashed these grand hopes and sent waves of indignation through the political parties.

The hardliners, who advocated a strong and autonomous foreign policy, made the rounds of the *mintō* leaders to drum up a protest movement. In late April antigovernment leaders like Inukai Tsuyoshi, Ōzaki Yukio, Suematsu Kenchō, and Shiga Shigetaka began to attack the cabinet's response to the Triple Intervention. While they failed to pull together a coalition to demand that the government accept responsibility for the Triple Intervention, in mid-June thirty-three Diet hardliners announced their intention to present a Diet resolution calling for the expansion of military expenditure, the reform of foreign policy, the clarification of the cabinet's responsibility for the return of the Liaotung concession, and the maintenance of Japanese influence in Korea.[7] The Jiyūtō, having secretly promised Diet support to Itō in shaping postwar policy, decided in July not to question the government's handling of the Triple Intervention, but the hawks held public rallies castigating the government and called for an emergency session of the Diet to debate its responsibility for the foreign policy fiasco.[8]

Under this heavy public attack for "diplomatic failures," the Itō cabinet decided not to convene an extraordinary session of the Diet in the fall. Since the granting of a ¥3 million "contribution" to the Korean government required the approval of the Diet, the proposal was put on

6. Omachi, *Hakushaku Gotō Shōjirō*, 749; Ōtsu, *Dai Nihon kensei shi*, 4:450–58.
7. Sakeda, *Taigai undō no kenkyū*, 77–80.
8. Ōtsu, *Dai Nihon kensei shi*, 604–10, 610–16, 623; Sakeda, *Taigai undō no kenkyū*, 83–84.

hold. In early September Foreign Minister Saionji informed Inoue, who had been importuning the government for weeks, that even though the government was not opposed to the idea of a "contribution," it lacked Diet support. Jolted by this bad news, Inoue replied that failure to make the contribution would leave his newly appointed successor, Miura Gorō, with no ground to stand on. Ominously, he warned that Japan's prestige would suffer a grave loss and that "untold turmoil and confusion" in Korean politics would follow if the contribution were not made.[9] He did not have the nerve to pass this bad news on to the royal couple. At his final audience on September 16 he told the king and queen that the money would be coming once the Japanese government straightened out its financial situation. But the "contribution" never arrived, and less than a month later the assassination of the queen brought an abrupt deterioration of Japanese influence in Korea.

THE ASSASSINATION OF QUEEN MIN

In mid-September 1895 Minister Sill reported to Washington that Inoue had "left a clear field for the cultivation of friendly relations with Korea."[10] Rarely has a diplomatic crystal ball been more clouded. Inoue had left hardly anything clear except Japan's inability to find stable allies in Seoul, and his successor, Miura Gorō, succeeded in cultivating enmity, not friendship. The choice of Miura as minister to Korea was a curious one. Very likely Itō was attempting to mollify his hawkish critics in the Diet by making the appointment. Although a native of Chōshū, Miura had long been a vocal opponent of the Sat-Chō leadership. A conservative and a jingoist, he was hardly an apt candidate for dealing with the complex and sensitive situation in Korea. Miura admitted as much in August, when he noted that to put someone like himself, poorly versed in affairs and without diplomatic experience, in charge of formulating and carrying out national policy on Korea was like setting a ship to sail without a compass or stars in the night sky to guide it.[11] But Tani Kanjō, a long-time ally and an equally hawkish former general, urged Itō to appoint Miura, in part on the curious grounds that he was a good friend of Pak Yŏng-hyo. Itō agreed to do so, expecting that Miura would follow the low-posture policy outlined in the June 4 cabinet decision, and Inoue seconded his choice, expecting that Miura would

9. NGB, 28.1, pp. 367–68.
10. NA, Dispatch Book, U.S. Legation to Seoul, no. 146, Sill to Olney, Sept. 18, 1895.
11. NKGS, 10:252–54.

pursue a more positive and active policy than a regular diplomat would.[12]

To be sure, Miura was not without his own opinions about what to do in Korea. Ostensibly to elicit guidance from his superiors, he had outlined three alternative policies in an August memorandum. The first was a "benevolent" (onkeiteki) policy of recognizing Korea as an independent monarchy allied to Japan, which would undertake responsibility to defend and reform Korea; the second was an "intimidating" (kyōhakuteki) policy of cooperating with "fair-minded" Western powers to make Korea an independent country under their joint protection; the third was a "passive" (mokujū) policy of partitioning Korea with another power and occupying one part of it. It was clear, however, that Miura favored the first option, even though it might involve war with one or two of the other powers. The "intimidating" policy, essentially a joint protectorate policy, would work only if rights and responsibilities were made absolutely clear and the cooperating powers did not harbor concealed intentions to gobble Korea up; and the "passive" policy might lead to a clash with the other partitioning power. The "benevolent" policy, by contrast, would eventually turn Korea into a Japanese protectorate.[13]

On the eve of his departure in early September Miura told the press, "The post of Japanese Minister is one of great difficulty but I believe it is a fit place to try my own theory of diplomatic methods."[14] Just what those methods might be were revealed within a month of his arrival in Seoul. Since neither Foreign Minister Saionji nor anyone else had given Miura instructions on how to proceed, he seems to have felt that he had freedom to respond to the situation as it developed. Like many politicians back home, and many of the resident Japanese in Seoul, including members of the legation staff and Japanese advisers to the Korean government, the new minister feared that the queen's comeback augured a deterioration of Japanese influence. The Min faction had been consistently hostile to the Japanese, and it seemed likely that they would turn for help to the Russians or the Americans. The capital was rife with rumors of plots against the pro-Japanese moderate reform cabinet headed by Kim Hong-jip. Miura later said that he expected trouble was not far off, whether in the form of rebellion in the provinces, a mutiny by the Japanese-trained hullyŏndae, or a plot by the Taewŏn'gun himself.

12. Sakeda, "Nisshin sengo gaikō," 7–9.
13. NKGS, 10:252–54.
14. Japan Mail, Sept. 5, 1895.

Within a few weeks of his arrival in Seoul, Miura found help from an
unexpected quarter. The Taewŏn'gun, eased out of power by Inoue
Kaoru the year before, continued to fulminate against his old rivals, the
Min. As relations between the court and the Japanese legation deteriorated, he apparently saw a new opportunity to strike back. In late
September, using Horiguchi Kuman'ichi, a legation staff member, as a
go-between, he let Miura know that he was willing to let bygones be
bygones. With the help of the Japanese, he said, he would like to reform
the court. After some hesitation Miura decided to pursue these overtures. Sugimura Fukashi, who had witnessed Ōtori's dismal dealings
with the Taewŏn'gun the previous year, suggested that the Japanese insist on certain conditions before agreeing to help the wily old regent:
first, the Taewŏn'gun should promise not to interfere in official appointments; second, he should agree to keeping Kim Hong-jip, Ŏ Yun-
jung, and Kim Yun-sik in power to continue the reform program with
vigor; third, the Taewŏn'gun's elder grandson would be appointed as
minister of the royal household; and finally, the Taewŏn'gun's youngest
grandson would be sent off to Japan for three years of study. These
conditions were intended to keep the reform program on course while
allowing the Taewŏn'gun to return to a position of influence.

After discussing these terms with his grandsons, the Taewŏn'gun
agreed to accept them. Assured that the Taewŏn'gun would serve as
front man, Miura—together with Okamoto Ryūnosuke, a legation staff
member, and Kusunose, a military attache—made plans for a coup to
overthrow the Min. To convey the impression that the Japanese-backed
coup was a purely Korean affair, the main force to be used was the
hullyŏndae. The only Japanese involved were to be Okamoto, who was
to escort the Taewŏn'gun to the palace when the coup took place, and
the Japanese interpreters attached to the *hullyŏndae*. On the morning of
October 7 War Minister An Kyong-su brought Miura news that the king
planned to dissolve the *hullyŏndae* because of clashes with the police and
to put Min Yŏng-ik, a pro-Russian official, in charge of court affairs.
Although October 10 had been the original date picked for the coup,
Miura decided to strike right away. "The time is imminent," he told
Sugimura. "If we lose an hour the court will take the initiative." In a cable
home Miura notified Saionji of this turn of events but neither asked for
instructions nor suggested that he was about to make a move himself.[15]

15. *NKGS*, 5:71. For a detailed study of the assassination plot, see Pak Jong-keun,
Nisshin sensō to Chōsen, 255–67.

Although the original plan relied solely on the Korean troops to provide force, on the evening of October 7 Miura began to worry whether the *hullyŏndae* would be able to carry it off by themselves. He invited two patriotic society activists, Adachi Kenzō, the editor of the *Kanjo shinpō*, and Kunitomo Shigeaki, a well-known advocate of an aggressive Asian policy, to mobilize help for an attack on the palace. When the coup finally took place early the following morning, the Taewŏn'gun was escorted to the palace by members of the Japanese legation guard as well as *hullyŏndae* troops. Japanese policemen dressed in Korean police uniforms scaled the wall to open the palace gate, and the attack party that rushed into the palace included several Japanese civilian toughs (*sōshi*) recruited by Kunitomo and Adachi. In the melee that followed Yi Kyŏng-sik, the minister of the royal household, was killed, and a party of Japanese burst into the queen's chamber, where they stabbed to death the queen and two of her ladies-in-waiting. The queen's corpse was dragged immediately into the nearby garden, doused with kerosene, and cremated. With the Taewŏn'gun ensconced in the palace and Japanese troops in control of the court, a new set of pro-Japanese ministers Ŏ Yun-jung (finance), Yu Kil chun (home affairs and education), and Cho Hŭi-yon (military affairs) were installed in office. When Consul Uchida visited Miura shortly after the coup, the minister told him, with evident satisfaction, "Well, Korea is finally in Japan's hands [*Nihon no mono ni natta*]. I'm relieved."

The hideous event, crudely conceived and brutally executed, was not the product of policy made in Tokyo. It was purely the outcome of Miura's own "diplomatic methods." Indeed, Miura attempted to conceal the real facts not only from the diplomatic community in Seoul but from his own home government. The earliest reports of the event were sent by the military and naval attachés at the legation to the army and navy general staffs. Only late in the morning of October 8 did Miura cable Saionji, reporting the incident as a plot hatched by the Taewŏn'gun and the *hullyŏndae*, in which the Japanese intervened only to protect the king and prevent fighting between rival Korean forces. But the cover-up did not work. Court ladies had witnessed the Japanese intruders dragging off the queen, and the American military adviser, General William Dye, had seen Japanese with drawn swords in the palace compound. On his way to the palace the American diplomat Horace Allen encountered a group of thirty "evil-looking Japanese with disordered clothes, long swords, and sword canes" running away from the palace. When confronted with this testimony, the legation informed the foreign diplomatic community that "the murders were committed by Koreans dressed as Japanese in European clothes," an assertion that Allen dismissed as a "statement too absurd to need contradiction."[16] Within a few days, when the full details became known in Tokyo, Miura was dismissed and shipped back to Japan, where he and some forty other Japanese suspected of collusion in the queen's murder were arrested and jailed for questioning.

KOMURA TO THE RESCUE

In the wake of the queen's assassination, the burden of maintaining Japanese influence rested on the shoulders of Komura Jūtarō, chief of the foreign ministry's political bureau, who was dispatched as minister to replace Miura. Komura was very different in outlook from his predecessors, Ōtori, Inoue, and Miura, all of whom were members of an older generation. Komura was only fifteen years old when the *bakufu* fell, and his memory of the foreign threat was dim. Like other ambitious early Meiji youths, he had plunged into the study of English, hoping to absorb the "new knowledge" of the West. After taking a law degree at Harvard, where he shared lodgings with Kaneko Kentarō, he returned to Japan to embark on a bureaucratic career, joining the Ministry of Justice. In 1884 he moved to the Ministry of Foreign Affairs, starting a climb up the official ladder that eventually led to ambassadorships in Washington (1898) and Moscow (1900), and then to the post of foreign minister itself (1901).[17]

No doubt one key to Komura's stunning rise in the diplomatic corps was his unvarnished and outspoken advocacy of "concession imperialism." Possessed of a broad vision of Japan's economic future in East Asia, he advocated staunch pursuit of Japan's material interests there. On the eve of the Sino–Japanese War, as chargé d'affaires in the Peking legation, he urged Foreign Minister Mutsu to take "strong and decisive action" to prevent European intervention or Chinese military action in Korea. In mid-July 1894 he cabled Tokyo arguing that since war was inevitable, Japan ought to send China an ultimatum to withdraw its troops before it went any further in its military preparations. During the war, as diplomatic liaison on Yamagata's staff, he followed the First Army into Manchuria, working with the local population

16. NA, Dispatch Book, U.S. Legation to Seoul, no. 156, Allen to Olney, Oct. 10, 1895.

17. Gaimushō, *Komura gaikōshi*, 1:20–42.

to secure logistical support. In his spare time he read a biography of Sir Harry Parkes, the uncompromising British champion of free-trade imperialism.

When peace negotiations with the Chinese began, Komura, perhaps inspired by Parkes's example, advised his superiors to squeeze as many concessions from Li Hung-chang as possible. Not only should Japan enjoy the same treaty privileges in China as the Western powers did, he said, but it should also demand the opening of new ports, a Peking–Tientsin–Chefoo railway concession, and internal navigation rights on the Yangtze and other major rivers. What he envisioned was the opening of the vast China market to the products of Japan's newly burgeoning manufacturing industries. All this reflected his confident sense of Japan's political and economic capabilities, and it was undoubtedly this confidence that prepared Komura to play such a key role in the establishment of the late Meiji empire.

The Japanese position in Korea in late 1895 offered little opportunity for Komura to exercise his vision. Rather, his task was to keep a badly deteriorating situation from becoming worse. After hustling Miura and the other Japanese involved in the queen's assassination back to Japan, Komura did his best to reassure everyone that Japan had no sinister designs to seize Korea by force. He quickly made the rounds of the other diplomats at Seoul to assure them that the government in Tokyo had nothing to do with the murder of the queen and that it did not intend to interfere in Korea's internal affairs. The Japanese government's only concern, he said, was the safety of the king, who remained a captive in his own palace. And while Komura was trying to spread calm in Seoul, the Itō government ordered its representatives in the major Western capitals to let the powers know that it planned to withdraw its troops from the Liaotung peninsula and from Korea once the political situation had stabilized there.[18]

What the Japanese leaders continued to fear was a foreign, most likely a Russian, intervention that would force Japan to withdraw not only its troops but also its advisers from Korea, destroying all chance to influence Korea's future. It was urgent to get a reform program guided by Japanese advisers back on track. For Komura, the top priorities were military and fiscal reform. The existing Korean military forces were sufficient to deal with internal rebellion and banditry, he thought, but

18. Sakeda, "Nisshin sengo gaikō seisaku," 9–10; Gaimushō, *Komura gaikōshi*, 1:69–72.

the army needed to be modernized and government finances to be put on a stable basis.[19] And the only hope for reform was to keep the government of Kim Hong-jip in power.

Despite effusive Japanese denials of any interest in intervening in Korean internal affairs, Western diplomats in Seoul remained deeply suspicious of Japanese intentions, and they continued to voice concern about the safety of the king and the maintenance of order in the capital. At a meeting of the foreign diplomats on October 25, the Russian minister urged that since *hullyŏndae* members had been involved in the murder of the queen, the unit should be dissolved. Komura, arguing that this was more likely to encourage disturbances than prevent them, instead persuaded the Korean court to form a new palace guard from the most reliable *hullyŏndae* and *taiuidae* troops in late October. Anxious to spread oil on troubled waters, he also told Kim Hong-jip to punish those Koreans who had been involved in the assassination and to have the king rescind his edict demoting the late queen to a commoner rank.[20]

However conciliatory Komura may have been toward the Koreans and the other powers, he was still intent on keeping Korean politics under Japanese influence. In early November, after the arrival of Inoue Kaoru, who had come to Korea to convey the condolences of the Meiji emperor to the Korean king, Komura cabled Tokyo for authorization to deploy Japanese legation troops to guard the royal palace if requested by the Korean king. His request was backed by Inoue, who felt that Japanese military force was necessary to shore up the pro-Japanese government of Kim Hong-jip. But the cabinet in Tokyo refused despite a further flurry of cables from Inoue and Komura, and Itō ultimately decided to order Inoue home, fearful that his more aggressive posture might harm relations with both the Western powers and the Koreans.

THE FLIGHT OF THE KING

By the late fall of 1895 the fate of Japanese influence in Korea, and the future of reform, seemed to rest on the survival of the Kim Hong-jip government. Its chances for survival, and with it chances for a dominant Japanese position in Korea, grew dimmer and dimmer as the end of the year approached. The cabinet was doubly tainted by its association with

19. Gaimushō, *Komura gaikōshi*, 1:78.
20. Ibid., 1:76–77.

the Japanese and by its commitment to reform. Rival factions connived against it behind the scenes, and its reform program was seriously impeded by its inability to restore local order and stability in the wake of war and the Tonghak risings.

In late November word reached Komura that a plot against the Kim government was being fomented by Yi Pŏm-jin and other members of the queen's faction who had taken refuge in the Russian legation at the time of the assassination. The plan was to attack the palace with a force of two hundred troops and forty swordsmen, kill off the incumbent ministers, and put a new cabinet in place. When Komura informed Kim Hong-jip what was afoot, Kim asked for Japanese troops to defend the palace and to arrest the conspirators. Komura, still anxious not to provoke the powers, suggested that it would be better to warn off the plotters. The plotters moved ahead anyway. In the early morning of November 28 a small force attacked the palace. The new palace guard held them off, and several conspirators fled once more to the Russian legation. Yi Pŏm-jin, the mastermind, escaped the capital and was spirited out of Inchon on a Russian warship to Shanghai.

In the end, however, it was not conspiracy but the zeal of its reform-minded members that brought an end to the Kim Hong-jip cabinet. On December 30 the government issued a royal edict ordering all Korean men to cut off their topknots. Yu Kil-chun, the acting home minister, proclaimed that the measure was advantageous to health and the transaction of business.[21] While that view might seem eminently reasonable to an outsider, the topknot decree inflamed popular sentiment against the government and its Japanese allies. In nineteenth-century Korea, as in nineteenth-century Japan and China, hair was a matter of substantial cultural and political significance. To cut one's hair was to cut off ties with the past, to reject time-honored social attitudes and forms.[22] Precisely for that reason the cutting of topknots had been advocated by reform-minded Koreans, especially those who had been refugees or students in Japan and the United States. For them the topknot was a sign of barbarism and backwardness.

The more moderate and conservative members of the Kim government were well aware of the gravity of the topknot decree. Although

21. Bishop, *Korea and Her Neighbours*, 2:178; Kasuya, "Shoki gihei undō ni tsuite," 27ff.

22. At the time of the Meiji Restoration, letting a forelock grow or cutting a *chonmage* was a statement of progressiveness, and in late Ch'ing China the cutting of the queue was a declaration of revolutionary intent.

willing to change the government structure or to open civil service examinations to all classes, they had hesitated to issue the decree for fear
of public outcry. The topknot was not simply a symbol of national or
cultural identity; it was a symbol of manhood itself. Only when a young
male was betrothed and ready to assume adult responsibilities was he
permitted to tie his hair in a topknot. A Korean male without a topknot,
no matter what his age or status, was a half-man, treated at best as an
irresponsible juvenile. In effect, the topknot decree infantilized the entire
male population at a stroke, humiliating them and violating the memory
of their ancestors. When it was announced that the king had cut his hair
short, personal shame was amplified into national shame. In the eyes of
many Koreans, who thought the edict inspired by outside advisers, the
king's haircut symbolically reduced Korea to a vassal of the "dwarf
barbarians" from Japan.

The enforcement of the decree began in the capital. "The click of the
shears was heard at every gate in Seoul, at the Palace, and at the official
residences," reported Isabella Bird Bishop. Peasants, merchants, and
officials who came from the provinces on business were shorn on their
way into the Seoul, and some decided not to return home for fear of
their lives. One newly clipped local official was met on his arrival by a
mob who said they did not want a "monk magistrate."[23] As enforcement spread to the provinces, so did local unrest. Japanese merchants
adventurous enough to travel in the interior noticed an immediate impact. Although trade had been going well for the handful of Japanese in
Konju, for example, it suddenly dropped off after the proclamation of
the topknot decree. Local police officials forced the townsmen or visitors
from nearby villages to cut their hair. Fewer and fewer outsiders came
into town for fear of losing their topknots. The great winter fair, which
usually drew people from all over the country, was sparsely attended.
And business grew worse for the Japanese as rumors spread that they
were responsible for the decree.[24]

In many provincial areas, where unrest had already been stirred by
the steady flow of reform decrees and news of the queen's assassination,
the topknot decree galvanized open rebellion. Tonghak rebel activities
in 1894 had been concentrated in the rich agricultural areas of the south
in Chŏlla, southern Ch'ungch'ŏng, Hwanghae, and southern Kyŏngsang but by the fall of 1895 unrest was more widespread, affecting

23. Bishop, *Korea and Her Neighbors*, 2:179–80.
24. *Nikkan tsūshō kyōkai hōkoku*, no. 7 (Mar. 1896): 6–13; no. 8 (Apr. 1896): 28–
30, 38–39.

Kangwŏn, northern Ch'ungch'ŏng, and northern Kyŏngsang as well. Local rebel leaders were invariably Confucian scholars or provincial *yangban*, the mainstays of the local elite. Almost everywhere that unrest occurred, rebel leaders voiced their anger over the death of the queen and the topknot decree, the two most concrete and vivid symbols of the assault on the old order. The leader of a "righteous army" in Jechon, for example, issued a manifesto accusing the Japanese of professing "neighborly relations" while infringing on the prerogatives of the king and slaughtering the queen. In February 1896 a "righteous army" (*ŭibyŏng*) organized by Yu In-sok stormed and occupied local government offices, attacked officials responsible for enforcing the topknot decree, and carried out other reprisals against proreform local officials.[25]

In other parts of the country "righteous armies" attacked Japanese military garrisons in the interior and cut the Seoul–Pusan telegraph line. The hostility of ordinary Koreans toward Japanese civilians in provincial towns was palpable. Those friendly one day were unfriendly the next; those who had once eagerly sought to buy Japanese goods no longer came around. In Kaesong the Japanese inhabitants decided to evacuate to the safety of Seoul or Inchon. Similar evacuations took place in Kunsan, Mokp'o, and other trading towns. In P'yŏngyang the Japanese were reluctant to leave lest the Chinese merchants regain their prewar position in the local market, but they departed obediently when a Japanese government vessel manned by a small armed contingent arrived to evacuate them. The only safe places for Japanese appeared to be Seoul and Inchon, but even there the unrest made itself felt. Korean merchants who had dealt with the Japanese were no longer as willing to make their way to the treaty ports.[26]

The unrest provoked by the topknot decree spurred fresh conspiracy against the Kim Hong-jip government in Seoul. Once again the leader was Yi Pŏm-jin, who managed to solicit help from the American and Russian legations. The king, who had been cowering in the royal palace supplied with food and watched over by General Dye, the American military adviser, and several missionaries, was deeply shaken by the death of his consort and fearful for his own life. He asked Horace Allen whether he should seek Russian help, and Allen agreed to arrange a meeting between the Russian minister and a military confidante of the king. On February 10 the Russians moved a force of two hundred mar-

25. Kasuya, "Shoki gihei undō ni tsuite."
26. *Nikkan tsūshō kyōkai hōkoku*, no. 8 (Apr. 1896): 28–30, 38–39.

ines from Inchon to the capital, ostensibly to increase security at the
Russian legation. Early the next morning the king and the crown prince,
spirited out of the palace in closed palanquins used by ladies-in-waiting,
arrived at the Russian legation, pale and trembling, to take up residence
in spacious apartments prepared for them there. The streets leading to
the legation were guarded by Korean troops, and within the Russian
compound Russian marines were posted with a small artillery piece on a
terrace below the king's window.

Within a few hours of the king's escape royal decrees were issued rescinding the topknot decree and denouncing the "principal traitors" involved in the affairs of July 1894. Later in the day Kim Hong-jip (the
prime minister), Ŏ Yun-jung (the finance minister), and Chŏng Pyŏng-
ha (the minister of agriculture and commerce) were dragged through the
street and beheaded in front of the Seoul police station. Their bodies
were mauled, mutilated, and torn to pieces by an angry mob. The king,
after consulting with Allen and Waeber, appointed a new cabinet
headed by the "pro-Russian" Yi Pŏm-jin, Yi Wan-yong, and Yi Yun-
yong. Several members of the new government had been sheltered by
Allen in the American legation after the queen's assassination.[27] This
palace coup, remarkably similar to the coups of 1882, 1884, 1894, and
1895, left the Russians in a dominant position in Seoul.

DEALING WITH THE RUSSIANS

The flight of the king to the Russian legation, where he became an exile
in his own country, and the appointment of "pro-Russian" and "pro-
American" officials to the cabinet knocked the props from under the
Japanese. Indeed, the new government moved rather quickly to erad-
icate all Japanese influence at the center of power. The Japanese advisers
appointed to the ministries in 1895 were dismissed, and the military
units trained by Japanese officers were disbanded. Rumors were rife that
diplomatic relations between Japan and Russia had been broken off,
that the Russians and the Chinese had formed an alliance to deliver
Korea from Japanese domination, and that the Japanese settlements at
Inchon, Pusan, and Seoul had been put to the torch. As Minister Sill
noted in the summer of 1896, the overthrow of Japanese authority was
"complete and absolute." "At this moment the nationals of any other
power could obtain [concessions] from Korea upon more favorable

27. Harrington, *God, Mammon, and the Japanese*; *Komura gaikōshi*, 81–82.

terms and with less question and objection than Japan could obtain them."[28]

The Japanese government was in no position to protest the coup, nor could it hope to reverse the situation by a show of force. And with the death of its chief collaborator, Kim Hong-jip, its alternatives were even more narrowly constrained than six months before. The two options still open, as Komura suggested in a cable a few days after the coup, were to place Korea under an international guarantee or to reach an agreement with Russia over the future of the country. Both were among ideas that Itō had been toying with since the fall of 1895. He had even proposed to make a trip to Europe to sound out the powers about several possibilities an Anglo-Japanese alliance, a Russo-Japanese alliance, or an international guarantee of Korean independence. Now there was little other choice. Since none of the other powers was inclined toward the proposal for an international guarantee, the only alternative was to work out a deal with the Russians. For the next two years, defining mutual "spheres of influence" with the Russians became the main focus of Japanese policy in Korea.

In Tokyo the main advocate of an accommodation with Russia was Yamagata Aritomo, who saw larger issues at stake than the future of Korea. Since the outbreak of the Sino-Japanese War, Yamagata had argued that Japan should press its interests in China, especially in the rich and populous south, while maintaining a postbellum status quo in Korea. This "protect the north, advance to the south" strategy rested on Yamagata's grand vision of building a railway trunk line that would span China, linking Japan through the continent to the borders of India. Since such an expansion of a Japanese presence in China would undoubtedly provoke friction with the British, Yamagata thought it made sense to align Japan with Russia, Britain's chief rival in Asia. An accord or alliance with Russia would achieve two purposes: in the short run it would protect Japanese interests in Korea; and in the long run it would prevent the formation of a Western coalition against a broader Japanese advance in Asia.[29]

But policy toward Korea had to take into account not only the realities of the balance of power in East Asia but also contrary pressures from the politicians and the public, both more inclined to chauvinistic resolutions of foreign policy issues than diplomatic ones. The idea of a

28. NA, Dispatch Book, U.S. Legation to Seoul, no. 226, Sill to Olney, July 17, 1896.
29. Sakeda, "Nisshin sengo gaikō seisaku," 20–21.

rapprochement with Russia did not play well with the Japanese public, which was still incensed over the Triple Intervention and deeply resentful of Russian meddling. Anti-Russian feelings were high in the Diet, where the opposition parties introduced a resolution attacking the government for failing to live up to the promises implicit in the declaration of war on China in 1894. In early 1896 the Itō government had to recess the Diet to prevent the issue from becoming a public embarrassment, and to secure cooperation in the lower house, Itō was forced to strike a bargain with Itagaki and the Jiyūtō. The new budget authorized an increase of the army by six divisions, clearly signaling preparation for a possible war with the Russians.

Attempts to strike a bargain with the Russians continued, however. In early March Komura and Waeber tried to resolve the tension in Seoul. Their negotiations made clear that each side wanted the other to give up its principal advantage. The Japanese wanted to get the king out of the Russian legation, and the Russians wanted to get Japanese troops out of Korea. In the end the secret memorandum worked out by Komura and Waeber on May 1 was not entirely to Japan's disadvantage. The Japanese had to recognize the political status quo: the incumbent cabinet would remain in power; the king would be allowed to stay in the legation until he felt it was safe to return to the palace; and the Russians were allowed to station four companies of troops on the peninsula. To counterbalance the Russian military presence, the Japanese were allowed to maintain four companies of troops in Korea, two of them stationed at Seoul, as well as a company of two hundred gendarmes to guard the Seoul-Pusan telegraph line.[30] While the Russians maintained the political upper hand, a Russo-Japanese military balance had been established.

The Komura-Waeber memorandum was basically reaffirmed at a higher level later in the month. On May 17 Yamagata Aritomo arrived in Moscow to attend the coronation of Czar Nicholas II, carrying secret instructions to negotiate a settlement with the Russian government to stabilize the political situation in Korea. The original draft agreement Yamagata presented to the Russians included a clause providing for a joint Russo-Japanese guarantee of Korean independence, but this clause did not appear in the final protocol. Instead of establishing a Russo-Japanese protectorate, the Yamagata-Lobanov agreement merely stated

30. Gaimushō, *Komura gaikōshi*, 1:83–89; Kajima, *Diplomacy of Japan*, 1:425–31.

a joint intention to encourage fiscal reform in Korea, promote the formation of modern police and military forces, and maintain telegraph lines. Secret clauses, however, provided (1) that both countries, after mutual agreement, could move troops into separate spheres within the country; (2) that the king could remain in the legation until a reliable Korean palace guard had been organized; and (3) that the troop strength agreed on in the Komura-Waeber memorandum would remain in force until adequate Korean military and police forces were organized.[31]

It is clear that throughout the negotiations Foreign Minister Lobanov-Rostovsky knew that Russia held the chief trump, the Korean king. And it is also clear that the Russians wanted to extend their influence ever more deeply into the peninsula by acquiring economic rights and by placing Russian advisers with the Korean government. Even as it was negotiating with Yamagata, the Russian government made a secret agreement with Min Yŏng-hwan, the Korean envoy to the czar's coronation, promising to protect the king after his departure from the legation, to dispatch a Russian military officer to discuss training of the army and the palace guard, and to send a Russian financial adviser as well. Sweetening the agreement was a vague promise of a loan and a commitment to build a telegraph line. In April the Russians also secured mining rights in northern Hamgyŏng near the Manchurian border, and in September Iulii Ivanovich Briner, a Vladivostok merchant, obtained timber-cutting rights on Ullŭng Island and in the Yalu River basin. The Russian General Staff had dispatched Colonel Strel'bitski as its military agent and D. D. Pokotilov as its financial agent in August, and the two arrived with a small detachment of Russian officers and non-commissioned officers to assist in reorganizing the Korean Army. The Russians, in sum, employed the same techniques to gain predominance over the Korean court and government that Inoue had pursued in 1894–95.

To many members of the Korean elite, Russian influence was no more desirable than Japanese influence. Concern over the king's sojourn in the Russian legation continued to mount. In July 1896 Sŏ Chae-pil, recently returned from his long exile in the United States, banded together with other repatriated young reformers to form the Independence Club, a loose grouping of Western-educated reformers not unlike the

31. Kajima, *Diplomacy of Japan*, 1:432–47.

Meirokusha.[32] This new group, fearful that the country's autonomy was being compromised and alarmed at the granting of railroad, mining, and timber concessions to the Russians, the Americans, and other foreigners, began to protest the steadily growing influence of the foreign powers in Korea. Rumors spread that several high officials had provided secret funds to start a petition movement urging the king to leave the Russian legation and that a campaign was being organized to shut down every market in Seoul until he returned to his own palace.

While a small clique led by Kim Hong-mok opposed the king's departure from the Russian legation, several elder statesmen urged him to do so. Despite the Russian minister's reluctance to see him go, in late February 1897 the king finally moved to a new palace in Chong-dong adjacent to the British and American legations.[33] The move did not lessen the Russian influence at the Korean court. Indeed, it began to escalate. In March 1897 Finance Minister Serge Witte, the key figure in the formulation of Russian East Asian policy, frustrated in his efforts to expand Russian influence in China by securing railroad rights in Manchuria and establishing a Russo–Chinese Bank, turned his attention to Korea. He decided that if a sphere of influence in China was out of reach, then he would create one in Korea. In June K. A. Alexeev, an official in the Russian customs service, was appointed financial agent to Korea, and in September Alexis de Speyer, former chargé d'affaires in the Russian legation at Tokyo, arrived in Seoul to replace the accommodating Waeber. This ambitious twosome promptly launched a brief but ultimately unsuccessful campaign to establish Russia's paramountcy in Korea by acquiring economic concessions and seizing control of the reform process.

The "arrogant and boisterous" Speyer, with the grace of a bear in a ballet shoes, initiated a purge of other foreign influence from the Korean court. He persuaded the king to fire all of his foreign advisers, including the Americans, and he arranged for the appointment of a new cabinet. The Russian minister wanted complete monopoly over access to the levers of power. "No Korean entertaining friendly sensations for America," he told Allen, "shall have a place in the government."[34] The mon-

---

32. The original activity of the group was to collect money for the construction of an Independence Gate, an ecclesiatical arch in search of a church, outside the West Gate of the capital, where traditionally the Koreans had welcomed the arrival of envoys from Peking; the group also converted the pavilion where the Chinese envoys had stayed into Independence Hall.

33. Kajima, *Diplomacy of Japan*, 1:448–50; *NGB*, 30:366–69.

34. Harrington, *God, Mammon, and the Japanese*, 298.

arch himself was placed under heavy-handed surveillance. In early October 1897 Horace Allen reported to Washington, "I am told that the King is so hedged in by the Russian party, as to be unable to speak privately with his friends. A Korean friend of mine tells me that [he] ... was unable to converse with him because of the constant presence of one of three Russian interpreters, who are said to be on duty in the King's rooms at all times."[35]

The Russian takeover did not proceed without incident, however. When Alexeev, the Korean government's new financial adviser, arrived in October, Speyer immediately began a campaign to have him appointed director of the Korean Customs Service, a powerful and influential position. Customs dues provided the government with its most stable and reliable source of income. When the finance minister refused, Speyer had the pro-Russian foreign minister make the appointment. Despite his dismissal, the incumbent customs director, McLeavy Brown, a feisty Englishman, refused to leave his post. Confident that he had the backing of his own government, he calmly continued at his duties, bolstered by the protestations of the British consul in Seoul. In late October the impasse was resolved after a squadron of eight British warships under Admiral Buller put in at Inchon to remind the Russian minister that his policy depended on more than an inside track at the Korean court. A compromise was reached: Brown was reinstated, and Alexeev was placed under him.

THE COLLAPSE OF RUSSIAN INFLUENCE

The ultimate success of Speyer's aggressive attempts to turn Korea into a Russian protectorate depended less on his maneuverings in Seoul than on the fundamental attitude of his government in Moscow. In the long run the Russian government was most interested in establishing a position in Manchuria, and the ventures in Korea were a weak alternative. Korea was the main ring for the Japanese, but for the Russians it was a sideshow. And when it appeared that the Korea problem was becoming a distracting irritant that compromised advances elsewhere in East Asia, St. Petersburg was willing to abandon a forward effort there. Despite his yeoman's service, by early spring 1898 Speyer found himself out of favor not only with the Japanese and the other powers in Korea but also with his home government.

35. NA, Dispatch Book, U.S. Legation to Seoul, no. 17, Allen to Sherman, Oct. 9, 1897.

Ironically it was Speyer's attempt to secure a warm-water naval base in Korea, long a goal of Russian policy in East Asia, that proved his undoing. In early 1898 Speyer approached the Korean government with a request to lease land for a coaling station on Juliyongdo (Deer Island), an island at the mouth of Pusan harbor. The new foreign minister, Yi To-jae, refused on the grounds that the proposed site occupied land that had been set aside for the building of an international settlement zone. Before he could respond, he said, he would have to consult with the ministers of the other powers. Speyer threw a fit, refused to accept Yi's answer, and demanded his dismissal. The king, surrounded by his Russian interpreters, caved in to Speyer's demands. When the news got out, the Independence Club mounted a protest campaign. It members signed a joint petition demanding an end to continuing foreign interference in Korean internal affairs.

During the next few weeks anti-Russian sentiments spread within the capital. In the midst of the confrontation over the dismissal of the foreign minister, a former interpreter at the Russian legation was attacked on February 22, 1898. The heavy-handed Speyer indignantly demanded that the king arrest and punish the culprits within three days. This maladroit blustering served only to fan further hostility toward Russia. Anti-Russian manifestos were posted on the streets of Seoul, orators denounced the Russians in the marketplaces, and the Independence Club intensified its protests. Speyer, frustrated by the anti-Russian mood, complained petulantly to Katō Masuo, the new Japanese minister to Seoul, that the Korean court was beyond hope and the country was incapable of independence; Japan and Russia ought to partition it, he said. Nevertheless, with characteristic obtuseness, he continued to pressure the court to round up the assailants. On March 7 he delivered an ultimatum to the king: within twenty-four hours he wanted to know whether the Korean court wished continued assistance from Russian military and financial advisers.[36]

The court sent a secret emissary to the Japanese minister for advice on how to respond. It was a moment that Katō must have been waiting for. If the Russians are so upset at the Koreans, he said, then why not dismiss the Russian financial and military advisers? The Korean court decided to take his advice. When Speyer came for a response to his ultimatum the next day, he was told that there was no need for continued Russian help. Speyer suddenly found himself twisting in the wind.

36. Gaimushō, *Komura gaikōshi*, 1:93–97; NGB, 31.1, 165–68.

Without a word of complaint, the government in St. Petersburg closed down the newly opened Russo-Korean Bank, called its financial adviser and military instructors home, and unceremoniously dispatched Speyer as minister to Brazil, where he could cause little further trouble. The sudden collapse of the Russian ascendancy in Seoul gave the Japanese a new opening to expand their influence.

The Russian government was willing to scrap the efforts of its irascible minister to Seoul since it had managed to obtain its long-cherished warm-water port in East Asia. After a long and complicated negotiation with the Chinese, including a "temporary occupation" of Port Arthur by a Russian naval squadron in December 1897 and a substantial bribe to Li Hung-chang in March 1898, the Russians had obtained a twenty-five-year lease on Port Arthur and the right to build branches linking the Chinese Eastern Railway to Talienwan and the Yalu River. This agreement was the culmination of Witte's grand design for creating a Russian sphere of influence in Manchuria.[37] It rendered superfluous Speyer's efforts to secure a coaling station at Pusan. The St. Petersburg government was now anxious to conciliate the Japanese, who had responded to the Russian "temporary occupation" of Port Arthur by concentrating their fleet at Tsushima.

The groundwork for a démarche had already been laid while Speyer was pressing his pursuit of Juliyongdo. In early January 1898 Hayashi Tadasu, the Japanese minister to St. Petersburg, sent word to Foreign Minister Nishi that the czar felt that "continual friction between the two countries is not conducive to the interests of both countries" and that the Russian foreign minister had suggested that an arrangement could be made to "avoid competition in the future." The Russians also made it clear that they recognized that Japan had a greater interest in Korea than Russia did.[38] As Hayashi observed, the "Russian government plainly shows their desire to conciliate us, in order to make an enemy less, if not a friend more."[39] In early February Hayashi presented Foreign Minister Muraviev a new proposal for a joint protectorate in Korea.[40]

Anxious to consolidate their new gains in Manchuria, the Russian government made a positive but guarded response to the Japanese overtures. On March 17 Muraviev suggested that Russia might pledge not to interfere in the internal affairs of Korea. Two days later the Itō

37. Malozemoff, *Russian Far Eastern Policy*, 101–4.
38. *NGB*, 31.1, pp. 109–16.
39. Ibid., p. 120.
40. Malomezoff, *Russian Far Eastern Policy*, 109.

government, putting the so-called *Man-Kan kōkan* (an exchange of Manchuria for Korea) formula on the table, proposed that Russia recognize Japan's freedom of action in Korea in return for Japanese assurance that Manchuria lay outside Japan's interests.

The upshot of the ensuing negotiations was the Nishi-Rosen convention of April 25, 1898, which signaled the demise of an activist Russian policy in Korea. The two countries recognized the independence of Korea, pledged not to interfere in Korea's internal affairs, and agreed not to nominate military instructors or financial advisers to the Korean government without notifying the other party. But the key provision as far as the Japanese were concerned was Russian recognition of Japanese economic interests in Korea. Under article 3 of the convention the Russian government agreed not to "obstruct the development of commercial and industrial relations between Japan and Korea." This meant that Japan, for nearly two years shut out of the game of concession diplomacy, could return to the playing field unimpeded by fear of Russian interference. The Russians, of course, did not intend to concede the game to the Japanese, or to the Americans and French either, but they were willing to back down from Speyer's attempt to replace Japan as the principal player.

Why did the Russian government decide to withdraw its bid to establish itself as the hegemonic power in Korea? Hayashi Tadasu, the Japanese minister to St. Petersburg, surmised that the Russians did not wish to alienate the Japanese on the Korean question when they were trying to secure control of an ice-free port in Manchuria. Katō Masuo, the minister to Seoul, took a more cynical view. The Russians were willing to make concessions to the Japanese because rising anti-Russian sentiments, from the king on down, eroded Russian influence in Korea, just as Japanese influence had eroded after the murder of Queen Min two years before.[41] Undoubtedly both factors were at work, but ultimately it was the success of the Russians in securing the Manchurian concessions that dampened their interest in Korea. The way was opened to link the trans-Siberian railway line through Manchuria to the ice-free harbors of Port Arthur and Talienwan, and through this transcontinental rail link St. Petersburg could now make its political and diplomatic weight felt in East Asia and could be assured that Russian goods would flow into the region. In this new context Korea was less important to the Russians.

41. *NGB*, 31.1, pp. 121–25.

THE STRENGTHENING OF THE COURT

With the departure of Minister Speyer in the spring of 1898, the Korean court and the Korean government were on their own, free from the influence of an outside power for the first time since the upsurge of Chinese influence in the 1880s. It was an opportune moment for the Korean leadership to reassert national independence and to launch a program of national self-strengthening. Indeed, some Korean historians refer to the years between 1897 and 1904 as the period of "Kwangmu reforms." In their view, these reforms marked an initiative by the Korean government, with foreign help, to grope its ways toward a program of modernization. In piecemeal and often tentative fashion, the government, sustained by new nationalist elements, made efforts to reform the land and tax systems, to modernize and expand the army, to create new central economic institutions and stabilize the currency, and so forth. Far from sensing that the end of independence was near, the Korean elite, unrestrained by the baleful influence of foreigners, began to build the foundation of a truly autonomous national state.[42]

Middle- and lower-ranking officials continued to carry out piecemeal efforts at modernization, primarily at the capital and its immediate vicinity. New army units were organized, reorganized, and reorganized yet again; a newly established officers' training academy began turning out graduates; a national cadastral survey was initiated under the supervision of an American adviser; stamps, patents, and land certificates were printed by a government printing office; students were sent abroad with government scholarships to study everything from sericulture to papermaking; academies were set up in Seoul to train postal and electrical technicians, Western-style doctors, sericulturists, mining engineers, and specialists in foreign languages; regulations for the prevention of contagious diseases were promulgated, and a Western-style hospital opened its doors in the capital; and so forth. In 1900 regulations were issued, orders requiring that all government officials wear Western-style clothes, and in 1902 the topknot-cutting decree, rescinded six years earlier in the face of public protest, was reissued, with government officials once again first in line to have their heads shorn if they had not already adopted the new hairstyle.

Just what the cumulative effect of these reforms would have been in the long run, or just how long they would have continued, is hard to

---

42. Cf. Kang Mang-il, *Kankoku kindaishi*, 198ff. Much of this section is based on this work and on *Hanguksa. 19. Kundae*, 44–109.

judge. It may well be that these changes were setting the country on the road taken by the Japanese in the 1860s and 1870s; or that they may have taken Korea no farther than the late Ch'ing self-strengthening efforts had taken China. There is no doubt, however, that the new reform projects put heavy demands on the government's budget, creating new opportunities for foreign leverage and new opportunities for corruption.

The symbolic assertion of Korean independence had begun, ironically enough, while the king was still ensconced in the Russian legation. Conservative officials and scholars sought to bolster his authority by calling for an elevation of the king's title. At the time of the Kabo reforms King Kojong had decided to call himself a *taikunju* [大君主] instead of *kukwang* [國王], but when the Kim Hong-jip cabinet had proposed to elevate his title from *kukwang* (king) to *hwangche* [皇帝] (emperor) and to address him as "His Imperial Majesty" (*p'yeha*) [陛下], the Western diplomats had objected. After his flight to the Russian legation, Kojong, still determined to acquire the new honorific, prompted his ministers to start a petition movement. Many petitions came flooding in after his return to the palace. On October 12, 1897, Kojong, solemnly vowing once again to his ancestors that he would protect his country's independence and promote his people's welfare, was formally coronated as emperor at a newly built Altar of Heaven, similar to the altar at Peking. The following day he announced that henceforth his country would be known as the Korean Empire (*Taehan cheguk*).

The Russian minister, Speyer, still actively attempting to turn the country into a Russian protectorate, acknowledged these changes as a sop to the amour propre of the Koreans, whose independence he was trying to circumscribe. For the Korean elite, however, the change in title marked a final symbolic cutting of Korea's vassal tie to the Ch'ing. Since Korea had become an independent country, it was no longer necessary for its ruler to accept a title that subordinated him to the Chinese emperor. If the Korean ruler assumed a title parallel to that of the Chinese ruler (*huang-ti*) and the Japanese ruler (*tennō*), it would assert his parity with both. And considering the damage that had been done to the prestige of the monarch by the murder of the queen, the topknot decree, and the flight to the Russian legation, it could only enhance the ruler's reputation among his people.[43]

43. Kang Mang-il, *Kankoku kindaishi*, 199–202. Within a few years, after much discussion and planning, the Korean empire acquired other accoutrements of a modern nation state—a system of official decorations (1900), a national anthem (1902), and flags for the king, the crown prince, and the army (1902).

The new monarchical pretensions were buttressed by attempts to re-centralize power and authority in the hands of the court. The Kabo reforms, following the model of the Japanese monarchy, had attempted to separate the court from the government and bring all official revenue under the control of the Ministry of Finance. To undo these changes, the conservative cabinet of Yun Yong-son not only restored the king's power to override the decisions of the cabinet (renamed the *uijŏngbu*) but also strengthened the court's financial independence. In June 1896 control over mines in forty-three counties as well as the monopoly over the production and sale of red ginseng was moved from the Ministry of Commerce and Agriculture to the royal household treasury. The court also regained control over income from taxes on fish, salt, boats, and other miscellaneous items, and various government-owned lands (temple lands, etc.) were turned over to the court. Many peasants, hoping to avoid the new money taxes levied by the government, commended their land to the court, to whom they paid rent. Quite apart from various illegal sources of income, such as bribes and the sale of office, these revenue sources enormously increased the financial powers of the monarch. By contrast, the government had to rely primarily on land tax revenues and income from the mint, while the customs revenues remained under the firm hands of the commissioner of customs, McLeavy Brown. Indeed, so well fixed was the court and so fiscally desperate was the government that occasionally the Ministry of Finance had to borrow money from the royal exchequer to pay official salaries.

No change in titles or reassertion of royal power could conceal the corrosion of authority, stability, or continuity at Seoul. The emperor's new clothes cloaked a confused and unstable political center. Between the enunciation of the new Korean Empire in October 1897 and the outbreak of the Russo-Japanese War in February 1904, the king appointed 27 prime ministers, 23 royal household ministers, 27 foreign ministers, 23 home ministers, 32 finance ministers, 33 military affairs ministers, and 28 ministers of justice. In 1898 alone he appointed 8 prime ministers and 10 foreign ministers. To be sure, there were re-cidivist ministers—Yun Yong-son served as prime minister eight times —but even so the ministerial turnover was unusually high. By late December 1898, a little over a year after the promulgation of the empire, Horace Allen wrote, "During the past fortnight or so, there has been, practically, no central government in Korea. Every day has witnessed the appointment of Ministers of State only to be discontinued the next day. The departmental offices have closed, and public business stopped, and the city practically turned over to the agitators.... Absolutely no taxes come in from the provinces, and the treasury is entirely exhausted."[44]

What prompted Allen's observation was the sudden explosion of intrigue, infighting, and conflict within the Korean elite following the departure of Speyer. It was as though the disappearance of a dominant outside force at Seoul uncorked a half-fermented jug of political rivalry long stoppered by foreign pressure. Plot and counterplot came bubbling out. The deepest lines of conflict were drawn between the relatively conservative ministers who controlled the cabinet and the returned reformist exiles like Sŏ Chae-pil, Yun Ch'i-ho, and Yi Sang-jae, who had formed the Independence Club in July 1896. Initially a catchall organization where conservative officials rubbed shoulders with reformist outsiders, the club became increasingly activist in 1897, holding demonstrations to protest the government's spineless acquiescence to growing Russian influence over the king. As its protests against foreign intrusion and the granting of concessions became more shrill, and conservative high officials resigned from its membership, leadership gravitated into the hands of the more radical leaders Sŏ, Yun, Yi, and Yi Sung-man, who mounted a campaign for the establishment of a national assembly to strengthen the bonds between monarch and people.[45]

In late October 1898 the club began to mount mass demonstrations and protest meetings in the capital, drawing the participation of thousands of urban *yangban*, students, monks, merchants and other commoners, and even members of the outcaste. The king appeared to be on the verge of giving in to the club's demands for an appointed assembly, half of which was to be elected by the Independence Club. When the club voted to recall Pak Yŏng-hyo from Japan and give him a seat in the assembly, the conservatives struck back. Cho Pyŏng-sik charged that the club was plotting to overthrow the king, and on November 5 seventeen club leaders were arrested. Demonstrations and riots continued as club supporters protested the arrests, and peddlers mobilized by the conservatives fought them in the streets. Bloody street battles in late November brought Seoul to a state of near anarchy, prompting Allen's lugubrious report home. At the end of December, however, the king ordered the dissolution of the club; four hundred of its members were arrested, and several of its leaders, including Yun Ch'i-ho, fled into exile.

44. NA, Dispatch Book, U.S. Legation to Seoul, no. 167, Allen to Hay, Dec. 23, 1898.
45. Kang Mang-il, *Kankoku kindaishi*, 219–25. For detailed treatment of the Independence Club, see Chandra, "Nationalism and Popular Participation."

The break-up of the Independence Club, the main nonofficial force for institutional reform, prompted a further consolidation of monarchical power. To inter any hopes of a popular assembly or popular representation, a government commission staffed by conservative officials began work on a new "constitution." In August 1899 it produced a nine-article document that transformed the Korean emperor into an absolute monarch who held all legislative, judicial, and executive power. Article 2 declared that the Korean empire was an "absolute government," and article 3 declared that the emperor possessed "unlimited monarchical authority" and that he was "an independent body in international law." Under the rest of the document the emperor was given command over the army and navy, the right to declare and suspend martial law, the right to grant pardons, the right to declare war, and the right to make treaties. In theory, no parliament, nor indeed anyone else, could curb the emperor's power.

Far from making Kojong absolute, however, the new constitution made him all the more vulnerable to factional rivalry and competition. The stamp of his seal could make or break official careers, fill or empty pockets, and grant concessions and contracts to foreigners. The monarch was the font not only of honors but of wealth, and his discretionary powers invited, not to say encouraged, favoritism. If the Japanese emperor had become an *omikoshi*, hoisted on the shoulders of his ministers, to be displayed to his people on special occasions but otherwise kept safely in his shrine, the Korean monarch was a working potentate with the power to decide the fate and fortunes of the men who served him. The king's favor was a source of income as well as a source of pride, and that made palace intrigue endemic. In certain ways the politics of the court reminded the Japanese of their own ancien régime: a "despotism" ruled by a personal monarch, the Shogun, surrounded by familiars and favorites.

Aware of the fragility of its independence, the Korean court pursued a foreign policy of the weak, attempting to keep the foreigners at bay by balancing one against the other. It was a variation of the strategy of "using barbarians against barbarians." If no single foreign power had a predominant interest in the country, then Korea would be able to maintain its autonomy. But as Independence Club members pointed out in 1897–98, this was a self-defeating strategy, for it drew the foreigners more deeply into the country, handing over to them sources of national wealth and suffocating Korea's own independent efforts at reform. It also opened the way for foreign intrusion into domestic politics.

During the period of the Kwangmu reforms each major power tried to cultivate a body of partisans within the Korean court and bureaucracy willing to use their influence or position to advance that power's interests. The government passed back and forth among high officials partial to one or another of the foreign powers. Diplomatic dispatches refer constantly to members of the "Russian party" or the "American party" or the "Japanese party." Just what held these bureaucratic factions together—ideals, interest, personal connections, or past experience —is difficult to assess. The Namierization of late Yi politics awaits the hand of a Korean historian able to make his or her way through a diverse body of materials in Korean, Japanese, Russian, and English. What is most important to note for our purposes is that no one faction seems to have dominated court politics for very long. As we have seen, the turnover in high office was kaleidoscopic. Factional leaders could gain only enough power to displace their rivals temporarily, but never enough to secure long-term influence over the government. For the Japanese, the atmosphere of intrigue was evidence that the Korean elite lacked an ethic of public duty or any sense of national interest. Nevertheless, the Japanese had little choice but to work within this chaotic cauldron of interest brokering.

The king himself increasingly relied on an inner circle of familiars in the royal household to act as his agents in dealing with the foreigners. Through Yi Yong-ik he dealt with the Russians; through Yi Kun-taek and Kim Yong-chun he dealt with the Japanese; and through Kang Sok-ho he dealt with the Americans.[46] Both the Americans and the Japanese ministers, however, disliked Yi Yong-ik, who by 1900 had so ingratiated himself with the monarch that he exercised extraordinary control over the royal finances. Yi, whom Horace Allen once described as possessed with "a passion for getting control of government funds," had made his way to high office from extremely humble origins. Although it is certain that he came from a commoner family in North Hamgyŏng Province, his family background is so obscure that neither his parents' names nor their pedigrees are known. During his youth, with a small stake earned as a peddler, Yi went into gold mining, first at Tanchon and then at Yonghung, where he struck it rich. Despite a meager education, Yi wanted to advance in the official world, and he was willing to spend his money to do so. Eventually he attracted the attention of Min Yŏng-ik, who used him as an emissary to carry messages to and from

46. Moriyama Shigenori, *Kindai Nikkan kankeishi kenkyū*, 58–60.

the queen when she took refuge in the provinces after the 1882 mutiny. With Min as his patron, he had climbed his way into the king's inner circle by the late 1890s, assuming the post of royal household treasurer in 1897, in part because of his earlier experience in mining. He also served in several other key economic offices—as minister of finance, minister of war, head of the mint, and president of the railroad bureau—gathering into his hands enormous power not only over the king's finances but also over many lucrative new government projects. Yi's methods often were neither scrupulous nor legal. In February 1898 members of the Independence Club filed a complaint alleging that he had wrongfully deprived peasants of their mining rights, illegally seized ginseng plantations, and misappropriated state assets. Whatever his personal ethics, Yi consistently resisted the encroachment of Japanese political influence. Advocating a policy of hostility toward close neighbors and friendship toward distant ones, he worked to increase Russian influence, hoping to counterbalance the Japanese. The Japanese authorities, who regarded him as "pro-Russian," were anxious to get rid of him.[47]

In any case, by the spring of 1898, Japanese leaders were far more optimistic about their prospects in Korea than they had been two years before, when the Korean king was literally in the hands of the Russians. Not only had Russian influence at Seoul faded, but political changes at the court gave Japan new opportunities for political leverage. Ironically, the newfound independence of the Korean court quickened its appetite for dependence on outsiders. Reform-minded officials saw the introduction of foreign investment, technology, and experts as a means of civilizing their country; corrupt and venal officials used competition among the foreigners to line their pockets with bribes and kickbacks; and the king and his circle hoped to shore up the monarchy by astute manipulation of the foreigners. The deepening complaisance of the Korean elite eased the pursuit of concessions. Competition from Western diplomats and businessmen remained strong, but the Japanese, unlike the British or the Russians or even the Americans, were not distracted by large and important concerns outside of East Asia. If patient and plodding like the tortoise, the Japanese thought themselves able to win over swifter hares less attentive to the race for concessions on the peninsula.

47. Biographical information on Yi Yong-ik may be found in Cho Ki-jun, *Hanguk kiopka sa*, 63–86.

CHAPTER 4

The Race for Concessions,
1895–1901

The failure to establish political hegemony did not diminish Japanese efforts to expand their economic interests on the peninsula. As Isabella Bird Bishop noted, "It must be borne in mind not only that [Japan's] diplomacy is secret and reticent, but that it is steady ... and the Japanese have as much tenacity and fixity of purpose as any other race."[1] During the late 1890s Japanese "fixity of purpose" meant tenacious pursuit of an economic foothold even as paramount influence over the Korean court and the government was preempted by the Russians. Persistently but often futilely, the Japanese legation in Seoul navigated the uncertain waters of Korean court politics and diplomatic rivalry in pursuit of railroad, mining, and other concessions. They met with little success during Speyer's aggressive drive for Russian advantage, but with Speyer gone and an accommodation reached with St. Petersburg, they found themselves in a much better position to press their claims.

Just as the Japanese leaders had emulated "free trade imperialism" in the 1870s, they were now following the practices of "concession imperialism." Their model was no longer Commodore Perry, whose gunboats had forced an "unequal treaty" on Japan, but Lord Cromer, whose manipulation of Egypt's finances had turned it into a protectorate. As Inoue Kaoru had noted while minister to Seoul:

> How was it that the British had an excuse to intervene in Egypt? Was it not that the British had established its position of interest by providing Egypt

1. Bishop, *Korea and Her Neighbors*, 2:289.

with capital? ... If our country wishes to firmly establish its position in Korea and to provide a basis for intervention in its internal affairs, then it is most urgent that we strengthen our position in terms of real rights, whether railroads or financial loans, and prepare the way to move from intervention in financial relations to other relations.[2]

As we have already seen, in 1894 and 1895 Inoue had tried but failed to "Egyptianize" Korea by bullying the Korean government to grant railway concessions and accept loans. But the failure did not deter others from continuing the effort.

The economic penetration of Korea required subtler tactics than Inoue had employed. Complex negotiations had to be carried on by both private and official groups. In a sense, the making of Korean policy was less a matter decided at the top of the political structure than a collective effort involving all the "Korean interests" that had developed since the 1880s. The overall aims of the Japanese leadership did not waver, but its tactical stance was often influenced by other parties: the military high command, the legation staff in Seoul, the domestic business and banking community, the political party politicians, the Japanese resident community, and even the domestic press. Incrementally, and in undramatic ways, this shifting coalition of forces provided much of the "tenacity" and "fixity of purpose" behind the pursuit of concessions. In sheer force of numbers and intensity of commitment, the Japanese were hard for the Americans, the French, or even the Russians to match.

Political and economic considerations, however, often checked the attempt to gain an economic foothold in Korea. First, the Japanese leadership was increasingly preoccupied with the "race for concessions" in China, an escalation in international rivalry that presented both dangers and opportunities. They appraised policy toward Korea for its impact on relations with the other powers in East Asia, and often they were in disagreement. Itō and Inoue preferred to proceed cautiously, avoiding offense to the foreign powers, particularly the Russians, while Yamagata, Matsukata, and Ōkuma wanted to pursue Japanese interests more aggressively, however the foreigners might react. Resolving these differences took time. Second, the pursuit of economic concessions such

2. Quoted in Cho, *Kindai Kankoku keizaishi*, 193–94; the document appears in *NGB*, 27.1, pp. 477–78. Interestingly enough, some Korean leaders were also aware that borrowing from foreigners could lead to control by foreigners. In October 1894, when Yu Kil-chun visited Japan on a mission to discuss a possible loan to ease the Korean government's temporary financial difficulties, he expressed the fear that if Korea were to default on its foreign debt, then it surely would suffer the fate of Egypt; perhaps he had overheard Inoue. Moriyama Shigenori, "Kabo kaikaku shakkan mondai," 115–16.

as railroad lines or the advance of loans to the Korean government required heavy Japanese investment. Raising capital was made difficult by a series of financial crises that hit the domestic capital market in the late 1890s. As the result of a bad harvest in 1897, a financial panic occurred in the first half of 1898, and the resulting recession continued into the first half of 1899. Another financial panic followed in 1900–1901. These temporary contractions in credit often made domestic business and banking interests reluctant to invest in or to make loans to Korea.

Nevertheless, by the eve of the Russo-Japanese War, the Japanese were well on the way to establishing economic hegemony on the peninsula. To be sure, the other powers held concessions as well, and on the northern border a group of Russian promoters were building up a position at Ryonganp'o (renamed Port Nicholas) across the border from Antung, where Russian troops were based. But the web of connections the Japanese had woven was tighter and finer, secured by the presence of a growing population of Japanese settlers. As we shall see in part 2, Korea was no longer simply a "dagger pointed at the heart of Japan" but a cornucopia pouring profit, large and small, into Japanese pockets.

RAILROAD CONCESSIONS

Few projects excited the imperialist imagination more than the railway construction. A strong navy and merchant marine might link a metropolis to its colonies, but networks of steel rails provided expansionists the most efficient means of securing territory, extracting resources, and opening markets. The significance of the railway as a tool for imperialist expansion was first appreciated by the British in India. In 1844 Rowland M. Stephenson, the chief promoter of rail construction in India, observed that a rail line was "a military measure for the better security with less outlay of the entire territory" as well as "the means of conveyance from the interior to the nearest shipping ports of the rich and varied production of the country, and to transmit back manufactured goods of Great Britain, salt, etc. in exchange."[3] An emblem of technol-

3. Thorner, *Investment in Empire*, 48–49. Sir Thomas Maddock, a senior officer in the Government of India, provided an even clearer exposition of the military-political significance of the railway in the late 1840s. "It seems to me that, quite independently of commerical considerations, railroads might have been invented and used as instruments of government. In India the importance of them for conveying troops and all that troops require, is incalculable.... The advantages which a civilized government will derive from improving the condition of its semi-barbarous subjects, and in resisting the aggression of its semi-barbarous enemies, are so great, that the Government of India might be very well justified in making railroads for the attainment of them." Ibid., 86–87.

ogy at the service of profit and power, the railway line was at once a highway for the spread of commerce and a rampart of military power.

In the last decades of the century fascination with the railway as a tool of imperialist expansion reached its peak.[4] Projects for the construction of transcontinental railway lines abroad proliferated during the 1870s. The Berlin-Baghdad line, originally conceived as a purely commercial project for a Sarajevo-Constantinople line through the Balkans, captured the imagination of German politicians and promoters and much of the German public as a means of driving German power eastward into the heartland of the Ottoman Empire and ultimately perhaps to the borders of India. In France plans for a trans-Saharan line, crossing the desert from Algeria to West Africa, were often mooted, though never executed, by visionary engineers and colonialists during the 1870s and 1890s. The master imperialist Cecil Rhodes promoted a project to build a Cairo-Capetown railway to link the British foothold in South Africa with its protectorate in Egypt, and his British South Africa Company did manage to construct a long stretch of line. The most ambitious project of all, and the one of most concern to Japan, was the trans-Siberian railway, laid down between 1891 and 1903. The economic value of linking European Russia with western Siberia was clear, but the continuation of the line to the Pacific, where the Russian economic presence was negligible, proclaimed Russia's future political and strategic ambitions in the region.

By the 1890s the economic and political significance of railway construction was abundantly clear to Japanese leaders. In 1892, for example, Yamagata expressed a deep anxiety about the trans-Siberian line: "Russia is unable to use force in the Balkans, so she will turn her eyes singlemindedly to the East and will want to give full play to her bestial greed. . . . Ten years from now, with the completion of the trans-Siberian railway, Russia will be in a position to invade Mongolia, and who can tell whether or not in the future she will reach China."[5] Yet Yamagata was also aware that the tools of Western expansion could be harnessed to Japanese power. Just two years later he projected his own vision of a great railway trunk line that would stretch from Pusan through north China, and perhaps one day across China to the very borders of India.

4. "Until now the world had known only thalassocracies: but they were now to be confronted with an imperialism founded on railroads. The railways were one of the essential conditions of the American thrust westward, the Russian thrust eastward, and the domination of all continents newly opened by Europe from the sea." Girard, "Transport," 250.

5. *YAI*, 215–22.

Yamagata's vision, like the Cape-to-Cairo and trans-Sahara lines, failed to materialize, but it shows how strongly the Western model kindled his political imagination.

RAILROAD CONCESSION SEEKERS, 1896–1897

The pursuit of railway concessions had the backing of several interests: the army high command, a group of Osaka promoters, treaty port businessmen and merchants, and a few large metropolitan capitalists. Each had a different motive, but all saw the advantage of working with the others, and despite differences in perspective, and sometimes in tactics, they cooperated in keeping the issue of railway concessions on the government's agenda. The leadership in Tokyo, often restrained by its diplomatic milieu, sometimes pushed the railroad construction projects forward with less enthusiasm than their promoters wished, but when conditions permitted, Itō, Yamagata, and others lent their weight to the effort.

The Japanese military, anticipating a land war on the continent, first showed an interest in Korean railway construction in the early 1890s. After an observation tour of China and Korea in 1891, Kawakami Sōroku, assistant chief of the army general staff, concluded that a railroad line should be built linking Seoul to Pusan, the most probable major port of disembarkation for Japanese troops on the continent. With a railroad line to speed deployment, the Japanese would be at an advantage. In response to a request from Kawakami in late 1892, the Japanese consul at Pusan mounted a secret mission, disguised by the delightful cover story that it was collecting unusual bird specimens for an American museum, to survey a possible Pusan-Seoul route. Copies of the mission's report went not only to the army general staff and the Foreign Ministry but also to Shibusawa Eiichi, whose Dai-Ichi Bank was central to the financing of Japan-Korea trade.[6]

The Japanese began to pressure the Koreans for railroad construction rights on the eve of the Sino-Japanese War. In August 1894 when Ōtori asked the Korean government for rights to build lines linking Seoul with Inchon and Pusan, the Koreans had put off the request, indicating that they had already made a commitment to build railway lines with the help of British merchants, but in order to get the Japanese out of the royal palace they finally signed a provisional agreement. The agreement

6. *Chōsen tetsudō shi*, 28–29; NGB, 29:628–35.

was no more than a promise, but it gave the Japanese a foot in the door. In November a survey team of one hundred technicians under the direction of Sengoku Mitsugu, a leading railroad engineer, arrived in Korea to investigate possible routes. According to a newspaper report in late 1894, the lines were to facilitate military use and to be constructed under the direction of Japanese military engineers at a cost of about ¥2 million.[7] As we have seen, the Korean government put off Inoue Kaoru's continuing demand for a railroad treaty during the winter of 1895. The Koreans were aware that they had neither the capital nor the technical expertise to build railway lines themselves, but they preferred that almost anyone but the Japanese do it for them.

When the war ended, the army lost its sense of urgency, but in the meantime a group of civilian concessionaires had become involved when it still appeared that Inoue might succeed in negotiating a railway treaty. In February 1895 Ōmiwa Chōbei, Takeuchi Tsuna, and Ōzaki Saburō drew up plans for a company to establish a new Korean central bank and to build both a Seoul-Pusan and a Seoul-Inchon line. Ōmiwa, president of the Fifty-eighth Bank in Osaka, was an old Korea hand who first came to Korea in 1891 as an adviser on currency reform. While his plan to convert Korean coinage from a copper to a silver base failed, he established connections with many high Korean officials, including some in the reform camp such as Kim Ki-jin and An Kyong-su. Takeuchi, a colorful veteran of the Tosa loyalist movement, was a familiar of Itagaki Taisuke and Gotō Shōjirō and a key figure in the Jiyūtō. He had first gone to Korea with Ōmiwa in the summer of 1894 at the behest of Foreign Minister Mutsu, a fellow Tosa man, on a private mission to sound out the mood of the Korean court. Takeuchi, who had been involved in a number of successful business ventures, including the Takashima coal mine, was an ideal middleman between the business and political worlds. Ōzaki Saburō, a former protégé of Sanjō Sanetomi, who had risen to become head of the cabinet legislative bureau, was well connected in bureaucratic circles. What prompted these promoters to put together a railway and banking company proposal was a chance to profit from inside political connections.[8]

Neither Itō nor Mutsu were averse to using the promoters for their

7. Pak Jong-keun, *Nisshin sensō to Chōsen*, 100–102; *Chōsen tetsudō shi*, 1:34–42.

8. According to one account, Ōmiwa had dismissed the construction of a Seoul-Pusan line as a "sophomoric pipe-dream" before the war, but once he learned that the Japanese government was pressing Korea for railway construction rights, he saw it as a golden opportunity. Nakai Kitarō, *Chōsen kaikō roku*, 13–15.

own purposes. In early 1896, as Japanese influence in Seoul was collapsing, Itō urged Takeuchi and Ōmiwa to visit Korea. While he was not optimistic that the Koreans would grant a railway concession, he still hoped that they might be induced to reform their banking system. When Ōmiwa arrived in Seoul in March, he found the political waters muddied by the flight of the king to the Russian legation. One of his Korean contacts suggested the possibility of a private loan of one million yen to finance a Seoul-Inchon line, but the pro-Russian foreign minister, Yi Wan-yong, indicated that he considered the 1894 provisional agreement void.

To the alarm of the Japanese military, and the disappointment of the Ōmiwa group, in early April 1896 construction rights for the Seoul-Inchon line were granted to James R. Morse, an American businessman who had served as Korean consul and commercial agent in New York. Morse, who ran a trading company with offices in Yokohama as well, had been thwarted in his efforts by the intervention of Yuan Shih-kai to secure a railway concession in 1892; but this time he had the support of the American minister, Horace Allen, whose stock had risen considerably after the flight of the king to the Russian legation. The Russian minister, Waeber, agreed to support Morse if he relinquished his timber-cutting concession in the north to a Russian concessionaire. As Allen later crowed, "We Americans never failed to profit by fishing in waters muddied by the Japanese."[9] When news reached the Japanese army general staff, it immediately urged the cabinet to buy the Seoul-Inchon concession from Morse. Despite Komura's continuing protests that the concession violated the provisional agreement of 1894, the Korean government stood by its commitment to Morse. To the dismay of the Japanese, the day after the grant of the concession to Morse was announced, the French minister asked that rights to build a Seoul-Ŭiju line be granted to a French company, Fives-Lille, and in July, once again with help from Waeber, an agreement was signed.

Looking for new allies, Ōmiwa turned to the Japanese resident community in Korea. At his invitation Yamaguchi Tabei, head of the Seoul Residents Association, agreed to send a delegation to Tokyo. Yamaguchi, who had already realized the need for railway construction in

9. In contrast to the Japanese general staff, Allen's interest in railroad rights was commercial and cultural, not strategic. The construction of railways, he said, would advance trade, enchance national finances, spread enlightenment among the population, and stimulate agriculture. New York Public Library, Allen Papers, Press Book no. 4, no. 37, pp. 52–53.

Korea, secretly offered Foreign Minister Yi Wan-yong ¥50,000 to persuade him to put off the French request for a concession until the fall of
1896. The Seoul Chamber of Commerce passed a resolution proclaiming the "urgent necessity" of securing the Seoul-Pusan railway construction rights, and similar resolutions were passed by local Japanese
chambers in Inchon, Pusan, and Wŏnsan as well.[10] While their interest
in rail lines was largely commercial, the local Japanese residents were
not immune to grand dreams of expanding Japanese influence. As
Yamaguchi observed in June 1896, "The port of Pusan ... will control
the lifeline of all the districts of Korea. When the trans-Siberian railroad is eventually completed, the [Seoul-Pusan] line will connect our
country with Russia, and [as] a main line piercing the European and
Asian continents, inevitably it will be of the utmost importance in the
intercourse between East and West."[11]

When Ōmiwa and his supporters from Seoul met with Itō and Mutsu
in early May, neither was enthusiastic about pressing the Korean government for a Seoul-Pusan concession. First, they argued, given the
current financial crisis in Japan, it would be difficult to raise capital for
such a risky venture. The Japanese had no experience building railroads
overseas, and since Korea was poor and sparsely populated, the line was
likely to be unprofitable. Few people were buying shares in profitable
domestic railroads, and they were less likely to invest in unpromising
Korean lines. Second, since other powers wanted to claim railroad rights
in Korea, the government had to act cautiously. Itō did not wish to antagonize either the Americans or the Russians by asking for a major
railway concession.[12]

But the prime minister was vulnerable to domestic political pressure.
Takeuchi warned Itō about the political consequences of caution. If
the government refused the promoters' request for support and the
Seoul-Pusan rights went to another country, the government's responsibility would become an issue in both houses of the Diet. Itō, who had
just beaten back an opposition attack on his "weak" foreign policy,
could hardly have welcomed that prospect. On May 11 he told Takeuchi that if he and his partners could assemble one hundred people to
act as "organizers" (hakkōjin) for a Seoul-Pusan railway line, he would
back their attempt to seek a concession.[13]

10. Chōsen tetsudō shi, 1:59.
11. Nikkan tsūshō kyōkai hōkoku, no. 10 (June 1896): pp. 63–64.
12. Gaimushō, Komura gaikōshi, 1:102.
13. Takeuchi Tsuna, "Takeuchi Tsuna jijoden," 449–50.

With this promise from Itō, the Ōmiwa group mobilized 150 backers, including financial and business potentates like Shibusawa Eiichi (Dai-Ichi Bank), Ōe Taku (director of the Tokyo Stock Exchange and vice president of the Tokyo Chamber of Commerce), Masuda Takashi (Mitsui Bussan), Maejima Hisoka (director of several companies), Nakano Buei (Tokyo Stock Exchange), and Inoue Kakugorō (Diet member). What attracted them was a mixture of national interest and self-interest. For a modest investment of ¥50 they were in on the ground floor of an important national enterprise. If they had been willing to underwrite bond issues during the Sino-Japanese War, they would have little hesitation to put up such a trifling amount for a patriotic cause. As Maejima observed in July 1896, "The railways from the eastern end of the Korean peninsula obviously form a starting point, a gateway to the great railways between Asia and Europe.... We now have a chance of spreading out our limbs a bit, but if we take no notice and let it pass, it will immediately pass into the hands of some other country, and this opportunity, once gone, will be lost forever."[14]

In early July 1896 Ōmiwa and Ōzaki were back in Seoul. Despite the support of Hara Takashi, the new Japanese minister, they were unable to win the Seoul-Pusan concession. Foreign Minister Yi Wan-yong assured them that the Korean government did not intend to cede the rights to the French concessionaire, M. Grille, but he added that for the moment political disturbances in the south made it impossible to grant a railroad concession through the region. In December 1896, after six months of lobbying in Seoul, Ōmiwa returned to Japan empty-handed. As he pointed out to a reporter, the promoters of the project were hesitant to proceed because of a domestic recession. But, he added, "the Seoul-Pusan railway is a national issue and [its fate] should not be determined by the ups and downs of the economy."[15] In fact, however, the project was to remain in abeyance until Russian influence had plummeted in Seoul and the Japanese had recaptured control of the Seoul-Inchon line.

RECAPTURING THE SEOUL-INCHON LINE, 1897–1898

Although the American businessman James Morse had stolen the march on the Japanese, he had trouble moving his Seoul-Inchon project for-

---

14. Quoted in Hunter, "Japanese Government Policy," 580–81.
15. *Tōkyō keizai zasshi* 34, no. 856, Dec. 17, 1896, p. 1096.

ward. His contract with the Korean government required that construction be completed by 1899, but with the Russians in control of the court and the Japanese waiting eagerly in the wings, Morse found American investors reluctant to put up capital. It was one thing to secure a concession, another thing to make use of it.[16] Aware of Morse's difficulties, Masuda Takashi, head of Mitsui Bussan, sent him word that Ōmiwa's group of Japanese investors would be interested in buying him out, and in early 1897 Morse let Shibusawa Eiichi know that he was willing to consider an offer.

The political atmosphere in Japan had changed too. The new prime minister, Matsukata Masayoshi, had long favored securing concrete economic interests in Korea, and the foreign ministry was in the hands of Ōkuma Shigenobu, who, like Vice-Minister Komura, wanted to regain the upper hand for Japan in Korea. Ōkuma was in favor of negotiations for a transfer of the Seoul-Inchon concession using H. W. Denison, an American adviser to the foreign ministry, as go-between. Since the Seoul-Inchon line was shorter and less expensive to build than the Seoul-Pusan line, and hence more likely to turn an early profit, it made more sense to acquire it first. With the help of Matsukata and Ōkuma, Shibusawa put together a new and larger syndicate to buy the concession. The plan was to let Morse, with his access to American technology and equipment, complete the line, then to buy it from him. The syndicate offered him ¥100,000 ($50,000) in earnest money immediately and ¥2 million ($1 million) for the completed line.[17] In July 1897 Morse, who continued to have trouble finding other backers, asked the syndicate for $300,000 in earnest money, but they decided instead to break their contract with him.

Foreign Minister Ōkuma was troubled when he learned of this new development: what if the Seoul-Inchon line were to fall into the hands of other foreign investors, the British, the French, or, worse yet, the Russians? It was in the national interest for the government to take action. Ōkuma arranged for the Yokohama Specie Bank to lend Morse $500,000 (¥1 million), guaranteed by the government, if Morse agreed to continue construction and to withdraw his demands to the syndicate. In effect, the government assumed the risk of a default by Morse in hopes of keeping the line out of hostile foreign hands. This sent a clear

16. NA, Dispatch Book, U.S. Legation to Seoul, no. 108, Allen to Sec. State, May 23, 1898.
17. *SEDS*, 16:516–24.

signal to the syndicate that the government had a compelling interest in what had started out as a purely business proposition.

In October 1897 the syndicate itself asked the government for direct financial support. What would happen, they said, if economic conditions at home did not improve and the syndicate was unable to raise the ¥2 million to buy out Morse when the Seoul-Inchon line was completed? The syndicate's leaders asked for a loan of ¥1 million without a fixed term. If the line showed a profit of less than ¥50,000 a year, the loan was to be interest free, but if more, then the interest was to be 5 percent per annum. In effect, the syndicate was asking for the government to assume the greater risk. Despite misgivings about violating the constitution, which required that all national loans be approved by the Diet, Matsukata, with Ōkuma's backing, agreed to this proposal, and a portion of the China indemnity money was deposited with the Yokohama Specie Bank as collateral for the loan. The principle of private enterprise at public risk was carried a step further.[18]

Well aware that the Seoul-Inchon line's political importance put him in the catbird's seat, Morse tried to squeeze a higher price for his concession by bringing the Russians into play. His negotiations with the Japanese syndicate took place as the Russian minister Speyer was aggressively pursuing a privileged economic position in Seoul. In the early fall of 1897 Speyer told Horace Allen that he wanted Morse to use Russian gauge on the line so that rolling stock and locomotives could be switched more easily to the projected Seoul-Ŭiju railway, creating a network linking Korea with the trans-Siberian line.[19] In January 1898, St. Petersburg rejected his suggestion that the Russian government purchase Morse's rights lest that give Japan an excuse to demand rights for a Seoul-Pusan line, so Speyer proposed that a private company buy out the Japanese loan to Morse, who would then hold the rights until the Russians could purchase them openly. The Seoul-Inchon concession, as Horace Allen observed, turned out to be "a most valuable property, for the Japanese and the Russians have been bidding against each other in such a lively fashion that Morse is going to realize handsomely on his little investment, and what started as a purely commercial proposition has by the added political force, become quite an important matter."[20]

In March 1898 Morse told the syndicate that a French group repre-

18. Nakamura Masanori, "Keinin Keifu tetsudō," 230–32; *SEDS*, 16:525–42.
19. New York Public Library, Allen Papers, Press Book no. 6, Allen to Morse, Sept. 12, 1897, p. 278.
20. Ibid., Allen to Rockhill, Jan. 30, 1898, p. 357.

sented by M. Grille had made an offer of ¥3 million for the Seoul-Inchon concession and that he would repay the Japanese loan with a portion of his profit from the sale. Alarmed by this news, Prime Minister Itō agreed to provide Shibusawa's syndicate a no-interest loan of ¥800,000 in addition to the ¥1 million already promised by Matsukata. Minister of Finance Inoue Kaoru, who wanted the line to be built by the Korean government with Japanese help, tried to block the ¥1 million by arguing that it was illegal; but Itō, bolstered by Komura's plea that the line was of great political importance, prevailed.[21] The syndicate told Morse it would hold him to the contract.

By the fall of 1898, however, Morse was beginning to feel the whole affair something of a nuisance. With the establishment of a foothold at Port Arthur, the Russians had lost interest in the line and could no longer be played off against the Japanese.[22] Work on the line was plagued with difficulties. According to Shibusawa, Americans working for Collbran, Morse's construction contractor, were treating the Korean laborers "like dogs," and the Japanese were worried that this ill treatment might have an adverse impact on the reputation of the line and on Japanese relations with Korea.[23] Anxious to unburden himself, Morse offered to sell the line to the Japanese syndicate immediately in October 1898. On December 13 the Yamagata government, more appreciative of the strategic importance of the line than Itō had been, promised the syndicate a loan of ¥1.8 million on the condition that representatives from the transportation, finance, and foreign ministries supervise construction and management of the line. The syndicate, reorganized as the Seoul-Inchon Railway Company, a partnership rather than a corporation, finally bought Morse out for ¥1,720,452.15 in May 1899, and by July 1900 construction of the line had been completed.[24]

While the initiative in recapturing the Seoul-Inchon concession had been taken by big metropolitan investors like Shibusawa Eiichi, the government had played a crucial, albeit reactive, role in assuring their success. Japanese investors, concerned about the unstable political situation in Korea and doubtful that the line would prove to be as profitable as domestic railroads, were reluctant to put up much of their

21. Inoue Kaoru Kō Denki Hensankai, *Segai Inoue Kaoru Kō den*, 4:678–79.
22. NA, Dispatch Book, U.S. Legation to Seoul, no. 108, Allen to Sec. of State, May 23, 1898; New York Public Library, Allen Papers, Press Book no. 6, Allen to J. Sloan Fassett, May 17, 1898, p. 417.
23. *Chōsen tetsudō shi*, 49–51; *SEDS*, 16:558.
24. KSH, Sakatani Yoshirō Papers, Folder 503, "Chōsen shotetsudō ni kansuru shorui"; Tokutomi, *Kōshaku Matsukata Masayoshi den*, 2:760–63.

own capital.[25] Rather, it was the government, drawing on the financial windfall of the Chinese indemnity, that put up the money to buy out the line. Given the favorable terms of the loan, the syndicate members, who put up only ¥470,000 of their own money, risked very little but stood to make substantial profits from a monopoly on the traffic between Inchon, the chief port for foreign trade, and the capital. The peculiarity of the line's financing did not go unnoticed. When it finally opened in July 1900, the Tōkyō keizai zasshi, a staunch champion of laissez-faire economics, recognized it as a milestone in Japan's economic expansion abroad but remarked how unfortunate it was that so much of the capital had come from the national treasury and so little from the capitalists themselves. "Thus, we cannot take complete pride in the completion of this enterprise," it editorialized. "However, perhaps in the future our nation's capitalists, taking the success of the Seoul-Inchon line as a model, will invest their capital abroad with more vigor."[26] In fact, however, the line served less as a model for capitalism than as an example of how much the Japanese government was involved in building an economic infrastructure in Korea.

THE SEOUL-PUSAN LINE, 1898–1903

The retreat of the Russians in the spring of 1898 paved the way for new negotiations on the Seoul-Pusan concession, but it is not entirely clear what induced the Korean government finally to grant it to the Japanese. According to the recollections of Takeuchi Tsuna and Ōe Taku, a critical role was played by Katō Masuo, the Japanese minister in Seoul who carried on a "certain special kind of maneuvering."[27] Both referred to Katō's cooperation in helping to curb the activities of the Independence Club. By ingratiating himself with the Korean court, Katō not only smoothed negotiations on the railway line but also managed to cultivate key Korean officials like Min Yŏng-sok, Min Yŏng-hwan, and Yu Kil-chun. Even so, other officials, claiming to be worried at the reaction of the Russians, said it would better for Korea to build the line itself with capital and other assistance from Japan or give the construction rights to an American concessionaire.[28]

Ironically, help from the American legation may have pushed the

25. SEDS, 16:565.
26. Tōkyō keizai zasshi, July 14, 1900, p. 60.
27. Saiga, Ōe Tenya denki, 638.
28. New York Public Library, Allen Papers, Press Book no. 6, Allen to Collbran, July 24, 1898, p. 439.

Japanese suit forward. Since it was clear that Morse was going to sell his interest in the Seoul-Inchon line to the Japanese at the best price he could get, Horace Allen decided to help the Japanese secure the Seoul-Pusan concession. In July 1898 he proposed two alternatives to the Korean finance minister: the government might borrow money from Japan and allow the Japanese to build and operate the line for a Korean company; or it might include the Seoul-Pusan line in the Seoul-Inchon concession and allow the Japanese syndicate to build it. In either case Allen hoped that the Japanese would buy construction materials, rolling stock, and the like from the United States.[29] The finance minister seemed to favor the second alternative, an outright grant of a concession to the Japanese.[30]

When Itō Hirobumi visited Seoul on his return from a trip to China, the Koreans finally agreed to give the Seoul-Pusan concession to the Japanese syndicate. According to one account, Minister Katō told a high Korean official that Itō was planning to chide the Korean king for lack of progress on the Seoul-Pusan line negotiations, and if that were to happen Katō would have to resign. Upset to hear that a trusted friend might leave, the king was persuaded to grant the concession.[31] According to Takeuchi's recollection, Katō urged the Koreans to make the concession as a token of "harmony between Japan and Korea," since Itō had worked so hard on behalf of Korean independence. In any event, Itō's visit became a festival of friendship, festooned with cordial speeches and a message of felicitations from the Meiji emperor to the Korean court. By the time Itō left, the Korean government had indicated its intention to give the concession to Japan.[32]

On September 8, 1898, the Korean government signed an agreement with the Seoul-Pusan Railway Company. The company was to begin construction on the line no later than September 1901 and to complete it within ten years. The Korean government was to provide the right of way on the condition that the railroad carry Korean military supplies, troops, and mail free of charge. Construction materials were to be brought into the country without customs duties, the construction work force had to be 90 percent Korean, and foreign technicians had to return home once the line was finished. Shares in the Seoul-Pusan Railroad

29. Ibid., Press Book no. 9, speech to Naval War College, p. 59.
30. Ibid., Press Book no. 6, Allen to Morse, July 28, 1898, p. 441.
31. Saiga, Ōe Tenya denki, 639–40.
32. Takeuchi Tsuna, "Takeuchi Tsuna jijoden," 452–54; Chōsen tetsudō shi, 1:163–64.

Company could be owned by Koreans or Japanese but not by nationals of any third country, and railway rights in the three southern provinces were not to be given to any other party. The Korean government could buy back the line fifteen years after its completion but could resell only to Japanese or Korean nationals. If no price was agreed on, the concession would be extended another ten years.[33]

In February 1899 Ōe Taku, one of the organizing group, arrived in Korea with a team of a dozen or so technicians and engineers to survey a possible route and to estimate construction costs. Travel funds were provided by the general staff, whose interest in construction of the line remained strong.[34] The plans that emerged from the survey, paying due attention to both the commercial and military uses of the line, projected a route parallel to the main road linking Pusan with the capital. To facilitate the movement of troops and materiel the line was to be narrow gauge, but the rolling stock was to be broad gauge; and the right of way was to be as wide as possible so that shops and warehouses to promote local trade could be built close to the stations.[35]

The estimate of construction costs turned out to be much higher than expected, so the promoters decided to capitalize the Seoul-Pusan Railway Company at ¥25 million, an amount much larger than the capitalization of the most successful domestic rail companies. How was this enormous sum to be raised in the midst of the severe recession that had begun in 1898? The boom in domestic railroad investment had come to a halt. Newly organized rail companies, unable to raise capital through stock sales, had been financed by high-interest bonds, and operating capital was often covered by loans and notes. Many of these companies collapsed in 1899 and 1900.[36]

With the mood for railway investment so bearish at home, investors were not likely to put their money into a foreign venture. One alternative was to turn to the government for help, and another was to seek foreign investors. The promoters considered both possibilities, but in November 1899, after considerable lobbying and public hand-wringing, Ōmiwa, Inoue Kakugorō, and Nakano Buei asked the government for assistance in reducing the investment risk. Under their proposal only ¥5 million of the ¥25 million capitalization was to be covered by public stock subscription; the remaining ¥20 million was to be raised

33. SEDS, 16:375–76.
34. Chōsen tetsudō shi, 1:163–64.
35. SEDS, 16:382.
36. Ōishi, Nihon sangyō kakumei no kenkyū, 2:187–202.

by the sale of government-guaranteed bonds. The government was also to guarantee a return of 6 percent on the entire capital for a period of fifteen years, in effect assuring investors that they had nothing to lose. While Prime Minister Yamagata was sympathetic to the proposal, there was considerable opposition inside and outside the government. Itō Hirobumi and Inoue Kaoru, the two senior leaders most intimately engaged with the Korean problem, were reluctant to push too fast on the construction of the line for fear of upsetting the Russians; bureaucrats in the Ministry of Finance were reluctant to subsidize such a foreign railroad enterprise in a time of financial stringency; and others argued it was absurd to plunge into an uncertain overseas venture when there was scarcely enough capital to build domestic lines.[37]

In February 1900, with the blessing of the Yamagata cabinet, the Diet passed a resolution urging a speedy completion of the Seoul-Pusan line, but the promoters were still short of funds. They had even been unable to come up with ¥50,000 needed to begin preparations for construction. When Shibusawa appealed for help the minister of the army, Katsura Tarō, agreed to supply money from army secret service funds. On New Year's Eve 1899 Shibusawa picked up a bundle of cash from an intermediary, making it possible to send another survey mission to Korea the following spring and summer. Interestingly, when Shibusawa offered to return the sum, Katsura suggested that instead he donate it to the Tōyō Kyōkai, a proexpansion society.[38]

The promoters were equally attentive to their political base in Korea. In April 1900, at the urging of Ōmiwa, the Korean government established a new bureau of railroads within the imperial household to oversee railway development; the new agency was headed by Min Yŏng-sok with Ōmiwa as adviser. Korean officials, scenting an opportunity for profit in the provision of the agreement with the Japanese that 90 percent of the workforce must be Korean, began to set up labor-contracting companies. While the Japanese were surveying the route, for example, a high government official organized a company to recruit construction foremen and workers along the prospective route. All the earnest money collected from the prospective workers, however, went for expenses, and the company collapsed, undoubtedly leaving its organizers wealthier for their pains. Another group of officials in the Imperial Household set up a company under Min Yŏng-kil and then

37. *SEDS*, 16:388, 396.
38. Ibid., 6:396–97; 16:387–88.

vigorously lobbied Takeuchi for a contract to undertake the entire construction job, a project with ample opportunities for moneymaking.
After considerable negotiation Takeuchi was finally able to put them
off.[39]

Takeuchi was far more worried about local reactions to the building
of a railway through the heart of the peninsula. Anti-Japanese disturbances were fresh in memory, and widespread popular hostility toward the "dwarf barbarians" was difficult to ignore. If suddenly a railway line were cut through the countryside, slicing paddy fields in two,
leveling valleys, displacing houses and graves, there were bound to be
protests that would delay construction of the line. In May 1900 Takeuchi set out from Seoul along the projected route, stopping at each local
military garrison and country *yamen* to explain the benefits the railroad would bring. Most local officials were curious about the project,
barraging him with naive questions about whether locomotives had
wings or could run as fast as a horse.[40]

Raising capital remained a problem. Foreign Minister Aoki was enthusiastic about seeking foreign investors, but the agreement signed with
the Koreans precluded the sale of stock to third-country nationals. In
January 1900 the promoters met with Yamagata, Matsukata, and
Katsura to urge that the agreement be changed to permit foreign investors. The Korean government resisted pressure to change this provision,
and so did some of the Japanese promoters. Ōe Taku argued that foreign capital would defeat a key goal of the Japanese government, which
was to prevent the line from falling under the control of foreign interests. The Russian government, for example, might try to buy up a substantial interest in the company through purchase of stock by proxies,
and the Japanese might find themselves losing control of the line as
earlier the French had lost control of the Suez Canal through the sale of
stock to British investors.[41] Takeuchi, by contrast, favored bringing in
foreign capital, and Shibusawa backed him, but the Korean foreign minister, Pak Che-sun, known to some of his colleagues as a "local agent
of the Japanese Foreign Ministry," refused to agree for fear of being
labeled "pro-Japanese."

The only course left was to rely on the domestic capital market. After
considerable lobbying the promoters convinced cabinet members that
given the parlous condition of the financial world, it would be difficult

39. Takeuchi Tsuna, "Takeuchi Tsuna jijoden," 459–60.
40. Ibid., 461–62.
41. *Chōsen tetsudō shi*, 1:97–102; *SEDS*, 6:403–9; Saiga, *Ōe Tenya denki*, 647–50.

to raise capital unless investors were guaranteed a high rate of return. Yamagata once again threw his support behind the project. In September 1900 the government issued regulations providing a 6 percent subsidy for dividends on the company's paid-in capital for a period of fifteen years; and early the following year the Diet passed a bill to appropriate the subsidy money. In June 1901, after nearly three years of lobbying, maneuvering, and persuasion, the promoters were finally ready for the formal organization of the Seoul-Pusan Railroad Company under the presidency of Shibusawa Eiichi.[42]

Since the panic of 1900–1901 made it difficult to raise capital in the big financial centers of Tokyo and Osaka, the company promoters decided to take their capital-raising campaign to the provinces, appealing to local chambers of commerce, provincial bankers, prefectural and county officials, and local businessmen. The home minister asked each prefectural governor to raise subscriptions for a quota of shares, and the promoters fanned out across the country to drum up support. To increase confidence in the company and to underline its "national" significance, the promoters induced the imperial household to buy shares. Shibusawa Eiichi and Maejima Hisoka worked the Tokyo area, appealing to members of the peerage, officials in the imperial household, ministry officials, and the representatives of the highest taxpayers in the House of Peers. Takeuchi, Ōzaki Saburō, and others traveled to Kyushu, Tohoku, central Honshu, and Shikoku in search of provincial shareholders.

Not surprisingly, the promoters tried to convince listeners that the enterprise made economic sense. Shibusawa assured a gathering of prefectural governors in April 1900 that the Seoul-Pusan line was certain to be profitable in the long term.

> Viewed from the standpoint of the Japanese economy, I think that [the Seoul-Pusan line] will not be an unprofitable venture.... Korea is an agricultural country.... Last year one million koku of Korean rice was sold in our country. If the price of this agricultural product is made cheaper, it will increase the wealth of Korea. If one asks what profit there might be in increasing the wealth of Korea, it is that more Japanese manufactures will be sold there.... I believe that making their agricultural products cheaper is a way to sell more of our manufactures there. If you ask how to make Korean agricultural products cheaper, the answer lies in the convenience of transportation and communication.[43]

42. *SEDS,* 16:382–87.
43. *SEDS,* 16:410–12.

In short, Shibusawa argued not only that profits would accrue to the owners of the Seoul-Pusan line but also that construction of the line would have a ripple effect benefiting domestic manufacturers as well as Japanese consumers of Korean rice. The successful opening of the Seoul-Inchon line in 1900 doubtless gave force to this kind of appeal.

The promoters also appealed to the patriotic sentiments of potential investors, often in the crudest fashion. Ōzaki Saburō, for example, argued in his speeches to local businessmen and notables that if the Seoul-Pusan line were not built, the lives and money expended in the Sino-Japanese War would have been wasted. Korea would come under the control of another power, and Japan would find its own independence threatened. "It is your duty as a citizen (*kokumin*) to buy our stock," he prodded. "If you cannot buy many shares, one or two will be fine. If you are devoted to your country, buy whatever you can."[44] With tension rising between Japan and Russia in the wake of the Boxer incident, this unabashed flag-waving may have struck a responsive chord.

Whatever the strength of patriotic appeals, in an uncertain financial climate the government guarantee of a 6 percent annual dividend made the investment attractive. The initial subscription drive was a great success. An offering of 100,000 shares (¥5 million) brought in subscriptions for 209,251, or more than two subscriptions for every share offered. While the promoters, the Japanese imperial household, and the Korean royal family accounted for about 18 percent of the subscriptions, the rest were bought by wealthy local landholders, provincial businessmen, and bankers. The average subscription by members of the organizing group amounted to 173.9 shares, or about ¥8,700, and the average for ordinary subscribers was 10.8 shares, or about ¥540. If we recall that the beginning annual salary for a public official was ¥600 in 1907, this was clearly a substantial amount, well beyond the reach of all but the most affluent.

Since subscribers did not have to pay in the full amount pledged, however, the company found itself with only ¥500,000 to begin construction by the deadline of September 1901. Of that amount, nearly a third went for preparatory expenses—administrative costs, gifts to Korean officials, surveying costs—with only ¥340,000–350,000 left to build the line. Since the estimated cost per mile was ¥80,000, this would allow construction to advance no more than few miles out of either Pusan or Seoul. A second subscription drive in the fall of 1901,

44. *Tōkyō keizai zasshi*, April 31, 1904, pp. 783–84.

which brought subscriptions for 335,684 shares, of which ¥1,687,000 was paid in, made it possible to begin work on the line, albeit slowly. In March 1902 the *Tōkyō keizai zasshi* sarcastically speculated that it would take twenty years to complete the line at the rate capital was being raised.[45]

The signing of the Anglo-Japanese alliance in January 1902 raised the promoters' hopes that the British might be willing to invest in the line. In April 1902 Shibusawa approached Prime Minister Katsura, Foreign Minister Komura, and other top officials with the idea of selling foreign bonds to raise capital for the line. While visiting England during the coronation of King Edward IV, he met with representatives from Baring Brothers, Samuel and Samuel, and other London financiers to discuss underwriting such a bond issue. The British bankers, more interested in a sure profit than in solidarity with their new allies, were unwilling to proceed on terms acceptable to the Japanese, and the search for foreign capital reached another dead end.[46]

As relations between Japan and Russia deteriorated in 1902–3, the problem of financing the Seoul-Pusan line through public sale of stocks became more urgent and more difficult. A third subscription drive in the spring of 1903, in the midst of talk about war with Russia, was far less successful. Only 64,216 shares were subscribed, reflecting considerable investor anxiety about the future of the peninsula.[47] But since a Japanese-controlled trunk line up the center of the peninsula was crucial to Japanese military operations, the army was anxious to complete construction as soon as possible. The civilian bureaucracy rallied around the company. During the summer of 1903 the Ministry of Finance put pressure on the Bank of Japan to help raise capital, and in August the Ministry of Transportation authorized the company to issue ¥4 million in short-term bonds at 5 percent. In contrast to his earlier reluctance to support the company, even Inoue Kaoru offered his services to act as a go-between in gathering investors for the bond issue. A syndicate of several city banks and semigovernmental banks—the Mitsui Bank, the Mitsubishi Bank, the Dai-Ichi Bank, the Fifth Bank, the Hundredth Bank, the Yasuda Bank, the Teikoku Shogyo Bank, the Japan Industrial Bank, and the Yokohama Specie Bank—each put up ¥200,000 to ¥500,000 to underwrite the bond issue.[48]

45. Ibid., Mar. 29, 1902.
46. SEDS, 16:456–58.
47. SEDS, 16:431–43, 497–98.
48. Ōishi, *Nihon sangyō kakumei no kenkyū*, 2:304–5.

Even with this new infusion of capital, work on the line proceeded slowly. By early December 1903 only about 70 miles out of 270 had been finished, and all of that was over flat terrain. The most difficult parts of the line, requiring bridging and tunneling, had still to be constructed. The probability of war with Russia was nearly certain. On December 1, 1903, Kodama Gentarō, the army vice chief of staff, announced that since time was of the essence, construction of the line should not be left in the hands of private capitalists but should be taken over by the government. Within the Katsura cabinet a consensus built behind this view. By the end of the month the company was completely reorganized under an imperial ordinance, in effect converting it into a quasi-governmental enterprise. The government agreed to provide the company with ¥1.75 million in construction subsidies and to guarantee a ¥10 million company bond issue, but in return the top executive positions in the company were taken over by government bureaucrats. An official from the railroad bureau in the Home Ministry was appointed president, and a new set of managing directors, including an incumbent Transportation Ministry official, a former Foreign Ministry official, and a former Bank of Japan official, was put in place. Of the original promoters, only the redoubtable Takeuchi remained in the top echelons of management. For all practical purposes the Seoul-Pusan concession had shifted out of the hands of private entrepreneurs into the hands of the government.[49]

THE FINAL LINK: THE SEOUL-ŬIJU LINE

By the end of 1898 the Japanese had secured concessions for two major trunk lines, but the final major link in a transpeninsular rail system, from Seoul to the town of Ŭiju on the Manchurian border, remained in the hands of a French concessionaire, M. Grille. Since the line ran through more difficult terrain, it was not expected to enjoy as profitable a traffic as the other two lines. The French syndicate was given three years to begin construction and ten to finish it.[50] The Japanese legation in Seoul, and the home government, were worried about who would control the line. Since it would connect with the rail network the Russians were building in Manchuria, and since the French were allies of the Russians, there was every likelihood that the Seoul-Ŭiju line might be

---

49. SEDS, 16:463–78; Nakamura Masanori, "Keinin Keifu tetsudō," 242–45.
50. NA, Dispatch Book, U.S. Legation to Seoul, no. 226, Sill to Olney, July 17, 1896.

used to carry hostile military forces south, unimpeded by the rivers and rugged landscape of the northwest.

Like Morse, M. Grille did not find it easy to raise capital, and like Morse he was well aware of the political value of the line. His timing was not as good, however. When he offered to sell the Seoul-Ŭiju construction rights to the Russians, he was rebuffed; their Manchurian enterprises were already well underway and their interest in Korea had diminished. Undaunted, Grille turned to a group of Japanese investors, but his terms were stiff: he demanded that a French construction company build the line, that materials be purchased from the company at 20 percent over market price, and that in addition the company be paid a 5 percent commission.[51] When the Japanese turned him down, Grille was unable to begin construction by the time specified in his contract, and he lost the concession.

In 1899 the Korean government decided to turn the Seoul-Ŭiju concession over to a group of Korean investors led by Pak Ki-jong, who had already established a company to build a short branch line near Pusan in May 1897. Pak, a Pusan native of humble origin, had learned Japanese in his youth while working in the Tsushima trade. He had gone to Japan in 1876 as an interpreter on the first Korean mission and then again in 1880. A convert to "civilization and enlightenment," he did his best to promote the introduction of new technological knowledge into Korea, sending two of his sons to mining and railroad schools in Japan. The railroad project in Pusan, organized while Pak was serving as chief of police, never got further than preliminary surveys, possibly because Pak lacked sufficient capital, possibly because the line promised little profit, possibly because it lost significance once the Seoul-Pusan project was underway. In any event, in early 1899 Pak and a group of other interested Koreans organized the Daehan Railroad Company to take over the Seoul-Ŭiju concession. The company did not hold on to it very long. When Yi Yong-ik, the monarch's favorite, became president of the railroad bureau, he decided that both the Seoul-Ŭiju and Seoul-Wŏnsan lines should be operated as royal enterprises.[52]

In 1900 the Northwest Railroad Company, established by Yi Yong-ik with financial support from the mint, took over the concession. Under pressure from the French minister, however, the company hired a French construction company on terms that Grille had earlier proposed

51. Chōsen tetsudō shi, 1:102–4.
52. Cho, Kindai Kankoku keizaishi, 89–104.

to the Japanese. A special construction office was set up in the imperial household under the supervision of M. Lefevre, formerly a secretary in the French legation, and in October 1901 a grand opening ceremony was held at the capital's West Gate. Lefevre, however, was not optimistic about the project's future. Too many strange things were happening. Palace geomancers predicted that since the line began at the West Gate, where the "eye of the dragon" was found, calamity would follow once construction started. When Takeuchi heard that Lefevre intended to resign, he lobbied Yi Yong-ik, Wang Sun-kun, Yi Chae-sun, and others to take over the construction rights. The Russian minister protested, demanding that the concession be turned over to a Russian company, but Minister Hayashi came to the rescue and discussions proceeded on course.[53]

In March 1903 Takeuchi, Ōe Taku, and a group of other Japanese businessmen gathered to organize a joint Japanese-Korean venture, the Seoul-Ŭiju Railway Company. Their plan envisaged construction costs of ¥25 million, a figure made high by the need to bridge the Yalu River, an engineering task of considerable expense and complexity. Before asking the Korean court to grant the concession, the promoters asked Foreign Minister Komura for the same loan guarantees given the Seoul-Pusan company. Komura, who had already proposed in the fall of 1902 that the Japanese government make a loan to the Korean court in return for the Seoul-Ŭiju concession, was favorably disposed, but negotiations with the Koreans collapsed in December 1903 when Takeuchi was called home to become one of the three managing directors of the reorganized Seoul-Pusan Railway Company. Once the war began, however, the Japanese army quickly got permission from the Korean government to build a military line on the Seoul-Ŭiju route, and construction was soon under way.

By 1904 the Japanese had acquired full control of what was to become the core of Korea's modern railway system. The Japanese success was the product of their "tenacity," but it was also the product of consensus among key figures in the Tokyo government, the military high command, and a small group of domestic promoters and investors. To be sure, there had been disagreement about how the railway lines should be built and by whom. Inoue Kaoru, who had pressed for railway concessions while minister in Seoul, wanted the Koreans to build the line themselves with the help of Japanese capital and technical assistance,

53. Takeuchi Tsuna, "Takeuchi Tsuna jijoden," 463–64.

a position he continued to hold as finance minister in the Itō cabinet. Neither Itō nor Mutsu favored Japanese-owned lines, in part out of fear of provoking the Russians, in part out of doubt about the ability of the promoters to raise the necessary capital. But army leaders like Kawakami Sōroku, Yamagata Aritomo, and Katsura Tarō consistently provided political and financial support to the Japanese promoters and concessionaires, and so did key figures in the foreign ministry, like Ōkuma, Aoki, and Komura, all advocates of a forward policy on the Asian continent. Eventually even Itō was won over, although he remained somewhat reluctant to support the civilian railroad promoters.

Why was it that until the eve of the Russo-Japanese War the Japanese leadership preferred to rely on private businessmen and financiers rather than to acquire railway construction rights directly? First, using unofficial proxies like Ōmiwa, Takeuchi, or Shibusawa lessened the possibility of diplomatic embarrassments. While it was clear to everyone in Seoul, and in the home capitals of the Western powers too, that the Japanese government was deeply committed to the various railroad ventures, it was useful to maintain the fiction that they were owned and managed by private investors and not the government itself. After all, the Russians also worked through proxies, including Frenchmen and Americans, in the hunt for concessions. Second, the Korean court may have found it easier to work with private capitalists, from whom "gifts" must have been forthcoming, and it was easier for the Korean government to turn down a request from a Japanese company than from the Japanese government itself. Finally, the businessmen and financiers hunting concessions in Korea were trusted and respected by the top government leaders. Key figures like Shibusawa and Maejima Hisoka had been present at the creation of the Meiji state—indeed, had once been officials themselves—and they could be relied on to work "for the sake of the country." The interests of the capitalists and the interests of the government leaders, while occasionally colliding in the short run, meshed neatly in the long run, and cooperation between them rested on working relationships that stretched back for decades.

LOANS TO THE KOREAN GOVERNMENT

Such cooperation proved more difficult in the case of loans to the Korean government. While financiers wanted to turn a profit, government leaders saw loans as a way of expanding Japanese leverage over the Koreans. The experience of the Western imperialists, of which the

Meiji leaders were well aware, had shown that a loan was a subtle but effective way to insinuate political influence over a weak state whose financial apparatuses were disorganized or whose appetite for spending had outgrown its revenues. The loan created a sense of obligation on the part of the borrowing government and made it more dependent on the lender; it provided the lender with an excuse to demand a greater voice in the borrowing country's affairs; it encouraged the borrower to buy goods in the lending country with the lender's currency; it often discouraged the borrower from turning to other outsiders for financial or other kinds of help; and in a capitalist world where contracts were sacrosanct, it provided an ultimate excuse for political intervention. Not only trade but power and influence followed the international promissory note.

In the 1870s and 1880s the French had demonstrated in Tunisia, and the British in Egypt, the political and strategic significance of the international loan. In 1875, for example, when the British government under Prime Minister Disraeli bought up nearly half of the shares in the Suez Canal, he explained his reasons to the House of Commons as follows: "I have never recommended and I do not recommend now this purchase as a financial investment.... I have always and do now recommend it to the country as a political transaction, and one which I believe is calculated to strengthen the empire."[54] By capturing a large stake in the ownership of the canal project, Disraeli intended to weaken French influence in Egypt and possibly forestall a French occupation of the country. Between 1876 and 1879 the British, working with the French, assumed control over the finances of the Egyptian government through the establishment of two controllers of receipts and expenditure, one British and the other French, but both appointed by the Egyptian government. Their function was to reform the financial system so that the Egyptian government could pay interest on the foreign debt as well salaries for its civil servants and soldiers. When the Khedive was threatened by a group of army officers led by Urabi Pasha in 1881, the British sent in a military force to protect it and the canal, and its military occupation eventually turned into a British protectorate under the guidance of Sir Evelyn Baring, later Lord Cromer. The British experience in Egypt was well known to the Japanese leadership, for whom it was axiomatic that financial influence and political influence went hand in hand.[55]

54. Quoted in Fieldhouse, *Economics and Empire,* 121–22.
55. Omachi, *Hakushaku Gotō Shōjirō,* 748.

If there were any doubt about that axiom, the Japanese leaders had only to look at how the international loan had become a vehicle for the expansion of European influence in China. Within a week of the signing of the Treaty of Shimonoseki, the Ch'ing government, already in debt for £6.6 million to foreign firms like the Hong Kong and Shanghai Bank for loans to cover war expenses, approached bankers and financiers in England, France, and Germany with a request for a joint international loan to pay the 200 million tael indemnity to Japan. Owing to disagreements among the three powers, the loan never materialized, but eventually the Chinese contracted three huge separate loans: a Franco-Russian loan of Fr 400 million in 1895, an Anglo-German loan of £16 million in 1896, and another Anglo-German loan of £16 million in 1898. As the race for concessions accelerated in China during the late 1890s, it was not difficult to conclude that the granting of economic rights and concessions was an inevitable quid pro quo to the foreign lenders.

The Japanese made few efforts to bind the Korean leadership by the purse strings after the failure of Inoue's attempts to arrange a ¥3 million loan in the summer of 1895. As we have seen, during the next four years they concentrated with some success on securing railroad concessions. In any event, under the terms of the Nishi-Rosen agreement the Japanese and the Russians had agreed that any loans to Korea should be made jointly. In November 1899, however, the loan question surfaced again when a court official informed Hayashi Gonsuke that the American and British ministers had approached him with a proposal to raise a ¥5 million loan mortgaged against mining rights on royal land. The purpose of the loan, he explained, was to permit Korea to issue a new silver currency. Hayashi's response was swift and predictable: the Japanese would not sit silently by if the Korean government borrowed such a huge sum from other countries. It might be conjectured that the Korean officials had anticipated this reaction when they leaked the news and that once again they were playing the foreigners against each other.

The loan question immediately became entangled with a long-standing Japanese interest in the reform of the chaotic Korean currency system. Coins came in a wide assortment, some minted privately, some minted by the government, and their value fluctuated considerably. Since the early 1890s there had been sporadic but unsuccessful attempts at reform. In August 1894, as part of the Kabo reforms, the government promulgated new currency regulations establishing a silver-standard decimal system of coinage modeled on the Japanese system, but the regulations were hastily drafted. Little or no provision was made for the exchange of old coins for new, no exchange offices were established, no standard of exchange was set, no schedule for the change was announced, and no means of publicizing the change was made. However, since the regulations allowed the circulation of foreign currency until new coinage was minted, the Japanese yen was soon circulating in Korea as legal tender. Ironically, the result was an inflation in the value of Korean copper cash. When the Japanese army tried to pay porters and buy provisions, the Koreans refused to accept the unfamiliar Japanese coins, so army paymasters had to acquire large quantities of Korean coppers, forcing a sudden appreciation of their value.[56]

After the war confusion in the currency system persisted: newly minted silver coins circulated side by side with the traditional copper cash, Japanese silver yen, and new nickel coins.[57] The situation irked Japanese merchants and businessmen. Not only was there neither a uniform coinage system nor any fixed standard for exchange transactions, but much of the coinage in circulation was of poor quality or counterfeit. In August 1897 Shibusawa Eiichi, anticipating Japan's shift to the gold standard, proposed his own plan for Korean currency reform. If the Japanese silver yen piece were withdrawn from circulation in Korea, Japanese traders would be forced to use the unstable and cumbersome Korean currency. Shibusawa persuaded Iwasaki Yanosuke, president of the Bank of Japan, to allow a specially stamped one-yen silver coin to continue circulating in Korea; but the Korean government, undoubtedly responding to pressure from the Russian financial adviser, forbade its circulation in February 1898. Undaunted, Shibusawa visited Korea in April, just as the Nishi-Rosen talks were coming to a successful conclusion, and with the help of Minister Katō Masuo he was able to persuade the king to lift the prohibition.[58] In July 1898 the new "pro-Japanese" minister of finance, Min Yŏng-gi, together with his predecessor, Sin Sang-hung, presented a new plan for currency reform: adopting the gold standard, issuing convertible notes, and lifting the prohibition on the circulation of the Japanese silver yen piece.[59] While the continued circulation of the silver yen worked to the advantage of

56. In April 1894 a string of one thousand copper cash cost ¥1.50 in Pusan; by November the price had risen to ¥2.00–2.50. Kang Mang-il, "Yi-shi Chōsen kaikō chokkei," 99–103.
57. Ibid., 104; Cho, *Kindai Kankoku keizaishi*, 211–33.
58. *SEDS*, 16:61, 70–84.
59. Moriyama Shigenori, *Kindai Nikkan kankeishi kenkyū*, 81–82.

Japanese, especially the Dai-Ichi Bank and its customers, the basic currency problem remained unsolved.

In this context the Koreans began to explore the possibility of a Japanese loan. On November 25, 1898, Yi Yong-ik, the king's trusted financial confidant, presented Hayaski Gonsuke a proposal to borrow ¥5 million to finance currency reform. If the loan were added to ¥1 million income from the royal ginseng monopoly and ¥1 million in government reserves, the Korean government could set up a new central bank and issue ¥7 million in new currency. Hayashi was enthusiastic. The loan was for a productive purpose, and the proposed currency reform would be to the advantage of Japanese trade. Uppermost in Hayashi's mind, however, were the opportunities for the further expansion of Japanese political influence. The loan proposed by Yi was not secured by any fixed collateral, but a Japanese syndicate could demand mining or railroad concessions or ask for an exclusive lien on customs revenues in return. Even without such guarantees, the loan would give the Japanese financial leverage over the court. At the very least it would provide an excuse to protest the grant of mining rights or other concessions to third countries; if Korea defaulted on the loan, Japan could demand rights and concessions in compensation. As Hayashi cabled Foreign Minister Aoki on December 13, "Whoever pours the most capital into Korea, after all, will be the one who has the largest and most influential voice in Korean affairs. If we respond to their hopes and ingratiate ourselves, thereby consolidating the basis of our influence here, it will not be necessary to worry about low interest rates, temporary defaults in payment, or the like."[60] In short, Hayashi thought about the loan to Korea in much the same way Disraeli thought about loans to Egypt. It had little to do with commercial or financial profit, and everything to do with political influence.

Foreign Minister Aoki did not warm to the proposal. Given the financial crisis in Japan, it was unlikely that a Japanese business syndicate could pull together a loan of this magnitude. Instead, he suggested that the loan be backed by an international syndicate including the American and British as well as Japanese. Hayashi opposed that idea. Foreign investors would not be content with an unsecured loan, he said; they would insist on economic concessions or rights. That would "destroy the raison d'être of our plan" to keep Western economic influence out of Korea. If private bankers and financiers could not come up with the

60. *NGB*, 32:320.

money, he asked, then what about the Ministry of Finance or the Bank of Japan? Or perhaps the Japanese government could make a "contribution" of ¥3 million to the Korean government, as Inoue had proposed in 1895.[61] Hayashi's blandishments met with little positive response. The Yamagata cabinet had its hands full trying to pull together domestic backing for the Seoul-Pusan railroad line, and it was not interested in taking on the loan project as well.

In March 1900 the Ministry of Finance proposed a new plan to expand Japanese financial influence in Korea. Sakatani Yoshio, head of the budget bureau, and Matsuo Shigeyoshi, head of the finance bureau, proposed to Finance Minister Matsukata that the manager of the Seoul branch of the Dai-Ichi Bank, be designated as the Japanese government's financial representative in Korea; his mission would be to buy gold ore and expand the circulation of Japanese convertible notes.[62] Matsukata, as we have seen, was interested in promoting Japanese economic interests in Korea if domestic financial conditions permitted. In May 1900 he expanded the ideas of his bureau chiefs by proposing the establishment of a central financial organ in Korea, under the direction of a Japanese national, to supervise currency reform and to negotiate foreign loans. In an early June meeting Foreign Minister Aoki, Shibusawa, and Yamamoto Tatsuo, president of the Bank of Japan, agreed with Matsukata that currency reform was desirable but concluded that the establishment of a central bank was premature. It would be better to persuade the Korean government to allow the Dai-Ichi Bank to issue convertible bank notes in Korea.[63]

In the meantime, the American firm of Collbran and Bostwick launched negotiations for a ¥5–7 million loan to the Korean government in return for a lien on the customs revenues, a concession to build waterworks for Seoul, and the rights to set up a special bank. The project had the support of William Sands, a recent Harvard graduate hired as a court adviser, and "pro-American" members of the Min faction, who saw the loan as a way of financing a general reform program. McLeavy Brown, head of the customs service, opposed it since a lien on the customs would curb his control and forestall his own plans for currency reform.[64]

To head off the American businessmen, in September 1900 Brown

61. NGB, 32:312–21.
62. Moriyama Shigenori, Kindai Nikkan kankeishi kenkyū, 87–88.
63. NGB, 33:140; SEDS, 16:95–96.
64. Moriyama Shigenori, Kindai Nikkan kankeishi kenkyū, 89–90.

and Hayashi worked out a new proposal: ¥3 million to establish a convertible currency backed by gold or some other metallic standard; ¥1 million to complete the Seoul waterworks; and ¥1 million for a system of lighthouses and buoys to make coastal shipping safer. The total loan of ¥5 million was to be repaid over twenty years at an interest rate of 6 percent with only the payment of principal required during the first five years. These terms were much more favorable than those offered by Japan in 1895. In return for the loan, the Japanese were to be given a lien on customs revenues, the Dai-Ichi Bank was to serve as the government "customs banker" handling customs transactions, and future appointments of the superintendent of customs were to be made after consultations with the British and Japanese ministers.[65]

Needless to say, Hayashi's cables in support of this new plan bubbled with enthusiasm. The loan would divert customs revenues to productive uses, block the influence of other countries, consolidate the position of the Dai-Ichi Bank, and finance reform measures that would have a positive influence on Japanese trade. Hayashi took pains to point out the political benefits as well. "Politically the advantages that redound to us will be great," he wrote. "If the present proposal succeeds, we will be able to acquire financial rights over and above currency reform. We will be able to extend the political influence of our empire into Korea, directly and indirectly, in other ways. And, this proposal, I believe, is in reality a kind of Anglo-Japanese alliance." Matsukata was equally enthusiastic. Indeed, he had already promised Shibusawa that the Bank of Japan would provide ¥2 million from government reserves.[66]

Domestic politics, however, again interfered. In September 1900 Itō Hirobumi organized a new majority party in the Diet, the Seiyūkai, with the intention of returning to power. He made it clear that he would not take over the cabinet if the loan to Korea were approved: he did not wish to provoke the Russians. On October 4 the cabinet considered a proposal by Sakatani to lend the Dai-Ichi Bank ¥2 million from the China indemnity through the Bank of Japan but finally decided against it, ostensibly because of the political situation in Korea, but probably to mollify Itō. Sakatani lamented the decision. In a letter to Hayashi he emphasized that the Ministry of Finance was doing what it could to advance Japanese economic interests in Korea.[67] Foreign Minister Aoki

65. KSH, Sakatani Papers, folder 502, "Chōsen shomondai ni kansuru shorui."
66. NGB, 33:147–48.
67. KSH, Sakatani Papers, folder 502, "Chōsen shomondai ni kansuru shorui," docs. 3, 5, 10, 16, 22.

also urged Hayashi to see if a loan could be arranged without government financial assistance, and he suggested that if opinion in the Diet shifted in favor of the loan, the government might very well reverse itself.[68]

Since local negotiations between McLeavy Brown and the manager of the Inchon branch seemed to be going well, Shibusawa decided to push ahead with the loan project. The bank's resources were limited, however, and it could not come up with the amount originally proposed. At first the bank offered the Korean government credit instead of cash. Rather than a ¥5 million loan, it proposed a ¥1 million overdraft. When Shibusawa visited Korea in November 1900, he made a new proposal to Brown: a loan of ¥2 million in return for the right to issue customs notes. But Shibusawa and Brown were unable to agree on a number of issues: how high the interest rate should be, how long the Dai-Ichi Bank would serve as customs bank, whether to include financing of the Seoul waterworks in the loan, and so forth. Ultimately Brown threatened to break off talks unless the bank put up either the ¥5 million loan originally proposed or the ¥1 million overdraft subsequently proposed.[69]

The indefatigable Hayashi pressed his case for renewing loan negotiations when he returned to Japan in January 1901. He suggested that the Dai-Ichi Bank issue banknotes which could be lent to the Korean government. This tactic had the advantage of making it easier for the Dai-Ichi Bank to put up a large loan, and it would also provide a partial solution for the currency problem. The Ministry of Finance objected that it would be illegal for the Dai-Ichi Bank to issue its own notes in Korea since banking regulations stipulated that only officially established banks (*kokuritsu ginkō*) could issue currency, and it would disrupt good diplomatic relations with Korea. The Dai-Ichi Bank, relying on the expert opinion of Professor Ume Kenjirō, an Imperial University professor who had helped draft both the civil and commercial codes, argued that the notes would circulate only if the Korean government agreed, and hence there would be no infringement of Korean sovereignty. And it made no difference that the circulation of privately issued bank notes was illegal in Japan, since they would circulate in Korea with

68. *NGB*, 33:154–55; KSH, Sakatani Papers, folder 502.

69. *SEDS*, 16:108–18; *NGB*, 33:165–67. The American and Russian ministers were beginning to complain about special favors for the Dai-Ichi Bank, and so were their allies within the Korean court. Moriyama Shigenori, *Kindai Nikkan kankeishi kenkyū*, 93.

the permission of the Korean government. Persuaded by these arguments, the Ministry of Finance finally gave the bank permission to present McLeavy Brown with a new proposition: in return for permission to the bank to issue ¥3 million in convertible notes, the bank would lend the Korean government ¥3 million, one third in convertible notes and one third in specie, to be secured by customs revenues.

Yi Yong-ik, however, was plotting to have McLeavy Brown fired as head of the customs service. Brown, who had carefully managed to build up a customs revenue surplus over the years, did not want it frittered away as collateral for loans by foreign speculators, and he insisted that the customs should be mortgaged only to support reform of the fiscal and economic systems. Yi, who had his own ideas about how customs revenues could be used, was undoubtedly irritated by this inflexibility. In early February 1901 the Korean government asked permission to fire Brown on the grounds that he had refused to move out of his official residence so that the imperial palace could be expanded. The American, British, and Japanese diplomats all recognized the hand of Yi in this effort, and they suspected that behind him lay the intrigues of Pavlov, the Russian minister, who was lobbying for the appointment of Alexeev, the erstwhile Russian financial adviser, to the post. In face of this diplomatic pressure, Yi's intrigues failed, and Brown was told to stay on.[70]

In the meantime Yi was busily pushing his own plan to establish a central bank using a foreign loan as capital. He was averse to borrowing from one of the major powers Russia, Japan, or the United States so he initiated discussions with a French syndicate, the Syndicat du Yunnan, represented by a Auguste Cazalis, a graduate of the École Polytechnique. By April 1901 a contract was struck to provide the Korean court with a twenty-five-year loan of ¥5 million at 5.5 percent interest and secured by customs revenues to be used for the minting of currency and the exploitation of mines in P'yŏngan Province. Two-thirds of the loan was to be made in gold ingots and the rest in silver. The French, Hayashi speculated, were interested in building their own power base in Korea, and the English backers of the syndicate hoped to make money from coal-mining rights. The Korean king, by contrast, may have hoped the loan would allow him to indulge his lavish spending habits, now crimped by financial reform, and he may also have wished to establish

70. Moriyama, *Kindai Nikkan kankeishi kenkyū*, 93–94.

ties with a third power like France to whom he could turn for help in case conflict broke out between Japan and Russia.[71] As might be expected, Hayashi, acting on orders from the new foreign minister, Katō Takaaki, protested the French loan contract, and so did the other foreign ministers in Seoul, including Horace Allen, who was still hoping to arrange a loan through American businessmen. Under foreign pressure, the Korean court backed out of its contract with the Yunnan syndicate in January 1902.[72]

The Korean government was still in desperate need of cash. Official finances had taken a turn for the worse in the late 1890s as new spending projects gobbled up revenues. The expenditures of the imperial household rose from 650,000 won in 1899 to 1.7 million won in 1903, and those on military development rose from 1.4 million won to 4.07 million won. Although the Kabo reforms of 1894–95 had attempted to put the court on a shorter fiscal leash, it steadily expanded its own independent income during the Kwangmu reforms. The royal household assumed control over mining rights and the ginseng monopoly, both important sources of income. In 1898, as part of a tax reform plan, land surveys were begun and deeds were issued to landholders. But since the surveys were partial, covering only two-thirds of the counties, increases in the tax rate in 1900 and 1902 had little effect on government revenues. To make matters worse, the profligate production of nickel coins caused rapid inflation, forcing up prices government had to pay for goods and services and cutting the value of taxes collected in the new coinage.[73]

To tide the government over, in August 1901 Yi Yong-ik approached the Dai-Ichi Bank for a short-term loan of ¥400,000 to pay for arms imports and other purposes. The bank imposed tough terms: the interest rate was 10 percent, and the loan was to be secured against land tax revenues. The Koreans, desperate for the money, agreed, and the loan was the first of ¥720,000 in short-term loans advanced to the Korean Ministry of Finance between 1902 and early 1905.[74] Probably as a tacit condition of these short-term loans, the Dai-Ichi Bank managed to get its own financial instruments into circulation. In October 1901 the Ministry of Finance authorized the bank to issue bearer demand notes and in November to issue bearer demand banknotes. By 1902 Dai-Ichi

71. NGB, 34:567–71.
72. NGB, 34:584–85, 594–95, 597; NGB, 35:435–40, 446–47, 451–53.
73. Moriyama Shigenori, Kindai Nikkan kankeishi kenkyū, 80–82.
74. NGB, 34, 565–66, 578–79.

banknotes began to circulate in Pusan and Mokp'o, adding one more layer of complexity to the anarchic currency system.[75] In the fall of 1902 the government issued an order prohibiting the circulation of the Dai-Ichi banknotes but rescinded it under pressure from Hayashi in February 1903.[76]

Despite continued lobbying by Hayashi and encouragement from the Katsura cabinet, the ¥3 million loan project went nowhere. The sticking point continued to be the use of customs revenues as collateral for the loan. Ultimately the negotiations foundered on disagreements between the Korean government and the Korean court, and among officials in each as well, over who had the authority to decide how to spend the customs receipts, the only stable and secure source of official revenues. In his final negotiations with the Dai-Ichi Bank, McLeavy Brown had agreed that customs revenues were not to be used as collateral for any other projects during the period of the loan, effectively closing the door to other foreign concessionaires, but the final terms were never resolved.

Undoubtedly the failure of the negotiations had to do with Yi Yong-ik's continuing search for other sources of foreign capital. In November 1902 it was rumored that Yi had reached an agreement with Baron Gunzberg, a large stockholder in the Russo-Chinese Bank who had made his fortune as a contractor in the development of Dairen. The contract was said to involve a loan of ¥5 million for five years at 5 percent. When Hayashi, acting on instructions from Tokyo, made a formal protest, he got only denials from the Korean foreign minister and the Russian minister that any such negotiations had taken place.[77]

During the spring and summer of 1903 two Japanese businessmen, with the backing of Hayashi, floated new loan schemes involving the appointment of a Japanese to supervise the use of the loan money. In April Soeda Nobuyuki, an Osaka businessman, discussed with Yi Yong-ik a loan of ¥3 million to start a new central bank. This plan collapsed when Yasuda Zenjirō, a potential member of the loan syndicate, decided that the proposed 6.5 percent interest rate was too low. A second and more grandiose plan to set up a central bank, involving a loan of ¥10 million, was discussed with Takagi Bunpei, president of the Kyoto Electric Railway Company; but it too was never consummated. In September Foreign Minister Komura finally told Hayashi that, given the unstable and uncertain situation in Korea, it was unlikely that many

75. *SEDS*, 16:129ff.
76. *SEDS*, 16:157–65.
77. *NGB*, 35:474–78.

private investors in Japan would be willing to risk their money there, and he urged him to put off any further efforts to negotiate a Japanese loan.[78]

In contrast to the maneuverings over railroad concessions, from which the Japanese had emerged as the clear winners, attempts to influence the Korean government through loans ended in futility. No major loan agreement was concluded despite the endless negotiations. The Japanese diplomats in Seoul managed to block their rivals from establishing financial domination over the Korean government and court but were unable to secure it for their own countrymen. Even the tireless Hayashi failed. To be sure, he was able to establish an informal working alliance with the British and, to a lesser extent, the American legations to counterbalance a similar alliance between the French and the Russians; but he was never able to secure the kind of fiscal control over the Koreans that he had sought since his arrival in Seoul.[79] The same factors that made the securing of railroad concessions difficult made the loan project impossible: recurring financial crises at home; the lack of sufficient private Japanese capital to finance large-scale projects in Korea, including major loans; and the reluctance of the top Tokyo leadership, including Yamagata, to upset the Russians by pushing Japanese economic interests in Korea too aggressively. In the meantime, the financial condition of the Korean government continued to deteriorate as the minister of finance papered over its budget shortfalls with short-term loans, tax-rate increases, and expanded minting of nickel coins. It was becoming clearer and clearer that the Korean elite, despite a growing commitment to reform and self-strengthening, was losing the fiscal ability to sustain reform. The "Egyptianization" of Korea was just over the horizon, but it was to come in a much more direct way than it had in Egypt.

78. *NGB*, 36.1, pp. 648–52.
79. Moriyama Shigenori, *Kindai Nikkan kankeishi kenkyū*, 98.

CHAPTER 5

Toward the Protectorate, 1901–1905

The competition for concessions in Korea played out against a headier drama—the "Far Eastern crisis" triggered by the German occupation of Kiaochow Bay in the fall of 1897. The territorial integrity of China, honored by tacit agreement among the treaty powers since the 1840s, was in question, and the balance of power in East Asia appeared on the verge of a drastic realignment. In the face of this crisis, the problem of Korea suddenly paled in importance. As Itō Hirobumi noted at an imperial conference in early 1898, "The problem of Korea's independence hardly seems worthy of notice. Not only is the independence of China in grave doubt, but the country may soon be on the verge of partition."[1] The question confronting the Japanese leadership was how to react to the rapidly changing situation in China, a larger, more complex, and more critically important issue than the future of Korea.

Like all crises, the race for concessions presented new opportunities for the Japanese. If the Ch'ing empire was about to break up, Japan could salvage its share of the wreckage. The crisis played into the hands of those who had argued since the end of the Sino-Japanese War that Japan should pursue a policy of "defending in the north, advancing in the south."[2] As the race for concessions accelerated, many Japanese

1. Quoted in Yoshida Kazuyuki, "Nihon teikokushugi no Chōsen heigō," 9–10.
2. During the debate over the peace treaty with China, for example, Matsukata Masayoshi, often a maverick on foreign policy issues, had argued strongly against acquiring the Liaotung peninsula, urging instead a "southern strategy" (*nanpō kei'ei*) centered on Taiwan. Tokutomi, *Kōshaku Matsukata Masayoshi den*, 544ff. This view ran against the

leaders thought the time ripe to put a "southern strategy" into practice. Advocates of the southern strategy saw the province of Fukien,
directly across the straits from Taiwan, as the most promising strategic
and commercial foothold for Japan. In early 1898, as the horse-trading
among the powers intensified, Admiral Yamamoto Gonnohyoe told
Prime Minister Itō that if Japan acceded to a British request to end its
occupation of Weihaiwei, presumably so that the British could ask for it,
then the Japanese government should ask in return that Fukien be designated as a Japanese sphere of influence.[3] War Minister Katsura supported the idea, and so did others like Yano Fumio, the Japanese minister to Peking. In April the Japanese managed to obtain a nonalienation
agreement from the Ch'ing government, who promised not to let any
other power obtain a foothold in Fukien Province.[4] Ōkuma Shigenobu,
briefly prime minister and foreign minister in the summer and early fall
of 1898, had grand dreams not merely of securing a Japanese foothold
in the south but of establishing Japan as the guide for the reform of the
Ch'ing court. The collapse of the Hundred Days reform, to say nothing
of the collapse of the Ōkuma cabinet, brought a sudden awakening, but
in 1898 the Yamagata cabinet continued to seek concessions in the
south, asking for the right to construct railroad lines there.[5]

The pursuit of a southern strategy peaked in the summer of 1900,
when the Boxer rebellion reached the Chinese capital. The rebels' cap-
ture of Peking, which revealed the weakness of the Ch'ing regime, em-
boldened the Yamagata government to extend Japanese power into
south China. Navy Minister Yamamoto argued that since Japanese
troops had provided most of the manpower for the expeditionary force
that relieved the besieged legations in Peking and put the rebels down, it
was due the largest reward. Yamagata agreed. "First we should pursue
the hare in the south," he said, "and once we catch it, it will not be too
late to chase the hare in the north."[6] To snare the "hare in the south,"
the Yamagata government mounted a secret operation to seize the port

main tide of opinion within the army, the Diet, and the press, but with the acquisition of
Taiwan it gathered support. The strongest backers of a "southern strategy" were to be
found in the navy and in the Taiwan colonial government. In July 1896, for example,
Katsura Tarō, the governor-general of Taiwan, urged that Japan pursue a policy on the
south coast of China similar to its policy in Korea; namely, it ought to plant its influence
and interests there so deeply that no other power could dislodge it.

3. Kaigun Daijin Kanbō, *Yamamoto Gonnohyoe to kaigun*, 100–102.
4. Nish, *Russo-Japanese War*, 51.
5. *NGB*, 33:261–62.
6. *NGB*, 33.3, pp. 951–53.

of Amoy with the help of anti-Ch'ing revolutionaries led by Sun Yat-sen, preparing the way for a Japanese military and territorial foothold in Fukien. Ultimately the plan aborted when the United States and Great Britain, both backers of an Open Door policy in China, warned the Japanese off, and the Chinese revolutionaries, bereft of Japanese military and naval support, were ousted by local authorities. In the wake of this fiasco enthusiasm for a southern strategy cooled, and a sense of crisis faded as it became clear that a partition of China was no longer in the offing.[7]

What effect did this temporary southward shift of priorities have on the Korean question? It did not mean that the Japanese had either abandoned interest in Korea or discounted the peninsula's importance. Advancing internal reform and Japan's economic interests in Korea remained fixed goals. Even in the midst of the Amoy operation Prime Minister Yamagata, urging the creation of a Japanese sphere of influence on the peninsula, noted that Korea occupied a "most important relationship with respect to national defense and economy."[8] Indeed, the aggressive stance of the Russians in Manchuria and north China served only to heighten Japanese fears that the diplomatic agreements reached with St. Petersburg in the spring of 1898 could not contain Russian ambition. The bear in the north still found the hare in the north attractive prey, perhaps more than before, now that it was roaming on the northern border of the Korean peninsula. As we have seen, the Russian minister in Seoul continued to spar with the Japanese over economic concessions, and the Korean court encouraged Russo-Japanese rivalry as part of its tactics for survival. As the crisis in China subsided, the Japanese leadership concentrated on how to deal with the persistent Russian threat to the peninsula.[9]

THE SEARCH FOR ALTERNATIVES, 1900–1903

Although the new foreign minister, Katō Takaaki, announced in October 1900 that Japan hoped to maintain the status quo in Korea and had

7. Yoshida Kazuyuki, "Nihon teikonkushugi no Chōsen heigō," 13–14; Jansen, *The Japanese and Sun Yat-sen*, 96ff.

8. *YAI*, 262.

9. In August 1900 Horace Allen reported that Hayashi Gonsuke had told the Korean monarch that "it was Russia's intention to annex Manchuria and that Japan would resist any such action to the extent of going to war." NA, Dispatch Book, U.S. Legation to Seoul, no. 275, Allen to Hay, Aug. 31, 1900.

no intention of taking any positive steps there,[10] a powerful segment of the Japanese leadership believed that given the political and moral bankruptcy of the Korean government, the best solution to the Korean problem was to make the country a protectorate. "Independence" was a sham unless Korea could defend itself, and it could not defend itself unless it acquired the institutions and infrastructure of a modern state. Given the experience of the Kabo reforms, however, Japanese leaders were pessimistic that the Korean elite could carry out any meaningful reform without outside help. A few months after the Sino-Japanese War, for example, Itō Hirobumi lamented to his old friend, Ernest Satow, that Korea was "quite incapable of reform from within" and that "those [reforms] which Japan had endeavored to introduce seemed a long way off from being realized." When Satow suggested that the war had at least gained independence for Korea, Itō demurred. The idea of Korean independence was quite impractical, he replied, and the country "must be either annexed, or be placed under the protection of some other Power." What power might that be? asked Satow. "The strongest," replied Itō laconically.[11]

By the turn of the century it appeared that Japan had emerged as the "strongest" power in Korea. According to Katsura Tarō's biographer, when Katsura took office as prime minister in 1901, the establishment of a protectorate in Korea became one of his government's goals.[12] A protectorate, widely used as a device for domination by the Western imperialists in the late nineteenth century, would provide the Japanese freedom of action to respond with force to an intrusion or occupation by a third power (i.e., the Russians); it would also allow the Japanese more direct involvement in reform—including the installation of Japanese advisers to shape and guide the reform effort, as the Japanese had done in 1894–95. The goal was easier to set than achieve, however. As the Japanese were acutely aware, the complicated tangle of international rivalries in the region, and particularly the growing Russian presence in Manchuria after 1900, precluded any precipitous unilateral action in Korea. To violate the agreements with the Russians would not only rob Japan of the moral high ground but would also require force.

10. *NGB*, 33:704.
11. Lensen, *Russian Push Toward Japan*, 44–45. One might surmise that Itō meant Japan, but it is also possible that he had Russia in mind as well. The main point is that at this juncture Itō did not hold out much hope for the independence of an unreformed Korea or the ability of an independent Korea to reform itself.
12. Tokutomi, *Kō Katsura Tarō den*, 2:995. I have not been able to locate any document that confirms this statement. It may be an ex post facto boast.

By contrast, it was by no means impossible for the Japanese and the Russians to strike a new bargain over Korea as they had after the flight of the king to the Russian legation. For their part, the Russians wanted to expand their foothold in Northeast Asia at low cost. In the wake of the Boxer crisis, with Russian troops and Russian capital consolidating the Russian presence in Manchuria, it made sense to reduce the possibility of conflict with Japan. During the years 1900–1903 the two countries traded proposals to solve the Korean problem without resort to the costly alternative of force. Three options were explored: (1) partition of the peninsula; (2) neutralization of Korea by international guarantee; and (3) an "exchange of Manchuria for Korea" (*Man-Kan kōkan*). None of these worked out, but the continuing effort to compromise suggests the reluctance of the Japanese to fight for their ascendancy in Korea unless absolutely necessary.

The first option, partition of the peninsula, was suggested by the Russians in the summer of 1900. In July Isvolsky, the Russian minister in Tokyo, proposed that the two countries establish separate spheres of influence in Korea, the Russians in the north and the Japanese in the south. The proposal may well have reflected the interests, and possibly the influence, of the so-called Bezobrazov faction, who sought to develop mining and timber-cutting concessions in north Korea along the Yalu border. The Japanese elder statesmen, whom Isvolsky approached directly, reacted positively. Inoue Kaoru, who had been leery of antagonizing the Russians ever since the end of the China war, thought it a good idea, and so did Itō. Yamagata even suggested drawing a line from Wŏnsan in the east to the Daedong River in the west, a proposal he had made to the Russians in 1896.[13]

The Russian proposal ran into heavy opposition from other quarters. Foreign Minister Aoki did not like the idea at all, nor did Komura, the Japanese minister at St. Petersburg. If the Russians intended to occupy Manchuria, then Japan should not divide Korea but try to protect it. A more appropriate solution, suggested Komura, would be the exchange of Russian recognition of Japanese paramountcy in Korea for Japanese recognition of Russian paramountcy in Manchuria, with the understanding that each would give the other commercial freedom in its sphere of influence.[14] When news of the proposal leaked, the Tō-A Dōbunkai, a vocal and influential pan-Asianist society founded by Konoe

13. *YAI*, 262–64.
14. Nish, *Russo–Japanese War*, 95–100.

Atsumaro in 1898, lobbied actively against it, visiting high government officials to urge its rejection. Faced with this opposition, and divided in its own counsels, the Japanese government was unable to formulate a response to the Russians, and the proposal died.[15]

The second option—the neutralization of Korea guaranteed by a consortium of powers—was also put forward by the Russians. The idea had already been suggested by Yamagata before the Sino-Japanese War, and Itō may have considered it a possibility as well. Certainly neutralization was the favorite alternative of the Korean monarch, for whom it was much preferable to partition or the paramountcy of a single power. Indeed, neutralization was a way of institutionalizing the balance of power, or the balance of rivals, that Kojong so assiduously tried to sustain. After consulting with Pavlov, the Russian minister in Seoul, Isvolsky proposed to Aoki that the neutralization of Korea be jointly guaranteed by Russia, Japan, and the United States. Foreign ministry officials were skeptical. As Komura, the Japanese minister in Peking, pointed out, the immediate result of such a neutralization agreement would be "to annul Japan's preponderating position in Corea [sic] and consequently preclude her from exercising any check against Russian action in Manchuria."[16] Neutralization, in other words, was simply a Russian expedient to gain time while it consolidated its position in Manchuria.

Isvolsky's suggestion died as quickly as the partition proposal had, but neutralization of Korea continued to appeal to the Russian leadership and to the Korean monarch, who kept pushing the idea. Finance Minister Sergei Witte backed it for precisely the reasons Komura had divined: as a short-term tactic rather than a permanent solution to the Korean problem. If the neutrality of Korea could be guaranteed by a consortium of powers, Russia would no longer have to worry about Japanese belligerence; however, once its strength in Manchuria was consolidated, Russia would be in a better position to think about moving into Korea again.[17] In January 1901 Isvolsky brought a new neutralization proposal directly to Prime Minister Itō and to Inoue, whom the Russians regarded as moderates. Once again the two men, hoping to reduce tensions with Russia, welcomed the idea, and once again the foreign ministry opposed it. Foreign Minister Katō Takaaki wanted to make Russian withdrawal from Manchuria the precondition for any

15. Moriyama Shigenori, *Kindai Nikkan kankeishi kenkyū*, 119–20.
16. *NKGS*, 9:305–7; Moriyama Shigenori, *Kindai Nikkan kankeishi kenkyū*, 124–25.
17. Malozemoff, *Russian Far Eastern Policy*, 163–67.

such proposal, and Komura suggested that if Korea was to be neutralized, then Manchuria should be as well.[18] Katō informed Isvolsky that Japan would postpone any discussions of the proposal until the status quo was restored in Manchuria by the withdrawal of Russian troops.[19] The Russians put forward another neutralization proposal in the fall of 1902, but the American government indicated that "as a matter of principle" it did not participate in such joint international guarantees, and with that the initiative collapsed.[20]

The third option an "exchange" of Korea for Manchuria was the one favored by Itō, who consistently worked to avoid confrontation with the Russians. This option was essentially an elaboration of the compromise reached in the Nishi-Rosen agreement of 1898. If each side recognized the other's sphere of influence in Northeast Asia, the potential for conflict between them would ease, and the Japanese would be able to consolidate their political and economic position in Korea without fear of Russian interference. While touring Europe in December 1901, Itō approached the Russians with an informal proposal that they recognize "Japan's freedom of action in its political, industrial and commercial aspects and her exclusive right to help Korea by giving her advice ... and military aid."[21] No mention was made of Russian rights in Manchuria, but Itō may well have expected a Russian counterproposal. If so, he was correct. The Russians responded by suggesting that Japan recognize Russia's superior rights and freedom of action in Chinese territory adjoining the Russian border in return for Russian recognition of Japanese "freedom of action in Korea in respect of industrial and commercial relations."[22] But the Russians also asked the Japanese to agree not to use Korea for military purposes, not to build military installations impeding the passage of the Korean straits, and to consult with the Russians before offering Korea active support or military assistance to quell internal disturbances.

The proposed "demilitarization" of Korea was not at all to the liking of the Japanese leadership, who saw Korea as a keystone of national defense. As Itō commented, it meant that "Japan should act as a sort of custodian and be relegated to the status of a party carrying out an ordinance on which both country's had previously agreed."[23] Prime Min-

18. NGB, 34:527.
19. Moriyama Shigenori, Kindai Nikkan kankeishi kenkyū, 127–30.
20. Ibid., 138–39.
21. NGB, 35:393–417.
22. NGB, 34:521–41.
23. Nish, Russo-Japanese War, 123.

ister Katsura and his foreign minister, Komura, felt that as long as Russia maintained troops in Manchuria, they would menace Korea and they perhaps had begun to think that one day Japan might be able to supplant Russia as the dominant power in Manchuria. In any case, while Itō was talking with the Russians, the Katsura cabinet was already considering another alternative—the offer of an alliance with Great Britain, Russia's principal rival in East Asia. Faced with the possibility that the British offer would be withdrawn if not acted on quickly, and the probability that even prolonged negotiations with the Russians might not yield an agreement that served Japanese interests, the Katsura government decided to sign the Anglo-Japanese alliance. The "exchange of Manchuria for Korea" was not revived until the Russo-Japanese negotiations of late 1903.

While these discussions were going on, the Japanese government was also exploring the possibility of a secret defensive alliance between Japan and Korea, a solution to the problem of Korean vulnerability that would exclude the Russians. The idea of such an alliance had been floated in the midst of the Boxer crisis by certain pro-Japanese Korean officials with the support of the Tō-A Dōbunkai. When Itō Hirobumi took office as prime minister once again in the fall of 1900, he rejected the idea, but Foreign Minister Komura revived it in the midst of discussions on the Anglo-Japanese alliance. If war were to break out with Russia, Japanese troops would have to be sent to Korea. Komura was anxious to put any such military expedition on a legitimate basis so as not to invite an adverse reaction by the other foreign powers. During the Sino-Japanese War the Japanese had signed a provisional agreement with the Koreans to legitimize military operations.[24] When Pak Che-sun, the Korean foreign minister, visited Japan in December 1901, the Japanese presented him with a draft defensive treaty that would have forged a tighter bilateral relationship between the two countries. In return for a Japanese guarantee to protect Korean territory and preserve the Korean royal house, the draft proposed that Korea agree not to alienate any part of its territory to another power, not to use its revenues as collateral for foreign loans without Japanese permission, and not to rely on any other powers for assistance. Pak was not particularly enthusiastic about the proposal, preferring an international guarantee of neutralization, and Pavlov, the Russian minister in Seoul, protested to

24. Moriyama Shigenori, *Kindai Nikkan kankeishi kenkyū,* 132–33.

Kojong that its real purpose was to justify the stationing of Japanese troops on the Korea-Manchuria border; thus, this initiative also died.[25]

CONTAINING THE KOREANS

By the spring of 1903 Russo-Japanese animosity had reached new heights. The Russians had failed to honor their promise to withdraw troops from Manchuria, and they were building what appeared to be an economic and strategic enclave on the south bank of the Yalu River. To the Japanese leadership it seemed that the Russians wanted to have their cake in Manchuria and to nibble at Korea too. When the military attaché at Seoul reported in May 1903 that Russian troops had established themselves at Yangamp'o on the Yalu border, the Japanese government began to gird for war. While the navy leadership, especially Admiral Yamamoto Gonnohyoe, remained cautious, the army high command—in particular, middle-level staff officers—was ready to fight. In May 1903 an army staff report prepared by Ōyama Iwao, the army chief of staff, suggested that even though there were deficiencies in Japan's state of military and naval preparedness, the Russians were weak militarily. If war were to begin immediately, the two countries would be on an equal footing, but if it were delayed for three or four years the Russians would be able to outmatch the Japanese through a military buildup. The moment was opportune, the report concluded, to settle the Korean problem.[26]

The Korean problem was not simply military; it was political as well. If war broke out, how could the Japanese be sure that the Koreans would not align themselves with the Russians? What would happen if the monarch took refuge in one of the foreign legations? And what if the Russians were to seize control of Seoul? It was imperative that Japan keep the Korean court on a short leash. The question was how to do so. Although military force would determine Japan's success on the battlefield, the Koreans had to be dealt with diplomatically. When Katsura and Komura discussed with Yamamoto how the Koreans might react if war broke out between the Japanese and the Russians, they concluded that Japan "must place [Korea] under our authority by real force, but the best policy would be to choose means that are nominally correct."[27]

25. Ibid., 135–36.
26. Tani, *Kimitsu Nichi-Rō senshi,* 69–70, 83–84.
27. Kaigun Daijin Kanbō, *Yamamoto Gonnohyoe to kaigun,* 143.

There were two ways to keep the Koreans under control if the Japanese went to war with the Russians: the first was to send in troops immediately to establish the superiority of Japanese force in Seoul; the other was to sign either a defensive alliance or a protectorate treaty with the Korean government.

Not surprisingly, army leaders favored the first solution. At the army's suggestion, the foreign ministry proposed to the *genrō* that the best policy would be to send a large and powerful military force to Korea before the Russians did; whoever got to Seoul first would be able to control the king and the government. When the proposal was discussed at the *genrō* conference on June 9, Yamagata Aritomo, who remembered what had happened in 1882, 1884, and 1894, urged the immediate dispatch of two divisions to Seoul before the Russians could bring forces down from Manchuria. But the navy balked. Yamamoto Gonnohyoe opposed a preemptive military action on two grounds: first, the dispatch of Japanese troops to Korea, an independent country, would provoke the foreign powers; second, the dispatch of troops during negotiations with the Russians would destroy international confidence in Japan, perhaps provoking international intervention; and finally, the Russians would regard it as a provocative act, tantamount to a declaration of war, and hostilities might begin before Japan's preparations were complete. Since the army could not send troops overseas without the cooperation of the navy, none of the other army leaders present at the meeting—Ōyama, Terauchi, or Kodama—spoke in favor of Yamagata's proposal; and even though Yamagata persisted, he was not able to win support so long as the navy leadership opposed the immediate dispatch of troops.[28]

The other solution—the signing of a defensive or a protectorate treaty with the Koreans—was likely to meet opposition from the Koreans. In a belated effort to maintain the country's independence, in March the Korean king had announced the institution of a conscription system, and in July the Korean minister of war proposed the establishment of a Korean navy. But so severe were the Korean government's fiscal problems that it simply could not afford to arm itself. The only alternative was to maintain Korean neutrality in the event of war between its two powerful neighbors. In August Kojong sent emissaries to Tokyo and St. Petersburg with a plea that Korea's neutrality be respected. Neither the Russians nor the Japanese took the request seriously. Komura, who had

28. Ibid., 143–50.

earlier proposed a secret defense treaty to the Koreans, used the Korean overture to suggest that they sign a bilateral alliance with Japan instead. Hayashi Gonsuke, who seemed to favor more forceful measures, did not think a secret treaty was a good idea. If negotiations were to proceed, he observed in October, then the Japanese government should be prepared to bribe the Korean government with loans or make direct payments to key Korean officials; he suggested an increase in the Japanese garrison in Seoul as well. On November 30 Komura ordered Hayashi to approach Kojong with a proposal for a secret alliance by a back channel, using an intermediary such as Ōmiwa Chōbei.[29]

It is clear that any treaty signed with the Koreans would have been intended to put a best face on the inevitable dispatch of troops to Korea. On December 30, 1903, the cabinet decided to "keep [Korea] under our influence under whatever circumstances," but it concluded:

> As it is advisable, if possible, for us to select a good justification for our actions, it would be most convenient if we could conclude with her an offensive and defensive alliance or an agreement for her protection as was the case at the time of the Sino-Japanese War of 1894–95.... Even if we succeed in this policy, it goes without saying that as we cannot expect the Emperor of Korea to observe such a treaty throughout, ultimate success will depend on military force. In short, as the policy towards Korea greatly depends, directly or indirectly, on military operations, we must decide the policy of our country in line with military considerations.[30]

The Japanese distrust of the Korean king was palpable, exceeded only by their distrust of the Russians.

In the meantime Hayashi, who nervously reported the arrival of 120 Russian soldiers to protect the Russian legation in early January 1904, was not having much luck in Seoul. Although he had managed to win some supporters—Yi Chi-yong, Yi Kun-t'aek, Min Yŏng-chol—by bribery and threat, powerful forces opposed a Japan-Korean treaty. The Russian minister, who had gotten wind of Japan's intentions, pressured the Korean king not to sign an agreement with the Japanese, and officials like Yi Chi-yong and Yi Yong-ik, the king's financial adviser, who believed that the Russians would win a war with Japan, advised against it as well. The talks continued, however. As a condition for agreement the Korean government insisted that the Japanese rein in Korean political refugees in Japan like Pak Yŏng-hyo and Yu Kil-chun, who they alleged had been involved in the assassination of Queen Min. The Japanese

29. Moriyama Shigenori, *Kindai Nikkan kankeishi kenkyū*, 142.
30. Kajima, *Diplomacy of Japan*, 2:113; NGB, 36.1, pp. 41–45; NGNSB, 1:219.

government, willing to abandon these erstwhile collaborators to mollify Kojong, agreed to do so, and the Korean monarch finally gave his assent to a secret agreement in late January 1904.[31] At the last moment, however, under pressure from Yi Yong-ik, Kojong decided not to sign until the Japanese acknowledged Korean neutrality. While the Koreans were willing to make a secret pact with the Japanese, they wished to hedge their bets by making a public declaration of their neutrality, a position that was logically contradictory but made good political sense. Faced with this recalcitrance, Komura decided to drop the matter. As he told Hayashi, "We can manage something without the secret agreement."[32]

What the Japanese managed was a surprise landing of Japanese forces on Korean territory before war was officially declared. On February 8, 1904, the same day that Japanese naval vessels launched a simultaneous attack on the Russian naval base at Vladivostok, cheering local Japanese residents watched a Japanese naval squadron—one armored cruiser, five light cruisers, and eight torpedo boats—bombard two Russian warships lying off Palmido Island at the mouth of Inchon harbor. As smoke from the sinking vessels spread across the sky, Japanese troops began coming ashore from four transport vessels. "Everything moved along like a machine," remarked one Western observer, "the quietness with which it was done being most noticeable." Within several hours the port was under Japanese control, with sentries posted at key points and squads of soldiers patrolling the streets. To the surprise and distress of the Korean court, several Japanese units began marching toward Seoul. In a letter home Horace Allen reminisced: "We have seen the Chinese drive out the Japanese, leaving the streets littered with the dead, which the dogs ate, as I frequently saw in passing. In 1894 we saw the Japanese drive out the arrogant Chinese, who seemed to fear the same treatment they had meted out the J[a]panese, but were mistaken. Today we saw the Japanese drive out the haughty Russians."[33]

Although the Japanese emperor finally declared war with Russia in early February, it still took nearly two weeks for Hayashi to cajole, intimidate, and manipulate the Korean leadership into signing a protocol permitting the Japanese to undertake military operations on Korean territory. The Korean king had perhaps expected that an "illegal" dis-

31. *NGB*, 37.1, pp. 314–16, 333–37; *NKGS*, 8:16–18; Tako, "Nichi-Rō sensō zengo," 42–45.
32. Kajima, *Diplomacy of Japan*, 2:146.
33. New York Public Library, Allen Papers, Box 3, Letters and Papers Relating to the Russo-Japanese War, 1904, Allen to his sons, Feb. 12, 1904.

patch of Japanese troops would invite foreign intervention, but that fragile hope collapsed quickly. The protocol, signed on February 23, pledged the Japanese to "guarantee the independence and territorial integrity" of Korea and to "take necessary measures" if the royal house or the territorial integrity of the country was "endangered by the aggression of a third Power or internal disturbances." In return, the Koreans agreed to let the Japanese occupy strategic areas, if necessary, to achieve these ends. In effect, the Japanese had managed finally to wrench agreement to a defensive alliance from a still reluctant Korean leadership. So secret were the negotiations, however, that the Japanese Privy Council, whose task was to scrutinize treaties with foreign powers, did not know about it until it had been signed, and a few days later the council formally complained to the emperor that they had not deliberated the matter before the fact.[34]

To forestall any backtracking, Hayashi arranged to remove the chief anti-Japanese leaders from the country. The obstructive Yi Yong-ik, the monarch's trusted financial confidante, was placed under confinement and sent to Japan on a government-chartered Japanese vessel the day the protocol was signed; a few days later Min Yŏng-chol, thinking he had been appointed minister to China, was shipped off as well; and Yi Kun-t'aek was dispatched in the same way. Nonetheless, there was strong public reaction to the protocol. When the Korean court leaked its contents to the *Taeguk shimmun*, a Korean-language newspaper, opponents mounted public rallies demanding that the agreement be abrogated and the officials who signed it be dismissed. On March 3 a dynamite bomb was thrown at the residence of Foreign Minister Yi Chi-yong, who was accused of betraying the country by signing the protocol. The charge was too small to do much damage, but resentment against the Japanese continued to seethe, particularly in the Seoul region, where small acts of sabotage disrupted telegraph lines, roads, and the railway.[35]

The Korean court, still uncertain who was going to win the war and mindful of the mood of the Confucian elite, played a nervous game of procrastination. Fortune-tellers, soothsayers, and diviners warned of Japanese defeat, and wild rumors spread at court that a Russian army of 500,000 was poised to surround Seoul. Not until May 19 did the monarch work up nerve to formally break diplomatic relations with Russia

34. Yamabe, *Nihon no Kankoku heigō*, 273–77.
35. Matsumiya, *Saikin no Kankoku*, 28–29.

and rescind the Russian timber-cutting concessions on the Yalu. This change of heart may have been prompted by a "gift" of ¥300,000 brought by Itō Hirobumi from the Meiji emperor as a token of appreciation to the Korean monarch for being "helpful" to the Japanese army. Itō also proffered a gift of ¥20,000 to Lady Om, the king's consort, who asked to share half of it with the two crown princes.[36]

It is not likely that the Korean ruler, however venal, would have sold himself so cheaply had Japanese military operations not been so successful. In early April General Kuroki's forces defeated a Russian advance force at P'yŏngyang, and in late April the Japanese engaged the Russians on the Yalu front, defeating them at Kiulengchien on May 1 and at Fengcheng five days later. The king sent Cho Pyŏng-sik as a special envoy to a victory celebration arranged by the local Japanese residents in Seoul, and along with several other Korean government ministers and luminaries he gave three banzai cheers for the Japanese emperor. When reports of a Russian counterattack at Anju, the confidence of the court wavered again; but when the counterattack was repelled, a pro-Japanese mood gathered strength. On May 17 the monarch summoned his ministers to discuss abrogation of Russian-Korean treaties.[37] Even if the Korean court was not enthusiastic about its new ties with the Japanese, the Japanese were relieved that the Korean government had finally chosen sides.

PLANNING THE PROTECTORATE

To many outsiders the February 23 protocol looked like a "protectorate treaty"—that was how Horace Allen characterized it in his dispatches to Washington.[38] For the Japanese, however, the agreement was no more than a foot in the door. It enabled Japan to deploy its troops "legally" on Korean territory, but it did not address the fundamental problem of reform, nor did it advance Japanese economic interests. These fundamental goals required a more sweeping intrusion and also a comprehensive plan of action. On May 31, 1904, the Katsura cabinet adopted a blueprint for Korea's future, already approved by the genrō, that was

36. NKGS, 9:503–4.
37. Matsumiya, Saikin no Kankoku, 41–45.
38. Burnett, Korean–American Relations, 3:125. As one British writer noted, "Susceptibilities are soothed, and possibly diplomatic difficulties are turned, by calling [Korea] independent; but in reality it is as much under Japanese protection as Egypt is under ours: all state-paper description to the contrary notwithstanding." Quoted in Ladd, In Korea with Marquis Ito, 247–48.

predicated on such an intrusion, and with remarkable precision that blueprint became reality in the succeeding months and years. The cabinet decision, a consensus document embodying the views both of moderates like Itō and Inoue and of advocates of a more aggressive policy like Katsura and Komura, envisaged a massive Japanese military presence, sweeping internal reforms, and the expansion of Japanese economic presence on the peninsula.

The document appears to have been based, to a certain extent at least, on a memorandum Hayashi Gonsuke provided Itō in late March. First, Hayashi recommended that a Japanese, with responsibility to carry out Japan's goals in Korea, be appointed either as minister to Korea or as supreme adviser to the Korean government. Second, to bring order to the Korean government's business and to improve Japanese trade, it was urgent to carry out a fiscal reform of Korea, including a new currency system and better tax collection. Third, "by unobtrusive means" the Japanese should gradually secure economic rights and concessions for their nationals—railroad concessions, mining concessions, coastal and inland navigation rights, mail and telegraph concessions, and the right to acquire land. Finally, the Japanese should obtain rights to land and maritime sites for permanent military and naval bases to defend the peninsula and Japanese rights there.[39]

No doubt this raw pursuit of Japanese advantage in Korea was not precisely to Itō's taste. His own conception of Korea's future was less self-interested and less pragmatic than Hayashi's, and it emphasized reform for its own sake as much as for the Japanese needs it might serve. When he had visited Korea in March 1904, he lectured Yi Chi-yong and other high officials on "constitutional theory" and the need for reform. At an audience with the Korean monarch a few days later, he held up the Meiji emperor as a paragon of reform and national self-strengthening whom the Korean ruler might well emulate. When Kojong pointedly reminded Itō that the Kabo reforms had been brought to a sudden end by an "unfortunate incident" (i.e., the murder of the queen), Itō replied that it was unwise to undertake hasty reform that might "upset popular sentiment and disturb order."[40]

It is worth examining the May 31 decision at some length, not only because it summarized the reasons why the Japanese leadership wanted great control over Korea but also because it outlined basic policies pur-

39. NKGS, 9:491–92.
40. Ibid., 9:494–503; Matsumiya, *Saikin no Kankoku,* 34.

sued during the protectorate.[41] The basic premise of the document was precisely the one that had guided Japanese policy in Korea since the 1880s: the fate of Korea so directly affected the security of the Japanese empire that no other country could be allowed to swallow it up. The document began by asserting that Japan at that moment was exerting its entire strength and wagering its national destiny to preserve the independence and integrity of Korea. After observing rather obtusely that the trust of the Korean nation, high and low, toward Japan was growing, the document went on to argue that the instability of Korean politics and the deterioration of popular sentiment meant that it would not be able to maintain its independence by itself for very long. Therefore, it was necessary that Japan gradually built its position in Korea politically, militarily, and economically to forestall the outbreak of future disturbances and accomplish the self-defense of the Japanese empire. While the protocol of February 23 had moved in the direction of a protectorate, it was necessary, by the signing of a treaty with the Koreans and the establishment of concrete facilities, to acquire full rights for a protectorate over Korea and to acquire key economic rights as well.

In specific terms, the cabinet decision proposed the following policies:

1. The establishment of permanent Japanese military and naval bases on the peninsula. To enhance Japan's own defenses and also to maintain order within Korea, it would be necessary to station Japanese forces in Korea even after the war with Russia ended. For that purpose Japan had to expropriate strategic inland and coastal areas. But it was also clear that a Japanese military presence was important to affirm "our [Japanese] power over Korean society, high and low."

2. The assumption of Japanese supervision over Korean foreign affairs. Under the February 23 protocol it was still possible for the Korean government to sign treaties with other countries or to assign rights and concessions to nationals of countries other than Japan. As experience had demonstrated, the Korean court was a "pit of intrigue," and Korean officials were wont to make promises to or agreements with foreigners that benefited themselves or their families without regard for the national interest. To end this deplorable state of affairs, it would be necessary for the Japanese to assume direct supervision of Korean foreign affairs, including assent to the signing of treaties with third powers.

3. The establishment of Japanese supervision over Korean govern-

41. The text may be found in NGNSB, 1:224–28.

ment finances. While the debacle of the Kabo reforms had taught the Japanese the sad lesson that hasty reform would invite resistance, both high and low, fiscal reform was of the greatest urgency. The Korean people suffered from abuses generated by the existing financial system, and without a sound and stable financial basis, it would be impossible to finance institutional and other important changes. To that end it would be necessary to provide Korea with a financial adviser to supervise the reform of tax collection, to change and rationalize the currency system, and perhaps eventually to put actual control of the financial affairs directly in Japanese hands.

4. The acquisition of Japanese control over the Korean railway system. The railroad system, the document affirmed, was the "marrow" of the management of Korea, essential to political, military, and economic control. The document urged the expeditious completion of the Seoul-Pusan line and the Seoul-Ŭiju line, both projects already underway, but added that agreement would have to be reached with the Koreans about how the Seoul-Ŭiju line was to be operated once peace was restored. It also proposed to secure Japanese rights for the postwar construction of a line from Seoul to Wŏnsan, then up the northeast coast to Unggi Bay, to link the capital with the Tumen River region; and it also urged the renegotiation of rights to build a branch linking Masan, a key commercial and military port, to the Seoul-Pusan trunk line at Sanlangjin.

5. The acquisition of Japanese control over Korean telegraph, telephone, and mail systems. Political and military prudence dictated the need to control the Korean telegraph system, and fiscal reasons suggested the desirability of taking over the fledgling Korean postal system, which lost considerable amounts of money every year. The ideal situation would be to merge the Korean mail, telegraph, and telephone systems into the Japanese system and to standardize facilities in both countries. Failing that, the Japanese ought to take over the important lines and run them independently from the Korean government.

6. The promotion of Korean economic development. In the past Korea had supplied Japan with food products and raw materials, and in exchange Japan had sold Korea its manufactured products. Since it seemed likely that the future economic relationship between the two countries would develop along these lines, the document proposed that the Japanese play a key role in the development of the primary sector of the Korean economy. To open new land to cultivation, Japanese settlers should be sent to the peninsula; Japanese settlers should be given the

right to own or lease land beyond the limited zone around the treaty settlements; the foreign timber concessions in the Yalu and Tumen Valleys should be turned over to Japanese nationals; new mining surveys should be undertaken to find promising sites for development by Japanese concessionaires; and Japanese coastal fishing rights should be extended to the three northern provinces.

This omnibus document addressed the concerns of the military high command, the proreform elements, the trading interests, and the civilian expansionists. It dealt with all the issues that had been bundled into the "Korea problem" over the previous decade—Korea's military vulnerability, its troublesome unilateral diplomacy, its disordered finances, its inability to push forward on reform, its unexploited economic potential. And it outlined a concrete set of actions to be taken. This was very much in contrast with policymaking during the Sino-Japanese War, when the Itō cabinet had never been able to decide what it wanted to do in Korea and had left much of the initiative there to envoys like Ōtori and Inoue, who often improvised. For the first time since the decision to open Korea in 1876, the Japanese leadership had committed itself unequivocally to assuming direct political control over Korea. All other alternatives had failed to protect Japan's strategic and economic interests on the peninsula. Yet even this decision was contingent. It could become reality only if the Japanese emerged victorious from the war and if the Korean leadership could be persuaded or compelled to sign a protectorate treaty.

Even before the formal establishment of a protectorate, however, the Japanese were making de facto inroads on Korean sovereignty. The Japanese military, for example, had begun to deal with small acts of popular resistance—the sabotage of roads, the cutting of telegraph wires, and the blocking of railroad lines by assuming a growing role in the maintenance of local law and order. The Korean police were either unwilling or unable to respond, so in early July the Korea Garrison Army announced military regulations cracking down on sabotage along the routes between Seoul and Wŏnsan, P'yŏngyang and Ŭiju, Seoul and Inchon, and Seoul and Pusan. Anyone who harmed military telegraph or rail lines, and anyone who knew of such acts but concealed them, was to be punished by death; anyone who captured the perpetrators of such acts was to receive a reward of thirty yen. Villages along railway or telegraph lines were held collectively responsible for their security, and village chiefs were ordered to set up committees that would guard the lines by rotation.

These regulations, which required local Korean authorities to administer punishments under the supervision of Japanese garrison commanders, were not provided for under the February 23 agreement, nor were they approved by the Korean government. But as the war progressed, the run of the army's writ widened, and the regulations were put into effect throughout the whole peninsula. The commander of the Korean Garrison Army informed the Korean government that it would assume police and security powers in Seoul and its surrounding area since he was no longer confident that the Korean police could guarantee the safety of Japanese forces.[42] In July 1905, after the war had ended, military regulations were revised to provide that anyone inflicting harm on the Japanese military could be dealt with either under Japanese laws and regulations or under the laws and customs of Korea.[43] In effect, the Japanese army was usurping the basic functions of local government.

At the same time, the dispatch of Japanese advisers opened the way to widening Japanese influence over the central government. In early August 1904 the Korean government signed an agreement to appoint financial and diplomatic advisers recommended by the Japanese government. Durham White Stevens, an American formerly employed by the Japanese foreign ministry, was named diplomatic adviser, and Megata Jūtarō, a bureau chief in the Japanese Ministry of Finance, became financial adviser. Eventually three other Japanese advisers were appointed: Maruyama Shigetoshi, a former Japanese home ministry official, became police adviser; Katō Masuo, a former minister to Korea, became adviser to the Korean court; and Nozu Shigetake, a Japanese army officer, became military adviser. The powers of these advisers were quite sweeping. Megata's contract, for example, gave him the right to approve all cabinet decisions on financial matters, to attend cabinet meetings related to finances, and to make recommendations to the cabinet through the minister of finance.[44]

In practice, then, if not in law, the Japanese were moving toward a protectorate at all levels of the Korean government well before the end of the war.[45]

<hr />

42. Matsumiya, *Saikin no Kankoku*, 48–58; Tako, "Nihon ni yoru Chōsen shokuminchi,"part 1, 48–56.

43. Tako, "Nihon ni yoru Chōsen shokuminchi," part 1, 49–53, 54–55.

44. *NGB*, 37.1, pp. 360–69.

45. In April 1905 the Japanese also secured an agreement with the Koreans transferring control over the Korean postal, telegraph, and telephone services to the Japanese government. The Japanese were obliged to report the financial condition of these communications networks to the Korean government and to share profits from their operation,

THE END OF KOREAN INDEPENDENCE

It was not until April 1905, when the war was going clearly in Japan's favor, that the Katsura cabinet formally decided to sign a protectorate treaty giving Japan full control over Korea's external relations and placing domestic affairs under the supervision of a Japanese resident. The decision was a cautious one. Having learned from the bitter experience of the Triple Intervention, the Japanese leadership was anxious to avoid provoking foreign intervention by precipitous changes. While foreign diplomatic representatives would be asked to leave the country once the agreement was signed, there would be no need to suddenly abrogate treaties that the Koreans had made with other powers, nor would the Japanese immediately cancel the other foreigners' treaty privileges—extraterritoriality and the like. It was important to proceed with prudence, waiting to ascertain the willingness of the foreign powers to accept a Japanese protectorate in Korea.[46]

Even before the fighting ended, the Japanese had begun to make their intentions clear. In January 1905 President Theodore Roosevelt assured the Japanese minister in Washington that the United States would not object if the Japanese were to provide Korea with "protection, supervision, and guidance," a sentiment that was reconfirmed by the Taft-Katsura agreement in late July. The British indicated that they would have no objection to a Japanese protectorate if Japan, in turn, agreed to extend the terms of the Anglo-Japanese alliance to include India; they also insisted that the Japanese maintain an "open door" in Korea, providing "equal opportunities for the commerce and industry of all nations." Even the Russians, with whom the Japanese had contested control over Korea for a decade, were finally compelled by the Treaty of Portsmouth to recognize Japan's "predominant interests" in Korea and to abjure themselves of any further interference in Japanese activities there. Throughout the summer of 1905 Hayashi Gonsuke dropped heavy hints that his government expected that the foreign legations in Seoul would be withdrawn in time, and at the end of August the other diplomatic representatives in Seoul agreed to ask their governments to recall them and appoint chargés d'affaires in their stead. Far from rallying to the side of the beleaguered Korean monarch or attempting

---

but otherwise they were free to manage the communications system, to expand it as they wished, and to appropriate state property or buy private property to do so.

46. The full text is to be found in *NGNSB*, 1:233–34.

to obstruct the Japanese, these three major powers were ready to abandon the country to the Japanese.[47]

As long as the Japanese guaranteed an "open door" in Korea, and as long as they confined their expansionist impulses to that country, the Western powers were willing to accept Japan as a partner in imperialism. In any case, except for the Russians, none of the other powers had as compelling strategic or economic interests on the peninsula as Japan did, and it was clear that little could be done to salvage the independence of the Koreans, who were demonstrably unable to defend themselves. The Westerners appeared to have reached a consensus that the Koreans were no worse off under Japanese rule than they were under their own. As Horace Allen told the American secretary of state on the eve of the Russo-Japanese War:

> We will make a real mistake if we allow sentimental reasons to induce us to attempt to bolster up this "Empire" in its independence. These people can not govern themselves. They must have an overlord as they have had for all time.... Let Japan have Korea outright if she can get it.... I am no pro-Japanese enthusiast, as you know, but neither am I opposed to any civilized race taking over the management of these kindly Asiatics for the good of the people and the suppression of oppressive officials, the establishment of order and the development of commerce.[48]

With the other powers squared away, the Japanese leadership agreed that the "appropriate moment" had arrived to establish a protectorate. The man chosen to negotiate the treaty was Itō Hirobumi, a distinguished elder statesman, well known to the Korean leaders, who had treated him like visiting royalty during his stay at Seoul in March 1904. (The Korean emperor had permitted Itō to take dinner at the same table and saw him off at the door of the palace.) If anyone could persuade the Korean monarch to surrender the very basis of his sovereignty, Katsura and Komura decided, it was Itō. But the task was not likely to be an easy one. Kojong, who clung to the right of diplomatic representation as his only weapon against final absorption by Japan, was not likely to accept a treaty without a struggle.

When Itō met with the Korean monarch on November 15, he made it clear that the treaty was not negotiable: it had to be accepted as proposed. If the Korean government refused to sign, the Japanese were prepared to accept their decision, he said, but in that case Korea would

47. Kim and Kim, *Korea and the Politics of Imperialism*, 125–28.
48. New York Public Library, Allen Papers, Press Copy Book, Allen to Rockhill, Jan. 4, 1904, p. 829.

find itself in a far more difficult situation. When the monarch said that he wanted to consult his ministers and determine the will of the people, Itō warned that he wanted no delays. It was perfectly reasonable to consult ministers, he replied, but it was remarkably strange that the monarch wanted to consult the "will of the people." After all, under the new Korean constitutional structure, the emperor was an absolute monarch, with the power to decide everything, was he not? And was not the proposal to consult the people, who were "childlike" and ignorant of "trends in the world," intended to foment popular opposition to the Japanese? Cowed by Itō's stiff response, the king promised to consult with his ministers.[49]

The next day Itō himself met with several ministers to explain why Japan needed to take control of Korea's external affairs. If Korea were left to its own resources, he told them, complicated intrigues would create opportunities for other foreign powers to take advantage of; were that to happen, the region would once again be plunged into conflict. "Your country does not have the power to defend itself, and it depends on us for its national defense." He was quick to add that the Japanese had no intention of destroying Korea as a nation. "I am not insisting that your country commit suicide, nor do I believe that your country cannot progress to a position similar to our own. I expect that if you thrust forward boldly, the day will come when you will advance to a position of equality with us and we will cooperate with one another." To that end he urged the Koreans to build the nation's wealth and power by reforming its internal administration and cultivating knowledge.[50]

The stage was set for the final act with a script carefully crafted by Itō and Hayashi. On November 17 the entire Korean cabinet was to be invited to lunch at the Japanese legation. If discussions went well at lunch and the ministers agreed to the treaty, an audience would be arranged with the monarch; if not, the ministers would solicit the emperor's decision. Hayashi would accompany the ministers to the palace, and if the need arose, he would call Itō to come as well. Since some ministers, anxious to dissociate themselves from the treaty decision, might try to escape on the way from the legation to the palace, Hayashi asked General Hasegawa Yoshimichi, commander of the Japanese garrison forces, to post troops along the route, ostensibly as a "protective guard." And since there was danger of popular demonstrations or disturbances if one

---

49. NKGSS, 6.1, pp. 25–26; Tako, "Nihon ni yoru Chōsen shokuminchi," part 1, 63.
50. NKGS, 1:30.

of the ministers committed suicide in protest or if word of the negotiations leaked, armed Japanese troops were to be posted around the palace, with sentries at the legation and other key points in the city. Units equipped with machine guns and field pieces were posted at each of the capital's main gates. The whole city was to be put in a state of military alert. On the morning of November 17 Hayashi also dispatched an agent to the foreign ministry to keep watch on the custodian of the king's seal to make sure that it would be available when needed to sign the treaty.[51]

As Itō and Hayashi anticipated, the king's ministers were unable to reach a decision during lunch discussions. Deeply divided, they wanted the monarch to make the final decision. At about three in the afternoon, accompanied by Hayashi, the cabinet left the legation for the palace. Kojong, they discovered, was "ill." While the ministers continued their discussions in the library on the first floor of the royal palace, the monarch, who still hoped to retain the outward forms of independence and keep open communication with the other powers by retaining legations abroad, remained sequestered in his rooms on the second floor. When Hayashi, told by an informant in the palace interior that the king had dispatched the imperial household minister to Itō's lodgings with a request to delay the discussions for two or three days, he decided the time had come to bring Itō into play.[52]

After Itō arrived at the palace, accompanied by General Hasegawa and a bodyguard of kenpei, he immediately asked each minister to indicate whether he assented to the treaty or rejected it. The acting prime minister, Han Kyu-sol, who appeared to Hayashi to be in a state of extreme agitation, was adamant in his opposition. Even though he admitted that "our country cannot maintain its independence by its own strength," he said that he would defy an imperial command to sign a protectorate agreement even if it meant resignation and imperial punishment for "disloyalty." With that Han rose from his seat and walked unsteadily in the direction of the royal quarters as if he personally intended to stop the monarch from agreeing to the treaty. A few moments later the group heard the sound of women's screams and running feet in the palace interior. What terrible thing had happened? In his excited state Han had blundered into the women's chambers. Overwhelmed by his heinous breach of court etiquette, he fainted dead away. When

Hayashi learned the cause of the uproar, he muttered, "Throw some water on his face to calm him down." The discussion continued without the prime minister.[53]

One by one the other ministers gave their views. Foreign Minister Pak Che-sun, shortly to replace the hapless Han as acting prime minister, said he opposed the treaty and refused to negotiate, but he would do so if the monarch ordered him to. Finance Minister Min Yŏng-gi also said that he opposed the treaty in general. The rest of the cabinet—soon to be known as the "five traitors"—seemed to give their assent to the treaty. Minister of Education Yi Wan-yong wanted to make several amendments, but he basically accepted the Japanese argument for a protectorate:

> Our country's diplomacy to date has been endlessly inconstant. As a result Japan has fought two great wars and suffered heavy sacrifices, but in the end it has guaranteed Korea's position. Should our diplomacy once again result in the disruption of the Orient, it would be unendurable, so the [Japanese] demands are unavoidable. Our country has brought this on itself. . . . Japan is determined to achieve its goals, and since Japan is strong and Korea weak, we do not have the power to refuse them. Today, when there is no clash of feelings, and no crisis threatens, we should reach a harmonious understanding.

War Minister Yi Kun-t'aek had earlier expressed agreement with the education minister, but since the acting prime minister had expressed opposition, he felt the cabinet should take joint responsibility and follow the prime minister's decision. Minister of Justice Yi Ha-yong waffled heroically: while a new treaty was not necessary, he said, since the Korean government had already signed the February 23, 1904, protocol and other agreements, the Koreans had violated its obligations several times and so had no choice but to accept the protectorate treaty. Minister of Home Affairs Yi Chi-yong, who had signed the February 23 protocol, expressed full agreement with Yi Wan-yong, and so did Kwon Chong-hyun, the minister of agriculture and commerce.[54]

By Itō's count, a majority of 5–2 expressed agreement with the treaty. While he had the monarch informed of the results, the ministers tried to insinuate some last-minute amendments into the document. They failed to limit the power of the Japanese resident-general to "interfere in internal affairs," but they did succeed in adding a clause com-

---

53. Hayashi Gonsuke, *Waga nanajū nen o kataru*, 226–30; Yamabe, *Nihon no Kankoku heigō*, 290–98.
54. *NKGSS*, 6.1, pp. 41–49.

mitting the Japanese government to "maintain the welfare and dignity of the Imperial House of Korea" and a preamble that held out a possibility that Korea could regain control over its external affairs "when it is recognized that Korea has attained national wealth and power." With that the "negotiation" came to an end.

What happened next is not entirely clear. While the Japanese official account claimed that the Korean emperor finally agreed to the protectorate treaty, Homer Hulbert, a British journalist acting as an agent and publicist for the emperor, asserted at the time that the emperor and every one of his ministers had stood firm against the treaty and that it was only out of fear of "personal injury" that "at last a paper was signed by a majority of the ministers present."[55] By contrast, an unpublished letter written to Horace Allen in early 1906 by Durham W. Stevens, an American whom the Japanese chose as an adviser to the Korean government, tells a different story:

> You know and I know that the Emperor would not have yielded willingly. But he did assent to all that Marquis Ito asked at the private audience three days after the Marquis' arrival. What he hoped to accomplish secretly by the opposition of the Cabinet, and by other means of avoidance in which he is adept, you who know him much better than I can guess. But the cabinet failed him. Pak Chai Soon [Pak Che-sun] would never have signed the treaty if the Emperor had not given him express command to do so. He did sign the treaty and the seal was brought from the Foreign Office by his express orders. The stories about soldiers in the palace, and concessions forced at the point of the bayonet and all the rest of the skull and cross bones yarns are silly rot. The man who made the settlement possible on the Corean side was Yi Wan Yong [Yi Wan-yong]. He stood for it from the beginning. I talked the whole matter over with him and Pak Chai Soon before Itō came and it was plain from what they told me that they had no intention of yielding to palace influences or being used as catspaws.[56]

Since neither Hulbert nor Stevens was present at the conclusion of the treaty, and since both repeat *ex parte* accounts from Korean informants, neither can be cited as a completely reliable witness, although both suggest that the treaty was finally signed.

The recent discovery of new documentary evidence, however, calls this into question. Lee Tai-jin, curator of the Kyujangkak archives at Seoul National University, has recently asserted that the original text of the protectorate treaty bore neither the king's signature nor his seal.

55. Cf. Hulbert, *Passing of Korea*, 221–22.
56. New York Public Library, Horace Allen Papers, Box 1, General Correspondence, Letters to Allen, 1906, D. W. Stevens to Allen, Jan. 10, 1906.

A Hungarian scholar, Karoly Fendler, also discovered a letter written three days after the conclusion of the treaty by the German chargé d'affaires at the legation in Seoul, who was told by Korean sources that the emperor had refused to sign, that he had not authorized Foreign Minister Pak Che-sun to sign, and that the official seal had probably been seized by force and put on the treaty by members of the Japanese legation.[57] While the latter report is probably no more or less reliable than the hearsay accounts provided by Hulbert and Stevens, Professor Lee's discovery, if correct, does suggest that the Japanese may have used fraud if not crude coercion or threats against the personal safety of the king and his ministers to secure a signed treaty. This is the conclusion of Shin Yong-ha, a distinguished Korean historian, who has argued on the basis of Lee's discovery that the Japanese unilaterally proclaimed that the pact had been concluded without any official Korean ratification.[58]

Whatever really happened in the palace on November 17, two things are clear. First, as Yi Wan-yong suggested, the Korean leaders really had few diplomatic options other than to sign the treaty. The other foreign powers had, in effect, abandoned Korea to the Japanese, and it was no longer possible to use the foreigners against one another as Kojong and his ministers had so skillfully done after the Sino-Japanese War. Even the claims circulated by the monarch and other high officials that the Korean government was coerced into signing the treaty went unheeded officially.

Second, resistance to the treaty began to spread from the palace into the streets. When news of the agreement was published in the *Hwang-sŏng simmun*, the reaction in the capital was outrage and anger. A crowd of several thousand gathered in front of the royal palace demanding an immediate abrogation of the treaty, and throughout the city smaller groups milled in the streets, shocked at the announcement. Over the next several days the Chongno merchants shut their shops and schools in Seoul were closed. Crowds continued to assemble at the palace, and patriotic agitators circulated among them handing out anti-Japanese pamphlets or haranguing them with speeches. A petition to the monarch signed by two hundred Korean officials and former officials, headed by Cho Pyŏng-se, several times a cabinet minister, called for abrogation of the treaty on the grounds that it had been signed under duress; it also called for the dismissal of Foreign Minister Pak Che-sun.

57. These reports are summarized in *Newsreview*, June 23, 1992, pp. 26–28; June 22, 1992, pp. 6–7.
58. Ibid., June 22, 1992, pp. 6–7.

Chang Chi-yon, the president of the *Hwangsŏng simmun*, summed up the reaction of the "educated classes in general" in an editorial on November 20. "Ah, how wretched it is. Our twenty million countrymen have become the slaves of another country! Should we live, should we die! Has not the spirit of our people, enduring for four thousand years, been annihilated in a single night! How wretched it is, how wretched it is! My countrymen, my countrymen!"[59]

The Japanese were not surprised. Hayashi, who had warned about the reaction of "conservative officials and Confucian scholars," worried that rallies, petitions, and pamphlets against the treaty might affect broader popular opinion; otherwise, he reported, it did not really amount to much. Indeed, much of the protest was led by conservatives intent on "defending the orthodox, rejecting the unorthodox." Nevertheless, the Japanese authorities took no chances. From the day of the negotiation Japanese forces throughout the peninsula had been on the alert, and the Japanese police reacted quickly to the outbreak of anti-treaty agitation. The authorities arrested Chang Chi-yon for not clearing his editorial through the censors, and the Japanese police tried to open up shops closed by the merchant boycott.[60] But the most urgent task was to cut off the monarch and his familiars from outside contacts. Police under the supervision of Maruyama Shigetoshi, the Japanese adviser, guarded the palace, keeping close watch on the Koreans permitted to enter and leave. No member of the Korean military forces was allowed to meet with the monarch without permission from the minister of war. Clearly, the Japanese did not intend to let Kojong pursue the intrigues that had undone them so often before. But containing the king, as we shall see, proved easier than containing popular anger.

THE GOVERNOR-GENERALSHIP

While the Japanese government's intention to establish a protectorate had been clear since the spring of 1904, the questions of who would represent Japanese authority in Korea and how that authority should be exercised had not been fully resolved. In February 1904, shortly after war broke out, Major General Ichiji Kosuke, commander of the legation guard at Seoul, proposed the establishment of a "government-general"

59. Matsumiya, *Saikin no Kankoku,* 53.
60. Tako, "Nihon ni yoru Chōsen shokuminchi," part 2, 2–3.

(*sōtokufu*) to expedite military operations, especially in the north. It should be headed by a lieutenant general or a full general with power to command not only military forces but the legation staff in Seoul, he said, and it should supervise not only military operations but overall reform of Korea. Once the war was over, the Japanese would have in place an instrument for placing the peninsula under Japanese protection. In effect, this new structure would be a protectorate government under the control of the army.[61]

Needless to say, Minister Hayashi was not enthusiastic about the proposal, nor was the foreign ministry. The relationship between Japanese military and civilian authorities remained complicated and strained. When the army assistant chief of staff visited Korea in late August, he reported that there was little coordination among all the Japanese agencies on the peninsula—the army, the legation, the *kenpei*, the consular police, and so forth. To resolve the confusion, he recommended the abolition of the legation and the establishment of a new unified political agency under the command of a military man. In the meantime, Prime Minister Katsura tried to resolve the bureaucratic infighting by working out a compromise with Foreign Minister Komura and War Minister Terauchi Masatake. The reorganized Korea Garrison Army was placed under the command of Lieutenant General Hasegawa Yoshimichi, who was to report directly to the emperor, thus outranking the Japanese minister; however, Hasegawa was to have no control over the legation staff. The compromise assuaged the army's amour propre, but it did not resolve the larger question: who was to control the protectorate when it was established?[62]

In November 1905, when the protectorate treaty was finally signed, General Hasegawa made a new pitch for military control of the peninsula. The new "managerial organ" in Korea, he said, should be based on parallel military and civilian hierarchies, but the overall leader should be a military man. His argument was simple: force was the only way to control the Koreans.

> I cannot help but believe that in dealing with [the Korean masses], who are nearly barbarians in their level of knowledge, in their want of any conception of the state, and in their worship of the strong, it will not be effective to use means that do not rely on force.... In dealing with disturbances that are inevitable in a period of transition, one can not rely on ordinary police to deal

61. Ibid., part 1, 46–48.
62. Tako, "Nichi-Rō sensō zengo," 118ff.

with them before the fact or to suppress them after the fact. No, on the contrary, we must rely solely on the power of the military police and the army.[63]

The argument, while pessimistic, did provide a realistic forecast of how the Koreans would react to the loss of national sovereignty.

The pessimism expressed by Hasegawa was shared by military leaders at a higher level. In August 1905, just before the signing of the peace treaty with Russia, Yamagata Aritomo expressed an equally gloomy view about the prospects for reform in Korea:

> It goes without saying that Korean politics are corrupt and disorderly, and its people lack the ability or the spirit to make progress.... Hoping that Korea will institute sudden changes as our country did during the Restoration is like trying to catch fish in a tree. At the time of our Restoration nearly all who took part in the most important affairs of state realized the need for the country to make progress, and knowledgeable men outside the government vied to introduce the country to Western things.... Korea has neither the basic knowledge nor sufficient capacity to absorb the new civilization. The Korean people, high and low, are indecisive and rather indolent.[64]

It was precisely such a view that licensed the iron hand tactics advocated by Hasegawa and other army leaders.

Ultimately the character of the protectorate government—*tōkanfu*, or "residency-general" as it was termed—was determined by Itō, the first resident-general (*tōkan*), who wanted a free hand in Korea with no domestic bureaucratic interference from either the military or the foreign ministry. In accepting his appointment, Itō insisted that he report directly to the emperor and that he be given full control over all military forces in Korea. His prestige, and his rivalry with Yamagata Aritomo, carried the day. While Yamagata was reluctant to place any military forces under the control of a civilian, he was also anxious to have Itō accept the residency-generalship, a position that would reduce his influence in domestic politics. The emperor issued a rescript clearly lodging the right of command over military forces in Korea in the hands of the resident-general, who was also empowered to conduct Korea's foreign affairs, to oversee all Korean government business, and to supervise all Korean and Japanese government officials on the peninsula. The arrangement left many army staff officers unhappy, including Tanaka

63. Tani, *Kimitsu Nichi-Rō senshi*, 591–93.
64. *YAI*, 283–84.

Giichi, who felt that putting a civilian in command of military forces violated the army's right of direct access to the emperor.[65]

In early March Itō arrived in Seoul for his first visit as resident-general, ready to tackle the job begun unsuccessfully a decade before by his ally, Inoue Kaoru. His basic task, as he announced time and time again, was to bring about fundamental institutional and economic reform. As he pointed out to Korean audiences, Japan had been compelled to turn Korea into a protectorate to guarantee its own security. His argument was that the Koreans, who had docilely submitted to Chinese suzerainty for centuries, had not taken advantage of the independence the Japanese had won for them in the Sino-Japanese War, and that the Japanese therefore had to step in to help put their country in order.[66] But it is clear that Itō thought that reform involved not only the national interest of Japan but was a positive goal in itself. The Japanese were to be a civilizing force, bringing to the Koreans the benefits of modernity that they enjoyed at home. "What Japan asks of Korea today," he told one audience, "is to join their strength to change the status quo in Korea, to advance the knowledge of its people, and to bring it the same blessings of civilization that Japan enjoys."[67]

During his years as governor-general, Itō was often in a nostalgic mood. In his conferences with the Korean cabinet, he sometimes reminisced about the days when Japan had found itself in circumstances not so different from Korea's, forced to open itself to the outside world and unlikely to survive if it clung to a seclusion policy but beset with reactionaries opposed to any change. He was fond of telling them how, almost by force of will, his generation had brought about the meteoric rise of their country to the ranks of the powers, a process he sometimes looked back on with astonishment. Indeed, at times he seemed to suggest that modernization was as much a matter of character as of circumstance. The problem with Korea, he thought, was the corruption and backwardness of the Korean elite, who looked after their own interests rather than those of the nation, and a major task was to wipe out that corruption and backwardness.[68]

One is struck by Itō's lack of "racist" contempt for the Koreans.

---

65. Tako, "Nichi-Rō sensō zengo," 120ff.; Conroy, *Japanese Seizure of Korea*, 335–38.

66. Hiratsuka, *Itō Hirobumi hiroku*, 2:230.

67. Ibid., 2:231 (speech to Confucian scholars in Taegu).

68. Ibid., 2:220–21.

Certainly he expressed a far more optimistic view of their potential for change than either Yamagata or Hasegawa did. "From what I have seen," he told an audience of Koreans officials in early 1909, "the Koreans are in no way inferior to the Japanese. In their physical and mental strength, they are not inferior in comparison to the Chinese; there is no reason that they should be inferior to the Japanese in the development of their spiritual instincts." But that raised an interesting question. "If they are of the same race, then why should one [people] slide into impotence, while the other increases in national prestige and grows stronger and more prosperous each day?" The answer was clear to Itō: the Korean people had been misled and misgoverned. The cause of the backwardness and weakness of Korea lay not in the inherent character of the Korean people but in the corruption and conservatism of the Korean elite.[69]

When he met with Korean leaders, Itō made it clear that the reform process would work only with the collaboration of the Koreans themselves. Indeed, he saw it as one of his tasks as governor-general to prod the Korean leadership into surmounting the failure of political will that had, he thought, held back reform. At his meetings with the Korean cabinet Itō urged them to face their responsibilities. There were bound to be differences of opinion about the direction of reform, and even much opposition to it, but if those in power faced their tasks squarely and produced results that demonstrated the advantages of reform, then in the end the populace would support them. "Reform of public affairs is the work of the foresighted," he told them. " ... You must realize that it is more than natural for the people to oppose reform, and from the beginning you must decide to succor the people by sacrificing yourselves in the execution of affairs."[70]

In sum, if military officers like Hasegawa had defined Japan's task as coercing the Koreans to change, Itō, who took a more optimistic view of their potential for reform, was willing to try the tactics of guided change. Yet guided change would work only if the Japanese could succeed at a task they had failed so far—the forging of a reliable and effective set of Korean collaborators. No matter how many Japanese advisers were appointed to nurse along the reform process, no matter how hard they exhorted change, and no matter how many reforms were promul-

69. Ibid., 2:233–34.
70. NKGSS, 6.1, p. 219.

gated, ultimately the game would be decided by the reaction of the Koreans to the reform process and by their participation in it. In the end, the success of the protectorate, from the Japanese point of view, would lie in finding reliable partners. Should such partners not emerge, then it would be easier for advocates of more complete control to argue that Korea could not be changed unless it came fully under Japanese sovereignty—in short, that it be annexed by the Japanese directly, without the mediation provided under the protectorate.

CHAPTER 6

The Politics of the
Protectorate, 1905–1910

In early 1906 Kiuchi Jūshirō, a high official in the residency-general, wagered Durham White Stevens, the Korean government's foreign affairs adviser, that it would take only three years for Japan to annex Korea. Stevens, who thought it would take five, was almost exactly right.[1] Four years and ten and a half months after the protectorate treaty was signed, the Japanese government announced to the world a new agreement that brought Korea directly under the sovereignty of the Japanese emperor. Why was this decision reached so soon after Korea had been made into a protectorate? What caused the Japanese leadership to change their minds? Why did they decide that the benefits of direct control outweighed the costs, and how easily were they able to reach such a consensus? What most influenced their final decision: domestic politics, the situation in Korea, the international context, or something else?

For those who argue that the Japanese had annexation in mind all along, even as far back as 1873, these questions are superfluous: the Japanese were simply fulfilling a long-term goal. But if one takes the position that the Japanese leaders did not make any serious attempt to extend direct political dominance or control over Korea until the mid-1890s, then these questions are fruitful to explore. After all, taking full administrative responsibility for Korea involved costs as well as benefits,

1. Baba, *Kiuchi Jūshirō den*, 162.

and the decision was not taken lightly. No one was better aware of the costs than Itō. As he told the Korean cabinet in 1906, "If at present Japan wanted to swallow up Korea, it could achieve that goal without much effort. That notwithstanding, the reason that Japan does not do so is that we wish to preserve our own security not by pursuing the foolish business of annexing Korea, spending great sums of money, and controlling it ourselves, but rather by supporting Korea, leading it toward prosperity, having the Korean people take complete charge of their own defense, and then allying ourselves with it."[2] In short, building Korea into an independent and reliable ally under Japanese guidance was a more cost-effective policy than putting it directly under Japanese colonial rule. While there may have been compelling reasons to dominate Korea, there were also good reasons for not annexing it.

To be sure, there were strong advocates of annexation within Japan. Most notable were the leaders of pan-Asianist patriotic societies like the Genyōsha or the Kokuryūkai, who advocated the expansion of Japanese political domination throughout East Asia. Men like Toyama Mitsuru and Uchida Ryōhei, as well as lesser-known figures like Sugiyama Shigemaru, were often at work behind the scenes, lobbying political party leaders, seeking alliances with Diet members, and even presenting their case to cabinet ministers and top military leaders. They were most successful in finding allies in the Diet, where a vocal band of foreign policy hawks had come into prominence by calling for a more aggressive stance toward Russia in 1903–4 and castigating the Katsura government's "weak diplomacy" at the Portsmouth treaty negotiations. With the encouragement of the chauvinist societies, prominent Diet leaders like Kōno Hironaka, Ōtake Kan'ichi, and Ogawa Heikichi launched a bitter attack on Itō's "soft policy" and called for sterner measures before the Koreans got completely out of hand.[3]

These political gadflies, however, remained at the edge of a larger policy struggle that aligned Itō and Inoue Kaoru against more powerful advocates of annexation at the highest levels of the civilian and military

2. Moriyama Shigenori, *Nikkan heigō*, 112; NKGSS, 6.1, p. 267. At a press conference with reporters in Seoul early in 1906, Itō made a similar point: since the difficulties of annexation were legion, it would be necessary to bring Korea to self-rule under Japanese guidance.

3. On the patriotic societies and the Diet hawks, see Jansen, *Japanese and Sun Yat-sen;* Okamoto, *Japanese Oligarchy.* For a brief discussion of the role of the Diet in Korea policy, see Maejima, *Nihon teikokushugi to gikai,* 116–32.

bureaucracies, particularly among the members of the Yamagata faction. In the wake of the Russo-Japanese War, Yamagata Aritomo had emerged as the elder statesman with the most influence over external policy. His network of *kobun* included not only key army leaders but also civilian figures like Hirata Tōsuke, Ōura Kenmu, and Den Kenjirō. By contrast, Itō had begun to lose influence before the war, particularly since he took what appeared to be a tentative and vacillating attitude toward the Russians. When he resigned from his fourth premiership in 1901, he was succeeded not by his comrade, Inoue Kaoru, but by Katsura Tarō, a protégé of Yamagata. The Russo-Japanese War had been fought with Yamagata and his political clients at the helm—Yamagata as army chief of staff, Katsura as prime minister, and Terauchi Masatake as war minister. After the war it was natural that he should command considerable respect. The declining influence of Satsuma leaders, none of whom had headed a cabinet since Matsukata in 1898, strengthened Yamagata's position as well.[4]

The question at dispute between Itō and the Yamagata faction was not whether Japan should pursue an expansionist policy but rather what kind of expansionist policy it should follow. While Yamagata and his followers were concerned primarily with security issues, Itō and Inoue wanted to promote Japanese economic and cultural influence on the continent. The contrasting orientations were revealed in the debate over whether or not to end the Japanese military occupation of Manchuria in 1906. The army leadership, with the backing of Yamagata, wanted troops there out of apprehension over the Russian threat; but Itō and Inoue, more attentive to the economic potential of the empire, feared that continued occupation would alienate Britain and the United States, whose support and capital were needed for Japan's colonial enterprises. It was not only shortsighted but stupid to violate international treaties and obligations to maintain a slight military advantage in Manchuria. "It seems that Chief of Staff Kodama fundamentally misunderstands Japan's position in Manchuria," said Itō angrily. "The 'management of Manchuria' is a phrase that was on the lips of our people during the war, and even now officials, and naturally merchants and others too, often use it, but Manchuria is not our territory. It is purely part of China's territory. There is no logic (*dōri*) in exercising our sovereignty over a place that does not belong to us." In the end a compromise was

---

4. See Kitaoka, *Nihon rikugun to tairiku no seisaku*, 60–62.

reached and the military occupation ended, but the episode reveals the abiding tension between Itō and the Yamagata faction.[5]

With the death of Kodama Gentarō in the summer of 1906, Terauchi Masatake, who served as war minister from 1902 until 1911, a period longer than anyone but Ōyama Iwao, emerged as the most powerful leader within the army. Other generals had more seniority and more distinguished war records, but Terauchi had the backing of Yamagata and Katsura. If Katsura was Yamagata's foremost *kobun*, Terauchi was his second. Terauchi filled top posts in the general staff and the war ministry with his own protégés, and he worked to strengthen the war ministry vis-à-vis the general staff. As army leader, Terauchi also backed Yamagata's advocacy of a more aggressive "continental" policy. Before the war Japan's military stance had been basically defensive, albeit based on the notion of *défense à outrance*, but after 1905 the army took the position, embodied in the Imperial Defense Policy of 1907, that the maintenance and expansion of Japan's rights on the Asian continent should be the highest objective of national defense policy.[6] Not surprisingly, Terauchi emerged as one of the strongest supporters of annexing Korea.

The debate over the future of Korea revolved around how best it could serve Japan's national defense needs. The Russo-Japanese War had not only turned Japan into a "continental power" but had also put Korea in a new and larger strategic context. The new Korean railway system, for example, could be linked with the railway systems in Manchuria and China, enabling Japan to move troops and supplies across the continent quickly. Korea assumed new significance as a territorial base from which Japan might extend political and economic influence over north and northeast China. It was not merely a territory to be kept out of the hands of any hostile power. The question was: should Japan continue to follow Itō's policy of reform and uplift in hopes of transforming Korea into a reliable ally or buffer state, or was greater political control needed to make Korea a more usable strategic asset? In the end, the issue was resolved less by the victory of Itō's opponents than his own growing pessimism about the practicality of a more moderate policy. In sum, the annexation of Korea came after Itō's default.

5. Inoue Kiyoshi, *Nihon teikokushugi no keisei*, 300. Itō continued to advise against policies that might alienate Great Britain, the United States, or Germany. As he warned the cabinet in November 1907, "If we repeatedly follow selfish principles, the Western countries will come to doubt our sincerity and to place no trust in us. As a result they may cut off the advance of capital, and our economic society would bear the direct brunt. Our government finances would suffer difficulties." Ibid., 315.

6. Kitaoka, *Nihon rikugun to tairiku no seisuku*, 9–13.

PURGING THE COURT

When Itō took up his duties as the new resident-general, he was aware that the protectorate would work only if the Japanese had the cooperation of the Koreans themselves. It was essential, he told reporters in January 1906, that both the Korean people and Korean officials be won over to the reform effort. In the end, no matter how many Japanese arrived on the peninsula, no matter how hard they exhorted change, and no matter how many reform decrees were promulgated, the final outcome would be decided by Korean cooperation. The search for reliable collaborators was central to Itō's strategy of reform through "self-rule."

So too was removing one of the central obstacles to change, the Korean monarch, whose relations with the Japanese had continued to deteriorate. As Hayashi Gonsuke reported to Katsura shortly before the protectorate treaty was signed, "If we can clean up the court, and then cut the weeds from their roots, we can achieve success in improving government administration in Korea as a whole."[7] From the very beginning Itō's audiences with the Korean emperor crackled with mutual animosity. Kojong was not reluctant to criticize the resident-general for lapses in protocol, nor to recall, with righteous indignation, the misdeeds the Japanese had perpetrated in Korea from the murder of Queen Min onward. For his part Itō, with an anger more often calculated than spontaneous, never hesitated to remind Kojong of how precarious his hold on power was. The audiences often deteriorated into verbal sparring matches, with neither man inclined to give ground to the other.

The source of tension was Kojong's continuing effort to play the other foreign powers off against the Japanese, a tactic he had pursued since the opening of the country in the 1870s. Given the readiness of the Western powers to wash their hands of Korean independence in the spring and summer of 1905, this was a futile game, but Kojong had no other to play. During the war he had continued to send secret emissaries abroad to appeal for foreign intervention against the Japanese. According to a report from the Japanese consul in Shanghai, his agents even handed the former Russian minister to Korea a letter asking the czar for help in expelling the Japanese, a fruitless request given the progress of the war.

In the fall of 1905 the emperor turned to the Americans for support.

---

7. Quoted in Conroy, *Japanese Seizure of Korea*, 334.

An agent of the emperor approached E. A. Elliott, an employee of the American firm of Bostwick and Collbran, asking him to enlist the help of Horace Allen in recruiting a prominent American lawyer to plead the Korean case with President Theodore Roosevelt. The Korean ruler hoped that other powers could be represented in the protectorate, to act as a "restraining influence" on the Japanese.[8] This initiative came to naught. Although Collbran considered success of the plan "exceedingly remote," his partner Bostwick thought it would be "like refusing an oar to a drowning man" not to give it a try. Bostwick got in touch with Allen, who in turn got in touch with Joseph Choate, the former American ambassador to London. Allen was willing to take a $500 retainer for his service, but he was not particularly encouraging. "I have long felt, and have so expressed myself," he wrote to Choate, "that Korea should have some overlord, and it has seemed to me that Japan was the natural and proper one." Not surprisingly, Choate declined to take the job, and Allen urged Bostwick to drop the matter since it was unlikely that the American government would reverse its decision to recognize the Japanese protectorate.[9]

Another back-channel approach to the Americans was equally unsuccessful. In October Kojong had dispatched Homer B. Hulbert, an American missionary teacher in Korea for nearly twenty years, to Washington with a letter asking President Roosevelt for help. The American minister in Seoul warned the secretary of state that Hulbert's judgment was "not infrequently colored by prejudice" and his message should be taken with a grain of salt.[10] When Hulbert met Secretary of State Elihu Root a week after the signing of the protectorate treaty, he was told that there was nothing the United States could do about it. A cable from Kojong, sent by way of Chefoo, claiming that the treaty had been signed under duress had little effect on the State Department, which ordered the American legation in Seoul to close down.

---

8. Elliot sent Bostwick four letters in cipher—one for each of the Korean legations in St. Petersburg, Paris, Berlin, and Washington—instructing the ministers to draw up letters conveying this hope to the sovereigns of these countries. With each ciphered letter was a blank sheet of paper bearing the emperor's seal to be used as the last page of the appeal. The Korean monarch also promised a payment of $10,000 to finance the approach to the American president. New York Public Library, Allen Papers, Subject Correspondence, Box 3, Correspondence and Documents Relating to the Attempt of the Emperor of Korea to Enlist the Aid of the United States Government Against the Japanese, 1905–1906 (hereafter cited as "Attempt"), E. A. Elliott to Bostwick, Oct. 10, 1905.

9. New York Public Library, Allen Papers, "Attempt," Collbran to Bostwick, Oct. 10, 1905; Allen to Choate, Dec. 18, 1905; Allen to Bostwick, Jan. 25, 1906.

10. Burnett, *Korean–American Relations*, 3:191.

Having failed to move the American government, Hulbert suggested that the Korean monarch bring Korea's case before the international tribunal at the Hague. In mid-January he cabled the emperor asking for documentary proof that the Japanese had extracted the treaty by force and for funds to support an appeal for international help. With the approval of Kojong, Hulbert engaged the services of a New York lawyer to supervise an investigation for the tribunal.[11] The emperor also continued to send secret emissaries pleading for help to both Russia and the United States, and he encouraged a foreign journalist, Ernest J. Bethell, to publish criticism of the Japanese in his English-language newspaper, the *Korea Daily News*.[12]

Irritated by these and other intrigues, in early July 1906 Itō chided the monarch for his reluctance to relinquish involvement in foreign affairs, even refusing to hand over to the resident-general original copies of foreign treaties from the court archives. The emperor, he said, had also failed to carry out a "rectification" of the court, ridding it of sorcerers, shamans, magicians, and other hangers-on, the like of which were "not to be seen among the courts of civilized countries," and he accused the monarch of consorting with those who were trying to obstruct friendly relations between Korea and Japan. Itō concluded his catalogue of grievances by saying that he had proof that the emperor had referred to him and General Hasegawa as "enemy barbarians," that the court had given funds to "seditious elements" (*bōtō*), that the court maintained secret relations with these elements, and that it had sent secret emissaries to Korean communities in Shanghai and Vladivostok. To put a stop to these intrigues against Japan, Maruyama Shigetoshi was to take charge of the palace guard and keep access to the palace tightly controlled.[13]

None of this deterred the monarch from his tactics of desperation. In early 1907 the *Taehan maeil sinbo*, a Korean-language newspaper edited by Bethell, published a letter from the emperor claiming that the protectorate treaty had been signed under duress—a letter that the emperor then emphatically denied writing. But what finally broke the patience of the Japanese was the dispatch of a secret delegation to the Hague Peace Conference in June 1907. The delegation, led by the helpful Homer B. Hulbert, included three former Korean high officials. In

11. New York Public Library, Allen Papers, "Attempt," Bostwick to Allen, Jan. 19, 1906; Hulbert to Rittenhouse, Jan. 12, 1906.
12. Moriyama Shigenori, *Kindai Nikkan kankeishi*, 205.
13. *NKGSS*, 6.1, pp. 232–38, 242–44.

late April, after selling all his possessions, Hulbert left Japan for Vladivostok, where he rendezvoused with the Korean members of the mission. After making their way across Russia to Europe, they arrived in the Hague, only to be refused the right of diplomatic representation. Since Korea was a protectorate, they were told, it was not possible to recognize their credentials.

The Japanese authorities, who had kept Hulbert under surveillance, suspected that the mission was financed by "dividends" paid into the royal treasury by the Korean-American Electric Company, a Bostwick and Collbran enterprise. The royal household minister denied this connection, but the police extracted an admission from a Korean official who had received $15,000 from Collbran to divide among Hulbert and the three Koreans for their trip to Europe.[14] Just why the Japanese authorities did not try to stop Hulbert, even though they knew what he was about, is an interesting question. Perhaps there was no way to control a foreign national protected by extraterritoriality, or perhaps the Japanese were looking for an excuse to rid themselves of Kojong once and for all.

In any event, the Hague mission proved the final straw for Itō. On July 3 he confronted Kojong: "Denying Japan's right to protect [Korea] in such an underhanded manner," he fumed, "is perhaps a quick way of declaring war against Japan." Later in the day he told Prime Minister Yi Wan-yong that the king's plotting was sufficient reason for Japan to declare war, and he urged Yi to take action. The Korean cabinet, meeting with the emperor the next day, asked him to apologize: the alternative was war and the destruction of the nation. The recalcitrant Kojong did nothing.

On July 7, in a cable to Prime Minister Saionji, Itō said that the emperor should be forced to abdicate and that a new treaty should give Japan greater power over Korean internal affairs.[15] The Saionji cabinet, not wishing "to lose the opportunity presented by the Hague incident to acquire full control over Korean affairs," discussed two possible alternatives: the first was to have the Korean monarch turn his sovereign powers over to the resident-general, whose assent would be required in all domestic affairs; the second was to have the emperor abdicate and to install the resident-general as regent or viceroy with the power to approve all actions of the Korean government.[16] In the end the cabinet,

14. Komatsu, *Meiji gaikō hitsuwa*, 389–93.
15. Tako, "Nihon ni yoru Chōsen shokuminchi," part 3, 177–78.
16. *NGB*, 40.1, pp. 455–56.

with the approval of the *genrō*, decided to let Itō proceed as he thought best. If possible, he was to secure full control over domestic administration; if that was not feasible, he was to assure that all important subcabinet appointments be subject to the resident-general's approval and that Japanese nationals be permitted to serve in such posts. In either case the change was to be achieved by a new Japan-Korea treaty rather than through the unilateral action of the Korean monarch.[17]

The government's decision rested on a strong consensus. Only Yamagata and Terauchi favored forcing the Korean emperor to abdicate to the Japanese emperor or to the crown prince, and only Terauchi wanted to move toward annexation. Otherwise, there was unanimity that the residency-general should abandon indirect control through advisers and place Japanese officials directly within the Korean governmental structure. Only if the emperor refused to agree to the new arrangements should the Japanese government carry out an annexation—that is, have the Korean emperor surrender his sovereign powers to the Japanese monarch.[18]

It is striking that the Saionji cabinet considered the possibility of annexation only as a fallback position. One reason for their hesitation was continuing concern over the possible reaction of the foreigners, especially the Russians. Since February 1907 the Japanese had been trying to reach an agreement with the Russians about arrangements in the region, and the Russians had made it clear that they would not recognize Japanese annexation of Korea without some compensation. But the Japanese leaders were also probably worried about the reaction in Korea. Elite opposition to the protectorate had found a voice early on, and it had become increasingly strident during the first year and a half of the protectorate.[19]

The task of forcing the emperor to abdicate was left to the Korean cabinet, who urged Kojong to step down. But the emperor had one last sad trump to play—Pak Yŏng-hyo. Shortly after his arrival in Seoul Itō had asked the monarch to pardon Pak and other political refugees for their crimes. Kojong at first refused, but after Pak returned to Pusan in June 1906, Itō persuaded him to grant Pak a pardon and permission to live in Seoul. Never hesitant to bite the hand that had fed him, Pak began to intrigue against the Japanese just as he had in 1894–95. Assured by his other ministers that Pak was no longer pro-Japanese and that he

17. *NKGSS*, 6.2, pp. 598–601.
18. Ibid.; Hara, *Nikki*, 3:75–76.
19. Moriyama Shigenori, *Kindai Nikkan kankeishi*, 213–14.

had the respect of the English and Americans, Kojong finally accepted his overtures. In the midst of the crisis, on July 17, the same day the cabinet censured him for the Hague incident, he suddenly appointed Pak royal household minister. Pak had urged him to step down in such a way that he would regain control over the throne as regent just as his own father, the Taewŏn'gun, had.[20]

On the morning of July 18 Kojong, advised that the situation was grave, finally agreed to abdicate, but Pak, who, like the Bourbons, never forgot anything and never learned anything, decided to block abdication by a palace coup such as those he had attempted in 1884 and 1895. The plan was to have palace guards assassinate the cabinet ministers at the abdication ceremony. On the night of July 18 a unit of palace guards broke into the palace, but the war minister and justice minister managed to escape to Itō's residence with a report of the attempted coup. Itō had General Hasegawa dispatch a Japanese infantry battalion to put an end to it. On July 19 the emperor stepped down, and the following day the new emperor, Sunjong, was installed on the throne. The mood in the capital was uneasy. When rumors of the planned abdication had reached the streets earlier, shopkeepers closed their stores and small crowds gathered on the street. In anticipation of further disturbances, Itō urged Tokyo to send a mixed brigade to the peninsula to help maintain order. On June 22 Pak and his fellow conspirators were arrested; while most were later released, Pak was exiled to Cheju Island for two years.[21]

With his abdication, Kojong was destined for apotheosis as a nationalist hero—a curious fate for an ineffectual sovereign who presided over the collapse of his country's independence. The docile new emperor Sunjong, a man of limited mental capacity, was an ideal ruler from the Japanese point of view. Unlike his father, he contentedly served as a ceremonial monarch. In November 1907 he declared at the ancestral temple his intention to pursue a reform policy. To establish a more visible link between the monarch and the people, the Japanese authorities arranged for the emperor to make public appearances, just as the

20. *NGB*, 40.1, pp. 480–82. Just why Pak returned to Korea is obscure. No doubt he wished to return to power, but it is not clear who encouraged his ambitions. According to one rumor, Itō invited him back with the intention of appointing him to the cabinet. Itō himself, however, was puzzled as to whether he had come in answer to a secret invitation from Kojong's party or some other Korean faction. He finally concluded that Pak had come back for personal reasons. Conroy, *Japanese Seizure of Korea*, 355–57. For more detail on the handling of the Korean political refugees in Japan, see *NGB*, 39.2, pp. 157–64.

21. *NGB*, 40.1, pp. 465–67; *NKGS*, 8:96–98; Togano, *Chōsen saikinshi*, 134–38.

Meiji emperor had in the 1870s. In early 1909 he made two grand tours of the south, feted with parades, fireworks, banquets, and local exhibitions. At his side were not only the usual court officials and chamberlains but also Resident-General Itō. One wonders whether the Koreans who witnessed these festivities came away with a new sense of intimacy with the emperor or a sense of despair that he had become a puppet of the Japanese. The new crown prince shipped off to Tokyo, almost as a cultural hostage, for education under the direction of the newly designated royal tutor, Itō Hirobumi.

The abdication of Kojong enabled the Japanese to depoliticize as well as denationalize the royal court. The key step was bringing the royal household treasury, long a source of funds for Kojong's private projects and intrigues, under the direct control of the central government. Even after the establishment of the protectorate Kojong had attempted to preserve his fiscal independence, complaining bitterly to Itō about Megata Jūtarō's attempts to infringe on his prerogatives. Seeking to mollify him, Itō had agreed to postpone the reform of royal finances, only to discover that the monarch used his fiscal independence to finance foreign and domestic opposition to the protectorate.[22] After the abdication, however, the court bureaucracy was overhauled, sinecures eliminated, and superfluous chamberlains, maids, servants, and guards released from their duties. The task of disposing of the court's landed property and other assets, such as the ginseng monopoly, was more complicated, but by the middle of 1908 most had been transferred to the national treasury. The central government budget continued to provide funds for the royal family (¥1.2 million annually) as well as an allowance for the former emperor (¥300,000), but the disbursement of those funds was no longer at the personal discretion of the monarch and his familiars, and hence could no longer be used to fund political machinations.[23]

THE SEARCH FOR COLLABORATORS

What enabled Itō to rein in the Korean court was his success in finding high-level collaborators willing to work with the new residency-general. From his arrival in Seoul, Itō relied on the support of a relatively small group of men who traded cabinet portfolios when major shifts in the

22. *Itō hirobumi den*, 3:715–22.
23. Baba, *Kiuchi Jūshirō den*, 199–200; NKGS, 8:122–36.

government took place in mid-1907 and again in mid-1908. While it is difficult to generalize, members of this group did share certain characteristics. First, all were in their late forties or early fifties; they were members of a generation that came of age when Korea was opened to the outside world in the 1870s. Second, nearly all had risen to prominence after the Sino-Japanese War, during a period of internal instability and intrigue, when cabinets rose and fell every few months. And finally, many had some experience abroad, whether as members of officials missions or as diplomats or as political refugees, and nearly all of those with foreign experience had visited Japan. Thus, these high officials were rather different from those who traditionally had dominated the central government, men who had never left home, had never seen the outside world, and had little appreciation of how backward Korea was in comparison with the Western countries or their neighbor Japan.

The first prime minister under the protectorate, Pak Che-sun, was typical of the high-level collaborators.[24] He had been involved either in foreign affairs or in the early self-strengthening reforms during most of his official career. After passing his examinations, Pak was assigned to the commercial section of the Tongmi Amun, the new "foreign office" established in 1883. After spending two years in Tientsin, the center of Li Hung-chang's self-strengthening efforts, he rose through a series of local and central government posts, including a stint at the government's new Western-style mint. By October 1898, when he was appointed foreign minister, Pak had a reputation for being a member of the "Japanese party." During the next few years Pak handled negotiations with Japan and China on a host of key issues—the return of Korean political refugees, the loan agreement, the Sino-Japanese commercial agreement, the opening of a new treaty port at Ŭiju, and the proposals for the "neutralization" of Korea. Known also as a China expert, with a good command of Chinese, Pak hoped to keep a harmonious balance among Korea, China, and Japan. After being posted to Peking as minister plenipotentiary, Pak returned to Korea on the eve of the Russo-Japanese War, then passed through a kaleidoscopic series of cabinet posts—minister of foreign affairs, minister of justice, minister of agriculture and commerce, and minister of education. Not only was he well known to the Japanese, but he was acknowledged by all domestic factions to be an adroit and subtle negotiator.

24. Biographical information on Pak Che-sun may be found in Hosoi, *Kanjo no fuun to meishi*, 29–33.

In early 1906 Itō assured the Pak cabinet that it would have exclusive control over internal affairs. His role, and that of the Japanese advisers, was to prod, cajole, and persuade the Koreans to adopt reform measures. To that end he began holding regular meetings with the cabinet to discuss reform policies. These meetings were much more tranquil than the audiences with Kojong, and Itō spent much time exhorting the cabinet ministers to act as well as talk.[25] Meanwhile the Japanese advisers like Megata Jūtarō and Maruyama Shigetoshi drew blueprints for new tax systems, land surveys, reorganization of the police force, development of a postal system, and other changes intended to bring Korea into the modern world. The Tokyo government offered the Pak cabinet a loan of ¥10 million to support the reform effort. A small portion was allocated for building new schools and reforming the elementary education system, but the bulk of the money was to be spent on economic infrastructure—roads, irrigation systems, docks, hospitals, bridges, and banks. As the annual reports of the resident-general document in great detail, the physical transformation of Korea was well underway by the end of the year.

The Pak cabinet, however, ran into political difficulties very quickly. The cabinet came under attack by a growing anti-Japanese nationalist movement, and the prime minister was vilified for having signed the protectorate treaty. By the spring of 1907, aware that his government was alienated from public opinion and dependent solely on Japanese support, Pak was ready to resign. Not only was he under fire from outside the government, but he was increasingly undercut by intrigue of his fellow collaborators. Minister of Education Yi Wan-yong was putting himself forward as an alternative to Pak; and Song Pyǒng-jun, leader of the recently organized Ilchinhoe, was lobbying Japanese officials to carry out a "reconstruction" of the cabinet. With nudging from staff members like Kiuchi Jūshirō, Kokubun Shōtarō, and Maruyama Shigetoshi, Itō finally decided to accept Pak's resignation and install a new cabinet resting on a coalition between Yi and Song.[26] Indeed, it was this cabinet that finally forced the king to abdicate.

Both Yi and Song were opportunists, but they represented quite different faces of Korean collaboration—one patrician, the other plebeian. If Song was an upstart eager to take advantage of the new opportunities created by the collapse of the old political order, Yi was a member of the

25. For example, see the minutes of the meeting of June 25, 1906, NKGSS, 6.1, pp. 219ff.
26. Baba, Kiuchi Jūshirō, 169–72.

old elite anxious to preserve as much of the status quo as possible.[27] Like his predecessor, Pak Che-sun, Yi Wan-yong spent much of his early official career involved in foreign affairs. After passing his official examination in 1882 and serving in a series of posts, he enrolled in an English-language academy in 1887. In the late 1880s he served in diplomatic posts as legation secretary in Washington, as consular official in Tientsin and Shanghai, and finally as chargé d'affaires in Washington. In July 1894 Yi was appointed minister to Japan, a post he never actually occupied, and in May 1895 he became minister of education in the cabinet dominated by Pak Yŏng-hyo.

During his rapid rise to prominence in the late 1890s Yi was known as a member of the "Russian party." When a "pro-Russian" cabinet came to power after the flight of the king to the Russian legation, Yi, who carefully cultivated ties with the Russian minister Waeber, first became foreign minister, then minister of finance. For this reason, Itō was initially reluctant to trust him. Unlike Pak, who was known for his scholarship and probity, Yi had a reputation as an intriguer, with an eye for the main chance. After the collapse of Russian influence he skittered through a series of posts, changing portfolios every few months as one cabinet resigned and another took office. By 1905, however, Yi had emerged as one of Japan's strongest allies in the central government. Despite the fact that he spoke no Japanese and only passable English, he attracted the attention of Itō, who judged him unusually "audacious" (*daitan*) for a Korean. Not only had Yi been the strongest supporter of the protectorate treaty, but he also shared Itō's view that Kojong ought to be removed from power. In December 1906 Yi told General Hasegawa that there was little hope that Kojong would change his attitude toward the Japanese, and he promised Hasegawa to work for abdication behind the scenes. From then on Japanese faith in Yi was practically unshakable.

Yi's motives in collaborating with the Japanese probably reflected both self-interest and principle. The factions that had dominated high politics before the Russo-Japanese War had all fallen apart, creating a power vacuum at the center. Nearly all old-line conservative officials had withdrawn from politics or lost influence. With the exception of Cho Pyŏng-sik, who had switched allegiance to Japan, leaders of the prewar "Russian party" had been relegated to powerless official posi-

27. Biographical information on Yi Wan-yong may be found in Hosoi, *Kanjo no fuun to meishi*, 21–29.

tions. Following the dramatic suicide of Min Yŏng-hwan to protest the protectorate, the "American party," whose influence was already fading, completely collapsed, and the imperial favorite Yi Yong-ik was assassinated in 1906. This power vacuum created an opportunity for Yi Wan-yong to achieve political ascendancy by ingratiating himself with the Japanese and driving the monarch from power. To the extent that he had any policy in mind, it was probably maintaining the position of the political elite—the *yangban* aristocrats—by accepting Japanese-sponsored reform. Less interested in reform per se than in not provoking the Japanese, he feared that Kojong's resistance to the Japanese might well push them toward full annexation, a change that would leave the traditional ruling class out in the cold.[28]

If Yi Wan-yong fit the mold of the traditional high official, Song Pyŏng-jun, leader of the Ilchinhoe, was more like Yi Yong-ik, the able but corrupt royal favorite who rose to power in the late 1890s. Song was a man from nowhere, a lower-class hustler and hanger-on who clambered to the political heights by dint of unscrupulous opportunism, sycophantic charm, good luck, and boundless ambition. His early years are shrouded in obscurity. According to one story, his father was a cattle dealer from Hamgyŏng and his mother a street prostitute; another alleged that he was the illegitimate son of an *ajŏn* tax collector in Hamgyŏng; and still another described him as the bastard son of a *yangban* official in Seoul. About all that can be said with certainty about his family background is that there is no certainty, a telling comment in a society whose elite could remember their ancestors tens of generations back.[29]

It seems likely that as Song rose higher in the world, he embroidered stories of his youth, making sure to emphasize cordial early ties with the Japanese. He claimed to have been a member of the entourage who met the Kuroda mission at Pusan in 1876, to have begun a small trading operation with Ōkura Kihachirō in Pusan, to have been forced into hiding at the time of the Imo mutiny because of his close ties with the Japanese, to have befriended Kim Ok-kiun as well as Pak Yŏng-hyo, to have saved a Japanese woman and her child at the time of the Kapsin coup and to have lost his house and property as a result, and so on.

The outlines of Song's career become clear only in the mid-1880s, when he served as a minor military functionary in a series of provincial

28. Moriyama Shigenori, *Kindai Nikkan kankeishi*, 208–11.
29. Biographical information on Song may be found in Hosoi, *Kanjo no fuun to meishi*, 116–28; Omura, *Chōsen kizoku retsuden*, 105–10.

posts. Through the patronage of the powerful Min clan, who were said to have taken him under their wing in the early 1870s, he secured military rank and adoption into a *yangban* family named Song. During the late 1880s and early 1890s he frequented the royal palace, enjoying the favor of Queen Min. According to one story, in 1894 he tried to join the ranks of the Tonghak rebels but failed because of his association with the Min. For reasons that are not entirely clear, but perhaps because of his association with the deposed Min clan, Song fled to Japan in 1895, spending the next decade there. Before leaving he secretly (and illegally) bought some ginseng shoots at Kaesong in hopes of starting ginseng cultivation in Japan. When he discovered that Japanese soil was not suitable for ginseng cultivation, he set up a sericulture training school for Korean students in Yamaguchi prefecture. With introductions from Pak Yŏng-hyo, he cultivated Japanese politicians, officials, and businessmen, no doubt with an eye to his future. In 1904, through the introduction of Ōkura Kihachirō, Song met War Minister Terauchi and managed to secure a position in the Seoul headquarters as an interpreter for General Ōtani Kikujō, the quartermaster. In fact, he worked as a contractor, running canteens for the Japanese troops.

In August 1904, probably as a means to mobilize laborers for the construction of the military railway between Seoul and Ŭiju, Song organized the Yushinhoe (Restoration Society). To expand its numbers, the group merged a few days later with the Chinbohoe (Progress Society) led by Yi Yong-gun, a former Tonghak leader who had spent three years in Japan after his release from prison. In a fawning letter sent to Japanese officials, including General Hasegawa and Minister Hayashi, the new organization, called the Ilchinhoe (Restoration Society), offered its support to the Japanese effort against the Russians. "Today," the letter said, "Japan is fighting with Russia to carry out its great duty of preserving peace in Asia and of protecting Korean soil and establishing her independence. For these reasons we Koreans all deeply appreciate the Japanese, and our thanks is far beyond the expression of these words.... We demand a more concrete Korean-Japanese treaty which we hope will soon be concluded. We also hope that the Japanese will untiringly advise us for our betterment and for the direction of our nation."[30]

From the outset the Japanese authorities viewed the Ilchinhoe with considerable ambivalence. Before leaving his post, Hayashi advised

---

30. Han, "Uchida Ryōhei," 161.

Itō to dissolve the organization. However, others like Kiuchi Jūshirō worked with the Ilchinhoe leaders and their Japanese friends behind the scenes. Itō Hirobumi was initially persuaded that the Ilchinhoe might be useful to the Japanese, but eventually he decided that the group was a liability. Much of this ambivalence stemmed from the ambition and aggressiveness of Song, who, after the war ended, decided to convert the Ilchinhoe into a political instrument, using its members, many of them manual laborers, to stage demonstrations in the capital, to surround the residences of high government officials with angry mobs, and to mount marches on the royal palace. Although the organization's political muscle could be yoked to the task of spreading Japanese influence, the agenda of its leaders, to assume control over the Korean cabinet, was not entirely compatible with the aims of the Japanese leadership.

The strongest Japanese supporters of the Ilchinhoe were Japanese patriotic societies and chauvinist groups looking for allies in the pursuit of their pan-Asian dreams. Song and Yi had paid court to the Kyushu patriotic leader Kōmuchi Tomotsune, who counseled them to follow moderate policies.[31] After the establishment of the protectorate, however, the most powerful patron of the Ilchinhoe was Uchida Ryōhei, founder of the Kokuryūkai, who arrived in Seoul in March 1906 to serve on Itō's staff. Uchida's goal was straightforward: he wanted to portray the ultimate annexation of Korea as the result of Korean initiative. For this purpose the Ilchinhoe seemed ideal. Over the next three years Uchida bombarded Itō, Yamagata, Terauchi, and Katsura with letters, reports, and proposals aimed at building the Ilchinhoe's credibility.

The alliance between Uchida and the Ilchinhoe was cemented in the fall of 1906 when Uchida became an official adviser to the society. In a lengthy report to Itō he pointed out that the Ilchinhoe was the largest political organization in Korea, with an alleged membership of one million, and the only one that was pro-Japanese. By early 1907 Uchida had managed to winkle a monthly subvention of ¥2,000 from the residency-general, and in May General Hasegawa, with Itō's assent, provided it with ¥100,000 from secret service funds. He also introduced Song to both Yamagata and Terauchi, the two Japanese leaders most favorable to the idea of annexation. It seems clear that Uchida wanted to install the Ilchinhoe leaders in power. Indeed, he suggested to Itō that the Pak Che-sun cabinet be replaced by a new cabinet made up of

31. Nishihara, *Yume no nanajū nen*, 20–23.

Ilchinhoe members. While Itō did not swallow that proposal, he thought the Ilchinhoe leaders could be useful as part of a coalition. When Pak Che-sun stepped down as prime minister in May 1907 after rejecting such a proposal, Itō arranged to have Song, whom he knew to be a supporter of abdication, included in the new Yi Wan-yong government.[32]

When Yi accepted the post of prime minister in May 1907, Itō urged him to organize a cabinet of men who would have "the courage not to stray from their goal even if they met opposition from the court or opposed the will of the court."[33] What he really meant was a cabinet that would agree to get rid of Kojong and allow the Japanese more control over domestic administration. In fact, Yi chose a cabinet of familiars, many of them related to him by blood or marriage. Yi's brother, Yi Yun-yong, a former protégé of the Taewŏn'gun who had served in the "pro-Russian" cabinets of 1896–97, became royal household minister. Im Son-jun, a model Confucian *yangban* scholar who served successively as home minister and finance minister under the Yi Wan-yong government, was the father-in-law of one of Yi's sons. Yi Yong-sik, a former member of the "Russian party" and also one of Yi's in-laws, was a minor figure in Seoul politics before his elevation to minister of education; he was so ill acquainted with the outside world that he allegedly told a Japanese audience on his first visit to Japan how surprised he was that their country seemed so peaceful and orderly despite their "not following the Way."[34]

The other ministers, who had close ties to Japan or reputations as reformers, were probably included in the cabinet at Japanese insistence. Cho Chung-ung, who served as minister of justice and then as minister of agriculture and commerce, was a disciple of Ŏ Yun-jung, an advocate of moderate reform. After spending much of the 1880s in domestic exile for having written a memorial offensive to pro-Russian elements in the court, in 1894 Cho was chosen, along with Yu Kil-chun, to accompany the Korean crown prince on his visit to Japan. After the murder of Queen Min, he was forced to flee into exile in Japan, where for nearly a decade he lived the shifting life of a political refugee, apparently with some financial assistance from the Japanese foreign ministry. In the summer of 1907 Cho returned to Korea to help organize the Korean

32. Kuzuu, *Nikkan gappō shi*, 1:41–46, 239–48.
33. *NKGSS*, 6.1, p. 494.
34. Cf. Matsumiya, *Saikin no Kankoku*, 48–58.

Agricultural Association. At the recommendation of Kokubun Shōtarō, Itō's secretary, he was made minister of justice in the Yi government and later served as minister of agriculture and commerce. Although not a very effective leader, Cho was clearly a man committed to "civilizing" Korea.

The other Japan hand in the Yi government was Ko Yong-hui, a member of the *chungin* class, who had first gone to Japan in 1876 in the entourage of Kim Ki-su, the first official Korean emissary. In 1881 he arrived in Japan again with the Pak Yŏng-hyo / Kim Ok-kiun mission. Forced to retire from office after the 1884 coup, Ko was protected from more severe consequences by his relatively low status. After working for the new Western-style government arsenal, he was appointed minister to Tokyo in 1895 as a result of Pak Yŏng-hyo's influence; he served there again on the eve of the Russo-Japanese War. Despite his long association with radical reformers like Kim and Pak, Ko had a reputation for being a career official, accustomed to adjusting to circumstances and never pressing his views strongly. But perhaps because of his association with Pak, he spoke against the abdication of the emperor after joining the cabinet in 1907.

This group of collaborators, while not completely malleable, passively presided over the steady encroachment of the Japanese on the central and local government. At the end of July 1907, under pressure from Itō, the Yi cabinet signed a new protectorate agreement giving the resident-general the right to approve the establishment of all laws and important administrative decisions of the Korean government; requiring the resident-general's approval for all appointments of high officials; permitting the Korean government to appoint Japanese nationals as officials on the recommendation of the resident-general; and prohibiting the appointment of other nationals as officials without the resident-general's approval. In effect, the agreement placed the resident-general in control of domestic affairs as well as foreign affairs. As Moriyama Shigenori has pointed out, the signing of the agreement "achieved a de facto annexation."[35] By late August 1908 many of the principal officials in the residency-general had been appointed as vice-ministers in the Korean government. Gradually Japanese nationals were placed in provincial government posts as well, and incumbent provincial governors were eased out of office to make way for the appointment of Koreans,

35. Moriyama Shigenori, *Nikkan heigō*, 140.

including former political refugees, "familiar with the Japanese language and Japanese conditions by virtue of long residence in Japan."[36]

Ironically, Itō called the shift a "policy of nurturing self-rule." This euphemism suggested that direct Japanese involvement in domestic affairs would accelerate the creation of an institutional infrastructure enabling Korea to stand "independent"—that is, independent of any foreign intrusion but Japan's. As Itō often observed, the Koreans had simply been unable to do this by themselves: "It was a fact recognized by the world at large that the misgovernment and corruption of the people were so widespread and deep-rooted that a very strong hand would be needed to turn over a new leaf in the life of the peninsula."[37] Certainly the Europeans—the British in Egypt, for example—had pursued a similar policy, and the Japanese intended to do the same.[38] In fact, during the period 1907–9 the Japanese pressed forward with plans for many reforms, including a new legal and judicial system to bring an end to extraterritoriality; a stable and uniform currency system to facilitate economic development; a central bank to better coordinate the national financial system; and agricultural stations and other ventures to introduce new kinds of technology.

FIGHTING THE "RIGHTEOUS ARMIES"

It seems likely that Itō hoped that the rest of the population would prove as malleable as high-level collaborators like Yi Wan-yong and his cabinet. No matter how the Korean people might resist at first, he may have thought, in the long run they could be brought into the "civilized" world. When one cabinet minister complained about popular resistance to the reform effort, Itō replied, "If you become alarmed at the voices of discontent and change your goals, all the hard effort you have made to this point will become fruitless. I am not surprised at the discontent of the Koreans. In Japan the advocates of a closed country policy often engaged in sedition. If you want to make the various institutions work in order to bring about the progress of the country, then you must carry on your affairs with determination."[39] The subtext of his comment was

36. Much more research needs to be done, particularly in Korean sources, to find out just who collaborated with the Japanese authorities. For obvious reasons, this line of investigation has not been pursued by Korean scholars, and so far it has not attracted the attention of Japanese researchers.

37. *Seoul Press*, July 27, 1907.

38. Ibid., Nov. 9, 1907

39. NKGSS, 6.1, pp. 448–49.

that if Korean leaders wanted to deal with conservative resistance, they should be as resolute as the Meiji leaders.

But Itō seriously underestimated the strength of popular antipathy toward the Japanese. An anti-Japanese movement emerged in the provinces as well as in Seoul in early 1906. The most dramatic expressions were rebellions or military uprisings led by conservative Confucian scholars and former officials morally outraged at the humiliation of the court and the intrusion of the foreigners. Having found that petitions, memorials, and other traditional peaceful methods of resistance and remonstrance had no effect, they turned to resistance by force. In March 1906 a former leader of the Min faction, Min Chong-sik, mounted an uprising in southern Ch'ungch'ŏng Province, hoping that it would spread to other provinces, plunging the country into such confusion that the other foreign powers would intervene and expel the Japanese. Rightly or wrongly, Min thought that he had the tacit support of the monarch and the court, whose power he hoped to restore. Min soon lost control of his supporters, and in November he was captured by the Japanese. In May another major rising broke out in northern Chŏlla under the leadership of Choe Ik-hyon, a man of enormous prestige who had served as governor of Seoul and as prime minister. The insurrection aimed at overthrowing the Pak Che-sun government and replacing it with a government that would build the country's strength and end official abuses of the people.[40]

Less visible than these dramatic acts of resistance was the spread of more diffuse popular hostility in the provinces. Far from supporting Japanese efforts at reform, many ordinary Koreans felt affronted and threatened by the sudden intrusion of the Japanese into their lives. Anti-Japanese sentiment often sprang from friction between the local population and Japanese settlers, who flooded into the country during and after the Russo-Japanese War. The Japanese brought with them customs and practices offensive to the sensibilities of the ordinary Koreans. The relative visibility of Japanese women, for example, shocked many Koreans, who regarded their behavior as lascivious.

But there was more to the friction than normal distrust of outsiders or ethnocentricity. Flush with confidence at their own superiority, particularly after the victory over the Russians, many Japanese, civilian or military, treated the Koreans with contempt, often physically abusing them. Laborers working on railroad construction were brutalized by

40. *Chōsen bōtō tōbatsu shi*, 10–27.

their supervisors, landowners found their property summarily appropriated for military installations or official facilities without full explanation, and merchants were fleeced by sharp-dealing Japanese who took advantage of constantly shifting exchange rates to swindle them. At best this caused smoldering resentment; at worst it could explode into violent retaliation.[41]

To take one example, the *Korea Review* reported that a young Japanese settler in Mokp'o, determined to take possession of a house in a nearby village, perhaps as payment for a defaulted loan or some other lien, had trussed up the owner, tied a stick with a heavy weight at each end across his shoulders, and then hung him from the rooftree of the house. After several hours of intense pain the Korean died. Frightened by what he had done, the Japanese fled, the dead Korean's son, armed with a knife, in hot pursuit. Finally captured at the riverside nearby, the Japanese was dragged back to the scene of the crime, where he was killed and eviscerated.

As the *Review* editor pointed out, this summary justice, while not the civilized way of doing things, reflected a deep distrust that justice would not otherwise be rendered. "The Korean knew, as all Koreans know and has been demonstrated more than once, that to have appealed to the Japanese authorities would not have secured the extreme penalty of the law. The Japanese would have been locked up for a time perhaps and probably deported back to Japan."[42] Conversely, the Japanese "had been led to think that against the Korean the crime would be condoned or that if he could get among his countrymen he could hide and defy prosecution. He knew that no Japanese court would take evidence of a Korean to the extent of pronouncing the sentence of death." In short, the Japanese settlers, confident of the backing of their own countrymen, often stepped across the boundaries of law and decency in pursuing their own narrow interests.

It is impossible to say how many similar incidents occurred, but it is clear that the reform process itself generated popular distrust, resentment, and apprehension. Just as there had been a wave of local protests against the reforms of the Meiji government in the 1870s, similar disturbances began in the Korean provinces in 1906. For example, the attempt to tighten control over tax collection in the fall of 1906 met with resistance in many areas. Rumors began to spread that the new tax

41. Cf. *Korea Review*, 1906, pp. 383–86. On the general problem, see also *NKGS*, 8:73–75.
42. *Korea Review*, 1906, p. 384.

regulations—"evil laws" trumped up by the Japanese authorities—were intended to enrich the Japanese, who would send all surplus revenue back to Japan after paying the expenses of the Korean government; other rumors alleged that the new tax revenues were to be used to pay off debts to the foreigners; and still others said that since all the money was to go into the Japanese government, the Koreans had no obligation to pay taxes. Many rumors may have been started by local officials, *yangban*, and *ajŏn*, whose interests and incomes were threatened by administrative rationalization, but they found believers among the population. In many areas taxpayers refused to pay their dues to the local authorities, and small riots and disturbances broke out in late 1906 and early 1907.[43]

The events of July 1907—the abdication of the emperor and the signing of a new protectorate treaty—intensified anti-Japanese discontent, but it was the disbanding of the Korean army in early August that escalated violent resistance and accelerated its spread into the provinces. The Japanese had been pushing the Korean government to reduce the size of its armed forces since the early days of the Russo-Japanese War. The Korean army was badly administered, chaotically organized, tainted by corruption, and poorly equipped, but still quite expensive to maintain. Megata Jūtarō insisted that military reduction was essential to fiscal reform. But the most compelling reason behind the decision to disband the Korean army was its political unreliability. In 1906, for example, the army leaders had declined to cooperate with the Japanese in putting down the risings of Min Chong-sik and Choe Ik-hyon, either ignoring Japanese orders or sabotaging them. Even more alarming, after the announcement of the king's abdication on July 19, Korean troops had joined with the mobs that raged through the streets of Seoul, attacking police boxes and torching the residences of cabinet ministers. To forestall more serious trouble, the Japanese military garrison seized the Korean army arsenal at Yongsan, cutting off its supplies of ammunition before it fell into the hands of insurrectionists. When the third Japanese-Korean agreement was signed on July 24, an additional secret agreement committed the Korean government to disbanding all its military forces save for one battalion of imperial palace guards.[44]

The disbanding of the army marked the emergence of a new phase of anti-Japanese resistance. Indeed, that phase began on August 1, 1907,

43. *NKGS*, 8:72–73.
44. Tako, "Nihon ni yoru Chōsen shokuminchi," part 3, 179–83; Matsumiya, *Saikin no kankoku*, 86–87, 107–10, 121–28.

the day of the dissolution ceremony. In an effort to split the officers and the troops, the Japanese authorities had informed the Korean officers that none would be dismissed and urged them to persuade the rank and file to accept dissolution peacefully. Several officers decided instead to resist. When the Korean troops were assembled at the training grounds, guarded by a forest of Japanese bayonets, they were told that they would receive a generous severance allowance: ¥80 for noncommissioned officers, ¥50 for enlisted men with more than one year's service, and ¥25 for those with less than a year. The ceremony was marred, however, by the absence of about 1,350 men, including two full battalions. The commander of the First Battalion, First Regiment, had shot himself to protest the dissolution, and his troops, joining with those of the Second Battalion, staged an insurrection, seizing weapons, attacking their Japanese instructors, and then pouring into the streets to fight Japanese troops. Indeed, when the gunfire sounded from the direction of Namdaemun, the Japanese hastened the dissolution ceremony. The fighting in Seoul was put down in a few hours, with seventy Koreans dead and a hundred wounded, but many of the cashiered officers and soldiers, carrying their weapons with them, fled to the provinces, where they became the nuclei of "righteous armies," local anti-Japanese guerrilla bands that plagued the Japanese for the next few years. Officers and soldiers from the Korean army garrisons at Kanghwa and Wonju also staged armed resistance to the dissolution, as did elements in other provincial units, and they too added to the ranks of the guerrilla insurgents.[45]

The insurgency gathered force during the next few weeks. Itō, who had returned to Japan, began to receive alarming cables from General Hasegawa. For example, on August 16 Hasegawa reported that while the leader of Kanghwa rising had been arrested in Seoul, on August 12 a band of forty insurgents attacked a police station in Kyŏnggi, killing two policemen, two women, and one merchant; the local Japanese residents and their families, including policemen and the postmaster, pulled up stakes the next day, retreating for the safety of Seoul. On August 13 Japanese troops, who had been landed from a Japanese gunboat at Kannung in Kangwŏn Province, advanced inland in response to reports of insurgent bands. At Chuksan in North Chŏlla, insurgents attacked

45. Tako, "Nihon ni yoru Chōsen shokuminchi," part 3, 184–89; *Chōsen bōtō tōbatsu shi*, 27–36.

Japanese settlers on August 14, and it was reported that one man had been killed and that five or six women were missing. The same day, hearing news of insurgents near Hongchon, the local postmaster and other Japanese fled to Chunchon. On the August 15 a band of about twenty men clothed in black began firing on the rail station at Suwŏn, expending a dozen or so rounds before fleeing. In response to reports that former Korean soldiers were causing disturbances south of Taejun, a company of Japanese troops was dispatched to deal with them, and Japanese troops were also sent to counter the activities of a group of cashiered Korean troops from the Kanghwa garrison who were operating near Haeju. Such reports, coming in daily, left the unmistakable impression that unrest was widespread.[46]

The guerrilla bands, sometimes a thousand or more strong but more often only several dozen men, waged a war of harassment against the Japanese for the next three years, attacking Japanese settlers and pro-Japanese Koreans in the provinces and staging armed assaults on the symbols of Japanese intrusion—police stations, telegraph lines, agricultural stations, railroad tracks, and the like. Much of the rebel activity was aimless and disorganized. Attacks were isolated and uncoordinated, mounted without much planning and without any overall strategy except driving the Japanese out. The guerrilla insurgents were more successful in harassing the Japanese than in damaging them, but they did cause momentary panic in the Japanese settler community. As a Japanese official reported to Itō in December 1907, "Ordinary people can not live on doing their daily work. Some are fleeing with their families, some have been killed, some have lost their homes. Now there is cold and starvation. It is a calamitous situation. Japanese residents are all retreating from the interior."[47] Indeed, many Japanese settlers packed and left for home.

The insurgency also threatened the interests of the landholding elites in Seoul, disrupting harvests and making the collection of rents difficult in many areas. The anti-Japanese "righteous armies" at the time of the Sino-Japanese War or the insurrections of early 1906 were usually led by traditional local elites; by contrast, more commoners participated in the new guerrilla movement. An investigation of 255 guerrilla commanders or assistant commanders in 1908-9 revealed that only 25 per-

46. For sample cables, see HL-Korea, File 265, pp. 11-14.
47. Quoted in Conroy, Japanese Seizure of Korea, 367.

cent were *yangban* or Confucian scholars; the majority were common peasants, bandits, hunters, miners, cashiered soldiers, or former army officers.[48] The motives that drove men to rebellion were complex and often ambiguous, and once committed to insurgency, the guerrillas found it difficult to turn back.

Surviving interrogation records open a small window onto the variety of motives that inspired the guerrilla leaders. A common theme was indignation at the "sad fate" of Korea. No Pyŏng-dae, a fifty-three-year-old *yangban*, said he became a *ŭibyŏng* leader to "wipe away the humiliation of the emperor and to avenge the foes of the motherland."[49] Very much the same feelings prompted An Chu-hong, a thirty-one-year-old illiterate agricultural laborer, to roam the marketplaces of his province, bewailing the fate of the nation and urging men to join him in the fight to end the unjust rule of the Japanese.[50] And a thirty-two-year-old illiterate inkmaker, Kang Sa-mun, joined a "righteous army" because he was upset that Japanese had become officials in the government, that the Japanese were grabbing Korean forests, rivers, and land for themselves, and that the Japanese were forcing men to cut off their topknots.[51] Whatever other motives may have been at work, a powerful patriotism, often tinged with a visceral xenophobia like that of *jōi* activists in *bakumatsu* Japan, was at the core of the guerrilla insurgency. Often other elements were at work too—thwarted ambition, youthful enthusiasm, adventurism, family pride, and even family problems.

Let us examine two rather different rebel leaders. Twenty-seven-year-old Yu Pyong-gi, the scion of a distinguished *yangban* family in South Chŏlla, was drawn into the rebel movement by patriotic idealism mingled with status consciousness and family pride. Yu was indignant that the Japanese "protectorate" controlled Korea, but he was also ashamed that neither he nor his two brothers had ever held an official post. The family name would be sullied if the sons of the *yangban* did nothing for their country: to do nothing was unmanly. Determined to throw out the traitors in the government at Seoul, set up a new government in their place, and restore national power, in the spring of 1908 Yu gathered a group of followers. His guerrilla force, consisting at its peak of seven hundred men and five hundred weapons, ranged over Chŏlla during the next several months. Yu's influence, or perhaps the size of his force, was

48. Kang Mang-il, *Kankoku kindaishi*, 229–30.
49. *CDU*, 1:34.
50. *CDU*, 1:72.
51. *CDU*, 1:74.

such that he could requisition food, grain, cash, and other supplies for his men simply by issuing written appeals.[52]

Yet how different Yu was from the second case, that of Hwang Sa-il, a thirty-five-year-old farmer with no official connections or elite family background. Hwang, who had no children of his own, paid a fellow villager, Yang, to take Yang's wife as his concubine. After the cuckolded Yang used up all the money, he came to retrieve his wife. When Hwang refused to return her, Yang threatened to kill them both and went off to join a guerrilla band. To escape harm, Hwang himself joined the same band but assumed (or perhaps bought) a rank that placed the husband under his command. In contrast to Yu, who retired from the struggle only after being seriously wounded in battle, Hwang, after splitting off with his own small band in March 1909, finally turned himself in to the authorities.[53] The two stories—one of noble patriotism and the other of bedroom farce—suggest a complex range of motives behind the insurgency.

The most dramatic challenge to the Japanese came in December 1907, when a combined force of nearly ten thousand (according to Japanese reports) "righteous army" guerrillas from all over the country, including three thousand former Korean soldiers, gathered at Yangju north of Seoul, armed with modern rifles and traditional muskets, for an attack on the capital. The force was led by Yi In-yong, a *yangban* scholar from Kyŏnggi Province, who had tried but failed to organize an anti-Japanese resistance movement after the Sino-Japanese War. Roused from retirement to a life of farming when he heard the news that the Korean army had been disbanded, his plan was to lead a "righteous army" against Seoul to confront the resident-general with Japan's transgressions against Korea. If Itō refused to accede to the insurgents' demands, then the insurgents would kill Yi Wan-yong and his cabinet of collaborators; in its place the "righteous army" would organize a new government dedicated to ousting the Japanese and establishing true independence for Korea.[54] In an unsuccessful attempt to win foreign support, Yi sent secret requests to the foreign consulates asking that the "righteous army" be given formal recognition as belligerents in international law. But advance elements marching toward the capital lost contact with their rear, then encountered stiff resistance from Japanese troops, and finally were forced to retreat. When Yi received news of his

52. *CDU*, 1:77.
53. *CDU*, 1:72.
54. *CDU*, 1:36–38.

father's death in early January 1908, he returned home and the combined army fell to pieces. The anti-Japanese guerrilla insurgents were
never again able to assemble such a large force, and for the next
two years their activities were confined to small-scale, local raids and
attacks.[55]

At first Itō seems to have been relatively optimistic that the insurrections could be put down quickly.[56] The Japanese garrison army, supported by both the *kenpei* and the police, mounted a campaign of suppression by force, often involving full-scale firefights and sometimes a
brutal scorched-earth policy, to put down the local guerrilla activities.
This forceful policy had the full backing of the Japanese community,
many of whom were more worried about their livelihoods than their
lives. In October 1907, for example, the Federation of Japanese Chambers of Commerce, worried that the disturbances would have an adverse
effect on trade by making it difficult for rice shipments to reach the
treaty ports, petitioned Itō not only to indemnify Japanese traders and
businessmen victimized by Korean violence but also to use military force
to bring the rebels under control.[57]

By early 1908 Itō was becoming increasingly pessimistic about the
anti-insurrection campaign. Indeed, it was becoming clear to General
Hasegawa that the insurgency had turned into a guerrilla war "more
difficult to fight than the Russo-Japanese War." Realizing that bringing
an end to the resistance would take years, not months, Itō asked War
Minister Terauchi to reinforce Japanese military units on the peninsula.
In October 1907 an additional cavalry regiment had been dispatched to
the peninsula, and it was joined by two more in 1908. To facilitate the
coordination of the antiguerrilla campaign, the Korea Garrison Army
was given full power over operations, with local Japanese *kenpei* and
police units under its command. The result was an intensification of the
antiguerrilla campaign in the latter half of 1908.[58]

According to statistics compiled by the Korean police, Japanese forces
fought with a total of 83,000 guerrillas in more than 1,900 separate
engagements. According to the reports of the Japanese Garrison Army,
between August 1907 and June 1911 a total of 141,815 guerrillas were
engaged by the Japanese army, the *kenpei*, and the police in a total of
2,852 engagements. Unlike post–World War II anticolonial guerrilla

55. Kang Mang-il, *Kankoku kindaishi*, 227–28.
56. Moriyama Shigenori, *Nikkan heigō*, 160.
57. *Keijō Nihon shōgikaigisho nenpō*, 1907, pp. 123–24.
58. Moriyama Shigenori, *Nikkan heigō*, 160–61, 170.

movements, the Korean "righteous armies" were at a considerable disadvantage. For one thing, like the Korean emperor they had little hope of foreign help, save for moral support. While foreign missionaries reported on the brutalities wrought against Korean peasants in the Japanese scorched-earth campaigns, no outside political help, and needless to say no foreign intervention, was forthcoming. This meant that the guerrilla forces had no way of replenishing their supplies of arms and ammunition except by buying them from foreign gunrunners or stealing them from other guerrilla units. In any case, their weapons were vastly inferior to the Japanese, and many rebels fought with old matchlock muskets.

Neither were the guerrillas particularly successful at coordinating their attacks or forming a nationwide underground organization. While guerrilla bands in particular locales might join forces from time to time, for the most part the resistance movement remained highly fragmented. Often men wandered from band to band as the spirit or circumstances moved them, and bands constantly fluctuated in size and strength. Perhaps a coherent ideology or a charismatic leader might have drawn them together, but they had little in common except for a common revulsion for the Japanese.

The result was that the Japanese, with their up-to-date weapons and ample supplies of munitions, enjoyed a superior force ratio, enabling them to crush the guerrillas in a long, cruel, but ultimately successful campaign. In dealing with the guerrillas, the Japanese military authorities pursued a campaign of indiscriminate retaliation, striking not only the rebels themselves but the general population. The Japanese were aware that in many areas plagued by "rebels," village headmen often sided with the insurgents by withholding information from the authorities or by other means, often out of fear of reprisals. To counteract this collaboration, the Japanese tried to demonstrate that it was even more fearful not to cooperate with them.

Frederick Arthur McKenzie, the only Western journalist to observe the fighting in the provinces directly, reported that in Ch'ungch'ŏng Province, Japanese soldiers laid to waste seven or eight villages to punish the villagers for not cooperating with the Japanese. A band of "righteous soldiers," one of them from the wasted villages, had torn down telegraph lines in the hills nearby. Japanese troops had been forced by the guerrillas to fall back, but then they marched down to the village. Since the villagers had neither stopped the guerrillas from tearing down the lines nor reported on them, said the Japanese, the villagers were the same as the "righteous army." The Japanese soldiers went from house to house, looting what they wanted and then setting the houses on fire. One villager, cutting grass with a knife, was killed by the soldiers, who mistook him for a guerrilla rebel. When the Japanese troops left, the village was a scorched plot, with not a single house or wall standing; the pots with winter stores were broken and the earthen *ondol* wrecked. As McKenzie commented, "In place of pacifying a people, [the Japanese] were turning hundreds of quiet families into rebels.... To what end? The villagers were certainly not the people fighting the Japanese. All they wanted to do was look quietly after their own affairs."[59] Indeed, the intensification of guerrilla activities in the late spring of 1908 may have reflected not only the economic desperation of "spring famine" that many peasants habitually faced but also the conversion of many innocent bystanders into active anti-Japanese guerrillas, venting their anger at the arbitrary ruthlessness of Japanese tactics. Even the official Japanese history of the suppression indicates that between July 1907 and December 1908 about 6,880 houses were destroyed and 1,250 Korean civilians killed in the antiguerrilla campaign.[60]

The policy of draconian reprisals against ordinary farmers and villagers reflected the belief of General Hasegawa and other Japanese officials that the general populace was sympathetic to the "rebels" and "bandits."[61] Itō, who was not averse to using the iron hand in dealing with the rebels, backed Hasegawa. In November 1907, when Foreign Minister Hayashi informed him that the British government was investigating Japanese military atrocities against the Koreans, Itō replied that he would order the army to modify its practices but suggested that the atrocities were bound to occur since the Japanese forces had to put down the rebels with limited strength. And Itō admitted that sometimes Japanese troops "resorted to burning a whole village because a few citizens were letting rioters stay in their houses" and that "military measures against riotous people had been too severe."[62]

The real success of the Japanese was due less to their intimidation of the general population than to their relentless pursuit of the insurgent forces, whom they ground down by constant small engagements, eroding their numbers and their morale; by 1909 and 1910 many insurgents, convinced of the "evil" of their cause, had given themselves up or were

59. McKenzie, *Tragedy of Korea*, 185–87.
60. Kim and Kim, *Korea and the Politics of Imperialism*, 204–5.
61. Ibid., 203.
62. Conroy, *Japanese Seizure of Korea*, 367.

betrayed to the authorities by local Korean residents. Popular support may also have declined because the insurgents more and more were forced to rob, steal, and loot in order to finance their operations. Many Koreans, especially the more well-to-do who were often objects of the attacks, must well have wondered if the Japanese could be any worse than the rebels.

In 1908 police officials in Chŏlla reported that while local people had been sympathetic to the rebels at first, disenchantment set in as the insurgency dragged on. "The damage they have suffered at the hands of both the insurgents and the pacification forces has been great, and as a result a tendency toward an aversion to the insurgents has emerged," they reported. "Since local officials are exerting themselves in response to the great pacification campaign, the common people often voluntarily report the whereabouts of the insurgents. Rebel leaders have been captured, and many of their fellows have turned themselves in." A bountiful harvest that year, including a cotton crop grown for export to Japan, also helped to restore local peace.[63]

The pressure of Japanese counterinsurgency measures took its toll. The diary of Sŏ Pyŏng-hui, a physician from South Kyŏngsang who became a rebel leader in late 1907 after an unsuccessful effort at buying office in Seoul, reveals how the rebels were slowly subdued. In February 1908 Sŏ commanded a force of sixty-eight men, armed with fifty-eight matchlocks, two Western-style rifles, and one sword. During the next three months he fought four engagements with Japanese troops, losing men and weapons in every one. By August, when he joined another band, he had only eighteen men left. In early 1909, with a force of about thirty, he staged daring attacks, apparently eluding detection by burying his weapons and dispersing his followers when danger threatened or disguising himself as a peddler to escape notice. By August 1909, however, his following had dwindled to fewer than twenty, and his raids were aimed not at the Japanese but at raising money by forcefully stealing from Korean landowners or local finance officials. He was finally captured in October after the arrest of several followers, who may have betrayed him.[64]

In contrast to the dogged and systematic antiguerrilla campaign of the Japanese military forces, the often-mentioned antiguerrilla activities of the Ilchinhoe were completely ineffective. The outbreak of popular

63. CDU, 1:34–36.
64. Ibid., 1:105.

unrest seemed to Uchida Ryōhei an opportunity to expand the organization's provincial base. In November 1907, after surveying conditions in the province and consulting with both Yi Wan-yong and the Ilchinhoe leadership, he proposed to Itō a plan to organize local "self-defense bands" in every village to protect "law-abiding" Koreans from the marauding guerrillas. The bands were to work with the local authorities, but they were not to be armed. "There should be no weapons in the hands of the people," said Uchida.[65] The main purpose of the local self-defense units was to make it easier to distinguish who was "law-abiding" and who was rebellious. Band members would investigate households, collect privately held weapons, patrol villages, report those with "rebel sentiments," and provide material assistance to the needy. The local bands were not to be autonomous but to be organized under the supervision of the police, the *kenpei*, and the Japanese military, in effect serving as auxiliary organizations intended to help the Japanese put down the guerrilla insurgency. For example, the self-defense units might report the names of guerrilla sympathizers to the Japanese authorities, but the tasks of interrogation and punishment were to be left to the latter. Eventually, Uchida suggested, the self-defense units might become the "foundation" for a system of local self-government in Korea.[66]

During the next two months, in a flurry of organizing activity, Ilchinhoe members fanned out through the provinces, collecting tales of guerrilla violence and atrocities and trying to persuade local village leaders to form self-defense bands. Yi Yong-gu himself took part in the campaign, setting off with Uchida on a tour to the north. In a memorial photograph taken before their departure to the provinces, the organizers looked quite grand in military-style overcoats, sporting gunbelts and shod in heavy boots. Uchida himself was armed with a Mauser-type pistol that Itō had given him. Despite this impressive start, the organizing campaign was cut short in December 1907, when Uchida received a letter from Vice Resident-General Sone expressing concern over reports that Ilchinhoe members, in their efforts to expand their own organiza-

65. Another question was whether the self-defense units should have official standing or whether they should be privately organized. If they had official standing, then their activities would have to be regulated and supervised by officials; by contrast, if they were purely private organizations, then it would be difficult for civilian or military authorities to provide them any support. Itō suggested that regulations for the organization of self-defense units should be drafted. Kuzuu, *Nikkan gappō hishi*, 1:372.

66. Ibid., 1:374–76, 475.

tional base, had stirred up trouble by intimidating others or forcing them to cut off their topknots. Rather than easing local unrest, Sone complained, the organizing effort was spreading unease and anxiety among law-abiding elements, and he asked Uchida to keep the organizers under control. After showing the letter to Yi Yong-gu, Uchida decided to hurry back to answer Sone's charges, and the organizing tour was suddenly cut short.[67]

Why did the residency-general look askance at the Ilchinhoe effort to organize self-defense units? Uchida later surmised that Korean rivals of the Ilchinhoe leaders had tried to undermine the organization's growth by playing on Sone's anxieties.[68] Perhaps this was the case. But there is evidence that the Japanese authorities had good reason for skepticism about the real purpose or the effectiveness of the self-defense bands. In December 1907 Kiuchi Jūshirō received a report summarizing the views of local Japanese police authorities at the county level. Less than half reported any success in getting self-defense units organized after calling in Korean country magistrates and village leaders to explain the purpose of the bands. And such success often amounted to little more than contacting the village authorities and issuing regulations. The greatest successes seem to have been achieved near the capital in Kyŏnggi, Kangwŏn, and North Chŏlla Provinces. The reports suggested that self-defense units were more likely to be organized in towns or villages where *kenpei* units were stationed, presumably because they offered protection against guerrilla retaliation. In Taegu, for example, it was decided to set up self-defense bands only in areas where there was no unrest.[69]

Many local Japanese police authorities reported that either there was no need to organize self-defense bands or that doing so would be counterproductive. Some suggested that in areas where there was little guerrilla activity, it would be unsettling to the populace to set up self-defense units; others reported that meetings to explain the purpose of the units were either sparsely attended by the local Korean authorities or not attended at all. It is not difficult to imagine that Korean village heads were not anxious to attract the attention of the guerrilla insurgents by cooperating with the Japanese authorities.

Many reports also complained about the activities of the Ilchinhoe

67. Ibid., 1:392.
68. Uchida Ryōhei, "Nikkan gōhō," in Takeuchi, *Ajiashugi*, 214–15.
69. HL-Korea, folder 283, pp. 95–108.

members. In Chŏnju, for example, it was said that the self-defense units were being organized mainly as a way to recruit Ilchinhoe members; in Chunchon and elsewhere that Yi Yong-gu traveled, he left the impression that he was simply out to attract followers; in Choungjin, Ilchinhoe organizers tried to extort funds from local county and village authorities when they ran out of expense money; in Sungjin, the Ilchinhoe organizers did little more than hang around the local Japanese authorities and never ventured forth to organize local villagers; in Unsan, rumors circulated that the real purpose of the self-defense units was to compel men to cut off their topknots; and in Sanwae, the Ilchinhoe organizers simply stirred up ill feeling.[70]

All of these reports suggest that Sone's cautionary letter to Uchida was prompted less by political intrigues at the capital than by apprehension over the hostility, suspicion, and distrust provoked by the Ilchinhoe involvement in the self-defense unit plan. Although Uchida continued to claim that the Ilchinhoe provided the only support the Japanese enjoyed in the provinces and that only by backing the Ilchinhoe would that support grow, Japanese officials were increasingly skeptical about the organization and its activities.[71] In December 1908 Ishizuka Eizō, a high-ranking civilian official, observed:

> Among the provincial members of the Ilchinhoe there continue to be scoundrels in pursuit of an easy life who flaunt the influence of the Ilchinhoe, pursue unsavory activities in flagrant fashion, and engage in lawless behavior. There are also officials associated with the Ilchinhoe who emptily brandish the banner of civilization and violate established custom. As a result their alienation from the ordinary populace has become more and more pronounced, and ill feeling toward the Ilchinhoe grows unabated.... Since last year not a few Ilchinhoe members have met their death at the hands of the insurgents or had their houses burned and their wives, children, and family subjected to persecution and cruelty.[72]

Not only was the Ilchinhoe losing members, but its leaders were increasingly turning against the pro-Japanese Yi Wan-yong government for failing to protect them. In July 1908, following a protest by provincial Ilchinhoe members in the capital, Itō suggested to Katsura and Terauchi that the organization be disbanded and its members be bought off with direct payments or offers of employment.[73]

70. Ibid.
71. For Uchida's views, see HL-Korea, folder 264 and folder 283, pp. 68–70.
72. NGB, 41.1, pp. 855–56.
73. Moriyama Shigenori, Kindai Nikkan kankeishi, 224; Kuzuu, Nikkan gappō hishi, 1:553–65.

TOWARD ANNEXATION

Popular guerrilla resistance was the last in the series of events that pushed the Japanese toward a full takeover of Korea. In early June 1909 Itō announced his resignation as resident-general, removing himself as an obstacle to annexation. Some have suggested he did so because his policy of "nurturing self-rule" had come under attack at home. Uchida Ryōhei, who was increasingly critical of Itō's "gradualism," orchestrated a behind-the-scenes campaign to ease Itō out of office. Arguing that it was time for Japan to exercise "direct rule" over Korea, Uchida sent a long memorandum urging annexation to Yamagata, Katsura, and Terauchi in January 1909.[74] Chauvinists in the Diet, like Ogawa Heikichi, who had been calling for the annexation of Korea since 1907, took up the cry against Itō. In a Diet interpellation, Ogawa lambasted Itō's "soft policy" as a detriment to national prestige and charged that the Korean government was riddled with corruption.[75] But Itō was too powerful and canny a figure to bow before this kind of political pressure, and he already indicated a wish to retire in the fall of 1908, well before the public attack was mounted against him.

The most plausible explanation for Itō's resignation is that he had concluded that his gradualist policy had reached a dead end.[76] The spread of the "righteous army" movement provided ample proof that the reform program had not won over the Korean populace but had instead alienated them. And if the policy of "nurturing self-rule" did not work, then the only way to assure that Korea would remain under Japanese control was to annex it formally. Itō had never ruled out annexation as a solution to the Korean problem. In early 1907, when Foreign Minister Hayashi Tadasu had asked him whether or not to mention the possibility of annexation in negotiations with the Russians over a new secret agreement, Itō had replied that it would be "good policy" to do so. "Since annexation will probably become more difficult as the years go by if conditions in Korea change as at present, perhaps we should make clear our intentions today and secure the assent of Russia in advance."[77] The answer reflected Itō's usual circumspection in dealing

74. Kuzuu, *Nikkan gappō hishi*, 2:6–42, 75–76. During the imperial tour of the southern provinces in January 1909, Song, apparently drunk, struck a court chamberlain during an argument. Forced out of office, he left for Japan under a cloud of opprobrium.

75. Much of the ammunition for these charges was supplied by Kiuchi Jūshirō, who was disgruntled at being shifted from his position as vice-minister of home affairs to vice-minister of agriculture and commerce. Moriyama Shigenori, *Nikkan heigō*, 174.

76. Gaimushō, *Komura gaikōshi*, 2:379, 382.

77. Ibid., 2:381.

with the Western powers, but it also indicates that he was not opposed to annexation in principle.

Even before his resignation Itō had given a go-ahead signal to the Katsura government. In late March 1909 Foreign Minister Komura submitted to Katsura an annexation proposal that became the basis for the government's decision the following July. As preparatory steps he recommended stationing a military force in Korea large enough to maintain the country's defense, the dispatch of increased numbers of police and *kenpei* to maintain law and order, the placing of the Korean railroad system under the Tetsudō-in, the linking of the Korean rail system to the South Manchuria railway to develop a unified continental rail system, the encouragement of more Japanese migration to Korea, and an expansion of the powers of Japanese working as officials in the Korean government. Katsura, long a supporter of Korean annexation, immediately agreed with Komura's proposal but thought it best to clear the matter with Itō before taking it to the cabinet. When Katsura and Komura visited Itō at his Oiso villa on April 9, they were delighted to find that, contrary to their expectations, Itō had no objection to the proposal. However, Itō was clearly not happy with the way things had turned out, and he continued to stress the difficulties involved in annexation in private talks with Yamagata and others.[78]

When Itō took leave of Korea, his sense of frustration was palpable. At a farewell meeting with local officials in Inchon he expressed disappointment that the living conditions of the Korean people had not improved much during his three and a half years as resident-general. "Perhaps," he said, "it was because my efforts were not sufficient, or perhaps it was that the Koreans did not apply themselves or exert themselves, or perhaps it was because there were sometimes elements who did not like being under the protection of a foreign country."[79] Whatever responsibility Itō seemed to take, it is clear that he laid the blame for the failure of his policies on the Koreans themselves. As he had said many times, the success of the reforms depended on their cooperation, and not much cooperation had been forthcoming. His final acquiescence to a policy of annexation indicated that he realized it was much easier to make enemies in Korea than friends.

Itō's departure opened the way for advocates of annexation in the Katsura government—Katsura, Terauchi, and Komura—to accelerate

78. Ibid., 2:376.
79. Ibid., 2:381.

preparations for a takeover. In July 1909, a month after Itō's resignation, the Katsura cabinet secretly adopted a formal decision to "annex Korea and make it part of the [Japanese] empire ... at an appropriate moment."[80] It remained only to work out the details: the drafting of an annexation decree, the treatment of the Korean royal house after annexation, the structure of the new colonial administration, the adjustment of the treaties with the foreign powers, and so forth. During the next year Prime Minister Katsura and Foreign Minister Komura, working in extreme secrecy, devoted themselves to these administrative tasks, waiting only for the "appropriate moment."

On the peninsula final preparations for annexation involved cracking down on both friends and enemies. In the fall of 1909 the Japanese military forces, under the command of General Ōkubo, launched "the great southern pacification campaign" in North and South Chŏlla Provinces. Enjoying the protection of the local population, rebel forces, more numerous and better organized than elsewhere, had boldly attacked the thinly spread Japanese military units in the area, capturing weapons and other supplies. The purpose of the campaign was twofold: first, to prevent erosion of Japan's "national prestige"; and second, to impress on the "the stubborn people" in the region the strength and effectiveness of the Japanese army. As the staff headquarters of the pacification forces observed:

> Since the people of North and South Chŏlla did not witness our army in action during the Sino-Japanese and Russo-Japanese wars, they do not yet understand its true worth. They are still lost in dreams of the Bunroku era [the period when the Koreans turned back Hideyoshi's invasion], and they hold our countrymen in contempt. So we should carry out a great pacification with determination, dispatch our expeditionary forces at full strength, scour the hills and plains, and root out the rebels.... We must make the Korean people everywhere fear and admire the sternness and bravery of the Imperial Army and restore Japan's fundamental historical honor.[81]

The Japanese military authorities had detailed intelligence on the rebel forces: the names of their leaders, the approximate size of their forces, and their operational bailiwicks. Altogether there were about sixty-six separate guerrilla bands operating in Chŏlla. The largest was a force of five hundred men, but most numbered fewer than a hundred. Against them the Japanese pacification force, consisting of two infantry battalions, was to cordon off the area pacified and to hunt down the

80. NKGSS, 6.3, pp. 1254-56.
81. CDU, 1:84-85.

rebels. The army troops were supported by a Japanese gunboat and a small fleet of other vessels operating off the Chŏlla coast; local *kenpei* and police forces provided additional manpower. The Japanese wished to deploy as large a force as possible since they had learned that splitting troops into small units was a waste of time and effort.[82]

The carefully planned campaign was to take place in three phases. Operations began on September 1, just as the weather was beginning to cool but before the autumn harvest. The timing was seen as most advantageous to the Japanese. Guerrillas often returned to their villages to help with the harvest, making it difficult to distinguish between "rebels" and "law-abiding people," and they made off with part of the crops as food supplies. The pacification forces proceeded in methodical fashion, hunting down the rebel forces village by village. The troops first surrounded a village, posting sentinels on its outskirts. The village headman was asked to produce a list or register of all male villagers, and the Japanese then checked the list against those males present. Anyone suspected of being an insurgent was detained and interrogated. Sometimes the Japanese troops dressed in Korean clothing, lulling the villagers's suspicions or tricking rebel sympathizers into betraying themselves. Since guerrillas often stayed in the hills and forest during the daylight hours, the Japanese troops often came back at night to hound out any rebels who returned to the village; they sometimes mounted several raids against the same village over the course of several days to root out all the insurgents. Captured rebels were interrogated to find out the names of their comrades or the location of concealed weapons caches.

The goal of this dull and methodical pacification campaign was not to terrorize the population, as some of the earlier antirebel operations had been, but rather to destroy the guerrillas themselves. The Japanese commanders were ordered to act toward the local population in such a way that "military force and mollification went hand in hand." If possible, the rebels were not to be killed but made to surrender and confess the error of their ways. Only those who resisted or tried to flee were to be killed. Evidently the authorities hoped to avoid the cycle of brutality and retaliation that had marked early phases of the antirebel campaigns. Indeed, much use was made of psychological warfare. Broadsides and broadsheets were circulated accusing the rebels of treason and destroying the prosperity of the region. The Japanese also mobilized the local administrative authorities to cooperate in the pacification. Not only did

82. *CDU*, 1:83–86.

they help in supporting the troops with provisions and lodging, but they also cooperated in the antirebel propaganda campaign. The governor of South Chŏlla Province toured the pacification areas twice, exhorting county officials and other lower-level officials to assist the Japanese in putting down the insurrection.

The results of the campaign must have been gratifying to the Japanese authorities. The leaders of 103 bands, totaling 4,138 men, were brought under control. The majority (61) were captured, 19 turned themselves in, and only 23 were killed.[83] While sporadic guerrilla activity continued for the next two years, its level and intensity declined.

Oddly enough, Japan's "friends" in the Ilchinhoe were to cause more political trouble in the final march toward annexation. In September Uchida Ryōhei, hoping to push the home government faster toward annexation, met with Yi Yong-gu to discuss how the Ilchinhoe might help. They discussed three possibilities: replacing the Yi Wan-yong government with one dominated by the Ilchinhoe; having the Korean monarch transfer administrative control of the country to the Japanese emperor; or mounting a massive rally of forty thousand to sixty thousand Ilchinhoe members to demand that the Yi Wan-yong cabinet support annexation. The first option was no longer likely, and the second was beyond their control; thus, Uchida urged the Ilchinhoe to mount a petition movement. To broaden its base, he tried to persuade two other large political associations to join the annexation petition movement as well—the Taehan Hyŏphoe (Great Korea Association) and the Suhbuk Hakhoe (Northwestern Scholarly Society). Neither organization wished to join, nor did Uchida get any encouragement from the new resident-general, Sone Arasuke. When Itō was assassinated in October 1909, Uchida thought the moment opportune to launch the petition campaign. (By his own account he had the backing of War Minister Terauchi.)[84] On December 4 Yi Yong-gu, claiming the support not only of the "one million" members of the Ilchinhoe but the twenty million people of Korea, presented petitions to Emperor Sunjong, Prime Minister Yi Wan-yong, and Resident-General Sone asking that the emperor abdicate and that sovereign control over Korea be given to Japan.

The result, as one might expect, was an immediate, vocal, and virulent reaction against the Ilchinhoe. The next day the Taehan Hyŏphoe and the Suhbuk Hakhoe staged a demonstration against the petition at

83. CDU, 1:88–89, 101–5.
84. Kuzuu, Nikkan gappō hishi, 2:116 ff., 203–5.

the West Gate of the city. The police forced the crowd to disperse lest it spark new disorders in the capital. Out of the cauldron of nationalist outrage bubbled petitions, memorials, broadsides, and editorials condemning the Ilchinhoe and its leaders as "villains," "bush snakes," or "national traitors." According to local police authorities, the reaction was less strong outside the capital, save among some *yangban*, Confucian scholars, and Christian converts. The public outcry upset Resident-General Sone, who issued a warning to organizations that disturbed the public peace and who assured the Koreans that there had been no change in Japanese policy on the question of annexation. He would have expelled Uchida from the country as well, but the military authorities objected.[85]

However useful the Ilchinhoe might have seemed to Japanese officials in 1905–6, by the beginning of 1910 it had become a political liability. The Katsura government, worried that its activities would impede annexation rather than facilitate it, pressured the organization to drop its petition movement. In February 1910 the prime minister told Sugiyama Shigemaru, a chauvinist activist who succeeded Uchida as an adviser to the organization, "The final decision on the annexation and when it will take place is a matter for Japanese government policy, and there will be no involvement by Koreans at all."[86] In early summer even Uchida, the Ilchinhoe's erstwhile patron, cabled Yi Yong-gu with instructions not to take any further action without his approval, and in August the new governor-general, Terauchi, once a sympathizer, ordered the Ilchinhoe to disband as all other political organizations had. To be sure, the Japanese were generous toward the Ilchinhoe: "dissolution expenses" in the amount of ¥150,000 were distributed to the organization's members, with the highest-ranking officers receiving up to ¥5,000 and the rank-and-file ¥10 each. But when Yi Yong-gu protested that his organization had followed the Japanese "through fire and water," he met with a cold rebuff from both Terauchi and Uchida.[87] Even the best of collaborators were no longer necessary.

On August 22, 1910, the advocates of annexation—Yamagata, Katsura, Komura, and Terauchi—saw their goal achieved. In a furtive ceremony at the resident-general's quarters, Prime Minister Yi Wan-

---

85. Kim Chong-myong, *Chōsen chūsatsugun rekishi*, 309–10, 314–25.
86. Kuzuu, *Nikkan gappō hishi*, 2:501–2.
87. Ibid., 2:676, 710–11, 726–34. On his deathbed several years later Yi Yong-gu told Uchida, "I am a fool. I am a traitor." Reassuringly Uchida replied, "The foolish man of today will become the wise man of tomorrow." Uchida was wrong; Yi was right. See Uchida, *Nihon no Ajia*, 317.

yong signed an annexation treaty that extinguished the sovereignty of
the Korean state. The signing, however, was not announced publicly for
a week as the Japanese secured themselves against a negative reaction.
The treaty, almost an anticlimax at the end of a year of secret planning
and preparation, signaled the ultimate failure of Itō's gradualist approach to "fundamental reform." The attempt to induce change rather
than force it on the Koreans had proved more costly than anticipated.
The Korean leaders who collaborated with the Japanese had proved incapable of commanding any public support, and the cost of containing
popular resistance to the Japanese presence proved as high as direct
political and administrative control. Itō had seriously underestimated
the unpopularity of the Japanese and the disruptive impact of reform, and he overestimated the intrinsic appeal of "civilization" to the
Korean populace. Contrary to his expectations, the Japanese had to
spend "great sums of money" even to maintain the fiction of Korean
"independence." For the same price Japan could enjoy full sovereignty
over the peninsula, free to turn it into a springboard for broader and
more aggressive actions on the continent. And it was for that reason
that Itō acquiesced, albeit reluctantly, to the plans for annexation.

The final incorporation of Korea into Japanese territory marked the
end of a long process that had begun with the attempt to "open" the
country in 1876. Over the decades the Japanese had shifted from one
form of imperialist enterprise to another—from free-trade imperialism,
to the securing of concessions and spheres of influence, to the establishment of a protectorate, and finally to full colonial rule. What propelled
the process was not simply the increased capacity of the Japanese for
expansion but their ultimate failure to build a stable collaborative
structure that might have enabled them to stop short of full colonial
control. The process was not unlike the experience of many Western
powers, who slid down the slippery slope of imperialism when confronted with an indigenous elite that refused to collaborate. Had the
Meiji leaders' anxieties been allayed by the emergence of a strong and
actively modernizing Korean elite willing to rely on Japan for help,
Korea might well have maintained its independence. But a tradition of
contempt toward the Japanese, and an entirely understandable suspicion of Japanese motives, scotched that possibility.

2. An 1884 *Marumaru chinbun* cartoon showing the partition of China (depicted as a pig) as a dinner party. The caption reads: "The foreigner talks in his sleep."

3. King Kojong and his son, Sunjong, ca. 1890.

4. The Japanese crown prince (later the Taishō emperor) on a visit to Korea in 1907. *Front row, from left*: Song Pyŏng-jun, Yi Wan-yong , Prince Yoshihito (Japanese crown prince), Prince Yŏngch'in (Korean crown prince), Prince Arisugawa, Itō Hirobumi (resident-general); *behind Prince Yŏngch'in*: Admiral Tōgō Heihachirō (*left*) and Katsura Tarō (*right*).

5. *Ŭibyŏng* ("righteous army") guerrillas surrendering at Mokp'o, South Cholla.

6. Japanese soldiers fighting the *ŭibyŏng* ("righteous army") guerrillas, February 1907.

7. Chongno, Seoul, ca. 1900.

8. The Japanese settlement at Namsan, Seoul, in 1895. (The Japanese legation and consulate are in the upper left corner; the resident association office is at left center; the other structures are residences, restaurants, and shops.)

9. Resident-General Itō Hirobumi (right center) greeting a group of Japanese primary school children in front of his official residence (the former Japanese legation) on the emperor's birthday, 1906.

10. Houses of settlers sponsored by the Oriental Development Company at Yongin, Kyŏnggi Province.

11.   Japanese sundries store at Kunsan, Chŏlla Province, mid-1910s. The store sold cotton cloth, dyes, sugar, flour, kerosene, matches, and other miscellaneous goods.

12. Sacks of soybeans ready for shipment, Inchon.

13. An 1878 *Marumaru chinbun* cartoon showing the countries of the world as a Doll Festival display.

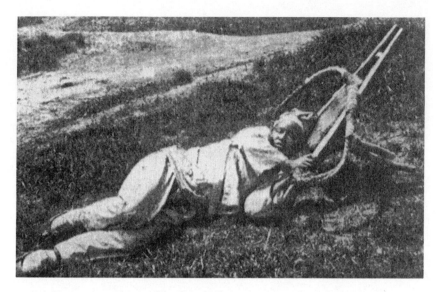

14. A Korean napping on his *chigi* (A-frame): a stereotypical image of the Korean male.

15. General Terauchi, the first governor-general of Korea, depicted opening the rock cave so that the "righteousness and justice" of the sun goddess, Amaterasu, shines on the Korean people. Cover of *Tōkyō Puck*, September 1910.

PART TWO

■   ■   ■

CHAPTER 7

Capturing the Market

Japanese Trade in Korea

During the late nineteenth century the question of how trade expansion was linked to political expansion provoked lively debate. Did trade follow the flag, or was the reverse true? As with most questions so starkly posed, the issue did not lend itself to an unambiguous answer. Few Japanese, however, believed that Japan could have acquired trading privileges on the peninsula without a show of force. As a writer in the journal of the Japan-Korea Trade Association noted in 1896, "To judge from the history of commercial development in the various countries of the world, it is indisputable that trade with a barbarian (*yaban*) or undeveloped (*mikaihatsu*) country cannot make progress without military force behind it. Certainly that is the case in Korea today."[1] Not only had the Korean market been opened by force, but it had been kept open by force in the early days. When local authorities attempted to block trade by a variety of stratagems in the late 1870s, the Japanese had no qualms about dispatching gunboats or naval vessels to back up official protests.

The Japanese political and military presence, however, was only a lever to wedge the market open; it could not guarantee that Japanese trade would succeed. That success depended rather on the shape and direction of Japanese economic development, particularly its overall relationship with the outside world. Indeed, one could argue that by the 1890s Japan's trade with Korea was determined largely, though not

---

1. *Nikkan tsūshō kyōkai hōkoku*, Apr. 1896, p. 24.

entirely, by that relationship. As the Japanese economy grew, so did Japan's economic dependence on the outside world. In 1885–86 imports and exports each amounted to about 6 percent of the gross national expenditure (GNE), but by 1898–1900 exports had risen to 10 percent and imports to 13 percent of GNE. The direction of trade had also shifted. In the mid-1880s Japan bought and sold mainly in the American and European markets, but by the turn of the century about half its trade was with Asia.

The transition in both the size and the direction of trade signaled a basic structural transformation in the Japanese economy. In the mid-1880s Japan was still a relatively backward, semicolonial society, selling agricultural products (silk yarn, tea, marine products, rice) or natural resources (copper and coal) to industrialized Western economies in exchange for machine-made consumer goods (cotton yarn, sugar, wool and cotton textiles, petroleum). By the turn of the century it had emerged as a newly industrializing country, increasingly able to sell the products of its light industry abroad, and increasingly impelled to buy raw materials and producer durable goods from the outside.[2]

From the viewpoint of the Japanese this structural change sorted the external market into two distinct spheres, a Western sphere and an East Asian sphere, each with its own pattern of trade. The pattern of trade with the advanced industrial countries of the West (Great Britain, Germany, and the United States) continued to be that of a semicolonial, peripheral, or late-developing country, exchanging products of the primary sector for manufactured goods. This trade was far more important to the Japanese than to its Western trading partners, for it provided inputs essential to Japan's own economic and industrial growth, and overall it was in deficit for the Japanese. By contrast, in its trade with the undeveloped countries of East Asia, Japan took the role of an advanced industrial country, buying raw materials or primary products and selling manufactured goods. This dual structure reflected the transitional character of the Japanese economy at the turn of the century.

From Europe came most of Japan's heavy industrial goods and semimanufactures. To build up the industrial sector, the Japanese imported locomotives, spinning machinery, steel rails, and steel plate from Great Britain and Germany. And since government arsenals were not able to keep up with the enormous expansion in demand for military hardware

2. Ōishi, *Nihon sangyō kakumei no kenkyū*, 1:63.

created by the Sino-Japanese and Russo-Japanese wars, Japan had to buy many instruments of war from Europe as well—steelclad warships, ammunition, explosives, and ordnance. Since all of these imports were costly, the products of advanced technology and capital-intensive production, Japan's trade with Europe was usually in deficit. The United States was Japan's second largest supplier of steel and heavy machinery, and it also supplied raw cotton for Japan's burgeoning cotton-spinning industry; but trade with the United States was in better balance and often in surplus for Japan. Although the surplus tended to decrease over time, from the mid-1880s through the post–Russo-Japanese War period, the Japanese continued to sell more to the United States than it bought there. Even at the turn of the century more than half of its silk yarn was sold in the United States.

In East Asia, Japan's chief market was China, a sprawling society of several hundred million people. To some extent trade with China involved an exchange of primary goods—iron products, copper, and coal from Japan in return for soybeans and soy flour from China. But trade revolving around the new Japanese cotton spinning and weaving industry steadily grew in importance. Not only was China a major source of raw cotton, but it also became the chief market for Japanese machine-spun cotton yarn.[3] The Japanese were less successful in penetrating the European colonial markets in Asia—British India, French Indo-China, and the Dutch East Indies. Although the Japanese bought raw cotton from India and rice from Indo-China, the domination of these colonies by metropolitan economies blocked the sale of Japanese manufactures there, and Japan's trade with these areas was usually in deficit.

In general, then, Japan acted like a developing country in its trade with the West and like a developed country in its trade with Asia. Japanese political and business leaders, mindful of this pattern, were keenly aware how tightly Japan's economic future was tied to outside markets. Expansion of foreign trade, especially the export of Japanese manufactures, was high on their agenda by the end of the Sino-Japanese War. Under pressure from the business community the Diet passed laws abolishing export duties on cotton yarn, abolishing import duties on raw cotton, subsidizing silk yarn exports, and subsidizing the construc-

3. Japan's chief competitors in China were the British; but more important, the Indian cotton industry, which originally developed as an import substitute industry, gradually came to dominate the cotton yarn and textile market east of Suez as the competitiveness of the British industry declined.

tion of merchant vessels and the establishment of long-distance ocean shipping lines. As Prime Minister Ōkuma observed in 1898, "Foreign trade has the largest connection with a country's national interests. It is so important that success or failure in foreign trade establishes a nation's success or failure."[4]

The Japanese leadership was also aware of Japan's comparative advantage as a country in the midst of a transition from backwardness to development. Kaneko Kentarō, a key figure in the Ministry of Agriculture and Commerce in the late 1890s, articulated a vision of Japan as an emerging industrial power. The country, he argued, could not hope to compete with Russia, the United States, or China as an agricultural exporter, but it was blessed with assets as an exporter of manufactured goods: it had ample supplies of coal, and its workers were superior in dexterity and mental skills to those in neighboring countries. The natural market for its manufactures lay not in Europe or the United States, where industry was more highly advanced than in Japan, but rather in Asia and the Pacific, where there was little or no indigenous industry and a growing demand for manufactured products, and where proximity enabled Japan to deliver its products at prices competitive with the West. It was here that Japan could sell the products of its growing light-industry sector—cotton yarn, cotton cloth, flannel, canned goods, cement, and the like.[5]

In the context of this overall pattern the growth in Japanese trade with Korea during the decade and a half before annexation was perfectly natural. One might even conclude that exactly such a trade relationship would have emerged, as it had with China, even if Japan had not extended its political hegemony over the peninsula. It may have been true that military force was necessary to open Korea to trade, but it by no means follows that political or military force was needed to expand it. As long as Japan could compete with Western manufacturers in the Korean market, and as long as the Koreans had agricultural surpluses to exchange for Japanese product, trade was bound to grow.

Trade was the economic magnet that attracted Japanese to the peninsula before annexation. For a variety of reasons, not the least important of which was the uncertain political atmosphere, big Japanese investors were reluctant to put their capital into large-scale manu-

4. Daisankai nōkōshō kōtō kaigiroku, 42.
5. Kaneko Kentarō, "Taigai kōgyō no hōshin," JNN 2.6 (June 1898): 5–8; 2.7 (July 1898): 6–10.

facturing or transportation enterprises in Korea without assurances of guaranteed returns. Investment in land or agriculture was hobbled by restrictions on the right of foreigners to buy land outside a narrow belt around the treaty ports. If profits were to be made in Korea, they were to be found in trade or activities in support of trade, and if there were economic incentives to go to Korea, these were to be found in the opportunity to engage in trade or to provide goods and services to those who did. In fact, the Japanese population in Korea was concentrated in the treaty ports, and its occupational structure was shaped by foreign trade. Whether one worked for a trading firm or a teahouse, a bank or a brothel, the flow of goods between Korea and Japan had a profound effect on one's livelihood.

In aggregate terms, trade with Korea was not of substantial importance to the metropolitan economy. It accounted for only a small proportion of Japan's external economic relations. Even during the years between the Russo-Japanese War and annexation (1906–10), a period when trade with Korea surged, on average the peninsula absorbed only 7 percent of all Japan's exports per year and provided only a little more than 3 percent of its imports. This put Korea far behind China, Japan's main trading partner, which absorbed about half of its exports and provided about one-third of its imports during the same period. The relative economic insignificance of Korea in contrast to China was generally recognized by Japanese officials. As Sakawa Tsuneaki, an official in the Ministry of Agriculture and Commerce, observed after an official tour to both countries in 1902, "After looking at China, looking at Korea is like looking at stones after looking at jewels. If one compares them in terms of weight, the difference is like that between a lantern and a temple bell. And if one talks in terms of value, it is like the difference between bones and meat." The feeling was shared by businessmen like Katō Masayoshi, president of the NYK steamship company, who said that "one cannot speak of Korea in the same breath with China."[6] However, Japan dominated Korean trade as it did not dominate China's. As Foreign Minister Komura pointed out, "There are those who ridicule our trade with Korea, but ridiculing creates a problem. Even though it amounts to only ¥8 million, the Korea trade differs from the China trade or trade with America in that the export and

---

6. *Meiji zenki sangyō hattatsu shi shiryō*, suppl. vol. 28:109–10; Katō Masayoshi, "Shinkoku ni oite kei'ei subeki jigyō," *JNN*, 1903, pp. 5–6. Similar comments, albeit with a bit more optimism about the economic future of Korea, can be found in *KSSH*, 25.

shipping of goods is handled entirely by the Japanese."[7] Thus, trade with Korea was an "important enterprise" not to be scorned.

THE BEGINNING OF JAPANESE TRADE IN KOREA

After the signing of the Treaty of Kanghwa, the Meiji government, anxious to consolidate a tangible Japanese presence on the peninsula, moved quickly to marshal trade in service of the flag. Since the Tsushima merchants and shippers involved in the traditional trade with Korea handled only a small volume of goods, and since older Osaka merchant houses like Mitsui, Shimada, and Ono showed little interest in the peninsula, the government took the initiative in promoting trade under the new treaty arrangements. By the mid-1870s top government officials like Ōkubo and Ōkuma had established working relationships with trusted businessmen like Iwasaki Yatarō, Ōkura Kihachirō, and Shibusawa Eiichi, all of whom had been involved in efforts to promote foreign trade through the establishment of shipping and trading concerns, participation in foreign trade expositions, the organization of chambers of commerce, and the like.[8] It was to these new businessmen that the government turned for help in establishing an economic foothold in Korea.

By the time the Japanese superintendent of trade arrived at Pusan in late October 1876, the government had already ordered the Mitsubishi Steamship Company, which had provided ships for the Kuroda-Inoue mission, to set up regular shipping service through Tsushima between Nagasaki and Pusan. The company, which assigned the steamship *Naniwa-maru* to the service, was provided with an annual subsidy of ¥5,000 for its pains. When Wŏnsan was opened in 1880, the company got an annual subsidy of ¥10,000 to open a Nagasaki-Wŏnsan route, and in 1881 it received a ten-year, no-interest loan of ¥80,000 to buy a new ship for a regular run from Nagasaki along the east coast of Korea through Wŏnsan to Vladivostok. Throughout the mid-1880s the government continued its subsidies to the company to maintain and expand service to Korea. The Mitsubishi monopoly on subsidized shipping routes ended only in 1887, when the Osaka Shipping Company was given an annual subsidy of ¥50,000 for a period of eight years to open service.

7. Gaimusho, *Komura gaikō shi*, 78.
8. Tiedemann, "Japan's Economic Foreign Policies," 118ff.

To prime the pump for trade, Ōkubo Toshimichi, the minister of the interior, turned to Ōkura Kichachirō, whose foreign trade company, the Ōkura-gumi Shōkai, was the first to set up a branch office in London. In late 1876 Ōkura sent off a shipment of miscellaneous goods, mainly modern foreign machine-manufactured textiles (wool cloth, cotton shirting, and Indian calicoes) and traditional Japanese handicraft products (silk brocade, simple utensils, and sundry goods).[9] Well aware that the government was anxious to promote trade with Korea, Ōkura sought the same special treatment that the Mitsubishi company enjoyed. In April 1877, shortly after the outbreak of the Satsuma rebellion, Ōkura petitioned the government for a no-interest loan of ¥150,000, secured by government bonds owned by the Ōkura-gumi, to purchase a vessel for a regular run to Korea and to set up a foreign exchange office and a trading office there. Pleading disingenuously that trade with Korea was not likely to turn a profit, he argued that the loan would help cover his losses. When top government leaders considered his proposal at a meeting in Kyoto, a majority opposed helping Ōkura as long as the fighting in Kyushu continued, but Ōkubo managed to push through a decision providing him with shipping.[10]

When a second petition for a ¥150,000 government loan failed to get approval later that year, Ōkura decided to recruit the help of the energetic Shibusawa Eiichi, president of the Dai-Ichi Bank and a protégé of Ōkuma Shigenobu and Inoue Kaoru. After each agreed to invest ¥25,000 of his own capital, Ōkura and Shibusawa asked the Ministry of Finance for a ¥100,000 loan to set up a foreign exchange office in Korea and the Home Ministry for permission to set up a thrice-monthly shipping run to Korea. The Ministry of Finance, where Shibusawa was well connected, agreed to make the loan once the Satsuma rebellion was over, but the Home Ministry, whose officials were partial to the Mitsubishi interests, turned down the request for the shipping route. With that came an end to Ōkura's efforts to build a predominant position in the

9. To market this first modest shipment of foreign goods, the newly established Ōkuraya at Pusan adjusted to local custom. Since the Koreans were not used to dealing with foreigners directly, a display of goods, more like a bazaar or fair than a shop, was set out at a local temple. Several hundred curious Koreans, many of them coming from some distance, flocked to the Japanese settlement to sightsee and buy, but Korean merchants still had difficulty understanding how the Japanese did business. Accustomed to haggling, they could not understand what the price tags on the Japanese goods were for, nor did they realize they could get discounts for large purchases. And when the Koreans paid for goods in cash, the Ōkura men suddenly realized that they had no safe place to store it. *SEDS*, 16:8–9, 639–42.

10. *Ōkura zaibatsu no kenkyū*, 50–55.

Korea trade by integrating shipping, banking, and marketing operations into a single enterprise.[11]

Despite the failure of the joint venture, Shibusawa decided to extend his own banking operations into Korea. In June 1878 the Ministry of Finance granted the Dai-Ichi Bank permission to set up a Pusan branch of the Dai-Ichi Bank; half of the branch's ¥100,000 capital came from a government loan. In return for this support, the Dai-Ichi Bank was to provide financial services for the Japanese engaged in trade—foreign exchange transactions, secured loans, acceptance of deposits, and the like. The government put up another ¥10,000 loan to provide the bank with circulating capital, and the Pusan consulate used it as a fiscal agent for the disbursement of funds. Since it also served as the local agent for the Tokyo Marine Insurance Company, the Pusan branch of the Dai-Ichi Bank, the only financial organ in the newly opened port, soon found business flourishing. When Wŏnsan and Inchon were opened in 1880 and 1883, respectively, the bank set up offices in both ports. The Inchon branch handled not only the local consulate's finances but also those of the legation at Seoul. During the 1880s the bank's importance as a facilitator of the Japan-Korea trade grew. Its reputation for honesty and efficiency attracted business from the Korean government as well. In 1883 the German-born superintendent of the newly established Korean Customs Service, Paul Georg von Mollendorf, agreed to let the bank handle the customs revenues, and in 1884 the bank began to buy up gold dust to supply the newly established Bank of Japan with metal to back its convertible notes.

Like the Mitsubishi Shipping Company, the Dai-Ichi Bank enjoyed the advantage of getting into the Korean trade on the ground floor. Other modern-style business enterprises, particularly those without close government connections, were less successful. In 1877, for example, the Sumitomo Trading Company exported to Pusan a test shipment of 10,000 kin (13,200 pounds) of copper ore from the Besshi mines. The following year the trading company set up a branch office in Pusan, and in 1880 one in Wŏnsan as well. Although Sumitomo had an advantage in controlling its own supplies of copper ore and shipped goods in its own ships, it had to buy and sell other goods—textiles, kanpyo, gold, rice, and so forth—in competition with other Japanese. When Hirose Saihei, the chief Sumitomo bantō, visited Korea in 1883, he concluded that prospects were not very promising and decided to close both

11. Ibid., 55–58.

branches.[12] Other banks and shipping companies began to move into Korea in the late 1880s as the volume of trade expanded, but the Dai-Ichi Bank and the Mitsubishi Steamship Company, both with substantial direct and indirect financial support from the government in Tokyo, dominated the infrastructure of Japan's trade with Korea.

In terms of sheer numbers, however, the managers and office workers of metropolitan banks, shipping companies, and trading companies were less important in the Korean trade during the 1880s and early 1890s than were small-scale merchants, skippers, wholesalers, contractors, peddlers, and warehousers. Few if any of these small-scale operators enjoyed the kind of government patronage or support that the metropolitan firms did. During the early days many were petty merchants and dealers from Tsushima who had been involved in the pre-treaty trade; others were laborers or artisans who drifted to Pusan from the main islands, mainly the western prefectures, in search of work or profit. For the most part the Japanese traders came to Korea as sojourners, with no intention to put down roots, interested only in turning a quick profit before returning home. Usually capital poor, often with only the barest resources, they would scramble for whatever business they could get, hoping to parley a meager stake into a small fortune. Many of them failed, went broke, and returned with their pockets as empty as when they arrived. A handful of these hustlers, by dint of good luck, hard work, unscrupulousness, or some combination of all three, succeeded in building small trading operations, buying and selling their way to positions of prominence in the small expatriate treaty port communities.

While government officials were willing to lavish support and subsidies on large-scale firms based at home, they sometimes took a dim view of the petty treaty port merchants.[13] However, these same mer-

---

12. Takashima, *Chōsen ni okeru shokuminchi*, 234–235; Shikata, "Chōsen ni okeru kindai shihonshugi," 162–64.

13. Often these expatriate treaty port merchants were not entirely fastidious in their methods. For example, Ōike Tadasuke, a native of Tsushima who arrived in Pusan when the port opened for trade and eventually became one of the richest men in the city, later recalled his early days as follows: "I was authorized to engage in official trade from 1876, but I was unable to make money in broad daylight, so I carried on my trade by smuggling goods in the dark, without control or punishment by the Korean authorities, while the Japanese officials openly tolerated my secret activity. After all I had to do it in a clandestine way, because this private trade brought me 200–300 percent profit.... In order to maintain smooth relations with the native merchants and to facilitate my commercial transactions I loaned money to them from time to time, but they would not pay their debts when called, so at night I traveled as far as Ch'oryang and Pusan-chin to collect the loans, when dogs barked at me and stones flew from all directions, putting me to flight with swellings

chants served as intermediaries between the Korean market and the trading interests at home. In contrast to the Western merchants in the treaty ports of China, the Japanese merchants did not rely much on native go-betweens like the compradores, shroffs, or linguists but dealt directly with Korean customers and suppliers. They were the shock troops of Japanese economic penetration, an aggressive rank and file busily reconnoitering new markets, scouting out new products, and building new economic networks. When they strayed beyond the limits of the treaty settlement, they often found themselves subject to official harassment and even physical abuse. The only government support they enjoyed was the continuing presence of Japanese gunboats in the ports and off the coasts, ready to come to their aid in case of trouble.[14]

The early arrivals in Pusan enjoyed a monopoly on Korea's foreign trade until the early 1880s. No other country had a trade treaty with Korea, nor were there any foreigners but Japanese at Pusan. Under the terms of the trade regulations the Japanese could carry on trade under the same set of rules they could at home: they paid no tariffs, they could use their own currency, they could travel to and from Pusan as they pleased, and they were subject to their own law, not Korean law. And they enjoyed an advantage that made for lucrative business. Since the Koreans had no knowledge of market conditions or prices abroad, and since the Japanese had no obligation to declare the cost of import goods as they would have had they been subject to customs, the Japanese could charge more or less what the market would bear without arousing the distrust of the Koreans, who were endlessly fascinated with the exotic Western goods the traders brought in. It was not uncommon for some importers to mark up prices by as much as 1000 percent, and similar profits were possible in the export trade as well. In the 1870s one *koku* of rice that cost ¥0.40–0.45 in Korea could be sold in Japan for ¥6.00–8.00. Little wonder that many who swarmed to Pusan dreamed of quick and easy riches.[15]

---

on my forehead, and yet this adventure had to be repeated again and again in order to save money." Quoted in Kim Ui-hwan, "Japanese in Pusan," 88. Ōike's perseverance was rewarded. By the 1890s his business was flourishing. His firm, with branches in Osaka, Wŏnsan, and elsewhere, employed a large number of clerks and workers, and it served as an agency for the NYK line. With the bumps on his forehead long since cured, Ōike had become an important personage in the treaty port, a man of considerable property, respected enough to serve not only as the head of the chamber of commerce but also as speaker of the local residents' assembly.

14. Kang Tok-sang, "Yi-shi Chōsen kaikō chokugo," 1–2.
15. Ibid., 1–3.

Since Japan had only just embarked on building up a modern manu-facturing sector, Japanese merchants engaged mainly in a carrying trade, marketing in Korea foreign goods bought from British merchant houses in Shanghai, then transshipped through Nagasaki to Pusan, Wŏnsan, and eventually Inchon. During the period 1876–82 Western-made goods, mainly cloth and woven goods but other cheap manu-factures as well, accounted for 88 percent of Japanese exports to Korea, and Japanese only 12 percent. Profits on these goods were lower than on the Japanese-made handicraft items like silk, sake, lacquer, and matches, but there was an insatiable demand for them.

The Japanese carried home mainly products of primary industry—rice, soybeans, and leather. Most of the rice, which was extremely cheap in comparison to Japanese rice, went to urban consumers at home, and demand eventually grew to the point that Korean rice prices were quoted in the market at Osaka, its main destination. The rice trade, however, was volatile, with volume and prices fluctuating markedly from year to year, depending on harvest conditions at home and in Korea. An abundant harvest in Korea and a poor crop at home meant big profits, but the reverse situation depressed the trade. Until 1882 rice was the biggest Korean export to Japan, but a sudden fall in Japanese rice prices, caused by the Matsukata deflation, hurt the trade. Soybeans, by contrast, were a sturdier crop, less susceptible to changing weather than rice. Similar to domestically grown Japanese beans in quality and moisture content, Korean soybeans were also easy to process into tofu. As the cheapness and quality of Korean soybeans became known at home, the demand grew, and when Korean farmers discovered that Japanese merchants were willing to pay a good price, they began to put more land into the crop.[16] When Japanese demand for rice slackened in the mid-1880s, soybeans became the most important staple exported from Korea to Japan.[17]

In the early 1880s the Japanese monopoly on Korean foreign trade was broken when the Western powers negotiated trade treaties with the Korean court. The main competition came not from the British, the Americans, or the French but from the Chinese. Traditional Sino-Korean trade across the northern border had suffered with the opening of Pusan and Wŏnsan to the Japanese. While few reliable statistics

16. *Genzan hattatsushi*, 1916, pp. 83–84.
17. Kang Tok-sang, "Yi-shi Chōsen kaikō chokugo," 5–8; Takashima, *Chōsen ni okeru shokuminchi*, 220ff.; Im Pyong-yun, *Shokuminchi ni okeru shōgyōteki nōgyō*, 36–38.

are available, one scholar has estimated that before the Kanghwa treaty its annual value was ¥3–4 million, more than twenty times as large as the Pusan-Tsushima trade (whose average volume for 1873–76 was ¥130,000.) By 1881, according to one report, imports from China had dropped to ¥395,000, or about one-fifth of the value of imports from Japan. Whatever the precise figures, the trend was unmistakable. The Japanese were able to deliver foreign manufactures more cheaply than the Chinese could. A length of machine-made shirting that cost ¥4.8 in the north could be had for only ¥3.8 at Pusan or Wŏnsan. And the Japanese were more eager than the Chinese to buy Korean products like rice and leather, and they were willing to pay higher prices for them.[18]

To break the new Japanese hold on the market, the Chinese persuaded the Korean court to accept a set of trade regulations with China. While Japanese trade continued to grow in absolute terms, by the late 1880s Japanese consuls were reporting (and lamenting) a relative decline in the face of Chinese competition. In 1885 the value of Japanese imports at the three main ports (Pusan, Wŏnsan, and Inchon) had been four times that of the Chinese, but by 1892 the Chinese had nearly pulled even. While the Japanese continued to hold their own at Pusan, the Chinese made serious inroads in the trade at Inchon and Wŏnsan, gradually supplanting Japanese domination of the markets there. There was little doubt that growing Chinese political influence at Seoul gave the Chinese merchants an advantage. Yuan Shih-kai did his best to promote trade. After the China Merchants' Steamship Company set up regular shipping service in 1883, Chinese merchants were discouraged from using Japanese bottoms, and Yuan provided funds to set up a shipping and freight company to carry goods from Inchon to the capital.[19]

Chinese merchants did not encounter the cultural hostility the Japanese often experienced. While the Koreans looked down on the Japanese as vulgar, money-grubbing "dwarf barbarians," they regarded the Chinese as bearers of civilization. Indeed, the lifestyle of many marginal small-scale Japanese traders invited the contempt of the Koreans. One old-timer later recalled that the Japanese settlement at the foot of Namsan in Seoul was a "nest of beggars" (*binbōjin no sukutsu*).[20] Japanese consuls also complained that the Japanese traders, who were in search of quick profits and had little interest in developing long-term

18. Kang Tok-sang, "Yi-shi Chōsen kaikō chokugo," 9–11.
19. *Keijō-fu shi*, 2:617–18.
20. Ibid., appendix, p. 29

trade, were often cold and brutal in their dealings with the Koreans. By contrast, the Chinese merchants were cordial and ingratiating, cultivating their customers and doing their best to accommodate them. All other things being equal, the Koreans were more inclined to deal with the Chinese than with the Japanese.

All other things were not equal, however, for the Chinese had certain economic and managerial advantages over the Japanese. First, under the trade regulations Chinese merchants were not confined to the treaty ports as the Japanese and the Westerners were. They were permitted to settle in the interior, giving them superior access to Korean marketing networks and more direct contact with Korean customers and suppliers. Chinese import goods were often better suited to Korean tastes, and the Chinese did their best to offer favorable credit. Second, the Chinese merchants could sell foreign manufactured merchandise at lower prices than the Japanese. While the Japanese brought in foreign textiles by way of Nagasaki, where a Japanese trademark was often added, the Chinese merchants brought them in directly from Shanghai. Fewer middlemen were involved, and transaction and shipping costs were lower. According to one contemporary estimate, by the 1880s it cost a Chinese merchant only ¥2.00 to bring in a bale of calicoes that cost a Japanese merchant ¥4.00. Third, the Chinese were willing to take lower profits. Whereas a Chinese merchant might take a ¥0.07 commission on a length of calicoes, a Japanese merchant, interested mainly in a quick profit, might charge ten times as much. Finally, the Chinese had lower capital costs than the capital-poor Japanese traders, who had to borrow from private moneylenders to finance their operations since their credit rating was low with the Dai-Ichi Bank and other banks operating in Korea. Rates were high, often 10–20 percent, in contrast to the 5–6 percent rate most Chinese enjoyed. Had the Japanese traders pooled their resources as the Chinese did, suggested a Japanese consul at Wŏnsan, they might have been able to do better, but instead they simply undercut one another by their aggressively self-aggrandizing methods.[21]

The reaction of the Japanese trading interests in Korea to the rise of Chinese competition was mixed. While the increase in Chinese competition occasioned concern both in the treaty ports and at home, it does not appear to have generated much demand for aggressive political action. For example, in September 1893 the commercial section of the Osaka Chamber of Commerce, in proposing ways to expand the

21. Pak Jong-keun, "Nisshin sensō to Chōsen bōeki," 1–3; NGNSB, 1:123–25.

Korean trade, focused on managerial and economic measures: better market information from the Japanese chambers of commerce in the treaty ports; better information from Japanese consuls about the prices, types, and quality of goods that sold well; better information about local products, taxes, currency, and finances in Korea; and measures to encourage Japanese banks in Korea and Shanghai to facilitate foreign exchange transactions so that the Japanese could buy Western goods more easily in Shanghai for reexport to Korea.[22] This was a relatively mild set of tactics for overcoming Japan's disadvantages in the Korean market, predicated on the assumption that these disadvantages were economic rather than political.

However, both treaty ports merchants and Japanese officials were very much concerned about embargoes imposed by local Korean officials on the rice trade. Embargoes were a traditional Korean method of dealing with local grain shortages. Drought, early frost, or floods might bring a poor harvest, and a poor harvest forced up grain prices. In times of want, when the danger of popular unrest, peasant risings, or military insurrection increased, officials would respond by prohibiting trade in grain, confiscating rice bought or sold, or banning the transportation of rice out of the province. Grain embargoes, in other words, traditionally served as a social safety check to overcome temporary local shortages in the food supply.

With the opening of the ports, many local Korean officials saw grain export embargoes as a way of restraining the commercial activities of the Japanese. The terms of the Kanghwa treaty, however, prohibited the practice. In 1881 the Korean government attempted to renegotiate the treaty to permit the Korean government to embargo the export of rice, barley, and soybeans, but the Japanese rejected the idea. The Japanese position softened when the 1882 treaty between the United States and Korea included a provision permitting grain embargoes. When the trade regulations with Korea were renegotiated in 1883, the government in Tokyo, reluctant to antagonize the Korean court in the wake of the 1882 incident, agreed that in the event of food shortages caused by military disturbances, floods, or other natural disasters, the Korean authorities could ban the export of grain if they gave the local Japanese consul a month's notice.

After the Koreans recovered this small fragment of their sovereignty, grain embargoes became a persistent problem between the two govern-

22. *Ōsaka shōgyō kaigisho geppō* 14 (Oct. 1893).

ments, particularly after 1885, as more and more Japanese merchants began making their way into the interior when restrictions on travel outside the treaty settlements were lifted. Local officials, intent on keeping the Japanese out of their turf, would often impose embargoes without following the procedures laid out in the trade regulations, and the Japanese merchants would respond by calling on local Japanese consuls to protest the embargoes and by demanding indemnities from the Korean government for their losses. The consuls and the legation at Seoul backed the merchants' demands, and nearly all of the incidents were resolved by the willingness of the Koreans to lift the embargoes and dismiss local officials who issued them. But the demands for indemnities for merchant losses were more troublesome, and they often led to long and acrimonious negotiations, such as those that resulted from three grain embargoes imposed in 1889–90—two in Hwanghae and one in Hamgyŏng—involving claims of ¥215,000 by forty-seven Japanese merchants, all but two of them treaty port residents.[23]

By the end of 1892 the indemnity question had drawn the attention of the political opposition in the House of Representatives. Anxious to placate the Jiyūtō, Foreign Minister Mutsu Munemitsu began to press the Koreans more vigorously for a settlement of the indemnity issue. In November Hara Takashi, chief of the commerce bureau, even suggested sending gunboats to seize customs revenues or local tax revenues if the Korean government did not settle the matter. When Ōishi Masami, a prominent Jiyūtō leader for whom the indemnity issue was a matter of "national prestige," was appointed minister to Seoul, he too recommended summoning gunboats. The more cautious Mutsu, anxious not to stir up the other powers, tried to get the Chinese to intervene instead. When that failed, he decided to present the Koreans with an ultimatum. After a stormy audience with the Korean king in early May, when the king became so incensed at Ōishi for bringing up the indemnity matter to him personally that he pronounced a death sentence on the interpreter, the Japanese finally delivered an ultimatum demanding a settlement within two weeks and prepared to call Ōishi home.[24] On May 19, 1893, the Koreans agreed to an indemnity of ¥110,000, and the matter was settled.[25]

The embargo issue was not dead, however. In October 1893 the

23. Yoshino, "Yi-chō makki."
24. NA, Dispatch Book, U.S. Legation to Seoul, Heard to Gresham, May 5, 1893.
25. It was later rumored that the Korean official investigating the Japanese claims had been bribed to make a favorable judgement. Ibid., Heard to Gresham, Aug. 26, 1893.

Korean king issued a decree prohibiting the export of all rice from the country. Because of long and unseasonable rains, crop failure throughout the country had been predicted and the price of rice had begun to rise. Ostensibly the king announced the embargo to prevent further food shortages and price rises. But many, including the American diplomat Horace Allen, suspected that Yuan Shih-kai was behind the ban. As Allen reported to the State Department, "It has long been known that the Chinese used the prospective famine to get in a master stroke against Japanese trade."[26] Since the Koreans could not sell their grain to the Japanese, they could not buy Japanese imports. "The result," speculated Allen, "will be the failure of the Japanese banks and merchants here, and the withdrawal of the steamship lines, unless the Koreans act reasonably."[27]

The local Japanese chambers of commerce in Inchon, Pusan, Wŏnsan, and Seoul vigorously complained to the foreign ministry and to the Seoul legation about the ban. There was no good reason for the decree, they said. Investigations in the interior indicated that the harvest would be a fair one, except in several parts of Chŏlla and Kyŏngsang. If the harvest really was bad, prices would rise higher than prices in Japan and the Koreans would be reluctant to sell to the Japanese. If the crop was abundant, as seemed likely, then the embargo would inflict hard times on the countryside by artificially forcing prices down and reducing the buying power of the Korean peasants. In either case, the ban would bring stagnation in trade, to the detriment of both Koreans and Japanese.[28] Under pressure from the Japanese and the Americans, the grain embargo was withdrawn in January 1894, and the grain embargo problem remained dormant until a new round of bans was issued in the late 1890s.[29]

Disputes over indemnities to Japanese grain merchants were unlikely to provoke a "bean war" with Korea, but they did leave a residue of tension and uncertainty among the Japanese trading interests in Korea. Despite rising competition from the Chinese, the Japanese still remained

26. Ibid., Allen to Gresham, Dec. 20, 1893; see also Allen to Gresham, Nov. 20, 1893.
27. Ibid., Allen to Gresham, Nov. 7, 1893.
28. Keijō-fu shi, 1:554–58.
29. There is some evidence to support the Japanese claim that the famine conditions did not exist. In April Horace Allen reported that the Chinese had begun shipping rice to Korea to relieve the famine conditions. "Rice began to come in from China by the shipload. There was no room at the Port, and it is piled high in the streets.... The Japanese are buying it and shipping it to Japan." NA, Dispatch Book, U.S. Legation to Seoul, Allen to Gresham, Apr. 6, 1894. This comment suggests that the Chinese deliberately attempted to manipulate the market to the advantage of Chinese merchants.

Korea's most important trading partner. But that position was vulnerable to political intervention, and the national embargo promulgated by
the king in October 1893 deepened anxiety that Japanese trade might be
undermined by Chinese intrigue if not Chinese competition. Events,
however, soon swept these anxieties away. The approach of hostilities in
1894 brought boom times for the Japanese traders in Korea. Competition from the Chinese, which had so upset treaty port residents and
consuls in the early 1890s, suddenly vanished, leaving the field open for
the Japanese. With rumors of war in the air, the Chinese began to pack
their goods. In late July, when news of Yuan Shih-kai's stealthy exit
from Seoul spread through the city, the Chinese merchant community
scrambled to leave before the fighting began. And even though many
Chinese remained in interior towns and cities, trade with China came to
a near standstill.[30] As the Japanese consul in Seoul observed, the war
provided a "golden opportunity" to expand trade.

THE GROWTH OF THE KOREAN TRADE, 1894–1910

The influx of Japanese troops in the summer of 1894 created a sudden
increase in demand for Japanese sundries, but the deflection of merchant
shipping for military use meant shortages in supply. The price of ordinary Japanese goods leapt upward in Inchon, the main point of disembarkation for the Japanese army. A *kin* (1.32 pound) of sugar went
from ¥0.08 to ¥0.17; a loaf of wheat bread from ¥0.70 to ¥1.20; a can
of kerosene from ¥1.20 to ¥2.50; a ton of coal from ¥6.50 to ¥15.00.
Rice, meat, eggs, and other foodstuffs were also scarce since the Japanese merchants in the port had nothing to barter for them. As a result,
a steady stream of Japanese civilians from the home islands began to
arrive in Inchon, their bags stuffed with sake, tobacco, sugar, shirts,
gloves, and cold-weather gear on which they hoped to make a quick
profit. By the fall they were pouring in at a rate of one thousand a
month, putting a heavy strain on the resources of the port. When the
front line moved north into Manchuria after the battle of P'yŏngyang in
mid-September, the military procurement boomlet died down, but there
were still opportunities to be exploited.[31]

The departure of the Chinese from the peninsula opened the market
for cotton goods. From September 1894 the sale of calicoes imported

30. Pak Jong-keun, "Nisshin sensō to Chōsen bōeki," 6–7; *Keijō-fu shi*, appendix,
pp. 22–23; Hulbert, *History of Korea*, 2:265.
31. Pak Jong-keun, "Nisshin sensō to Chōsen bōeki," 3–5.

from Japan began to improve markedly. Since no supplies were coming from China in time to make winter clothes, the Koreans turned to Japanese suppliers. To meet the increased demand for calicoes, the Tokyo government freed merchant ships to carry cotton goods to Korea, and the Yokohama Specie Bank facilitated the ordering of calicoes directly from Manchester with a single telegram by putting up guarantee money. Big Osaka merchants began to ship not only foreign cotton goods but Japanese manufactures as well. The army quartermaster allowed treaty port merchants to set up shops at Japanese supply bases in the interior to sell calicoes to local Koreans. Nearly everybody in the treaty ports—not only the regular foreign trade firms but bakers, barbers, and laundrymen—tried to get into the calico trade. In the rush to make money, many shoddy goods were shipped to Korea. The Ministry of Agriculture and Commerce, fearing that the reputation of Japanese goods would be damaged in the long run, sent an official to visit chambers of commerce in the cotton-manufacturing districts to counsel against this practice.[32]

The increase in demand for Japanese imports was also stimulated by an increase in the circulation of Japanese currency on the peninsula. The Korean porters, coolies, and suppliers hired by the Japanese military were paid in Japanese yen. Since many Koreans had little confidence in this unfamiliar foreign currency, they converted it quickly to Korean currency, often at very low rates of exchange. Many also got rid of their yen by buying goods from Japanese merchants. All of this produced sudden wealth, and suddenly money poured into Japanese banks in Korea. Between March 1894 and March 1895 deposits in the Inchon branch of the Dai-Ichi Bank rose from ¥26,500 to ¥232,000; and the total deposits in all three main Japanese bank branches in Inchon (the Dai-Ichi, the Eighteenth, and the Fifty-eighth Banks) quadrupled between May 1894 and November 1895. And as credit built up, interest rates came down.[33]

The growth in Japanese trade did not end with the war. Between 1895 and 1904 Japanese exports to Korea grew from ¥3.8 million to ¥20.4 million, and imports from ¥2.9 million to ¥6.4 million (table 2). In 1895 Korea had bought only 2.8 percent of all Japanese exports; by 1904 it bought 6.4 percent; and by 1908, 8.0 percent. Indeed, between 1908 and 1910 Korea rose to become the fourth largest customer of Japan after the United States, China, and France, all much larger and

32. Ibid., 5–10.
33. Ibid., 11.

TABLE 2   JAPAN–KOREA TRADE, 1876–1911

| | Japan–Korea trade | | | | | Korea–Japan trade | |
| | Commodity exports | | Commodity imports | | Gold and silver imports | Commodity imports | Commodity exports |
Year	¥000s	%[a]	¥000s	%[a]	¥000s	%[b]	%[b]
1876	20	0.1	13	0.1			
1877	315	1.4	124	0.5			
1878	245	0.9	205	0.6	22		
1879	567	2.0	677	2.0	54		
1880	974	3.4	1,256	3.3	114		
1881	1,945	6.0	1,372	4.2	468		
1882	1,587	4.1	1,202	3.9	530		
1883	2,167	5.7	1,010	3.4	564		
1884	213	0.6	276	0.9	324		
1885	462	1.2	471	1.6	810	81.5	98.6
1886	829	1.7	563	1.8	1,078	81.9	96.8
1887	552	1.1	1,010	2.3	1,222	73.7	97.6
1888	707	1.1	1,042	1.6	1,214	71.9	91.6
1889	1,093	1.6	1,273	1.9	886	67.6	91.1
1890	1,251	2.2	4,364	5.3	369	65.0	98.0
1891	1,466	1.8	4,033	6.4	299	60.0	95.9
1892	1,411	1.5	3,046	4.3	396	55.3	93.0
1893	1,301	1.5	1,999	2.3	525	50.2	90.0
1894	2,365	2.1	2,183	1.9	556	62.5	88.8
1895	3,831	2.8	2,925	2.3	1,231	72.2	95.3
1896	3,368	2.9	5,119	3.0	838	65.8	93.0
1897	5,197	3.2	8,864	4.0	1,006	63.9	90.2
1898	5,844	3.6	4,796	1.8	1,063	57.4	79.2
1899	6,996	3.3	4,976	2.3	2,434	65.1	84.2
1900	9,953	5.0	8,806	3.4	2,970	75.3	76.6
1901	11,373	4.5	10,052	3.9	4,844	61.6	87.5
1902	10,554	4.1	7,958	2.9	6,049	64.2	78.8
1903	11,761	4.1	8,912	2.8	5,422	63.4	80.2
1904	20,390	6.4	6,401	1.7	5,142	70.9	82.2
1905	26,619	8.3	6,151	1.3	5,418	73.7	78.1
1906	25,210	5.9	8,206	2.0	5,861	77.3	85.1
1907	32,792	7.6	16,372	3.3	5,452	66.0	76.7
1908	30,273	8.0	13,718	3.1	5,027	58.6	77.8
1909	26,998	6.5	14,139	3.6	6,400	59.6	74.4
1910	31,450	6.7	16,902	3.6	10,797	63.7	77.2
1911	41,688	8.5	15,802	3.0	15,117		

[a] Imports and exports with Korea as a percentage of overall Japanese foreign trade.
[b] Imports and exports with Japan as a percentage of overall Korean trade through the treaty ports.

SOURCE: Murakami Katsuhiko, "Shokuminchi," in Ōishi Kaichirō, *Nihon sangyō kakumei no kenkyū*, 2:233.

more populous countries. From 1898 onward the trade balance shifted in Japan's favor. While the Japanese were not able to reestablish the trade monopoly they had enjoyed until 1882, they did manage to recapture the market share lost to the Chinese before the war.[34]

The bulk of trade flowed through the ports of Inchon and Pusan. In Japan, Osaka and to a lesser extent Kobe gradually supplanted Nagasaki as the main ports of departure for Japanese manufactures and the main ports of entry for Korean rice and other goods. In 1905 an official report observed, "The Japan-Korea trade really ought to be called the Osaka-Korea trade."[35] From the early 1890s the Osaka business community had shown increased interest in the prospects for trade with Korea, and more Kansai enterprises began to engage in trade. In July 1890 the Osaka Shipping Company established a regular run from Osaka to Pusan; the Osaka-based Fifty-eighth Bank set up a branch office in Pusan in 1893 and another in Seoul in 1895; and the chief Japanese trading firms in Korea set up their main offices in Osaka as well.[36] In 1904 a special mission sent by the Osaka Chamber of Commerce to explore economic and trading conditions in Korea came back with a report filled with optimistic prognostications about the future of Korea as a market and source of supply.

The remarkable growth in imports from Japan undoubtedly was influenced by the Japanese military and political presence, but, as we have seen, that presence was still rather fragile immediately after the Sino-Japanese War. A rise in Korean demand for foreign goods in the late 1890s was probably a more significant factor. The Korean government's halting program of reform in the late 1890s increased government need for everything from police uniforms to building materials. Exposure to the outside world also created a vogue for Western-style clothing—suits, hats, umbrellas, and shoes—much like the faddish pursuit of "civilization and enlightenment" in Japan during the 1870s. In the countryside as well, commercialization of agriculture, accelerated both by the collection of taxes in money and the growth of the rice trade with Japan, brought well-to-do peasants and landlords new wealth, and doubtless some of this new wealth shaped new patterns of consumption as well.

The Japanese advance into the Korean market depended on certain advantages enjoyed over foreign competitors. First, in contrast to the Westerners, the Japanese enjoyed the advantage of proximity to Korea.

34. Ōishi, *Nihon sangyō kakumei no kenkyū*, 2:233–36, 241–45.
35. Nōshōmushō Shōkōkyoku, *Kankoku jijō chōsa shiryō*, 78.
36. Yamada Shōji, "Meiji zenki no Ni-Chō bōeki," 65–68.

While Western countries might supply heavy industrial goods that Japan could not—railroad rails, rolling stock, heavy machinery, and the like—other Western products could not compete so well. The Korean market was several weeks from Europe and the United States but only a day or two from Japan. As a result, Western manufacturers and traders did not attach much importance to the Korean market, and they usually marketed products like kerosene, flour, and sugar through Chinese merchants. Second, in contrast to the Chinese, who were equally close to Korea, the Japanese had the advantage of a growing industrial base, particularly in the production of cotton yarn and cloth, and they had a wider range of goods to sell. While tɪ e Chinese continued to engage in a carrying trade for foreign manufactures, the Japanese were able to sell their own domestic manufactures. Consumer goods imported to supply the Japanese residents educated the Koreans, especially the upper classes, to new possibilities for consumption. Third, the Japanese also came to dominate the infrastructure of Korean trade. Most of Korea's foreign trade was carried in Japanese bottoms, most of the established treaty port trading houses were Japanese, and the most important trade currency was the Japanese yen. After Bank of Japan convertible notes were recognized by the Korean government as legal tender, their circulation began to spread from the ports to the interior, easing transactions for the Japanese.[37] Finally, one should not forget that Japanese merchants and businessmen worked hard to build the Korean trade, aggressively and persistently exploring new markets, new products, and new sources of supply. As Isabella Bird Bishop noted, the Japanese were "the most nimble-witted, adaptive, persevering and pushing people of our day. It is inevitable that British hardware and miscellaneous articles must be ousted by the products of Japanese cheaper labor, and that the Japanese will continue to supply the increasing demand for scissors, knives, matches, perfume, kerosene lamps, iron cooking pots, nails, and the like."[38]

THE SUNDRY TRADE

Nowhere was the enterprise of the Japanese more evident than in their attempts to penetrate the interior market for sundry goods. As many foreign observers remarked, the main vehicle for retail consumer trade

37. Nōshōmushō Shōkokyoku, *Kankoku jijō chōsa shiryō*, 155–56.
38. Bishop, *Korea and Her Neighbors*, 2:214.

in Korea was not the small retail shop but the periodic market held on regular days in village or town centers.[39] Market centers were usually two to six *ri* apart, and market days were staggered so that native peddlers could make their rounds carrying goods in carts or on their backs in A-frames (*chigi*). Local residents traded their agricultural or handcrafted products and bought goods carried to the market by the itinerant merchants. Two great national fairs at Taegu and Kongju in the spring and fall attracted merchants from all over the country, but even at these fairs most buying and selling was carried out by barter. In 1904 the Osaka Chamber of Commerce mission was surprised to discover that very little cash passed hands at the great market in Taegu. One man would exchange his rice for another man's cloth, and everyone seemed determined to sell or barter everything they had brought to the market, even if it meant selling cheap and buying dear.[40]

The observant Isabella Bird Bishop provides us with a lively description of a Korean market day:

> At the weekly market the usual melancholy dullness of a Korean village is exchanged for bustle, colour, and crowds of men. From an early hour in the morning the paths leading to the officially-appointed center are thronged with peasants bringing in their wares for sale or barter ... while the main road has its complement of merchants, *i.e.* pedlars, mostly fine, strong, well-dressed men, either carrying their heavy packs themselves or employing porters and bulls for the purpose. These men travel on regular circuits to the village centers, and are industrious and respectable. A few put up stalls.... But most of the articles ... are exposed for sale on low tables or on mats on the ground, the merchant giving the occupant of the house before which he camps a few *cash* for the accommodation.[41]

By the end of the Sino-Japanese War many Japanese were convinced that the long-term success of Japanese trade, especially the sale of Japanese manufactures, depended on their ability to penetrate this interior trade network. Chinese merchants, for example, traveled to the interior, moving from market to market like the native peddlers, sometimes buying houses to set up small shops or retail operations. As a writer in the journal of the Japan-Korea Trade Association noted, this gave the Chinese great advantage as did the fact that the Koreans "respect the Chinese, and dislike our fellow countrymen."[42] It was natural to conclude that if they wanted to compete with the Chinese, the Japanese

39. Cf. Percival Lowell, *Chōson*, 218–19.
40. *KSSH*, 35.
41. Bishop, *Korea and Her Neighbors*, 2:106.
42. *Nikkan tsūshō kyōkai hokoku*, Sept. 1895, p. 99.

themselves should engage in the interior peddler trade. In a country still lacking railroads, telegraph lines, paved roads, or even good riverine shipping, what better way was there to learn about local markets and products?

During the Sino-Japanese War some venturesome small merchants began to move into the interior. The presence of the Japanese military forces made travel safer than it normally was. As a result of the fighting in P'yŏngyang, for example, much of the city had been vacated by its inhabitants, and a number of Japanese traders simply moved into empty houses to set up shop selling sake, tobacco, sugar, and other goods to the Japanese soldiers. When the Koreans returned to find Japanese intruders occupying their homes, nasty confrontations occurred, but even after the war ended the Japanese managed to maintain a foothold in the city. The same thing happened at Taegu, Kaesong, and Chŏnju, where commercial camp followers stayed on to sell their wares to Korean buyers instead of military customers. When *ŭibyŏng* risings broke out in late 1895 and 1896, however, many Japanese merchants in the interior were forced to retreat to Seoul or Inchon.[43]

In late 1895 the Inchon Chamber of Commerce recommended that the Japanese organize bands or associations of traveling peddlers, based in Seoul, Inchon, P'yŏngyang, and Kaesong, to carry Japanese goods to nearby market towns. Travel in groups was safer than traveling alone, the chamber argued, and an association would reduce needless competition among the small-scale Japanese merchants.[44] In April 1896 the Keirin Shōgyōdan, an itinerant merchants' association, was organized in Inchon, with branches in Seoul, Pusan, and Wŏnsan. Its announced purpose was to promote trade, which had suffered as a result of the disturbances in late 1895 and early 1896, and to overcome the disadvantages of individualistic peddling in the interior. The head of the Inchon Chamber of Commerce, invoking patriotic rhetoric, called the new association a "national enterprise" (*kokkateki jigyō*) that deserved "adequate protection and support from the state."

As was so often the case, patriotic rhetoric was the prelude to a request for subsidy. With the support of the consul at Inchon, Ishii Kikujirō, the Keirin Shōgyōdan asked the Japanese government for a capital fund to support its operations.[45] In the spring of 1897, with the encouragement of Foreign Minister Ōkuma, the Ministry of Agriculture

43. Ibid., Dec. 1895, pp. 42–46.
44. Ibid.
45. *NGB*, 30:1167–69.

and Commerce provided the group with a subsidy of ¥100,000 to investigate local market conditions—what kind of products the Korean preferred and what kind of competition the Japanese faced from foreign goods.[46] By 1898 the organization boasted 1,380 members in branches at P'yŏngyang, Kaesong, Seoul, Wŏnsan, Taegu, Mokp'o, and Chinnamp'o and 998 members at Inchon.[47] Its reputation deteriorated rather quickly, however. The consulate at P'yŏngyang reported that local Korean officials thought the association was "a kind of military group with administrative powers" and that most of the Japanese in the city regarded it as "useless." After observing the group in operation, Ishii, earlier one of its supporters, concluded that while its purpose was splendid, it was not at all effective in promoting trade; on the contrary, it seemed to have a negative impact. Unlike Chinese merchants, who built good relationships with Korean buyers, members of the Keirin Shōgyōdan were little better than "confidence men," backpacking useless patent medicines and phony panaceas into the interior and swindling poor Koreans out of their money. The consensus among the Japanese consuls in Korea was that the group might be useful if properly organized, but it needed supervision. Not surprisingly, the association not only lost its subsidy but was eventually disbanded. The Japanese authorities wanted to avoid unnecessary trouble with the Koreans.[48]

While this effort to send bands of peddlers to the interior proved short-lived, more and more adventurous Japanese traveled inland in search of quick profits. The number applying to the Inchon consulate for internal travel passes jumped from 88 in 1893 to 385 in 1895, 600 in 1896, and 700 in 1897.[49] Their work was anything but easy. Merchants traveling to the interior were warned to carry pistols in case they met "ignorant fellows," and they were advised that wearing a uniform would be useful since anyone who looked like a soldier was bound to be treated with respect.[50] Apart from safety, travel to the interior involved enormous discomfort and inconvenience. Korean inns were small, cramped, dirty, and poorly ventilated, made up of a kitchen, a bedroom for the innkeeper and his family, and another bedroom for guests, who were crammed together like pieces of sushi with a single chamberpot

46. *NGB*, 30:1175, 1191.
47. Cf. FMA, Files 3.2.3.1 and 3.3.2.8.
48. Only the consul in Pusan gave the group a favorable report. He pointed out that most of the important merchants in the port belonged to the group, and its members were not like the fly-by-night cheats who operated out of Inchon and Seoul. *NGB*, 30:1172–82.
49. Ibid.
50. *Nikkan tsūshō kyōkai hōkoku*, Jan. 1896, pp. 40–41.

shared by all. The Japanese traveler could expect to be assaulted by strange smells and attacked by armies of bedbugs. Food was plentiful at the inns, but pots and pans were rarely washed, and the pungent pickled vegetables served with meals were not to Japanese tastes. "The faint-hearted are likely to feel nauseous before they put food in their mouths," warned the journal of the Japan-Korea Trade Association.[51]

Advocates of interior trade argued that Japanese peddlers would have an uplifting influence on the local Korean population, spreading enlightenment as they hawked their pots and pans, their matches and soap, their cotton yarn and bolts of shirting. And there was hope that once the Koreans got to know the Japanese better, their hostility and contempt would be overwhelmed by admiration. In fact, the presence of the Japanese peddlers in the interior may well have increased cultural friction. The Korean upper classes, particularly the local *yangban* and officials whom Japanese merchants tried to cultivate as a way of facilitating entry into local markets, were extremely meticulous about proper dress, deportment, and language. The pitfalls were legion even when the Japanese tried to ingratiate themselves by small pleasantries. In Japan, for example, when greeting a man it was natural to ask after the health of his parents, his wife, and his children, but in Korea, where the sexes were rigidly segregated from childhood onward and where it was regarded as improper for a woman to be seen in public with a man, asking after a man's wife or mother was a gross impropriety. Such gaffes invited hostile reaction.[52]

The mainstay of the interior peddler trade was daily consumer goods. Japanese peddlers moved from market to market selling cheap Japanese-made mirrors, eyeglasses, hair oil, teacups, rice bowls, chamberpots, buckets, pots and pans, needles, knives, and the like. The more successful interior merchants also acted as agents for export houses in the treaty ports, buying rice and other agricultural products while selling their own wares on the side. Although it was illegal for the Japanese to own land before 1906, many peddlers acquired small plots and earned a living farming part-time and selling part-time. When work began on the Seoul-Pusan rail line, many petty merchants plied their trade in the construction zone, selling to the Japanese construction crews and setting up lodging houses, eating places, sake shops, sundries stores, and even brothels catering to a strictly Japanese clientele.

51. Ibid., Nov. 1895, pp. 83–86.
52. Ibid.

No doubt, as the mission of the Osaka Chamber of Commerce noted in 1904, most Japanese in the interior were honest and hardworking, but there were also hustlers and petty profiteers, willing to turn their hand to anything to make money. At the great fair in Taegu, for example, the Osaka mission saw at least ten booths running a primitive kind of roulette, *bunmawashi*, where customers could win bread or cigarettes by spinning a top on a sheet of paper sectioned off in numbers. Gambling, of course, was not illegal but smuggling was, and because of its risk it was also profitable. Many Japanese residents were tempted by the opportunity it offered. When a new nickel currency was introduced in the 1890s, there developed an active trade of smuggling counterfeit nickels manufactured in Japan; a number of Japanese also tried to smuggle ginseng, over which the government exercised a monopoly. The Japanese authorities, however, tried to discourage this kind of activity, cracking down on smuggling when they discovered it.

THE RICE TRADE

The Japan-Korea trade was not built on the sundries trade or on the sharp practices of itinerant peddlers. Rather, it rested on a natural division of labor between Japan as a newly industrializing economy and Korea as a preindustrial agrarian one. The staples of the trade were Korean agricultural products (rice and soybeans) and Japanese manufactures (principally cotton yarn and textiles). Indeed, one Japanese economic historian has suggested that the trade could be called an "exchange of rice for cotton." Both sides in the trade were pursuing comparative advantage, and participants on both sides profited. To understand why and how the Japanese dominated the Korean market, it is necessary to examine the structure and institutions involved in the staple trade.

Following the Sino-Japanese War, the overwhelming bulk of all Korean exports went to Japan. Perhaps 80 to 90 percent of this export trade was accounted for by rice and soybeans. Owing to price fluctuations in Japan, the rice trade was more volatile than the soybean trade and quite competitive, but it was also relatively safe, easy to finance, and highly profitable. The rice trade began to take off before the Sino-Japanese War. In 1890, when bad harvests created severe rice shortages in Japan, Korea enjoyed an abundant harvest and exports to Japan suddenly jumped. By the mid-1890s rice was the principal Japanese import from Korea. The main market was the Kansai region, where the demand for cheap rice was growing as the region industrialized. Two structural changes sustained this growth: an increase in urban population and a long-term rise in the price of domestic rice.

Some businessmen argued that there was a close link between rice imports and national prosperity. In 1901 the Hakata Chamber of Commerce, complaining about a recent Korean rice embargo, observed:

> The amount of rice produced in Japan has not kept pace with the development of manufacturing. Since the population is increasing every year, this naturally causes an inflation in rice prices. . . . Because rice prices are high, the wages of factory workers do not fall. The basic costs of manufacturing stay high, and this is one reason for a decline in business. We therefore believe that it is of the utmost urgency for our country's economy that we should stop the inflation of rice prices by importing foreign grain at low cost, thereby keeping manufacturing wages low.[53]

While it is easy to discount the hyperbole of chamber of commerce rhetoric, the argument had considerable currency. As one writer put it in 1911, the importation of foreign rice was "a crucial problem for the survival of our people."[54]

Although British India and French Indo-China remained the main sources of Japanese rice imports after the Russo-Japanese War, the share of Korean rice began to grow again (see table 3). The peninsula also supplied rice to Kwantung Territory and southern Manchuria when a Japanese colonial presence was established there after the Russo-Japanese War. The Manchurian market, once dominated by Chinese rice shipped in from Shanghai, relied more and more on Korea rice, and by the time of annexation an active trade had grown up between Inchon and the Manchurian ports of Dairen, Chefoo, and Niuchiang.[55]

The major port for the rice export trade was Pusan, located close to the rich and fertile rice-growing regions of the south. Since the rice trade was relatively stable and profitable, Japanese banks were more willing to finance rice merchants than dealers in import goods. The Dai-Ichi Bank, the Eighteenth Bank, and the Fifty-eighth Bank all competed for borrowers in the rice trade by providing attractive terms.[56] The rice dealers obtained their supplies in a variety of ways: sometimes they bought from Korean wholesalers (*kaekchu*) in the treaty ports who were connected to local wholesalers in the interior by their own networks of

53. Yoshino, "Yi-chō makki," 102–3.
54. Okada, *Chōsen yūshutsumai jijō*, 36.
55. Ibid., 39–42.
56. *KSSH*, 26.

TABLE 3   JAPANESE RICE IMPORTS, 1902–1910

	China	French Indochina	British India	Siam	Korea	Total rice imports
1902						
¥000s	342	4,651	7,225	1,266	3,961	17,751
%	1.9	26.2	40.7	7.1	22.3	100.0
1903						
¥000s	2,045	14,207	27,428	3,499	4,781	51,960
%	3.9	27.3	52.8	6.7	9.2	100.0
1904						
¥000s	818	15,789	35,858	5,578	1,579	59,792
%	1.4	26.4	60.0	9.3	2.6	100.0
1905						
¥000s	1,471	8,503	32,959	3,773	1,269	47,981
%	3.1	17.7	68.7	7.9	2.6	100.0
1906						
¥000s	271	6,482	15,131	2,709	1,579	26,172
%	1.0	24.8	57.8	10.4	6.0	100.0
1907						
¥000s	421	7,493	13,204	1,816	7,995	30,931
%	1.4	24.2	42.7	5.9	25.8	100.0
1908						
¥000s	291	6,885	7,341	2,134	6,036	22,689
%	1.3	30.3	32.4	9.4	26.6	100.0
1909						
¥000s	87	5,245	1,791	2,019	4,442	13,586
%	0.6	38.6	13.2	14.9	32.7	100.0
1910						
¥000s	56	3,533	1,708	1,951	1,386	8,644
%	0.6	40.9	19.8	22.6	16.0	100.0

SOURCE: Naikaku Tōkeikyoku, *Nihon teikoku tōkei nenkan*, vols. 21–29 (1902–10).

intermediaries; sometimes they sent their own buyers directly into the interior; and sometimes they bought rice from independent Japanese traders working in the interior.

Japanese rice traders in the treaty ports advanced cash or goods to Korean middlemen there to make rice purchases. Sometimes the Japanese lender would charge interest and ask delivery of a specified amount of rice; the final settling of accounts would be decided by the price of rice on delivery. This arrangement protected the Korean agent against loss if the price of rice rose. Often, however, the Japanese rice merchants would simply advance a fixed amount of money to purchase a fixed amount of rice, shifting the risk to the Korean middleman. If the price of rice rose above the price fixed by the Japanese dealer, the Korean dealer would take a loss and the Japanese dealer would profit; if the price were lower, the Korean agent would take the profit.

By the turn of the century rice exporters had developed a new method of financing trade with official cooperation. The post-1895 government reform program brought a shift to the collection of taxes in money rather than in kind, but the machinery for forwarding money to the central government remained cumbersome because of the bulkiness of Korean currency. When tax revenues had to be remitted directly to Seoul, local officials preferred to convert Korean currency into the more convenient and portable Japanese currency, and they relied on private Korean merchants to remit tax receipts to the capital. The Ministry of Finance would order powerful merchants in Seoul to collect tax monies from local officials in October for delivery to the ministry in April, in effect allowing the merchants to use the tax money as interest-free loans for six months. County-level officials often made similar arrangements with influential local merchants, and wholesale merchants (*kaekchu*) dealing with Japanese rice traders in Pusan took advantage of such arrangements to finance their transactions. Instead of relying on advances from the Japanese, they would use the tax monies entrusted to them to buy rice or soybeans for sale to the Japanese; they would take their payments in Japanese yen, remit enough yen to Seoul to cover the contracted tax payment, and then keep the rest as profit.

Japanese rice dealers at Pusan and Masan made similar arrangements with local officials, sometimes through the mediation of Japanese banks. Local officials would lend the Japanese tax money collected in Korean currency; the Japanese, dealing directly with producers or local intermediaries, would buy up rice and other goods with the Korean money; these goods would be sold for Japanese yen; and the Japanese trader would repay the Korean local officials in yen at the current rate of exchange, often to the profit of both parties.

In 1899, for example, a group of five Japanese residents at Taegu formed a trading company, the Sanyū Shōkai (Three Friends Trading Company), to sell import goods at the Taegu market and to buy rice for export with the returns. The company soon ran short of capital, so the partners hired a Korean go-between to contract with local county officials to exchange tax money collected in Korean currency for Japanese yen to be remitted to Seoul. They used the Korean currency to buy rice, which they then sold for yen to Japanese exporters in Pusan, forwarding an appropriate amount of the yen receipts through a Japanese agent to the Ministry of Finance in Seoul. In December 1899 the failure of a transaction involving 4,400 *won* of tax money delayed payment to the capital, and the Korean go-between was arrested. The Japanese partners eventually made good on their obligation, but the company folded and the "three friends" presumably parted company.[57]

As the rice trade grew, treaty port rice merchants relied less and less on Korean middlemen in the ports and more and more on direct contact with the suppliers in the interior. They dealt with two types of Korean merchants: the *kaekchu* and the *yŏgak*. The *kaekchu* was a commercial jack-of-all-trades, engaged in everything from wholesaling to banking: he might use his own capital to buy goods in the interior for wholesale to retail merchants or peddlers; he might act as a commission agent for others; or he might engage in financial transactions like issuing or discounting bills, accepting deposits, making loans, and exchanging currency. When dealing with the Japanese rice traders, the *kaekchu* took rice on consignment from the producer for sale in the treaty ports in return for a commission. The *yŏgak*, by contrast, was usually a specialized large-scale dealer in agricultural products such as rice and other grains, salt, fish, fruit, and tobacco; his establishment consisted of a large residence, storehouses for goods, and stalls or barns for horses and oxen. The *yŏgak* made his money by charging commissions to both the buyer and the seller of rice.[58]

By the eve of annexation Japanese rice merchants in the treaty ports were bound to Korean producers and middlemen by a variety of networks (figure 1). In some transactions the Japanese merchants remained sedentary, operating out of a shop in the treaty port, waiting for Korean agents to bring in rice. *Kaekchu* usually handled rice arriving at the port in bulk by riverboat, while rice arriving by land was usually marketed by smaller Korean operators or sold to Korean middlemen. The Korean seller, whether a *kaekchu* or a smaller operator, would make the rounds of the Japanese dealers with samples, trying to strike the best bargain possible. Other Japanese rice merchants sent their agents into the interior at harvest time, where they made the rounds of local markets, buying rice for shipment to the treaty ports. Sometimes these agents would rely on the help of a local *kaekchu*; sometimes they would post notices at the houses of local notables announcing that they were in the village

57. Yoshino, "Yi-chō makki," 104–7.
58. *KSSH*, 63–65.

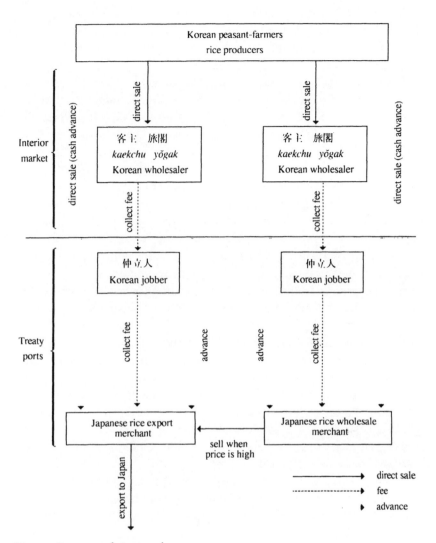

Fig. 1.   Patterns of rice purchase.

to buy rice. This aggressive pursuit of rice by direct purchase in competition with Korean wholesalers created a sellers' market, and as a result the profits for rice dealers were often slim.

Some Japanese rice dealers tried to eliminate the middleman completely by making advance payments or extending low-interest loans to Korean farmers at planting time to buy seed or tools; in return, the farmers would pledge their harvest as collateral. The Japanese rice merchant might use his own capital or money borrowed from a Japanese bank to make these loans. When the harvest came, the Korean farmer would receive the difference between the value of the harvest and the amount of the loan, and the Japanese lender would get the remainder of the rice together with a fixed amount of interest. Since the lender put up the loan on the basis of a rice price much lower than the market price, the advantage was on his side: if the harvest were poor, he would not lose, and if the harvest were good, he stood to profit greatly. At first the Korean farmers welcomed the cash in the spring when they needed it, but gradually, as they began to understand the financial transaction a little better, they tried to take advantage of the lender. Sometimes they would use the loan for their own small investments. When harvest time came, the farmers either failed to make good on their contracts with the lenders or sold their rice to other dealers from whom they got better prices, and the lender took a loss. Japanese merchants, aware of the growing riskiness of the practice, gradually abandoned it except for special areas where they would make advance payments to individual farmers, associations of farmers, or even whole villages, with the village head acting as guarantor of the loan.[59]

Within the treaty ports a further layer of transactions took place among the Japanese merchants. Wholesalers, who bought from Korean suppliers, often speculated by holding onto their rice stocks until the price peaked. Export merchants in turn bought from the wholesalers for shipment and sale to Japan. More often than not, however, individual traders or trading companies would carry on both types of business or would switch back or forth from one line to another as market conditions changed.

The chain of transactions bringing rice from the interior to the ports varied from place to place. In Inchon, where imports provided the bulk of business and export constituted a second line of business for most Japanese traders, rice merchants rarely ventured on buying missions in

59. Okada, Chōsen yūshutsumai jijō, 66–70.

the interior, preferring instead to buy rice brought to the port by Korean merchants. In Kunsan a similar situation prevailed until the end of the Russo-Japanese War. But as the number of Japanese dealers grew and competition with other ports became more intense, the Kunsan merchants began to send agents into the interior to buy directly. It was in Kunsan that large dealers specializing in rice exports, like the Fujimoto Company, made their appearance. In Pusan most dealers bought from Korean merchants bringing rice from the interior, and many continued the practices of making advances to farmers through Korean intermediaries, though less and less frequently. In Mokp'o many dealers began to imitate the practices of their neighbors in Kunsan, moving to buy in the interior, while in Chinnamp'o buying practices resembled those in Pusan.[60]

Most Japanese involved in foreign trade tried at one time or another to deal in rice, and in several ports rice merchants formed export traders' associations to bring order to the market. Such associations were established in Pusan, Inchon, Chinnamp'o, Kunsan, and Mokp'o. The associations were intended to cushion risk for their members by setting up reserve funds, to improve the quality of rice produced by the establishment of rice inspection systems, or to reduce competition. But none seemed to work very well, and often they fell apart within a few years. Many dealers, preferring to operate on their own, simply refused to join, and often those who did ignored the association regulations. Some export associations, like the Mokp'o Rice Dealers' Association, simply dissolved themselves; others found their functions taken over by the local Japanese chambers of commerce.[61]

The rice arriving at the ports was either unhulled rice (perhaps 30–40 percent of the total) or unpolished rice (*genmai*). The Japanese found Korean threshing and polishing processes crude, and this difference in quality standards opened a profitable niche for rice mills using Japanese machinery to turn unhulled rice into *genmai* and *genmai* into polished rice. Japanese dealers, possibly hoping for another opportunity to make a profit, increasingly preferred to buy unhulled rice for processing at Japanese-owned rice mills in the treaty ports. Polished rice was sold locally to Japanese port residents or was shipped to Dairen and north China. *Genmai*, by contrast, was mainly exported to Japan. Japanese merchants preferred it to Korean polished rice, which brought a lower

60. Ibid., 70–73.
61. Ibid., 87–91.

price than domestic polished rice in the Japanese market. Given the high cost of transport and the prospect of low profits, hardly any unhulled Korean rice was shipped to Japan.

The trade in rice and other agricultural staples like soybeans doubtless had an important economic impact on the hinterlands of the ports, often prompting a shift in local production patterns. Determining the nature of that impact requires further research in Korean as well as Japanese sources, but it seems likely that increased commercialization of farming in response to the growth of agricultural exports created new wealth for those Koreans engaged in the trade. Growing demand from the Japanese meant that prices tended to rise as trade expanded, competition increased among Japanese traders, and the relatively higher prices of rice in Japan exerted upward pressure on the rice market in Korea. Korean consumers of rice—town dwellers, for example—were probably hurt by rising rice prices. Those who best stood to profit were Korean rice dealers, wholesalers, and buying agents or well-to-do landowners with sufficient reserves to withhold rice from the market until they could get the best price. Small producers were less likely to benefit. Under pressure to convert their rice to cash in order to pay debts or taxes, they often had to sell at lower prices in the fall to meet their obligations, and sometimes subtle pressures were exerted on peasants to sell at lower prices to local merchants with close ties to the local *yamen*.[62]

THE IMPORT TRADE:
COTTON GOODS AND SUNDRIES

In contrast to the rice trade, where a growing metropolitan market for Korean rice guaranteed steady long-term profit, the import of non-agricultural manufactured goods to Korea was a riskier business. Import merchants, for example, found it more difficult than rice merchants to obtain financing from Japanese banks. Profits from the import trade were smaller than those from the rice trade, and importers dealt in goods that banks were reluctant to accept as collateral. A grain exporter, by contrast, could secure a loan by putting up as collateral his stocks of rice or soybeans, which would find a ready market at home. The import merchant was often a much smaller operator than the ex-

62. Im Pyong-yun, *Shokuminchi ni okeru shōgyōteki nōgyō*, 42ff.; Yoshino, "Yi-chō makki," 104–14. For an interesting treatment of the impact of foreign trade on the late Yi economy, see Eckert, *Offspring of Empire*, 7–26.

port merchant, often capital poor, running his business on a hand-to-mouth basis.

The import of cheap consumer goods attracted avaricious small-timers, interested in making quick profits by sharp dealing or by hawking shoddy goods at high prices rather in building a long-term market and clientele. On their visit to Korea in 1904 the Osaka Chamber of Commerce mission noticed grit in the evening meal they had just cooked. On closer inspection the grit turned out to be enamel coating that had flaked off a Japanese-made pot they had just bought in Pusan. When one member of the party picked up the pot to throw the meal out, the handle bent out of shape in his hand.[63] Their experience was not unique. Complaints about cheap Japanese goods were common in Korea: canned goods only half full; stacks of plates sold with good ones at either end and seconds in the middle; matches that did not light or broke when struck and packed in boxes that fell apart; bottled perfume with no fragrance; and so forth. Although high-quality Japanese sundry goods were imported into Korea, they were sold mainly to Japanese residents. For the Korean consumer, ignorant of products and easily duped by sharp-dealing Japanese, the main consideration was cost, not quality, and it was easy for the unscrupulous to unload shoddy goods.[64]

The cooking pot the Osaka mission bought at Pusan may well have been brought to the peninsula by dealers from their own hometown. These dealers, operating without much capital, would bring samples of high-quality goods to Korea, pick up orders throughout the country, and then return to Osaka to have cheap imitations made of the samples. The goods ordered were secured by cash deposits, and when the shoddy imitations arrived, the Korean buyers could do little but take delivery since they had already paid for them. Merchants involved in this kind of activity claimed to be competing with Chinese merchants who brought similar goods from China, but they hurt the reputation of Japanese manufactured products.[65]

Concern over shoddy trade goods worried the resident Japanese, particularly after the Russo-Japanese War. In late 1907 the Federation of Japanese Chambers of Commerce in Korea sent various business associations, chambers of commerce, and government agencies in Japan a resolution calling for an end to the practice. If poor-quality goods continued to come into Korea, the resolution predicted, "not only will the

63. KSSH, 26–38.
64. Arakawa, Saikin Chōsen jijō, 175ff.
65. Kajikawa, Jitsugyō no Chōsen, 564–68.

reputation of our trade and manufactured goods in Korea completely collapse, but it will have a substantial impact on Japan-Korea trade."[66] An Osaka Korea Foreign Traders Association (Osaka Chōsen Boeki-sho Kumiai) was eventually established to control the quality of goods shipped to Korea and to check the credit ratings of merchants there.[67]

The staple of the import trade, however, was not cheap sundry goods but Japanese-made cotton yarn and textiles. Korean consumption habits assured these products a stable long-term market, not an opportunistic one. While the *yangban* had new garments made from silk, the ordinary Korean farmer or townsman wore clothing made of cheaper cotton cloth. The demand for cotton textiles was satisfied traditionally by domestic homespun goods, but during the 1880s several types of foreign-made cotton goods began to encroach on the market: machine-made calicoes (known as unbleached muslin in American usage and as *kanakin* in Japanese); machine-woven sheeting (a rather heavy cloth made with coarse yarn); and Japanese homespuns (narrower than machine-made cloth). In warmth and durability sheeting was superior to *kanakin*, and it was closer in quality to Korean homespuns. However, narrow-bolt Japanese homespuns manufactured on traditional handlooms or modified looms in small workshops or in cottage industries were closest to indigenous Korean homespuns in size and quality.[68] The demand for imported cotton goods was differentiated by status. Most of the demand for Western-manufactured *kanakin* or calicoes, especially bleached goods, came from the upper classes, who fancied their finer weave and luster even though they did not wear well under the brutal washing techniques of Korean housewives. Most demand for imported sheeting came from the middling strata, while the lower classes preferred the more durable narrow-width homespuns.[69]

As we have seen earlier, by the early 1890s, with help from the Ch'ing government, Chinese merchants had gained the upper hand in the calico trade, bringing into Korea goods woven in either India or England. A government-subsidized shipping route from Shanghai through Chefoo to Inchon cut transportation costs dramatically: it cost only half as much to bring a bolt of calico by that route as it did by the Shanghai-Nagasaki-Inchon route. And while individual Japanese merchants operated independently with few assets, dealing in cash and un-

66. *Keijō Nihonjin shōgyō kaigisho nenpō*, 121–22.
67. Kajimura, *Chōsen ni okeru shihonshugi*, 120–21.
68. Ibid.
69. Murakami Katsuhiko, "Nihon shihonshugi ni yori Chōsen mengyō," 126–36.

able to extend credit, the Chinese importers formed trading associations that pooled large supplies of capital available at low interest.[70] Japanese goods also had difficulty competing with cheaper Korean homespuns. Japanese consular officials, concerned over the failure of Japanese goods to penetrate the market, urged Japanese merchants to cease cutthroat competition among themselves and pay attention to quality.

In the early 1890s some small-scale Japanese entrepreneurs attempted to recapture a share of the market by importing "imitation homespuns" manufactured in Japan to resemble Korean homespuns in quality and bolt width. In 1889 Yahashi Kanichirō, a Pusan merchant, brought a Korean weaver to Japan so that Japanese weavers could study his style and technique, and 1891 he began to export "imitation homespuns" to Korea. Imitators soon followed. Small weaving sheds to produce this "imitation homespun" (mosei momen) for the Korean market were set up in Aichi, Osaka, Nara, Ehime, Yamaguchi, and Fukuoka.[71] As they competed with one another, however, these small weaving operators, like the producers of other cheap trade goods for the Korean market, began to cut quality. The resulting product was often inferior to the Korean homespuns. It was thinner and wore out faster under daily washings. The Japanese "imitation homespuns" acquired a reputation for being cheap but poor in quality. As a result, dealers in Pusan would often mix bolts of the "imitation homespuns" with higher-priced native homespuns from Wŏnsan, hoping to fool their customers by concealing the origins of the Japanese product. The Japanese also began to experiment with producing inexpensive "trade cotton" (bōseki momen) woven from machine-made cotton yarn instead of handspun yarn on handlooms and equal in quality to the Korean product. By the time of the Sino-Japanese War this new product had begun to penetrate the Korean market with great success.[72]

As we have already seen, the disruption of the Chinese trade networks as a result of the Sino-Japanese War opened the way for a sudden surge of Japanese-made yarn and textile sales in Korea. Between 1895–99 cotton products on average accounted for 52 percent of all Japanese exports to Korea. Although the average dropped to 40 percent in 1900–1904 and 30 percent in 1905–10, cotton goods still remained a staple of the import trade. Indeed, Korea was the second largest market for Jap-

---

70. *Nikkan tsūshō kyōkai hōkoku* 3 (Nov. 1895): 14ff.
71. *Nikkan tsūshō kyokai hōkoku* 4 (Dec. 1895).
72. Im Pyong-yun, *Shokuminchi*, 43–46; Kajimura, *Chōsen ni okeru shihonshugi*, 120–24; Murakami, "Nihon shihonshugi ni yori Chōsen mengyō," 125–26.

TABLE 4   EXPORTS OF JAPANESE COTTON YARN AND
FABRIC TO KOREA AND CHINA, 1885, 1896, 1908

	Korea		China							
			China		Kwantung		Hong Kong		World total	
	¥000s	%	¥000s	%	¥000s	%	¥000s	%	¥000s	%
1885										
Cotton fabric	20	11	154	87					177	100
1896										
Cotton yarn	404	10	3,524	88			86	2	4,029	100
Cotton fabric	880	40	548	25			547	25	2,226	100
Total	1,284	21	4,072	65			633	10	6,256	100
1908										
Cotton yarn	2,696	13	16,361	79	300	2	955	5	20,724	100
Cotton fabric	5,523	38	4,534	31	2,110	14	424	3	14,611	100
Total	8,219	23	20,895	59	2,410	7	1,379	4	35,335	100

SOURCE: Murakami Katsuhiko, "Shokuminchi," in Ōishi Kaichirō, ed., *Nihon sangyō kakumei no kenkyū* (Tokyo: Tōkyō Daigaku Shuppanbu, 1975), 2:246.

anese-made cotton goods after China. To be sure, with its much smaller population it was a much smaller market (table 4). Between 1901 and 1910 Japan sold an annual average of 49,000 piculs of yarn to Korea in contrast to 2,350,000 piculs to China, and an annual average of ¥7.1 million worth of cotton textiles to Korea in contrast to ¥102.4 million to China. At least until 1914, though, the Japanese did not face the same competition in Korea that they faced in China, where British and Indian goods dominated the market. In Korea the Japanese managed to establish a monopoly on the yarn import market, providing 90–100 percent of all cotton yarn imports to Korea by the late 1890s; and by 1914 Japan accounted for 97 percent of Korea's cotton textile imports.[73]

In the years between the Sino-Japanese and Russo-Japanese Wars, narrow-width homespuns made the greatest gains in the Korean market (figure 2). During the period 1892–1908 Korea absorbed 90–100 percent of all Japanese homespuns exported. In 1901 the production of narrow-width homespuns, woven on handlooms in rural workshops or weaving sheds, was concentrated in Aichi (39% of total production), Osaka (25%), Ehime (10%), Nara (8%), and Saitama (4%), but exports to Korea came mainly from workshops in Aichi, Osaka, Nara,

73. Yoshino, "Yi-ki makki."

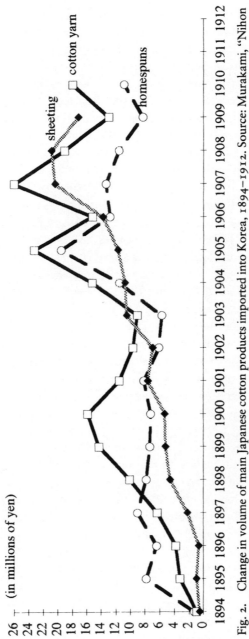

(in millions of yen)

cotton yarn
sheeting
homespuns

1894 1895 1896 1897 1898 1899 1900 1901 1902 1903 1904 1905 1906 1907 1908 1909 1910 1911 1912

Fig. 2. Change in volume of main Japanese cotton products imported into Korea, 1894–1912. Source: Murakami, "Nihon shihonshugi," 1979.

Kagawa, and Yamaguchi. In Aichi, an area typical of homespun production, the producers were usually small-scale, with few capital reserves, often unable even to maintain inventories of yarn. The weavers were typically low-wage rural women, working at home as a by-employment, just as women weavers did in Korea. But the productivity of the Japanese workers was higher than the Korean weavers—about two or three times as high according to one estimate—since they used the faster *battan* loom. Around the turn of the century several small-scale weaving sheds, employing perhaps three or four dozen weavers, were established in Aichi to produce specifically for the Korean market, but these operations probably used power looms, not hand looms.[74]

After the Russo-Japanese War, sales of machine-made sheeting, specially woven for the Korean market, moved ahead of sales of Japanese-made homespuns. Japanese manufacturers began to be attracted to the Korean market immediately after the Sino-Japanese War. The export of sheeting to Korea was pioneered by the Kanakin Weaving Company, which began marketing its brand there in 1895. Within two or three years it had secured a near monopoly position. Success, as always, attracted imitators. In 1897 the Kyoeisha, a company formed by a group of Japanese merchants in Inchon and Seoul, contracted with the Osaka Spinning Company to import sheetings and competed fiercely with Kanakin over the next several years. By 1902–3 the chief companies selling machine-manufactured goods in Korea were Osaka Spinning Company, Kanakin Weaving Company, Mie Spinning Company, and Okayama Spinning Company. To get a leg up on the other firms, in 1905 Mie Spinning signed a contract with Mitsui Bussan and Takase Trading Company in Inchon to market its products. By the end of the Russo-Japanese War Japanese cotton manufacturers were waging a fierce price war in Korea, intensified by a falloff in demand at home.

In any event, Japanese cotton manufactures began to make steady gains against British and American woven goods, particularly in the market for sheetings, for several reasons. First, the Japanese companies gathered better market information than did their foreign competitors. The redoubtable Isabella Bird Bishop, for example, was impressed by the care with which the Japanese studied the Korean market. Unlike the British, who did little or nothing of the kind, the Japanese investigated local tastes in colors, patterns, and widths of cloth. "The Japanese success," she wrote,

---

74. Murakami, "Nihon shihonshugi ni yori Chōsen mengyō," 118–26.

putting the advantages of proximity aside, is, I believe, mainly due to the accuracy of the information obtained by their keen-witted agents, who have visited all the towns and villages in Korea, and to the carefulness with which their manufacturers are studying the tastes and requirements of the Korean market.... On the report of the agents of the importing firms, the weavers of Osaka and other manufacturing towns with adroitness and rapidity closely adapted the texture, width, and length of their cottons closely to those of the hand-loom cotton goods made in south Korea, which are deservedly popular for their durability, and have succeeded not only in producing an imitation of Korean cloth, which stands the pounding and beating of Korean washing, but one which actually deceives the Korean weavers themselves as to its origin, and which had won great popularity among Korean women.[75]

Second, production costs of Japanese woven goods were lower than for Western manufactures. The main competitive advantage of the Japanese cotton industry lay in its marriage of low-cost labor to capital-intensive technology. The development of sophisticated raw cotton mixing techniques also enabled the Japanese weaving companies to keep the cost of raw materials down. The more expensive raw cotton imported from the United States could be blended with cheaper Chinese and Indian cotton to produce a strong but cheap cotton yarn. And since most sheeting was woven in mills of large-scale firms that integrated spinning and weaving operations, transaction costs were reduced. Sheeting could be woven from yarn manufactured by the firm, not purchased from another company. Even the Kanakin Weaving Company used yarn spun in its own plant. And, of course, since Japan was closer to Korea, the cost of shipping and handling goods was lower than for American, British, or Indian manufactures.[76]

Third, the Japanese domestic manufacturers were intensely competitive. Ironically, competition was stimulated by the efforts of one group of firms to establish oligopolistic control through an orderly marketing arrangement in Korea. In 1906 the three major exporters of sheeting (Osaka Spinning, Mie Spinning, and Kanakin Weaving) organized an export cartel, the San'ei Cotton Textile Export Association (San'ei Menpu Yūshutsu Kumiai) to reduce competition through price cutting and to present a united front against foreign competition. While Japanese manufacturers at first had competed through quality, once Mie Spinning entered the Korean market, price competition became intense, and the price of a bale of sheeting began to drop sharply. Shibusawa

75. Bishop, *Korea and Her Neighbors*, 2:216.
76. Murakami, "Nihon shihonshugi ni yori Chōsen mengyō," 115–18.

Eiichi, an adviser to both the Osaka and the Mie spinning companies, urged an end to their senseless and self-destructive rivalry. The manager of the Osaka office of Mitsui Bussan, Fujino Kamenosuke, offered his services as a go-between, and in 1906 the export cartel, promising "Triple Prosperity" (San'ei) for its three member firms, was organized. (Not coincidentally, the same three companies founded an export cartel —the Nippon Menpu Yūshutsu Kumiai—to compete with American textile imports to Manchuria, where the pattern of demand was very similar to that in Korea.)[77]

The agreement provided that the three companies would sell their products under a single brand name. Each company was to have a sales quota based on its loom capacity, and the Osaka Spinning Company label was to be used on the product. Every effort was to be made to establish uniform quality. The Dai-Ichi Bank offered to provide the association with short-term foreign exchange at low cost, and Mitsui Bussan, which agreed to supervise quality control, was designated as the association's marketing agent in Korea. In turn Mitsui designated ten Japanese-owned wholesale outlets in the Inchon-Seoul area. The designated wholesalers, who were not permitted to deal in any other kind of textile goods, all got the same allotment of goods, regardless of their credit or sales records. The intent was clearly to shut out the competition and to establish a monopolistic position in the Korean market. Rather quickly the cartel cut the quality of its product and jacked up the price of a bale from ¥105 to ¥130. During the period 1908–10 it managed to secure a 70 percent share of Japan's sheeting exports to Korea.[78]

The organization of the export cartel served to stimulate competition. To break its dominant position, other associations were pulled together. A group of about ninety Korean merchants excluded from the cartel's marketing system formed their own association to import sheetings manufactured by Fuji Gasu Spinning Company, then the Amagasaki Spinning Company.[79] Eventually this group was replaced by the Kyoekisha, a group organized with the help of Nishihara Kamezō. This association signed special agreements to market the output of the Kanegafuchi Spinning Company, whose Kyushu mill specialized in the

77. The formation of these export cartels may have paved the way for a merger of the three firms. In 1906 Kanakin Weaving merged with Osaka Spinning, and in 1914 Osaka and Mie Spinning merged into Tōyō Spinning (often referred to as Tōyōbō).
78. Murakami, "Nihon shihonshugi ni yori Chōsen mengyō," 138–42.
79. Kajikawa, *Jitsugyō no Chōsen*, 564–68.

production of cotton textiles for the Korean market. Importing the Kanegafuchi products through the Itō Chū Company, the association negotiated special low freight rates with the Korean railway, and it soon managed to compete with the San'ei association. The Wakayama Spinning Company made a special trading agreement with the Takase Trading Company, but the Naigaimen Company, also interested in breaking into the Korean market, was unable to find a suitable marketing agent.[80]

The net effect of this sharpened competition was to boost the sale of Japanese cotton textiles in the Korean market. Prices fell and the Japanese market share expanded steadily. Imports of Japanese shirtings (*kanakin*) and sheeting to the Korean market quadrupled between 1906 and 1912. Finer and better-quality British woven goods, occupying a higher niche in the market, continued to hold their own, still accounting for 37.1 percent of Korea's cotton textile imports in 1910, but with the outbreak of World War I, they were finally driven out of the market. In 1914 Japan cloth accounted for 97 percent of all Korean cotton textile imports.

In contrast to China, where the Japanese aggressively marketed cotton yarn, Korea was primarily a market for woven goods. In 1908 Japan exported about twice as much cotton textiles as cotton yarn to Korea, whereas in China it sold nearly seven times as much yarn as cloth. The reason seems obvious: Japanese weaving manufacturers did not want to compete with themselves by selling the Koreans yarn that could be woven into cloth on native looms. Horace Allen had seen this as a possibility in 1896. "The nicely spun cotton yarns of Japan," he wrote to an American businessman, "are being bought by the Koreans to be woven into cloth on their old time looms. They can in this way get a cloth a little cheaper than an imported article, while it [lasts?] at least six times as long and admits of pigment washing, which the highly sized imported cloth will not do."[81] It made no sense for the Japanese to sell cotton yarn in Korea when higher profits and a surer market existed for woven goods.[82]

The Japanese cotton manufacturers came to dominate the Korean cotton textile through astute and aggressive marketing tactics rather than as a result of the Japanese political presence. To be sure, the polit-

80. Nishihara Kamezo, *Yume no nanajū nen*, 36–40.
81. New York Public Library, Allen Papers, Press Copy Book no. 4, Allen to C. W. Everett, Jan. 22, 1896, p. 89.
82. Ōishi, *Nihon sangyō kakumei no kenkyū*, 2:246–50.

ical presence helped. The widening circulation of Japanese currency, the growing number of Japanese on the peninsula, and the building of a trade infrastructure under Japanese political auspices undoubtedly promoted trade in tangible ways. Yet had the Japanese cotton industry been unready or unwilling to take advantage of these new conditions, it is unlikely that the Japanese would have come to monopolize the Korean market for cotton goods. The expansion of Japanese imports, indeed, underlines the synergistic nature of imperialist penetration, where efforts of one set of Japanese with one set of motives reinforced the efforts of another set of Japanese with another set of motives. Penetration was not the result of one decisive stroke but of a slow accumulation of actions and initiatives, coming from the bottom up as well as the top down.

CHAPTER 8

Dreams of Brocade

Migration to Korea

By the time of annexation the Japanese residents on the Korean peninsula had grown into the largest overseas community of Japanese in the world (table 5). The rapid inflow of migrants was dramatic. On the eve of the Sino-Japanese War there were altogether about 9,354 Japanese in Korea, most of them crowded into the two chief treaty ports, Pusan and Inchon. With the Japanese victory in 1895 the inflow of Japanese gathered force, and by the end of the Russo-Japanese War the trickle had become a flood, overflowing the boundaries of the foreign settlements, spilling out of the ports to interior towns and cities, following the channels carved by the expanding Japanese political presence. As surely as water flows downhill, Japanese settlers followed the spreading ambit of Japanese power. By 1910 their number had grown to 171,543.

This influx, however, was a series of uneven waves rather than a driving flood. The first wave came with the outbreak of the Sino-Japanese War. A boom in the procurements trade offering opportunities for quick profit prompted hundreds of adventurous small traders, camp followers, and carpetbaggers to scrape together fare for the crossing to Korea, grab their passports, and load themselves with food and warm clothes for the journey. As news of Japan's early victories in the war reached home, the numbers of migrants increased. Even the weak and vulnerable settlers who had left the peninsula when war broke out—wives, children, and old people—began to return. Through the fall of 1894 incoming vessels disgorged newcomers, severely straining the re-

TABLE 5   JAPANESE RESIDENTS OVERSEAS,
1880–1920

	1880	1890	1900	1910	1920
Korea	835	7,245	15,829	171,543	347,850
Taiwan			37,954	98,048	166,621
Kwantung				11,077	78,721
Manchuria	} 166	864	3,243	18,097	97,962
China				7,355	35,968
Karafuto			413	28,688	89,257
Vladivostok		374	2,208	1,953	5,072
Hawaii		12,675	57,486	70,764	112,221
U.S. (mainland)	23	1,979	32,493	21,875	115,533
Canada		98	2,651	10,274	17,716
Brazil			9	1,559	34,258
Peru			694	4,933	10,199
Australia	7	92	3,296	3,061	5,261
Total	1,031	23,327	156,276	449,227	1,116,639

SOURCE: Kimura Kenji, "Meijiki Nihonjin no kaigai shinshutsu to imin-kyoryūmin seisaku," *Shōkei ronshū* (Waseda), no. 35 (Sept. 1978).

sources of the foreign settlements. In Inchon alone nearly one thousand new arrivals were reported between September 20 and October 22. And as the war moved north, so did many of the new arrivals.

The majority were petty merchants, peddlers, construction workers, artisans, and porters. Many came to make a quick profit selling sundries to Japanese troops. Newspapers reported that at Ŭiju on the Manchurian border, a hundred or so camp-following peddlers and merchants had spread their wares—straw sandals, eggs, vegetables, winter clothing, stockings, and the like—for sale at outrageous prices to Japanese troops, porters, and construction workers. Others sought jobs as porters or coolies with the Japanese forces' quartermaster operations. Indeed, an enterprising Osaka publishing house issued a pamphlet offering advice to those interested in working for the Japanese army: how to sign up for jobs, what clothes and supplies to bring, what to expect on arrival, and how much to get in wages. The pamphlet also suggested bringing along a pistol or knife for personal safety.[1]

This swarm of penny capitalists and carpetbaggers was loose and

1. *Chōsen jūgun tosen annai.*

undisciplined, bent only on making the most of a brief opportunity. Often rapacious and dishonest, they were ready to charge their fellow Japanese what the market would bear, and if looting could turn a profit, they were ready to loot as well. Their treatment of the Koreans and their property was brutally high-handed. To provide fuel for their campfires, they tore down houses abandoned in the midst of the fighting, and they stole livestock, chickens, vegetables, and even household goods from unoccupied houses to eat or to sell. The local military authorities, distressed at this disorder, issued regulations to bring the camp followers under control.[2]

While many wartime migrants returned home with their pockets full once the fighting had ended, others stayed. By the end of 1895 most Japanese settlements were much larger than they had been a year before. Between 1894 and 1895 the population of Inchon, for example, grew so much—from 2,500 to 4,500—that the settlement zone could no longer hold them. The majority of the newcomers had to crowd into the native quarters, where they paid often exorbitant rents. An eight-mat room went for ¥8.00, a native-style house for ¥10.00, and a Western-style house for ¥12.00. As in any boomtown, the number of small retail stores, restaurants, drinking shops, inns, entertainment places, and even ice merchants mushroomed. The atmosphere of the settlement, where money was made and spent easily, was unsettled and ebullient. The Japanese residents in Inchon, clucked an editorialist of the Tōkyō keizai zasshi, were footloose and spendthrift, dreaming of the "adventurer's success [achieved] through exceptional abilities or exceptional opportunities" rather than through safe and steady hard work, perseverance, and thrift.[3] Ōkuma Shigenobu, a supporter of commercial expansion on the peninsula, feared that the migration of "corrupt, coarse, arrogant, rough, violent, fraudulent, and bullying" Japanese to Korea, and not diplomatic ineptitude, represented Japan's real failure there.[4]

The postwar influx did not create a stable community. Many migrants were temporary sojourners with no thought of permanent settlement. Many went home when jobs with the Japanese military forces disappeared, and few had the capital or resources to stay if their dreams of quick money met with disappointment. Petty capitalists engaged in retail trade, importing, or peddling were competing intensely in an expanding but limited market, and the failure rate was high. Some made

2. Higuchi, "Nisshin sensōka Chōsen," 36–43.
3. Tōkyō keizai zasshi, no. 838 (Aug. 15, 1897).
4. Nikkan tsūshō kyōkai hōkoku 15.11 (Nov. 1896): 5.

TABLE 6   TURNOVER OF JAPANESE RESIDENTS
IN TREATY PORTS, 1896–1899

Treaty port	Population as of Jan. 1 (A)	Immigrants	Outmigrants	Total (B)	% (A/B)
Seoul					
1896	1,592	476	508	984	61.8
1897	1,588	470	324	794	50.0
1898	1,734	557	306	863	49.8
1899	1,985	707	577	1,284	64.7
Inchon					
1896	3,904	1,770	1,725	3,495	89.5
1897	3,949	1,829	1,477	3,306	83.7
1898	4,301	1,807	1,890	3,697	86.0
1899	4,218	1,520	1,523	3,043	72.1
Pusan					
1896	5,433	2,915	2,281	5,196	95.6
1897	6,067	2,957	2,775	5,732	94.5
1898	6,249	2,484	2,407	4,891	78.3
1899	6,326	2,215	2,445	4,660	73.7
Wŏnsan					
1896	1,299	85	86	171	13.2
1897	1,423	43	117	160	11.2
1898	1,560	41	82	123	7.9
1899	1,600	36	53	89	5.6

SOURCE: *Kankoku shutchō chōsa hōkokusho* (Yokohama: Yokohama Zeikan, 1907) 15–16.

several trips to and from Japan before deciding to put down roots. To judge from migration statistics, the population turnover was high, particularly in the immediate postwar period, and it was significantly higher at Inchon and Pusan than at Seoul or Wŏnsan, where trade was less important (table 6). Between 1896 and 1902 the overall Japanese population in Korea tended to flatten out, with a slight upturn in 1903.

When Japanese troops landed in Inchon in the winter of 1904, a boom was on again as it had been ten years before. Prices began to shoot up madly, sometimes doubling overnight. When this news reached home, a new swarm of adventurers and opportunists jammed into ships departing for Inchon, often paying two or three times the regular fare or bribing deckhands to squeeze them on board, to brave a five- or six-day journey on the freezing deck amid piles of freight and gear. There were far too many arrivals for the settlement to absorb, and many pressed on to Seoul, ending up at the door of the Japanese consulate begging for work. The consulate asked the Foreign Ministry to staunch the inflow of Japanese, but still they came, putting an immense strain on the food supplies, lodging, and finances of the Japanese settlement.[5]

While the size of the settlement at Inchon decreased once the war ended, the number of Japanese soared both at Seoul, where the resident-general was now firmly established, and at Pusan, the other terminus of the new Seoul-Pusan railway line (see figure 3). Between 1898 and 1907 the Japanese population at Pusan grew from 6,249 to 18,481, and that of Seoul from 1,734 to 13,416. At Seoul only a few arrived with jobs already assured through arrangements. Many migrants carried letters of introduction from friends or *senpai* at home; others had relatives or friends and acquaintances from the same hometown who had already settled in Korea; and still others came empty-handed, hoping that something would turn up. But letters of introduction were often useful for little more than attesting to one's identity, and relatives and friends were often not as helpful as expected. Many migrants, their expectations betrayed and unable to find work, departed for home when they ran out of money, leaving a trail of unpaid restaurant and lodging bills.[6] It was only the persistent, the diligent, or the fortunate who managed to tide themselves over once the war boom collapsed, and only the exceptional managed to make money as quickly or spectacularly as they had hoped.

Except for a handful of adventurous souls—peddlers, grain buyers, sellers of patent medicines or cheap confections, and the like—few Japanese ventured into the interior before the Russo-Japanese War. For one thing, it was not legal to live outside the foreign settlement zones, and for another life was often dangerous and uncertain in the interior. The outbreak of anti-Japanese incidents in 1895–96 had demonstrated that. Even after the establishment of the protectorate, the spread of the anti-Japanese guerrilla movement, especially during 1907–9, put Japanese in the interior in harm's way. While some Japanese settlers set up shop along the Seoul-Pusan line, especially near the large stations, most new arrivals continued to flock to the larger settlements—Pusan, Seoul, and Inchon—and in smaller numbers to Masan, Mokp'o, Kunsan, and Wŏnsan. Life was safer, more secure, and certainly more familiar in the ports, and there was comfort in numbers.

5. Nakai, *Chōsen kaikō roku*, 115.
6. *JNN*, 9.16, Aug. 1, 1906, pp. 33–36; 7.9., Apr. 15, 1904, 700–703.

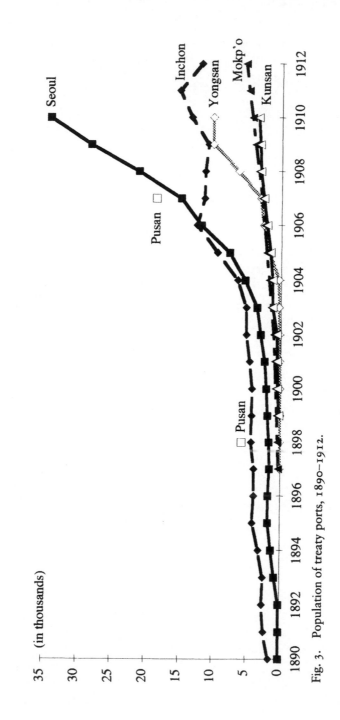

Fig. 3. Population of treaty ports, 1890–1912.

MIGRATION AND GOVERNMENT POLICY

The promotion of migration to the peninsula had become an unquestioned axiom of Japanese policy by the time of the Russo-Japanese War. The May 1905 cabinet decision stressed the importance of migration, and four years later, in its policy on annexation, the government once again proposed to "settle as large a number of our countrymen inside Korea as possible, deepening the foundation of our power and at the same time bringing closer economic relations between Korea and Japan."[7] At once a political and economic vanguard, Japanese migrants to the peninsula were to serve the national interest even while pursuing their own. What government leaders had in mind, however, was not sojourners or transients of the sort who flocked to the peninsula during the wartime booms but rather permanent residents ready to put down roots in the Korean soil. As one writer put it, the ideal Japanese migrant was someone for whom Korea would become a second homeland, which he would be as determined to defend as he would his place of birth.[8] In short, the government wanted settlers in Korea to be "colonists" (shokumin), not "emigrants" (imin.)

During the last two decades of the Meiji period it was common to distinguish between "emigrants" and "colonists."[9] Although he did not use these terms, Itagaki Taisuke described the distinction between them succinctly in 1892: the colonist was "one who goes abroad to develop land and cultivate production with the intention that his heirs will live there permanently"; the emigrant was "a poor person who moves away from home, whether inside the country or outside, and contracts his labor to a powerful capitalist."[10] Emigration was thought of as a movement of the poor and the weak, primarily an economic act with little political meaning since the main beneficiary was not the state but the migrant, who might find a better livelihood. Colonization, by contrast, was invariably linked with national purpose, national power, and national interests. It implied the controlled movement of people, often under official auspices or with official protection and encouragement,

---

7. NGNSB, 1:315–16.
8. Samura, Tō-Kan no susume, 25. The most suitable emigrant, one writer had observed several years earlier, was "one with the determination to take his household, pick up his family, and move to Korea, ready to end his days there." Kojima Kisaku, Chōsen no nōgyō, 78.
9. Cf. Okawa, Nihon iminron, 11–17.
10. Itagaki, "Shokuminron," 1:71.

from the home country to a less developed society where they would establish prosperous and independent communities.

Tōgō Minoru, a young theorist of colonialism, described the colonist as a person who settled permanently away from his homeland, living in a country less advanced or developed than his own, together with large numbers of his fellow countrymen, but who maintained the institutions of his homeland, followed its customs, and did not lose his national uniqueness.[11] The emigrant might be oppressed, assimilated, or rejected by the host society, but the colonist was not; he was an outsider on the inside, dominating the host society, not being dominated by it. Colonization, with all that it implied—political influence, institution building, and the export of culture, laws, customs, and even language— excited and tantalized the political imagination in a way that emigration did not. It was seen, as emigration was not, as a means of expanding national power.

When the early Meiji government did anything at all to promote the movement of Japanese abroad, it was more positive about colonization than about emigration. Indeed, largely because its early experiments in encouraging emigration failed, the government tightly restricted movement out of the country during the 1870s. The first emigrants, sent to work on the sugar plantations in Hawaii, were treated badly by the plantation owners, who fought with them over wages, hours, and working conditions, until many of the emigrants returned home, bitter and resentful about their experiences. The government response was to suspend the issuance of passports for overseas travel except for travelers pursuing the tasks of *fukoku kyōhei*—government officials, students, merchants, and businessmen. Not until the Matsukata deflation brought agrarian distress in the early 1880s did the government loosen its restrictions on emigration. In 1885 limitations on residence abroad were lifted, and the government signed a treaty with the kingdom of Hawaii to provide laborers under strictly regulated terms.[12]

The change in policy did not dispel the negative connotations of emigration. It was seen primarily as a response to falling farm income and spreading rural discontent and secondarily as a means of earning foreign exchange and developing a pool of disciplined laborers—the returning contract laborers—with direct knowledge of Western agricultural techniques. Neither did the policy involve active efforts to promote emi-

11. Tōgō, *Nihon shokumin ron*, 9.
12. Alan Takeo Moriyama, 1-13.

gration. While the government attempted to protect the emigrants from exploitation by unscrupulous employers or go-betweens, it provided no subsidies for emigration as it did for colonization. According to one estimate, between 1885 and 1905 the government expended only ¥150,000, a trifling amount, on emigration.[13]

By contrast, colonization—the planting of settlers in territories of strategic or economic significance—enjoyed the enthusiastic, sometimes desperate support of the Meiji government. During the early Meiji years colonization policy was directed mainly at the "threat from the north." To shore up its northern borders against encroachments by the Russians, the government attempted to move settlers into Hokkaido and Sakhalin.[14] In 1868 Okamoto Kansuke, the official responsible for Sakhalin affairs, began to lead groups of colonists to Aniwa Bay on the southern end of the island. The government offered settlers various inducements: cash, special allowances, and tools as well as land and fishing rights and spent more than ¥400,000 on the program between 1870 and 1873. The effort was abandoned when a treaty signed with the Russians, who outnumbered and outgunned the Japanese on the island, recognized their sovereignty over Sakhalin, but the government had managed to move in about three thousand settlers—many of them, to be sure, Ainu displaced from Hokkaido. And when Japan regained control over southern Sakhalin under the Treaty of Portsmouth, the government once again tried to lure settlers there by offers of free land, houses, tools, seed, tax exemptions, and low-interest, long-term loans from the Hokkaido Colonial Bank.[15]

Official interest in colonizing Hokkaido, the "northern gate" to Japan, was even more intense. The Hokkaido Colonization Office (*kaitakushi*) was established in 1869, and in August 1871 the government drew up a ten-year development plan for Hokkaido. Between 1872 and 1881 the colonization office was allotted an annual budget of ¥1 million, an enormous sum, to build roads, rail lines, coal mines, food mills, and other facilities. At first few were interested in settling in the harsh climate, with its long, hard winters, nor were they eager to undertake the burden of clearing the land. To populate the island, the government recruited *tondenhei* (military colonists), mainly from the unemployed former samurai in the Tohoku region, offering assistance to get them settled. The plan, suggested by Kuroda Kiyotaka, was inspired

13. Okawa, *Nihon iminron*, 240.
14. Ando, *Hokkaidō iminseisaku shi*, 25–54.
15. Stephan, *Sakhalin*, 56–64, 86–90.

by the traditional Chinese practice of setting up colonies of "farmer-soldiers" to defend its northern frontiers against the "barbarians"; the *tondenhei* were to build up the northern island economically while providing its defense. Indeed, the *tondenhei* represented the ideal model of what a "colonist" should be, ready to defend the land he was reclaiming and turning productive.[16]

It was only in the 1890s that a number of influential officials, politicians, and journalists—men like Enomoto Takeaki, Itagaki Taisuke, and Taguchi Ukichi—began to argue that the encouragement of migration outside Japan (as opposed to internal colonization) might strengthen the nation. In 1891 Foreign Minister Enomoto Takeaki, putting aside opposition within the Matsukata cabinet, established an emigration section (*iminka*) in the foreign ministry with the task of encouraging emigration and finding new potential territories for Japanese settlement. Two years later, after leaving the government, he helped to establish a private organization, the Colonial Association (*Shokumin Kyōkai*), to promote not only external trade and colonization but also emigration.

This more positive attitude toward emigration reflected a new sense of Japan's possibilities in world affairs. Older apprehensions about foreign encroachment were giving way to confident dreams of peaceful expansion into the outside world. In 1891 Taguchi Ukichi suggested that two urgent tasks faced the nation: the first was "to expand foreign trade and increase our national wealth," and the second was to "transplant our people abroad and erect a bulwark for our state."[17] The movement of Japanese people overseas, like the movement of Japanese goods, was linked with expanding power and influence in the world. For Taguchi, emigration was associated not with the export of poor laborers or excess population but with commerce and naval power, and he saw the overseas migrant as more colonist than immigrant.[18]

Itagaki Taisuke, another advocate of overseas migration, also stressed the link between migration and national strength. "I believe that if we vigorously pursue a policy of overseas settlement not only will our countless emigrants living abroad greatly increase our exports by their demand for goods from the home country but they will also enrich our country by what they save from their wages." The experience with

---

16. Enomoto and Kimi, *Hokkaidō no rekishi*, 1:130.
17. *Tōkyō keizai zasshi*, Oct. 24, 1891.
18. Mori Hisao, "Taguchi Ukichi no shokuminron," in Kojima Reiitsu, ed., *Nihon teikokushugi to Higashi Ajia*, 3–47.

contract laborers in Hawaii had demonstrated that it was possible to turn the export of the rural poor into national profit: during the period 1885–92 the twenty thousand emigrants to Hawaii had managed to save $1,530,000 from their wages, a substantial sum. Emigration was also a way of dealing with a population growing at the rate of four to five hundred thousand a year, creating heavier pressures on the country's land and resources. Finally, Itagaki argued, the expansion of Japanese people abroad paved the way for Japanese trade, for the emigrants educated foreigners about Japanese goods. "If our intercourse with the outside flourishes and our relations with foreign countries deepen, we will join the ranks of the world's great powers, thereby emerging as the leading power in the Orient (*Tōyō no meishu*). Indeed, it can be said that our policy of national wealth and strength lies in emigration policy."[19]

Despite the spread of such views the government did very little to promote emigration. Instead, it adopted a laissez-faire policy of protecting the emigrants against exploitation but leaving management and promotion to private companies (*imingaisha*). If anything, in the official world the distinction between "emigration" and "colonization" was becoming more precisely conceptualized in class and geographical terms. First, emigration was linked to occupations with low prestige. The Emigrant Protection Law of 1896 defined an "emigrant" (*imin*) as a person who went abroad for the purpose of labor; in 1901 foreign ministry regulations defined "labor" as either manual work (farming, animal husbandry, fishing, mining, manufacturing, construction, and transportation) or menial service (cooking, laundry, sewing, domestic service, and care for the sick). Second, in 1902 the law was amended to exclude from the legal definition of "emigrant" those traveling to Korea or China, suggesting that those going to the continent were in a different category from those headed toward Hawaii, the United States, Canada, Australia, or Latin America.[20]

The assumptions reflected in this legal distinction are clear: the migrant heading east across the Pacific was a humble toiler, a transient, a person of low prestige; the migrant heading across the Straits of Korea and the Yellow Sea was a pioneer, a settler, a bearer of Japan's destiny. These images were reinforced by the torrent of books, articles, and

19. Itagaki, "Shokuminron," 74–75, 81.
20. Okawa, *Nihon iminron*, 17–18.

pamphlets on the migration question that poured off the presses after the Russo-Japanese War, works that were suffused with a new sense of Japan's place in the international order. On the Asian continent the victory over Russia assured Japan the role of a major player in the competition for markets and political influence; in America, though, its triumph had excited suspicion and resentment, and rivalry with the United States was intensifying. Migration to Hawaii and the United States was likely to create international friction; migration to the continent was likely to enhance Japanese power. The emigrant laborer, looked down on by his white masters and living in modest conditions, tarnished national prestige; the continental settler, protected by Japanese political and military power and bringing a higher standard of living to the host country, enhanced it.[21]

For example, in 1906 Tōgō Minoru, a recent graduate of Sapporo Agricultural School, published *Nihon shokumin ron*, an influential work that argued for channeling the flow of Japanese overseas migration, especially agricultural settlers, to Korea, Manchuria, China proper, and eventually other rice-producing countries in order to relieve population pressure and develop new food supplies. "The future colonies of the empire must be sought nowhere but on the Asian continent."[22] Migration to Hawaii and the United States, he suggested, was not necessarily to Japan's advantage since the emigrants were likely to assimilate, becoming Americans as other immigrants there did. Responding to the kind of rosy arguments advanced in the 1890s by Taguchi and Itagaki, he wrote, "The expansion of a nationality is not necessarily the same as the development of a state."[23] If the expansion of national power was the goal of migration overseas, then it was better to send migrants to countries where the government was weak and the populace backward; in such countries it would be easier for the migrants to maintain their identity, to dominate the local inhabitants, and to expand the home country's influence. Settlers, particularly the agricultural settlers, brought with them the habits, culture, and institutions of their homeland: they were bearers of civilization as well as power. "Going to the aid of neighboring peoples, fulfilling our responsibility to mankind by leading them to enlightenment, showering on them the blessings of civilization—is that not our empire's great mission?" Tōgō urged the government to encourage migration to continental Asia by distributing

21. Ono, "Nihon teikokushugi to iminron," 347–48.
22. Tōgō, *Nihon shokumin ron*, 377–80.
23. Ono, "Nihon teikokushugi to iminron, 321.

unowned or uncultivated land to settlers so that they could set down roots.[24]

What Tōgō advocated for Asia in general, Katō Masao, a professor in the law faculty at Kyoto Imperial University, advocated for Korea in particular. From the turn of the century Katō called on the government to send independent cultivators to Korea not simply to deal with Japan's demographic problems but also to lay down the foundations for the expansion of Japanese influence and the development of the Korean economy. Like other advocates of an active migration policy, he argued that it was a means of alleviating the social problems created by population pressure on the land—unemployment, intensification of the struggle for economic survival, the widening gap between rich and poor. Avenues of migration to Hawaii, North America, and Australia were being narrowed as the influx of Japanese laborers met with local resistance, and China, with its own problems of overcrowding, was not a suitable destination for Japan's excess population. In Katō's view the only attractive alternative was Korea, sparsely populated, close to home, and blessed with a good climate and rich land, where Japanese settlers could maintain their own lifestyle, wearing Japanese clothes, living in Japanese houses, and eating Japanese food. He urged the government to assist agricultural settlers willing to develop uncultivated land there by paying all or part of their ocean fare, supplying them with seeds and tools, and providing land and houses to rent or own. The results would be an improvement in Korean agriculture as the Japanese brought in more advanced techniques, an increase in trade as the Koreans became more prosperous through agricultural growth, and the development of new sources of food for Japan.[25]

SPONSORED IMMIGRATION

The promotion of migration to Korea had already been mooted at the highest levels of the government in the 1890s. In the fall of 1894 Yamagata Aritomo thought that the dispatch of colonists to north Korea was, along with the building of a trunk line traversing the peninsula, one of the most urgent policies for Japan. Just as the railway would link Japan with the rest of continental Asia, so the colonists

24. Ibid., 319–23; Tōgō, *Nihon shokumin ron*, 365–77, 390.
25. Katō Masao, "Kankoku imin ron," 10–12; see also Kurose, "Nichi-Rō sengo no 'Chōsen kei'ei,'" 101–2.

would set down roots for Japanese influence in Korea.[26] By the time
of the Russo-Japanese War the promotion of emigration to Korea had
become an unquestioned element in government policy. The May 1904
cabinet decision committed the Katsura government to promoting
migration of agricultural settlers. Sending large numbers of Japanese
farmers to the interior of the peninsula would reduce the pressure
of excess population at home while promoting the development of
agricultural resources in Korea. Two birds could be killed with one
stone.

Agricultural migration was hindered primarily by treaty provisions
restricting foreign ownership of land to a zone within one *ri* of the treaty
settlements. As we shall see below, the Japanese attempted to ease land
ownership regulations and to secure control over land in the interior
from 1904 onwards. In 1905 the government sent a mission of agricultural experts to investigate agriculture and land ownership in Korea.
While its report in January 1906 focused on measures the Korean government might take to improve agricultural techniques and yields, it also
urged the Japanese government to do what it could to facilitate migration by confirming the right of Japanese to own land and settle in the
interior, permitting wider use of government-owned land by Japanese,
discounting train and steamship tickets for immigrants, and setting up a
mechanism to provide guidance for agricultural enterprises.[27]

The expanding political role of Japan in Korea and Manchuria after
the war added urgency to the promotion of migration to the continent,
where colonists were needed to buttress its strategic presence. General
Kodama Gentarō, as head of the organizing committee of the South
Manchuria Railway Company, urged that 500,000 settlers be sent to
Manchuria to discourage the Russians from starting a war of revenge,
and Gōtō Shimpei, the first president of the line, advocated erecting a
barricade of settlers in Manchuria as part of his policy of "military preparedness by civilian means" (*bunsoteki bunbi*).[28] Others argued that it
was especially urgent to move Japanese settlers into Korea to counterbalance residual Korean nationalism.[29] At the same time, since Japanese

26. *YAI*, 223–25.
27. *Tōkyō keizai zasshi*, Jan. 13, 1906, p. 35.
28. Inoue Kiyoshi, *Nihon teikokushugi no keisei*, 302–3.
29. Kōbe Masao, an agricultural expert who urged promoting agricultural migration,
pointed out that it was far more important to move Japanese settlers into Korea than into
Taiwan. "Whereas Taiwan is an island, Korea is part of the continent. The inhabitants of
Taiwan place importance on the practical, they hold benevolent government dear, and
they lack a concept of a state. While [the Taiwanese] are an itinerant (*dekasegi*) people, the

immigration had become an irritant in relations with the United States, Canada, Australia, and Great Britain, deflecting migration to the continent made diplomatic sense as well. If Japanese settlers went westward rather than eastward across the Pacific, relations with the Anglo-American powers were likely to be more cordial.[30]

By the fall of 1908 the Japanese government had adopted a policy of "concentrating overseas migration in Manchuria and Korea" (Man-Chō imin shūchūron). The decision was prompted less by anxieties over internal social and economic difficulties, a theme frequently found in the writings of those outside government, than by a clear desire to consolidate and expand Japan's commercial, economic, and political influence abroad. First and foremost, the government wished to prepare for possible resistance to Japanese expansion by Russia or China, two powerful neighbors whose future attitudes toward the Japanese presence in Korea and Manchuria remained ambiguous. But equally important, the policy would remove impediments to good relations with the Anglo-Saxon countries, with whom Japan was trying to develop trading and manufacturing ties. Instead of forcing these important economic partners to accept large numbers of unwanted immigrants whose presence created "anti-Japanese fever," it made more sense for the government to direct the flow of emigration to Asia instead. Not only would such a policy reduce friction and eliminate the diplomatic crises caused by the immigration issue, but it would also remove hindrances to the development of trade and industry—the "principal goals of our external policy." Obviously, the policy of "concentrating migration in Manchuria and Korea" also provided a graceful way to justify its acceptance of the humiliating American demand that Japan curb emigration. If it could be argued that emigration to Asia was in the national interest whereas emigration to Hawaii and the United States was not, then acceptance of these demands was a matter of statecraft, not a diplomatic failure or national humiliation.[31]

In a Diet speech in February 1909 Foreign Minister Komura, chief advocate of the policy, argued that Japan could hope to hold its own with such population giants as China, Russia, and the United States

---

inhabitants of Korea, even though their country is a vassal state or a protectorate, had their own state and possessed a long and unique history and unique customs." To hold them under control, it was important to bring over Japanese setttlers. Kōbe, Chōsen nōgyō iminron, 2.

30. NGNSB, 1:284–305; Ono, "Nihon teikokushugi to iminron," 317–18.
31. NGNSB, 1:308–9.

by spreading its people into nearby Asia. "As a result of the Russo-Japanese War, the position of the empire has changed, and we have seen an expansion of the territory under our control. We have come to the point where we must avoid dispersing our nationality (*minzoku*) in distant foreign lands and concentrate them in this new territory, managing them with complete solidarity and unity."[32] This rationale for promoting "colonization" in Korea as well as other parts of Asia focused on strategic and political ends. It made no mention of domestic problems like excess population, food shortages, or unemployment; indeed, it suggested that a large population was a source of national strength for countries like China and the United States.

Just what did the commitment to "concentration of emigration in Manchuria and Korea" mean in practical terms? How was the policy given shape and form? The answer is that the government attempted to encourage migration to Korea in much the same way it had encouraged migration to Hokkaido—by subsidizing the costs of emigration. The main vehicle was to be the Oriental Development Company (Tōyō Takushoku Kaisha), established in 1908. Although the company later expanded into a quasi-official multinational corporation presiding over a complex set of investments and enterprises in Manchuria and other parts of Asia, it began as an organization to send agricultural colonists to Korea. In effect, the company's goal was to put into practice the policy recommendations of the May 1904 cabinet decision, as ratified by the 1905 mission of agricultural experts.

In the immediate postwar years promotion of emigration to the peninsula was left in the hands of several private companies organized in 1905 and 1906 to buy land in Korea for Japanese settlers. But Katsura, after stepping down as prime minister, launched a more systematic effort. The moving force behind the establishment of the Oriental Development Company was the Tōyō Kyōkai (the Oriental Association), originally organized by Katsura as the Taiwan Kyōkai (Taiwan Association) in 1898 and renamed in 1907. The organization supported a variety of activities, including a training school for colonial officials, which later became Takushoku Daigaku, but its main function was to provide a vehicle for Katsura to influence the shape of continental policy while out of power.[33]

In May and June 1907 Komatsubara Eitarō, a former Home Minis-

32. Ono, "Nihon teikokushugi to iminron," 315–16.
33. Kirishima, "Tōyō shokutaku kaisha," part 2; Kurose, "Nichi-Rō sengo no 'Chōsen kei'ei' "; Moscowitz, "Oriental Development Company," 73–75, 81–85.

try official who served as secretary-general of the association, toured Korea and Manchuria to investigate the possibility of promoting agricultural development by sending over agricultural migrants. He reported back, as everyone else had, that the treaty restrictions limited the ability of Japanese to buy land, but he also observed that those Japanese who did buy land had little or no interest in the improvement of agriculture and were simply content to live off rents from Korean tenants. Komatsubara, echoing what so many others had already written on the subject, proposed that the government directly encourage farmers to migrate by offering discounts on fares to Korea and by providing tools, other domestic implements, and farmland through a system of subsidies and loans. "In managing Korea," he said, "we must first carry on colonization, thereby aiming at improving the development of agriculture, deepening the friendly relations between the Japanese and Korean people, and bringing about the development of economic relations between them."[34]

The Komatsubara report set in motion planning for a colonization company. Two committees put together plans: the first group included Matsuzaki Kuranosuke, a professor of economics at Tokyo Imperial University, and Nakanishi Joichi, a landholder in Kunsan Province recommended by Ōkura Kihachirō; the second included Iwai Hachirō, Hirata Tōsuke (a prominent member of the Yamagata faction), and Komatsubara. Both committees assumed that the company would be a quasi-governmental enterprise (kokkateki keiei) operating with government subsidies, run by state-appointed managers, and authorized to sell bonds to the public, and both also assumed that land under the company's control would be leased or bought from the Korean government. But there were slight differences in their separate proposals. The Matsuzaki committee proposed an immigration company whose function would be to buy land in Korea to turn over to Japanese immigrants and whose goal would be to produce a class of small Japanese landholders in Korea. The Iwai committee, by contrast, thought the company should be involved in a much wider range of activities—the sale oι seed, fertilizer, and tools, the marketing of agricultural products, the development of forestry and animal husbandry, and even transportation; in short, they projected an agricultural conglomerate.[35] The Matsuzaki plan left more to market forces; the Iwai plan involved more bureaucratic guidance.

---

34. *Tōyō Takushoku Kabushiki Kaisha sōritsu tenmatsusho*, 2.
35. Kirishima, "Tōyō shokutaku kaisha," 41–42.

In September 1907 the two committees put together a final proposal calling for the establishment of an emigration company capitalized at ¥10 million, subsidized by a government-guaranteed 6 percent dividend.[36] This arrangement, intended to provide a risk-free return on capital, was the same employed in the organization of the Seoul-Pusan Railway. To build support, the plan was presented to a gathering of key financial, industrial, and political leaders in late September and also circulated to the Saionji cabinet, Resident-General Itō Hirobumi, the Korean Prime Minister Yi Wan-yong, and Korean Agricultural and Commerce Minister Song Pyŏng-jun. By late December a draft bill to establish the company was approved by the Saionji cabinet.

Although there was general support for the plan, there were competing ideas as well. As an alternative way to promote agricultural migration, Finance Minister Sakatani Yoshio proposed to set up a colonization office (*shokuminkyoku*) in the residency-general. Many members of the business community, though, favored a company with a broader mandate, able not only to acquire land and promote immigration but also to engage in other activities, including mining operations. The businessmen also favored a higher guaranteed dividend. The reclamation and development of cultivated land was an expensive investment, they argued, and if profits were too low, investors would be reluctant to buy the company stock. These and other reservations were accommodated in the bill presented to the Diet in the winter of 1908.[37]

More substantial objections came from Resident-General Itō Hirobumi, who feared that the project was politically insensitive and perhaps too ambitious. The goals of the company—the colonization of Korea and the improvement of Korean agriculture—were unobjectionable, but its politics were a problem. For one thing, since the company was to operate independently in Korea, it might pose a threat to the authority or influence of the residency-general. Itō feared that the Oriental Development Company might become a tool of the Yamagata faction and that it might become an autonomous power in Korea as the British East India Company had become in India. Beyond that, he objected to the exclusion of Korean participation in the company. Given the sudden outburst of indigenous resistance in 1907–8, Itō was not anxious to fuel the fires of Korean nationalism. He argued that unless the Koreans were involved in the company, they would see the company as just another at-

36. Proposals relating to the founding of the company may be found in FMA, file 3.3.2.29, and KSH, Shoda-ke Archive, reel 41 (vol. 71).
37. Kirishima, "Tōyō shokutaku kaisha," 47.

tempt, like the Nagamori plan (see chapter 10), to grab their land. When he returned to Tokyo in early March 1908, Itō insisted that the company be established under Korean law as well as Japanese, that Koreans be included among the company managers and stockholders, and that Korean farmers as well as Japanese be settled on the company's land. These objections were met by further amendments to the bill, which finally passed the Diet with little objection in March 1908.

Initial projections about the number of migrants to be settled in Korea were quite grandiose. Noda Utarō told a Diet committee considering the bill that 30,000 to 50,000 agricultural emigrants were to be sent during the first decade of operation, and that by 1920 the total number would reach from 350,000 to 500,000. The planners, however, were more modest in their expectations. The compromise plan drawn up by Matsuzaki and Iwai in September 1907 proposed a schedule of 10,000 migrants during the first year of operations, 20,000 the second year, 30,000 the third year, and 10,000 a year after that.[38] The drafters of the Oriental Development Company Law appear to have used these figures as well. Their report proposed that the company acquire 253,000 chō (about 620,000 acres) of land during its first decade: 10,000 to be farmed by Korean tenants, 3,000 to be worked by hired labor, and 240,000 to be turned over to the 240,000 migrants brought in on the schedule outlined above. In practice, this projection would have required the company to acquire 14 percent of all the cultivated land in Korea.[39] The emigrants were to be provided with enough to support themselves through self-cultivation, and as much as possible they were to be sent in groups and widely dispersed over the country to minimize Korean resistance to a perceived "land grab."

By the time of annexation the Oriental Development Company had not sent a single emigrant household to the peninsula, and its plans for promoting migration had been scaled down considerably. The company regulations approved by the new government-general in September 1910 set no fixed quota for the first year. For 1911–14 an annual migration of 1,000 to 1,500 households was projected, considerably less than originally planned. Even so there were few takers. In 1911, when the annual quota was set at 1,300 households, only 1,235 applications were received; and of those only 160 were accepted. The same pattern

38. Ibid., 42.
39. It was assumed that paid-in capital on company stock sales would provide the capital to buy the land and the loans to immigrants would be financed out of the sale of company bonds. Kurose, "Nichi-Rō sengo no 'Chōsen kei'ei,'" 104–7, 117.

TABLE 7   RECRUITMENT OF IMMIGRANT
HOUSEHOLDS BY THE ORIENTAL
DEVELOPMENT COMPANY, 1911–1920

Year	No. of applicants	No. accepted	No. actually migrated (A)	No. in Korea after 10 years (B)	% (A/B)
1911	1,235	160	160	117	73.1
1912	1,714	720	421	337	80.0
1913	2,086	1,167	814	624	76.7
1914	3,472	1,330	796	532	66.8
1915	1,964	1,108	586	400	68.3
1916	1,284	774	386	260	67.4
1917	1,101	542	295	209	70.8
1918	1,553	650	475	313	65.9
1919	1,282	598	481	319	66.3
1920	2,111	967	688	417	60.6

SOURCE: Kurose Ikuji, "Nichi-Rō sengo no 'Chōsen kei'ei' to Tōyō shokutaku kabushiki kaisha,"
Chōsenshi kenkyūkai ronbunshū 12 (Mar. 1975): 120, 124.

continued over the next decade (table 7). Among those accepted, the attrition rate was high. Prospective immigrants often changed their plans before departure because of sickness, a death in the family, a lack of funds, and various other reasons. Even in the peak year of 1914, when 1,330 households were accepted, only 796 eventually migrated to Korea.[40] And many households that did migrate eventually returned home.

Why did government-sponsored migration fail? First, as a company official later observed, the initial plans of the company were based on quite unrealistic projections arrived at by *soroban* calculations, not by investigation of what was really possible, and they vastly overestimated the amount of uncultivated land available to turn over to the settlers. By 1913, for example, the company had acquired only 60,000 *chō* of land, or about one-quarter the amount projected in 1907–8.[41]

Second, soon after its organization the Oriental Development Company shifted its goals from national purpose to private profit. Its management was reluctant to invest in low-profit activities like the immigration program. As Noda Utarō, vice-president of the company, told a

40. Tōyō Takushoku Kabushiki Kaisha, *Tōtaku jū nen shi*, 92–93.
41. Kurose, "Nichi-Rō sengo no 'Chōsen kei'ei' "; see tables 12, 14, 15, pp. 114, 116, 117.

reporter in 1914, the company had to answer to stockholders, not the public; if dividends were not high, stockholders would complain. Most domestic companies offered dividends of 10 percent, but the Oriental Development Company was unable to distribute even 7 or 8 percent. Promoting emigration and developing irrigation works were necessary activities, but the company could not raise the capital to carry out such projects without turning a higher profit. "In a newly developed territory like Korea, the first principle is, above all, to produce a return.... If profits are no greater than at home, and one cannot make more money, then Korea will never develop no matter how much time passes." Instead of investing substantial capital in irrigation works, forestry development, or immigration, the company promoted them indirectly, lending money to private individuals to carry them on much as a bank would, to the happy benefit of the stockholders.[42]

Third, and perhaps most important, there was no great rush by rural households in Japan to sign up for the company's emigration program. During its early years financial support was rather meager. According to its report for the year 1911, the company offered emigrants "indirect protection" rather than "direct aid." Migrant families were provided travel information, offered discounts on train and boat fares, given discounts at designated inns or hostels, and helped with shipping their luggage. Once in Korea, immigrants could borrow funds from the company—up to ¥200 from the company for start-up costs such as building a house or buying seed, fertilizer, and tools, up to ¥500 for improvement of land, and up to ¥500 to tide them over periods of bad harvest or other natural disasters.[43] But no direct subsidies were provided to buy land or cover living expenses.

The majority of households applying to the company were tenant farmers at home, and most arrived in Korea with little or no operating capital of their own. The main assistance they received was loans to purchase land. As a result, the migrants rather quickly became stratified between those with few resources, who were often forced to the margin economically, and those with some funds of their own, who gave up cultivation to become the landlords of Korean tenants and invested their

42. Noda, "Chōsen kaitaku," 18–21.
43. Tōyō Takushoku Kabushiki Kaisha, Chōsen ijū tebiki; Tōyō Takushoku Kabushiki Kaisha sanjū nen shi, 175–79. For those migrating in groups of more than ten households, the company also promised to assist in the construction and maintenance of a school, to support day care centers (hoikusho), to arrange for free dental or medical help at nearby kenpei or army facilities, to dig wells, to build roads, and to construct bridges to make transportation and communication easier.

profits in moneylending. The first group—the marginal self-cultivators—was the larger, and the gap between the two grew in the period of
falling rice prices before World War I. Many of the poorer migrants,
who hardly had enough for subsistence, suffered from malnutrition and
associated ailments like night blindness and physical debilitation, which
left them unable to work. To make ends meet, many took on side jobs,
engaging in petty commerce or *dekasegi* employment, hauling timber
and stones while their wives made straw goods. Some simply broke their
contracts and decamped. As one company report indicated, many immigrants found themselves in desperate conditions when rice prices
dropped suddenly before they had a chance to settle in and consolidate
themselves: "Many earn only the bare minimum, just enough to sustain
life.... There are those who suffer from malnutrition, who lose their
power to see at dusk and who do not have the strength to work without
reducing their cultivation."[44] Indeed, in 1914 the company changed its
regulations to discourage the migration of poorer tenant farmers who
lacked "an ability to adjust" or "an independent spirit."[45]

Quite apart from the lack of adequate financial support, emigration
involved an enormous social and cultural wrench for rural families.
Rumors about the difficulty of life in Korea abounded: the country was
extremely poor, the Japanese authorities were cavalier and tyrannical,
children could not get a good education, rural emigrants had a hard
time and often lost all their money, and so forth.[46] Emigrants had to
pack their worldly goods and gather their families for a trip to an unknown country; they had to travel into remote and often inaccessible
areas, often isolated villages, hauling their luggage and goods by horse
over miles of unpaved road, to settle in the midst of strangers who
neither spoke their language nor welcomed their presence; and they
had to give up what had come to be accepted amenities even in rural
Japan—schools, clean and safe drinking water, hot baths, midwives,
and doctors—all the things that gave Japan a higher standard of living.
Only the truly desperate, the incurably optimistic, or the hopelessly
misinformed could have been attracted by such prospects.

As agricultural conditions improved at home during the World War I
boom, economic incentives for rural migrants diminished. The inflation
of rice prices during the latter stages of the war brought rural prosperity

44. Tōyō Takushoku Kabushiki Kaisha, *Shokumin jigyō kakuchihōbetsu seiseki.*
45. Aoki Kayoko, "Tōyō kaitaku kabushiki kaisha."
46. Shiba Anshikuro, "Naichi nōmin no kon to Man-kan ijū," *Chōsen,* June 1916,
p. 26.

and visible improvement in rural living conditions. Between 1914 and 1919 the number of domestic applicants for the Oriental Development Company's emigration program dropped steadily, and a larger proportion of applicants came from households already living in Korea. During the peak boom years (1917–19), about 40 percent of those applying were settled in Korea, and about 25 percent of those accepted were. These figures suggest that the program had become less significant in promoting migration to the peninsula and more important as a way of providing a financial stake to those already there. In effect, as Noda pointed out, the company was serving primarily as a bank to finance land purchases.

In any event, immigrants sponsored by the Oriental Development Company never constituted more than a minority among the Japanese agricultural households in Korea—even in 1919, only about one-third of the total. The program not only fell far short of its original goals but was far less effective than other less costly programs sponsored by a number of prefectural governments. Eleven prefectures, mainly in Kyushu and western Japan, provided subsidies and other forms of financial assistance to move fishing families to Korea. By 1910 there were more than eleven hundred fishing households in several dozen communities on the peninsula, all established at far less cost than households sponsored by the Oriental Development Company program.[47] By contrast, some prefecture-sponsored immigration and land development companies seem to have faced the same problems as the Oriental Development Company. The Ishikawa Prefecture Agricultural Company (Ishikawa-ken Nōgyō Kabushiki Kaisha), which the prefectural legislature provided with guaranteed loans, a subsidy to guarantee dividends at 6 percent, and the help of technical experts, purchased several tracts of land in Korea between 1914 and 1918. Starting modestly with one household in 1910, it had managed to send more than sixty-seven by 1915; but like the Oriental Development Company it found hiring Korean tenants more profitable, and in the early 1920s the company abandoned its efforts at encouraging agricultural migrants.[48] In the end, officially sponsored migration, whether sponsored by the quasi-official Oriental Development Company or by local gov-

47. For example, Okayama prefecture helped to set up a community of emigrant fishermen on a small island off the southern coast of Kyŏngsang by providing modest subsidies to help buy land, set up an elementary school, and develop uncultivated plots. KSSH, 70–80; see also Okayama-ken, Chōsen Okayama-mura jissekisho, 1–15.

48. Tanaka Yoshio, "Meiji kōki 'Chōsen takushoku.'"

ernments, was not very successful, and the vision of a peninsula densely populated by industrious Japanese small landholders gave way to the reality of a peninsula sparsely populated by petty Japanese entrepreneurs and functionaries.

VOLUNTARY MIGRATION

With the exception of those in the military or in official employment, nearly all of the Japanese who arrived in Korea before 1910, and most of those who arrived afterwards, came without any official help or encouragement. In other words, the vast majority of Japanese settlers were voluntary and self-supporting migrants who moved to Korea because they wanted to. As demographers point out, voluntary emigration sometimes occurs because the migrants seek to escape religious, political, or ethnic persecution at home. In such cases the uncertainties of migrating are counterbalanced by the greater risks of staying at home. Few if any Japanese went to Korea for such reasons. They were not fleeing for their lives as Jews fled the pogroms in Russia and Poland or Armenians fled the massacres in Turkey; nor were they forced to uproot themselves by the political upheavals that sent waves of Muslims to Pakistan and Hindus to India at the time of partition. Nor were they faced with major natural disasters at home, like the potato blight in Ireland or the crop failures in Germany that prompted inhabitants of those countries to come to the United States before the Civil War.

Rather, as most models of modern free migration suggest, the movement of Japanese from the home islands to Korea was prompted by a desire for economic improvement. It would make little sense for migrants to move to a new land where their economic circumstances were likely to be diminished. To be sure, in reality the immigrants often found themselves little better off than at home, but the motives of the migrants, not the consequences of their movement, concern us here. The key question demographers ask is, Were the migrants "pushed" by circumstances in their own society or "pulled" by opportunities in the society to which they migrated? Were the migrants in flight from adverse economic circumstances, or were they in pursuit of better ones?

Some historians, both Japanese and Korean, argue that Japanese migrated to Korea to escape deteriorating social and economic circumstances at home. Emigration, in other words, was read as one more evil wreaked by burgeoning domestic capitalism on Japanese society. No doubt capitalism was accompanied by unpleasant consequences, and no doubt the process of industrialization, internal migration, shifts in internal markets, and the like affected emigration to Korea. But it is difficult to make a general case that increasing misery of the Japanese working population had a very great impact on decisions to migrate to Korea or indeed to any other part of the world. During the years between 1894 and 1910, a period of enormous emigration not only to Korea but to Taiwan, Hawaii, and the United States, overall economic conditions were good—and getting better. Although it is true that the Japanese economy suffered several recessions during the period 1894–1910, especially in the wake of the Russo-Japanese War, production and employment in the modern sector expanded steadily. Between 1900 and 1909 the number of workers employed in private factories, government-owned factories, and mining increased from 528,642 to 1,153,441. Employment in the modern transportation and communication sectors expanded as well—from 166,000 in 1900 to 366,000 in 1909. In other words, in 1909 there were 824,799 more workers in the modern sector than there had been in 1900—more than double the number of jobs. Most of the job expansion took place in the Kinki region (Osaka, Kyoto, Hyogo, Nara, Shiga, and Wakayama), northern Kyushu (Fukuoka, Oita, Saga, and Nagasaki), and southern Kanto (Shizuoka, Aichi, and Mie.) In Kinki and southern Kanto employment grew in the textile industry, which relied heavily on female workers, but in northern Kyushu, which produced many migrants to Korea, new employment was concentrated in mining, a heavy employer of male workers.[49] In sum, lack of expanding employment opportunities does not provide a convincing explanation for migration to Korea.

Perhaps a better case can be made that a stagnating agricultural sector was a factor "pushing" migrants to Korea. For example, agricultural employment remained more or less constant during this period—14,186,000 employed in 1894 and 14,020,000 in 1910 and so did the number of farm households—5,446,000 in 1894 and 5,518,000 in 1910. But it is also important to note that although the number of farm households increased in eastern Japan, they declined in western Japan, where emigration was heaviest. The amount of arable land per farm household was growing in western Japan, however, while it was declining in the east. This means that farm households in eastern Japan were becoming slightly less well off in terms of assets, and those in the west slightly better off; but the overwhelming bulk of migrants to Korea,

49. Ōishi, *Nihon sangyō kakumei no kenkyū*, 2:134–38.

as we shall see, came from western Japan, not eastern Japan.[50] While this is a rather crude measure of well-being in the countryside, these trends argue against any notion that overall agricultural hardship was a strong motivating factor in prompting migration. Indeed, there were substantial cultural barriers to migration that made it difficult for the Oriental Development Company to recruit settler households.

To be sure, adverse local economic circumstances or short-term economic dislocation may well have affected many individual decisions to migrate, but at the macroeconomic level there is little evidence to suggest that deteriorating economic conditions were a major reason for the flow of Japanese settlers to Korea and the rest of the outside world in the last years of the Meiji period. In other words, it seems difficult to discover "push" factors—economic desperation or decline in economic opportunities—that might explain migration overseas in general or migration to Korea in particular. It seems much more likely that "pull" factors were more significant, especially with respect to migration to Korea. One "pull" factor was proximity; another was the opening up of new and attractive types of employment. Both suggest that migration to Korea was simply an extension of the same processes that led to internal migration from the countryside to the cities during the same period.

PROXIMITY AND CHAIN MIGRATION

If one tries to sort the various factors that influenced migration to Korea, place of origin in Japan may have been the most significant. To put the matter simply, the closer one lived to Korea along the sea lanes linking the home island to the peninsula, the more likely one was to become a migrant. The majority of the Japanese residents in Korea at the time of annexation came from Kyushu, Chugoku, and Kinki. Indeed, these were the areas from which most Japanese emigrants came (table 8). While Taiwan and the Kwantung Territory drew slightly more from Kanto, and Hawaii drew more from western Honshu, the concentration is striking but not surprising. After all, if distance is a barrier to migration, then it stands to reason—not always a reliable guide in the study of human behavior—that the probability of migration between two places increases as the distance between them decreases. And once a process of migration has begun, it tends to draw on the same population. What-

---

50. Mataji, ed., *Nōringyō*, vol. 9 of Ōkawa, Shinohara, and Umchara, eds., *Chōki keizai tōkei*, 218–19.

TABLE 8   REGIONAL ORIGINS
OF OVERSEAS MIGRANTS

	Korea (1908)		Taiwan (1905)		Kwantung and railroad zone (1906)	
	No.	%	No.	%	No.	%
Kyushu	42,388	33.6	18,749	32.7	4,584	35.8
Chūgoku	33,570	26.6	8,728	15.2	1,756	13.7
Kinki	14,992	11.9	7,755	13.5	2,275	17.8
Shinkoku	9,820	7.8	3,655	6.4	739	5.8
Kantō	8,667	6.9	6,244	10.9	1,436	11.2
Tōkai	5,125	4.1	3,141	5.5	768	6.0
Hokuriku	4,740	3.8	3,188	5.6	420	3.3
Tōhoku	3,418	2.7	2,566	4.5	350	2.7
Tōsan	2,802	2.2	2,049	3.6	407	3.2
Hokkaidō	618	0.5	435	0.8	54	0.4
Ryukyu	28	0.0+	779	1.4	3	0.0+
Total	126,168	100.0	57,289	100.0	12,792	100.0

ever prompted the pioneer migrants to move in the first place is likely to persist, at least in the short term, and the migrants who come later can readily follow routes and networks already established.

Japan's contacts with the Asian continent had traditionally passed through western Japan. During the Edo period China trade had been based in Nagasaki, trade with the Ryukyus in Kagoshima, and trade with Korea in Tsushima. While none of these areas played a significant role in trade with Europe and the United States, western ports continued to be important in the continental trade throughout the Meiji period. Nagasaki remained the principal entrepôt in this trade until the 1890s, when it was displaced by Osaka. It is therefore not surprising that in the early stages of settlement the vast majority of the Japanese residents in Korea came from five prefectures, three in northern Kyushu (Nagasaki, Oita, Fukuoka) and two in western Honshu (Yamaguchi, Hiroshima). In 1893, 84 percent of the Japanese in Pusan and 76.4 percent of those in Inchon came from those five prefectures. The largest number came from Nagasaki prefecture, which included both Tsushima, the traditional intermediary in the Korean trade, and the port of Nagasaki. Many of the Nagasaki prefecture natives appear to have been involved in foreign trade as owners of trading houses, as small shopkeepers, or as workers in other miscellaneous trades. By contrast, migrants from Yamaguchi tended to be manual laborers—carpenters, plasterers, masons, boatmen, day laborers, fishermen, or female servants. The same was true of migrants from Fukuoka, Oita, and Hiroshima.[51]

By the time of annexation the concentration of migrants from western Japan was diluted by an influx of Japanese drawn from farther afield. In 1910 the five prefectures mentioned above still ranked at the top of the list but accounted for only 47 percent of all the Japanese population in Korea. As time went on there was a small shift in the rankings of the prefectures, and a shift in percentages as well, but the patterns established by the time of annexation seemed to persist in a general way. One can attribute this to what sociologists call "chain migration," a process by which migrants tend to come from the same communities or set of communities over time. The process is quite common in many parts of the world. Voluntary migration takes place in a social context, and individuals who live in a community where others have gone abroad and found success are more inclined to leave home than persons who live in a community where most others have stayed put. The dynamic of "chain migration" depends on the flow of information from early migrants back to their home community. An adventurous pioneer goes abroad, establishes himself in a foreign society, and prospers; he encourages his close relatives, perhaps his siblings or cousins or even his former neighbors and friends, to join him; he may offer them jobs or employment if they come; he reports home on the opportunities for jobs or business he has discovered; as the news spreads, uncertainties or anxieties about conditions abroad are dispelled and more distant friends or relatives are tempted to migrate; when they arrive, they find familiar and friendly faces; and they in turn establish their own networks of communication. To the extent that networks of information tend to be highly local, migrants tend to come from highly concentrated areas.[52]

Since no consistent aggregate statistical information is available on the place of origin of Japanese migrants to Korea at the village or sub-prefectural level, it is difficult to make firm generalizations about the importance of chain migration. Anecdotal evidence suggests that mi-

51. Yamada Shōji, "Meiji zenki no Ni-Chō bōeki," 62–63.
52. A good example of chain migration can be found among the Japanese migrants to Hawaii. Immigrant workers from the same villages often ended up working on the same plantations, speaking their own local dialects, shring the same network of friends and acquaintances, marrying within the same population, and even preserving many of the home village customs, from food to entertainment.

grants to Korea often came from the same villages or communities at home. As one contemporary suggested, the Japanese had a national "urge to cluster" (*banji yoriaishugi*). "When they hear someone has started up a business somewhere, they rush out immediately and get into the same business as the other fellow."[53] A Japanese journalist who visited Kaesong on the eve of the Russo-Japanese War found that of the seventy Japanese residents, thirty had come from Fukuoka. When he inquired why, he was told that a few years earlier a man by the name of Ishibashi had come to the city from Fukuoka and had great success in business; the others had come from Fukuoka in hopes of doing the same.[54] It also appears that many of the agricultural migrants who came to Korea with the help of the Oriental Development Company came from the same villages.

The only microlevel study of migration to Korea, undertaken by Kimura Kenji, focuses on the village of Marifumura, Kumagu-gun, in eastern Yamaguchi prefecture.[55] The village, consisting of several hamlets, including Befu and Umajima, was located on the Inland Sea along the main shipping route between Kansai and Kyushu, and beyond Kyushu to Korea. The study suggests (1) that migrants to Korea were likely to come from areas where overseas migration was common in general and (2) that migrants to Korea were likely to come from specific hamlets or villages. In 1917, for example, 9,662 (or about 9 percent) of the 106,983 persons registered in Kumagu-gun were resident abroad: 4,080 in Korea, 2,545 in Hawaii, and 906 in the continental United States. In the village of Marifumura most of its registered overseas population (829 out of 868) were resident in Korea; and Umajima, one of the hamlets within the village, was known as the "island of the Korea *narikin*," since many of the families resident in Korea maintained houses there to which they retreated during the cold Korean winters.

In the hamlets of Befu and Umajima there were few farm families but a rather large number involved in commerce, particularly in the coastal shipping trade. During Tokugawa times, shipping households had carried tax rice for sale to Osaka and charcoal and dried sardines from Kyushu to ports on the coastal route in the Inland Sea. By the *bakumatsu* period their routes had expanded to include trade between Satsuma and Chōshū, trade with the Ryukyus, and even trade with

53. Sakamaki, *Kaigai risshin annai*, 16.
54. Nakai, *Chōsen kaikō roku*, 54.
55. Kimura Kenji, "Meijiki Nihonjin"; republished in Kimura Kenji, *Zai-Chō Nihonjin no shakaishi*, ch. 2.

Pusan by way of Tsushima. In short, even before the opening of Korea these two communities were already involved in trade contacts with the continent. When the *bakuhan* system collapsed, the local economy was hit by the ensuing change. The shipping of tax rice to Osaka ended, as did the trade between Satsuma and Chōshū, and modern shipping firms with better vessels began to compete for routes along the Inland Sea. These political and economic changes, coupled with the levying of new taxes on fishing rights, led many of the local shipping households in Marifumura to seek opportunities elsewhere.

When Pusan was opened as a treaty port, the leading shipping families from Marifumura, taking advantage of their earlier experience in the Korea trade, moved there to set up shipping enterprises. The Marifumura shippers plied a route from Pusan via Marifumura to Osaka, carrying soybeans, rice, and other grains for sale in Japan and returning with cargoes of sake, cotton cloth, lumber, salt, matches, and other sundries from Osaka and regional products from ports along the route to Korea. Eventually they began to modernize their fleets, buying Western-style sailing ships to replace their more traditional vessels. The changeover was financed by borrowing operating capital from the Dai-Ichi Bank, the principal bank involved in trading operations with Korea, with a number of large Osaka foreign trade merchants as cosigners. As their operations became established more or less permanently at Pusan, shipping family members, clerks, apprentices, and servants began to settle there. By 1889 about 20 percent of the population and 20 percent of the households from Umajima had moved abroad.

Once regular steamship service expanded after 1888, the sailing vessels owned by the Marifumura shipping households began to lose business; but since these households had settled more or less permanently in Korea by then, they adjusted to the new competition by shifting to the coastal trade in Korean waters or by turning to exclusively commercial activities within the treaty ports. As the Japanese presence in Korea deepened and solidified, so did migration. Between 1889 and 1903 there was a spurt of new arrivals in Korea, and by the time of the Russo-Japanese War nearly half the households registered in Umajima were living in Korea. It appears from figures on births and deaths in Korea that families rather than individuals were involved in the migration and that males who moved there tended to be household heads or eldest sons. This suggests that the migrants moved to Korea with the intention to stay more or less permanently.

Just how typical was the case of Marifumura? It is difficult to say in the absence of other similar studies. On the one hand, the case study does lend support to the generalizations that can be made from macro-level statistics, and it confirms the importance of proximity to Korea, traditional patterns of contact with the outside world, and the influence of previous migration in affecting the decision to migrate to Korea. On the other hand, it does not seem to explain very well the temporal pattern of migration, particularly the acceleration of migration after the Russo-Japanese War, since much of the migration from Marifumura took place before that. One can better explain the timing of the flow by looking at the second "pull" factor: the opening up of new opportunities for profit and employment.

THE LURE OF WORK

The ebb and flow of migration to Korea corresponds very closely with the opening up of new opportunities there. During the 1890s, when the number of Japanese residing in Hawaii, Taiwan, and the American mainland jumped from 23,327 to 156,276, an increase of 670 percent, the number of Japanese residing in Korea, where employment opportunities still remained quite limited, merely doubled. By contrast, between 1900 and 1910, when the overall number of Japanese emigrants increased a little less than 300 percent, the Japanese population in Korea rose tenfold. The most plausible explanation for this sudden surge is that the establishment of the protectorate, and then the final decision to annex the peninsula, created a whole new structure of economic opportunities for Japanese seeking to better their lives.

The impulses that drew Japanese to Korea, particularly after 1905, were not unlike those that drew others to the gold fields of the Yukon or the open spaces of California—the hope of quick success and a better life. It was clear that Korea was on the verge of economic development and change and with that came the possibility of new and better employment. The growing trade with Korea opened new opportunities for merchants large and small; the creation of a Japanese state within a state opened up jobs for policemen, mailmen, clerks, petty functionaries, and technicians; the expansion of a modern transportation, communication, and financial infrastructure made jobs for better-educated white-collar workers and engineers; the transformation of the landholding structure paved the way for land acquisition; and the influx of people to fill this new employment structure created the need for shopkeepers, barbers, teahouse owners, and brothel keepers to provide services enjoyed at home.

As we have already seen, the adventurers, carpetbaggers, and penny capitalists who streamed to Korea in 1894–95 and 1904–5 were drawn by the lure of quick money. The networks of information available to potential emigrants all stressed how easy it was to make money there. Before the Russo-Japanese War, for example, it was widely rumored that money was to be made not only in honest and ordinary trades but also in land speculation, mining, moneylending or usury, and even illegal activities like ginseng smuggling and importing counterfeit coinage. Indeed, the success stories of many early migrants, who arrived in Korea even before the Sino-Japanese War, turned on such freewheeling activities. After the Russo-Japanese War, with the imposition of new regulations and institutions by the residency-general, the days of quick money were on the wane, and the ordinary migrant could no longer hope to be rewarded with miraculous profits. As a writer in *Jitsugyō no Nihon* noted, things were settling down in Korea, and it was no longer possible to make it there unless one was willing to put down roots and pursue a safe and steady trade. The unproductive and unskilled could not hope to find a place; only those with capital or a skill could.[56] And those who did succeed often had to take second jobs, leaving their wives to tend their shops, while they dealt in land or lent money or worked for someone else or carried on small-scale workshop production.

The post–Russo-Japanese War influx was doubtless encouraged by a growing shelf of books singing the praises of migration to Korea. These belonged to the literature of success so vividly described by Earl Kinmonth,[57] and often they were put out by the same publishers. For example, the company that published *Kaigai risshin annai*, a general introduction to opportunities overseas, also put out *Risshin no Tōkyō* (Making It in Tokyo), *Kanpi gakkō nyūgaku annai* (How to Get into School at Government Expense), *Kugaku seikō annai* (How to Work One's Way Through School), and *Tetsudō shusshin annai* (How to Get Ahead in the National Railway.) The audience for all these books, we may assume, was very much the same. It was an audience of young men —prospects for women were not discussed—seeking to improve their lot by migrating to places where new chances for employment and educa-

56. *JNN*, 9.16, Aug. 1, 1906, pp. 33–36.
57. Kinmonth, *The Self-Made Man in Meiji Japan*, passim.

tion beckoned. And some of these books suggested that the most promising beckoned abroad. In 1911, for example, the author of *Kaigai risshin annai* portrayed Japan as a land of declining opportunities. "At present, for half our population, nay for 80 or 90 percent of it, the means to rise in the world and succeed (*risshin seikōhō*) are outmoded." Young men could no longer model themselves on the successful heroes of an earlier day: the Iwasakis and the Shibusawas who made their fortunes in early Meiji. And so he exhorted his readers: "Go! Go abroad! Abroad! Go!"[58]

The Japanese who traveled to Korea in the 1890s walked an ill-charted path, relying on hearsay or the advice of friends and relatives. Those who flooded into the peninsula at the time of the Russo-Japanese War could find nearly all they needed to know in these new guidebooks, which were packed with practical information for the would-be emigrant: how much boat and train tariffs were, what it would cost to ship luggage, what the weather was like in various parts of the country, how much it cost to buy everything from postage stamps to soybeans, what rents were like, how much it would cost to hire a maid, where to find a Buddhist temple, and how to speak a few Korean words. If the adventure had gone out of a decision to go to Korea, so had much of the uncertainty.

The underlying message in these guidebooks was that emigration to Korea had great advantages over emigration to other parts of the world. While many Japanese regarded the United States as a land of golden opportunity, the guidebook writers pointed out that Japanese emigrants to the United States faced formidable obstacles. Since the Japanese government had become increasingly reluctant to encourage emigration to America, it was difficult to obtain a passport. And even if one did manage to get there, it was difficult to find employment except as a menial cook, servant, waiter, or railroad worker—which meant having to bow and scrape to a Caucasian boss. The prospects were even less inviting elsewhere. In Hawaii there were job opportunities only for those willing to undertake backbreaking toil in the canefields; the climate was unpleasantly tropical in South America, and the cost of getting there high; and Australia, ostensibly an immigrants' paradise, rich in undeveloped and uninhabited land, simply did not welcome nonwhites. In short, the guidebooks told their readers, the Japanese emigrant who crossed the Pacific was doomed to become a low-status manual worker with little hope of improving his circumstances or status in life.

By contrast, what awaited the emigrant to Korea, said the guide-

58. Sakamaki, *Kaigai risshin annai*.

books, was the opportunity to be one's own master. The independent, ambitious, and aggressive individual with an appetite for hard work and long hours could make it. As one guidebook observed, "In Korea one can carry on some kind of independent enterprise with oneself as master, freely able to employ Koreans at low wages and tell them what to do."[59] And even if one did not want to become a boss or a small entrepreneur, as the development of Korea under the aegis of the protectorate-general took shape after the Russo-Japanese War, those aspiring to acquire or maintain middle-class or lower-middle-class status were likely to find opportunities as well. "As the development [of Korea] progresses, it will need construction workers and architectural technicians, it will need clerks to keep records and accounts, it will need manufacturers, it will need talent in all fields from commerce to agriculture.... The future demand for people is optimistic in the extreme."[60] What Korea offered was not simply lucrative employment but an opportunity to rise in the world, perhaps to improve oneself socially as well as materially, and to become one of the masters, not one of the servants.

The guidebooks did not eschew the hard sell. In 1909 one author of one guidebook wrote:

> Success comes to those who seize the opportunity. We must not ignore the great opportunity available today. Those who are not troubled by ill health, who have the spirit of adventure and the energy and ambition to work for themselves, and who have high goals and hopes for success, should not coop themselves up in Japan complaining about their livelihood or their employment difficulties. Without hesitation they should come to Korea as soon as they can to take advantage of this golden opportunity. [Korea] is a place where there are green hills everywhere; it is a place rich in resources; it is a place where there is freedom; this is our homeland (*waga kokyō*).[61]

While the ordinary migrant to Korea might not have waxed so lyrical— particularly about the green hills, which most Japanese found conspicuous by their absence—many were lured by similar sentiments, if not similar rhetoric. One author even called Korea the "paradise next door."[62]

These guidebooks were clearly not intended for the very poor or the economically marginal. Their advice was aimed at those with enough wherewithal to make emigration to Korea possible—the penny capitalist, the small shopkeeper, the small landowner or owner-cultivator. In 1910

59. Yamamoto Kōtarō, *Saishin Chōsen ijū annai*, 9.
60. Ibid., 11.
61. Ibid., 13.
62. Sakamaki, *Kaigai risshin annai*, 13.

Jitsugyō no Nihon, one of the principal organs of the late Meiji success philosophy, published a guidebook compiled by staff members of the *Chōsen nichinichi shinbun* marvelously titled *Hyaku-en no shoshihon to-Kan seikoho* or *How to Make It in Korea with Only ¥100.* Based on the case histories of Japanese settlers, the book was crammed with very concrete and practical advice on how to get a start in Korea with a small hoard of cash, enough to tide over settling in and starting up a new enterprise under highly competitive conditions. The examples were all modest—a cotton wadding merchant, a used clothing dealer, a soy sauce maker, a medicine peddler, a restaurant proprietor, a barber, a carter, and even a *rikisha* man. No tales of fabulous wealth were told, only accounts of how to make a steady, respectable, and comfortable living in the peninsula. The book enjoined modest commercial virtues as well— honesty, reliability, hard work, effort, patience. Migrants to Korea should not try to squeeze excess profit but settle for modest profits in order to assure that customers would come back. And above all there were injunctions to exert effort: "You must look after your customers from morning till night" (*Asa kara ban made hisshi to narite tokui mawari*); "You can't sit on your haunches" (*Shiri ga omokute ikenu*); "The struggle for survival is fierce" (*Seizon kyōsō ga hageshii*).[63]

In sum, the appeal of emigrating to Korea lay in the "pull" of new opportunities rather than the "push" of declining opportunities at home. Yet one might seek these new opportunities for a variety of reasons. In analyzing voluntary migration, sociologists and demographers often distinguish between "innovative" and "conservative" (or "defensive") migration. "Innovative" immigrants try to improve their circumstances by obtaining higher wages, an easier lifestyle, a more salubrious climate, a higher social status, or wider renown. In a sense, innovative migrants see a move abroad as a means of upward mobility. "Conservative" migrants, by contrast, try to maintain their circumstances or to recover what they have lost by moving abroad, and for them emigration is a check against downward mobility. Unless one can collar emigrants and subject them to survey research, however, this distinction is more heuristic than operational, more suggestive than practical. In most cases it is difficult to find aggregate statistical information determining what proportion of a migrant population is "innovative" and what proportion is "conservative," and in the case of Japanese migration to Korea it is impossible.

63. Chōsen Nichinichi Shinbun, *Hyakuen no shoshihon.*

CHAPTER 9

Strangers in a Strange Land

The Settler Community

By 1910 only a few settlers had made their way to the station stops along the new trunk railway lines, and fewer still had ventured into the countryside. Most Japanese—at least 70 percent and perhaps more—were living in urban areas, settled in two dozen or so large towns and cities.[1] This settlement pattern, not unusual in most colonial societies, should not surprise us. Before the Russo-Japanese War migration to Korea was restricted to the treaty ports, and residence in the interior was prohibited. To be sure, these restrictions were sometimes violated, but on the whole there were few reasons to do so. The main opportunities for enterprise and employment were to be found in the growing trade that passed through the ports. And even after the protectorate was established in 1905, it was safer and more comfortable to live in urban areas, where there were schools, doctors, hospitals, shops, restaurants, and nightlife. It was also in the cities that the most promising opportunities for making a living were to be found, whether in foreign trade, in the service and retail business, or in government service. Although the Tokyo government had hoped for an occupation of the peninsula by an army of agricultural colonists, because of economic reasons the Japanese settler community was almost entirely urban.

1. This calculation is based on figures in Tokio, *Saikin Chōsen chishi*, 3–4. According to these figures, in March 1911 the total Japanese resident population was 178,946, 130,627 of whom lived in thirty "principal cities."

A TOUR OF THE SETTLER COMMUNITIES

By the time of annexation the largest Japanese settlement was to be found at Seoul, the old capital of the Yi dynasty and the new administrative center of the Japanese colony.[2] The first Japanese residents of Seoul—a contingent of forty-odd legations officials, servants, and guards —had arrived there in April 1880, when Hanabusa, the first minister, took up his post at a legation building near the West Gate (Sodaemun). There were no other Japanese in the city, and even two years later their ranks had been swelled only by a dozen or so Japanese merchants who served as official purveyors to the legation. It was only when Seoul became a treaty port in 1883 under the Chinese and British treaties that the Japanese settlement began to grow. The English treaty permitted mixed residence, giving foreigners the freedom to settle anywhere they wished within the city, but the Japanese and—the other foreigners as well—felt more comfortable in relatively compact communities. After the failure of the pro-Japanese coup in 1884 the Japanese residents huddled under the reassuring shadow of the Hinomaru flag flying over the Japanese chancery built on the slope of Namsan, a low mountain in the southern quarter of the city. Under the Tientsin Convention of 1885 the Japanese were given the right to station two companies of army troops to guard the legation, as well as a company each in Pusan and Inchon. The legation buildings were unpretentious white wooden structures, and below them spread an array of shops, restaurants, teahouses, and even a theater.[3] When Isabella Bird Bishop visited the city in the early 1890s, she was much impressed by the Japanese settlement. "There, in acute contrast to everything Korean, are to be seen streets of shops and houses where cleanliness, daintiness, and thrift reign supreme, and unveiled women, and men in girdled dressing gowns and clogs, move about as freely as in Japan."[4]

In 1910 Seoul was not a very impressive city by Japanese standards. Its population of about 250,000 made it larger than a provincial Japanese city like Hiroshima but smaller than the major metropolitan centers like Tokyo or Osaka. Except for the city gates and walls and a cluster of royal palaces and residences in its northern half, the city boasted few monumental structures. Most residential buildings were

2. Unless otherwise indicated, this description of the main Japanese settlements is based on ibid., 420–52; *Shin Chōsen oyobi shin Manshū*, 373–422; Arakawa, *Saikin Chōsen jijō*, 190ff.

3. Nakai, *Chōsen kaikō roku*, 117.

4. Bishop, *Korea and Her Neighbors*, 2:41.

one story tall. The skyline was as flat as a rice field. On the west and
south sides of the city, where the foreign legations had clustered, bright
new red-brick structures poked their heads incongruously above the sea
of surrounding roofs—the Roman Catholic cathedral most incongruously of all. Several broad thoroughfares like Chongno sliced through
the city, but most back streets were narrow and cramped, hardly wide
enough for horses or ox carts to pass one another. During earlier days
even the main thoroughfares were lined with temporary shops and
stalls, lively with petty trade but chaotic to the eye, and the garbage-
filled streets were a whirl of unpleasant filth in the eyes of the Japanese
newcomers.[5]

The most conspicuous signs of modernity were to be found in the
expanding Japanese section that stretched from the South Gate (Namdaemun) along the foot of Namsan. It very much resembled a town at
home, with familiar-looking shops and housefronts. The signboards
were all in Japanese, and the shops purveyed the most up-to-date consumer goods and fashions to be found in the city. There were also a
middle school, a girls' school, and several elementary schools where
lessons were taught in Japanese; and the residents, perhaps emulating
British colonial habits, had founded their own Nihon Club. Following
the urge to transform the unfamiliar, the Japanese had staked out their
own geography. The main thoroughfare through the Japanese settlement became Motomachi, and other areas where the Japanese residents
lived were transformed into Nanzan-chō, Kotobuki-chō, Hayashi-chō,
Sakurai-chō, and the like. The northern half of the city, where the
yangban residences had concentrated, resisted the renaming.

The economic structure of the city was a curious mixture of old and
new. Here and there sprouts of the modern poked through the crust of
traditional society. Municipal gas and electric works supplied up-to-
date power for those who could afford it, and electric streetlights, which
first made their appearance along Chongno, had spread to much of the
city. For a time electric illumination was so associated with the Japanese
that small children pelted electrified Korean residences with stones.[6] The
technological pride of the city was the electric streetcar line that ran
along a route from the East Gate (Tongdaemun) to the West Gate

5. Traditionally, whenever a royal progress was to be made down Chongno, the stalls
were pulled down and their proprietors chased away so that practice processions, and the
real one, could proceed unimpeded; but once the progress was over, the stall owners came
bustling back, shoving and clamoring for a new site better than the old one. Ōsaka
Mainichi Shinbunsha, *Rōkaitakushi*, 209–14.
6. Yi Kyu-tae, *Modern Transformation of Korea*, 300.

(Sodaemun) and linked the city with the southern suburb of Yongsan along the Han River. Built in 1899 by the American firm of Collbran and Bostwick, the line had become a tourist attraction, goggled at by travelers from the countryside. More significantly, the city had become a major rail junction, where trunk lines converged from Pusan in the south, Inchon in the west, and Sinŭiju in the north. A few modern manufacturing plants had been built—a cigarette factory, a brick kiln, a mint, and a small iron foundry—and many new small workshops owned by Japanese residents produced daily consumption goods for other Japanese residents: miso, soy sauce, sake, soap, tatami mats, furniture, paper boxes, polished rice, tailored clothing, and the like.

For the most part, local demand for food and other consumer products was filled by traditional goods brought in from outside the city. As in the rest of the peninsula local trade still followed the rhythms of the agricultural cycle. When the Han River froze over in December, many shops and other enterprises closed down, and local commerce fell off substantially, only to revive with the thawing of the river in late March and early April. As new hints of green bloomed on the hills around the city, the market revived and construction work could begin. During the heat of the summer months, outside merchants stopped coming to the city again, and the dealings of the Japanese residents with Korean customers and suppliers fell off until the harvest months from late August through October.

More radically up-to-date was the sprawling new suburb of Yongsan built to the south of Seoul along the banks of the Han River. Originally it had been a river port where goods for Seoul were off-loaded. Soybeans, rice, hemp, firewood, coal, lumber, mat reeds, and pottery came downstream from the upper reaches of the Han River valley, and imported foreign goods came upstream from Inchon on the coast. Even during the winter months when boat traffic ceased, it was still possible for men and horses to cross the ice. The Japanese established themselves at Yongsan rather early, and by the end of the Sino-Japanese War enough had gathered there to set up their own local residents' association. The town had experienced a boom during the Russo-Japanese War, when the military railroad construction staff had set up shop and Japanese workers and technicians had poured in. After the war Yongsan served as a major garrison base for the Japanese forces in Korea. By the time of annexation it was one of the fastest-growing Japanese communities. Its streets were laid out in straight and precise lines, and modern barracks, office buildings, and warehouses were going up rapidly.

While the Japanese residents at Seoul and Yongsan constituted the largest single community on the peninsula, they were a minority surrounded by a much larger native Korean population. Such was not the case at Pusan, the next largest settler community, where nearly half the town's population of 50,000 were Japanese. Indeed, the town was built mainly by the Japanese. It had been the terminus of Japan's trade with Korea since the mid-fifteenth century, when an official or quasi-official trade first developed between Korea and Tsushima. In 1672 the *waegwan*, a residential "factory" for Tsushima officials and others involved in the trade, was established, and after the signing of the Treaty of Kanghwa Pusan became one of the first treaty ports opened. In the late 1870s the Dai-Ichi bank had opened a branch office there, and so had a number of major Japanese trading firms: the Ōkura-gumi, the Kyōdō-sha, the Tsushima-based Risshin Shokai, and several others. Around this nucleus gathered small shops catering to the needs of the Japanese settlers, offering everything from tofu and senbei to barrels and casks. Many of the petty shopkeepers were so poor, the *Chōya shinbun* reported in 1878, that even the Koreans looked down on them. And the Koreans must also have looked down on the Japanese porters, day laborers, and roustabouts willing to work for as little as twenty-five *sen* a month.[7] An English visitor in 1884 noted that the population of the foreign settlement, which he estimated to be about eighteen hundred souls, consisted "chiefly of the 'scum' of Japan and emigrants from Tsushima." "All the trade is in the hands of the Japanese," he continued. "They 'bully' the natives just as our enlightened countrymen, conscious of their immense superiority, formerly treated the natives of China and Japan."[8]

By 1910 Pusan had put its disreputable past behind it. As the port closest to Japan, the city became the main destination for Japanese migrants. Steerers from the local Japanese inns greeted disembarking passengers with a cacophony of shouts, and Korean porters clamored to handle their baggage on their A-frames. Otherwise, the town looked comfortingly Japanese, not all that different from a port town at home. A cluster of Japanese inns, some of them three stories high, were visible from the docks, and several dozen large Japanese-style shops lined the downtown streets. In the center of town not a single Korean-style dwelling was to be seen. Only the white-garbed Koreans on the docks

7. Yamada Shōji, "Meiji zenki ni Ni-Chō bōeki," 60–61.
8. A. W. D., *Notes on Korea.*

and in the street revealed the unfamiliar. In fact, the new arrival did not have to deal with Koreans at all, except to get his bags to the inn.

A deep, well-protected harbor located at the terminus of the major trunk line to Seoul, Pusan was a major gateway to the Korean market. Mail service with Japan began in 1876, an underseas cable to Japan was laid in 1884, and regular shipping routes connected the port with Shimonoseki and other Japanese ports. Until the Russo-Japanese War Inchon had handled about the same volume of trade, but by the time of annexation Pusan was beginning to pull ahead. Goods passed through the port to and from the great markets at Taegu and Chinju. So did commercial traffic coming down the Naktong River and the catches brought in by fishermen along the southern and eastern coasts. The city bustled constantly, indifferent to the seasonal rhythm that affected the more northerly ports and cities. Its Japanese population grew rapidly, spilling out of the official settlement zone into filled-in marshy areas to the north and new building lots pushing out into the farmland to the east. The city was affluent enough to support the construction of a hydroelectric plant, and by the time of annexation plans were being laid for an electric streetcar line as well.

The third-largest Japanese settlement was Inchon, Pusan's main rival as port. Close to the capital, Inchon had strategic as well as economic significance. It was the gateway to Seoul in much the same way that Tientsin was the gateway to Peking. But Inchon was a far less desirable harbor than Pusan. A mouth of the Han River immediately to the north poured a constant flow of silt into the sea. The bay was shallow, subject to sudden and extreme changes in tides. A broad stretch of shoreline was exposed at low tide, making navigation difficult for oceangoing steam vessels. Before the opening of the country this bleak and deserted stretch of coast had been covered with wild grass, host only to a small village of Korean fishermen whose houses were scattered along the shore.[9] The port acquired sudden fame in Japan when Minister Hanabusa and his entourage fled there from Seoul after the 1882 coup, but it was not opened as a treaty port until 1883. The Japanese initially preferred sites farther to the south, such as Mokp'o, Kunsan, and Ansanmen, which were closer to Japan and to the agricultural surplus areas, but it seems likely that political rather than economic considerations governed their final choice.

In its early years the port was as raw and rough as a frontier town.

9. Jinsen-fu, *Jinsen-fu shi*, 100–120.

It stretched along an east-west axis, pressed against the sea by surrounding low hills. The Japanese occupied the center of the town, with
the Chinese later filling in the city to the west and the other foreign settlements to the east. The Korean population lived on the outskirts of town,
as it did in Pusan. In the 1880s, with the exception of a handsome
Japanese consulate, the town structures, some of them built in Korean
style, others in Japanese style, had a temporary look. As one foreign
observer noted, "Altogether the settlement resembles very much one of
the 'mushroom' cities which spring up in the American kerosene district
... or like a rapidly built town in a new gold field."[10] Even in the early
1890s it remained a scruffy seaport scraped out of the coast like an open
wound. However, since the town was built from scratch, its streets were
broad and regular, easy for carts to navigate, with everything laid out
neatly at right angles.

The port grew rapidly in the 1880s as it developed as the main terminus for Chinese trade with Korea. The China Merchants' Steam
Navigation Company opened a direct line to Shanghai in 1883, and a
number of Japanese merchants at Pusan, sensing a shift in trade opportunities, relocated to the port.[11] By 1891 the Japanese community had
grown to 3,331, about ten times larger than in 1883, and it underwent
another spurt of growth during the Sino-Japanese War. The foreign
settlement zone was soon crowded, and shoreline had to be filled for
expansion. After establishment of the protectorate, however, Inchon
had a run of bad luck. The Seoul-Inchon line, which had briefly enjoyed
a monopoly over rail connections with Seoul, was bypassed by the construction of the Pusan-Seoul-Ŭiju trunk line, making it easier for goods
to enter the Korean market at Pusan. In March 1907 a great fire broke
out in the Shinmachi section, and a worldwide drop in trade hit hard
later in the year. By the time of annexation the port seemed to be in
decline.

The other Japanese communities in Korea were much smaller than
those in Seoul, Pusan, and Inchon. The oldest was Wŏnsan, a treaty port
opened even before Seoul and Inchon were. In 1880 a Japanese consulate had been established there, and soon the port boasted a modern
infirmary, a branch of the Honganji temple, and branch offices of the
NYK shipping line, Dai-Ichi Bank, and the Ōkura-gumi.[12] The harbor
was perhaps the best on the forbidding western coast of the country, but

10. A. W. D, *Notes on Korea.*
11. Deuchler, *Confucian Gentlemen and Barbarian Envoys,* 178, 188.
12. Takao Shinzaemon et al., *Genzan hattenshi,* 215–17.

trade never flourished. The regions to its west and northwest were sparsely settled, and the port was connected across the peninsula to key cities like Seoul and P'yŏngyang by miserable, potholed roads. When Inchon and Seoul opened, many Japanese firms packed up and left for these new locations. Trade at Wŏnsan dropped off, revived briefly in the 1880s, and then fell victim to the rice embargoes in 1889. Even after the Russo-Japanese War the small Chinese merchant community seemed to do as much business as the Japanese.[13] Although Wŏnsan remained a port of call for coastal shipping and shipped out the best soybeans in Korea, it remained a commercial backwater.[14]

The main Japanese settlement on the northern border was in P'yŏngyang, known to the Japanese as the site of important military victories —the defeat of Korean troops by Konishi Yukinaga in 1592, the defeat of Ch'ing troops in 1894, and the first clash between Russian and Japanese troops in 1904. Japanese did not arrive in large numbers until after the Sino-Japanese War. Even then the population was transient, mainly peddlers or itinerant merchants. From December through March, when the weather was severely cold, they would leave the city for more comfortable locations like Seoul and Inchon to await the spring thaw. Most of these early settlers were attracted by the prospect of quick profits, and they were less interested in building long-term trade than in taking advantage of passing opportunities. After the city was opened as a treaty port in 1899, and a consulate was established, a more permanent settlement began to grow.

The Russo-Japanese War gave P'yŏngyang a great boost. The Japanese army established a quartermaster headquarters there, and the city became a major depot on the newly built military railway. With the restoration of peace the city became a garrison for the Fifteenth Division, whose barracks and storehouses sprouted on a vast tract to the southeast. Drawn by the expanding military presence, migrants began to increase, settling in a newly developed residential area on the flat land south of the old native city. Many of the newcomers were suppliers for the military and their fellow Japanese settlers. Although the garrison was reduced from division to brigade size in 1907, the civilian population remained relatively stable. The military rail line by this time had

13. Arakawa, *Saikin Chōsen jijō*, 13.
14. Its small Japanese community was attractive to foreign visitors. Mrs. Bishop, who had a sharp eye for neatness, found the Japanese settlement to be the "neatest, trimmest and most attractive in all Korea" with "broad and well-kept streets, neat wharves, and fairly substantial houses, showing the interior dollishness and daintiness characteristic of Japan." Bishop, *Korea and Her Neighbors*, 1:200–201.

become part of a peninsula-wide system, and freight traffic developed after 1908. A small steam packet provided service down the Taedong River to Chinnamp'o. The city was ideally situated to become the chief commercial center in the northwest corner of Korea. Its only disadvantages were a four-month winter season, during which the river froze, and a primitive road system connecting it with the interior.

On the coast downstream from P'yŏngyang was the port of Chinnamp'o, originally an insignificant little fishing village not unlike the early Inchon. When the Sino-Japanese War broke out, the port became a major disembarkation point for Japanese troops and an anchorage for Japanese naval vessels. The army quartermaster corps built a light railway to handle the transport of military goods and materiel. When Chinnamp'o became an open port in 1898, it began to attract Japanese residents. During the war with Russia the port once again became a key point in the military's logistical system, and by the end of the war nearly three thousand Japanese had established themselves there. Many moved to P'yŏngyang, Ŭiju, and even across the border to Manchuria in search of new opportunities, but after a brief slowdown in growth the town was repopulated by new Japanese migrants. By 1910, when a new branch line connected the port to the Seoul-Ŭiju trunk line at P'yŏngyang, it had become the principal outlet for rice and other agricultural produce from the Taedong and Chaeryong River valleys. It shipped milled white rice to Dairen, millet to Wŏnsan, and rice and other grains to the Osaka region at home. Since there were fewer Japanese in the area than in the other ports, the volume of imports was smaller than in Inchon or Pusan, and much of it consisted of sundry goods for Korean consumption.

In the south there was another heavy concentration of Japanese residents at Taegu, a major regional market city. The city was the site of two great fairs that took place in February and August, drawing thousands of merchants from all over the peninsula. A few adventurous Japanese peddlers and merchants had made their way to Taegu around the time of the Sino-Japanese War, setting up shops and stalls to trade in the regular market, but Japanese migrants did not really begin to flow into the city until immediately before the Russo-Japanese War as construction of the Seoul-Pusan railway was beginning. By the end of the war the community was large enough to support the establishment of a Japanese elementary school with thirty pupils. Pusan merchant houses, mindful of the traditional commercial importance of the city, set up branch stores or offices in the city, and by the time of annexation the

Pusan Japanese dominated trade there. Taegu was an excellent outlet for Japanese manufactured goods—*kanakin*, cotton yarn, and sundries —as well as a source of rice and other grain. A few Japanese moved into the area to start agricultural ventures, growing commercial crops like tobacco, fruit, and vegetables, but the main business of the Japanese community was trade, which was busiest at harvest time. Since the city was a tight and narrow traditional settlement, its streets teeming with people and livestock on market days, the new Japanese community had to squeeze itself between the old city quarters and the new railway station, and in 1911 the city walls were pulled down to make way for expansion.

The other larger Japanese settlements in the south—Masan, Mokp'o, and Kunsan—were all of a piece. They had been opened as ports in the late 1890s to tap the riches of the agriculturally productive southern provinces. Masan, the largest of the three, was the port from which the Mongols had launched their ill-fated armada in the thirteenth century. Opened as a treaty port in May 1899, it was linked to the Seoul-Pusan line at Samlangjin. The town began to grow after the Russo-Japanese War, although not as rapidly as many had hoped, perhaps because it was too close to Pusan, or perhaps because it had been oversold and oversettled in its early years. To the west of Masan lay Mokp'o, which filled up quickly as settlers rushed in from Pusan, Inchon, Wŏnsan, and Seoul as well as from the home islands. Located close to the valley of the Yongsan River, a major cotton-growing area, Mokp'o quickly became a port for exporting raw cotton as well as rice and marine products. To the north of Mokp'o, at the mouth of the Kum River, was Kunsan, which opened in 1899. Connected by coastal shipping routes to Inchon to the north and Mokp'o and Pusan to the south, it shipped out export rice harvested from the Chŏnju plain. Being so dependent on the agricultural trade, its rhythms followed the annual production cycle, with the peak season for trade coming between October and March, after the harvest was in. Its prosperity was hostage to the size of the harvest, and because of a series of poor harvests after the Russo-Japanese War it did not flourish as much as other Japanese settlements.

In sum, we can think of the Japanese resident community at the time of annexation as a grid of points and lines laid down on the traditional political economy. The points were the major ports and urban centers, and the lines were the new trunk railway system and the network of coastal shipping. In nearly every place the Japanese settled they constituted a community physically separated from the mass of the Korean population. In places like Pusan, Masan, Mokp'o, Inchon, or Sin-ŭiju, where they made up 40 to 50 percent of the population, they could keep the Koreans at bay simply by sheer force of number and density. But even in cities like P'yŏngyang, Seoul, or Taegu, where the Koreans vastly outnumbered them, they clustered together in well-defined neighborhoods and communities, surrounded by familiar names, familiar faces, and familiar artifacts. With few exceptions, they remained strangers in a strange land.

THE OCCUPATIONAL STRUCTURE
OF THE JAPANESE COMMUNITY

The concentration of Japanese emigrants in towns and cities ran counter to the hopes of many colonial theorists and government officials that the peninsula would be colonized by an army of sturdy farmers bringing civilized ways and superior technology to the Korean countryside. In fact, as we have seen, even after annexation very few Japanese farmers uprooted themselves to go to Korea. According to an official occupational census, at the end of 1908 only about 4 percent of the Japanese residents in Korea were engaged in agriculture. By far the majority of Japanese residents were employed in tertiary occupations (commerce, government, and service), with a much smaller proportion engaged in secondary occupations (table 9). All of these occupations, of course, were urban.

A survey undertaken by the residency-general in June 1906 gives a more detailed and concrete sense of how Japanese in Korea made their living (table 10). The figures should be handled with some care. First, the information gathered was not consistent. While seven of the Japanese settlements reported the total number of persons in the jobholder's household, three (Pusan, Wŏnsan, and Sŏngjin) did not; further, not all the settlements used the same categories in reporting occupations. In other words, the survey conveys false precision. Second, it should be remembered that in the middle of 1906 the Japanese community was still expanding rapidly and administrative reform was only beginning. By the time of annexation the distribution of occupations must have altered significantly, particularly with the influx of Japanese officials, functionaries, policeman, constables, and the like to run the rapidly expanding new central and provincial state apparatus. Nonetheless, the survey does give a sense of what the Japanese community was and was not.

TABLE 9   OCCUPATIONAL STRUCTURE
OF JAPANESE RESIDENTS IN KOREA, 1907

Occupation	Number
Primary	
Agriculture	4,889
Fishing	2,956
Subtotal	7,845 (6.3%)
Secondary	
Manufacturing	11,763 (9.4%)
Tertiary	
Commerce	47,389 (37.9%)
Officials	15,681
Laborers	15,237
Geishas, waitresses	4,253
Professionals[a]	2,849
Subtotal	85,409 (68.3%)
Unknown	
Miscellaneous	15,681
Unemployed	4,424
Subtotal	20,105 (16.1%)
Total	125,122

[a] Doctors and midwives 1166, teachers 918, reporters 379, priests and missionaires 278, lawyers 108.
SOURCE: Tōkanfu Chihōbu, *Kyoryūmindan jijō yōran* (1908).

Few Japanese went to Korea to work as unskilled laborers. The Korean population provided a ready and nearly inexhaustible reservoir of unskilled workers, willing to work for lower daily wages than the Japanese would accept (table 11). Even Korean women, traditionally kept at home, began to enter the unskilled labor force. And as Korean laborers became accustomed to the work rhythms and demands of their Japanese employers, they acquired the kind of discipline the Japanese demanded at home—more inclined to work regular hours, less likely to show up late, and less apt to malinger. Those Japanese who did fall into the category of laborer were either artisans or craftsmen who had skills the Koreans could not provide or who acted as supervisors directing the work of Korean laborers. For example, craftsmen in the construction trade (carpenters, plasterers, masons, bricklayers, and the like) able to build according to Japanese or Western specifications were much in demand as the treaty settlements expanded and cities began to modernize. Skilled workers were also needed for large-scale engineering projects

TABLE 10   OCCUPATIONS OF JAPANESE RESIDENTS IN KOREA, 1906 (N = 55,342)

Commerce		Artisans and manual workers		Service		White collar and professional	
Sundry goods	5,279	Carpenter	3,996	Food & drink shop	1,471	Company employee	1,985
Confectioner	1,795	Hired hand (hiyatoinin)	3,429	Restaurant	1,134	Physician	437
Foreign trade	554	Longshoreman	1,676	Geisha	1,107	Bank employee	320
Pawnbroker	521	Building contractor	1,299	Waitress	1,064	Railroad employee	288
Pharmacist	514	Laborer (dokata)	1,085	Barber	676	Teacher	274
Tofu merchant	499	Sailor/seaman	1,054	Freight	640	Journalist	229
Fishmonger	497	Mason	826	Jinrikisha	559	Religious, missionary	143
Liquor store	419	Plasterer	619	Seamstress	474	Public scribe, notary	81
Rice merchant	399	Coolie/laborer (kufu)	603	Entertainment	368	Lawyer	55
Middleman	383	Bricklayer	573	Moneylender	299	Total	3,812 (6.9%)
Japanese clothier	272	Sawyer	512	Public bath	288		
Lumber merchant	225	Blacksmith	436	Laundry	275		
Poultry merchant	219	Laborer (dokō)	382	Boarding house	238		
Secondhand goods	214	Factory worker (shokkō)	289	Messenger	192		
Vegetables	186	Tatami maker	250	Photographer	165		
Meat	155	Tinsmith (buriki)	186	Masseur/acupuncture	103		
Clocks/watches	138	Barrelmaker	161	Middleman	84		
Hardware	129	Dyer	86	Public entertainer	84		
Peddler	126	House painter	72	Mail service	78		
Tobacconist	120	Shoemaker	69	Midwife	68		

Hairdresser	118	Cook	62	Nurse	68	
Western clothier	80	Gardener	56	Ship salvage	60	
Footwear	77	Lantern maker	50	Customs clearance	56	
Street stall	73	Total	17,771	Bargeman	50	
Wood/charcoal	64		(32.1%)	Total	9,601	
Furniture	63				(17.3%)	
Kitchenware	61					
Groceries	60					
Stationery	59					
Total	13,299					
	(24.0%)					

Officials and gov't service		Farming and fishing		Manufacturing		Other	
Gov't official	2,010	Fisherman	1,740	Sake brewery	175	unemployed	1,531
Adviser to Korean gov't	624	Farmer	1,660	Soy sauce	116	Other	1,566
Korean gov't office employee	374	Total	3,400	Print/engraving	106	Total	3,097
Postal official	280		(6.1%)	Rice milling	102		(5.6%)
Public official	171			Print/binding	93		
Military	144			Water purification	87		
Total	3,603			Dairy/creamery	80		
	(6.5%)			Total	759		
					(1.4%)		

TABLE 11   COMPARISON OF DAY WAGES:
JAPAN (1907) AND KOREA (1909)

	Japanese			Korean
	Carpenter	Blacksmith	Shoemaker	Carpenter
Japan (national average)	¥.86	¥.82	¥.75	—
Nagasaki	.93	1.15	.67	—
Ōsaka	1.30	1.30	1.03	—
Tōkyō	1.10	1.55	1.55	—
Hakodate	1.10	1.35	.50	—
Korea (national average)	¥1.40	¥1.74	¥1.36	¥.86
Seoul	1.50	1.45	—	1.00
Inchon	1.45	1.60	1.46	.95
P'yŏngyang	1.50	2.00	.90	.90
Chinnamp'o	1.60	2.50	—	.90
Kunsan	1.50	1.40	1.60	.75
Pusan	1.30	1.30	1.50	.70
Taegu	1.15	—	1.20	.70
Masan	1.35	1.80	—	—
Mokp'o	1.30	—	—	1.20
Wŏnsan	1.50	1.80	1.50	.50

SOURCE: Kōbe Masao, *Chōsen nōgyō iminron* (Tokyo: Yūhikaku Honten, 1910), 27–28.

like the Seoul-Pusan railway or harbor improvement in Pusan and Inchon.[15] Indeed, Japan was the principal source of modern skilled or
semiskilled labor in the 1890s and early 1900s, and even Western firms
hired Japanese to supervise their projects or staff their offices.

Those engaged in the direct manufacture of goods were also relatively
limited in number. Most traditional consumer goods were produced by
Koreans themselves, and those goods demanded by the Japanese and the
modernizing Korean elite were brought in from the outside world. The
main manufacturing enterprises operated by Japanese were small-scale
operations, requiring only modest amounts of capital, usually in processing food products that did not travel well—sake, *shōyu*, milk, and
pickles. Only in Seoul did larger manufacturing firms begin to make an
appearance by the time of annexation, but often they functioned more
as model factories or experimental enterprises than as firms catering to a
wide market.

If there was a "typical" settler, it was a person engaged in commerce
or a service occupation. He might be the proprietor of a large-volume

15. Kōbe, *Chōsen nōgyō iminron*, 19–24.

import-export house, but more often he was a small operator, a retail merchant or a jobber, with little capital, serving a small local market. In fact, some argued that the petty capitalist, rather than the farmer-cultivator, would be the vanguard of Japanese influence in Korea. In 1904, for example, the Osaka Chamber of Commerce mission urged building Korea as a "colony [whose people] have habits of food, clothing, and shelter similar to those in our own country and who will [therefore] demand our manufactures, while supplying the resources necessary for our manufacturing industries." This kind of colonization did not involve big capitalists and businessmen at home but "tens of thousands of small capitalists developing [Korea] through their individual labor and effort." Large-scale construction projects like railroads could be left to the government, and other high-risk ventures requiring large amounts of capital could be left to the English and the Americans. Basic development would be the work of the small capitalist ready to turn his hand to small-scale commerce or to become "half-farmer, half-merchant." North America might be the land of opportunity for the landless migrant, but Korea was for the petty bourgeois entrepreneur.[16]

To be sure, the mission's argument had its self-serving side: the Osaka business community needed agents to open the Korean market for its wares. But the report underlined the social realities behind migration to Korea. There was little vacant cultivable land in Korea, and the Koreans farmed the rest themselves. It was mainly in the realm of trade, especially trade in Japanese manufactured goods, that a Japanese settler could expect a competitive advantage over the Koreans. As roads were improved and new ones opened, as shipping service became more frequent, and as railroads were constructed, petty capitalists and small traders pressed into the interior, looking for markets where Japanese goods were a novelty and no one yet knew proper prices, exploiting the market ignorance of the local Koreans. And as the settlements of Japanese grew in the treaty ports, it was not Koreans but fellow Japanese, with easy lines of communication to Japan, who provided them with the goods and services they required. Within the treaty port enclaves, small-scale commerce was dominated not by indigenous merchants, as it had been in the treaty ports of China and Japan, but by outsiders.

For the Japanese it was simple to get into trade. As we have seen, by the late 1890s foreign trade was mainly trade with Japan. Japanese familiar with sources of supply, commercial practices, and markets in

16. *KSSH*, 1–6.

Japan obviously had an advantage over Korean entrepreneurs. The Japanese settlers could provide the Koreans with newfangled consumption goods better than their countrymen could, and often more cheaply than foreign competitors like the Chinese could. It was also easier for Japanese settlers to procure short-term financing for operating expenses than it was for Koreans. And, of course, the Japanese community itself became a market that created a separate set of demands and a separate set of tastes more easily catered to by other Japanese. The Japanese traveler to Korea preferred to stay in a Japanese inn than a Korean hostel; he wanted to eat Japanese food, not Korean; and for entertainment he wanted familiar songs and drink, not exotic ones. Providing services and goods to other Japanese in the treaty settlements was an economic niche that even the humblest of entrepreneurs could fill.

The range of employment in commercial and service activities was considerable. At the top of the social scale were the managers and officials of the large metropolitan firms like the Dai-Ichi Bank, the Eighteenth Bank, the Fifty-eighth Bank, the NYK and OSK steamship lines, Mitsui Bussan, and the Ōkura-gumi. Below them came the representatives of large Osaka merchant houses, the big wholesalers and jobbers, the owners of treaty port real estate, and big construction contractors. Then came the smaller retail merchants and peddlers, all the way down to jinrikisha haulers and laundrymen. Running a sundry goods shop or a confectionery store was among the most common occupations (see table 10), but there were also pharmacists and fishmongers, lumber and hardware merchants, retailers of furniture and kitchenware, barbers and photographers, proprietors of sake shops and restaurants, seamstresses and geisha.

Many classified as engaged in "commerce" were also involved in moneylending. Although some moneylenders were full-time, most Japanese settlers pursued lending as a side occupation while doing business as small shopkeepers, itinerant merchants, or even public officials. Public credit institutions were few and far between in Korea at the time of annexation, and most banks handled transactions for foreigners or the Korean elite but not for the hoi polloi. The ordinary Korean in need of short-term or long-term funds usually sought them from native moneylenders or mutual aid associations. In short, there was a strong domestic demand for small loans, and interests rates were high. An official report of the Korean Finance Ministry indicated that in extreme cases interest on loans made by private individuals could run over 10 percent per month (120 percent per annum), and even minimum rates could be as

TABLE 12   MONTHLY INTEREST RATES
CHARGED BY MONEYLENDERS IN KOREA

Loan	Interest
From Japanese to Japanese	
High	3.7%
Low	1.7
Ordinary	2.5
From Korean to Japanese	
High	3.3
Low	2.0
Ordinary	2.5
From Japanese to Korean	
High	3.9
Low	2.2
Ordinary	2.8

SOURCE: Kōbe Masao, *Chōsen nōgyō iminron* (Tokyo: Yūhikaku Honten, 1910), 11–12.

high as 3 percent per month (36 percent per annum). Indeed, as one Japanese expert observed, moneylending in Korea bordered on usury (table 12).[17] The threshold for entry into moneylending was not formidable: a capital of ¥200–300 was sufficient to get into the business, and lending out that amount produced enough income not only to support ordinary living expenses but also to accumulate a larger stock of funds.

In the countryside loans were most needed at the beginning of the agricultural season in the spring, when the farmer had to repair tools or buy new ones, hire work animals to plow fields, and obtain day laborers for extra help. Often farmers met these needs by promising to exchange their own labor for the services of others or by paying part of their harvest to the lender. The demand for funds seems to have been greater at harvest time. Many small farmers and tenants by then had consumed their store of the previous year's harvest but had not yet gathered in the new harvest, and they simply needed funds to make ends meet. Often they borrowed money using their current crop as collateral.[18]

Many Japanese merchants, traders, and owners of small service establishments in Korea were drawn from the middling or lower middling reaches of the "old middle class." After the Russo-Japanese War, how-

17. Kōbe, *Chōsen nōgyō iminron*, 10.
18. Ibid., 9–14.

ever, reform of the administrative system and the growth of the modern economic infrastructure produced a demand for members of the "new middle class" technicians, engineers, administrators, and clerical workers with literate and specialized skills. Their numbers grew in Seoul and other large settlements, such as Pusan and P'yŏngyang. Before the Russo-Japanese War the Korean government had employed only a few Japanese, but by 1908 more than fifteen thousand residents were counted as having official employment, either with the residency-general or the Korean government. The creation of modern police, mail, and tax-collecting systems created not only high-level jobs for figures like Megata Jūtarō but also low-echelon positions for postal officials, local policemen and constables, tax officials, office clerks, and interpreters. These posts were filled by new migrants recruited from Japan, but often Japanese already resident in Korea, especially those with some skills in Korean, were hired as well.

In short, under the protectorate the Japanese resident community became solidly urban middle or lower middle class. A substantial number of migrants came as families. Although male residents outnumbered female, this was mainly because public officials stationed in Korea often left their families at home, and males employed in the transportation sector were often unmarried. This made the Japanese resident community in Korea quite different from the Japanese migrant community in Hawaii and the continental United States, where most jobs were to be found in agriculture or menial service and where single men dominated (table 13). However, the pattern in Korea was not so very different from that in other parts of continental Asia, including the leased territories in Kwantung and the treaty ports of China. The occupational structure of the resident community in the Kwantung territory, for example, almost exactly paralleled that of the resident community in Korea (table 14). The guidebook writers at home were correct: migration to the continent did offer opportunities that migration east across the Pacific did not.

SOME PORTRAITS

While statistics give a good overall picture of the Japanese resident community, a few case histories might convey a better sense of what its members were like. For the sake of variety, let us look at those both at the top and the bottom of Japanese society in Korea.

TABLE 13 OCCUPATIONS OF JAPANESE RESIDENTS OVERSEAS, 1909

	Agriculture, animal husbandry	Fishing	Manufacturing	Commerce	Transportation	Public official	Professional	Student	Other	Total
China (including Kwantung Territories)										
Male	210	131	7,184	14,180	1,900	4,191	1,191	355	15,306	44,648
Female	100	114	4,034	8,743	1,153	2,583	837	16	13,888	31,468
Total	310	245	11,218	22,923	3,053	6,774	2,028	371	29,194	76,116
%	0.4	0.3	14.7	30.1	4.0	8.9	2.7	0.5	38.4	100.0
Korea										
Male	2,755	1,811	7,096	25,529	—	10,023	1,561	—	21,370	80,168
Female	2,134	1,145	4,667	21,869	—	5,561	1,288	—	19,359	61,584
Total	4,889	2,956	11,763	47,398	—	15,584	2,849	—	40,729	141,752
%	3.9	2.3	9.3	37.6	—	12.4	2.3	—	32.2	100.0
U.S. (mainland)										
Male	2,732	293	2,186	1,884	38	1,909	107	464	9,348	18,961
Female	527	15	131	662	20	119	48	58	457	2,037
Total	3,259	308	2,317	2,546	58	2,028	155	522	9,805	20,998
%	15.5	1.5	11.0	12.1	0.3	9.7	0.7	2.5	46.7	100.0
Hawaii										
Male	25,562	787	2,524	4,727	727	11	331	—	9,978	44,647
Female	10,057	434	1,437	3,493	442	1	195	—	5,084	21,143
Total	35,619	1,221	3,961	8,220	1,169	12	526	—	15,062	65,790
%	54.1	1.9	6.0	12.5	1.8	0.0	0.8	—	22.9	100.0

SOURCE: Naikaku Tōkeikyoku, *Nihon teikoku tōkei nenkan* (Tokyo: 1910), 29:86–99.

TABLE 14   OCCUPATIONAL STRUCTURE OF
JAPANESE RESIDENTS IN KWANTUNG
TERRITORIES, END OF JUNE 1910

Occupation	Number
Primary	
Agriculture	67
Fishing	248
Subtotal	315 (0.9%)
Secondary	
Manufacturing	4,304 (12.0%)
Tertiary	
Commerce	6,209
Officials	4,901
Mantetsu employees	4,173
Laborers	5,398
Geishas, waitresses	1,276
Miscellaneous[a]	8,991
Subtotal	30,948 (85.9%)
Unknown	
Unemployed	428 (1.2%)
Total	35,995

[a] Doctors, lawyers, bank employees, public scribes and notaries, innkeepers, restaurant owners, newspaper reporters, pawnbrokers, bathhouse operators, etc.
SOURCE: Takushokyoku, *Shokuminchi imin gaikyō*, n.d., n.p., pp. 3–4.

THE COMPANY REPRESENTATIVE

Ibukiyama Tokuji, manager of the NYK line's Inchon branch office, had followed the predictable path of the late Meiji elite.[19] Born in 1868, the son of a Morioka merchant family, he had entered the First Higher Middle School in 1886 and then gone on to the law faculty of Tokyo Imperial University in 1892. The normal course for most law faculty graduates was entry into the official world, but Ibukiyama, worried about the "immaturity" of the Japanese business, decided to choose a career that would help promote and develop it. When he graduated in 1895, he entered the NYK Shipping Company, which at the time was expanding its worldwide long-distance routes. Ibukiyama was one of five employees sent to staff the new London office. For a year and a half he studied British maritime history, trying to understand the secrets of Britain's great success. On the ship home, hoping to inspire "maritime

19. This biographical sketch is based on Yanagihara, *Kei-Jin jitsugyōka retsuden*, 3–4.

thought" among his countrymen, he wrote an outline history of the British merchant marine. In late 1897 he was sent to the NYK Shanghai office, and for the next two years he spent his time investigating water transportation on the Yangtze and in south China in preparation for opening NYK routes. From there he moved back to the company home headquarters, then to the Chefoo office, and then back to the home company, where he was placed in charge of operations on the Chefoo line.

During the Russo-Japanese War Ibukiyama managed arrangements with foreign vessels temporarily hired by the NYK line. In March 1905 he was appointed manager of the Inchon branch office, where he remained for several years. He must have seemed slightly out of place to many fellow residents. Imperial University graduates were not in great supply in Korea at the time, and most of them were in Seoul, working in the legation or as advisers or technicians in the Korean government. As a biographical sketch noted, Ibukiyama "was not a businessman but an idealist." In his spare time he devoured his favorite books, and he submitted essays and articles to learned publications like the *Kokka gakkai zasshi*. Following the precept "sound mind, sound body," he was also an accomplished oarsman, a sport he had practiced in his university days and shared with Hayashi Gonsuke, three years his senior at Teidai.

Like most representatives of large-scale metropolitan firms, Ibukiyama did not come to Korea by his own choice, nor did he intend to become a permanent resident. He was a sojourner, albeit a high-level one, who would serve his term in Inchon, as he had in London and Shanghai, before moving on to another assignment. He did not intend to put down roots or to "bury his bones" in Korea any more than the local Japanese consul did. As such, his position in the community was ex officio, ascribed by virtue of representing a large metropolitan firm. One suspects that in the long run his reputation as "idealist" rather than "businessman" may have slowed his rise in NYK.

THE WEALTHY FOREIGN TRADE MERCHANT

One of the principal movers and shakers in the Japanese resident community at Inchon was Okuda Teijirō, a grain exporter who also served as a member of the local residents' association assembly, as a member of the local chamber of commerce, as head of the Grain Exporters' Association, as auditor for the Inchon rice and soybean exchange, as a director of the Japan Soy Sauce Company, as general manager of the

Inchon Petroleum Association, as head of the Export Association, and as director of the Pusan Wharf Company.[20] While he was by no means the richest Japanese in Inchon, there were few businesses that his activities and decisions did not affect.

Like many of the older residents in Korea, Okuda was a native of Nagasaki, born into a family of medicine and drug merchants in 1858. He was seven years old when his father died; thereafter, he was raised by his grandfather. After inheriting the family headship at the age of twenty, Okuda decided to go into business. The country was in the midst of its early infatuation with new technology imported from the "civilized" world, and Okuda chose a new and untraditional line of business—the production of fire bricks. He embarked on a study of the art of fire-brick making, invested family money in producing sample bricks, and entered several contract competitions sponsored by the Ministry of Commerce and Agriculture. No matter how hard he tried, however, he was unable to produce bricks better than those imported from the West. His failure did not deter him. Using books on Western brickmaking supplied by the ministry, he finally mastered the technology and began production in 1887. Unfortunately, the market for fireproof bricks was limited to three customers—the government-operated Osaka Arsenal, the Osaka Mint, and the Miike Coal Mine Company—none of whom were interested in Okuda's output. His hard-won knowledge of brickmaking had no commercial value, and in acquiring it he had nearly exhausted all his assets.

Facing a dead end at the age of thirty-five, Okuda turned the family headship over to his younger brother and boarded a ship for Inchon, where he got a job as a clerk in a trading company. As one can well imagine, the master of fire-brick technology was not content to remain an underling. In early 1889 he urged his employer to send a trial shipment of soybeans to Chefoo using Mitsui Bussan as an agent. The first shipment turned a small profit of ¥0.20 per *koku*; a second shipment ran into trouble. The Chinese merchants in Chefoo, wanting to discourage this new competition, colluded to force the price down, threatening Okuda and his employer with the considerable loss of ¥1.00 per *koku* on a shipment of 50,000 *koku* of soybeans. But Okuda worked hard to turn the situation around. Since the oil presses of Chefoo were unable to obtain soybeans from other sources, the price finally rose again, and Okuda was able to turn a profit of ¥3.00 per *koku*. The episode won

20. This sketch is based on ibid., 27–28.

him a considerable reputation among the still tiny Japanese community in Inchon.

In 1891 Okuda managed to rescue his employer from another disaster—the establishment of an unsuccessful branch office in Osaka—by borrowing money from two foreign firms in Inchon. The following year he formed a partnership with the Townshend Company to set up the first rice-polishing mill in Korea, and in 1893 he quit his employer to open his own grain shop. The Sino-Japanese War gave him his biggest break. By the end of the war he had accumulated profits of ¥20,000, enough to give him an independent base of capital. With this stake he began to diversify, becoming the general agent for the American petroleum imported by the Townshend Company, then going on to organize the Inchon Petroleum Association and the Inchon Rice Exporters Association. Clearly a man of considerable tenacity, drive, and intelligence, Okuda managed to surmount his failure in the fire-brick industry by deploying these qualities in Korea. Perhaps he might have been equally successful at home if earlier he had developed an enthusiasm for some marketable technology or stuck with the family's traditional trade in drugs and pharmaceuticals.

THE POLITICAL FIXER

Although trade lured most to the peninsula, the game of imperial politics lured others—the *tairiku rōnin* and *sōshi* involved in the murder of Queen Min, for example. A rather different sort was Nishihara Kamezō, a businessman with important political connections who achieved notoriety as go-between in the negotiation of a Japanese government loan to the Chinese warlord president, Tuan Chi-jui, in 1917.[21] His background was not so different from that of many other migrants to Korea. His father was a small farmer from the northern part of Kyoto prefecture who pursued a variety of by-employments—silk spinning, lumbering, oil pressing—but had an unfortunate penchant for spending more than he earned. Nishihara, born the eldest son in 1873, was a clever child who skipped grades three times in elementary school, graduating at the age of eleven. By the time he was thirteen he had read the *Nihon gaishi*, the Analects, and Mencius. A big and husky lad, he was by his own account a natural leader—a *gaki taishō* able to hold his own in fights with older boys.

21. This sketch is based mainly on Nishihara, *Yume no nanajū nen.*

The young Nishihara was consumed by a wanderlust described quite vividly in his memoirs:

> I thought to myself how dull (*tsumaran*) it would be to be stuck forever in a backwoods village like Kumohara. I thought I would like to study some more. I had a boy's irrepressible and ardent desire to leave the village and go to the city. But there was nothing I could do about it. When I was I thirteen I ran away from home to go to Kyoto. On the way I fell in with a Buddhist priest and talked with him about my future. When I got to Kyoto the priest found me a comfortable place to stay, then let my father know where I was. My father came to fetch me and took me straight home without a word. After I got home I helped around the house, but I kept thinking how terribly dull it is, how dull it is, and I was always on the lookout for a way to break out. One day when I was fourteen, I went to [a neighboring village] to collect money for some silk yarn we sold to a weaving shed. I stuck the money in my wallet and set off for Kobe, my second attempt to run away from home. At Kobe, while working as a shop apprentice, I studied Spanish. About that time I read Nakae Chōmin's *On Population* and had an urge to travel abroad. I thought I would like to sail off to Mexico. My father, who thought it would be awful for his son and heir to go off to a foreign country, came to fetch me.... He led me, protesting, back home.[22]

After his father died Nishihara was able to satisfy his wanderlust. He left home for good in 1889 at the age of seventeen to seek his fortune, supported by a network of countrymen who had moved away from the village. First he worked in a Kyoto print shop, then as a merchant sailor on the NYK line between Kobe and Okinawa; from there he moved to Osaka, where he clerked in a rice shop owned by a fellow villager; then he left for Tokyo, where he moved from job to job—print shop apprentice, newspaper deliveryman, and the like. After briefly attending a law night school and a private academy run by an independent scholar, he concluded that a knowledge of law or economics was not going to be particularly useful to him.

What set him on the road to Korea was a meeting with Kōmuchi Tomotsune, a politician from Tango region who had won a seat in the first election of 1890 after a successful career in the early Meiji bureaucracy. "My mother and father gave me birth," Nishihara later wrote, "but it was through Kōmuchi-sensei that I became a human being and that I was able to do what trifling work [I have done] as a human being." With the help of Kōmuchi, who had good business connections, and the financial backing of two local capitalists, Nishihara set up a small cotton textile company at Fukuchiyama, where he served as

22. Ibid., 9–10.

manager for two years until a flood destroyed the mill, its inventory, and its raw material in 1896. Nishihara decided to move into the real estate business instead. It was rumored that the government was planning to garrison an army regiment and build a naval base in Fukuchiyama. Surmising that the price of land was likely to rise, Nishiyama, with local backers as well as some investors from Kyoto and Tokyo, began to buy plots. Since construction demand was likely to grow, Nishihara also raised ¥300,000 from backers in Kyoto and elsewhere to start a brick factory in Kamisaki. In 1898, when the navy found it difficult to recruit local laborers for the construction of a new facility at Maizuru, Kō-muchi asked Nishihara to take on the job. After scouring the Japan Sea coast as far away as Tottori, Nishihara managed to assemble a crew of five hundred workers, many of them *burakumin*, and served as their boss until 1902.

It was as a result of Kōmuchi's political activities that Nishihara went to Korea. In 1900 Kōmuchi, an anti-Russian hawk, had become involved in organizing the Kokumin Dōmeikai, a group formed to protest the Russian occupation of Manchuria. The organization dissolved in 1902, and its members joined Konoe Atsumaro's Tai-Rō Dōshikai, another anti-Russian patriotic group. Nishihara served as a fund-raiser for the organization, and he worked for Kōmuchi's successful campaigns for a seat in the House of Representatives in 1903 and 1904. After the signing of the Japan-Korea agreement of February 1904, Kōmuchi decided to visit Korea, taking Nishihara with him. An advocate of a paternalistic policy toward the peninsula, he urged Nishihara to do something for the benefit of the Koreans.

During the war Nishihara stayed on in Korea to assist in the organization of the Ilchinhoe. As a political agent Nishihara quickly developed a network of pro-Japanese Korean acquaintances, but he also continued to be interested in business opportunities. Indeed, in September 1905 he became a *sōdanyaku* of the Seoul Chamber of Commerce, an organization designed to give Korean merchants and businessmen a voice in policy. Working with the chamber, Nishihara lobbied against Megata's currency reforms and urged the Koreans to resist the efforts of the residency-general to expropriate land to extend railway lines or build military bases. In 1907, with a capital of ¥10,000, he helped set up the Kyoekisha, a trading company to import Japanese cotton goods to Korea. Half businessman, half political fixer, Nishihara was well connected with both the Korean collaborator community and the upper echelons of the Japanese official establishment. He remained in Korea until 1916, eventually serving as a close confidant of Governor-General Terauchi.

A SUCCESSFUL MANUFACTURER

Toshima Yūtarō, acknowledged by a local magazine in 1916 to be the "pickle king of Korea," was younger than either Ibukiyama or Okuda.[23] His arrival in Korea was almost accidental. The eldest son of a half-farmer, half-merchant household in Shiga prefecture, he was born in 1883. His father engaged in agriculture but was also a jobber dealing in silk cocoons and rice. Yūtarō finished ordinary primary school, but his parents did not encourage him to continue; trade was more important than education, they said. Like many farm boys of his generation, he migrated from the country to the big city. At age thirteen he was apprenticed to the Shimaya, a well-known purveyor of groceries and pickles in the Kanda section of Tokyo. By the time he was eighteen he had been put in charge of the grocery section, a position that required him to be well acquainted with what was going in both the city and provincial markets. As he learned more and more, he concluded that Hokkaido was a promising place to expand the business. His employer agreed with him but pointed out that it would be a waste of time for Yūtarō to start a venture until he had satisfied his military obligation.

Shortly after the outbreak of the Russo-Japanese War the twenty-one-year-old Yūtarō was recruited into the Second Infantry Regiment of the Fourth Division. Appropriately enough, he served behind the lines in Korea and Manchuria in the quartermaster's headquarters. Two years later, in March 1906, he returned home with an Order of the Rising Sun (eighth class) and a ¥200 government award for his services. His experience on the continent turned his ambitions in a new direction. Opportunity, he decided, lay not in Hokkaido but in Korea, where he had seen conditions with his own eyes. By his later account, he was moved by patriotic motives to set up a business there: although Japan had won a military victory in Korea, it still needed to win the commercial war with the foreigners.

In any event, Yūtarō arrived in Seoul in June 1906, found lodgings in small inn along Motomachi, and set up a small store selling pickles and groceries. Small retail operations, as we have seen, were numerous, and competition was intense. Business was slow, and to attract customers

23. Based on an article in *Chōsen kōron*, June 1914, pp. 100–103.

Yūtarō generously extended credit. During the first four or five months hardly any of his customers paid their accounts; when he went to collect, they turned him away with the excuse that they would not have bought from him in the first place if he had not been selling on credit. Not surprisingly, his business collapsed, and the ¥10,000 lent him by a Tokyo backer when he came to Korea was gone. He had learned his lesson: in the mushrooming Japanese community trust did not work the same way that it did at home; the only way to do business there was cash-and-carry.

Nearly bankrupt after eight months in Korea, Yūtarō sold off his remaining stock, shop equipment, and even the formal haori he had brought with him. With the tiny stake he managed to scrape together, he set himself up in a street stall at the morning market near Nandaemun, selling fresh fruits and vegetables for cash, not credit. Profits were small but operating expenses were low, so his small capital grew fast. After a year as vegetable peddler he had enough saved to quit. Instead of going back into the retail grocery business or going into moneylending or investing in a speculative venture, he set up his own retail/wholesale pickle business. By 1909 he had made enough to pay off his debts, and he began to prosper.

In 1915 Yūtarō put the Namdaemun store in the hands of a younger brother and bought a thousand-*tsubo* site in Furuichi-chō to set up a pickle factory, warehouse, and residence. Selling his own pickles and miso as well as imported miso, *takuwan*, *narazuke*, and salt from the government monopoly, his career as "pickle king of Korea" was underway. His story was not so different in its fundamentals from that of Okuda. His first failure came earlier and in Korea rather than in Japan, but like Okuda he was not defeated by his experience. By the early 1920s he had become head of the Seoul Pickle Producers Association and director of the Seoul Soy Sauce Producers Association.

THE SALARYMAN

Iizumi Kanda, roughly a contemporary of Toshima, came to Korea in quite a different way. In 1901, after graduating from his course in French law at Tokyo Imperial University, he decided to find a job that would take him to Korea.[24] The establishment of the Seoul-Pusan Rail-

24. Based on Iizumi Kanda, "Watakushi no shūshoku undō," *Zuihitsu Chōsen*, 1935, 60–64; Chōsen shinbun, comp., *Chōsen jinji kōshinroku* (Seoul), 1922, p. 40.

way Company was in the news, and Iizumi decided to find out who was running it. Armed with a letter of introduction from a *senpai* who headed the company's accounting section, he visited one of the company's directors, Kusaka Yoshirō, a former diplomat and prefectural governor who had left the official world to become a businessman. The initial interview lasted three minutes. Only after several months of bombarding Kusaka with his name card was Iizumi finally taken on as a member of the company's stock-selling campaign. Iizumi traveled in the provinces, lecturing on conditions in Korea to local audiences, persuading prefectural assemblymen and other local officials that the venture was safe, and convincing everyone of the urgency and importance of the project to Japan's future. Of the forty-odd members of the team, only a handful, Iizumi among them, were kept on as permanent employees. In 1902 he became head of the accounting and warehouse sections of the Seoul office. But when the Seoul-Pusan Railway Company was bought out by the Japanese government in 1906, Iizumi decided to look for employment in private business rather than become a bureaucrat. He tried to approach an influential *senpai*, Hayashi Gonsuke, the minister in Seoul, for an introduction to Megata Jūtarō, the Japanese financial adviser to the Korean government. Since Hayashi was too busy, Iizumi decided to get in touch with Megata directly. When Megata asked him about his language ability, he admitted that he could not speak French and that his English was not much better. Even so, Megata eventually found him a position as manager of a new warehouse company, and Iizumi quit his job at the railway.

Just what attracted Iizumi to Korea is difficult to discern from his later recollections. In his case, as in Toshima's, timing seems to have been important: he graduated from the university just when opportunities were opening up with the new railroad venture in Korea. Perhaps he was also influenced by the "old boy" network he used to secure a post. In any case, one thing led to another, and Iizumi eventually went on to a career in banking, first as manager of the Taehan Tenil Bank (Tai-Kan Ten'ichi Bank), then in 1907 as a section chief in the newly organized Chōsen Bank. The capital he brought to Korea was not material but consisted rather of the intellectual skills and personal connections that he had picked up in the university. These made him useful as a manager in the expanding modern business sector—railroads, warehousing, and banking.

THE "AVERAGE" RESIDENT

It is easier to find out about the more successful residents than the less successful, who are less apt to leave a trace in the historical record. Fortunately, however, the reminiscences of Urao Bunzō, one of the less successful and perhaps more typical colonists, gives considerable insight into the lives of ordinary Japanese residents. To be sure, much in Urao's experience parallels that of well-to-do businessmen like Okuda Seijirō, Nishihara Kamezō, or Toshima Yūtarō, but he seems not to have been as bright, as aggressive, or as lucky.

A native of Dannoura in Yamaguchi, Urao Bunzō came from a family that had seen better days.[25] Although four generations of the family had served as village headmen (*shōya*), Bunzō's grandfather had squandered the family wealth in pursuit of pleasure, and his father had inherited only the family house. Although not in good health, his father was adept at the abacus and managed to make a living as a village banker and moneylender, accepting deposits from country folk and lending money to shopkeepers and merchants in town. Bunzō did not inherit his father's talent for numbers, however, and did very poorly at arithmetic in school. In fact, his grades were so bad that he had to leave public school and go to a private academy. When he was fourteen or fifteen, he began to work, more or less as a servant. When Bunzō turned twenty, his father died, and the following year his older brother, a construction contractor, went bankrupt and took to drink. Bunzō was left at home with his widowed mother, who gave him a small allowance to visit a brothel three times a month; nevertheless, he felt bored and hemmed in. For a time he toyed with the idea of going to Hokkaido, where one of his friends had moved, but his mother would not let him. Instead, she gave him the boat fare to travel to Korea, where his older sister, Kichi, ran an inn at Seoul. In 1893, at the age of twenty-one, he sailed for Inchon.

His sister's house, a Korean-style dwelling with an *ondol*, was so small it surprised Bunzō, but attached to it was a more substantial forty-*tsubo* building (about 1,400 square feet) let out to four tenants and a small vegetable plot rented by a Japanese man whose wife worked as a maid at the Russian legation. With the rent and her income from sewing, Kichi managed to support herself. She was less successful at moneylending. When Bunzō tried to collect some loans she had made, he found her debtors were unemployed and unable to pay. To make a little

25. Based on Muramatsu, *Chōsen shokuminsha*.

extra money, the sister set up a "medicinal bath," but customers were few and business languished. Bunzō found life with his sister as constricting as life with his mother, but there was little for him to do since he had neither money to spend nor capital to invest in a business. To get out of the house, he began taking Korean lessons with a Korean physician.

Then came the war in 1894 and with it the chance to make a quick yen. The outbreak of the war brought a sudden inflation in food prices at Seoul: rice doubled in price, and eggs quintupled. A Dai-Ichi Bank employee suggested to Bunzō that there was money to be made in selling eggs, so Bunzō set off to nearby Suwon, where he collected a hundred-odd dozen (as well as twenty turtles suitable for *suppon*) in two days. By the time he got back to Seoul a good many of the eggs had spoiled in the August heat, but he was able to break even by selling the rest at a mark-up of 200 to 300 percent. The war provided other opportunities. Bunzo got a contract to provide bathing facilities—perhaps the remnants of the "medicinal bath"—for Japanese soldiers garrisoned at Yongsan, and when the troops moved north, Bunzō signed on as an interpreter. Unfortunately, at P'yŏngyang he came down with typhus and had to be shipped back to Inchon.

After the war ended, the physician who had been teaching Bunzō Korean suggested that he could make great profits by dismantling old Korean houses and selling the material. After two months of pleading, he received a loan of ¥600 from his sister to buy a large and handsome Korean house with an eight-hundred-*tsubo* lot. Within a month he had managed to sell all the materials of the dismantled house, including stonework the Japanese legation wanted to buy, and he still had a lot worth ¥600. For ¥400 he had the Ōkura-gumi construct him a large two-story dwelling, later converted to an inn, and he went home to Yamaguchi to find a bride. Even though he was not clad in brocade, his feet were firmer on the ground than they had been when he left home. His next venture, dealing in ginseng, was less successful. The Korean from whom he bought his first shipment was, unfortunately, not the owner of the ginseng plantation but its manager. After Bunzō paid him, the manager absconded to Pusan, leaving Bunzō with the obligation to pay the real owner. Even with the double payment, Bunzō and his associates managed to turn a profit of ¥500 each.

By this time Bunzō apparently had accumulated enough capital to set up a more stable business. In the spring of 1898 he opened a charcoal business in Seoul, hiring a graduate of the Shimonoseki Commercial

School to manage the shop while he investigated other ventures. When he heard that the American firm of Collbran and Bostwick had gotten permission to build an electric light and electric trolley system in Seoul, he decided to become a supply contractor for the project. Buying up a load of pine logs for ¥0.12 to ¥0.18 per log, he contracted to sell them to Collbran and Bostwick at a healthy mark-up of ¥0.30 per log. Once again there were problems. The Korean who had purchased the logs for him proved "unreliable," and many of the logs turned out to be unusable, so he turned a profit of only ¥0.05 per log instead of ¥0.12.

Dreams of quick profit continued to beckon. Bunzō decided to try his hand at smuggling counterfeit nickel coins. His partners in the venture were his store manager, a young merchant from Osaka, and a Korean. Each put up ¥2,000 to finance the venture, and the young merchant said he could borrow ¥20,000 at home. In late January 1899 Bunzō and the Korean partner set off for Japan, where they loaded a rented boat with barrels of counterfeit coins wrapped in straw. The load cost ¥20,000, but the face value of the coins was three times that. Bad weather delayed their arrival at Inchon, and as they made their way upstream to Seoul with their contraband, a Japanese police constable hailed them for a ride. Once on board he turned to Bunzō and said, "Urao-san, make no mistake. We know everything, so hand over the goods quietly. If you do I'll try to do the best I can for you with my superiors." Bunzō quietly turned over the counterfeit coins. In May 1899 he and fourteen other smugglers were ordered to leave Korea within three months and not to return for three years. His sister refused to put up ¥500 as warranty for his good behavior, so in late 1899 he closed up his charcoal store and left with his family for Japan, where he spent the next few years running a small mail packet and passenger service to Oki Island.

The dream of making it in Korea was still in his blood. When the Russo-Japanese War broke out, Bunzō sold out his business, packed up his family, and bought passage on a boat to Korea. When he arrived in Seoul, he found the city packed with Japanese subcontractors who had arrived to work on the construction of the Seoul-Pusan railway. One of them, who had set up headquarters in his sister's inn, asked Bunzō to buy him a house. Bunzō did so, and then he bought another, earning a handsome commission. But in early 1905 his wife died. Leaving his young daughter with his sister, he took a job as an instructor of Japanese at a school run by the Jōdō sect at Kangjin. The county magistrate sometimes came around for a visit, and so did the chief of the new police branch office at Kunsan, but otherwise it was a lonely life. When he heard that the residency-general was looking for interpreters to work in the new post office system, he borrowed money from the policeman and headed for Seoul, where he passed the examination for the job. After a brief stint at the Seoul post office, in 1907 he was sent off to a post at Ichon, a small town on the road between Seoul and Wŏnsan. His salary was ¥30 a month and his living expenses only ¥15, which allowed him to put a good bit of money aside. He stayed at Ichon for four years, with a new wife, lending money on the side, until he had accumulated enough capital to start his own moneylending business.

Bunzō was perhaps typical of the early migrants to Korea, the petty capitalists with dreams of quick and easy money, who took advantage of every opportunity, legal and illegal, to build a small stake into a big one. Most never realized their dreams of returning home clad in brocade, and instead they stayed on, permanent expatriates in a colonial society where they were assured of a secure and superior position, if only because they were not Koreans. Bunzō himself managed to make a trip to Tokyo, where he ordered a frock coat at Mitsukoshi Department Store and bought new gold-rimmed glasses at the Hattori Clock Shop, another *haikara* establishment. (And although he did not have the nerve to try the entertainment at Shinbashi, he did manage to visit to Yoshiwara.) But success was short-lived. Still on the lookout for new opportunities, in 1916 he moved south to set up a lumber business at Ch'ŏngju in North Chŏlla Province, then at Sinŭiju. Eventually he went bankrupt. In 1927 he moved across the border to Antung in Manchuria, where he and his third wife, a former geisha, ran a cafe until his death in 1935.

COMMUNITY INSTITUTIONS

The diverse and often unruly settler community was occasionally brought together by a need to lobby the metropolitan government. Since what was good for the Japanese trading community in Korea was good for the Japanese government too, there was usually little friction on questions of trade or foreign policy, except when the local residents were impatient at the sluggishness of the government in responding to what they regarded as obstacles placed in their way by the Koreans. But by the turn of the century, and especially at the time of the Russo-Japanese War, as more staid and stable middle-class elements moved to the peninsula, they demanded a protective cocoon of social institutions and a voice in controlling and regulating their own communities. On these mundane issues, particularly on the question of how much self-rule they should be allowed, the settlers' relationship with local Japanese officials and the home government was tinged with antagonism.

At first the treaty port chambers of commerce served as the principal political voice of the resident community. The first was established at Pusan in 1879, shortly after the port was opened, and others were set up in Inchon in 1885 and in Seoul in 1887. These chambers, especially those in Pusan and Inchon, were not intended to represent the small merchant, shopkeeper, or innkeeper but only the larger metropolitan firms involved in Korea-Japan trade. Membership was limited to those engaged in banking, shipping, foreign trade, or luxury goods. In practice, this meant that leadership was monopolized by the local managers of big metropolitan enterprises like the Dai-Ichi Bank or the NYK line or the more substantial trading houses. Only in Seoul, where the Japanese settler community was quite small and not many were merchants, were there no restrictions on membership; even women could join.[26]

Smaller and less well capitalized wholesalers, jobbers, and small retail merchants, resentful of their exclusion, began to demand fairer representation. In Inchon, for example, where membership fees were fixed for banks and shipping companies but were levied on foreign trade firms in proportion to their volume of business, the merchants complained. So did those completely left out of the associations, particularly the wholesalers and jobbers, who mediated transactions between the Korean market and the export firms. In 1887, just a few years after its organization, disagreement within the Inchon chamber had reached the point that it was ready to vote itself out of existence until dissuaded from doing so by the local Japanese consul, who reminded them to think about their long-term interests. Eventually, different fees were charged to different classes of members, and the membership was broadened to include all sorts of merchants, except artisans, restaurant owners, and sake shop operators. In 1894 sake merchants, brewers, and confectioners were allowed to join, and in 1895 anyone who was engaged in commerce as defined under the Japanese Commercial Code was permitted to join.[27]

The expansion of their membership enabled the chambers to present

26. FMA, File 3.3.5.4, "Chōsen kaikō ni okeru shōgyō kaigisho enkaku genzai no sōshiki torishirabegata takushokumusho yori ikken."

27. Kimura Kenji, Zai-Chō Nihonjin no shakaishi, 81–89; Jinsen Shōkō Kaigisho, Jinsen shōkō kaigisho gojū nenshi.

a united front to local authorities and the home government on issues of concern to the resident business community. Collective appeals to the local consuls, the legation at Seoul, or even the Foreign Ministry in Tokyo were more likely to bring results than individual petitions. Representatives from the local chambers often gathered at "national" meetings to deal with urgent issues, and sometimes they sought support from domestic interest associations like the Osaka Chamber of Commerce. By the turn of the century they could also turn for help to a small "Korean lobby" in the Diet, including one or two old Korea hands like Inoue Kakugorō, who had gone to Korea in the 1880s to assist the reform faction. While these Diet members did not constitute a massive bloc in the lower house, they could raise questions on behalf of the Japanese community in Korea.

Predictably enough, the chambers of commerce spoke out almost entirely on economic and trade issues, protesting currency regulations, local taxes, grain embargoes, or strikes by porters and coolies that hindered trade, or urging the creation of a Japanese-financed and Japanese-dominated economic infrastructure. During the 1890s they lobbied for harbor improvement, the construction of a Seoul-Pusan railway line, the easing of restrictions on migration to Korea, and the circulation of Dai-Ichi Bank notes as legal tender. After the Russo-Japanese War, an annual peninsula-wide convention of chambers of commerce issued resolutions calling for reduced domestic tariffs on rice imported from Korea, the building of new roads, bridges, railroad lines, and agricultural stations, and the suppression of anti-Japanese "banditry."[28]

As the Japanese communities grew in size and complexity, local residents became concerned about issues other than trade, particularly for public amenities that they were accustomed to at home, but the chambers of commerce did not become involved. In the early 1890s local consuls had issued regulations permitting the election of local residents' assemblies (kyōryūminchi kaigi) and local resident headmen (sōdai), but these had very limited powers. The local consul could dissolve or suspend them, and he could also issue regulations of his own.[29] Neither did the assemblies have any legal status or authority. Since they were not

28. Kimura Kenji, Zai-Chō Nihonjin no shakaishi, 89ff.
29. Law 80, Apr. 11, 1896. Consuls could also expel residents. Those expelled had to leave the country within fifteen days unless they could prove that they could not leave for business or other reasons; they were required to put up a forfeitable deposit if they stayed on. During the summer of 1899 another emergency ordinance forbade Japanese subjects to travel to Korea without permission of both the Foreign Ministry and the local Japanese authorities.

legally incorporated, they could not issue bonds to finance local improvement projects. Neither could the associations compel local residents to pay taxes or other fees. They could simply pack their bags and leave for home if they did not want to pay. Without authority under Japanese law to raise money for education, sanitation, public transportation, and other common facilities, the resident communities and their representatives lacked any stable fiscal base.[30] Everything had to be financed by the assessment of voluntary contributions. Although this worked well enough, for example, when the Japanese residents in Seoul had raised ¥10,000 in bonds to improve streets, put in drains, and dig gutters for rainwater, it was unsatisfactory in the long run.

The need for public utilities was acute. In the Japanese settlement in Seoul, for example, there were about three hundred wells, but not one of them provided potable water for ordinary residents. Only the military had access to reliable drinking water, and the civilian population had to buy it from private entrepreneurs at a high cost. Most households paid about eight yen a month, and even then water quality was not very good. In Inchon water was in such short supply that even the consulate staff was able to take baths only every two or three days, and in Pusan there were often water shortages owing to drought. The lack of adequate water supplies increased health risks. At the time of the Sino-Japanese War there had been a brief outbreak of bubonic plague, and in the summer of 1904 an epidemic of scarlet fever hit the Japanese in Seoul but did not touch those in the homeland. In addition, medical services were far less accessible in Korea than in Japan.[31]

It is particularly interesting that Japanese residents were almost equally concerned about the education of their children. With the influx of new migrants during and after the Russo-Japanese War, the local resident community simply lacked the resources to build schools to meet the demand even in the larger Japanese communities, let alone in more remote areas. Nakai Kitarō, head of the residents' association in Seoul, reported that during a trip on the new Seoul-Pusan line he saw school-age Japanese children playing by the station when they should have been in school because they had no schools to go to.[32] The residents wanted the Japanese government to recognize resident community schools as equivalent to those at home, and they wanted help in sup-

30. FMA, File 3.8.2.193, "Kyōryūmindanhō narabi doshiko kisoku seitei iken."
31. Nakai Kitarō, "Kankoku ni okeru Nihonjin kyōryūchi," *Tokyo keizai zasshi*, Feb. 4, 1905, pp. 164–71.
32. Ibid.

porting them. Petitions suggested that a program be set up to train teachers for schools outside the home islands; that prefectures sending the most migrants to Korea employ schoolteachers to work in the schools in Korea; that resident communities in Korea wanting schools send funds to the Ministry of Education, in return for which the ministry would appoint recent graduates from teacher training schools or volunteers who had finished their obligatory service; that teachers in Korea be given higher wages; and that the Ministry of Education regularly inspect schools in Korea.[33]

In the summer of 1904 the heads of all the local residents' associations from Mokp'o, Inchon, and Seoul met to formulate an agenda of requests to the Japanese government. They agreed on the following priorities: establishing a local government system for Japanese residents that would give local communities the power to tax; requiring Japanese consuls, diplomats, and military personnel to pay taxes supporting shared public facilities; and providing funds for the establishment of middle schools.[34] The following winter Nakai Kitarō went to Tokyo to lobby for the establishment of a local residents' organization law (kyoryūmindanhō). As he argued in an article in the Tōkyō keizai zasshi, the Japanese residents in Korea were "nameless heroes" advancing the cause of Japan with little or no help from the government. "This is, I think, true national development or real racial expansion.... But since neither the government nor the Diet has done anything to help the Japanese living in the treaty ports in Korea their progress and development has been slow." What the Japanese residents needed was direct government support in making life easier through better schools, better water supplies, better sanitation facilities, better medical support, and so forth.[35]

While Nakai got a sympathetic hearing from his old classmate, Ishii Kikujirō, chief of the commercial bureau of the Foreign Ministry, the cabinet legislative bureau was slow in drafting a bill. With the Diet session passing quickly, he put pressure on the bureaucracy by having a Diet member interpellate the government about treaty settlement ad-

---

33. The local residents had other demands as well. As the treaty settlements became more crowded, the number of legal disputes and criminal cases also increased. The dockets of the local consular courts were crowded, and all appeals had to go through the Nagasaki court of appeal (Nagasaki Kosoin); one group of residents asked that appeals be directed to Tokyo and Osaka.
34. Nakai, Chōsen kaikōroku, 121–22.
35. Nakai Kitarō, "Kankoku ni okeru Nihonjin kyoryūdan," Tōkyō keizai zasshi, Feb. 4, 1905, p. 170.

ministration, forcing responses from the foreign, education, and agriculture and commerce ministries. This tactic ruffled official feathers, and Nakai was eventually ordered to leave Tokyo, but Ishii and Vice Minister of Foreign Affairs Chinda promised to get a bill through the Diet. As Ishii argued before a lower house committee, the residents had relied on "public spirit" so far, but they would not be able to do so in the future; hence, they had to be recognized as legal bodies similar to local government bodies at home.

The law, finally passed in March 1905, authorized residents' associations to incorporate under the supervision of public officials and to function within the provisions of Japanese law and the treaties with Korea. The foreign minister was empowered to specify where associations could be organized, and the Foreign Ministry could determine whether associations were divided, merged, abolished, or altered in other ways. The organization of the residents' associations and the appointment of their officers and their assemblies as well as the raising of revenues, accounting for property, handling operating expenses, and the like were subject to official regulations. Their activities were to be supervised by the local consuls, the ambassador or minister at Seoul, and the foreign ministry, in that order.

By the time the law was put into effect, the protectorate had been established. Instead of coming under the control of the Foreign Ministry, the residents' associations were put under the supervision of the residency-general. Under new regulations issued in July 1906 each association was to have a chief (*minchō*), appointed for a three-year period, to be elected by the association assembly (*minkai*) and approved by the resident-general. The local assembly was to have from eight to twenty-four members, elected by male residents over twenty-five years of age who had paid ¥25 or more in taxes the previous year; those entitled to vote also had the right to stand for election unless employed as public officials, priests, or schoolteachers. The assembly had the right to make decisions on proposals presented by the *minchō* concerning the regulations of the association, expenditures, annual budget, disposition of association owned real estate, disposition of basic property and reserve funds, and legal suits. Not only did the associations have their own assets, but they also had the power to levy taxes, user fees, commissions, and labor services.

In terms of functions, the residents' associations resembled local government units in Japan, but ultimately their actions could be overruled by the *rijikan*, the local representative of the residency-general.

The *rijikan* could cancel any legislation passed by the *minkai* or void any election he deemed "contrary to law or regulations of the assembly" or "harmful to the public interest." He could also issue whatever orders he deemed necessary for the administration or supervision of the association, and he could prorogue the local assembly. The *rijikan* also had to approve all association regulations, all enterprises on which the organization spent money, the disposition of assets and reserves, the raising of special levies, and the incurring of loans. In sum, the local representative of the residency-general could block or undo almost anything the local assembly did. The local residents' "self-government" was tightly confined in a straitjacket of bureaucratic discretion.[36]

Among settlements with one thousand or more Japanese residents, associations (*kyoryūmindan*) were established in Seoul, Inchon, Pusan, Kunsan, Chinnamp'o, and P'yŏngyang in August 1906; in Masan and Wŏnsan in September 1906; in Mokp'o in October 1906; and in Taegu in October 1906. In settlements with fewer than one hundred Japanese residents, Japanese associations (Nihonjinkai) were organized to deal with educational facilities and sanitation. Usually these associations, like the chambers of commerce, were headed by representatives of large firms, especially the large metropolitan banks. They worked at providing the settler communities with public amenities like city streets, sewer systems, wells, parks, bridges, schools, hospitals, and fire brigades. The Japanese settlers wanted to be no less comfortable and safe on the peninsula than they would be at home.

The residency-general was uncomfortable with even this limited degree of "self-government." Its goal was a system that would subject all residents of the peninsula, Japanese and Korean, to the same sort of administrative control, and it was particularly worried that eventually the Koreans would demand the same kind of "self-government" as the Japanese. In 1908 the residency-general issued new rules requiring the *minchō* to be appointed by the residency-general itself, not chosen by public election. Needless to say, the settler community and the local Japanese press protested vehemently. The residency-general mollified public resentment by reappointing the elected incumbent headmen to their posts.[37] With annexation and the assumption of full control by the government-general, however, Japanese officials in Seoul began to talk of abolishing the whole self-government system. The revision of foreign

36. Tōkanfūrei no. 21, July 14, 1906.
37. Kimura Kenji, *Zai-Chō Nihonjin no shakaishi*, 78–79.

treaties in 1911 put an end to the treaty ports and the foreign settlements, undermining the raison d'être of residents' associations.

The associations showered Governor-General Terauchi with petitions urging that the associations be replaced by some other system of self-government; when they received no reply, they dispatched a delegation to Tokyo to plead with members of the cabinet, the head of the cabinet legislative bureau, the head of the colonial office, and members of both houses of the Diet. But Terauchi was determined to end the settler organizations, and in early 1913, after negotiating the disposition of the treaty settlements of the other foreign powers in Korea, he announced his intention to abolish the *mindan*. All their functions were to be given over to agencies of the government-general. As one observer put it with some bitterness, the Japanese residents were "to be put under the same bureaucratic administrative control as the Koreans, whose cultural level is low and who are weak in the ability to rule themselves."[38]

The local residents were not happy with the change, but given the constraints placed on public expression, it was difficult to push their opposition any further. The unwillingness of the colonial government to countenance any degree of settler self-government reveals the voracity of its appetite for control. Even the modest degree of local autonomy granted villages and towns at home was unacceptable to the colonial officials. The colonial regime adopted a style of bureaucratic autocracy that was under growing attack in domestic politics. The conflict between the resident community and colonial officials also reminds us that their interests were not always congruent. If the economic objectives of the abacus and the sword often matched, that did not mean that their political interests always meshed as well. Whether and how this tension continued to express itself is a question deserving further study.

38. *Shin Chōsen oyobi shin Manshū*, 427.

CHAPTER 10

The Korean Land Grab

Agriculture and Land Acquisition

"In any country where economic conditions are still primitive, the possession of land offers bright prospects indeed, and such is the case with Korea." So advised one guidebook to Korea.[1] Although most migrants at first turned their hands to trade, they soon discovered the advantages of landowning. Few economic opportunities in Korea seemed as risk free, and few as lucrative. "There is no sweeter way to make money," observed a member of the Osaka Chamber of Commerce mission. For a person with a small stake of capital, a steady and reliable source of income was within easy reach. And what made sense for the small investor made equal sense for the big one. Big metropolitan investors in Osaka and Tokyo, as well as in some provincial cities, saw the purchase of land in Korea as a relatively safe way to make profits in a country that otherwise afforded limited opportunities for investment.

Government officials, from top leaders down through the middle- and lower-echelon officials in the Ministry of Foreign Affairs or the Ministry of Agriculture and Commerce, did their best to promote Japanese land ownership in Korea. Missions sent to investigate economic opportunities in Korea before the Russo-Japanese War came back with optimistic estimates of the possibilities. Often inspired by a vision of thousands of Japanese small farmers settling on the peninsula, men like Katsura and Itō promoted plans for land acquisition by quasi-governmental agencies like the Oriental Development Company. Even a

1. Yamamoto Kōtarō, *Saishin Chōsen ijū annai*, 202.

number of prefectural governments, particularly along the Japan Sea, explored various migration and land development schemes. The motives behind these official efforts were mixed; for some, acquisition by Japanese subjects was a way of establishing a weightier social and political presence in Korea; for others, it was a means of alleviating population pressure at home by creating economic opportunities overseas; and for still others, it was the most efficient way to stimulate the improvement of Korean agriculture.

Promoting the idea of land ownership in Korea was not difficult. For one thing, arable land in Korea was quite cheap compared to Japanese arable land, but it was just as profitable to cultivate. In the vicinity of Taegu, for example, it was possible to buy one *tan* of paddy land for ¥1.50, or one-fifth to one-tenth of what it would cost in Japan. A man who sold his holdings in Japan could use the money to buy five times as much in Korea. And as a number of guidebooks observed, it was easy to find Koreans willing to sell their land for prices that might seem cheap to the Japanese but were handsome to the Koreans. The soil itself, it was generally thought, was as fertile as in Japan, and if the same amount of capital and labor were invested in a plot in Korea, it was likely to yield as much harvest as a similar plot in Japan. Even if rice prices were lower in Korea, the rate of return on the purchase price of land was likely to be at least as high as in Japan. The Osaka Chamber of Commerce mission estimated that it might run as high as 30 percent per year—a sweet profit indeed.[2] And those Japanese who became landlords rather than self-cultivators, it was reported, could clear at least 15 percent, and sometimes over 20 percent, in net profits.[3]

The bullish outlook on land investment in Korea was buoyed by overly optimistic views about the availability of land. In the many guidebooks and government reports on Korea published during the decade before annexation, one discovers a widely shared belief that vast tracts of virgin land awaited ambitious and energetic Japanese settlers. Some authors argued that much land went uncultivated because Korean peasants feared they would lose any profit from reclamation to corrupt officials or rapacious landlords. Others argued that the Koreans were simply too lazy to make use of the land. "It seems that the Koreans work when they are not playing rather than playing when they are not working," wrote Yamamoto Kōtarō. "If hard-working Japanese farmers

2. *KSSH*, 51–58.
3. Satō Seijirō, *Chō-hantō to shin Nihon*, 33.

were to shoulder their hoes, come to Korea, improve agricultural techniques, and farm the land according to Japanese methods, they could easily increase the harvest by twofold or threefold."[4]

The myth of untrammeled wastes awaiting the hoes of sturdy Japanese migrant farmers rested on the flimsiest of evidence. Before the completion of a national land survey under the Japanese colonial government in 1918, no reliable nationwide figures on cultivated land area or land ownership existed. The few observers who reported on Korea before the Russo-Japanese War had not seen very much of the country. To visitors accustomed to the densely settled agricultural areas of Japan, especially in the Kansai region or along the Inland Sea, the Korean landscape seemed quite barren of habitation. The Seoul-Inchon railroad line, which was as much of the country as many Japanese saw, ran through much undeveloped meadow and bottomland. It was natural for visitors to extrapolate these conditions to the rest of the country's interior, and often they did so.[5] Others made estimates of land available for reclamation, settlement, and cultivation not by any direct observation but simply by gleaning information from other guidebooks and reports.

One Japanese scholar has suggested that the myth of available land was propagated deliberately by those with an interest in encouraging an optimistic vision of Korea's agricultural potential. Government officials anxious to promote emigration to Korea obviously had a stake in doing so, and so did private business interests. For example, to attract investors, the promoters of the Seoul-Pusan Railway Company argued that the line would be profitable because it would run through the richest and most fertile areas of Korea. When they importuned government officials and Diet members for government subsidies, however, they argued that operation would not be profitable in the short run. What better way to resolve the contradiction than to suggest that the interior was filled with rich and uncultivated tracts, likely to be productive in the long run, but in need of investment for improvement in the short run.[6] While it is difficult to prove that Machiavellian designs lay behind the myth of available land, there is no question that the myth inflated the economic attractiveness of Korea, especially in the agricultural sector. After all, the Southern Pacific Railway encouraged Midwestern farmers to move to California by publishing paeans to sun and soil, not dreary geographical surveys.

4. Yamamoto, *Saishin Chōsen ijū annai*, 74–76.
5. Kobayakawa, *Chōsen nōgyō hattatsu shi*, 2:10.
6. Yamaguchi Muneo, "Kobuchi kaitaku mondai."

By the time of the Russo-Japanese War more realistic evaluations about the availability of untilled arable challenged earlier rosy estimates. After touring the southern agricultural provinces and the Seoul region, the Osaka Chamber of Commerce mission concluded that there was by no means as much uncultivated wasteland as reported, and certainly not as much as in Hokkaido or the undeveloped regions of South America. Most arable land was already under cultivation, and on fields without enough water to irrigate rice Korean farmers grew barley. The only lands fit for reclamation, the report concluded, were low-lying meadowlands along rivers left unprotected by dikes and so often flooded that they were left for pasture and livestock. Reclamation required heavy investment as well as cooperation among neighboring communities, and it was certainly beyond the resources of the individual buyer. Acquisition of such land was likely to be profitable only if undertaken by a group of investors or subsidized by the government. The best opportunities for the small investor, the report concluded, were to be found in the purchase of land already under cultivation.[7]

The settlers already in Korea did not have to be told that. Well before the Russo-Japanese War, Japanese settlers in the treaty ports had begun to purchase arable land. As early as 1884 some Japanese residents in Inchon had raised fruit trees and green vegetables on plots within the settlement zone. By the turn of the century, as the ports filled with new immigrants, Japanese settlers started buying land farther afield, often illegally. Under its treaty with the British the Korean government had limited the right of foreigners to buy land more than ten Korean *ri* (or one Japanese *ri*) from the boundaries of the foreign settlement zones. In effect, this put nearly all the peninsula beyond the reach of would-be foreign land buyers. Under the Kabo reforms the prohibition of foreign land purchases was reaffirmed, and during the late 1890s the government at Seoul repeatedly enjoined local officials to enforce it strictly. In 1898 the government also promulgated a law barring Koreans from offering land to foreigners as collateral for loans. These legal restraints, however, did not deter a handful of intrepid Japanese from buying land beyond the treaty limit.

According to Japanese consular reports, the pace of land purchases accelerated as the war with Russia approached. In 1903, for example, the Japanese consulate at Kunsan reported that Japanese owned about four hundred *chō* in the vicinity of the port; in the following year the

7. *KSSH*, 46–51.

amount jumped more than tenfold to five thousand *chō*.[8] In the Kunsan region a group of Korean go-betweens had even emerged to arrange land sales for a fee. Japanese also bought land in the Pusan and Mokp'o areas and along the right-of-way for the Seoul-Pusan line. Most Japanese buyers were familiar with local conditions in Korea, and most bought land within one *ri* of the settlements, as permitted by treaty, so few experienced any difficulty with their transactions.[9] The real land rush began during the Russo-Japanese War, as Japanese political control tightened. An initial wave of land buying came with the signing of the agreement in the spring of 1904. A second, beginning after annexation in 1910 and tapering off slightly during World War I, more than doubled the cultivated land owned by Japanese from 69,312 *chō* (1910) to 169,007 *chō* (1915).[10] Some buyers were intent on reclamation and cultivation; others were simply interested in speculation.

THE NAGAMORI PLAN

The acceleration of Japanese land ownership after 1904 was a direct consequence of Japanese government efforts. By the time of the Russo-Japanese War the agricultural development of Korea had become a central goal of Korea policy. The May 1904 cabinet decision made this policy quite clear:

> The most promising enterprise for our nationals in Korea is to engage in agriculture. As an agricultural country Korea in the past has provided our country mainly with foodstuffs and raw materials and in return received supplies of our manufactured goods from our country. We believe that future economic relations between the two countries must develop in accord with this principle. Furthermore, the population of Korea is small in comparison with its land area. If large numbers of emigrants from our country are permitted to move there and our farmers can penetrate the interior, we will acquire at a single stroke an emigration colony for our excess population and sufficient supplies of foodstuffs.[11]

8. Pak Chong-pin, "Ri-chō makki in okeru Nihonjin no kome to tochi no shudatsu," in Tsunoyama, *Nihon ryōji hōkoku no kenkyū*, 372. See also *Chōsen nōkaihō*, 1935, 82.

9. Satō Seijirō, *Kankoku seigyōsaku*, 38–39.

10. An U-sik, *Tennō to Chōsenjin*, 259. In Seoul officials of the government-general were sufficiently worried about the purchase of land by speculators who had no intention of cultivating it that in August 1913 the governor-general called on provincial governors to monitor local land sales. Kobayakawa, *Chōsen nōgyō hattatsushi*, 2:13.

11. NGNSB, 1:224–28.

The encouragement of both agricultural migration and agricultural development required the acquisition of land by Japanese nationals, and this in turn required changing the legal status of foreign landholding in Korea.

The Katsura cabinet proposed two ways of getting around the treaty restrictions on foreign land ownership. One was to change the treaties to secure recognition of the right of foreigners to buy, sell, or permanently lease privately owned land beyond the one-*ri* limit. The other was to persuade the Korean government to grant a leasehold or special rights to carry on agriculture or grazing of livestock on government-owned wasteland to a Japanese national who would manage it under the supervision of the Japanese government; in effect, this would amount to a concession to develop government-owned wasteland and uncultivated land for agriculture. Over the next few years the Japanese authorities pursued both alternatives.

In early 1904 Hayashi Gonsuke negotiated a secret agreement with Foreign Minister Yi Ha-yong allowing Japanese nationals to make mortgage loans to Koreans secured by usufruct rights on their land, which would permit a de facto if not de jure transfer of ownership in the event of default.[12] The Japanese minister also backed the efforts of Nagamori Fujiyoshirō, a former Ministry of Justice and Ministry of Finance official, to acquire rights to develop lands under the control of the Korean court. During an official trip to China and Korea in 1903 Nagamori had been impressed by how successful the Westerners were in securing economic concessions and privileges and how unsuccessful the Japanese were. After his return to Japan he floated a plan to acquire a concession for developing Korean "wasteland." According to some reports, Nagamori gained the support of Foreign Minister Komura, who instructed Hayashi to help in his negotiations with the Korean government.[13] After resigning his Ministry of Finance post in December 1903 Nagamori visited Seoul, where Hayashi suggested that it would not be appropriate to approach the Korean court while negotiations between Russia and Japan were still underway. In late January 1904 he returned to Seoul, just ahead of the Japanese troops, to begin negotiations as a private individual with Korean court officials.

The Nagamori plan, presented to the Korean court in early June

12. *NGB*, 37.1, pp. 345–46; see also Gregart, "Land Ownership in Korea," 139.
13. Matsumiya, *Saikin no Kankoku*, 66.

1904 after several months of preliminary negotiations, aimed at gaining more or less permanent control over the use and development of most uncultivated land on the peninsula.[14] Under the proposed agreement all forest, meadow, and other lands not clearly under private or government ownership or set aside for use by the court (including temple lands, graveyards, and restricted forests) were to be designated as "wasteland." The term was vague and hence expandable. The Korean government was to retain formal ownership over the "wasteland," but it was to entrust its reclamation, improvement, rearrangement, and settlement to a designated Japanese trustee or concessionaire, presumably Nagamori. It was important that the Korean government retain direct ownership of the land since other foreign powers might claim similar privileges under the "most favored nation" clauses of their treaties if the land were turned over to the Japanese directly. The Japanese trustee could use the land for a variety of purposes from rice cultivation to the hunting of wild animals. He was to provide capital for its development, and the land was to remain tax free for the first five years after development began. After twenty-five years the contract could be terminated by the Korean government, but it would be obliged to reimburse the Japanese trustee for all capital invested in the land with an additional payment of a 5 percent per annum interest.[15]

The content of the proposal was known to both Foreign Minister Komura and Itō Hirobumi, with whom Komura consulted on the matter. Indeed, Komura suggested that the lease be extended beyond twenty-five years and that the concessionaire or his heirs be given the option of taking over the land when the lease terminated. There can be little doubt that the May 1904 cabinet decision on Korea incorporated the Nagamori proposal as one of the alternatives to circumventing treaty restrictions on Japanese ownership of land outside the settlement zones.

The advantages of the Nagamori plan to the Japanese government were obvious. First, the establishment of a protectorate, the eventual goal of the Katsura cabinet, would not give the Japanese power to dispose of Korean land as they saw fit or to deny exploitation of land resources to other foreigners. A privately held agricultural development

14. Documents on the Nagamori plan can be found in *NGB*, 37.1, pp. 569–612; KSH, Inoue Papers, File 59, Documents 674-2, 674-5. See also Yamaguchi, "Kobuchi kaitaku mondai," 74–77; Kirishima Kazuhiko, "Nichi-Rō sensōka ni okeru tochi ryakudatsu keikaku to sono hantai tōsō," in Hatada Takashi Sensei Kinenkai, *Chōsen rekishi ronshū,* 2:269–88.

15. *NGB*, 37.1, pp. 582–83. See also Kirishima, "Nichi-Rō sensōka," 269–74.

concession was an indirect way of accomplishing those ends. As Hayashi Gonsuke pointed out, the alternative, a revision of the treaty restrictions on foreign land holding would make it difficult for the Japanese to monopolize the development of uncultivated land.[16] Second, the development of uncultivated wasteland by a quasi-official concessionaire had political advantages over the purchase by small independent investors. As the consul at Mokp'o pointed out, "social clashes" might arise if too many Koreans lost their land to Japanese owners or if too many Korean tenants found themselves under the domination of Japanese landlords.[17]

The Japanese residents were predictably enthusiastic for the Nagamori plan. The concession, the Japanese press in Korea argued, not only lay at the core of Korea's future development but would profit both the Japanese and the Koreans. At least one Japanese observer pointed out the myriad benefits the Koreans would enjoy: reclamation of wasteland would turn the useless into the useful; capital for development would flow into Korea; work would be provided for unemployed Korean tenants; rice production would increase; increased rice production would increase rice exports and customs revenues; the amount of cultivated land would expand dramatically; taxes from the reclaimed land would flow into the government treasury; roads and communications within the country would be improved as the cultivated area expanded; the introduction of Japanese tools and techniques would spread to the Korean peasantry; new industries and manufactures would spring up everywhere; and the value of the land reclaimed would increase by tenfold or more, bringing in new revenues for the Korean government.[18] In short, the plan was a panacea for all the ills of the agricultural sector.

The Korean court responded slowly, perhaps in hopes of drumming up public outcry. Indeed, when word of the Nagamori plan leaked outside the palace, an opposition movement gathered momentum. Memorials from *yangban* and scholars in the capital began to flood in, protesting that Japanese settlers would swarm in to occupy the tracts of "wasteland," disrupting law and order in the provinces and depriving Korean peasants of their traditional rights to gather hay and kindling on public lands. Broadsides attacking the plan circulated in the provinces as well. Opponents within the government also expressed a deep and legitimate fear that the Nagamori plan would amount to confiscation of

16. *NGB*, 37.1, pp. 571–72.
17. Ibid., 569–71.
18. Matsumiya, *Saikin no kankoku*, 70–72.

vast areas of Korean territory in the name of developing "wasteland." The Korean foreign minister pointed out that since nearly two-thirds of Korea was unused mountain and forest land, the Nagamori plan would turn most of the national territory over to a foreigner. There can be little doubt that a sense of threatened economic interest contributed as much to public opposition as national pride did. Much land listed on the registers as "wasteland" was in fact under cultivation, but the owners, in collusion with corrupt local officials, managed to have them so designated in order to avoid taxes. The Nagamori plan would have meant confiscation of this land by the Japanese.[19]

In light of the mounting public protest, the Korean cabinet decided in late June to turn down Nagamori's request for a contract. To forestall further Japanese attempts at a land grab, on July 11 the royal household minister granted a group of high government officials permission to establish a new company, the Korea Agriculture and Mining Company, capitalized at 10 million *won*, to reclaim wasteland, construct irrigation works, develop forest land and cut timber, and conduct mining operations. Clearly intended to shut the Japanese out, the company regulations prohibited foreigners from holding stock in the company and even forbade stockholders from selling or pawning their shares to anyone but close relatives. Stock sold outside the immediate family would not be recognized, and the seller would have to pay thrice the value of the stock to the company. In the event that foreigners tried to interfere with the operations of the company, the government would intervene strongly. The only foreign involvement permitted would be the hiring of foreign engineers and technicians. Given the amount of capital to be raised and the limited foreign involvement, it was clear that the company was organized less to develop land and other resources than to pacify public protest against the Nagamori plan.[20]

The Japanese chargé d'affaires, Hagiwara Moriichi, rallying help from the British and Italian ministers, immediately protested that important development concessions should not be granted exclusively to Koreans. The Korean court backed down, abolishing the office that had granted the company charter and thereby voiding it. The government's announcement, in effect rescinding the land-development concession to a Korean company, added new momentum to the anti–Nagamori plan movement. Peddlers, Christian converts, and others from all parts of the

---

19. Ibid., 72–73.
20. Kirishima, "Nichi-Rō sensōka," 280–88.

country began to gather in the capital. On July 22 a crowd of nearly two thousand protesters gathered on Chongno in Seoul, disrupting electric tram service. The Korean police were unsuccessful in bringing order, and the crowd remained unmoved even after appeals by representatives of the king. The Japanese *kenpei* had to be called in, and it took them until late evening to disperse the crowd.[21] On July 24 the entire Korean cabinet offered their resignations. Protest groups led by local *yangban*, Confucian scholars, and former officials continued to circulate pamphlets and broadsides, and there were even minor armed attacks on Japanese troops. The Korean foreign minister, accompanied by the head of the Korean constabulary, visited Hayashi to urge that he withdraw his demands, and in August the legation at Seoul recommended that the Nagamori proposal be withdrawn lest it further antagonize the Koreans. It was becoming clear to the Japanese that the political costs of the Nagamori proposal would exceed its advantages. By the end of September it was dead. But the idea of developing Korean wasteland under Japanese auspices did not die, and it was shortly to be revived in the plan to organize the Oriental Development Company.

THE LEGALIZATION OF LAND OWNERSHIP

Bombarded by petitions from the Japanese chambers of commerce and residents' associations, the Japanese government continued to work for the legalization of land ownership rights outside the treaty limit. To be sure, as we have seen, clandestine purchase of land in the interior was already underway before the Russo-Japanese War. Local authorities often turned a blind eye to these transactions, formally requesting the foreigners to get off the land but doing nothing if they refused.[22] As one guidebook writer pointed out, "Because the right to buy land is not legally and properly recognized [under the treaties], one might think that it is extremely difficult to buy or own land.... Traditionally in Korea the establishment of rights in land has been extremely vague, and from our point of view rather primitive.... But if you avoid Japanese-style fastidiousness and follow Korean-style customs, there is no reason to worry once you embark on the process."[23]

Following Korean-style customs meant obtaining Korean land deeds for land purchased. There were two types: "old deeds" (*kumun'gi*),

21. Matsumiya, *Saikin no Kankoku*, 77–80.
22. Shikata, "Chōsen ni okeru kindai shihonshugi," 28–33.
23. Satō Seijirō, *Kankoku seigyōsaku*, 34–42.

documents dating from the original reclamation of the land, drawn up by the reclaimer of the land and presented to the county officials to establishment his right of possession; and "new deeds" (*sinmun'gi*), certificates of sale drawn up when a new owner acquired the land from a previous owner. Each plot of land came with a bundle of *mun'gi*, which was passed on from one owner to the next; if the *mun'gi* were lost or destroyed, then testimony from neighboring landowners was required to establish ownership. If the buyer of a piece of land received all of the documents, he could establish clear title to the land. A guarantor had to sign the "new deed," but that was usually done by the village headman.[24] In practice, of course, these documents were worthless to the Japanese buyer unless there was implicit or explicit agreement by the local authorities to recognize the transactions. But such informal or quasi-legal arrangements did not offer much security, and the limitation on landholding continued to have a chilling effect on those reluctant to transgress the law.

Full legalization of land purchases by Japanese and other foreigners had to await the establishment of the protectorate. In October 1906, acting on advice from Ume Kenjirō, a professor in the law faculty of Tokyo Imperial University, the Korean government finally issued regulations permitting foreigners to hold land in the interior or to hold mortgages against such land. In presenting a draft of the law to the Korean cabinet in July 1906, Itō explained that it was merely to prevent fraud or deception in land transactions. In Japan, he pointed out, foreigners sometimes held land under the name of a Japanese, but if possession were contested in a court of law, the foreigner would not be able to sustain his right of ownership. In Korea, by contrast, foreign ownership of land had been tacitly recognized by the authorities. This history put Korea in a much different position from Japan. Since it would take enormous sums of money to buy out the foreign landholders, sums that the Korean government was very unlikely to raise, it made more sense to openly recognize the right of foreigners to own land, placing them under the same rights as the Koreans themselves. Professor Ume pointed out that foreign owners would not only have to pay taxes to the Korean government but would have to obey the laws of the land. The Korean ministers made no objection to the draft law, save to clarify technical language here and there.[25]

24. Ibid.; Gregart, "Land Ownership in Korea," 86–87.
25. NKGSS, 6.1, pp. 326–31.

Only when the new land regulations were made public, and domestic protest stirred once again, did some Korean cabinet ministers begin to have second thoughts. In April 1907 the Korean minister of justice complained to Itō:

There are not a few county officials (*kunchu*) who are quite discontent with the promulgation of these regulations. The people get together secretly and make pacts that when someone wants to sell land he will not sell it to the foreigners but to other Koreans. The reason is that when Japanese come into the village and farm the land they monopolize the common water rights for themselves and obstruct the irrigation of the Koreans. These people attack me, saying that even though the Koreans are meeting with such bad treatment the minister of justice has issued the land registration regulations permitting the foreigners to own land openly.

Itō, who repeatedly pointed out that the problem would never have arisen in the first place if Korean officials had not tacitly recognized foreign ownership of land, did not show much sympathy. "I am not surprised at the discontent of the Koreans. In Japan too the advocates of a closed country often started sedition."[26]

Under the new regulations, if one party to a land transaction was a Japanese (or other foreigner), the land sale contract was to be certified not only by the local county (*kun* or *pu*) magistrate but also by the Japanese consulate (or other foreign consulate); when both parties were foreigners, then it was sufficient to have the transaction certified only by the diplomatic authorities. As even the pro-Japanese Professor George Trumbull Ladd realized, the effect of these regulations was "the practical opening of the whole country to the foreigners."[27] The regulations also put land transactions between foreigners (and for all practical purposes that meant between Japanese residents) beyond the reach of Korean law. Since the 1906 land regulations covered only transfer of land, not existing land rights, another set of regulations issued in 1908 provided for the registration of all land transactions, removing any residual ambiguities.[28]

Early in 1907 regulations permitting the lease of unreclaimed government-owned land were also issued. Foreigners as well as Koreans were allowed to apply to the Ministry of Agriculture, Commerce, and Industry for ten-year land development leases. If the promised work was

26. Ibid., pp. 447–48.
27. Ladd, *In Korea with Marquis Ito*, 343–44.
28. Kobayakawa, *Chōsen nōgyō hattatsushi*, 2, p. 104.

completed, the land could be sold or granted outright to the lessees, and for the first five years after its sale the developed land was to be taxed at one-third the lowest rate in the province. These regulations, like those legalizing real estate transactions outside the treaty settlements, were obviously intended to remove any remaining legal impediments to Japanese land ownership. As the official explanation asserted, the uncertainty of tenure rights and the forging of traditional land documents had discouraged "responsible businessmen" from investing in Korean land, to the detriment of the country's agricultural development.[29]

When Korea came under the writ of Japanese law after annexation, legal ownership of land became unambiguously secure for the Japanese residents. Under the civil code promulgated by the government-general in 1912, ownership and transfer of all land was to be registered with the authorities. The registration process was based on real estate registration law in Japan, but since a national land survey was not completed until 1918, land registers remained provisional. The new code mandated the same procedures for both Japanese and Koreans, and it made land tenure legally enforceable.[30] The land registration in Korea system differed slightly from Japan, where land certificates (*chiken*) rather than registration constituted proof of ownership and where survey maps were based on smaller and more accurate subdivisions than those in Korea. But as one settler observed in 1935, the system was "the basis for the creation of farming operations based on large investment that have progressed so much today."[31]

JAPANESE LANDLORDS IN KOREA

For the Japanese, land ownership in Korea involved few extraeconomic values. Land had none of the associations of family, place, or ancestors that it often did at home. The Japanese bought land in Korea principally as an investment, and farming was strictly a commercial enterprise. One early agricultural settler explained, "At the time land in Korea was wonderfully cheap, about one-fifth of what it was in Japan. If you spread a bit of fertilizer on it, the rice came popping up. And since the land was cheap, you still came out ahead even if you sold the rice

29. Ibid., 2:107.
30. Ibid., 2:341.
31. *Chōsen nōkaihō*, 1935, pp. 79–80.

cheaply."[32] Usually it was not the Japanese landholders who did the farming but their Korean tenants, and quite often they were absentee landlords living in a town or city. This made Japanese landlords in Korea quite different from the typical village landlords at home, who resided in the same community where they owned land and whose holdings were often quite small.[33]

By the eve of annexation Japanese owners had acquired 62,268 *chō* of cultivated land, or about 2.7 percent of all the cultivated land in Korea (table 15). These holdings were concentrated in a belt that stretched along the south and southwest coasts mainly in South Chŏlla and North Chŏlla, with lesser concentrations in South Kyŏngsang, South Ch'ungch'ŏng, Kyŏnggi, and South Hwanghae—where the land was rich, communications were good, rice production was high, and access to Japanese markets was easy. The primary concentrations of ownership were in the fertile riverine plains of North Chŏlla, South Chŏlla, and South Kyŏngsang, near the ports of Pusan, Masan, Mokp'o, and Kunsan. A secondary concentration was to be found on the northwestern coastal plain in the hinterland of P'yŏngyang and Chinnamp'o. Within these areas Japanese holdings tended to cluster as islands in a sea of Korean land. For example, in North Chŏlla, the province with the largest concentration of Japanese-owned land, most Japanese holdings, especially those with investments of over ¥10,000, were concentrated in two districts.[34] With annexation land acquisition accelerated, and by 1915 Japanese-owned cultivated land had more than doubled to 171,053 *chō*.

In a sense, it is a mistake to speak of a homogeneous Japanese landlord class in Korea. Many Japanese landowners in Korea were not individuals but institutions or corporations. The Japanese "landlord class" in Korea included everyone from a village postmaster with a small truck garden farmed by a Korean tenant to the colonial government itself. Indeed, in 1910 if one added the holdings of the Oriental Development Company and public land under the control of the government-general to the total of individual owned holdings, perhaps 7 to 8 percent of all arable was under Japanese control. The methods by which the Japanese owners acquired land, and their reasons for doing so, differed, and it will be useful to review each major category.

TABLE 15   AGRICULTURAL LAND OWNED BY JAPANESE IN KOREA, 1910

Region	Land owned per capita (*chō*)	No. of agricultural managers	Agricultural land owned by Japanese (*chō*) (A)		Province	Arable land (*chō*) (B)	% (A/B)
Pusan	48.1	225	10,824.4	⎫ 12,547.4	S. Kyŏngsang	125,738.3	10.0
Masan	132.5	13	1,723.0	⎭	N. Kyŏngsang	158,661.8	0.5
Taegu	9.5	87	827.9		S. Hamgyŏng	217,415.2	0.1
Wŏnsan	6.9	46	315.4				
Inchon	19.7	38	748.1	⎫ 4,957.5	Kyŏnggi	146,957.2	3.4
Seoul	37.6	112	4,209.4	⎭			
Mokp'o	124.4	105	13,057.4		S. Chŏlla	280,433.9	4.7
Kunsan	298.4	66	19,696.7		S. Ch'ungch'ŏng, N. Chŏlla	189,194.1	10.4
P'yŏngyang	535.8	17	9,109.0	⎫ 10,816.8	S. P'yŏngan, Hwanghae	460,532.5	2.3
Chinnamp'o	90.0	19	1,707.8	⎭			
Sinŭiju	2.4	9	21.2		N. P'yŏngan	347,317.3	0.0
Ch'ongjin	2.2	13	28.0		N. Hamgyŏng	64,977.1	0.0
					N. Ch'ungch'ŏng	137,196.7	—
					Kangwon	175,850.0	—
Total	83.0	750	62,268.3			2,304,274.1	2.7

NOTE: Figures are from December 1909, except for the Seoul area, which are from June 1909. Figures do not include amounts for the Oriental Development Company. Area of land owned by Japanese includes uncultivated land. Arable land includes fallow land and slash-and-burn fields.

SOURCE: *Dairyoji Chōsen sōtokufu tōkei nempō*: table 211: Chōsenjin nōgyōsha oyobi kōchi menseki; table 228: Naichijin nōji keieisha.

THE GOVERNMENT-GENERAL

At the time of annexation the single largest holder of cultivated land was the colonial government itself, the self-designated heir to land previously under control of the Korean court and the Korean government. The consolidation of public land resulted from the reform of the official finances in 1908. In contrast to the early Meiji policy of building the monarchy's landholdings to buttress its power and prestige, Japanese officials in Korea pursued the opposite tack. Appalled at the corruption of the court and convinced of its involvement in "anti-Japanese" activities, they were intent on reducing both the prestige and the fiscal independence of the royal family. During the early years of the protectorate, as we have seen, Itō feared that funds were flowing from the court to rebellious elements in the countryside or to anti-Japanese exiles in Shanghai and elsewhere. The reform of royal finances undertaken in 1908 after the Hague incident was aimed at bringing order, uniformity, and predictability to public finances, but it was also intended to close the king's political purse.

One by-product of reform was a decision to hand over to the Korean government all land registered in the name of a royal palace or government institution. In June 1908 these lands (designated as yŏktunt'o) became public land (kokuyūchi), and all revenues from the land became public revenues. Some of the land had been post land (yŏkt'o) set aside to support post stations, horses, keepers, and stables used by officials traveling on official business or by official couriers carrying public documents; some of it had been garrison land (tunt'o) set aside for the support of local constabulary or militia units; and the rest was palace land (kungjangt'o), which supported members of the royal family as well as the families of royal consorts and concubines. Since the royal family and government officials had not exercised self-restraint in commandeering resources for their needs, much of the land was quite fertile. Most palace land was concentrated near Seoul in Kyŏnggi, northern Ch'ungch'ŏng, and Hwanghae Provinces, and together with other government land constituted an estimated 4 to 5 percent of the cultivated land in the country. To increase government revenues, the Taewŏn'gun had tried to convert this land back into taxable land during the 1860s, and under the Kabo reforms taxes from the land had been paid to the royal household ministry; nevertheless, it remained outside the control of the government until the reforms of 1908.[35]

35. Gregart, "Land Ownership in Korea," 105–12.

No one was clear just how much *yŏktunt'o* there was, what income it produced, or even where it was located. The land had not been accurately surveyed, and the collection of rents from tenant farmers was often haphazard. According to a 1907 estimate, the land amounted to 90,409 *chō* (about 6 percent of all registered land) and was farmed by more than 28,400 tenants. A cadastral survey supervised by the Japanese in 1909–10 uncovered much unregistered land and reassessed its total extent at 126,432 *chō*, or 36,023 *chō* more than originally thought.[36] When the Oriental Development Company was established, part of the public land was exchanged for shares, but the rest was handed over to the government-general in 1910. On the eve of annexation the land was the second most important source of government revenue after the land tax.[37]

The newly established colonial government found the public land a troublesome real estate portfolio to deal with. Holdings, scattered all over the peninsula, were not susceptible to easy centralized management. The collection of rents was cumbersome, and title to the land was often disputed. Some holdings were private land that had been commended to the Korean court as a means of evading taxes, and their original owners contested title when they discovered that had been inadvertently expropriated by the transfer of the land to the government-general. While the colonial administration relied on the land as a source of income, raising rents two or three times as prices rose, over the years it gradually moved toward divestment. In 1912 regulations permitted the lease or sale of *yŏktunt'o* to private developers, the Oriental Development Company, or even the tenants occupying it.

The colonial administration tried to improve the productivity of the land by setting up tenant cooperatives, particularly when parcels were contiguous, and it subsidized them by providing cash, seed, and tools. But the plan for improvement did not work well since it was managed through the regular administrative structure by officials with other things to do. Tenants, eager to assume full control over the land, petitioned the colonial government for permission to buy it. By 1919 the land was producing annual revenues of only ¥2 million (out of a total budget income of ¥125,803,000). The colonial administration decided to sell it off over a ten-year period, using the income from the sales to help the tenants become self-cultivators by improving local schools,

36. Kobayakawa, *Chōsen nōgyō hattatsushi*, 2:120.
37. Asada, *Nihon teikokushugi to kyūshokuminchi jinushisei*, 114; *Chōsen Kindai Shiryō Kenkyūkai shūsei*, May 18, 1960.

developing irrigation facilities, and constructing local light railway systems.[38]

THE ORIENTAL DEVELOPMENT COMPANY

The other major Japanese landholder in Korea was the quasi-official Oriental Development Company, originally organized to encourage the migration of agricultural settlers to Korea. Although Korean resistance had killed the Nagamori plan, the motives behind the plan were still compelling, and at the highest levels of government there was consensus that Japanese farmers should be sent to the peninsula. The earliest plans for the company called for settling Japanese migrants on 240,000 *chō* of land, or about 14 percent of all the cultivated land in Korea, over a period of ten years.[39] As we have already seen, the company's achievements fell far short of these ambitious goals, but its acquisition of land for potential settlers turned the company into a landlord with sprawling holdings throughout the peninsula.

Out of deference to the concerns of Itō Hirobumi, the Oriental Development Company was established as a joint Japanese-Korean enterprise, managed and owned by nationals from both countries. Needless to say, the Koreans were junior partners. The company president was Japanese, as were two-thirds of its directors and two-thirds of its auditors, placing effective decision making into Japanese hands. From the Japanese point of view binational ownership was the most important aspect of Japanese-Korean cooperation. In addition to allaying Korean fears of a land grab, it offered financial advantages to the Japanese. Korean stockholders were allowed to acquire stock in exchange for land, making it possible for the company to acquire land controlled by the royal family; and the Korean government was allowed to exchange land under its control for company bonds. In other words, joint ownership made it possible for the company to acquire holdings of public or quasi-public land with little or no direct outlay of capital.

The original agreement reached between the residency-general and the Korean Finance Ministry, which was controlled by Japanese financial advisers, committed the Korean government to put up 5,700 *chō* of publicly owned arable in return for 60,000 company shares worth ¥3 million. Since the land was not accurately surveyed and was scattered

38. Kobayakawa, *Chōsen nōgyō hattatsushi*, 2:516–20. See also *Chōsen Kindai Shiryō Kenkyūkai shūsei*, May 18, 1960.
39. Kurose, "Nichi-Rō sengo no 'Chōsen kei'ei,'" 104–5.

throughout the country, it was not entirely clear to the company just what it owned. Nor was there any accurate way of assessing the value of the land even if its boundaries had been clear. The transfer was at first largely formal, and the land acquired was of mixed value. The paddy land the Korean government traded for company stock was appraised at a lower value than its quality or productivity warranted, giving the company a bargain, but the government-owned dry fields turned out to be of poor quality. After 1910 these dry fields were exchanged for better-quality paddy fields, and in subsequent exchanges of land for stock the company insisted on getting land of good quality. By 1913 it held 12,523 *chō* of former public land, much of it concentrated in Kyŏnggi, Hwanghae, and South Kyŏngsang. In effect, the exchange of government land for Oriental Development Company stock accomplished the goals of the Nagamori plan, albeit on a much diminished scale. Government land turned over to the company amounted to only a small portion of former public land, and indeed to only about 29 percent of the company's total holdings.[40]

Most of the company's cultivated land was acquired through purchase. Although the original plans called for setting aside ¥30 million out of a ¥50 million bond issue to purchase land for the 240,000 prospective Japanese settlers, these projections were confounded by financial realities. As with other colonial ventures calling for heavy capital investment, it was simply not possible to raise the money needed in the domestic capital markets. Despite a heavy oversubscription of the first issue of Oriental Development Company stock, the post–Russo-Japanese War recession created a tight credit market, and by 1910 a certain amount of disillusionment about the prospects of the company had set in. The company was forced to tap two other sources to finance its ventures: ¥10 million in loans from the Postal Savings Deposit Bureau and ¥20 million in foreign debentures. Even with this war chest the company was still unable to fulfill the original goal of buying 240,000 *chō* of cultivated land.

The company's attempts to purchase land were often resisted by Korean landholders who resented and distrusted the intentions of the Japanese. Other difficulties arose too. Land-buying agents did not always get the company its money's worth. Sometimes they were duped by go-betweens who sold land without clear and unencumbered titles, and sometimes they took bribes from sellers to purchase land at arti-

40. Ibid., 114, 116, 117.

ficially high prices. The onset of the postannexation land rush also
brought a rapid inflation of prices. Not only were other buyers hustling
in from Japan to pick up good land at low prices, but Korean aristocrats
and officials rewarded with grants for their collaboration with the Japanese began to invest in land as well. Between 1910 and 1913 the price
of land more than doubled. As a result, by 1913 the company controlled
only about 2 percent of the estimated arable land in Korea, not 14 percent as originally contemplated. By 1915, as the company shifted its
interests away from Korea to Manchuria and from promoting immigration to investment and finance, its land purchases slowed down.
Although it continued to acquire forest land on the peninsula, during
the 1920s its arable holdings began to shrink.[41]

Many historians have emphasized the importance of the Oriental
Development Company in the transfer of land rights into Japanese
hands, but it is clear that the company never came even close to mo-
nopolizing the land market. Even in 1918, when its holdings were near
the peak, the company did not control more than 30 percent of all land
held privately by the Japanese, and often the cultivable land it held was
less productive than that of other Japanese landowners. Indeed, the fact
that it had relatively fewer holdings in areas where Japanese landholding was normally high suggests that it did not always take best advantage of the market, nor did it acquire the most desirable land.[42]
While its capital resources were considerable, diseconomies of scale and
lack of adequate market information may have undercut its success as a
landlord.

METROPOLITAN INVESTORS

In Japan large-scale land investment was rare. It was not unknown in
Hokkaido, a newly developed territory, but it was not typical of most of
the country. As Tobata Seiichi argued in the 1930s, agricultural development in Korea was much more "capitalistic." It centered not on the
small cultivator and cooperative irrigation systems but on heavy capital
investment, large-scale irrigation works, and large-scale corporate
management. What Tobata referred to was the large number of land

41. Ibid., 115–17. Gregart reports that during the early years of colonial rule Jap-
anese-held land tended to be less productive than Korean-held land. But as the Japanese
introduced new inputs such as fertilizers or improved irrigation systems, the average
quality rose and surpassed that of Korean land. Gregart, "Land Ownership in Korea,"
199–200, 214–15.
42. Mabuchi, "Chōsen nōgyō no tokushitsu," 151–55.

development or agricultural companies operating as corporate land-lords in Korea. To be sure, a full-blown corporate system of agricultural development did not emerge until the 1920s, but even before annexation metropolitan capitalists began to invest in Korean land. By the end of 1908 at least twenty-two land development or agricultural companies were operating on the peninsula, two-thirds of them capitalized at over ¥100,000 and three at over ¥1 million. In addition, many unincorporated individual investors had large holdings, some in excess of one thousand *chō*. By contrast, the Homma family, one of the largest landholding families in Japan, controlled only about 1,840 *chō* in 1935.

Land ownership was, in fact, one of the few opportunities open to large-scale investors in Korea. Apart from buying shares or debentures in the Seoul-Pusan Railway or the Oriental Development Company, there were few opportunities to invest in modern enterprises. Indigenous manufacturing was small-scale and technologically backward, and the demand for machine-made goods was satisfied by imports from Japan and elsewhere. The market for products of capital-intensive enterprises was thin, limiting the opportunities for investment. Even investment in the production of basic consumer goods—food products, clothing, and sundry goods—was not very promising. For example, one Tokyo businessman, who arrived in Korea intending to set up a brewery capitalized at ¥2 million, eventually abandoned his plans after concluding that there would be no market for its output. The only outlet for large-scale direct investment was land and land development.

There were two main spurts of heavy metropolitan investment in land: the first came during the protectorate period, and the second during the early 1920s, when the colonial government announced plans for a massive increase in rice production. Obviously the political context of investment was of considerable importance to metropolitan capitalists, whether they were wealthy individuals or groups of stockholders. The consolidation of Japanese political influence stimulated the earlier burst of investment. The Osaka Chamber of Commerce mission noted a sudden rush of land buyers to Korea in the spring of 1904, shortly after the outbreak of the war, especially in the Kum River valley in South Ch'ungch'ŏng and the Nakdong River valley in Kyŏngsang. Japanese already resident in the treaty ports acted as brokers, collecting fees from Korean landowners wishing to sell. Some investors were migrants who came to Korea intending to trade but soon discovered the profitability of land; others were speculators who hoped that the land boom would force up prices and produce windfall profits; and still others were pure investors shifting capital from other enterprises. Perhaps eight out of ten of these would-be landowners went home without buying, reported the mission, and those who stayed rapidly bid up the price of land. Near Kunsan prices rose 25 percent during the first six months of the Russo-Japanese War.[43]

Large-scale metropolitan investors had a purely commercial interest in buying land. Most often they were absentee landlords whose land was farmed by Korean tenants under the supervision of Japanese technicians and managers. Sometimes they engaged in subsidiary operations like moneylending or mortgage brokering. Their goal was to turn a profit by combining superior Japanese technological and managerial know-how with cheap Korean land and labor.

Among the early metropolitan investors were *zaibatsu* with existing connections in Korea and privileged political access. The Ōkura-gumi, which had been active in Korea trade since its beginning, began to buy land in Korea in 1904. Iwasaki Hisaya, head of the Mitsubishi interests, whose son-in-law was an official in the residency-general, acquired land tracts in North and South Chŏlla through the Toyama Agricultural Company (Toyama Noji k.k.). Not surprisingly, the *zaibatsu* leader most deeply involved in Korean land investment was Shibusawa Eiichi. In 1904 the Shibusawa interests organized the Chōsen Development Company (Kankoku Kōgyō k.k., later renamed Chōsen Kōgyō k.k.), a land company capitalized at ¥1 million and set up to deal in land mortgages and real estate loans as well as to purchase land for lease to tenants and to improve agricultural techniques in Korea. According to its official history, the company was established to remedy the lack of credit institutions in Korea offering long-term, low-interest agricultural loans at a time when capital was needed to introduce new farming techniques. In 1903 Hayashi Gonsuke discussed the establishment of a land mortgage company with Odaka Jirō, manager of the Dai-Ichi Bank's Inchon office. Shibusawa Eiichi took a personal interest in the project, and the Ministry of Agriculture and Commerce sent a mission to Korea to investigate the possibilities.[44] When the company was finally organized in 1904, about a quarter of its initial stockholders were associated with the Dai-Ichi Bank (including, of course, Shibusawa Eiichi himself, who held 10 percent of the stock), and its management was

43. *KSSH*, 51–58.
44. *Chōsen Kabushiki Kaisha*, 1–2.

dominated by former Dai-Ichi Bank officials. In effect, it was a semi-subsidiary of the Shibusawa interests.

Initially the company set up a temporary office in Seoul, offering loans in return for land as collateral; it also announced plans to set up an agricultural experimental station on court-owned land to introduce the Japanese agricultural techniques. In April 1904 the company began to buy land near P'yŏngyang, and within six months it had acquired three thousand *chō*. After the war ended, it bought plots along the Seoul-Pusan Railway line and near the port of Mokp'o. Between 1908 and 1915 its holdings grew from six thousand *chō* to twelve thousand *chō*. As a hedge against local variations in rice prices and land productivity, the company's holdings were not consolidated but scattered in tracts averaging about one thousand *chō*. As with most other land development companies, management was less interested in unreclaimed land or wasteland than in land already under cultivation. The company also acquired subsidiary businesses, absorbing the Korea Warehouse Company (Kankoku Soko k.k.) in 1909 and the Korea Development Company (Kankoku Kaitaku k.k.) in 1910.[45]

Most metropolitan land investors had no direct links to the *zaibatsu*. First, there were aristocratic rentier investors—former daimyo families like the Hosokawa, the Okabe, the Nabeshima, and the Tokugawa—who acquired holdings at the time of the Russo-Japanese War to diversify their portfolios. Second, there were large-scale landlords with several hundred *chō* of land, mainly from western Honshu, like Kamata Shotaro, a *gōnō* from Kagawa prefecture, who founded the Chōsen Enterprise Company (Chōsen Jitsugyō k.k.), or the group of landed and commercial investors from Ishikawa prefecture who founded the Ishikawa Agricultural Company with a subsidy from the prefectural government in 1907. Third, there were provincial urban mercantile, money-lending, or shipowning interests in Kyushu (mainly in Nagasaki and Fukuoka) or in the Kansai region (Osaka and Kobe) already involved in the Japan-Korea trade, who took advantage of their knowledge of economic conditions on the peninsula to get in on the ground floor when land purchase became legal and safe. Fourth, there were domestic mining and manufacturing companies that bought land not for profit but for its output. The Katakura spinning interests bought land to grow cheap rice for its millworkers and silkworms for its looms, and Kyushu mine owners like Yasakawa Keiichirō and Matsumoto Kenjirō invested

45. Ibid., passim.

in land to feed miners working in their Korean mines. Finally, others invested in Korean land simply as a matter of felicitous timing. The Murai interests, originally a small manufacturer of cigarettes in Japan, who found themselves with a large amount of liquid capital after being bought out by the government tobacco monopoly in 1904, invested in Korean land as a current profitable opportunity.

The motives of metropolitan investors, in other words, ranged from seeking rentier profits to reducing production costs in other enterprises. But the majority of large-scale investors were provincial commercial interests in Osaka and Kyushu or larger domestic landlords who aimed at making profits from the sale of rice and other agricultural commodities produced by their Korean tenants. The biggest private metropolitan landlord, not atypical of the majority, was the Fuji Development Company (Fuji Kōgyō k.k.), founded in 1914 with the backing of a group of Osaka merchants and shipowners. Fujii Kantarō, the major entrepreneur behind this venture, had begun his career as an apprentice at Fujimoto Shoten, an Osaka trading firm.[46] Placed in charge of rice dealing at the company's Kumamoto branch at the age of seventeen, he had beaten out the competition by purchasing a brand-new rubber-tired bicycle from Yokohama to make his rounds, a move that reduced his transactions costs considerably by eliminating the need for a *rikisha* or overnight stays in local inns. By the time he was twenty Fujii had become manager of the Kumamoto branch, which by his own later account he built into the foremost rice dealer in the prefecture. After the head of the firm died, the new partners decided to dissolve it; with help from the firm's principal employees and the Fujimoto family, Fujii managed to raise ¥20,000 to keep it going as a limited partnership. Shortly after the outbreak of the Russo-Japanese War, Fujii decided to set up branch offices in Inchon and Kunsan.

Fujii became interested in buying land in Korea because of the heavy rains that had fallen during the winter and spring of 1903, causing considerable water damage to the Korean crop. Fearing a recurrence of bad weather, he decided to guarantee his firm a supply of rice by buying two thousand *chō* of land in North Chŏlla during 1904–5. Much of it was marginal, beset with both drainage and irrigation problems. Anxious to increase the land's productivity, he experimented with various improvements to the irrigation system, from Japanese-style waterwheels to Chinese-style water ladders. Since nothing seemed to work, in frus-

46. The following account is based on Fujii Kantarō, "Fujii Kantarō jijoden."

tration he finally decided to convert the land to dry-field crops and orchards. At a chance meeting with Megata Jūtarō, the chief Japanese financial adviser, he urged the government to encourage the development of irrigation in Korea. In 1907 the Ministry of Finance issued regulations permitting the organization of local irrigation associations. With technical help from a Japanese agricultural expert at Kunsan, Fujii set up one of the first in the area, and by 1910 he had a new irrigation system in place on the company's land. In 1912 he purchased four thousand *chō* of land for reclamation in North P'yŏngan Province, near the mouth of the Yalu River.

Much of his capital was generated by a real estate trust and management business that Fujii set up to act as an agent for land buyers in Japan. Persuading friends and acquaintances of the profitability of land investment, he offered the services of the Fujimoto firm to handle all transactions, from buying the land through managing it. The firm collected a 10 percent fee on the purchase price, and it offered two arrangements for managing it. The first was subcontractual management, which guaranteed investors a 10 percent return on their investment even in bad years but allowed the company to keep any profits over 10 percent in good years; the second was ordinary management, under which the company deducted an agreed-on percentage (up to 20 percent) of the harvest in return for management services. The majority of Fujii's investors, who knew nothing about Korea but trusted Fujii, opted for the first option, which guaranteed a fixed return at a generous rate. But this arrangement also allowed Fujii to earn high profits in good years, which he could then reinvest in expansion and development of his own enterprises. When the enthusiasm for land investment died down in 1909–10, many investors decided to let go of their holdings, and the company bought the land back at the original price on long-term payments. As land and rice prices went up again, more profit rolled in; it was almost like getting the land for free, Fujii later recalled. In any event, by 1914 Fujii was in a position to consolidate his operations in a joint-stock company, capitalized at ¥1 million, partly with his own capital and partly with capital raised at home.

SETTLER LANDLORDS

Although most privately owned land was in the hands of absentee owners in Japan, far and away the majority of Japanese landowners in

Korea were settlers, most of whom came to Korea for other reasons but bought land when they discovered how profitable it could be. To be sure, some landowners came, ready to farm the land they bought. But more typical was the landowner whose attachment to the land was purely monetary, someone who wanted a small but safe investment to supplement other income. According to one estimate, in the early 1920s 43 percent of all Japanese landowners in Korea held plots of less than one *chō*, not sufficient to provide a comfortable household income but adequate to provide a family with fresh produce for the market or the table and income from rent.[47] The typical Japanese landlord, in other words, was an absentee smallholder, often living in a nearby town, where he made his living as a shopkeeper, policeman, moneylender, innkeeper, schoolteacher, or even priest.

Land hunger was intense even among the early migrants who came before the Russo-Japanese War. When settlers did not have sufficient capital to buy land as individuals they pooled their resources. In Mokp'o, for example, the local Japanese residents had already formed a land-buying cooperative in the summer of 1902. By the end of the Russo-Japanese War its forty-odd members had managed to acquire eighty *chō* of paddy and dry fields, yielding a return of 20 percent a year on their investment. Similar cooperatives were later organized in Inchon and Seoul.[48] The settlers' land hunger was not satisfied by houselots or farming plots within the treaty settlements or in their immediate periphery. As we have already seen, Japanese residents bombarded the consulates and even the legation with demands for the legalization of land ownership outside the treaty limit.

In the early days there were two main ways to acquire land: through direct purchase or through loans secured by mortgages on farm land. The second method was easier for the settler with a small stake in capital and was probably more profitable. Many Korean landowners were cash hungry, burdened by the inflation of coinage, increased taxes, and the rapacity of local officials. *Yangban* landowners were in need of funds to support their social pretensions, and ordinary farmers needed money to make ends meet. Usually they would turn to Korean moneylenders for consumption loans, a perennial need in most agrarian societies where incomes are subject to vagaries of weather and harvest. But by the time

47. Mabuchi, "Chōsen nōgyō no tokushitsu."
48. Fukuzawa, *Kankoku jitsugyō kanken*, 35.

of the Russo-Japanese War, Japanese settlers, who rather quickly discovered the ease of making profits from moneylending, had become an alternative source of credit for rural borrowers.[49]

Acquiring land through moneylending was often a pro forma transaction. When approached by a Japanese buyer, Korean landowners would sometimes refuse to sell at first, mainly out of a desire not to lose face or offend their neighbors; later, though, a landowner might ask for a loan through a Korean go-between. In other cases, Japanese buyers did not propose a purchase at all but rather offered to lend money to the potential seller with the land to be held as collateral. In either case, the terms of the loan were usually quite favorable to the lender; the land put up as collateral might be assessed as low as one-third of its value, and the loan might have a monthly interest rate of 5 percent and a period of three to six months. Borrowers often defaulted, probably by design, and they made no protest when the lender claimed the mortgaged land. If the local Korean authorities knew that the lender was Japanese, they would not interfere, as they had every right to before the issuance of new land regulations in 1907, and transactions of this sort were usually not disputed. Of course, some Japanese moneylenders tricked their borrowers into forfeiting their land by sharp practices, for example, by evading attempts at repayment of the loan until the local period had ended or by laying claim to more land than had been mortgaged.

An alternative way to acquire land through moneylending was to offer a loan with a portion of the harvest or usufruct rights, sometimes for decades or even centuries, as security. Such terms allowed borrowers to get larger loans, and it also afforded them greater opportunities to cheat Japanese lenders by secretly diverting part of the harvest to the market. But it also afforded greater legal security for the lenders, particularly if the land were outside the treaty limit zone. This practice was not uncommon in the Naktong River valley, where a Japanese settler named Kōnō Kisaburō had pioneered the method before the Russo-Japanese War and managed to have his rights recorded on the public land register.[50]

The direct purchase of land involved fewer ambiguities than acquiring it through defaulted loans, but it also involved certain risks in the period before land was properly surveyed, registered, or assessed. It was

49. Yamamoto, *Saishin Chōsen ijū annai*, 205–9.
50. Satō Seijirō, *Kankoku seigyō saku*, 34–42.

the method more likely to be used by Japanese migrants or settlers who came to Korea to farm the land. The prospective Japanese buyer would contact a Korean go-between, often a village notable, who would find a seller and act as agent. Once a sale was agreed on, the Japanese buyer would receive Korean land deeds designating him as the owner. The transactions, illegal and unenforceable if involving land outside the treaty limit, had to rest on trust. The Korean authorities usually ignored them. While they sometimes raised objections, they would also often levy taxes on the Japanese owner, a de facto recognition of property rights.

Japanese buyers, especially if they were newcomers to the peninsula, were wise to follow the principle of caveat emptor. There were as many sellers and their agents, both Japanese and Korean, who were ready to take advantage of Japanese land hunger as Japanese there were ready to take advantage of Korean prices. As Fujii Kantarō later recalled, the land rush was like "market day in front of the temple." In some cases, the Koreans involved thought they would be able to swindle the Japanese with impunity. During the Russo-Japanese War land rush, many Koreans were convinced that even though the Japanese appeared to be winning at first, they would eventually be defeated, as Hideyoshi's armies had been three centuries before. Even if a Korean sold his land honestly, the chances were that the Japanese would eventually abandon it, so it made sense to take the money and run.

Before the issuance of the 1907 land registration regulations it was not unusual for gullible or careless Japanese buyers to find themselves duped. The transfer of land was validated by the handing over of traditional land deeds, but frequently these documents were produced by forgers who soaked a freshly drafted "old deed" in urine to give it a convincing patina of age. In extreme cases there might be four or five deeds, all forged, for the same piece of land, and four or five Japanese "owners" would show up at harvest time to collect their rents. Often the seller would have no deed at all, either because the seller's plot was too small or too poor in quality to be taxed or because the Korean owner had failed to register it, or even cultivate it, in order to evade taxes. Sometimes a wayward son would sell land that belonged not to him but to his father, his uncle, or his cousin; it was also common for Korean sellers to unload infertile, swampy, or poor-quality land on unsuspecting buyers. The land-buying agents working for metropolitan investors or land companies would find themselves swamped with offers of such land.[51] It is easy to forget, in light of later developments, that the Japanese land rush brought short-term profits for the Koreans and their agents as well as long-term profits for Japanese buyers.

Japanese settlers sometimes tried to deal with sharp land-selling practices collectively. In May 1905 settlers at Kunsan, an area of heavy land buying, formed the Kunsan Nōji Kumiai to protect would-be purchasers against fraudulent land practices. The association kept records of land purchased by its members in order to avoid multiple sales of the same plot, and it also registered the purchases with the Japanese consulate in Kunsan. Although this approach did not provide absolute protection against either fraud or expropriation, it did provide a buffer against the perils involved in buying land in the interior.[52]

It is also easy to forget that before annexation the purchase of land, particularly land in the interior, was a chancy proposition for the settlers. "You didn't know what was going to happen.... People said that even your life was in danger, so it was hard to get in the mood to buy land. Starting a farm was a real adventure."[53] Not only did prospective buyers have to avoid being swindled by Korean sellers, but they also had to endure isolation and loneliness among unfriendly Korean neighbors, face the danger of attacks from the anti-Japanese guerrilla movements active in the years before annexation, and often invest considerable time, effort, and energy in making the land productive. The return on the investment was not always as simple or as automatic as guidebooks and official propaganda made it seem.

One early agricultural settler recalled the difficulties of getting started:

> On the basis of a visit I made in 1905, I settled in my present place in March 1906, bringing with me all my family property and two laborers, and in July I brought my family over. Since there was a lot of anti-Japanese sentiment at the time, only two Japanese families lived in the area, and roads and communication were very poor. Words cannot express how desolate and difficult it was. In 1907 insurgency broke out all over. Everywhere Japanese were killed or their houses were burned down. That kind of disaster twice struck the village where our farm was. Each time we suffered from arson, and although we were lucky enough to escape bodily harm, my family had to flee. Only the men stayed behind with weapons to keep order. In 1911 we began to raise purple vetch, but during the first three years we had a lot of trouble because the Korean children would steal it or the village cattle would graze in

51. Kobayakawa, Chōsen nōgyō hattatsushi, 2:110–12.
52. Tanaka Shin'ichi, "Tochi chōsa jigyōshi," 297–311.
53. Chōsen nōkaihō, 1935, pp. 80–81.

it. Finally everyone understood what we doing, and after that many people even came around to ask for seed.[54]

Finally, we should not forget that a few Japanese landowners did not intend to become absentee landlords or purely commercial investors but wanted to cultivate the land they owned. An extreme example was the romantic Hayashi Seizō, a Bible-toting idealist who quit the Salvation Army in 1911 to become an agricultural settler in the colonies.[55] Seizō, fed up with his life as a professional Christian, originally decided to sell his bicycle for the fare to Sakhalin, where he planned to find whatever work he could, perhaps as a delivery boy for a noodle shop, until he made enough to buy some reclaimable land. A friend suggested that he go to Korea instead. "There was big money in the future if you bought land right away," he later recalled. "Everyone was full of talk about it." When Seizō told the friend that he had no money, the friend offered to put up ¥500 to buy land if Seizō agreed to farm it. The friend would get 70 percent of rent income from the land, and Seizō would get 70 percent from the profit of farming.

In March 1911 Seizō arrived in Pusan, blissfully unencumbered by any knowledge of Korea or even farming. Armed with a letter of introduction to the brother-in-law of Yamamuro Gumpei, the Japanese Salvation Army leader, he made his way by train to Masan, then seventy kilometers by foot to Chinju, where the brother-in-law worked as an agricultural technician. After visiting the agricultural experimental station at Seoul, perhaps to get bearings for his new career in agriculture, he decided to settle near Pusan, where many Japanese had already bought land. Few actually farmed, as he hoped to do, but rather earned their livings as rentier landlords, land brokers, retail tradesmen, or moneylenders. "Don't buy land," he was told. It was better to lend money with land as collateral; the Koreans never repaid their debts and the lender got the land anyway. But Seizō wanted to be close to the land, farming during the day and reading books—including the Bible, of course—at night. Clearly he was not acting out of pure economic rationality. That made him an easy mark for Koreans wanting to capitalize on the local land rush.

While hiking through a village several stops out from Pusan on the Seoul-Pusan line, Seizō met Kim Dae-gi, the son of the local headman, who told him that the land and house of a recently deceased old couple

54. Kobayakawa, Chōsen nōgyō hattatsushi, 2:22–23.
55. The following account is based on Hayashi Seizō, Kōya no ishi.

was for sale. "After a time, through Kim's mediation, I bought some dry field. Since I didn't understand anything, they did not sell me good land, but palmed off some barren rock-filled soil, scattered in small plots, with a little bit here, and a little bit there, and not a single piece as large as one *tan*. I can safely say that there was no good land whatsoever for sale near the village." The plots he bought were good for neither barley nor soybeans. About all he could grow was potatoes. Even to do that he had to walk several miles to reach all of his plots.

A native of Tokyo, Seizō was hardly acquainted with rural life, much less with farming. With book and hoe in hand, and his Korean neighbors watching with some amusement, he set out to make his rocky patches bloom. Hopelessly unequipped for his new life, he understood neither the terms in the farming manuals nor the advice he got from other Japanese settler farmers. He forgot his tools in the field, the vegetables he set out to dry got damp and moldy from the evening dew, and his crops were stolen before they could be harvested. But he remained undaunted. "As I worked furiously, the sweat and the burden were heavy. But in the midst of it all, I always had a dream, always a poem, always a song. And so I had the good luck to overcome it all." He also had a backer. No one else wanted to buy his hardscrabble land, so he returned to Tokyo to borrow another ¥500 from his friend. With this new stake he bought better land in the Naktong River valley from a Japanese settler who had decided to return home; there he started an apple orchard, which eventually proved quite profitable.

In his naïveté, and with his ready access to capital, Seizō may have been exceptional among those Japanese who chose to farm the land they settled—and for that reason he is more interesting. A more typical owner-cultivator was Ōse Yūhei, the son of a tenant farmer too poor to send him beyond primary school. When the Russo-Japanese War broke out, Ōse read that it was easy to find work as a laborer in Korea, where wages were higher than in Japan; he scraped together boat fare for Inchon, arriving in August 1904. With the help of a hometown friend he got a railway construction job, and by the spring of 1906 he had managed to save ¥200 from his wages. Like many other settlers he set himself up in the sundries business, only to fall prey to dishonest suppliers, who cheated him out of his money, leaving him once again jobless and without money. Like Urao Bunzō, Ōse took a job as a mail carrier, first at Inchon, then in Yunan in Hwanghae Province. The next few years were not easy. During the anti-Japanese disturbances he fended off hostile attacks while making his appointed rounds, and despite scrimping and saving he had to spend his little nest egg on doctor's bills when he fell seriously ill. But in 1909 he got another post office job at Ch'ungju in Ch'ungch'ŏng province at a wage of ¥35 a month, from which he manage to save ¥30 by limiting his living expenses; in short order he saved ¥300, which he used to start buying land.

After annexation Ōse invited his brother to join him, and the two began to trade in livestock, buying calves and piglets, which they let Korean peasants raise and sold after they matured. This side business turned a tidy profit. A calf that cost ¥5 could be sold two years later for ¥25. Income from the livestock trade, added to savings from his post office salary, gave Ōse enough capital to snap up little parcels of land here and there, and soon he had enough to bring over the whole family. In 1912, seven years after he had arrived at Inchon looking for a laborer's job, he had become the owner of 3.4 *chō* of dry field land, 1.2 *chō* of paddy land, 1.8 *chō* of mountain land, and a house. Having become a man of property, he quit his job as mail carrier to become a full-time farmer, the very model of the migrant settler that the highest Japanese leadership had hoped to encourage. Ōse was neither a usurer nor a petty capitalist but a sober, hardworking young man with Franklinesque virtues, whose advice to others was a primer of *nōhonshugi* precepts.[56]

The pattern of Japanese land acquisition in Korea did not disturb traditional patterns of landholding or agricultural production. The Japanese did not try to abolish traditional laws for landholding so much as to systematize them through reform of landowning regulations, nor did they try to eliminate traditional small-scale peasant production. Even large-scale landowners like the Oriental Development Company or the Fuji Development Company did not attempt to introduce plantation-style production. Most of the land owned by these companies was farmed either by Korean or Japanese tenants or by Japanese small-holders. Likewise, the "public land" taken over by the new government-general after 1910 continued to be run as a giant landlord operation, collecting rents from Korean tenants who continued to rely on family labor and traditional technology.

In this respect, the Japanese experience in Korea was not all that different from the experience of many other colonial powers. As D. K. Fieldhouse has pointed out, large-scale plantations were less important in most colonies than traditional small-scale peasant production. Plan-

56. Ōse Yūhei's story (and advice) may be be found in Ōhashi, *Chōsen sangyō shishin*, 354–56.

tations made sense where the imperialists wished to introduce new crops, requiring new agricultural technologies and efficiently organized workforces, such as tea in India, rubber in Malaya, or sugar in Hawaii, but there "was little or no incentive to establish plantations where indigenous production of an export commodity was already established or where it was readily adopted by indigenous land owners."[57] Since rice continued to be the principal crop exported to Japan and the main crop of interest to Japanese land buyers, the large plantation was superfluous. Interestingly enough, in the one case where the Japanese did try to introduce a new crop—upland cotton—they chose to rely on the existing structure of peasant landholding and cultivation, inducing Korean peasants to grow it by distributing seeds and tools and subsidizing fertilizer and freight costs.

Even though Japanese landholding did not involve extraeconomic relationships and rewards between landlord and tenant, the pattern was not all that different from that at home, where small-scale production and small-scale landlordism were the rule rather than the exception. From the point of view of the Japanese authorities, the acquisition of land in small scattered holdings, most of them farmed by Korean tenants, had the advantage of avoiding the social upheaval and dislocations that wide-scale expropriation of land would have entailed. It also provided an economic base for a large number of Japanese settlers, who were able to invest in land and to profit from the expanding market for Korean agricultural products without a large amount of capital. Although most of the Japanese landowners were quite different from the army of agricultural settlers the Tokyo government had hoped would flock to the peninsula, they had a stake in remaining there over the long term, as the authorities hoped they would. But this pattern of landholding also made it more difficult to modernize Korean agriculture. Most cultivated land remained in the hands of Korean landholders, and the colonial government would have to resort to more indirect and inefficient means of inducing change in the countryside than would have been the case had an army of Japanese agricultural migrants been at their command.

57. Fieldhouse, *Colonialism, 1870–1945*, 78–81.

CHAPTER 11

Defining the Koreans

Images of Domination

When Europeans expanded into the tropical and semitropical regions of Africa, they encountered, in Hannah Arendt's words, "human beings whom no European or civilized man could understand and whose humanity so frightened and humiliated [them] that they no longer cared to belong to the same species."[1] The enormous gap between the colonizer and the colonized made it easy for the Westerners to construct images of subject peoples that licensed massacres and sanctioned suppression and control of a kind intolerable at home. For the Japanese, who could hardly ignore substantial similarities between the Koreans and themselves, the situation was quite different. While some Japanese might call the Koreans "Ainu with fancy clothes" or "monkeys who stand and walk upright," it was difficult to dismiss the Koreans as subhuman or even racially distinct. After all, the Japanese and the Koreans shared a past, a culture, and even an ethnic heritage.[2] These commonalities precluded easy justification of domination by a brutal and unheeding racism, but they posed a disturbing paradox: how could a people so close and so similar to the Japanese remain so distant and alien?

Nowhere was this paradox more clearly expressed than in the observations of Arakawa Gorō, a Diet member and newspaper editor from

1. Arendt, *Origins of Totalitarianism*, 184. Even Charles Darwin found it hard to believe that those "poor wretches," the Fuegians, were "fellow-creatures, and inhabitants of the same world." Quoted in Stocking, *Victorian Anthropology*, 105.
2. Onjōji, *Kankoku no jitsujō*, 87.

Hiroshima who visited Korea immediately after the Russo-Japanese War. "What kind of people are the Koreans?" he asked.

> There is nothing especially different about them. They all look just like the Japanese, of the same Oriental race, with the same coloring and physique, and the same black hair. Those who crop their hair and wear Western clothes, like railroad station attendants or students, are not a bit different from the Japanese. If you ... did not look carefully, you might mistake them for Japanese. Considering that the appearance and build of the Koreans and Japanese are generally the same, that the structure and grammar of their language are exactly the same, and that their ancient customs resemble each other's, you might think the Japanese and the Koreans are the same type of human being.

But, he went on, superficial resemblances were quite misleading.

> If you look closely [at the Koreans], they appear to be a bit vacant, their mouths open and their eyes dull, somehow lacking.... In the lines of their mouths and faces you can discern a certain looseness, and when it comes to sanitation or sickness they are loose in the extreme. Indeed, to put it in the worst terms, one could even say that they are closer to beasts than to human beings.[3]

The rhetorical sweep of this passage is astonishing: in the space of a paragraph or two the familiar-looking Koreans are dehumanized, their exterior stripped away to reveal a beast within. The paradox of Korean identity, expressed with exceptional starkness in Arakawa's observations, complicated all attempts to construct clear relationships between the Japanese and the Koreans.

Since the identity of the Koreans so complexly overlapped that of the Japanese, images of domination in Korea had to take into account the similarities between Japan and Korea as well as the differences. In a sense, Japanese attitudes toward the Koreans were more akin to nineteenth-century English attitudes toward the Irish than toward the Indians. However low their esteem for the ability of the Irish to rule themselves, most Englishmen would have admitted a greater kinship with them than with the "Hindoos," and their arguments for dominating the Irish were accordingly different.[4] Although the Irish could be dismissed as "Celts" displaced by more vigorous "Anglo-Saxons," the

---

3. Arakawa, *Saikin Chōsen jijō*, 86–87.
4. J. S. Mill might write to friend, "I myself have always been for a good stout despotism, for governing Ireland like India," but as a practical matter he knew that Ireland had to be governed as a part of the United Kingdom. Sullivan, "Liberalism and Imperialism," 606.

justification for English domination of Ireland rarely invoked more radical distinctions. Indeed, many Victorians argued for a positive side to the "Celtic genius." Matthew Arnold thought that "Celtic" emotion, sensuality, and sentimentality inoculated English national character against the "humdrum, the plain and ugly, the ignoble" qualities of the "Saxon."[5]

The Japanese constructed images of the Koreans that denied them parity with the Japanese through asymmetrical comparisons measuring Korean backwardness against Japanese modernity. By branding the Koreans as less "civilized" than themselves, the Japanese could claim the right to demand that they alter their institutions and folkways or submit to Japanese political control. In this respect, Japanese images of Korea resembled those constructed by European colonizers of their subject peoples. But the Japanese differed from the European colonist who stressed "those things which keep him separate, rather than emphasizing that which might contribute to the foundation of a joint community."[6] History, language, and culture set limits on the degree to which the Japanese could distance themselves from the Koreans. It was inescapably apparent not only that the Japanese and the Koreans looked like one another, as Arakawa pointed out, but that they shared a common tradition. This awareness militated against the most blatant forms of racism but not against an ideology of subjection. Indeed, when the concept of race was deployed, it was usually to embrace the Koreans rather than to disown them. By stressing a common history and a common cultural heritage, the Japanese could cloak domination of the Koreans in the language of amalgamation, merger, and assimilation or suggest the "naturalness" of annexation. In short, the Japanese tried to have it both ways—to justify the construction of a "joint community" while emphasizing the differences between those to be conjoined.

FILTH, SQUALOR, AND INDOLENCE: TRAVEL ACCOUNTS OF KOREA

Albert Memmi asked of European colonialism, "How can usurpation try to pass for legitimacy? One attempt can be made be demonstrating the usurper's eminent merits, so eminent that they deserve such compensation. Another is to harp on the usurped's demerits, so deep they

5. Curtis, *Anglo-Saxons and Celts*, 36–48.
6. Memmi, *The Colonizer and the Colonized*, 52–53.

cannot help leading to misfortune."[7] The demerit that the Japanese chose to harp on was Korean backwardness or low "cultural level" (*mindo*). In the 1870s the Japanese had already constructed a cultural hierarchy that divided the world into "civilized" and "uncivilized" and separated themselves from their Asian neighbors. For example, an 1878 cartoon in the *Marumaru chinbun*, the leading satirical journal, presented the nations of the world in a Doll Festival display, at the foot of which were three emblems of progress—a hot-air balloon, a steamship, and a locomotive (Plate 13). At the top were emperor and empress dolls; on the next tier, where ladies-in-waiting were usually placed, were two rifle-carrying foreigners, a Frenchman on the left and an Englishman on the right; below them five more Westerners—a Dutchman, an Italian, a Russian, a Belgian, and an American took the place of the usual musicians; and on the bottom tier, in place of the servants, were a top-knotted Korean and a pigtailed Chinese. Whereas the Western dolls stood or sat in dignified poses, the Korean and the Chinese, bowing obsequiously with averted eyes, were the very picture of subservience. The cartoon was a mandala of world politics as the enlightened Meiji gentleman saw it, with the "civilized" peoples (including Japan) enjoying higher prestige and the "uncivilized" Chinese and Koreans relegated to positions of subordination.

Throughout the Meiji period the visual vocabulary of political cartoons portrayed the Korean as a stock figure clad in a white suit with a black horsehair tophat perched on his head, a wispy beard straggling down from his chin, and a long Korean pipe clenched between his teeth (Plate 14). The cartoon Korean was very much a figure of fun, like the fat and pigtailed "John Chinaman" who stood for China, neither dignified nor threatening as images of Westerners often were. He was sometimes portrayed as a victim but more often as a dupe. His face might show surprise, naive curiosity, horror, anger, or stupidity, but never serenity or nobility. The Korean might be lampooned or exoticized but was never romanticized. Indeed, it is interesting to note that the Japanese political and economic penetration of Korea produced no writers like Rudyard Kipling or H. Rider Haggard, who wove enticing tales of adventure in strange and unfamiliar lands, nor any fiction at all in which Koreans appeared as major characters.[8] What impressed the Japanese was not that the Koreans were strange, but they were strange *and* backward.

7. Ibid., 71.
8. Tsurumi, *Senjiki Nihon seishinshi*, 105.

The backwardness of the Koreans was most vividly portrayed in travel accounts and guidebooks. From the turn of the century, but especially after the outbreak of the Russo-Japanese War, a small army of Japanese visitors descended on Korea, most of them first-time visitors. Some were journalists, others politicians, scholars, and officials. In the pages of their travel accounts appeared caricatures of Korea that gained the authority of eyewitness reports by their specificity and detail. The writers of travel accounts did not rely on their eyes alone. Often they spoke with Japanese already living in Korea, and they read what others had already written about the country. The result was less a set of direct observations than a set of interpretations remarkably uniform in tone. Their recurrent theme was the enormous cultural and material gap that set Korea apart from Japan. The Korea portrayed in travel accounts was bizarre or grotesque, if not downright repellent, leaving a palpable impression that Korea was in need of change spurred from the outside.

The reader of travel accounts and guidebooks would be struck by differences at so many levels—language, emotions, architecture, food, social divisions, political structure—that it might seem difficult to believe that people who lived so close should be so strange. When new arrivals landed at Inchon and Pusan, their first encounter with Korean society was the mob of Korean porters at dockside, shouting for attention. If they wandered to the edges of the foreign settlement, they were bound to glimpse what the rest of the country must be like. They would see a scattering of scruffy thatch-roofed dwellings or shops displaying their simple wares—tobacco, pipes, cheap cakes, straw sandals, or dried fish —in haphazard array; they would encounter a crowd of white-suited Koreans milling about, chattering, shouting, and sometimes screaming in their strange tongue; and the visitors' noses, and their sensibilities, would be assaulted by a stew of pungent smells. Nine out of ten newcomers, wrote one journalist in a burst of exaggeration, immediately retreated to the familiar territory of the foreign settlement without wanting to see any more of this strange and backward country. But the physical or material exterior that first presented itself to the gaze of the outside observer—buildings, clothing, landscape, or the physical appearance of the natives—took on meaning as a metaphor exemplifying what was wrong with Korea.

An extreme but not entirely atypical travel account was Okita Kinjō's *Rimen no Kankoku* (*Korea Behind the Mask*), an extraordinary compendium of cultural slurs, which concluded that the "seven major products of Korea" were "shit, tobacco, lice, *kaesang* [courtesans], tigers, pigs, and flies." This crude yet vivid inventory, mingling the exotic with the disgusting, was echoed again and again in Okita's account, whose vocabulary drew heavily on the lexicon of contempt. He found Koreans happy-go-lucky, smelly, dirty, pitiful, weak, disorderly, asocial, poverty stricken, barbarous, immature, lazy, dissipated, suspicious, and withdrawn; their vices encompassed swindling, larceny, gambling, bribery, adultery, viciousness, and intrigue; and their impoverished living conditions little or no better than those of primitive aborigines.[9]

Like travelers everywhere, Okita was fascinated by the native houses, finding in them an emblem and an explanation of Korean poverty and backwardness. As Okita noted, "If you want to learn about pigs, you must first look at pigsties." Housing literally shaped national character. The cramped, dark, and dirty dwellings—"pigsties for people"—had weakened the minds and bodies of the Koreans. How could children help but suffer when they spent their days secluded in these tiny hovels, sprawled on the *ondol*-heated floors? How could their lives be anything but warped and stunted? In Okita's view the cramped and inconvenient Korean houses were "the biggest reason" why the Koreans acted the way they did. "The living conditions in the interior of their houses, where one can hardly move about freely, help us understand why the Koreans are so gloomy, and why they have fallen behind the progress of the world and remain so indifferent to social activity." Living in these tiny, murky, airless huts "inhibited" their development, isolating them from one another and turning Korea into a society of atomistic individuals, oblivious to the needs of society. Like the Chinese, from whom they had acquired their worst habits, the Koreans had become "believers in pure individualism." In the vocabulary of late Meiji Japan, "individualism" implied a callous and self-concerned indifference toward the state, the society, and the public good.[10]

Other travel writers reported that Korean houses looked like the "huts of beggars and *hinin* at home"; or that the Korean had the worst houses in the world "except for the aborigines in the South Seas and Africa or the Eskimos"; and that they looked like the little huts thrown up at the edge of fields in Japan to house "honeypots" filled with night soil.[11] Onjōji Kiyoshi could hardly believe that human beings lived in such grimy dwellings. "They are not houses, they are caves," he wrote.

9. Okita, *Rimen no Kankoku*, 33.
10. Ibid., 28, 41–42.
11. Katō Seinosuke, *Kankoku no kei'ei*, 40; Okita, *Rimen no Kankoku*, 25; Arakawa, *Saikin Chōsen jijō*, 95.

"During the era of cave-dwelling, caves were dug horizontally into the ground on a slant, but it would not be wrong to think of the houses of the Korean people as caves set on top of the ground." In these dismal dwellings a family of perhaps five or six, and at least three or four, adults and children would live, sleeping, eating, and defecating in the midst of squalor and filth. "There is no way that the Korean people could produce human beings extraordinary in spirit and rich in vigor when they live in such narrow, ugly, and filthy cavelike houses.... After seeing these miserable houses everywhere as we passed along the Seoul-Pusan line, even in Seoul near the foreign settlement, I suddenly blurted out that the best thing would be to burn them all down."[12]

With almost pathological delight in the pervasiveness of filth and dirt, travel accounts described in clinical detail the excretory practices of the Koreans. The "defecatory habits" of the Koreans, wrote Okita, ranked among the wonders of the world. The Koreans showed no reluctance to relieve themselves anywhere and everywhere in the streets, in the front of house gates, in ditches and moats, even in front of the royal palace. The city of Seoul, he said, was the "shit capital" of the world. Everywhere one looked, the streets of the capital were fouled with human or animal dung. The stench assaulted the nose, stung the eyes. Every family dumped its excreta into the street, whence it found its way into the streams and small rivers running through the city, turning them yellow and clogging them with filth. There was no clean drinking water to be had in the city, yet the Koreans did not seem to mind, nor did they hesitate to wash their clothes in these "rivers of shit." As one writer put it, "The Koreans don't care how cloudy the water is. Even worse, they drink it without a second thought, even with piss and shit mixed into it. In truth, the Korean can't tell the difference between bean paste (*miso*) and shit (*kuso*)."[13]

Travel accounts and guidebooks propagated bizarre lore about the uses the Koreans found for their own excrement. Horse manure, it was reported, was mixed with mud plaster to harden housewalls, and urine was used as a kind of cleaning fluid to remove dirty spots on utensils or was daubed on the faces of small children as a cosmetic. More startling, and less plausible, were reports that excrement was put to medicinal use. "Urine is said to be efficacious for the treatment of kidney stones, tuberculosis, fever and the like, and even those in good health drink it as a

12. Onjōji, *Kankoku no jitsujō*, 69–72.
13. Arakawa, *Saikin Chōsen jijō*, 89.

kind of fortifying tonic," reported Arakawa Gorō. "I have also heard
that when an illness becomes serious and the patient seems close to
death, he is often made to eat feces. What an astonishing thing."[14] Astonishing indeed! No wonder that one writer concluded that Korea was
the "dirtiest country in the world" or that the Koreans behaved like
"pigs and dogs."

Filth, dirt, and disease registered again and again in the pages of the
guidebooks: Korean men never washed their hands after urinating and
thought it quite strange that the Japanese did; flies and maggots crawled
over Korean food; Korean houses stank of unwashed bodies and
crawled with bedbugs; epidemics were rampant. According to several
observers, the effects of filth could literally be read on the faces of the
population. One hardly saw a pockmarked face in Japan, but in Korea
one or two out of every half-dozen faces were pitted. "Everywhere one
goes there are an extraordinarily large number of pockmarked faces,
both men and women. I have even seen young girls whose sores have
not yet healed walking blithely down the street." Indeed, according to
some reports, the Koreans were indifferent to illness. "They have no
conception of sanitation. As medicine they use lots of urine or plant
roots and tree bark. Being the place it is, when someone gets sick, he is
left alone. No special treatment is given. Children are almost completely
neglected. Their upbringing is left to nature so they can resist rain and
wind, heat and cold." If they died, it was unfortunate; if they lived, they
would be strong.[15]

In the travel accounts, laziness ranked with backwardness, poverty,
and filth among the most salient characteristics of Korean life. "In general the Koreans lack the idea of industriousness and the idea of thrift,"
said Arakawa. "Everywhere one sees them smoking their long pipes,
lounging about with nothing to do.... They appear to have no conception of the importance of time."[16] The Koreans woke late in the morning, they quit early in the evening, and they never worked when it
rained. (One writer even alleged that the Koreans did not have um-

14. Ibid., 90; a similar passage may be found in Onjōji, *Kankoku no jitsujō*, 77.
15. Onjōji, *Kankoku no jitsujō*, 77–78.
16. Arakawa, *Saikin Chōsen jijō*, 92, 87. Okita even went so far as to argue that the
habit of smoking was an important cause of the Koreans' "disease of laziness." Their "lack
of mettle," their "lack of spirit," and their "general indifference" was due in large measure
to "nicotine poisoning." Sitting in cramped, dim quarters, shut off from sunlight and fresh
air, in a miasma of pipe smoke that gave ordinary Japanese a headache, they let nicotine
seep into their nervous systems and erode their spirit. Okita, *Rimen no Kankoku*, 62.

brellas or other raingear since they always stayed inside when it rained.)
When the Koreans did work, they appeared not to exert themselves.
"The amount of work that the most industrious of them can finish in a
day does not even amount to what a Japanese can finish in a half-day.
Since they have bigger physiques than the Japanese, and an absurd degree of endurance and boldness, it cannot be that they are unable [to
work]. It is simply their inherent laziness that keeps them from doing
so." In contrast to the Japanese, who were inclined to save time by
doing in one or two days what could be completed in two or three, the
Koreans tried to put things off as long as possible.[17] It was laziness
that made the Koreans easy prey to the vices of drunkenness, gambling,
swindling, stealing, and adultery, and laziness compounded by vice
that eventually would lead Korea to "national destruction."

The Koreans were portrayed as lacking ambition, living one day to
the next, never looking toward the future, never thinking about con-
tingencies, and never trying to accumulate enough to tide them over
hard times. "If they have enough to eat for the day, they are satisfied,"
wrote Onjōji. "Until something interferes with getting their daily meals,
they wander aimlessly about. That is why there is such an astonishing
number of idlers even in Inchon and Pusan."[18] Neither did the Koreans
have any sense of thrift. "To put it another way, as a people they simply
do not care about anything if they can eat, drink, and sleep from one
day to the next."[19]

All this did not mean that the Koreans were incapable of work. On
the contrary, as nearly all the writers agreed, the Koreans were strong,
patient, and enduring: in sum, perfect beasts of burden. Indeed, as they
walked slowly down the street, heedless of time and getting into everyone's way, they seemed not unlike oxen. "If you want to use [Korean
workers], they are extremely useful," wrote Arakawa. "First of all, the
Koreans have great strength for carrying things; indeed, they carry
things heavier than a Japanese horse could. I hear that it is not unusual
for a Korean to carry a load weighing sixty or seventy *kanme* [490–570

---

17. Okita, *Rimen no Kankoku*, 55, 58.
18. Onjōji, *Kankoku no jitsujō*, 79.
19. Okita, *Rimen no Chōsen*, 57. Their lack of thrift was plain from the pattern of
trade in agricultural goods. "For the first five or six months after the harvest, commercial
transactions with the Koreans go on at a great pace, but after that they completely come to
a halt.... The reason is that at the time of harvest the Koreans sell all they can and buy all
the things they need, but three or four months after the harvest is over all the grain they
had to sell is sold, and all their reserves are gone." Katō, *Kankoku no kei'ei*, 42.

pounds]. If you encourage them and put them to work under supervision, they are quite useful at carrying things. But the key is supervision
so that they work hard and keep their promise not to slacken their efforts."[20] Under proper (that is, Japanese) supervision, conceded one
travel writer, their "working power surpasses the Japanese."[21]

Although suited to hard physical labor, the Koreans were not
thought capable of more complex tasks, particularly those requiring
complicated mental effort. It was hard for them to perform even such
simple jobs as punching tickets at railroad wickets. Indeed, it was reported that Korean railroad employees required to do more demanding
work often became quite ill, contracting tuberculosis and other diseases.
"Even those who have been to Japan and received a substantial education there are not up to the demands of the job." And they were hopeless
at adding up how many tickets they had punched or calculating what
the fares were, no matter how much they were chided and scolded.
"Like most barbarians (yabanjin), they can not understand precise arithmetic," wrote Onjōji. "When one recalls that the Ainu in the depths
of Hokkaido do not know what year it is or that the barbarians in
Africa know how to count only as high as the number of their fingers
and toes, one feels quite sorry [for the Koreans]."[22]

Travel accounts and guidebooks did not so much dehumanize the
Koreans as infantilize or primitivize them, likening them to the Ainu, the
Eskimos, or African aborigines. The overwhelming message was that
the Koreans were no more capable of taking care of themselves than
were any backward people; they were to be treated like children rather
than adults. While some concluded that the Koreans were beyond re-
demption, many travel writers felt that they merely required the firm
hand of the Japanese to lift them out of their poverty, filth, and lassi-
tude. Even Okita, with his anal-obsessive attentiveness to Korean defe-
cation, felt there was hope. What the country needed, he said, was a
"clean-up," a "grand laundering," a "sanitization of the slough of in-
iquity that produces so many vices and abuses." Once such a thorough
cleansing was done, he said, "bright sunshine and air" would be let into
the country.[23] Needless to say, "bright sunshine and air" were met-
aphors for modernity and civilization, and the scrubbing away of squalor was a metaphor for Japanese domination.

20. Arakawa, Saikin Chōsen jijō, 87, 93.
21. Katō, Kankoku no kei'ei, 42.
22. Onjōji, Kankoku no jitsujō, 85–86.
23. Okita, Rimen no Chōsen, 30.

PASSIVITY, CORRUPTION, AND TOADYISM: IMAGES OF KOREAN POLITICS

At the simplest level images of domination rested on obvious contrasts between the clean, hardworking, up-to-date Japanese and the dirty, lazy, backward Koreans. But to see the Koreans as inferior did not necessarily lead to the conclusion that domination was necessary or appropriate. Two questions were implicit in the negative images found in travel accounts of Korea. The first was whether the filth, squalor, and indolence of Korean society were endemic or remediable. Were the Koreans backward by nature or by virtue of historical contingency? Were these qualities the consequence of an essential racial character or of structural constraints? The second was what if anything the Japanese should do about Korean backwardness. Why not let the Koreans wallow in their own filth and indolence while the Japanese improved their own lot? What need was there to establish Japanese domination over Korea in order to help the Koreans? Why not simply take advantage of their weakness to promote Japan's own gain? The discussion of these issues led to a more nuanced rationale for Japanese domination that urged the transformation of Korea society in the name of fraternal obligation.

What licensed optimism that Japan could "clean up" or "sanitize" Korea was the view that structural impediments were responsible for Korean backwardness. Implicitly or explicitly, Japanese journalists, travel writers, and visitors often argued that institutions, history, and politics rather than an ineluctable or inherited national character created stagnation in Korea. In other words, the roots of backwardness were to be found not in the Korean people themselves but in their social and political environment. If liberated from that environment, they could make progress toward "civilization." This view, essentially a rationalistic and liberal one, held out the possibility of reform if history could be reversed, politics transformed, and institutions changed. It also justified Japanese domination by suggesting that change in Korea depended on Japanese intervention.

"There are two ways that the Japanese look at the Koreans," wrote Yamamichi Jōichi in 1911. "The first view is that the Koreans are a degenerate people full of lies, bereft of moral sense, weak in endurance and courage, who will never raise themselves up as civilized people. The second view says that while they may lack a moral sense and courage they are a people by no means inferior to the Japanese in industry and endurance, who, if they have the proper leadership, will have a bright future." Like most Japanese observers, Yamamichi took the second view, with the operative emphasis on the need for "proper leadership" by the Japanese. "If there were an appropriate person or powerful country to control and properly lead [the Koreans], with the intention of reforming them, then there is no doubt that they can be turned into good, law-abiding people sooner or later."[24] The future of Korea need not be foreclosed by backwardness if only the Japanese took charge.

Many Japanese expressed sympathy for the social and political oppression of the Korean population. Kikuchi Kenjō, a Minyūsha correspondent who visited Korea in 1893, observed that the common people in Korea were as unfortunate as "African slaves" or "untouchables in India." He was not consigning them a lesser humanity but suggesting that they were victims of a reprehensible social system.

> No matter how much reason is on their side, there is no way for them to protest against the aristocracy. No matter how much ability they might have, they have no right to hold political power. They are kept down in the lower levels of society.... Even if the peninsula were to become a small nation, they would not be its citizens. They groan under the abuses of the aristocracy.... When one sees how shackled are their livelihood, their language, their transportation, their food and clothing, their very lives, one must conclude that they exist only to be oppressed. As members of society, they are no better than animals.

Ground down by the upper classes, the commoners had neither freedom nor hope. "A people without hope," concluded Kikuchi, "does not make progress."[25]

What consistently struck and appalled most Japanese observers was the Koreans' apparent lack of public spirit or patriotism. The Koreans tolerated a degree of foreign interference in their affairs that most Japanese would have regarded as national humiliation. It astonished Japanese observers that the Koreans could not rouse themselves to "drink gall and sleep on nettles" in response to national humiliation as the Japanese did in response to the Triple Intervention. "In the face of danger they protected the fate of their country by relying on the power of others," noted Tanaka Hozumi, a *Yomiuri* reporter. After the Sino-Japanese War, ministers and high officials became "cat's-paws for the

24. Yamamichi, *Chōsen hantō*, 61.
25. Kikuchi, *Chōsen ōkuku*, 194–96.

foreigners," and the Korean king fled into the arms of the Russians. The Koreans, he concluded, were "a pitiful people who responded to military pressure but rejected civilized interference in their affairs."[26]

Neither did the general populace appear to have any inclination to sacrifice themselves for king or country. As Arakawa Gorō put it, the ordinary Korean viewed the royal house as a traveler might—with indifferent curiosity.[27] Time and again Japanese reporters and travel writers remarked on the popular indifference to the burning of the Kyŏngbok Palace. The citizens of Seoul had gathered in front of the palace gate, puffing on their long pipes, laughing and chatting like spectators watching an interesting spectacle, not the destruction of their political center. Japanese also reported that top ministers were often discourteous or disrespectful to the monarch even in his presence, and that often they did not obey his orders.[28] For the late Meiji Japanese, disobedience to the wishes of the monarch, tantamount to sedition if not blasphemy at home, underscored the moral and social bankruptcy of the Korean political system.

Many writers argued that the Koreans had no patriotic or public sentiment because they lacked any public life. Government was monopolized by the aristocracy, the *yangban* elite. As a consequence, the common people had no understanding of what politics was. "They have no concept of the state, nor any notion of loyalty to the sovereign," wrote Kikuchi. "Their only aspiration, it seems, is to fulfill their animal wants and live out their lives. As long as they are able to get food and clothing and to live a peaceful life, they do not deeply question who it is that rules them."[29] With no sense of involvement in politics there could be no commitment to the nation, and with no commitment to the nation there could be no patriotism.

Many writers argued that economic oppression severed any moral integuments that might have bound the people to their rulers. "The *yangban* misuse their aristocratic privileges and treat the people cruelly. The peasants have their fruits of their hard labor wrung from them for the sake of the *yangban*. In other words, the relationship between

26. Tanaka Hozumi, *Tai-Kan shigi*, 21, 25–26.
27. Arakawa, *Saikin Chōsen jijō*, 64.
28. Katō, *Kankoku no kei'ei*, 73–74.
29. Kikuchi, *Chōsen ōkoku*, 74. Cf. the observation of Yamaguchi Toyomasa, a Japanese employed by the Korean Ministry of Finance before annexation: "The collective spirit between Koreans, high and low, has been weak from the beginning, and from every perspective patriotism has been inadequate." Yamaguchi, *Chōsen no kenkyū*, 64.

[people and *yangban*] is little more than the relationship between tyrannical landlords and pitiful tenants."[30] Exploitation was compounded
by official corruption. As one Japanese observer put it, in their dealings
with the people local magistrates and intendants were like "a pack of
dogs fighting over meat."[31] Local officials tried to recover the costs of
bribing their way into office (and to build their family fortunes) by
ruthlessly squeezing the populace. Corruption crushed any incentive for
the common people to save or store for the future. "The reason that the
Koreans lack a sense of thrift is not simply that they are indolent. It has
long been the custom for tyrannical and corrupt officials, generation
after generation grasping all that they can, to arrest anyone who accu-
mulates a little bit of property, to force him into prison without any
cause, and to rob him of the property he has acquired through his labor.
Contrary to common sense, accumulating property through hard work
is a way to put oneself at risk."[32] It was safer to spend what one had
than to attract the attention of rapacious officials through the accumulation of surplus wealth. The habits of indolence so often remarked on
by Japanese travelers were thus linked to structural causes.

In the view of many Japanese observers, politics in Korea was a
meaningless struggle for personal ambition or family gain. "In Korea,"
wrote Arakawa, "there are no factions that can be called public parties
(*kōtō*); there are only private cabals (*shitō*)." High officials were locked
in intense factional struggles over privilege, interest, and power without
reason, substance, or content. "The only principle [of ministers and of-
ficials] is to pursue prestige and interest, and they align themselves and
decide on national affairs by constantly dividing and realigning themselves."[33] And while the aristocratic factions fought for favor and pre-
ferments, the monarch tried to maintain his own position by pitting one
aristocratic faction against another. In contrast to Japan, where the imperial family had ruled "in an unbroken line" above the political fray, in
Korea there was no sense that "the royal house and the state were united
as one."[34] The ruler did not stand above petty intrigue, corruption, favoritism, and all the other ills that plagued the government; he was right
in the middle of them. A number of observers took the Kwangmu reforms of the late 1890s as a step in the wrong direction since they

30. Yamaguchi, *Chōsen no kenkyū*, 63.
31. Tanaka, *Tai-Kan shigi*, 27.
32. Katō, *Kankoku no kei'ei*, 44; see also Arakawa, *Saikin Chōsen jijō*, 65, and Tanaka, *Tai-Kan shigi*, 28–29.
33. Tanaka, *Tai-Kan shigi*, 27.
34. Yamaguchi, *Chōsen no kenkyū*, 64.

strengthened the court at the expense of the country and enlarged the king's capacity to line his own pockets.[35]

In the final analysis, "toadyism" or "worship of the powerful" (*jidai shisō*) was presented as the fundamental characteristic of Korean social and political life. "The Koreans, who always follow the strong and powerful, consistently believe that if one asserts himself he will be broken, but if one acts weak he can take advantage of the other." This was why the habit of "placing officials above the people" (*kanson minpi*) was so prevalent and so intense.[36] It also explained Korea's dealings with the outside world. Since early times the Koreans had been content to live in the shadow of their powerful neighbor, China. Unlike the Japanese, who had maintained a truculent independence from China, the Koreans had accepted status as a "dependent state" or "vassal state" of the Chinese "suzerain." For Meiji Japanese, engaged for a generation in securing national independence and autonomy in the face of outside pressure, this aspect of Korean political culture was particularly incomprehensible. Although it might be possible to liken the relations between *yangban* and populace to the relationship between samurai and commoner in pre-Restoration Japan, there was no precedent in the Japanese past for subordination to an outside power.

It will be immediately apparent that Japanese analysis of structural impediments to progress in Korea rested on an asymmetrical (and unfavorable) comparison with the Japanese institutional structure. If the Korean people were passive and oppressed, unable to recognize or defend their own rights, by contrast the Japanese were patriotic, aware of duties and rights, and therefore willing to sacrifice themselves for the national good; if officials in Korea were incompetent and ruthlessly corrupt, by implication those in Japan were men of talent dedicated to the public good; and if the king of Korea was a superstitious political retrograde, viewed with contempt by his ministers and indifference by his people, then the emperor of Japan was a beloved national paterfamilias leading his people to "civilization and enlightenment." In short,

35. Katō, *Kankoku no kei'ei*, 56–57. As for King Kojong, most Japanese writers were lavish in their criticism. In their view the problem of the monarchy was not simply structural but personal. The king was invariably portrayed as relentlessly and recalcitrantly backward-looking, content to follow the old customs, prey to superstition, and surrounded by corrupt ministers, political favorites, eunuchs, soothsayers, sorcerers, and other sinister persons. Even worse, he was deeply and emotionally anti-Japanese, using every opportunity he could to obstruct them, even if it meant relying on other powers and thwarting reform. Cf. ibid., 69–70.

36. Yamaguchi, *Chōsen no kenkyū*, 64–66; see also Arakawa, *Saikin Chōsen jijō*, 74.

the strengths of Japanese society mirrored the weaknesses of Korean society.

Interestingly enough, these asymmetrical comparisons were precisely those made between the "New Japan" and the "Old Japan" by liberal writers like Tokutomi Iichirō and Takekoshi Yosaburō in the late 1880s and 1890s. Substitute "Korea" for "Old Japan" in their dichotomies, and the contrasts still work. But what did this mean? It suggested that Japan and Korea had a recent historical experience in common. Although the Japanese might view Korean politics and society from a "civilized" or "enlightened" perspective, they were aware that the Korean ancien régime might undergo the same kind of sudden and dramatic change that their own had. In rebuking the flaws of the Korean state, Japanese were consciously or unconsciously rebuking their own immediate past. And knowledge that they had overcome that past made them sensitive to the possibility that the Koreans might do so as well. Even those most critical of corruption, aimlessness, and backwardness in Korean political culture were not inclined to throw up their hands in dismay. It was clear that when Koreans migrated outside their borders, away from the debilitating social customs and political institutions that ensnared them at home, they could become as industrious and frugal as the people of any country; thus, if those institutions could be changed, Korean society might be reformed.

The critical question was not whether the Korean state could be transformed into a modern polity but rather whether the Koreans could accomplish that task by themselves. The consensus was that they could not. As many writers observed, the Korean populace was politically submissive and inert, unable or unwilling to resist pressure from above. "The people submit themselves to tyrannical repression, and they never imagine crying out for the protection of their rights or carrying out a glorious revolution."[37] Nor was it likely that the entrenched ruling class; the royal family, the aristocracy, and the *yangban* would undertake the reforms required to pry the country out of backwardness. But that did not mean reform was out of question. Indeed, the conclusion drawn by most Japanese who analyzed the structural impediments to progress was that Korea could be changed only with their help.

This justification of domination echoed the early French notion of a *mission civilatrice*, which asserted that, with the help of France, backwardness could be overcome in North Africa and other colonial areas.

37. Tanaka, *Tai-Kan shigi*, 22–23.

The *mission civilatrice* assumed that all men were equal in potential and therefore equally capable of becoming "civilized." The concept drew no sharp racial boundaries between the French and those they sought to dominate, nor did it regard backwardness as a permanent condition. In a similar fashion, many Japanese, who in the 1890s could still remember a pre-Restoration Japan that resembled contemporary Korea, had little doubt that the Koreans would be able to uplift themselves with Japanese guidance. All that was required was to export Japan's own post-Restoration experience with modernization. This task would not necessarily be an easy one. As Yamamichi Jōichi noted, "It will take a rather long time for [the Koreans] to reach the point where they can cut free of their bad habits and customs of their own free will."[38] But that was all the more reason for controlling Korea with a firm hand and staying as long as needed to raise the "cultural level" of the Koreans and bring them into the fold of "civilization."

COMMON CULTURE, COMMON ANCESTRY: HISTORICAL PERSPECTIVES

Even with its universalistic assumption of a common humanity, the French notion of a *mission civilatrice* still recognized fundamental ethnic, religious, and cultural differences between the French and their subject peoples. In the long run, recognition of these differences prompted a shift in French colonial policy away from "assimilation" toward "association." The Japanese, by contrast, could find ethnic, cultural, and religious similarities that propelled them toward ever closer relations with the Koreans. The Koreans might be "backward" or "uncivilized," but ancient racial and historical ties linked them to the Japanese in a way that the French were not linked to the Arabs of Algeria. By invoking these bonds, historians, anthropologists, and journalists justified domination through annexation and assimilation.

Although Westerners often deployed the concept of race to justify the custody or stewardship of more advanced "races" over the less advanced, it was also a means of projecting an imagined commonality. As such, "race" was a powerful tool for the construction of political entities, especially national identities. In nineteenth-century Europe, nationalist movements contended that people of one "race" or one "nationality"—the terms were often interchangeable—should gather

38. Yamamichi, *Chōsen hantō*, 73–74.

into one nation or federation of nations. Racial or ethnic affinity, not rational choice or common purpose or historical accident, became the basis for the legitimacy of states, and in establishing such affinities, the question of historical origins was crucial.

The concept of race as an analytical category was introduced into Japan only at the beginning of the Meiji period. When Japanese scholars had debated the origins of the Japanese people in the eighteenth century, for example, the matter of race was not at issue. Questions of race and origin became linked only with the arrival of Westerners like Morse, Baelz, Aston, and Chamberlain, men from societies intensely concerned with questions of race and nationality.[39] Indeed, it is difficult to find these words in common use before the Meiji period. The 1867 edition of Hepburn's dictionary provides entries for *jiyu* and *biyodo* but not for *jinshu* (race) or even *minzoku* (race; nationality) and *kokumin* (people; nationality). Rather quickly, however, the idea took hold.[40] By the turn of the century race had become a standard yardstick to measure Japan in relation to the rest of the world. The concept was cloaked in the respectability provided by its use as an instrument for "scientific" understanding in the West.

Some ardent promoters of "civilization" and "enlightenment" like Taguchi Ukichi and Takekoshi Yosaburō used the concept of race to distance themselves from their Asian neighbors. Proclaiming a kind of racial *datsu-A ron*, they argued that racial affinities linked the Japanese and the Westerners. Taguchi, for example, advanced the curious post hoc propter hoc argument that the alacrity and adaptability that the Japanese had shown in taking over elements of Western civilization provided irrefutable evidence that the Japanese were of the Aryan race. So superior were the Japanese to the Chinese and other Asians in intelligence that they must be related to the Europeans and the Americans instead.[41] Such assertions afforded a rationale for domination over

39. Cf. Kudō, *Nihon jinshuron*, 49–79.

40. The very first lesson in the basic reader published by the Ministry of Education in 1873 began with the observation that the world was divided into "five types": the Asian race (*jinshu*), the European race, the Malay race, the American race, and the African race. Mombusho, *Shogaku dokuhon*, 1–2.

41. Kudō, *Nihon jinshu ron*, 158–60; See also Hashikawa Bunsō, *Ōka monogatari*, 40–50. In a similar vein, Takekoshi Yosaburō, another liberal journalist, put forth the theory that the original Japanese had migrated to the archipelago from the south, bringing with them the seeds of a civilization synthesized from Aryan and Semitic elements. Phoenician (Semitic) civilization, he argued, had spread to India, where it mingled with Aryan elements before spreading to the islands of the South Seas and then to Japan. As carriers of a superior civilization from the West, the original ancestors of the Japanese had a headstart

other Asians by asserting that the Japanese not only had a mandate to uplift their neighbors but, as a superior race, could hardly help doing otherwise.

The more common view, however, was that the Japanese were in fact an amalgam of subraces or ethnic groups related to the Koreans and the Chinese. "It goes without saying," wrote the well-known archaeologist and physical anthropologist Tsuboi Shōgorō, "that 'nation' (*kokumin*) and 'race' (*jinshū*) are separate things.... It is not necessarily the case that those who live in one country and make up one nationality (*minzoku*) are of one sort; some are formed from the mixture of two or even more elements. As in the case with the Japanese nationality (*Nihon minzoku*), ... one must realize that it is made up of those who resemble Ainu, those who resemble Malayan natives, those who resemble people from continental Asia, and those who mix the characteristics of all of these."[42] The assumption that the Japanese nationality was not "racially pure" suggested that the Japanese were adept at assimilating different ethnic groups into a seamless whole.

Interestingly, some argued that it was the *kokutai* that had made racial amalgamation possible over the course of Japanese history. Kita Teikichi, an influential historian employed by the Ministry of Education, asserted that the "Yamato nationality" (*Yamato minzoku*) was the result of the "blending" (*dōka*) and "fusion" (*yūgō*) of many peoples into one nation "loyal to the Throne." The Japanese were a "magnanimous people" who did not treat conquered people cruelly but tried to assimilate them. The Ezo, for example, were not exterminated by the superior Yamato peoples but transformed into loyal and happy subjects of the emperor. The Japanese

> moved as many [Ezo] as possible to the main islands, provided them with food, and gave them fields so that they became no different from ordinary farmers. They called themselves by the same names as the Yamato nationality (*minzoku*), they adopted the same customs, they intermarried with the Yamato people, and they became almost indistinguishable from them.... Today, after nine hundred years, all traces of them as Ezo have disappeared, and they survive only to the degree that their blood is passed on hidden among the Yamato people.

---

over their neighbors and quickly overcame a "Mongol" or "Chinese" people who had already brought continental civilization to the islands. The unspoken assumption of these arguments was that if it was all right for fellow Aryans like the English and the Germans to conquer "lesser breeds," it must be all right for the Japanese as well. Kudō, *Nihon jinshu ron*, 167–70.

42. Tsuboi Shōgorō, *Rekishi chiri*, Nov. 3, 1910, pp. 141–42.

What was true of the Ezo was also true of other aboriginal people the Japanese had conquered—the Kumaso, the Hayato, the Tsuchigumo, and so forth.[43]

In arguing for racial or ethnic affinities between the Koreans and the Japanese, writers relied on two set of evidence: physical and cultural. For physical anthropologists humankind could be divided into natural categories on the basis of physical characteristics such as height, hair color, the shape of the head, and facial features such as eyes, nose, and mouth. According to Tsuboi, examination of skeletal remains in Korea suggested that three basic types were to be found there: a northern type resembling the Tunguistic people, a southern type resembling the Japanese, and an intermediate type resembling elements of both. Like many others, Tsuboi argued that there was a strong family resemblance between Koreans living in the southern part of the peninsula and the inhabitants of the Japanese archipelago. Korean males tended to be a little taller than the Japanese, but their facial features were the same. Comparisons were difficult if one believed, as Tsuboi did, that the Japanese were a racial mixture themselves, but he allowed himself the cautious conclusion that "the physique of the principal element among the Koreans is the same as that of some elements of the Japanese or bears a strong resemblance to it. From the standpoint of race one cannot say that we and they are the same, but one can say that the majority of them are closely related to one of the elements which are part of our make-up."[44]

Others were willing to assert even stronger ethnic bonds between Japan and Korea. Kita Teikichi wrote: "I myself believe that one must come to the conclusion that our Yamato nationality (*Yamato minzoku*) fundamentally is no different from the Koreans. No one relying on ordinary eyesight can look at a Korean in either Japanese clothing or Western clothing and clearly distinguish him from the Japanese nationality. The only way we can discern differences is by language, customs, and the like, but as far as appearance goes one can see that [Japanese and Koreans] are almost the same." Admittedly, Kita said, there were wide variations in the appearances of the Japanese, so great at the extremes that one might wonder if all belonged to the same "Japanese nationality." But for Kita, as for Tsuboi, the "Japanese nationality" was an amalgam of racial groups blended into one "nationality" over the

43. Kita, *Kankoku no heigō to kokushi*, 66, 69–71.
44. Tsuboi, *Rekishi chiri*, 145–46.

course of centuries. The main point was that both Japanese and Koreans, in all their variety, sprang from the same racial stock. "In general, I believe that there is no reason not to state positively that Japan and Korean are of the same racial identity (*dōshu*). This is not something that is being said for the first time today. In the past our ancestors recognized that the people of Japan and Korea were of the same race."[45]

Those who most strongly insisted on ethnic affinities of the Koreans and the Japanese relied on historical and linguistic evidence rather than physical similarities to make their case. In a 1913 essay Yamaji Aizan, a leading popular historian and journalist, wrote: "Today it is accepted with hardly any room for dissent that Koreans and Japanese are a people of the same culture and race (*dōbun dōshu no minzoku*).... It is an indisputable fact that in primitive times Japan, Korea, and Manchuria had a common way of life." Yamaji found abundant evidence for this commonality in myth, language, customs, and material culture. Mounted archery, sumo, matrilocal marriage, ritual suicide (*junshi*), the use of "flutes" to trap birds and animals, flattening of the skulls of young infants, origin myths involving heavenly descent, rain-calling rites, rock-throwing contests, dog hunting, wearing of white clothing, local priesthoods, the carrying of burdens on the head—all were culture traits shared by the Japanese and the Koreans in "primitive times." Yamaji even asserted that the prehistoric Japanese, like the early peoples of Korea, ate beef and drank milk. The only uncertainty was whether the ancestors of the Japanese people had developed on the Korean peninsula or whether these cultural traits were brought to Japan from Korea—in other words, whether the commonality resulted from migration or from diffusion.[46]

The argument that Koreans and Japanese shared a common ancestry had achieved academic and intellectual respectability at least by the 1890s. Kume Kunitake adumbrated the idea in an 1889 article in *Shigaku zasshi*, and Hoshino Hisashi elaborated it the following year in the same journal. These young historians, trained in Western historiographical techniques, were engaged in an attack on nativist (*kokugaku*) historians for their naive and uncritical acceptance of the Nihongi and Kojiki as factual and for their obsession with the *kokutai*. But it is clear that both had a political agenda of their own: establishing historical grounds for Japanese domination in Korea. In examining the ancient

45. Kita, *Kankoku no heigō to kokushi*, 64–69.
46. Yamaji, "Nissen dōzoku no shiteki shosa," 81.

texts, they discovered not only that the Japanese and the Koreans spoke a common tongue but that the "Imperial ancestors" exercised dominion over the peninsula during "the age of the gods" as well as during the reign of the Empress Jingo; it was for that reason that "our countrymen regard Chōsen as a subject state (*zokkoku*)."[47] In 1893 Yoshida Tōgo published an influential work, *Nikkan kōshi dan*, that gave the common ancestry idea wider currency. In his view the Korean peninsula was divided into two racial types, a "continental race" (*rikushu*) settled mainly in the north and an "island race" (*tōshu*) settled in the south. The "island race," with its strong links to Izumo and Chikushi, was identical with the Japanese "race," and the primal act of creation, mythologized in the story of Izanagi and Izanami, included the creation of Korea (*Karakuni no shima*) as well as the Japanese archipelago.

The notion that Korea was, like Japan, a racial amalgam became another avenue to link ancient Japan and Korea. The ambiguity of the historical record, however, generated considerable debate over just how racial mixing took place. Most of these debates, like debates over Japan's strategic policies, revolved on a "north-south" or a "continental-maritime" axis. The basic question was whether the ancestors of the Japanese had come to the archipelago from the south and then spread to the Korean peninsula or whether they had first established themselves on the peninsula and then moved to the islands. In his *Nihonjinshi*, for example, Yamaji Aizan argued that the Japanese islands were originally inhabited by three "races": the Ainu, the Hayato, and the Yamato. The Ainu were the original inhabitants; the Hayato, related to the Malaysians, arrived in Kyushu from the west coast of Korea, whose people they resembled, but eventually lost their "vigor"; and both were eventually overrun by the stronger and more civilized Yamato people, who established the Japanese state after pushing the Ainu north and the Hayato into southern Kyushu. The Yamato, he surmised, were a branch of the "Turanian" race who reached Japan after they had founded the "Korean" states of Koryŏ, Silla, and Paekche as they migrated south on the peninsula before crossing the Japan Sea.[48] The Turanian race was

47. Quoted in Kudō, *Nihon jinshu ron*, 144. Hoshino Hisashi, "Honpō jinshu gopen ni tsuite niko o nobete magokoro aikokusha in shissu," *Shigaku zasshi*, 11 (October 1893), 19–43.

48. Kudō, *Nihon jinshu ron*, 59. Later Yamaji changed his mind. In a 1913 article he wrote: "It is an indisputable fact that in ancient times the Malaysian race, accustomed to a maritime life, had sailed from afar across the Indian Ocean and landed near the Yellow River. The interpretation that seems closest to the facts is that these Malay people moved into Shantung Province, then gradually spread south into Korea, and eventually crossed into Japan." Yamaji, "Nissen dōzoku no shiteki shosa," 95.

a dynamic one, for it included the Manchus, who brought order to China; the Turks, who created a vast multiracial empire; and the Mongols, who once created an empire that stretched from Asia to Europe.

By contrast, in *Chōsen kaika shi* (1901) Tsuneya Moriyuki posited the migration of a "Heaven-descended race" (*amakudari jinshu*) carried by sea currents from the Philippines north through Taiwan to Okinawa and Kyushu. He surmised that this race came from the southeast corner of the Asian continent. It was further subdivided into four subraces—the Yamato (or Amakudari), the Izumo, the Fuyo, and the Okinawans—all of whom shared a common history, a common mythology, a common language, a common material culture, and a common "racial character." Eventually they spread over the Korean peninsula and the Liaotung peninsula as well. In Tsuneya's view there had been several waves of migration: the Fuyo were first established in Korea, then displaced by the Izumo, who in turn were displaced by the arrival of the Yamato/Amakudari from the Japanese islands. This historical ethnography, like Yamaji's, reflected a "struggle for existence," with a stronger race or subrace eventually triumphing over weaker ones. In the racial mix of contemporary Korea, the Fuyo represented the largest component, with a substantial mix of Izumo, some Amakudari, and other aboriginal tribes.[49]

Advocates of the "common ancestry" or "common race" argument had to confront an important question: If the Koreans and the Japanese had a common racial ancestry, how could one explain their contemporary differences? The "biological" answer was that it was the result of mixing with inferior indigenous peoples, with "strong" blood diluted by "weak." By implication, the process of racial "dilution" was less complete or thorough in Japan, or at least involved a lesser admixture of "weak" blood. There was also an "environmental" explanation: lack of geographical contiguity between Korea and Japan meant that as the members of the original common race became more widely dispersed or scattered, they lost contact with one another, and their culture, customs, and character differentiated. "If Korea and Japan had remained a unified country," wrote Kita Teikichi, "that would have been splendid, but in ancient times transportation was poor and it was not as easy to go back and forth as it is today. As a result, even though Korea has the same roots [as Japan], it gradually drifted away."[50] While

49. Tsuneya, *Chōsen kaika shi.*
50. Kita, *Kankoku no heigō to kokushi,* 139–40.

the Japanese maintained their independence, the Koreans, living in the shadow of a more powerful China, became enmired in that country's conservative cultural tradition, acquiring traits that inhibited progress.[51]

To be sure, some suggested that the racial mix in Korea was of an entirely different character from that in Japan. Ayukai Fusanoshin, a lecturer at the *Tōyō Kyōkai Gakkō*, argued that the Koreans were made of the remnants of at least a dozen different subraces or tribes, all of them "weaklings who lost out in the struggle for survival and fled from their own countries." Korea was a country created not by the triumph of the strong over the weak but by the weak over the weaker. All of the subraces or tribes in Korea depended on outside power, with the result that there had never been a unified state of affairs within the country.[52] Since the Koreans were a "weak" people, they were susceptible to the influences of nature that had profoundly shaped the national character, making them more arrogant than the Japanese, more narrow-minded than the Chinese, as well as emotionally unbalanced and volatile, prone to sudden changes in mood, prematurely sexual, easily swayed, likely to stampede in crowds, and so forth. When Koreans were removed from their natural environment, they could change; but as long as they remained in that environment, they were likely to remain backward.

The logical implication (if not the hidden agenda) of the "common ancestry" or "common race" argument was that the separation of the Japanese and the Koreans was unnatural. After all, the doctrine of race as the basis of nationhood urged that related ethnic groups be united in political units. "It is the trend of the world today for those who are similar to ally and to resist those who are different, and to measure their interests and welfare on the basis or national and racial origin," wrote Yoshida Tōgo in 1910. "Somehow or other, against all reason, the people of the [Korean] peninsula, despite ties of geography and race, have ignored their destiny to become united with Japan and have remained independent." For him, the logic of history and the logic of race called for the unification of the "island race" who originally inhabited both Japan and southern Korea.[53] In 1913 he argued that the annexation of Korea could be read simply as the reuniting of two peoples long separated. It marked the reestablishment of the "unity of the island

51. Miura Hiroyuki, "Nikkan no dōka to bunka," *Rekishi chiri*, Nov. 3, 1910, pp. 163–73. Cf. the views of Ōkuma Shigenobu, "Senjin no dōka," 291–93.

52. Ayukai Fusanoshin, "Shizen yori uketaru Chōsenjin no seijō," in Aoyagi, *Chōsen*, 133. Ayukai was alleged to have been involved in the assassination of Queen Min.

53. Yoshida Tōgo, *Nikkan kōshi dan*, 85, 92.

race," and it ended a long and "unnatural" independence for the people of the peninsula.[54]

Support for assimilation or annexation was often phrased in terms of family or kinship ties. "I would suggest that Korea is a branch family (*bunke*) that shares ancestors with our country," wrote Kita Teikichi. When Korea fell into straitened circumstances, bullied and buffeted by her continental neighbors, Japan could not remain an idle bystander.

> That is why the Sino-Japanese War broke out. That is why the Russo-Japanese War broke out. As a result, we have witnessed the amalgamation of Korea and Japan. The time had come, it seems, for the branch family to return to the main family. If the branch family had been able to maintain a splendid independence, there would have been no need for the main family to interfere. But since things did not go so smoothly, it was inevitable that in order to help [Korea], Japan, the main family, made it into a protectorate.

Eventually the two countries were merged. "The branch family returned to the home of the main family. It did not disappear: it merged with the main family. Korea was not destroyed, and the Koreans are not a destroyed people. They have truly returned to their source."[55]

What were the implications of the "common race" or "common ancestry" argument? One, of course, was that Japanese domination over Korea was qualitatively different from Western domination over their colonial territories. "There are some commentators," wrote Miura Hiroyuki, "who try to explain the relations between Korea and Japan by reference to the annexation and control of territory in East Asia, the South Seas, and Africa by the Western countries. But can we believe that all these countries had the same close and deep historical ties that Korea and Japan have had from ancient times?"[56] For Japan the Koreans were not strangers or aliens or subject peoples as the colonial peoples of Asia and Africa were for their Western overlords. Miura, like many others, referred to them as "new countrymen" (*shinpu kokumin*), a term implying commonality, not separation. Indeed, there was a great reluctance to refer to Korea as a colony at all, and the word was hardly

54. Ibid., 83–85, 92–93. Cf. similar remarks by Kita Teikichi in 1910: "Fundamentally I think that [Korea] ought to be one part of our empire. But no, let me go further to insist that originally Korea was the foundation of our empire and that the people of Korea, in the main, are no different from our own Yamato nationality [*Yamato minzoku*]." Kita, *Kankoku no heigō to kokushi*, 231. This comment suggested that the annexation of Korea was not so much the incorporation of another society into Japan as the bringing together of two societies with a common origin.

55. Kita, *Rekishi chiri*, Mar. 11, 1910, pp. 139–40. See also Kita, *Kankoku no heigō to kokushi*, 77–79.

56. Miura, "Nikkan no dōka to bunka," 176.

ever used. Instead, the peninsula was usually referred to as a "new territory" or an "extension of the map," terms that avoided the issue of who dominated whom.

The other implication of the "common race" or "common ancestry" argument was that the Koreans were eminently capable of being assimilated. Indeed, they could excel at being Japanese. The most salient example were the *kikajin*, the Korean settlers who came to Japan during the Nara and early Heian periods. Not only were they welcomed by the Japanese, but they proved capable of blending into their new society without trouble. As Miura Hiroyuki pointed out, "Not only did they and their descendants become assimilated with us, in no way inferior as loyal subjects of the emperor, not a few of them were even people of exceptionally distinguished service." Indeed, famous historical figures, Japanese heroes like Sakaue Tamaro or Ōuchi Yoshitake, were descendants of the *kikajin*. "They became completely pure Japanese, both in the civil realm and in the military."[57]

These arguments revealed a persistent confidence that the historical ties between Korean and Japan, especially the "racial" affinities, would allow the Koreans to shed quickly their cultural thralldom to the Chinese. Certainly assimilation would be easier there than in Taiwan, which was more closely linked to China than Korea had been and which had never enjoyed any degree of political independence. And certainly it would be easier for the Japanese to assimilate the Koreans than for the Westerners to assimilate their subject peoples. The British, as Miura Hiroyuki pointed out, were able to integrate themselves into a unified state with the Indians, with whom they shared a common "Aryan" ancestry. If the British had been able to to do this, how much easier it would be for the Japanese in Korea, where there was a much stronger cultural and spiritual foundation for political unity.

Although the "common ancestry" theory represented a near consensus among the scholars, historians, politicians, educators, and journalists writing about Japanese-Korean relations, some doubters felt, largely on racial grounds, that assimilation could not be achieved very easily or very quickly. Yamamichi Jōichi saw the annexation of Korea as a Darwinian struggle between two races rather than as the reuniting of one divided race. As he observed of colonization in general, "The migration and aggression of superior peoples which accompanies the growth of population is a natural right that reflects the historical record

57. Ibid., 166, 176.

of human survival; when weak, small countries are absorbed by super-ior, large countries, it is a development fully in accord with the princi-ples of evolution."[58] While admitting great similarities between the Japanese and the Koreans, Yamamichi also pointed out that many of these were quite superficial. On the whole, he thought, the customs and manners of the Koreans were much closer to those of the Chinese. Ya-mamichi was deeply pessimistic that genuine "assimilation" would take place as quickly as many of the proponents of the "common ancestry" theory seemed to think. It could work only if the Japanese used "racial selection" as its method. By this he meant a policy of nurturing and protecting "superior" Koreans and weeding out the weaker or inferior, those "without the ability for economic development." Not surprisingly, he also thought it important for economic progress to send large num-bers of Japanese migrants to develop the peninsula.

What is most interesting about discussions of racial and historical origins of the Koreans and the Japanese is that all of them arrived ulti-mately at the same conclusion: that the Japanese annexation of Korea was natural, rational, and perhaps inevitable. For some the takeover was the upshot of a Darwinian struggle between weak and strong, but for most it was the result of a long and complex historical process of separation and reunion that stretched back into the realm of myth. This made it possible to portray the annexation (heigō) of Korea as an act of national integration rather than an act of imperialist subjugation. As Resident-General Terauchi told Prime Minister Yi Wan-yong on the eve of annexation, the two countries had long enjoyed an "inseparable re-lationship" (bunri subekarazaru kankei) and ought to reunite into "one body" (ittai).[59] Indeed, the term heigō is probably not best translated as "annexation," which implies the addition of one thing to another; it really means "amalgamation," a process of merger rather than a process of accretion. The colonial takeover, legitimized as an act of reunion, was thus hidden behind a façade of putative commonality between the dominator and the dominated.

58. Yamamichi, Chōsen hantō, 4.
59. Tokio, Chōsen heigōshi, 549.

Mimesis and Dependence

The residency-general headquarters, nestled on the slope of Mount Namsan overlooking the city of Seoul, was a fitting emblem of Japanese imperialism. With its mansard roofs and jutting wings, it was neither Japanese nor Korean in style but a distinctly Western structure that would not have been out of place in a European colonial capital. This resemblance should not surprise us. After all, Japanese imperialism, like so many other aspects of Meiji development, was an act of mimesis. The Meiji leaders, who avidly monitored world politics, crafted their expansionist policies along Western lines, deployed the same gunboat tactics to establish domination in Korea, and appealed to the same legal justification to legitimize it. In the same way, residency-general officials poured out annual reports filled with complaisant statistics on new roads laid, hospitals built, trees planted, crops harvested, railway lines extended, and trade promoted that were not so very different from reports produced by their counterparts in Western colonial regimes. And Japanese settlers, like Western colonials, carefully cordoned themselves off in segregated neighborhoods named after places back home and even established in Seoul a Nihon Club much like the clubs that dotted the British empire.

Indeed, one could argue that Korea was a laboratory where the Meiji leaders experimented with the various models of imperialism. In a sense, the Japanese experience in Korea recapitulated the process of slowly escalating domination that Ronald Robinson has described for the Western colonial experience.[1] First came the initial penetration through the establishment of a treaty structure; then a shift to more intrusive policy of concession diplomacy; next the establishment of indirect rule through the protectorate; and finally a full colonial takeover. Like the European colonial powers, the Japanese were seen from the Korean side not as bearers of the benefits of "civilization" but as predatory aggressors bent on compromising Korean sovereignty. And as was so often the case with the European colonialists, the Japanese failed to find Korean "friends" or create an effective collaborative structure. Ultimately, it was this failure that prodded the Japanese leadership to establish a permanent political and economic presence on the peninsula. Had the anxieties of the Meiji leadership been allayed by the emergence of a strong and actively modernizing elite willing to turn to Japan for help, perhaps the annexation of Korea might never have taken place.

To be sure, such a counterfactual argument can never be proven or disproven. It is also at variance with the view that the Meiji leaders were intent on making Korea into a colony, regardless of the difficulties or consequences, and that nothing would have stopped them, not even the emergence of an effective Korean reformist or modernizing regime. The view continues to be held by many nationalist historians in Korea and by anti-imperialist historians in Japan. But to me the historical record suggests much greater tentativeness in Japanese policy. The process of reaching consensus on what to do about Korea took several decades. Indeed, it could be argued that until the cabinet decision of May 1904 the Meiji leaders did not really make up their minds. Before that many alternatives were still possible, and if the Japanese had not won the Russo-Japanese War, these alternatives would have continued to be debated.

What ultimately enabled the Japanese to mimic Western imperialism was their simultaneous mimesis of other aspects of Western "wealth and power." By building a modern-style nation-state and a modern manufacturing sector, both buttressed by modern military and industrial technology, the Japanese acquired the material and social infrastructure needed for empire building. But however much Japanese practices of imperialist domination resembled those of the Western powers, it should be remembered that the Japanese arrived at them by a quite different historical route and under quite different historical circumstances.

---

1. Robinson, "Non-European Foundations of European Imperialism," in Owen and Sutcliffe, eds., *Studies in the Theory of Imperialism,* 117–42.

Indeed, Japan became an imperialist power while still subject to imperialist intrusion and bound by imperialist restraints. Memories of Western gunboat diplomacy remained vivid in the minds of the Meiji leaders, and reminders of Japan's "humiliation" persisted into the early years of the new century. It was not until early 1911, after the annexation of Korea had taken place, that Japan finally shed itself of the last vestiges of the "unequal treaties" imposed by the Western powers in the 1850s. In a formal sense Japan remained a "semicolony" even as it was acquiring a colonial empire of its own. Until the turn of the century, and even after that, many Westerners (and even many Japanese) thought of Japan as a "backward" society. And just as this historical experience put its imprint on the way Japan industrialized or constitutionalized itself, so too did it put an imprint on the way Japan became an imperialist power.

First, the military "backwardness" of Meiji Japan gave its imperialism a defensive cast. As suggested earlier, the encounter with Western imperialism nurtured in the Meiji leaders a "paranoid" vision of the international order. The Japanese justified the extension of political influence, and ultimately political sovereignty over Korea, as a means of protecting their country or, more grandiosely, "protecting the peace of the Orient" by preempting opportunities for Western territorial expansion and removing the Korean pawn from the Western rivalries in East Asia. At the same time, the Japanese leaders were acutely aware of their relative weakness toward the Westerners, whom at first they saw less as rivals than as powerful interlopers to be kept at arm's length. And since they saw Japan as still vulnerable to Western pressure, they knew that they had to have the cooperation of the Western powers if they wished to promote the further expansion of their power in East Asia. For example, in Korea the early attempt to build an informal empire had failed in large measure because the arrival of the Western powers limited the Meiji government's ability to act autonomously on the peninsula and encouraged the Korean elite to resist Japanese intrusion aggressively by using the other foreigners as a counterbalance. Rather than collaborate with the Japanese, the Korean court attempted to protect Korean independence by turning for help to the Chinese and then to the Russians. This strategy in turn increased Japanese anxiety about the future of Korea, anxiety that was resolved only by the victory over Russia.

The Meiji leaders, aware of Japan's position as a relatively weak latecomer, did their best to cultivate and encourage support from the most powerful of the advanced nations, especially the British, the premier colonial power and a keen rival of the Russians. In their negotiations with the Chinese after the Sino-Japanese War, for example, the Japanese not only attempted to acquire the same treaty privileges as the Western powers but to expand their treaty rights as well. Professor Nakatsuka has argued persuasively that the Japanese secured the right to establish manufacturing plants in the treaty ports, a privilege that the British had long sought, in order to win British support for the peace settlement. The British were well aware of what was happening. Indeed, a March 1895 cartoon in *Punch* showed a plucky little Japanese lad pulling the queue of a portly old Chinese and demanding that the "pig-headed old pigtail" give him the "keys of trade" to open up his shop.

From the Sino-Japanese War onward, but particularly after the Triple Intervention reminded them of their continuing vulnerability, the Japanese leaders continued to tread cautiously, appropriately solicitous of Western imperialist interests in East Asia. Although they had come to see the Russians as their new rivals for influence over Korea, the overall thrust of Japanese policy toward the czarist regime was conciliatory, at least until the military and naval buildup had been completed after the Sino-Japanese War. The attentiveness of the Japanese to defining clear spheres of interests in Korea and Manchuria, their acceptance of the Open Door note, their prompt dispatch of the largest military contingent to relieve the besieged legations during the Boxer Rebellion, their negotiation of bilateral treaties recognizing Western colonial rights and spheres of influence, and their willingness to keep markets open in Korea and Taiwan—all bespoke a strong sense that the success of territorial expansion in East Asia was dependent on the direct or indirect support of the Western powers.

These gestures of cooperation met with a positive response from the other imperialists, initially from the British and the Americans, later from the French and the Russians. As we have seen, for example, the American minister in Seoul, Horace Allen, had concluded by the time of the Russo-Japanese War that no harm would come to American interests as a result of Japanese domination of Korea. In a manner that echoed the Japanese justification of political intrusion, he argued that since the Koreans were clearly incapable of governing themselves, they needed an outside power to straighten them out and Japan was as suitable to that role as anyone else. As long as the Japanese maintained an "open" empire, which by and large they did through the 1910s, the Western powers saw them as no threat. Indeed, it was only during the 1920s, when the Japanese turned their attention to China, that the Americans and the British began to see them as hostile to their interests. But in Korea, where investment and trade were of only marginal importance, the Western powers were quite content to see the Japanese engaged in the "uplift" of the country.

Second, the relative economic "backwardness" of Japan made its imprint on the character of Meiji expansionism. As we have seen, Japan was still in the earliest stages of industrial development when its overseas expansion began in the 1890s. The agricultural sector of the economy still accounted for more than half of gainfully employed workers and for a little over 40 percent of the net domestic product.[2] At the time of the Sino-Japanese War the economy also bore the heavy imprint of incorporation into a world economy dominated by the Western industrial economies. In 1894 most of Japan's foreign trade was still handled by Western trading companies in Yokohama, Kobe, and the other ports, and most of it was still carried in Western bottoms. While the country was well on its way to self-sufficiency in light-industry products (cotton yarn and cloth, silk yarn and cloth), it was still heavily dependent on the import of foreign-made machinery and other producer durables. Most of Japan's iron and steel, steel steamships, railroad engines and rolling stock, pig iron, and so forth came from abroad. If not exactly undeveloped, Japan still remained well to the rear of the Western imperialist economies.

As a result, the Japanese were technologically and financially dependent on the West to sustain their expansion. In part, this dependence was manifest in the importation of military technology that Japan could not produce itself. While the country was on its way to becoming self-sufficient in the production of small arms and ordnance by the mid-1890s, so rudimentary was its industrial development that these weapons had to be produced with imported iron and steel. And weapon design lagged behind the most advanced technologies of the Western countries. During the Sino-Japanese War Japanese troops fought with nonrepeating Murata rifles and old-style artillery pieces cast in bronze; they possessed only ninety-six Maxim guns. Even more important was the lag in naval construction. The warships that made possible the victories over China and Russia were built not at home but in British and European shipyards. During the period 1896–1905, 88.6 percent of the

2. See Ohkawa and Shinohara, *Patterns of Japanese Economic Development*, table 2.1, p. 35.

tonnage of the Japanese Imperial Navy was of foreign manufacture, and only in 1910 did the first domestically produced battleship, the *Satsuma*, come off the ways.[3]

Although the Meiji leaders had been extremely reluctant to borrow abroad before the turn of the century, they relied heavily on foreign capital markets to finance the development of the empire. Between 1904 and 1913 the Japanese raised more than ¥2 billion in the money markets of New York, London, and Paris. About half of this sum went to pay the costs of the Russo-Japanese War; about 10 percent helped to finance two major government-sponsored colonial enterprises (the South Manchurian Railway Company and the Oriental Development Company); and another 30 percent was borrowed for railway development, including the Korean railway system.[4] So at least 60 percent (and possibly more) of Japan's foreign borrowing during this period supported imperialist expansion, including expansion in Korea. And there were other abortive attempts to attract foreign investment in the colonial empire: proposals for railway development in Taiwan, a plan to have an international consortium build railways in Korea, and the Katsura-Harriman plan for railroad development in Manchuria.

The relative backwardness of the economy, as we have seen, also limited the ability of Japanese capitalists and businessmen to exploit its economic opportunities overseas. While a small group of big firms like the NYK, the Dai-Ichi Bank, and the Ōkura-gumi early on played a role in developing Japan-Korea trade, for the most part big, capital-rich enterprises were reluctant to invest in the colonial territories like Korea or even to do a great deal of business there. Large-scale firms, whether banking or manufacturing, were content to invest their capital at home, much to the frustration of government leaders. In 1898 Ōishi Masami, the minister of commerce and agriculture, complained, "In China, as you know, the English, the Italians, and the French are turning their hand to railroad building, opening mines, constructing water control works, and getting permission to undertake manufacturing. But even though the citizens of these powers are moving ahead ... we do not hear of many Japanese turning their hands to such activities."[5] The only real investment bargain in Korea was land, but the most active investors, and the most numerous, were petty capitalists in the Japanese settlement

3. Fujii Shōichi, "Kindai gijutsu no dōnyū," in *Kindai (4)*, vol. 17 of *Iwanami kōza: Nihon rekishi* 85.
4. Feis, *Europe*, 422–29.
5. *Daisankai nōshōkō kōtō kaigiroku*, 652–53.

community. Even in China, with its vast potential market, it was not until World War I that large private firms like the major spinning companies began to make direct investments.

State capital rather than private capital played the principal role in developing an economic infrastructure in Korea. Although the government had withdrawn from direct manufacturing investment during the retrenchment of the 1880s, state investment remained important in the domestic economy, whether through the operation of enterprises like arsenals, steel foundries, railroads, and telegraph and telephone lines or through the management of a complex network of special banks. In 1897, 29.3 percent of the paid-in capital and capital reserves in manufacturing, mining, and transportation was invested in government-owned or government-operated enterprises; by 1902 the proportion had dropped to 27.2 percent; but after the nationalization of the railway system it rose again to 51.2 percent in 1907. In that year government-managed special banks also accounted for 38.5 percent of all the paid-in capital and deposits in banking.[6] It was only natural, then, that the government step in to support enterprises it considered essential to the construction of a colonial empire. After attempting to develop a railway network in Korea by giving indirect support to private capitalists, the government finally opted to take over the whole enterprise itself, and most of the road building, harbor development, and other infrastructural development on the peninsula after 1905 was financed by state capital. The quasi-governmental Oriental Development Company, although it ultimately proved a failure as an immigration company, likewise relied on heavy inputs of official capital and management.

The relative indifference of large-scale capitalists to the development of the colonial territories contrasted sharply with the activities of the petty capitalists and entrepreneurs who became the main force behind the development of trade with Korea. Trade developed not through a few large investments in an enclave but rather through the collective efforts of a large number of small entrepreneurs. As we have seen, adventuresome and often unscrupulous migrants swarmed to the peninsula after the Sino-Japanese War to seek their fortunes. Some brought a small stake of capital; others, like Conrad's Kurtz—"reckless without hardihood, greedy without audacity, cruel without courage"—arrived ready to exploit any opportunity that came their way. As the Osaka Chamber of Commerce mission quite correctly predicted, the main op-

6. Ishii, *Nihon keizaishi*, 191–92.

portunities on the peninsula were to be found in small, capital-poor enterprises, not in large, capital-intensive ones. And while the matter remains to be studied in greater detail, the postal deposit system at home, a mechanism for absorbing, accumulating, and aggregating the savings of the small farmer, the local landlord, and the small shopkeeper, likewise played a role in imperial development. These small deposits, channeled through the Industrial Development Bank, became an important source of capital for colonial enterprises. In other words, the shock troops of Japanese imperialism in Korea were not powerful metropolitan business interests but restless, ambitious, and frugal elements from the middle and lower strata of Japanese society.

Finally, the experience of the Japanese as the objects of Western imperialism made it possible for them to see themselves as victims even as they were victimizing others. Even in the 1890s, when foreign journalists began to write of the Japanese as the "Yankees of the Pacific" or the "Anglo-Saxons of the East," the Japanese were well aware of the cultural and social distance that separated them from the Westerners. If not quite Caliban, Japan was not yet Prospero. This ambiguous status led the Japanese to define their superiority over the Koreans as cultural or circumstantial rather than inherent or racial. The Japanese claim to superiority (and to "civilization") rested on the experience of their immediate past—their ability to overcome the backwardness that had once engulfed their own society. Indeed, Itō Hirobumi often invoked that experience to inspire the Korean cabinet and other members toward more vigorous reform efforts. Most members of the older generation, including the Meiji leaders themselves, realized that the "inferiority" of the Koreans was the product of history rather than race.

What created the difference between the Japanese and the Koreans, it was easy to conclude, was not some unbridgeable racial or cultural gap but simply political and social will. As a writer in the Chōsen shinpō pointed out in 1903, the Japanese had won the admiration of the foreigners by adapting their strengths and learning from them. "Does that mean, however," he asked, "that among the yellow race only the Japanese are superior in talent and wisdom or that they surpass others in insight and understanding? No, not at all. It is just that [the Japanese] exert themselves diligently, day and night, without ceasing."[7] If the Koreans were able to pull themselves together in a united effort to uplift their country, they too could achieve the same results as the Japanese,

7. Chōsen shinpō, Mar. 27, 1903.

and they too could become the object of foreign admiration. In short, what the Japanese had done was not beyond the reach of the Koreans—if only the Koreans started behaving like Japanese.

In other words, Japan's own historical experience was often cited as proof that it was possible for Korea to modernize too. While this view shared with the notion of a *mission civilatrice* a faith in the improvability of the human being, the Japanese, sharing a common ethnic background with the Koreans and other Asian peoples, were able to see themselves as having a special mission or special responsibility to help the Koreans overcome their backwardness. By suggesting that the Japanese were better able to introduce the Koreans to "civilization" than the Westerners, the Japanese privileged their own earlier "backwardness." As the first Asian people to break free of the thrall of Western imperialism, the Japanese had a kind of "yellow man's burden" to help their fellow Asians acquire the new knowledge and technology that would make them strong. To be sure, this sense of a pan-Asianist mission was not necessarily altruistic. It was justified on the grounds that Japan needed strong neighbors for its own self-protection. But altruistic or not, the fact that Japan had a unique experience in learning and assimilating lessons from the West made its justifications of domination rather different from those of the Western colonialist regimes.

The assimilationist doctrine of the new colonial government after 1910 very much reflected this vision of a pan-Asianist mission for Japan. When Korea was annexed in 1910, the Meiji emperor announced that the two peoples, the Japanese and Koreans, would live together in brotherhood. The implication was that the Japanese would treat the Koreans as members of the same family, an essentially nonracist conception of the colonial relationship. Indeed, the family metaphor was a recurring element in the rhetoric of the colonial administration, for it suggested that assimilation was natural. After all, what could be more totally fused, more totally consolidated, or more totally inseparable than a family?

The adoption of assimilationist rhetoric allowed the Japanese to argue that Korea was not a colony at all, at least not in the sense that European overseas possession were. In European colonies the rulers were completely alien, with no basis for commonality with the dominated peoples; hence, in the Japanese view, they tended to be rapacious, selfish, and exploitative. But in a territory like Korea, where the people not only shared culture and history with the Japanese but were also part of one common "family," exploitation was ipso facto impossible. As a Diet member observed in 1910:

> As you well know, what the British are doing in India and what the French are doing in Annam is far from what our country is doing in Korea. I do not need to tell you that Korea and our empire have had a common history for tens of centuries, and that they are countries sharing a common language and a common race. The relationship ... is deep, like the two wheels of a cart. Since each is individually weak, neither can stand by itself.

The conclusion was obvious: Japan was helping the Koreans to improve themselves; it was not exploiting them. The relationship was not oppressive but reciprocal or complementary like the two wheels of the cart or like two brothers in a family.

The family metaphor, however, suggested that the relationship between the two societies was vertical and asymmetrical as well. In a Japanese family, or indeed in a Korean family, older brother and younger were not equals, nor were brothers and sisters. Even though the Koreans might be described as members of the same family as the Japanese, that did not necessarily imply that they should be treated as having full parity with the Japanese. A sense of hierarchy was implicit in the family metaphor, just as it was implicit in the "family state" metaphor that was becoming current in Japanese politics in the 1890s. An assimilationist policy justified by a family metaphor thus permitted the Japanese to subordinate the Koreans, politically and socially, while explaining this differential treatment as natural—just as it was natural that an older brother command the respect of a younger brother.

The ideology of Japanese imperialism in Korea thus took on forms that had a distinctive cultural cast. The "yellow man's burden" was not quite the same as the "white man's burden," and the "enlightenment" of the Korean people was not quite the same as the *mission civilatrice*. The shared history, culture, and ethnic background permitted the Japanese to imagine a degree of commonality with the Koreans that Western colonialists could not establish so facilely with the natives whom they ruled. In the final analysis, this imagined commonality did not make much difference to the Koreans, but it may have encouraged the Japanese to offer opportunities to the Koreans within the colonial structure that were not available to other colonial peoples. The Korean subalterns working for the Japanese colonial state may have been more numerous if not more powerful than those in Western colonial regimes, and some have pointed out that many played a pivotal role in the post-1945 reconstruction of Korea as an independent state.

In sum, although the Meiji Japanese mimicked the imperialist culture system that developed in the West, Meiji imperialism was the imperialism of a backward or follower country. It was characterized by a psychology of inferiority vis-à-vis the West, a desire to catch up with the more advanced economies, limited foreign contacts, dependency on the import of capital goods, a lack of political leverage over the advanced powers, and a high degree of state involvement in economic development.

This conclusion is not exactly novel. Ever since the 1920s Japanese analyses of Meiji imperialism have stressed the difficulty of fitting it into the Western model. In the late 1920s Takahashi Kamekichi, a young economic critic, precipitated a controversy over the nature of Meiji imperialism by denying that the Leninist hypothesis fit the Japanese case.[8] In two provocative essays written in 1927 he argued that although Japanese capitalism had reached a "dead end," it had not yet reached the final stage of "monopoly capitalism" or "imperialism." If Japan was an imperialist country, it was a "petty imperialist" whose interests were closer to those countries under Western control than to the imperialist countries themselves. The wars that Japan fought to build its empire in the Meiji period were not "imperialist wars" but "nationalist wars" intended to maintain Japan's independence.[9] The "deadlock" that the Japanese economy faced was to be explained not by the internal contradictions that characterized the "imperialist" stage but by other factors, such as the evaporation of advantages Japan had enjoyed during the Meiji era (unexploited natural resources and cheap labor), or by changes in the international environment (competition from countries like China, the maintenance of the international status quo by the Western nations, dependence on the outside world for industrial resources).

The implication of Takahashi's argument was that Japan expanded in response to external circumstances, not as the result of internal economic changes, and that its expansion was an appropriate response to Western intrusion in Asia. Over the next decade rejoinders to Takaha-

8. A useful survey of the debate within the Left may be found in Hoston, *Marxism and Prewar Japan*, esp. chs. 4 and 7. See also Fujii, *Nihon teikokushugi*, 9–43.

9. "Japan's wars with China and Russia were all wars [waged] for the sake of Japan's independence and self-support," he wrote. Quoted in Hoston, *Marxism and Prewar Japan*, 87.

shi's "petty imperialism" thesis, and rejoinders to those rejoinders, generated a massive literature on the nature of Japanese imperialism. The counterattack, led by two Marxist scholars, Norō Eitarō and Inomata Tsunao, rested on a search for evidence to support the explanatory value of the Leninist hypothesis.

Since the Meiji economy offered scant evidence of having reached the stage of "finance capital" or "monopoly capitalism," it became necessary to deploy alternative interpretive approaches. One approach was to push Japan's entry in the "final stage of capitalism" forward in time to the post–World War I period, when there was stronger evidence for the emergence of finance capital, the acceleration of monopolization, and the export of capital, and to dismiss Meiji expansion as "premature," that is, not a good fit for the Leninist model. Another approach was to present Lenin's criteria for "the stage of imperialism" as attributes of world capitalism rather than of any specific national capitalism. This tactic allowed scholars to site Meiji Japan in the "final stage of capitalism" without arguing that it was "imperialist" in the Leninist sense. In an interesting essay that anticipated the Wallersteinian categories (core, periphery, and semiperiphery), Inomata suggested that there were three types of political economies in the world: the imperialist economies, in which finance capital had emerged as the dominant force; the colonial and semicolonial economies under imperialist control; and intermediate or developing (*hasseiteki*) economies that had not yet reached the stage of finance capital but had adopted imperialist policies in reaction or resistance to the intrusion of the imperialists. Japan, of course, fit into the last of these categories but was trying to become part of the first.[10]

The debate shifted ground with the promulgation of the 1932 Comintern theses on Japan. This document attempted to explain the peculiarities of Japanese imperialism rather than to fit Japan into Leninist theory. What prompted the 1932 theses was the need to devise a political analysis of the rising influence of the militarists in Japan. Instead of stressing Japan's development, the theses stressed Japan's backwardness, explaining Meiji imperialism not by the emergence of capitalism but by the persistence of remnants from the past. The theses argued that Japan was ruled by a "special sort of imperialist class" an alliance of "Asiatic feudalistic exploiters" and "capitalist investors who acquire astounding wealth at an astounding rate of speed." This alliance sup-

10. Inomata, "Teikokushugi riron to botsuraku katei."

ported the creation of an absolutist state and the buildup of a strong military, which pursued an aggressive foreign policy. Meiji imperialism could not be explained simply by internal "needs" or "demands" of the capitalist class. The interests and motives of the militarists had to be taken into account as well.[11] In other words, Meiji imperialism was not "modern imperialism" (i.e., imperialism as Lenin defined it) but "feudalistic-militaristic imperialism."

In this interpretation "state capital," as opposed to "finance capital," played a crucial role in expansion. In 1941, for example, Hosokawa Karoku argued that "state capital" enabled Japan to overcome its lag behind the Western countries, which had reached the stage of "finance capital." In order to industrialize rapidly, Japan had to move directly from handicraft production to modern industrial production, skipping the stage of "manufacture" that Western capitalism had traversed. Capital accumulated by the Tokugawa merchant class was inadequate to the task of rapid industrialization, so the Meiji state accelerated capital accumulation by adopting a new land tax system, establishing a nonconvertible currency, and issuing public bonds. "State capital" played a critical role not only in internal economic development but also in expansion abroad. Private capital was involved in expansion, to be sure, but it was "industrial capital," not "finance capital." Since feudal exploitation of the peasantry persisted in the agricultural sector, peasant households remained impoverished and the domestic market remained limited. When the cotton-spinning industry, the vanguard of industrial capitalism, found itself faced with a crisis of excess production in 1890, the cotton spinners sought to escape from this crisis by expanding markets in Korea and China.[12]

As Japan launched on a new phase of expansion in the late 1930s, interpretations of Meiji imperialism as a response to Western intrusion gained currency. To explain contemporary foreign policy plausibly, Japanese scholars and intellectuals constructed a narrative of Japan's modern history that put "Western pressure" or "Western aggression" at the center. To be sure, there was abundant evidence that the Westerners represented a hostile, intrusive, and disruptive force in mid-nineteenth-century Asia and that the Meiji leaders had attempted to defend themselves by an aggressive foreign policy. It was more difficult to explain why it was that the Meiji leaders had expanded into the rest of Asia as a

11. "The Situation in Japan and the Tasks of the Japanese Community Party," *Communist International* 9.7 (1932).
12. Hosokawa, *Shokuminchi*, 39–41.

way of responding to Western intrusion. To do so required explaining why Japan's neighbors were even more backward than itself.[13]

Postwar discussion of Japanese imperialism has tended to focus on the post–World War I period, which offers a more suitable match between Leninist theory and Japanese evidence, but a rough scholarly consensus emerged that Meiji imperialism was not "modern imperialism" but a "feudalistic-militaristic imperialism" associated with the establishment of the "emperor system." For example, Inoue Kiyoshi, doyen of the historiographical left in the 1950s and 1960s, argued that

> the modern emperor system was expansionist even as it was coming into being. It goes without saying that the external aggression of the emperor system possessed none of the characteristics of modern imperialism.... Japanese capitalism, of course, was not yet at the stage of monopoly capitalism, and industrial capital was not yet firmly established. The demands of capital were not the motive force that brought on the Sino-Japanese War. As we have pointed out in detail, the starting point was the peculiar expansionism of the semifeudal authoritarian emperor system, and it was the same as the "feudalistic, militaristic imperialism" that constituted one aspect of the external policies of Russian czarism.

Only after the Sino-Japanese War did there emerge a "dual structure imperialism," combining elements of both "modern imperialism" and "feudalistic-militaristic imperialism" and reflecting the coalition between "bourgeois" and "absolutist" elements on which the Meiji state rested.[14] Ironically, this line of interpretation is much closer to Schumpeter than to Lenin.

It is tempting to assert, as the Japanologist is so often tempted when making cross-cultural comparisons, that these characteristics made Meiji imperialism "unique." But the appearance of "uniqueness" may depend on an inappropriate comparison. Instead of measuring Japanese imperialism against British or French, we should measure it against the imperialist enterprises of other follower countries—perhaps most appropriately, as Inoue Kiyoshi pointed out, Japan's chief rival in East Asia, czarist Russia. Like the Meiji leaders, the late-nineteenth-century Russian leadership was intensely concerned about the activities of the more advanced countries on its borders; they too were haunted by a sense of cultural and political insecurity toward the West, particularly after their defeat in the Crimean War; they too invoked pan-nationalist slogans to

---

13. Ibid., 32–35.
14. Inoue, *Nihon teikokushugi no keisei*, 26, 150–51.

justify their incursions into the Balkans and Northeast Asia; they too presided over an economy that still remained largely agrarian; and they too relied heavily on state investment to develop their spheres of influence. While these comparisons are superficial, they do suggest that the analysis of nineteenth-century imperialism needs to develop a more complex morphology that will disaggregate it into "advanced" and "backward" forms—and perhaps start with Japan as a model for the latter.

Bibliography

Ajia Keizai Kenkyūjo Tosho Shiryōbu, comp. *Kyū shokuminchi kankei kikan kankōbutsu sōgō mokuroku (Chōsen hen)*. Vol. 2. Tokyo: Ajia Keizai Kenkyūjo, 1974.

Allen, Horace N. "An Acquaintance with Yuan Shih-kai." *North American Review*, July 1912.

——. *Korea: Fact and Fancy*. Seoul: Methodist Publishing House, 1904.

——. *Things Korean: A Collection of Sketches and Anecdotes, Missionary and Diplomatic*. New York: Revell, 1908.

An U-sik. *Tennō to Chōsenjin*. Tokyo: Sanichi Shobō, 1977.

Ando Sōjirō. *Hokkaidō iminseisaku shi*. Tokyo: Seikatsusha, 1941.

Aoki Kayoko. "Tōyō kaitaku kabushiki kaisha no seiritsu." *Chōsen kindaishi shiryō kenkyū shūsei* 3 (May 1960).

Aoki Koichi. "Fukuzawa Yūkichi no Chōsenron." *Ronsō* (Yokohama Shiritsu Daigaku) 32.1 (1981).

——. "Pak Yŏng-hyo no minponshugi shinminron minzoku kakumeiron." Parts 1 and 2. *Chōsen gakuhō* 80 (July 1976); 82 (Jan. 1977).

Aoyagi Tsunatarō. *Chōsen tōchi ron*. Seoul: Chōsen Kenkyūkai, 1923.

——. *Kankoku shokuminsaku*. Seoul: Nikkan Shobō, 1908.

——. *Shin Chōsen*. Seoul: Chōsen Kenkyūkai, 1916.

——. *Sōtoku seijishi ron*. Seoul: n.p., 1928.

——, ed. *Chōsen*. Seoul: Chōsen Kenkyūkai, 1913.

Arakawa Gorō. *Saikin Chōsen jijō*. Tokyo: Shimizu Shoten, 1906.

Arendt, Hannah. *The Origins of Totalitarianism*. New York: Harcourt, Brace, 1951.

Asada Kyōji. "Kyūshokuminchi Chōsen ni okeru Nihonjin ōjinushi kaikyū no henkō katei." *Nōgyō sōgō kenkyū* 20.1 (Jan. 1966).

————. "Nihon shokuminshi kenkyū no kadai to hōhō." *Rekishi hyōron*, no. 308 (1975).

————. *Nihon teikokushugika no minzoku kakumei undō*. Tokyo: Miraisha, 1973.

————. *Nihon teikokushugi to kyūshokuminchi jinushisei*. Tokyo: Ochano-mizu Shobō, 1968.

————. "Saikin ni okeru Nihon shokuminshi kenkyū no mondaiten." *Shakai kagaku shigaku* 42.3 (1976).

Ash, James Kenneth. "The Tonghak Rebellion: Problems and Interpretations." *Journal of Social Sciences and Humanities* (Bulletin of the Korean Research Center) 32 (March 1970).

A. W. D. *Notes on Korea*. Shanghai: Shanghai Mercury, 1884.

Baba Tsunego. *Kiuchi Jūshirō den*. Tokyo: Herarudosha, 1937.

Bannō Junji. *Kindai Nihon no gaikō to seiji*. Tokyo: Kyūbun Shuppan, 1985.

————. *Meiji kenpō taisei no kakuritsu*. Tokyo: Tōkyō Daigaku Shuppankai, 1971.

Barzun, Jacques. *Race: A Study in Superstition*. New York: Harper and Row, 1965.

Beasley, W. G. *Japanese Imperialism, 1894–1945*. Oxford: Clarendon Press, 1987.

Best, Gary Dean. "Financial Diplomacy: The Takahashi Korekiyo Mission of 1904–1905." *Asian Studies* 12.1 (Apr. 1974).

Bishop, Isabella L. Bird. *Korea and Her Neighbors: A Narrative of Travel with an Account of the Recent Vicissitudes and Present Condition*. 2 vols. London: John Murray, 1897.

Brierly, J. L. *The Law of Nations*. Oxford: Clarendon Press, 1955.

Brown, Sidney Devere, and Akiko Hirota, trans. *The Diary of Kido Takayoshi*. 2 vols. Tokyo: University of Tokyo Press, 1983, 1985.

Brudnoy, David. "Japan's Experiment in Korea." *Monumenta Nipponica* 25 (1970).

Burnett, Scott S. *Korean-American Relations: Documents Pertaining to the Far Eastern Diplomacy of the United States*. Vol. 3, *The Period of Diminishing Influence, 1896–1905*. Honolulu: University of Hawaii Press, 1989.

Bury, J. P. T., ed. *New Cambridge Modern History*. Vol. 11, *Material Progress and Worldwide Problems: 1870–1898*, ed. F. H. Hinsley. Cambridge: Cambridge University Press, 1962.

Center for East Asian Cultural Studies. *Meiji Japan Through Contemporary Eyes*. 3 vols. Tokyo: Center for East Asian Cultural Studies, 1969–70.

Chandra, Vipan. "The Independence Club and Korea's First Proposal for a National Legislative Assembly." *Occasional Papers on Korea* 4 (Sept. 1975).

————. "Nationalism and Popular Participation in Goverment in Late Nineteenth Century Korea." Ph.D diss., Harvard University, 1977.

————. "An Outline Study of the Ilchin-hoe (Advancement Society) of Korea." *Occasional Papers on Korea* 2 (Mar. 1974).

Chien, Frederick Foo. *The Opening of Korea: A Study of Chinese Diplomacy, 1876–1885*. Hamden, Conn.: Shoestring Press, 1967.

Cho Ki-jun. *Hanguk kiopka sa*. Seoul: Pakyongsa, 1974.

————. *Kindai Kankoku keizaishi*. Trans. Suh Yon-dal. Tokyo: Kōrai Shorin, 1981.

Ch'oe Lew-pyong. "Kankoku no bōeki dōkō 1877–1911." *Ajia keizai* 15.1 (Jan. 1974).

Choi, Kyung Ju. "Korea: The Politics of Survival, 1894–1905." Ph.D. diss., University of Pennsylvania, 1978.

Choi, Woonsang. *The Fall of the Hermit Kingdom*. Dobbs Ferry, N.Y.: Oceana Publications, 1967.

Chōsen Bōeki Kyōkai, comp. *Chōsen bōeki shi*. Seoul, 1943.

Chōsen bōtō tōbatsu shi. Yongsan: Chōsen Chūsatsugun Shireibu, 1913.

Chōsen jūgun tosen annai. Osaka, 1894.

Chōsen Kaitaku Kabushiki Kaisha, comp. *Chōsen kaitaku kabushiki kaisha enkaku*. 1937.

Chōsen Kenkyūkai, ed. *Shin Chōsenshi nyūmon*. Tokyo: Ryūei Shosha, 1981.

Chōsen kōgyō kabushiki kaisha sanjū shūnen kinenshi. Tokyo: Chōsen Kōgyō Kabushiki Kaisha, 1936.

Chōsen Menshifusho Rengōkai, comp. *Chōsen mengyō shi*. Seoul, 1929.

Chōsen Nichinichi Shinbun, comp. *Hyakuen no shoshihon: Tōkan seikōhō*. Toyko: Jitsugyō no Getsu Honsha, 1910.

Chōsen nōkaihō. 1935.

Chōsen Shinbun, comp. *Chōsen jinji kōshinroku*. Seoul, 1922.

Chōsen Shinbunsha, comp. *Chōsen tōchi no kaikō to hihan*. Seoul, 1936.

Chōsen Shōkō Kaigisho, comp. *Shisei nijūgo nen kinen: Kaikō shōkō zadankai roku*. 1935.

Chōsen Sōtokufu, comp. *Chōsen Sotokufu tōkei nenpō*. Seoul, 1912–43.

————. *Shisei nijūgo shūnen shi*. Seoul, 1935.

Chōsen tetsudō shi. Seoul: Chōsen Sōtokufu Tetsudōkyoku, 1915.

Chōsen Tōkanfu Sōmubu, ed. *Zai-Kan honpōjin jōkyō ichiranpyō*. Seoul, 1907.

Chōsen Zasshisha. *Saikin Chōsen yōran*. Seoul: Nikkan Shobō, 1910.

Chung, Henry. *The Case of Korea: A Collection of Evidence on the Japanese Domination of Korea, and on the Development of the Korean Independence Movement*. New York: Revell, 1921.

Clark, Donald N. "Yun Ch'i-ho (1864–1945): Portrait of a Korean Intellectual in an Era of Transition." *Occasional Papers on Korea* 4 (Sept. 1975).

Clark, Grover. *A Place in the Sun*. New York: Macmillan, 1936.

Conroy, Hilary. *The Japanese Seizure of Korea, 1868–1910: A Study of Realism and Idealism in International Relations*. Philadelphia: University of Pennsylvania Press, 1960.

Cook, Harold Francis. *Korea's 1884 Incident: Its Background and Kim Ok-kyun's Elusive Dream*. Royal Asiatic Society Korea Branch Monograph Series, no. 4. Seoul: Taewon Publishing, 1972.

————. "Pak Young-hyo: Background and Early Years." *Journal of Social Sciences and Humanities* (Bulletin of the Korean Research Center) 31 (Dec. 1969).

Curtis, L. P., Jr. *Anglo-Saxons and Celts: A Study of Anti-Irish Prejudice in Victorian England*. Bridgeport, Conn.: University of Bridgeport, 1968.

Curzon, George Nathaniel. *Problems of the Far East: Japan, Korea, China*. London: Longmans, Green, 1984.

Daisankai nōshōkō kōtō kaigiroku. N.p.: n.p., n.d.

Davis, Lance E., and Robert A. Huttenback. *Mammon and the Pursuit of Empire.* Abridged ed. Cambridge: Cambridge University Press, 1988.

Denny, Owen N. *China and Korea,* Shanghai: Kelly and Walsh, 1888.

Deuchler, Martina. *Confucian Gentlemen and Barbarian Envoys: The Opening of Korea, 1875–1885.* Published for the Korea Branch of the Royal Asiatic Society. Seattle: University of Washington Press, 1977.

Dong, Chon. "Korea and the Russo-Japanese War." *Koreana Quarterly* 1 (winter 1959).

Eckert, Carter J. *Offspring of Empire: The Koch'ang Kims and the Colonial Origins of Korean Capitalism, 1876–1945.* Cambridge: Harvard University Press, 1991.

Egi Tasuka. *Shokumin ronsaku.* Tokyo: Shūseido, 1910.

Enomoto Morie, and Kimi Nobuhiko. *Hokkaidō no rekishi: Kenshi shirizu.* Vol. 1. Tokyo: Yamakawa Shuppansha, 1970.

Feis, Herbert. *Europe, The World's Banker, 1870–1914: An Account of European Foreign Investment and the Connection of World Finance with Diplomacy Before the War.* New Haven: Yale University Press, 1930.

Fieldhouse, D. K. *The Colonial Empires: A Comparative History from the Eighteenth Century.* 2d ed. London: Weidenfeld and Nicholson, 1966.

———. *Colonialism, 1870–1945.* London: Weidenfeld and Nicholson, 1981.

———. *Economics and Empire, 1830–1914.* Ithaca: Cornell University Press, 1973.

Fujii Kantarō. "Fujii Kantarō jijoden." Unpublished MS. (1940?). Library of the Yūho Kyōkai, Tokyo.

Fujii Shōichi et al., eds. *Nihon teikokushugi.* Vol. 19 of *Shinpojiamu Nihon rekishi.* Tokyo: Gakusei Shuppan, 1975.

Fujimura Michio. "Meiji ishin gaikō no kyū kokusai kankei e no taiō: Nisshin shūkō jōki no seiritsu o megutte." *Nagoya Daigaku Bungakubu ronshū: Shigaku* 14.3 (1966).

———. "Meiji shonen ni okeru Ajiya seisaku no shūsei to Chūgoku: Nisshin shuko jōki sōan no kentō." *Nagoya Daigaku Bungakubu ronshū: Shigaku* 15.3 (1967).

Fujimura Michitaka. *Nisshin sensō.* Tokyo: Iwanami Shoten, 1973.

Fujimura Tokuichi, ed. *Kyoryūmin no mukashi monogatari.* Seoul: Chōsen Nisekikai Jimushō, 1927.

Fujiwara Akira. *Gunjishi.* Tokyo: Tōyō Keizai Shinpōsha, 1961.

Fukuzawa Masanobu. *Kankoku jitsugyō kanken.* Nagano: Fukuzawa Masanobu, 1906.

Furuya Tetsuo. *Nichi-Rō sensō.* Tokyo: Chūō Kōronsha, 1956.

Gaimushō, ed. *Komura gaikōshi.* 2 vols. Tokyo: Shinbun Gekkansha, 1953.

———, ed. *Nihon gaikō nenpyō oyobi shuyō bunsho.* 2 vols. Tokyo: Gaimushō, 1965–66.

Gaimushō Tsūshōkyoku, ed. *Kankoku jijō.* Tokyo, 1904.

———, ed. *Ryoken kafusu oyobi imin tōkei.* Tokyo, 1921.

Gallagher, John, and Ronald Robinson. "The Imperialism of Free Trade." *Economic Review,* 2d ser., 6 (1953): 1–15.

Genzan Shōkō Kaigisho, comp. *Genzan shōkō kaigisho rokujū nen shi.* Wŏn-san, 1942.

Girard, L. "Transport." In *The Industrial Revolution and After.* Vol. 6 of M. Postan and H. H. Habakkuk, eds., *The Cambridge Economic History of Europe.* Cambridge: Cambridge University Press, 1965.

Gotō Akira et al., eds. *Jiyū minken shisō.* Vol. 1 of *Shiryō: Nihon shakai undōshi shisōshi: Meiji ki.* Tokyo: Aoki Shoten, 1968.

Gotō Shinpei. *Nihon shokumin seisaku ippan: Nihon bōchō ron.* Tokyo, 1944.

Gregart, Edwin Harold. "Land Ownership in Korea under Japanese Colonial Rule, 1900–1935." Ph.D. diss., Columbia University, 1982.

Hagiwara Hikozō. *Kankoku zaisei no seri kaikaku.* Tokyo: Yūhō Kyōkai, 1966.

Han, Sang-il. "Uchida Ryohei and Japanese Continental Expansionism, 1874–1916." Ph.D. diss., Claremont Graduate School, 1974.

Hanguksa. 19. Kundae. Taehan cheguk ui chongmalkwa uibyong hangjaeng. Seoul: Kuk'sa P'yonch'an ui Wonhoe, 1978.

Hara Kei. *Nikki.* Ed. Hara Shuichirō. 8 vols. Tokyo: Kengensha, 1950–51.

Harada Katsumasa. "Chōsen heigō to shoki no shokuminchi kei'ei." *Nihon rekishi.* Vol. 1 of *Gendai.* Tokyo: Iwanami Shoten, 1963.

Harada Tamaki. "Chōsen no kindaika kōsō—Yu Kil-chun to Pak Yŏng-hyo no dokuritsu shisō." *Shigaku kenkyū* (Hiroshima Daigaku), no. 143 (June 1979).

———. "Jūkyū seiki no Chōsen ni okeru taigaiteki ishiki." *Chōsenshi Kenkyūkai ronbunshū* 21 (Mar. 1984).

Haraguchi Munehisa, ed. *Meiji ishin.* Vol. 9 of *Ronshū Nihon rekishi.* Tokyo: Yuseido, 1973.

Harrington, Fred Harvey. *God, Mammon, and the Japanese: Dr. Horace N. Allen and Korean-American Relations, 1884–1905.* Madison: University of Wisconsin Press, 1944.

Haruyama Meitetsu and Masahiro Wakabayashi. *Nihon shokuminshugi no seijiteki tenkai: 1895–1934.* Tokyo: Ajia Seikei Gakkai, 1980.

Hasegawa Zensaku, ed. *Kaigai ijū shinhattenchi annai.* Tokyo: Naigai Shuppankyōkai, 1911.

Hashikawa Bunsō. *Ōka monogatari.* Tokyo: Chikuma Shobō, 1976.

Hatada Takashi. "Kindai ni okeru Chōsenjin no Nihonkan." *Shisō,* no. 520 (Oct. 1967).

———. "Nihonjin no Chōsen kan." In Hatada, ed., *Nihon to Chōsen.* Tokyo, 1960.

———. *Nihonjin no Chōsenkan.* Tokyo: Keisō Shobō, 1969.

Hatada Takashi Sensei Kinenkai, comp. *Chōsen rekishi ronshū.* 2 vols. Tokyo: Ryūkeisha, 1979.

Hatori Yoshihiko. *Chōsen ni okeru shokuminchi kahei no keisei.* Tokyo: Miraisha, 1986.

Hayashi Gonsuke. *Waga nanajū nen o kataru.* Tokyo: Dai-Ichi Shobō, 1935.

Hayashi Seizō. *Kōya no ishi: Utsukushiki shinjū o sagasu shōnin monogatari.* Tokyo: 1964.

Hayes, Carleton J. H. *A Generation of Materialism, 1871–1900.* New York: Harper and Bros., 1941.

Headrick, Daniel R. *The Tentacles of Progress: Technological Transfer in the Age of Imperialism, 1850–1940.* New York: Oxford University Press, 1988.
———. *The Tools of Empire: Technology and European Imperialism in the Nineteenth Century.* New York: Oxford University Press, 1981.
Henderson, Gregory. *Korea: The Politics of the Vortex.* Cambridge: Harvard University Press, 1968.
Higuchi Yuichi. "Nisshin sensōka Chōsen in okeru Nihonjin no katsudō." *Kaikyō* 8 (Dec. 1978).
Hirata Kenichi. "Chōsen heigō to Nihon no yōron." *Shirin* 57.3 (May 1974).
Hiratsuka Atsushi, ed. *Itō Hirobumi hiroku.* 3 vols. Tokyo: Shunjunsha, 1929–30.
Hirose Kiyoko. "Kanghwa jiken no shūhen." *Kokusai seiji,* no. 37 (Oct. 1968).
———. "Kanghwa jōyaku no seiritsu o megutte." *Kokusai seiji,* no. 41 (Apr. 1970).
———. "Nisshin sensōzen no Igirisu kyokutō seisaku no ichi kōsatsu: Chōsen mondai o chūshin to shite." *Kokusai seiji* 51 (Oct. 1974).
Hiroshima Chōsen Shisatsudan. *Chōsen shisatsu gaiyō.* Hiroshima: N.p., 1913.
Hisama Ken'ichi. *Chōsen nōgyō keiei chitai no kenkyū.* Tokyo: Nōgyō Sōgō Kenkyū Kai, 1951.
———. *Chōsen nōgyō no kindaiteki yōsō.* Tokyo: Nishigahara Kankōkai, 1935.
Ho Taku-shu. "Chin-Futsu sensōki ni okeru Nihon tai-Kan seisaku." *Shirin* 43.3 (May 1960).
Hobsbawm, Eric. *The Age of Empire: 1875–1914.* New York: Pantheon, 1987.
Hobson, J. A. *Imperialism.* Ann Arbor: University of Michigan Press, 1971.
Hokkaidō Daigaku Fuzoku Toshokan, comp. *Kyūgaichi kankei shiryō mokuroku: Chōsen, Taiwan, Manshū.* Sapporo: Hokkaidō Daigaku Fuzoku Toshokan, 1975.
Honda Kosuke. *Chōsen nōgyō yōkō.* N.p.: n.p., 1905.
Hori Washō. "Nihon teikokushugi no Chōsen ni okeru nōgyō seisaku—1920 nendai shokuminchi jinushisei no keisei." *Nihonshi kenkyū,* no. 171 (Nov. 1976).
Hōsei Daigaku Bungakubu Shigakubu Kenkyūshitsu, comp. *Nihon jinbutsu bunken mokuroku.* Tokyo: Heibonsha, 1974.
Hosoi Hajime. *Gendai Kanjo no fuun to meishi.* Seoul: Nikkan Shobō, 1910.
Hosokawa Karoku. *Shokuminchi.* Vol. 10 of *Gendai Nihon bunmeishi.* Tokyo: Tōkyō Keizai Shinpōsha Shuppanbu, 1941.
Hosono Kōji. "Tōyō meishūron to 'Datsu-A' ron no riji." *Shakai kagaku tōkyu* 27.1.
Hoston, Germaine. *Marxism and the Crisis of Development in Prewar Japan.* Princeton: Princeton University Press, 1986.
Hulbert, Homer B. *The History of Korea.* 2 vols. Seoul: Methodist Publishing House, 1905.
———. *The Passing of Korea.* New York: Doubleday Page, 1906.
Hunter, Janet. "Japanese Government Policy, Business Opinion, and the Seoul–Pusan Railroad, 1894–1906." *Modern Asian Studies* 11.4 (Oct. 1977).
Iizumi Kanda. "Watakushi no shūshoku undō." In *Zuihitsu Chōsen.* 1935.

Im Chong-guk et al. *Souru jōka ni Han-kō nagareru: Chōsen fūzoku shi yawa.* Tokyo: Heibonsha, 1987.

Im Pyong-yun. *Shokuminchi ni okeru shōgyōteki nōgyō no tenkai.* Tokyo: Tōkyō Daigaku Shuppankai, 1971.

Imamura Takeshi. "Hanseikizen no Chōsen Nikkan heigō zengo no omoide." *Chōsen kindai shiryō kenkyū shūsei* 3 (May 1960).

Inada Shunosuke. *Shokumin seisaku.* Tokyo: Yūhikaku, 1918.

Inomata Tsunao. *Teikokushugi kenkyū.* Tokyo: Kaizōsha, 1928.

———. "Teikokushugi riron to botsuraku katei." *Shakai kagaku: Teikokushugi kenkyū,* Apr. 1927.

Inoue Kaoru Kō Denki Hensankai. *Segai Inoue Kaoru Kō den.* 5 vols. Tokyo: Naigai Shoseki Kabushiki Kaisha, 1933–34.

Inoue Kiyoshi. *Nihon teikokushugi no keisei.* Tokyo: Iwanami Shoten, 1968.

Ishii Kanji. *Nihon keizaishi.* Tokyo: Tōkyō Daigaku Shuppankai, 1980.

———. "Nisshin sengo keiei." *Iwanami kōza: Nihon rekishi* 16 *(Kindai* 3). Tokyo: Iwanami Shoten, 1976.

———. "Seiritsu-ki Nihon teikokushugi no ichi danmen." *Rekishigaku kenkyū* (Apr. 1972).

Itagaki Taisuke. "Shokuminron." In Itagaki Morimasa, ed., *Itagaki Taisuke zenshū.* Tokyo: Bunshunsha, 1933.

Itō Chōjirō. *Kankoku oyobi Kyūshū dan.* Tokyo: Itō Chōjirō, 1905.

Itō Hirobumi and Hiratsuka Atsushi, eds. *Hisho ruisan: Chōsen kōshō shiryō.* Rev. ed. 3 vols. Tokyo: Hisho Ruisan Kankōkai, 1934–36.

Itō Hirobumi den. Ed. Shunpō Kō Tsuishōkai. 3 vols. Tokyo: Tōseisha, 1943.

Itō Hirobumi Kankei Monjo Kenkyūkai. *Itō Hirobumi kankei monjo.* 9 vols. Tokyo: Hanawa Shobō, 1973–81.

Itō Seizō. *Kankoku shokumin kanken.* Tokyo: Zenkoku Nōjikai, 1907.

Jansen, Marius B. *The Japanese and Sun Yat-sen.* Cambridge: Harvard University Press, 1954.

———. "Modernization and Foreign Policy in Meiji Japan." In Robert E. Ward, ed., *Political Development in Modern Japan.* Princeton: Princeton University Press, 1968.

Japan, Government-General of Chōsen. *Annual Report on Administration of Chosen.* Keijō (Seoul), 1907–37.

———. *Thriving Chosen: A Survey of Twenty-Five Years' Administration.* Keijō (Seoul), 1935.

Jien Fukunaka Seijirō-O den. Seoul: Takase Gomei Kaisha, 1943.

Jinsen-fu. *Jinsen-fu shi.* Inchon: Jinsenfucho, 1933.

Jinsen Shōkō Kaigisho, comp. *Jinsen shōkō kaigisho gojū nenshi.* Inchon, 1934.

Jo, Yung-hwan, ed. *Korea's Response to the West.* Kalamazoo: Korea Research and Publications, 1971.

Kaigai Kōgyō Kabushiki Kaisha, comp. *Kaigai kōgyō kabushiki kaisha shoshi.* N.p.: 1931.

Kaigun Daijin Kanbō, ed. *Kaigun gunbi enkaku.* Tokyo: Kaigunshō, 1922.

———, ed. *Yamamoto Gonnohyoe to kaigun.* Tokyo: Hara Shobō, 1966.

Kajikawa Hansaburō. *Jitsugyō no Chōsen.* Seoul: Chōsen Kenkyūkai, 1911.

Kajima Morinosuke. *The Diplomacy of Japan, 1894–1922.* Vol. 1, *Sino-Japanese War and Triple Intervention.* Tokyo: Kajima Institute of International Peace, 1976.

Kajimura Hideki. *Chōsen gendaishi no tebiki.* Tokyo: Ryūkei Shosha, 1981.

———. "Chōsen kara miru Nichi-Rō sensō." *Shinchō* 7.8 (1980).

———. "Chōsen kindaishi to Kim Ok-kiun no hyōka." *Shisō*, no. 510 (October 1966).

———. *Chōsen ni okeru shihonshugi no keisei to tenkai.* Tokyo: Ryūkei Shosha, 1977.

———. "Shokuminchi Chōsen no Nihonjin." In Samon Kimbara, ed., *Chihō demokurashii to sensō.* Tokyo: Bunichi Sōgō Shuppan, 1978.

Kamigaito Kenichi. *Nihon ryūgaku to kakumei undō.* Tokyo: Tōkyō Daigaku Shuppankai, 1982.

Kaneko Kentarō. *Keizai seisaku.* Tokyo: 1902.

———. "Taigai kōgyō no hōshin," *Jitsugyō no Nihon* 2.6 (June 1898): 5–8; 2.7 (July 1898): 6–10.

Kang Chae-on. *Chōsen kindaishi kenkyū.* Tokyo: Nihon Hyōronsha, 1970.

———. *Kindai Chōsen no shisō.* Tokyo: Kinokuniya Shoten, 1971.

Kang Dong-jin. *Nihon genronkai to Chōsen.* Tokyo: Hōsei Daigaku Shuppankyoku, 1984.

Kang Chae-on. *Chōsen jōi to kaika: Kindai Chōsen ni totte no Nihon.* Tokyo: Heibonsha, 1977.

———. "Kwangwha jiken zengo." *Sanzenri* 3 (Aug. 1975).

Kang Mang-il. *Kankoku gendaishi.* Tokyo: Kōrai Shorin, 1985.

———. *Kankoku kindaishi.* Tokyo: Kōrai Shorin, 1986.

———. "Yi-shi Chōsen kaikō chokkei ni okeru Chō-Nichi bōeki no tenkai." *Reikishigaku kenkyū*, no. 265 (June 1992).

Kang Pyong-tae. *Chōsen kindaishi.* Tokyo: Heibonsha, 1986.

———. *Chōsen shakai no kōzō to Nihon teikokushugi.* Tokyo: Ryūkei Shosha, 1977.

Kang Tok-sang. "Yi-shi Chōsen kaikō chokugo ni okeru Chō-Nichi bōeki no tenkai." *Rekishigaku kenkyū*, no. 265 (June 1962).

Kang Tong-jin. *Nihon no Chōsen shihai seisaku shi kenkyū.* Tokyo: Tōkyō Daigaku Shuppankai, 1979.

Kang, Younghill. *The Grass Roof.* New York: Scribner's, 1931.

Kankoku Seifu Keimu Kōmonbu, comp. *Kankoku.* Scoul, 1907.

Kankoku shutchō chōsa hōkokusho. Yokohama: Yokohama Zeikan, 1907.

Karasawa Takeko. "Bōkotsurei jiken." *Chōsenshi kenkyū ronbunshū* 16 (Dec. 1973).

Kasuya Ken'ichi. "Shoki gihei undō ni tsuite." *Chōsen kenkyūkai ronbunshū* 14 (Mar. 1977).

Katō Masao. "Kankoku imin ron." *Taiyō*, Jan. 5, 1901.

Katō Seinosuke. *Kankoku kei'ei.* Tokyo: Jitsugyō no Nihonsha, 1905.

Kawasaki Saburō. *Chōsen kakushin saku.* Tokyo: Hakubunkan, 1894.

Keijō-fushi. 3 vols. Tokyo: Shonandō Shoten, 1934, 1936, 1941.

Keijō Nihon shōgikaigisho nenpō. 1907.

Keijō Nihonjin shōgyō kaigisho nenpō. Seoul: Keijō Nihonjin Shōgyō Kaigisho, 1907.

Keijō Shōgyō Kaigisho, comp. *Zai-Sen naichijin jinkō shirabe: Chōsen kōsanbutsu shirabe.* Seoul, 1921.

Keijō Teikoku Daigaku Hōgakkai. *Chōsen keizai no kenkyū [dai-san].* Tokyo: Iwanami Shoten, 1938.

————. *Chōsen shakai keizai shi kenkyū.* Tokyo: Tōkō Shoin, 1933.

Kikuchi Kenjō. *Chōsen ōkoku.* Tokyo: Min'yūsha, 1896.

Kim, Chŏng-myŏng. *An Chung-an to Nikkan kankeishi.* Tokyo: Hara Shobō, 1979.

————, ed. *Chōsen chūsatsugun rekishi.* Tokyo: Gannando, 1967.

————, ed. *Chōsen dokuritsu undō.* 6 vols. Tokyo: Hara Shobō, 1967–.

————, ed. *Chōsen tōchi shiryō.* 10 vols. Tokyo: Kankoku Shiryō Kenkyūjo, 1970–71.

————. *Itō Hirobumi ansatsu kiroku.* Tokyo: Hara Shobō, 1972.

————, ed. *Kankoku heigō shiryō.* 3 vols. Tokyo: Hara Shobō, 1978.

————. *Nikkan gaikō shiryō.* 10 vols. Tokyo: Hara Shobō, 1979–81.

————. *Nikkan gaikō shiryō shūsei.* 8 vols. Tokyo: Gannando, 1962–67.

Kim, C. I. Eugene, and Han-Kyo Kim. *Korea and the Politics of Imperialism, 1876–1910.* Berkeley: University of California Press, 1967.

Kim, C. I. Eugene, and Doretha E. Mortimore, eds. *Korea's Response to Japan: The Colonial Period.* Kalamazoo: Center for Korean Studies, Western Michigan University, 1975.

Kim Hung-chan. "Yu Kil-Chun: A Korean Crusader for Reform." *Korea Journal* 12 (Dec. 1972).

Kim Il-mun. *Tennō to Chōsenji to sōtokufu.* Tokyo: Tahata Shoten, 1984.

Kim, Key-Hiuk. *The Last Phase of the East Asian World Order: Korea, Japan, and the Chinese Empire.* Berkeley: University of California Press, 1980.

Kim, Kyung-t'ae. "A Survey of Domestic and International Conditions Relating to the Opening of Ports in 1876." *Journal of Social Sciences and Humanities* 42 (1975).

Kim, Richard E. *Lost Names: Scenes from a Korean Boyhood.* New York: Praeger, 1970.

Kim, Ui-hwan. "Japanese in Pusan (Fusan) after Opening of Port." *Journal of Social Sciences and Humanities* 40 (Dec. 1974).

Kim, Young-ho. "Yu Kil-Chun's Idea of Enlightenment." *Journal of Social Sciences and Humanities* 33 (Dec. 1970).

Kim, Young-sop. "Absentee Landlord System During the Nineteenth and Twentieth Century in Korea—Aggravations in the Landlord and Agromanagerial Means in Chaeryong, Totaku Farmlands." *Journal of Social Sciences and Humanities* 37 (Dec. 1972).

Kimura Kenji. "Meijiki Nihonjin no Chōsen shinshutsu no shakai keizaiteki haikei." *Tochi seido shigaku*, no. 101 (Oct. 1983).

————. "Meiji Nihonjin no kaigai shinshutsu to imin kyoryūmin seisaku." *Shōkei ronshū* (Waseda), no. 35 (Sept. 1978).

————. *Zai-Chō Nihonjin no shakaishi.* Tokyo: Miraisha, 1989.

Kimura Shōtarō. *Kankoku naichi no iri.* Nara: Kimura Shōtarō, 1903.

Kinmonth, Earl H. *The Self-Made Man in Meiji Japan: From Samurai to Salary Man.* Berkeley: University of California Press, 1981.

Kirishima Yoshihiko. "Tōyō shokutaku kaisha no setsuritsu katei." Parts 1 and 2. *Rekishi hyōron*, no. 282 (Nov. 1973); no. 285 (Jan. 1974).

Kita Teikichi. *Kankoku no heigō to kokushi.* Tokyo: Sanseido, 1910.

Kitaoka Shin'ichi. *Nihon rikugun to tairiku seisaku.* Tokyo: Tōkyō Daigaku Shuppankai, 1978.

Kitazaki Fusatarō. *Tōtaku sanjū nen no ashiato.* Tokyo: Tōhōtsu Shinsha Shuppanbu, 1938.

Ko Pyong-un. *Kindai Chōsen keizaishi no kenkyū.* Tokyo: Yūsankaku, 1987.

————. *Kindai Chōsen sōkaishi no kenkyū.* Tokyo: Yūsankaku, 1987

Ko Sung-je. *Shokuminchi kin'yū seisaku no shiteki bunseki.* Tokyo: Ochanomizu Shobō, 1972.

Kobayakawa Kurō, ed. *Chōsen nōgyō hattatsu shi.* 3 vols. Tokyo: Yūhō Kyōkai, 1959–60.

Kobayashi Hideo. "'Kaisharei' kenkyū nōto." *Kaikyō* 3 (Dec. 1975).

————. "1910 nendai kōhanki Chōsen keizai jōtai." *Nihonshi kenkyū*, no. 118 (Apr. 1971).

Kōbe Masao. *Chōsen nōgyō iminron.* Tokyo: Yūhikaku Honten, 1910.

Kojima Kisaku. *Chōsen no nōgyō*, Tokyo: Kinkodo, 1905.

Kojima Reiitsu, ed. *Nihon teikokushugi to Higashi Ajia.* Tokyo: Ajia Keizai Kenkyūjo, 1979.

Kokuritsu Kokkai Toshokan, comp. *Chōsen kankei shiryō mokuroku.* 4 vols. 1966–75.

Kokuritsu Kokkai Toshokan Sankō Shoshibu. *Inoue Kaoru kankei monjo mokuroku.* Tokyo: Kokuritsu Kokkai Toshokan, 1975.

Komatsu Midori. *Chōsen heigō no rimen.* Tokyo: Chūgai Shinronsha, 1920.

————. *Itō-kō chokuwa.* Tokyo: Chikura Shobō, 1936.

————. *Meiji gaikō hitsuwa.* Tokyo: Chikura Shobō, 1936.

————, ed. *Itō-kō zenshū.* Tokyo: Shōwa Shuppansha, 1928.

Ko Megata Danshaku Denki Hensankai, ed. *Danshaku Megata Jūtarō.* Tokyo, 1938.

Kondo Ken'ichi, comp. *Saitō sōtoku no bunka tōchi.* Tokyo: Yūhō Kyōkai, 1970.

Kondo Yoshio. *Inoue Kakugorō sensei den.* Tokyo: Inoue Kakugorō Sensei Denki Hensankai, 1943.

Koyama Hirō. *Nihon gunji kōgyō bunseki.* Tokyo: Ochanomizu Shobō, 1972.

Kudō Masaki. *Nihon jinshuron.* Tokyo: Yoshikawa Kobunkan, 1979.

Kuroda Ken'ichi. *Nihon shokumin shisō shi.* Tokyo: Kōbundō, 1942.

Kuroda Koshirō, ed. *Gensui Terauchi hakushaku den.* Tokyo: Gensui Terauchi Hakushaku Denki Hensanjo, 1920.

Kuroki Yukichi. *Komura Jūtarō.* Tokyo: Tosho Kenkyūsha, 1941.

Kurose Ikuji. "Nichi-Rō sengo no 'Chōsen kei'ei' to Tōyō shokutaku kabushiki kaisha." *Chōsenshi Kenkyūkai ronbunshū* 12 (Mar. 1975).

————. "Sōgyōki ni okeru Tōyō takushoku kaisha no keiei kōzō." *Ronshū* (Kagoshima Keizai Daigaku) 23.2 (1974).

Kuzuu Yoshihisa, ed. *Nikkan gappō hishi*. 2 vols. Tokyo: Kokuryūkai Shuppanbu, 1930.

Ladd, George Trumbull. *In Korea with Marquis Ito*. New York: Scribner's, 1908.

Lee, Bae-young. "Competitive Mining Survey by Foreign Powers in Korea—With Emphasis on the 1880s." *Journal of Social Sciences and Humanities* 36 (Dec. 1972).

Lee, Chong-sik. *The Politics of Korean Nationalism*. Berkeley: University of California Press, 1965.

Lee, Hoon K. *Land Utilization and Rural Economy in Korea*. Chicago: University of Chicago Press, 1936.

Lee, Ki-baik. *A New History of Korea*. Trans. Edward H. Wagner and Edward J. Shultz. Cambridge: Harvard University Press, 1984.

Lee, Young Bum. "The Annexation of Korea—Japanese Policy: 1905–1910." *Koreana Quarterly* 7 (1965).

Lee, Yur-bok. *West Goes East: Paul Georg von Mollendorf and Great Power Imperialism in Late Yi Korea*. Honolulu: University of Hawaii Press, 1988.

Lensen, George Alexander. *The Russian Push Toward Japan, 1697–1875*. Princeton: Princeton University Press, 1959.

——, ed. *Korea and Manchuria Between Russia and Japan, 1895–1904: The Observations of Sir Ernest Satow*. Tallahassee: Diplomatic Press, 1966.

Lew, Young-Ick. "An Analysis of the Reform Documents of the Kabo Reform Movement, 1894." *Journal of Social Sciences and Humanities* 40 (1974).

——. "Korean-Japanese Politics Behind the Kabo-Ulmi Reform Movement, 1894–1896." *Journal of Korean Studies* 3 (1981).

——. "Minister Inoue Kaoru and the Japanese Reform Attempts in Korea During the Sino-Japanese War, 1894–1895." *Journal of Asiatic Studies* 7 (1984).

——. "The Reform Efforts and Ideas of Park Young-Hyo, 1894–1895." *Journal of Asiatic Studies* 1 (1977).

Li, Mirok. *The Yalu Flows: A Korean Childhood*. Trans. H. A. Hammelmann. East Lansing: Michigan State University Press, 1956.

Lichtheim, George. *Imperialism*. New York and Washington: Praeger, 1971.

Limb, Ben Quincy. "Sei-Kan Ron: A Study in the Evolution of Expansionism in Modern Japan, 1868–1873." Ph.D. diss., St. John's University, 1979.

Lin, T. C. "Li Hung-Chang: His Korean Policies, 1870–1885." *Chinese Social and Political Science Review* 19 (1935).

Lindley, M. F. *The Acquisition and Government of Backward Territories in International Law*. London: Longmans, Green, 1926.

Lone, Stewart P. "General Katsura Tarō and the Japanese Empire in East Asia, 1874–1913." Ph.D. diss., Australian National University, 1989.

Lowell, Percival. *Chöson: The Land of the Morning Calm—A Sketch of Korea*. Boston: Ticknor and Co., 1888.

Mabuchi Sadatoshi. "Dai-ichi taisenki Chōsen nōgyō no tokushitsu to sanichi undō." *Chōsenshi Kenkyūkai ronbunshū* 12 (Mar. 1975).

McCune, George M. "The Exchange of Envoys Between Korea and Japan During the Tokugawa Period." *Far Eastern Quarterly* 5 (May 1946).

——. "The Japanese Trading Post at Pusan." *Korean Review* 1 (June 1948).

McGrane, George A. *Korea's Tragic Hours: The Closing Years of the Yi Dynasty.* Ed. Harold F. Cook and Alan M. MacDougall. Seoul: Taewon Publishing, 1973.

McKenzie, Frederick Arthur. *Korea's Fight for Freedom.* New York: Revell, 1920.

———. *Tragedy of Korea.* London: Hodder and Stoughton, 1908.

McNamara, Dennis Louis. "Imperial Expansion and Nationalist Resistance: Japan in Korea, 1876–1910." Ph.D. diss., Harvard University, 1983.

McNeill, William H., and Ruth S. Adams. *Migration: Patterns and Policies.* Bloomington: Indiana University Press, 1978.

Maejima Shōzō. *Nihon teikokushugi to gikai.* Kyoto: Mineruvā Shobō, 1976.

Malozemoff, Andrew. *Russian Far Eastern Policy, 1881–1904.* Berkeley: University of California Press, 1958.

Matsumiya Shun'ichirō. *Saikin no Kankoku.* Tokyo: Hakubunkan, 1905.

Matsumura Shosei. *Zai-Man-Chōsen dōhō.* Seoul: n.p., 1926.

Matsushita Yoshio. *Meiji gunsei shiron.* 2 vols. Tokyo: Yūhikaku, 1956.

———. *Meiji no guntai.* Tokyo: Yoshikawa Kobunkan, 1963.

Matsuura Rei. "Bakumatsuki no tai Chōsen ron: Dōmeiron to sei-Kan ron." *Rekishi kōron* 6.8 (1980).

Mayo, Marlene J. "The Korean Crisis of 1873 and Early Meiji Foreign Policy." *Journal of Asian Studies* 31.4 (1972).

Meiji nyūsu jiten. 9 vols. Tokyo: Mainichi Komyunikeshonzu, 1983–86.

Meijishi Kenkyū Renrakukai, ed. *Minkenron kara nashonarizumu e.* Tokyo: Ochanomizu Shobō, 1957.

Memmi, Albert. *The Colonizer and the Colonized.* Boston: Beacon, 1972.

Miyachi Masato. *Nichi-Rō sengo seijishi no kenkyū.* Tokyo: Tōkyō Daigaku Shuppankai, 1973.

Miyajima Hiroshi. "Chōsen kango keikaku igo no shōgyōteki nōgyō." *Shirin* 57.6 (1974).

———. "Chōsen 'tochi chōsa jigyō' kenkyū josetsu." *Ajia keizai* 19.9 (Sept. 1978).

———. "'Tochi chōsa jigyō' no rekishiteki zentei jōken no keisei." *Chōsenshi kenkyūkai ronbunshū* 12 (Mar. 1975).

Mizuno Naoki. "Nihon no shakaishugisha to Chōsen." *Rekishi kōron* 8.8 (1980).

Mizuta Naomasa. *Tōkanfu jidai no zaisei—Chōsen kindai zaisei no jikatame.* Tokyo: Yūhō Kyōkai, 1974.

Mochiji Rokusaburō. *Nihon shokuminchi keizai ron.* Tokyo: Kaizōsha, 1926.

Monbushō. *Shogaku dokuhon.* Tokyo: Shihan Gakkō, 1873.

Mommsen, Wolfgang J. *Theories of Imperialism.* Trans. P. S. Falla. Chicago: University of Chicago Press, 1977.

Mommsen, Wolfgang J., and Jurgen Osterhammel. *Imperialism and After: Continuities and Discontinuities.* London: Allen and Unwin, 1986.

Mori Hisao. "Taguchi Ukichi no shokuminron." In Kojima Reiitsu, ed., *Nihon teikokushugi to Higashi Ajia.* Tokyo: Ajia Keizai Kenkyūjo, 1979.

Mori Toshihiko. *Meiji roku nen seihen.* Tokyo: Chūō Kōronsha, 1979.

————. *Meiji roku nen seihen no kenkyū*. Tokyo: Yūhikaku, 1978.

Moriyama, Alan Takeo. *Imingaisha: Japanese Emigration Companies and Hawaii, 1894–1908*. Honolulu: University of Hawaii Press, 1985.

Moriyama Shigenori. "Chōsen ni okeru Nihon to Berugi shindeiketto." *Nenpō kindai Nihon kenkyū* 2 (1980).

————. "Kabo kaikaku ni okeru shakkan mondai: Inoue Kaoru no kanyo shita dainiji kaikaku to Chōsen shidōso taiō o chūshin to shite." *Tōyō gakuhō* 52.2–4 (Mar. 1976).

————. *Kindai Nikkan kankeishi kenkyū*. Tokyo: Tōkyō Daigaku Shuppankai, 1987.

————. *Nikkan heigō*. Tokyo: Yoshikawa Kobunkan, 1992.

Moscowitz, Karl. "The Creation of the Oriental Development Company: Japanese Illusions Meet Korean Reality." *Occasional Papers on Korea* 2 (Mar. 1974).

Mosse, George L. *Toward the Final Solution: A History of European Racism*. New York: Howard Fertig, 1978.

Moulder, Frances. *Japan, China, and the Modern World Economy*. Cambridge: Cambridge University Press, 1977.

Murakami Chūjirō. *Yūbō naru iminchi*. Tokyo: Kaigai Imin Tsūshin Annaisho, 1911.

Murakami Katsuhiko. "Dai-Ichi Ginkō Chōsen shiten to shokuminchi kin'yū." *Tochi seido shigaku* 61 (Oct. 1973).

————. "Nihon shihonshugi ni yori Chōsen mengyō no saihensei." In Kojima Reiitsu, ed., *Nihon teikokushugi to Higashi Ajia*. Tokyo: Ajia Keizai Kenkyūjo, 1979.

————. "Shokuminchi." In Ōishi Kaichirō, ed., *Nihon sangyō kakumei no kenkyū*, vol. 2. Tokyo: Tōkyō Daigaku Shuppanbu, 1975.

————. "Shokuminchi jigane suikyū to Nihon sangyō kakumei." *Keizaigaku kenkyū* 16 (Dec. 1973).

Muramatsu Takeshi. *Chōsen shokuminsha: Aru Meijijin no shogai*. Tokyo: Sanseido, 1972.

Mutsu Munemitsu. *Kenkenroku: A Diplomatic Record of the Sino-Japanese War, 1894–1895*. Trans. Gordon M. Berger. Tokyo: University of Tokyo Press, 1982.

Nagaoka Shinkichi. "Nisshin sengo no zaisei seisaku to baishōkin." *Nihon seisaku shiron* 1 (1973).

Nahm, Andrew Changwoo. "Reaction and Response to the Opening of Korea, 1876–1884." *Studies on Asia* (1965).

————. "Russia's Policy Toward Korea, 1854–1904: A Re-examination." *Journal of Social Sciences and Humanities* 64 (Dec. 1986).

————, ed. *Korea under Japanese Colonial Rule: Studies of the Policy and Techniques of Japanese Colonialism*. Kalamazoo: Center for Korean Studies, Western Michigan University, 1973.

Naikaku Tōkeikyoku. *Nihon teikoku dai-29 tōkei nenkan*. Tokyo, 1910.

Nakada Konosuke. *Zai-Kan jinshi meikan*. Osaka: Mok'po Shinpōsha, 1905.

Nakai Kitarō. *Chōsen kaikō roku*. Tokyo: Tōgyō Kenkyūkai, 1915.

Nakamura Masanori. "Keinin-Keifu tetsudō kensetsu o mejiru kanryō to buru-joaji no dōkō." In *Yamasaki Yoshi kyōjū kanreki kinen ronbunshū hensen iinkai*. Tokyo, 1972.

―――. "Nihon teikokushugi seiritsushi joron." *Shisō*, no. 1,574 (Apr. 1972).

Nakatsuka Akira. *Kindai Nihon to Chōsen*. Tokyo: Sanseidō, 1968.

―――. *Nisshin sensō no kenkyū*. Tokyo: Aoki Shoten, 1968.

Nelson, M. Frederick. *Korea and the Old Order in Eastern Asia*. Baton Rouge: Louisiana State University Press, 1945.

Nihon gaikō bunsho. Tokyo: Nihon Kokusai Renmei Kyōkai, 1936–.

Nihon Kokusai Seiji Gakkai. *Nikkan kankei no tenkai*. Tokyo: Yūhikaku, 1963.

Nikkan Shobō Henshūbu, ed. *Saishin Chōsen chishi*. Seoul: Nikkan Shobō, 1912.

Nish, Ian. *Japanese Foreign Policy, 1869–1942: Kasumigaseki to Miyakezaka*. London: Routledge and Kegan Paul, 1977.

―――. *The Origins of the Russo-Japanese War*. London and New York: Longman, 1985.

Nishihara Kamezō. *Yume no nanajū nen: Nishihara Kamezō den*. Tokyo: Heibonsha, 1987.

Nishio Yotarō. *Kim Yu-gi shoden: Uragirareta Nikkan gōhō undō*. Tokyo: Hara Shobō, 1977.

Noda Utarō. "Chōsen kaitaku ni taisuru shokan no hitotsu." *Chōsen oyobi Manshū* 84 (July 1914).

Nōshōkō Kōtō Kaigi, comp. *Dai-ichi kai nōshōkō kōtō kaigi giji sokkiroku*. N.p., 1897.

Nōshōmushō Shōkōkyoku, comp. *Kankoku jijō chōsa shiryō*. Tokyo, 1905.

Odagiri Masunosuke. *Chōsen*. Keijō, 1890.

Ōe Shinobu. *Nichi-Rō sensō no gunjishiteki kenkyū*. Tokyo: Rippū Shobō, 1976.

―――. "Shokuminchi ryōyū to gunbu." *Rekishigaku kenkyū* (Sept. 1978).

Oh, Bonnie Bongwan. "The Kabo Kaengjang of 1894 in Korea and the Policy of Mutsu Munemitsu." *Journal of Social Sciences and Humanities* 44 (Dec. 1976).

Ōhashi Seizaburō, ed. *Chōsen sangyō shishin*. Seoul: Kaihatsusha, 1915.

Ohkawa, Kazushi, and Miyohei Shinohara, eds. *Patterns of Japanese Economic Development: A Quantitative Appraisal*. New Haven: Yale University Press, 1979.

Ōishi Kaichirō, ed. *Nihon sangyō kakumei no kenkyū*. 2 vols. Tokyo: Tōkyō Daigaku Shuppankai, 1975.

Ōka Yasuichi. *Saishin Kankoku jijō*. 1903. Tokyo: Aokido, 1905.

Oka Yoshitake. "Meiji shoki jiyū minkenronsha no me ni eijiru tōji no kokusai jijō." In Meijishi Kenkyū Renrakukai, ed., *Minkenron kara nashonarizumu e*. Tokyo: Ochanomizu Shobō, 1957.

Okada Shigekichi. *Chōsen yūshutsumai jijō*. Tokyo: Dōbunkan, 1911.

Okamoto, Shumpei. *The Japanese Oligarchy and the Russo-Japanese War*. New York: Columbia University Press, 1970.

Ōkawa Kazushi, Shinohara Miyohei, and Umehara Mataji, eds. *Chōki keizai tōkei suikei to bunseki*. 14 vols. Tokyo: Tōyō Keizai Shinpōsha, 1965–79.

Ōkawa Shūmei. *Ōkawa Shūmei zenshū*. 5 vols. Tokyo: Ōkawa Shūmei Zenshū Kankōkai, 1962.

Okayama-ken, comp. *Chōsen Okayama-mura jissekisho*. Okayama, 1916.

Okita Kinjō. *Rimen no Kankoku*. Osaka: Kibunkan, 1905.

Okudaira Takehiko. "Chōsen no joyakukō to kyoryūchi." In *Chōsen kaikoku kōshō shimatsu*. Tokyo: Tōkō Shoin, 1935.

Ōkuma Shigenobu. "Senjin no dōka." In Aoyagi Tsunatarō, ed., *Chōsen*. Seoul: Chōsen Kenkyūkai, 1913.

Ōkura Zaibatsu Kenkyūkai, ed. *Ōkura zaibatsu no kenkyū: Ōkura to tairiku*. Tokyo: Katō Shuppansha, 1982.

Omachi Keigetsu. *Hakushaku Gotō Shōjirō*. Tokyo: Fuzanbo, 1914.

Ōmori Tokuko. "Nihon kinhon'isei to Chōsen sankin." *Rekishigaku kenkyū*, no. 428 (Jan. 1976).

Omura Tomoho. *Chōsen kizoku retsuden*. Seoul: Chōsen Kenkyūkai, 1910.

Oniwa Kan'ichi. *Chōsenron*. Tokyo: Tōhō Kyōkai, 1896.

Onjōji Kiyoshi. *Kankoku no jitsujō*. Tokyo: Rakuseisha, 1906.

Ono Kazuichirō. "Nihon teikokushugi to iminron." In *Sekai keizai to teikokushugi*. Tokyo: Otsuki Shoten, 1973.

―――. *Ryōdaisenkanki no Ajia to Nihon*. Tokyo: Ōtsuki Shoten, 1979.

Ōsaka Mainichi Shinbunsha Keijō Shikyoku. *Rō kaitakushi ga okuru hantō rimenshi*. Keijō: Ōsaka Mainichi Shinbunsha, Tōkyō Nichinichi Shinbunsha, Keijō Shikyoku, 1940.

Ōsaka Shōkō Kaigisho, comp. *Kankoku sangyō shisatsu hōkokusho*. Osaka, 1904.

Ōtsu Junichirō. *Dai Nihon kensei shi*. 10 vols. Tokyo: Hōbunkan, 1927–28.

Ouichi Kazuo. *Tōyō takushoku: Maboroshi no kokusaku kaisha*. Tokyo: Nihon Keizai Shinbunsha, 1982.

Ōyama Azusa. *Yamagata Aritomo ikensho*. Tokyo: Hara Shobō, 1966.

Owen, Roger, and Bob Sutcliffe, eds. *Studies in the Theory of Imperialism*. London: Longman, 1972.

Pak Ch'un-il. *Kindai Nihon bungaku ni okeru Chōsenzō*. Tokyo: Miraisha, 1972.

Pak Jong-keun. "Chōsen kindai ni okeru minzoku undō no tenkai." *Rekishigaku kenkyū*, no. 451 (1978).

―――. "Chōsen ni okeru 1894–95 nen no Kim Hong-jip seiken no kosatsu I, II: 1894 (Kabo) kaikaku to no kanren de." *Rekishigaku kenkyū*, no. 415 (Dec. 1974).

―――. "1894 nen ni okeru Nihongun teppei mondai to Chōsen 'naisei kaikaku' an tojō no haikei," *Chōsenshi Kenkyūkai ronbunshū* 5 (Nov. 1968).

―――. "Minpi satsu jiken no shorisaku o mejiru shomondai." In Ōtsuka Rekishi Gakkai, ed., *Higashi Ajia kindaishi no kenkyū*. Tokyo: Ochanomizu Shobō, 1967.

―――. "Nisshin kaisen ni okeru Nihongun no Chōsen ōkyū senryō jiken no kōsatsu." *Rekishi hyōron*, no. 302 (June 1975).

―――. "Nisshin kaisen ni okeru Nihongun no Chōsen ōshitsu senryō jiken ni taisuru Chōsenjinmin no hantai tōsō." *Rekishi hyōron* (Aug. 1976).

———. "Nisshin sensō to Chōsen bōeki: Nihon ni yoru Chōsen taigai bōeki no shinai taitei." *Rekishigaku kenkyū*, no. 536 (Dec. 1984).

———. *Nisshin sensō to Chōsen*. Tokyo: Aoki Shoten, 1982.

Palais, James B. "Political Leadership in the Yi Dynasty." In Dae-sook Suh and Chae-jin Lee, eds., *Political Leadership in Korea*. Seattle: University of Washington Press, 1976.

———. "Political Participation in Traditional Korea, 1876–1910." *Journal of Korean Studies* 1 (1979).

Palmer, Spencer J. *Korean-American Relations: Documents Pertaining to the Far Eastern Diplomacy of the United States*. Vol. 2, *The Period of Growing Influence*. Berkeley: University of California Press, 1963.

Park, Il-keun. "China's Policy Toward Korea, 1880–1884." *Journal of Social Sciences and Humanities in Korea* 53 (June 1981).

Park, Seoung-Rae. "Fukuzawa Yūkichi on Korea." *Journal of Social Sciences and Humanities* 45 (June 1977).

P'eng Tse-chou. *Meiji shoki nikkanshin kankei no kenkyū*. Tokyo: Hanawa Shobō, 1969.

Pusan Nihonjin shōgyō kaigisho nenpō. Seoul, 1906–10.

Quinones, Carlos Kenneth. "The Impact of the Kabo Reforms upon Political Role Allocation in Late Yi Korea, 1884–1902." *Occasional Papers on Korea* 4 (Sept. 1975).

Rich, Paul B. *Race and Empire in British Politics*. Cambridge: Cambridge University Press, 1986.

Rikugunshō, comp. *Meiji tennō godenki shiryō: Meiji gunjishi*. 2 vols. Tokyo: Hara Shobō, 1966.

Ro, Chung-hyun. "A Study on Administrative Reorganization in Yi Dynasty (Korea), 1894–1910." *Journal of Social Sciences and Humanities* 28 (1968).

Ryūmonsha, ed. *Shibusawa Eiichi denki shiryō*. Tokyo: Shibusawa Eiichi Denki Shiryō Kankōkai, 1955–65.

Sada Hakubo. "Sei-Kan ron no kyūmondan." In Yoshino Sakuzō, ed., *Meiji bunka zenshū*. Tokyo: Nihon Hyōronsha, 1927–30.

Saiga Hirochika. *Ōe Tenya denki*. Tokyo: Ōe Moto, 1926.

Sakai Yukichi. "Konoe Atsumaro to Meiji sanjū nendai no taigai kōha." *Kokka gakkai zasshi* 83 (1969).

Sakamaki Gentarō. *Kaigai risshin annai*. Tokyo: Seibunsha, 1911.

Sakeda Masatoshi. "Nisshin sengo gaikō seisaku no kosoku yōin." In *Nenpō kindai Nihon kenkyū*. Tokyo: Yamakawa Shuppansha, 1980.

———. *Kindai Nihon ni okeru taigai kōundō no kenkyū*. Tokyo: Tōkyō Daigaku Shuppankai, 1978.

Sakurai Yoshiyuki. *Chōsen kenkyū bunken shi: Meiji-Taishō hen*. Tokyo: Ryūkei Shosha, 1979.

———, ed. *Meiji nenkan Chōsen kenkyū nenken shi*. Seoul: Shomotsu Dōkōkai, 1941.

———. *Meiji to Chōsen*. Tokyo: Sakurai Yoshiyuki Sensei Kanreki Kinnen Kai, 1964.

Samura Hachirō. *To-Kan no susume*. Seoul: Chōsen Nichinichi Shinbun, 1909.

Sands, William F. *Undiplomatic Memories: The Far East, 1896–1904.* New York: McGraw-Hill, 1930.

Satō Seijirō. *Kankoku seigyō saku.* Osaka: Okujima Shoten, 1904.

———. *Chō-hantō no shin Nihon.* Osaka: Satō Seijirō, 1904.

Sawamura Tōhei. *Kindai Chōsen no mensaku mengyō.* Tokyo: Miraisha, 1985.

Schumpeter, Joseph. *Imperialism / Social Classes.* Trans. Heinz Norden. New York: Meridian, 1955.

Shibahara Takuji, Takaaki Ikai, and Masahiro Ikeda, eds. *Taigakan.* Vol. 12 of *Nihon kindai shisō taikei.* Tokyo: Iwanami Shoten, 1991.

Shikata Hiroshi. "Chōsen ni okeru kindai shihonshugi no seiritsu katei." *Keijō Teikoku Daigaku Hōbungakkai ronshū,* 1933.

Shimomura Fujio. *Meiji shonen jōyaku kaiseishi no kenkyū.* Tokyo: Yoshikawa Kobunkan, 1962.

Shin Chōsen oyobi shin Manshū. Seoul: Chōsen Zasshisha, 1913.

Shin-Kan shōkyō shisatsu hōkoku. Yokohama: Yokohama Zeikan, 1906.

Shinobu, Junpei. *Kan hantō.* Tokyo: Tōkyōdō Shoten, 1901.

———. *Komura Jūtarō.* Tokyo: Shinchōsha, 1942.

Shinobu Seizaburō. *Nihon gaikōshi.* Vol. 1. Tokyo: Mainichi Shinbunsha, 1974.

———. *Nisshin sensō.* Tokyo: Fukuda Shobō, 1934.

Shinobu Seizaburō and Chūichi Nakayama. *Nichi-Rō sensōshi no kenkyū.* Tokyo: Kawade Shōbō, 1972.

Shiokawa Ichitarō. *Chōsen tsūshō jijō.* Hachio Shoten, 1895.

"The Situation in Japan and the Tasks of the Japanese Communist Party." *Communist International* 9.7 (April 15, 1932).

Snyder, Jack. *Myths of Empire: Domestic Politics and International Ambition.* Ithaca: Cornell University Press, 1991.

Sōtokufu Shomubu. *Chōsen ni okeru naichijin.* Seoul, 1923.

Stephan, John J. *The Kuril Islands: Russo-Japanese Frontier in the Pacific.* Oxford: Clarendon Press, 1974.

———. *Sakhalin: A History.* Oxford: Clarendon Press, 1971.

Stocking, George W., Jr. *Victorian Anthropology.* New York: Free Press, 1987.

Strachey, John. *The End of Empire.* New York and Washington: Frederick Praeger, 1966.

Suematsu Kenchō. *Kōshi Itō-Kō.* Tokyo: Hakubunkan, 1911.

Suematsu Yasukazu, ed. *Chōsen kenkyū bunken mokuroku: 1868–1945.* 2 vols. Tokyo: Tōkyō Daigaku Tōyō Bunka Kenkyūjo Fuzoku Tōyōgaku Bunken Sentā, 1980.

Sugimura, Fukashi. *Meiji nanahachi nen zai-Kan kushinroku.* Tokyo: Sugimura Yōtarō, 1931.

Sugiyama, Shinya. *Japan's Industrialization in the World Economy, 1859–1899: Export Trade and Overseas Competition.* London and Atlantic Heights, N.J.: Athlone Press, 1988.

Suh, Sang-chul. *Growth and Structural Changes in the Korean Economy, 1910–1940.* Cambridge: Harvard University Press, 1978.

Sullivan, Eileen P. "Liberalism and Imperialism: J. S. Mill's Defense of the British Empire." *Journal of the History of Ideas* 44.4 (Oct. 1983).

Tabohashi Kiyoshi. *Chōsen tōchishi ronkō*. Seoul: Seishin Bunkasha, 1972.
———. *Kindai nissen kankei no kenkyū*. 2 vols. Tokyo: Bunka Shiryō Chōsa-kai, 1963–64.
Takahashi Kamekichi. "Makki ni okeru teikokushugi no henshitsu." *Shakai kagaku* (Apr. 1927).
———. *Nihon kindai keizai hattatushi*. 3 vols. Tokyo: Tōyō Keizai Shinpōsha, 1973.
Takahashi Tosen. *Zai-Kan seikō no Kyūshūjin*. 3 vols. Nagasaki: Koyogo Sho-ten, 1908.
Takao Shinzaemon et al. *Genzan hatten shi*. Wŏnsan: Takao Shinzaemon, 1916.
Takashima Masaaki. "Chōsen ni okeru shokuminchi ginkō no tenkai: Dai-Ichi Ginkō Chōsen shiten: Kankoku (Chōsen) ginkō no bunseki o chūshin tosh-ite." *Keizai riron*, nos. 142–43 (Jan. 1975).
———. *Chōsen ni okeru shokuminchi kinyū shi no kenkyū*. Tokyo: Ōhara Shinseisha, 1978.
———. "'Kankoku shokutaku ginkō' setsuritsu keikaku ni tsuite (shiryō)." *Keizai riron*, nos. 139–40 (July 1974).
———. "'Ni-Kan ginkō' kōzō to 'Kankoku takushoku ginkō' setsuritsu kei-kaku ni tsuite." *Keizai riron*, no. 122 (July 1971).
Takeuchi Tsuna. "Takeuchi Tsuna jijoden." In Yoshino Sakuzō, ed., *Meiji bunka zenshū*. Tokyo: Nihon Hyōronsha, 1929
Takeuchi Yoshimi, ed. *Kindai Nihon shisō taikei: Ajiashugi*. Tokyo: Chikuma Shobō, 1963.
Takeuchi Yoshimi and Karaki Junzō, eds. *Kindai Nihon shisō kōza*. Vol. 8. Tokyo: Chikuma Shobō, 1961.
Tako Keiichi. "Nichi-Rō sensō zengo ni okeru shokuminchi keiei no ippen ni tsuite." *Handai hōgaku*, nos. 116–17 (Mar. 1981).
———. "Nihon ni yoru Chōsen shokuminchi katei ni tsuite no ichi kōsatsu: 1904–1910 nen ni okeru." Parts 1–3. *Handai hōgaku*, no. 90 (Mar. 1974); no. 94 (Mar. 1975); no. 101 (Jan. 1977).
Takushokukyoku. *Shokuminchi imin gaikyō*. Tokyo, 1909.
Tanaka Hozumi. *Tai-Kan shigi*. Tokyo: Myōhōdo, 1899.
Tanaka Ichinosuke, ed. *Zensen shōkō kaigisho hattatsu shi*. Pusan: Pusan Nip-pōsha, 1936.
Tanaka Shin'ichi. "Chōsen ni okeru tochi chōsa jigyō no sekaiteki chii: Teikoku-shugi, shokuminchiteki tochi seisaku no tokushu Nihon-Chōsen teki seika-ku." Parts 1 and 2. *Shakai kagaku kenkyū* 29.3 (Oct. 1977); 30.2 (Aug. 1978).
———. "Kankoku zaisei seiri ni okeru 'chōzei daichō' seibi ni tsuite." *Tochi seidoshi kenkyū* 63 (Apr. 1974).
———. "Kankoku zaisei seiri ni okeru chōzei seido kaikaku." *Shakai keizai shigaku* 39.4 (Jan. 1974).
———. "Tochi chōsa jigyōshi no ichi danmen." In Hatada Takashi Sensei Kinenkai, comp., *Chōsen rekishi ronshū*. Vol. 2. Tokyo: Ryūkeisha, 1979.
Tanaka Yoshio. "Meiji kōki 'Chōsen takushoku' e no chihōteki kanshin." *Chōsenshi Kenkyūkai ronbunshū* 4 (Sept. 1968).
Tani Hisao. *Kimitsu Nichi-Rō senshi*. Tokyo: Hara Shobō, 1966.

Thorner, Daniel. *Investment in Empire: British Railway and Steam Shipping Enterprise in India, 1825–1849.* Philadelphia: University of Pennsylvania Press, 1950.

Tiedemann, Arthur. "Japan's Economic Foreign Policies, 1868–1893." In James William Morley, ed., *Japan's Foreign Policy: A Research Guide.* New York: Columbia University Press, 1974.

Tō-A Kangyō Kabushiki Kaisha, comp. *Tō-A Kangyō Kakubushiki Kaisha jū nen shi.* Tokyo, 1933.

Tōbata Seiichi and Ōkawa Kazushi. *Chōsen beikoku keizai ron.* Tokyo: Nihon Gakujutsu Shinkōkai, 1935.

Togano Shigeo. *Chōsen saikinshi.* Tokyo: Fusando, 1912.

Tōgō Minoru. *Nihon shokumin ron.* Tokyo: Bunbudo, 1906.

Tōkanfu. *Kankoku heigō tenmatsu sho.* Seoul: Kankoku Tōkanfu, 1910.

———, comp. *Kankoku shashin cho.* Seoul, 1910.

———, ed. *Zai-Kankoku Nihonjin sangyō dantai ichiran.* Seoul, 1907.

Tōkanfu Chihōbu. *Kyoryūmindan jijō yōran.* Seoul, 1908.

Tōkanfu Sōmubu Naijika, ed. *Kankoku jijō yōran.* Tokyo, 1906.

———, ed. *Zai-Kan honpōjin jōkyō ichi ranpyō.* Seoul: Tōkanfu, 1907.

Tokio Shunjō. *Chōsen heigō shi.* Seoul: Chōsen Oyobi Manshūsha, 1926.

———. *Saikin Chōsen chishi.* Seoul: Chōsen Ōyobi Manshūsha, 1918.

Tokunaga Isami. *Kankoku sōran.* Tokyo: Hakubundo, 1907.

Tokutomi Iichirō. *Kōshaku Matsukata Masayoshi den.* 4 vols. Tokyo: Kōshaku Matsukata Masayoshi Denki Hensankai, 1935.

———. *Kōshaku Yamagata Aritomo den.* 3 vols. Tokyo: Yamagata Aritomo Kō Kinen Jigyōkai, 1933.

———. *Rikugun taishō Kawakami Sōroku.* Tokyo: Dai-Ichi Kōronsha, 1942.

Tomita Seiichi. *Tomita Gisaku den.* Chinnamp'o, 1936.

Toyama Shigeki. "Chōsen ni taisuru minzokuteki henken ni tsuite." *Rekishi hyōron,* no. 152 (April 1963).

———. "Meiji shonen no gaikō ishiki." In Haraguchi Munehisa, ed., *Meiji ishin.* Vol. 9 of *Ronshū Nihon rekishi.* Tokyo: Yuseido, 1973.

Tōyō Sanshi. *Katsura Tarō.* Tokyo: Daiko Shobō, 1913.

Tōyō Keizai Shinpōsha, comp. *Nihon bōeki seiran.* Tokyo, 1975.

Tōyō Takushoku Kabushiki Kaisha, comp. *Chōsen ijū tebiki.* Seoul, 1915.

———. *Shokumin jigyō kakuchihōbetsu seiseki.* Seoul, 1918.

———. *Tōtaku jū nen shi.* Tokyo: Tōyō Takushoku Kabushiki Kaisha, 1918.

——— *Tōyō Takushoku Kabushiki Kaishi sanjū nenshi.* Tokyo, 1939.

Tsiang, T. F. "Sino-Japanese Diplomatic Relations, 1870–1894." *Chinese Social and Political Science Review* 17 (1933–34).

Tsuneya Moriyuki. *Chōsen kaika shi.* Tokyo: Hakubundo, 1901.

Tsunoda Jun. *Manshū mondai to kokubō hōshin: Meiji kōki ni okeru kokubō kankyō no hendō.* Tokyo: Hara Shobō, 1967.

Tsunoyama Sakae, ed. *Nihon ryōji hōkoku no kenkyū.* Tokyo: Dōbunkan Shuppan, 1986.

Ueno Yūzuma. *Sankoku ippenron.* Tokyo: Uchida Yoshibei, 1894.

Umezu Kazuo. *Nihon no bōeki shisō: Nihon bōeki seisaku shisō shi kenkyū.* Tokyo: 1963.

Underwood, Lillias Horton. *Fifteen Years Among the Top-Knots; or, Life in Korea*. Rev. ed. New York: American Tract Society, 1908.

Uyehara, Cecil H., comp. *Checklist of Archives in the Japanese Ministry of Foreign Affairs, Tokyo, Japan 1868–1945: Microfilmed for the Library of Congress*. Washington, D.C.: Library of Congress, 1954.

Wada Yachiho, ed. *Chōsen no kaikō*. Seoul: Chikazawa Shoten, 1935.

Waswo, Ann. *Japanese Landlords: The Decline of a Rural Elite*. Berkeley: University of California Press, 1977.

Watanabe Shirō. *Kaigai risshin no tebiki*. Tokyo: Minyūsha, 1902.

Wehler, Hans Ulrich. "Bismarck's Imperialism, 1862–1890." *Past and Present*, no. 48 (1970).

Wilkinson, William H. *The Korean Government: Constitutional Changes, July 1894 to October 1895, with an Appendix on Subsequent Enactments to Thirtieth June 1896*. Shanghai: Statistical Department of the Inspectorate General of Customs, 1897.

Wright, Mary C. "The Adaptability of Ch'ing Diplomacy: The Case of Korea." *Journal of Asian Studies* 17 (May 1958).

Yamabe Kentarō. *Nihon no Kankoku heigō*. Tokyo: Taihei Shuppansha, 1966.

———. *Nihon tōchika no Chōsen*. Tokyo: Iwanami Shoten, 1971.

———. *Nikkan heigō shoshi*. Tokyo: Iwanami Shoten, 1966.

Yamada Hideo. *Shokuminchi keizaishi no shomondai*. Tokyo: Ajia Keizai Kenkyūjo, Ajia Keizai Shuppankai, 1973.

Yamada Shōji. "Jiyūminken undō to Chōsen." In Tanaka Akira, ed., *Nihonshi: Kindai*. Tokyo, 1977.

———. "Jiyūminkenki ni okeru kō-A ron to datsu-A ron: Ajiashugi no keisei o megutte." *Chōsenshi Kenkyūkai ronbunshū* (June 1969).

———. "Meiji zenki no Ni-Chō bōeki: Sono Nihongawa no ninaite no kōzō ni tsuite." In *Kindai Nihon no kokka to shisō*. Ed. Ienaga Saburo Kyōjū Tōkyō Kyōiku Daigaku taikan kinen ronshū kankō iinkai. Tokyo: Sanseido, 1979.

Yamagata Isō. *Keijō Zappitsu*. Tokyo: Naigai Shuppankai, 1912.

Yamaguchi Muneo. "Kobuchi kaitaku mondai o mejiru tai-Kan imēji no keisei, rufu kaitei ni tsuite." *Shigaku zasshi* 87.10 (Oct. 1978).

Yamaguchi Sei. *Chōsen sangyō shi*. 3 vols. Tokyo: Hōbunkan, 1910.

Yamaguchi Toyomasa. *Chōsen no kenkyū*. Tokyo: Ganshodo, 1911.

Yamaji Aizan. "Nissen dōzoku no shiteki shosa." In Aoyagi Tsunataro, ed., *Chōsen*. Seoul: Chōsen Kenkyūkai, 1913.

Yamamichi Jōichi. *Chōsen hantō*. Tokyo: Nikkan Shobō, 1911.

Yamamoto Kōtarō. *Saishin Chōsen ijū annai*. Tokyo: Minyūsha, 1904.

Yamamoto Shirō. "Kankoku tōkanfu setchi to tōshiken mondai." *Nihon rekishi* 36 (1976).

———, ed. *Terauchi Masaaki nikki*. Kyoto: Dōmeisha, 1970.

Yanagihara Kō. *Kei-Jin jitsugyōka retsuden*. Inchon, 1905.

Yi, Kyu-tae. *Modern Transformation of Korea*. Trans. Sun Tong-mahn et al. Seoul: Sejong Publishing, 1970.

Yoshida Kazuyuki. "Nihon teikokushugi no Chōsen heigō: Kokusai kankei o chūshin ni." *Chōsenshi Kenkyūkai ronbunshū* 2 (Nov. 1966).

Yoshida Tōgo. *Nikkan kōshi dan*. Tokyo, 1893.

Yoshino Makoto. "Chōsen kaikokugo no kokumotsu yūshutsu ni tsuite." *Chō-senshi Kenkyūkai ronbunshū*, no. 12 (Dec. 1975).

———. "Yi-chō makki ni okeru beikoku yūshutsu no tenkai to hōkokurei." *Chōsenshi Kenkyūkai ronbunshū*, no. 15 (Mar. 1978).

———. "Yi-ki makki ni okeru menseihin yūnyū no tenkai." In Hatada Takashi Sensei Kinenkai, comp., *Chōsen rekishi ronshū*. Vol. 2. Tokyo: Ryūkeisha, 1979.

Young, John, comp. *Checklist of Microfilm Reproductions of Selected Archives of the Japanese Army, Navy and Other Government Agencies, 1868–1945*. Washington, D.C.: Library of Congress, 1959.

Yūhō Kyōkai Shiryō Kenkyūkai, comp. *Chōsen kankei bunken shiryō sōmo-kuroku*. Vol. 1. Chigasaki: Chōsen Shiryō Kenkyūkai, 1961.

Yūhō Kyōkai Shozo, comp. *Chōsen kankei bunken shiryō sōmokuroku*. Vol 2. Tokyo: Yūhō Kyōkai, 1972.

Yui Masaomi and Obinata Sumio, eds. *Kanryō Keisatsu*. Vol. 3 of *Kindai Nihon shisō taikei*. Tokyo: Iwanami Shoten, 1990.

Zai Chōsen naichijin shinshi meikan. Seoul: Chōsen Kōronsha, 1917.

Index